Best wishes
from
Cassie Nicholes

HISTORICAL SKETCHES OF SUMTER COUNTY

Volume II

By

CASSIE NICHOLES

Library of Congress Catalog Card Number 75-28632

Published by
THE SUMTER COUNTY HISTORICAL COMMISSION

Sponsored by
THE SUMTER COUNTY COMMISSION

Printed by
A PRESS, INC.
GREENVILLE, S.C.

INTRODUCTION

The author of **Historical Sketches of Sumter County – Volume I and II** – is Miss Cassie Nicholes with whom the writer has a very pleasant association as a member of the Sumter County Historical Commission. Born in Sumter County before the turn of the century, Miss Nicholes defies the accepted norms. Keeping house by herself at 83, she also served as associate editor of the **Sumter News** until recently, covering a wide territory and driving her own auto in search of features and news stories. She turns out a prodigious amount of copy – all by hand, since she never bothered to type.

Mike Karvelas, also a member of the Historical Commission, summarized Miss Nicholes' career as follows:

> "A native of the Privateer section of Sumter County, she is the daughter of Mr. and Mrs. I.M. Nicholes. She began her formal education in a one-room, one teacher school located in the woods near Bethel Baptist Church. At age 17 she entered Coker College at Hartsville, S.C., where she majored in Latin and minored in English to receive an A.B. degree.
>
> "She attended summer school at Furman University, Greenville, S.C., and the University of South Carolina, Columbia, and did her graduate work in English. She studied the Old and New Testaments and elementary Greek at Southern Baptist Theological Seminary in Louisville, Ky.
>
> "For 45 years Miss Nicholes taught Latin, French and English in schools in a number of South Carolina communities, among them Simpsonville, Easley, Turbeville, Mayesville, Cameron, Orangeburg and Sumter. She directed senior class plays for 20 years and was the adviser for the yearbook and newspaper at Edmunds High School in Sumter.
>
> "A member of Delta Kappa Gamma, a teachers' Honor Society, she is a past president of the Iota Chapter. She is a member of Mayesville Baptist Church and a resident of Sumter since 1975.
>
> "Miss Cassie has served the weekly newspaper, The **Sumter News**, as Mayesville correspondent, feature writer, feature editor and more recently associate editor."

This having been said, we the members of the Sumter County Historical Commission recommend this book to you. We wish that each of you could somehow be privileged to meet this vivacious little lady whom we all admire and love so well.

Robert B. Moise, Chairman
Sumter County Historical
Commission

Dedicated

to

MYRTIS GINN OSTEEN

In appreciation for her years of tireless effort in the preservation of Sumter County history.

FOREWORD

Historical Sketches of Sumter County, Vol. II is not a sequel to the first volume published in 1975 but rather it contains additional sketches of persons, families, churches, homes, organizations, old businesses, etc. that date into the past history of Sumter County. These sketches were published in **The Sumter News** over the period extending from 1967 to 1981. Therefore some of the earlier ones do not contain current information.

Sketches contained herein are what the name implies. They do not claim to give all information on a subject. They only pinpoint some of the highlights concerning each subject treated.

Information for these sketches has come from numerous sources, including books, magazines, family records, newspapers, and persons closely associated with the subject being treated.

Numerous persons have kindly given information, some more than others, but each one approached has been of great help. The author is deeply indebted to all who have furnished information either in written form or through personal contacts. Many places have been visited for the purpose of procuring information.

As much as I should like to do so, I cannot thank publicly everyone to whom I am indebted, and my sincere hope is that each will accept this expression of my appreciation.

My gratitude is here expressed to the Caroliniana Library in Columbia, the Department of Archives and History and the Sumter County Library for valuable assistance in collecting facts for this publication.

I wish to express special thanks to the committee from the Historical Commission for the hours they have spent in helping gather information, giving helpful suggestions, copyreading and in other ways. Those on the committee are Miss Catharine Bass, Mrs. C.B. Burns, Mrs. Myrtis Ginn Osteen and Mr. Robert Moise.

Thanks are also due the entire Historical Commission for their cooperation and to the County Council for making the publication possible.

Cassie Nicholes

Sumter, South Carolina Yesterday and Today

CONTENTS

PART III – PERSONS

ILLUSTRATIONS

PART I. EARLY LIFE IN SUMTER COUNTY

Recollections Of Main Street In The Past

Relaxing on one of the Charleston benches on the newly "furbished" Sumter Towne Mall, viewing the attractive new sidewalks that are now being laid, the restful spots where flowers are blooming in profusion, and watching shoppers as they hurry or saunter or walk purposefully in and out of the many fine stores where a variety of merchandise can be found, one may fall into a contemplative mood. He may recall from what he has read or from conversations with "old timers" the way Main Street was in years gone by.

In the early days of Sumterville, as the town was then called, Main Street was not paved. Those who wished to travel on this street must go through sand or, in case of rain, mud. A few of the merchants made brick entrances to their stores to accommodate themselves and their customers. In fact, it was not till 1908 that a beginning was made in the improvement of the streets. It was between 1908 and 1910 during the time when W.B. Boyle was mayor that Main Street was paved with brick from Bartlette to Canal.

As darkness came on each night, a lamplighter made his rounds on some of the streets, lighting the kerosene lamps, which were protected by glass covers and placed on eight-foot posts. This convenience was found as early as 1880, but only on a few streets. It was not until the late 1800's that electricity was available on Main Street through the efforts of a private company.

For fire prevention, large fire wells were placed at intervals in the downtown area, chiefly on Main Street. These wells, eight to ten feet square, were covered over by heavy timbers. Each had in the center a manhole where the hoses of the hand-pumped fire engines were attached.

As the daydreamer thinks back, he may recall hearing of the Carriage and Buggy Co. on the corner of Main and Dingle and the old boarding house known as the Curtis House. He may remember, too, hearing that the Negro Shiloh Baptist Church was on the block between Oakland and Bartlette and that the Church of the Holy Comforter (Episcopal) stood on the east side of the Main and Bartlette corner until it was moved to its present location in 1905.

On the northeast corner of Main and Bartlette was the Hurlburt home, the only brick home in the town at that time and north of this dwelling was a small brick store. On the same block on the east side of Main were two boarding houses known as the Davis and the Brunson houses.

A livery stable was operated by W.G. Ellis on one corner of Main and Dugan and on another was Hauser's steam mill, which ground corn and ginned cotton.

There were three homes on the east side of Main Street between Bartlette and Caldwell – one owned by a Mrs. Watson, one by Dr. A.J. China, one by John W. Dargan and later by Dr. George W. Dick. The last was the site of the present Federal Building.

On the northwestern corner of Main and Dugan stood the John F. Haynsworth house, which was occupied in the 1830's by Mr. and Mrs. George Kellogg, teachers in the Sumterville Academy and parents of America's first home-trained opera star, Clara Louise Kellogg.

On this block were the headquarters of C.T. Mason, Sr., watchmaker and inventor, Freeman Hoyt's jewelry store and a Mr. Pate. On the corner of Main and Liberty, the present location of McLellan's, was what was known as the Barrett building. This was a Charleston-type structure with a store on the first floor and family accommodations upstairs.

On the east side on Main (on the corner of Main and Caldwell) were the home and formal garden of Dr. Witherspoon. Also on this block were the home of Col. W.A. Colclough, the millinery shop of the Misses McElhouse and R.P. Monaghan's general merchandise store.

On the southeast corner of Main and Liberty was the A.A. Solomons dry goods and general merchandise establishment. This building still stands and is occupied by the Sumter Dry Goods Company, now known as Keiths.

Recalling the saying that the block between Liberty and Hampton was once the business center of the town, the dreamer decided to move up the Mall the better to visualize the long-ago activities in that section. With no difficulty, he found a bench near some lovely crepe myrtles in full bloom. After enjoying the attractive surroundings, he was again lost in the past.

Settling comfortably in his new position, he began to doze,

drifting off into his vision of what North Main Street was like almost a century ago.

On the northwest corner of Main and Liberty in 1880 was a large gaping hole, the cellar of a large store which had burned. However, two years later there stood on that spot the largest store building in Sumter, built by J. Ryttenberg and Sons. This later became a bank.

Next was A.J. China's drug store. Then there was an eating place run by Bill Andrews; and next, a junk shop. Following these was Sumter's first court house, which was designed by Robert Mills. It occupied a square extending from what is now Edwards to the present Berger building, which, together with a similar building (later destroyed) had been occupied successively by Theodore Solomons and Co., J. Ryttenberg and Sons, and Levi Bros.

H.F. Folsom had his watch and jewelry store next.

The lot on the northeast corner of Main and Liberty where the Skyscraper, recently demolished, once stood, was owned by Marx E. Cohen, grandfather of Herbert A. Moses. Next were three small stores and then one occupied by L.B. Hanks, later used for a number of years by B.J. Barnett Co. Jack's later was located in the Hanks building.

The next store on this block was that of Bultman Bros., shoemakers. Then came D.J. Winn's tailor shop and clothing store. Ducker and Bultman's Grocery Store occupied for a number of years the next location.

Next to an alley came the old Town Hall, erected in 1871, which replaced the first Town Hall, a remodeling of the first jail.

The ground floor of the 1871 Town Hall had a hall with two small rooms on the front, one occupied by a bar and the other, by a drug store. The rear was used as city market with a dozen booths for the butchers.

There was a narrow stairway leading to the second floor where the "Music Hall" was used for various forms of entertainment. It could seat approximately 500 in chairs that could be removed in the event of a reception or dance. There was a stage at one end with an adjoining dressing room.

The city clerk and treasurer had offices also on the second floor to which access was possible by an outside stairway.

This Town Hall burned in 1892 and the one that stands today was built the following year.

Next to the Town Hall was an alley furnishing access to two houses, where the fire engines were kept, to the city jail and guardhouse. The guardhouse was built of logs and covered with weatherboarding. It had three cells with heavily barred windows.

When a prisoner tried to escape in 1880, he set fire to the building. He was burned along with the guardhouse.

North of Town Hall was another brick store owned by J. Ryttenberg and Sons, later by the E.P. Ricker saloon.

Soon after the Civil War a brick building was erected on the next lot by Col. W.A. Colclough and was occupied for several years after 1887 by a number of businesses, including that of Schwartz Bros. The building was later in the possession of W.B. Burns & Sons Hardware.

Still another brick building on this lot was occupied by John Reid's dry goods store, and there were two one-story frame stores between this and the corner of Main and Hampton.

On the west side of Main between Hampton and Canal there were four buildings. First, was a two-story building in which the first floor was used as a harness shop run by a man named Wroten. On the second floor, J. Diggs Wilder operated a "Photographic Gallery" in 1880.

Next were two vacant lots in those early days but in time these were occupied. Beyond these was the law office of J.S.G. Richardson; and Dr. John S. Hughson had his office in the same building. On the southwest corner of Main and Canal was a large building known as Clark's Hotel.

On the northeast corner of Main and Hampton was the lovely garden of Chief Justice F.I. Moses and next to that was the law office of Joseph H. Earle. On the other side of the vacant lot, that came next, was the law office of Gen. E.W. Moise, adjutant general in Wade Hampton's administration. Beyond another vacant lot was the law office of W.F.B. Haynsworth and Thomas B. Fraser, Sr., which was built about 1820 by Dr. Joseph Cox Haynsworth.

It was rolled back from Main Street and is now the office of Geo. D. Shore at 12 Law Range, a street that did not exist as such in 1880. It was the driveway to the stables of the A.A. Solomons home, which stood with its spacious garden where the courthouse now stands.

Across Main Street from this home was the site of the home of John Gayle, where court was first held in Sumterville ca. 1800.

In those early days there were no plate glass windows and most of the buildings were in poor condition even in 1880. Most have disappeared altogether or greatly changed with only a few remaining.

As the soft lights along the Towne Mall began to dispel the shadows, the dreamer returned from his imaginary journey into the past. He viewed the many modern store fronts and signs along Main Street and thought "What a difference!" He could well have remembered, too, those who through the years spent their energies making Sumter the up-to-date city that it is today.

Browsing In Sumter's Past

In this day and time, when mail comes to Sumter several times each day, it is hard to realize that such service was once not even imagined.

Dr. Anne King Gregorie relates in her **History of Sumter County** that mail service was begun in 1801[1] for a place "designated as Sumterville from the name of the District" under order of the postmaster general of the United States, and the first postmaster was John Gayle.

The **Camden Gazette**, it seems, established in 1816 a private weekly mail route which would leave Camden on Friday and return on Saturday by Black River, stopping among other places at William Taylor's store in Sumterville.

About 1830 a route from Charleston to Camden began passing through the village as required by law since it was a courthouse town. Three years later, a daily stage route included Sumterville. Henry Haynsworth became postmaster at this time and held the position for 31 years.

Mail was frequently lost in those early days because of flooded streams. And since there was no registry service, there was no recompense for mail lost either accidentally or otherwise. It is said that in 1835 a man in Tennessee offered a reward for the return of "the right hand halves" of some notes on the Bank of the United States that a kinsman in Sumterville had sent and which he had never received.

When mails first came to the little community in 1801, the postage rate for a single sheet was eight cents up to 40 miles, increasing to 25 cents for 500 miles or more. However, rates changed at intervals. In 1846 it cost three cents to send a letter up to 300 miles and 10 cents for greater distances. Prepayment of postage was not required before 1855. Four times each year postmasters published a list of unclaimed mail.

For many years mail was carried by stage, but in 1850 a train mail service was begun between Sumterville and Wilmington, N.C., thus bringing mails from the north and south to Sumter District more quickly than by the Charleston route. At this time Sumter District had 20 postoffices: Bishopville, Bradford Institute, Bradleyville, Brewington, Clarendon, Friendship, Fulton, Lodibar, Manchester, Mechanicsville, Mill Grove, Mount Clio, Plowden's Mill, Privateer, Providence, Salem, Stateburg, Sumterville, Willow Grove, and Wright's Bluff.

Even with the new route by train, mail delivery was uncertain since railroads did not have adequate trestles for crossing swollen streams. Such was the case in 1852 when the editor of **The Watchman** is said to have complained because he had had neither northern nor southern mail for a week.

Ramsey in his **History of South Carolina** praised the healthful climate of the High Hills of Sumter, mentioning several residents who had passed the century mark. He tells of one 95-year-old lady who walked ten miles to church each Sunday, "attended by her descendants to the fifth generation."

Placed between news items was the following advertisement in a newspaper of some years ago when advertising consumed much of the space of a paper (even the front page):

"A tired stomach is very much like a sprained ankle. It needs a crutch . . . we must relieve it of all work for a time, or until it is restored to its natural strength." The "crutch" recommended was Shaker Digestive Cordial.

Recollections of Edwin Scott tells of the fact that indigo grew wild in the woods around his home. It had stalks one and a half feet tall, with bluish green leaves.

Cotton growing was limited in his day because there were no gins. Families and neighbors would sit before a large open fire, roasting potatoes and "pindars," chatting and removing the lint from the cotton seeds.

From an old record it has been established that Gen. Thomas Sumter sold to President Thomas Jefferson a tract of land as a site for a military academy; however, when the matter was brought before Congress there was such dispute concerning the location that it was decided by a majority of one that the academy would be built at West Point.

The land that was purchased by the President in South Carolina later became the location of the Great Falls Power Plant.

In 1913 a group of Sumter Volunteer Firemen won the State tournament in Abbeville. The group included Ryan White, Ormsby "Yank" Blanding, Al Keels, Herman Phelps, Eugene "Genie" Wilder (The Fire Chief), Cliff Brown, Harry Weeks and

J.H. "Jack" Forbes (Asst. Chief).

Francis Kinlock of Acton, Stateburg, published around 1800 a "Eulogy of George Washington." The book was published again 67 years later.

The Sumter Insurance Agency is the oldest established business in Sumter. It was organized in 1866 and has served its clients successfully since that time.

The Sumter Firemen won the Inter-State races held in Wilmington, N.C., July 13, 1930. The Delgars came in first in the Hose Wagon Race (in 37.15 seconds), and the Monaghans were in third place.

An editorial short appearing in a paper dated August 21, 1905, reads as follows: "The new stores to be erected on the Courthouse square will not be completed too soon to meet the demand. Every few days we hear of some business prospector looking for a place in which to open business."

Apparently in the early days the firemen had some interesting activities. In 1915 "The hose and hand reel" teams, some 20 of them, attended a firemen's Convention in Greenwood. The racing wagon and horses, Jeff and Jim, were placed in cars for the trip. They were accompanied by Messrs. Ryan White, Ormsby Blanding and Eddie Dunne.

Carolina Coca-Cola Plant was mentioned in one paper as the most efficient plant in the entire South. Its operations are said to extend into nine counties. It was started in Sumter with A.T. Heath as president in 1919.

The article goes on to say that the Sumter Plant is "a model of efficiency, sanitation and beauty."

These news items were found in old copies of **The Sumter Herald** and **The Sumter Daily Item.**

Echoes From Sumter's By-Gone Days

"How times have changed!"

This is an exclamation often heard. And yet as we listen to echoes of days gone by, we can detect some similarities of customs and trends. It is true, too, that human nature is much the same as in former days.

All through the years, education and schools have held the spotlight. From **The Sumter News** of 1866 comes the following announcement: "Miss Haynsworth will reopen her school on Monday, August 27, 1866. This is a most admirable school and should be heartily and liberally patronized." (This school, run by Miss Hortense Haynsworth, dates back at least 11 years prior to this for, according to the record in 1855, Miss Haynsworth was assisted by Miss S.W. Wells.)

In the same issue of **Sumter News** was the announcement of the opening of the Academy of Our Lady of Mercy, which is called in the article "a popular and valuable institution."

It was reported from Wedgefield in 1894 that Prof. D.D. Rambo of Philadelphia had arrived for the opening of Wedgefield High School.

In the personal items of one paper, there was an entry stating that Prof. Clarence J. Owens, president of Orangeburg College, was visiting in the homes of students in the Brogdon and DuRant neighborhoods.

Recreation and vacationing have always held importance in the life of man, though the forms have changed much through the years. In the past century, tournaments and cockfighting were the craze in the Sumter area. Horse racing was also popular in the old days and it continues to be of interest to many.

Camping sites were visited by vacationers in the past years, but the convenience of taking along a camper with sleeping and cooking accommodations was unheard of. However, many chose this type of vacationing in preference to others even with less convenient facilities. Around 40 years ago one of the most popular places for camping and swimming was Pocalla Springs, owned by M.H. Beck, who boasted that he had the "Best Swimming Pool in Seven States." In fact, it was said that it was one of the finest summer resorts in the South. The main building was a three-story stucco structure, containing modern and sanitary bathhouses, a spacious dance hall on the third floor and a large room for "games and amusement devices." Thousands of swimmers from all over the state crowded this pool each summer.

The mountains lured vacationers in the past just as they do today. The main difference is the mode of travel. Today one can go on a sightseeing trip to the Blue Ridge and return the same day if he so desires. Driving in the mountains in a modern automobile is a genuine delight. However, in the early days, folk traveled by train, often taking advantage of excursion rates to go on a vacation. One such excursion in 1900 came from Charleston through Sumter, where many from nearby areas boarded the train. This excursion was in two parts – one going to Asheville and one to Walhalla for the semi-centennial celebration of that little town.

Bicycles have for many years been a favorite means of transportation as well as vehicles for pleasure riding and racing.

In a notice in the press in the year 1894, it was predicted that the year '95 would give the bicycle business a boost because of two big cycle shows – one in Chicago and one in New York, each striving to surpass the other.

Two years later, however, it was reported that there was little prospect for bicycle races in Sumter during that season, because the track association had lost money the previous year. The article stated that track and stands were in bad repair and there was no money in the treasury for the work. Whether racing was revived at a later day is in no available record. Some who read this article may know the answer.

Today bicycling is still a popular hobby as well as a much-used mode of travel, especially in the city. Bicycle tours interest many. A group made a tour of South Carolina, observing especially sites made famous during the Revolutionary War. The party included cyclists from New York, Florida and Arkansas. They were joined by a number of South Carolinians, with a local citizen, Ray Guest, planning the itinerary.

From its beginning, Sumter has been the home of many music lovers. As far back as 1851 there was an organized class in vocal music which met at the Male Academy, with a Mr. Cuttino, a traveling voice teacher as instructor. (Though the record does not state this teacher's first name nor his home, he could well have been related to the many of the same family name who are now exceptionally fine musicians.)

In 1852[2] the Swiss Bell Ringers presented a "chaste, select and novel" entertainment at the remodeled jail known at that time as the Town Hall. This was only one of many traveling groups of various types that gave musical performances in Sumter. In 1855 two concerts were given at the Courthouse by two child prodigies – the "Infant Drummer" and the "American Mocking Bird."

It is said that during the 1880's many programs of a very high type were presented at the Music Hall, under the management of D.J. Auld, Sumter's postmaster. One outstanding performance of this decade was "The Mikado" done by the Bijou Opera Co.

Among numerous other groups bringing fine performances to the Music Hall were Star Opera Company and Monte Christo Company.

All the excellent musical programs were not given by outsiders, however, for Sumter had and still has numbers of accomplished musicians. One example of concerts presented in the early days by local artists was given by the pupils of Miss Ammie Teicher and Professor Schumacher. On the program were renditions by the Teichers (Ammie, Isadore, Francesca) and by Misses Ballough, Eddelman, Daisy, Munn, Welsh and Walsh.

Opera star Clara Louise Kellog stopped in Sumter, where she was born, for an appearance during one of her tours at the height of her career.

In 1896 voters seemed as indifferent in many elections as

they are today. In a municipal election of that year, few are said to have registered and of those only 105 votes were cast. Of these A.W. Suder received 45; J.F. Pack, 34; J.F. Laudhery, 26. Suder was elected with a plurality of 11.

The following notice in the press of 1866 might be of interest: "Application will be made at the next session of the legislature to renew and amend" the charter for the town of Sumter.

Activities of many kinds were reported in the newspapers then as they are today. A few personals will illustrate.

Morris Averbuck made the freshman basketball team at the University of Virginia in 1924. He had been a valued player on his team at Sumter High.

Mr. R.R. Singleton of Wedgefield killed a deer weighing 168 pounds and having a "full head of horns."

J.K. McElveen of New Zion planted two acres of tobacco and harvested 1,708 pounds, clearing $215.88 on the experiment. He planned to plant 15 acres in the following year.

From Greenville came the following item in 1924:

"Charles Cuttino, Jr., son of Mr. and Mrs. C.L. Cuttino of Sumter, has been elected president of one section of the Philosophian Literary Society, one of two such societies on the Furman University campus."

Sumter was "awarded places of distinction among the recent appointments by the Faculty of the South Carolina College. The first appointment was given to Mr. H.R. Garden of this town and the eighth to Mr. P.W. Mills of Salem" – **Sumter Tri-Weekly Watchman,** November 20, 1860.

"We learn, with much pleasure, that a Company of Mounted Police was organized at Bell's Mill, in this District, on the 14th instant. . . . The officers of this company are as follows: Captain F.M. Mellett; First Lieut. Jno. W. Dargan; Second Lieut. Richard B. Cain; Third Lieut. M.G. Ramsey." – **Sumter Tri-Weekly Watchman,** November 20, 1860.

In the same issue of this paper was a notice of an election of four delegates from the Claremont District to the "Convention of the People" in Columbia. Some of the managers who were "to meet at the Sumter Court House, count the votes, and declare the election were listed as follows:

Sumter – Thomas M. Baker, Henry W. Gardner, Thos. D. Frierson.

Swimming Pens – J.W. Montgomery, Leonard Brown, J.F.M. Michau.

Privateer – Thomas H. Osteen, Warren Wells, James W. Richardson.

Mayesville – W.E. Mills, W.W. Bradley, Benjamin F. Wilson.

"Among the admissions to the Bar, at the recent examination, we are pleased to see the name of Jos. F. Rhame. This young gentleman has taken a long and arduous course of studentship in the office of Messrs. Blanding and Richardson of our town. . . . We learn that it is his intention to settle in Manning . . . " – **The Sumter Watchman**, December 5, 1860.

According to the **Sumter Tri-Weekly Watchman** of September 18, 1860, the first bale of new cotton, grown on the farm of Daniel Brunson, "near this place," was sold three days earlier at 10½ cents.

A news item in the June 28 issue of the same paper called attention to an advertisement concerning a tract of land for sale. The ad, reads in part, as follows:

VALUABLE LAND
FOR SALE

"Seven hundred and forty-seven acres situated in Salem, Sumter District, S.C., about one mile from Mount Zion Church and about seven miles from Mayesville, W. and M. Railroad.

"I do not believe that a more healthy and desirable place can be found anywhere. The Mount Zion neighborhood has always been noted for its religion, intelligence, and refinement . . .

"For terms, apply to Mr. N.W. Copeland, on the place or to J.C. Witherspoon."

"This evening (Wednesday), all who are fond of good music (and who is not?) can gratify their taste for the 'concord of sweet sounds' and at the same time contribute to a most deserving object, by attending the concert at the Court House . . . "

This concert took place on April 13, 1864, for the purpose of raising funds for the "families whose supports have been withdrawn by the war." Another notice of the same concert gave the admission price as $2. It was also stated that if the weather was "too inclement" on Wednesday, the concert would be given on Thursday.

In the same issue of **The Sumter Watchman** (April 13, 1864), there was an item stating that no passenger trains would run for 60 days by order of the War Department, the roads to be used for the "transportation of mails, troops and stores."

The same paper carried a news brief telling of the attempted destruction of Bradford Springs Episcopal Church. Someone discovered the fire before much damage was done. The item concluded with this statement, "That man must be base indeed who would thus attempt to destroy a house of prayer."

In the **Sumter Tri-Weekly Watchman** of September 18, 1860, there is an interesting ad concerning a sure cure for cancer. It reads in part:

CANCER CURED

NO CURE – NO PAY

"Would respectfully inform the citizens of S.C. and other States, that he resided in Sumter District near the Court House, where he still continues to practice in the art of removing and healing that formidable disease, Cancer, without the use of knife or caustic."

He listed a number of people in and around Sumter who would testify to the "efficacy" of his practice.

From a report submitted to the Presiding Judge by M. Moses, chairman of the Commissioners of Public Buildings of Sumter District, an excerpt reads as follows: "The Commissioners advertised for sealed proposals for building a Jail of hewn timbers on the foundation of the burnt Jail; and on the 3rd July last the contract was let out to Mr. A.J. Moses; at the price of $5,999, he being the lowest bidder." This report was given in **The Watchman** of December 4, 1867.

Scrapbooks Reflect Personality Traits

In years gone by, it seems, keeping a scrapbook was a favorite hobby with ladies. Special pictures, poems, stories, songs, as well as important newspaper clippings were preserved in a large book, usually with a colorful cover, though sometimes the cover was plain, giving no indication of the "goodies" inside.

In leafing through one of these old treasure chests, one may see many characteristics of personality traits of the owner reflected in the choice of entries.

A scrapbook kept first by Marsena Brunson Loring in the 1830's or '40's, for instance, shows her great love for flowers as well as an unusual knowledge of the many varieties. Carefully pressed and pasted on the pages are numerous specimens, both wild and cultivated. Many of these are labeled with both the common name and the botanical name and classification. A few are listed as follows: Hydrange-quercifolia, Class 10th order 2nd (oak hydrangea); Castaneapumila (Chinquapin); Indigo-feria (Wild Indigo); Oxalisacetosella (sorrel); Achillea-mille-folium, Class 17th Order 2nd (Yarrow); Philaris Americana (Ribbon Grass).

Then there are numbers of specimens with only the common name, such as the potato flower, ferns of different varieties, hoar-hound, Jacob's ladder, lilac, haw, calico flower. And there are still others without names.

In addition to the flowers, gathered, pressed and preserved so lovingly by Mrs. Loring, there are many pictures of flowers in vivid colors, some coming no doubt from seed catalogues.

Later the daughter of the original owner, Anna Charlotte Loring, added to the book (in the 1860's and later). Among her souvenirs were lovely greeting cards – birthday, Christmas, Easter, etc. The personal messages and names on these, of course, are not visible. They must have been kept, however, as remembrances from dear friends or loved ones as well as for their beauty.

In a picture of Penn signing a treaty with the Indians in 1682 or 1683, he is offering to the chiefs a bottle of Ayer's Cherry Pectoral with the added guarantee that it would cure coughs, colds, etc. (Would this be an anachronism or was this product really known at that early time?)

These advertisements, only a few of the many represented in the scrapbook, must have come from calendars, magazines or some other method of selling wares, for surely it was before the day of color pictures in newspapers. But whatever the means of distribution these pictures were, no doubt, saved because of their beauty rather than as an endorsement of the products being sold.

Many marriage and death notices were included in this scrapbook, giving some indication of the numerous friends as well as relatives of these two who lived out their lives so many years ago in Sumter and vicinity. It may be of interest to many still living in this area to read the following wedding write-up:

"The marriage of Miss May Bossard, daughter of Sumter's distinguished citizen Dr. J.J. Bossard, and Mr. Percy Smith of Georgetown drew a large crowd to the Presbyterian Church, the interior of which was tastefully decorated with evergreens and hot house plants.

"Mendelson's Wedding March was played on the violin by Mr. John Moran, accompanied by Mr. David Winn on the organ.

"The ushers, Messrs. E.M. Wilson, R.L. Cooper, E.O. Ingram and Hugh Fraser, two in either aisle, proceeded (sic) the bridal party. The attendants were: Miss Zena Talley and Capt. W.P. Conyers.

"Miss Lena Colclough and Mr. Tom Smith.

"Miss May Holman and Dr. A.C. Dick.

"Miss Dora Richardson and Mr. J.N. Brand.

"Mr. James and Miss Mamie Fraser.

"Miss Fraser was the maid of honor and stood at the side of the bride during the ceremony. The bridesmaids came in two at a time followed by two gentlemen; they crossed in front of the pulpit and arranged themselves in a half circle on either side of the pulpit. The bride, who came in on the arm of her father, wore a beautiful costume of white satin, en train. The bridesmaids wore empire costumes of white organdie with ribbon trimmings. Each one carried a bouquet of yellow chrysanthemums. The ceremony was performed by Rev. N.W. Edmunds, D.D.

"After the ceremony the bridal party drove to the residence of Dr. J.J. Bossard, where an elegant reception was held until the young couple left on the 8:30 train for Columbia, from which city they went to Washington."

A very lengthy account of the death of Mrs. Pauline Brazilia Brownfield of Summerville has been preserved among other entries. It relates much of her life history, telling of her birth in Brazil in 1812, the daughter of Col. Thomas Sumter and Nathalie DeLage Sumter. The article includes the story of how Nathalie, daughter of a French countess, came to America and met Col. Sumter on her way back to France.

Pauline Brazilia spent some time in Paris before returning to the Sumter home at Stateburg, later marrying Dr. Brownfield. The date of her death is not given (so many old clippings do not include dates), but it was sometime after 1866 when she moved to Summerville.

The many selections of poetry kept over a period of at least 25 years reflect something of the religious fervor, the patriotic zeal, the romantic inclinations of those who lived in another day. Many of these poems had to do with the War Between the States. One very sad poem was written in the winter of 1863 by young Lt. William Alexander McQueen, son of the beloved pastor of Sumter's First Presbyterian Church. Entitled "The Soldier Boy's Dream," this poem was set to music by young comrades of the author in the Palmetto Battery fighting in Virginia, and sung often by the soldiers in this company. McQueen was killed in service. It is said that one stanza of the song is inscribed on a monument in a Boston cemetery.

Another poem called "In Memoriam" was dedicated by the author to holders of Confederate treasury notes. The lines were written on the back of a Confederate Treasury $500 bill, which was found in Richmond, Va., after the evacuation. The first and last stanzas read as follows:

"Representing nothing on God's earth now
And naught in the waters below it
As a pledge of the nation that is dead and gone
Keep it, dear friend, and show it.

"Keep it, for it tells our history o'er,
From the birth of its dream to the last,

Modest and born of the angel Hope,
Like the hope of success it passed."

Many prayers, hymns and religious poems demonstrated the deep spiritual inclination of those who made the collections. Here and there, too, are pictures of beloved churches and ministers. There is one especially good portrait of Bishop Francis Asbury, that great man of God to whom Methodists in Sumter and, for that matter in much of America, owe so much.

There are found also many lovely poems on nature such as "The Beautiful Snow," "Falling Leaves" and others.

Poems and stories with a sentimental flavor include such titles as "How He Was Crippled," "A Mother's Gift," "The Old Log House."

Wedding invitations were found in the book, but in few cases were there full dates.

Under miscellaneous items might be named a list of officers of Gamecock Co. Rifles: Captain – T.W. Lee; 1st Lieutenant – E.M. Pitts; 2nd Lieutenant – E.S. Kennedy; 3rd Lieutenant – L.D. Jennings: O.S. – B.F. Burkett.

There are many obituaries found on the pages of this old scrapbook. One of the lengthiest begins thus: "Seldom has the pen recorded the death of a woman more lovely than Mrs. Elizabeth A. Chambers, known to the literary world as 'Lizzie Clarendon,' daughter of Rev. Hartwell Spain of the South Carolina Conference."

The notice gives the date of her death as December 12, 1857, saying that she died in Sumter. The very flowery tribute praises the "sparkle of her mind" even in childhood. She was said to have advanced rapidly in school and she began publishing her writings at the age of 16. The writer of the article said of her talent, "She must take rank among the first female writers of the South . . . " She is also listed as one of Sumter's most gifted poets. Some of her poems are found here and there in the scrapbook, but they are too long to quote.

Notice of the death of two of the children of Henry and Sarah Haynsworth within four days is of unusual interest. William Henry, age 16, died on May 27, 1858, and Elizabeth, age 5, died on May 31.

A similar occurrence was the passing of the two daughters of Mrs. Hannah Bradford Jayroe and the late Andrew Brown Jayroe. Hannah Louisa Josephine, 13, died on March 22, 1856, and Rebecca Caroline, 14, on March 26.

Few of the death notices told anything of survivors, funeral services or places of burial, but were usually beautiful tributes to the deceased.

In the obituary of Mrs. Loring's mother, Mrs. W.L. Brunson, who died May 18, 1864, the writer, signed "D. Mc.," spoke most highly of her wonderful life. One paragraph will give the tone of the tribute: "She lived, for the most part, in the retirement of the family circle except when the duties of benevolence called her abroad. The sick and afflicted ever found in her a ready and sympathetic friend . . . and the house of God (was) her constant resort."

The notice of the death of Mr. W.L. Brunson notes him as "one of the oldest and most respected of our citizens." It is followed by an article telling of his great kindness to his slaves. So much did they love him that when they were freed they remained with him.

The death of one of Sumter's earliest merchants, Freeman Hoyt, is given as having occurred on January 11, 1869. One sentence tells something of the fine qualities of this man: "In all his family relations, our lamented friend was kind, considerate, devoted, – his home was ever made happy by his presence, and comfortable from the proceeds of his steady and successful industry."

There are numbers of other death notices of those who had lived in the area in the 19th century. These included Browns, Bradfords, Brunsons, Haynsworths, Wilsons, Col. John A. Colclough, Mr. and Mrs. Flowers, a Vaughn, Capt. Francis Sumter, the wife of Judge Fraser, Mrs. Posthuma Dick, Mary C. Mellette, Mrs. Alice Dargan Mitchell, Dr. McQueen, and numerous others.

Here and there throughout the scrapbook are many tidbits of general interest, of wisdom, of philosophy, of advice, of humor.

A story of the origin of the song, very popular around the turn of the century, "The Old Oaken Bucket," may be of interest to some older readers. It tells of a man named Woodworth, who was a printer in New York. One day he and some of his friends met at "Mallory's" where they could get a "good drink." After imbibing the drink, Woodworth remarked that "Mallory's eau de vie was superior" to any he had tasted. But one of his friends said, "No, you are quite mistaken; there was one thing which, in both our estimations, far surpassed this in the way of drinking."

When asked what the drink was, he said, "The draught of pure, fresh spring water that we used to drink from the old oaken bucket that hung in the well, after our return from the labors of the field on a sultry day in Summer."

Woodworth's eyes filled with tears and he said, "True! True!"

He returned to his office, picked up a pen and within a half hour he had written "The Old Oaken Bucket."

This old folk song, so beloved in the past, could well be

revived in this present generation as a reminder of the simple life enjoyed by the young people of days gone by.

A philosophical thought is found in a conversation between a hummingbird and a butterfly:

A humming-bird met a butterfly and was so impressed by its beauty that it suggested they become friends: "I cannot think of it," was the reply; "You once spurned me and called me a drawling dolt."

"Impossible," exclaimed the hummingbird. "I always entertained the highest respect for such beautiful creatures as you."

"Perhaps you do now," said the other, "but when you insulted me, I was a caterpillar. So let me give you a piece of advice: never insult the humble, as they may some day become your superiors."

Under the head "Gleanings" in the "Carolina Times" is a humorous incident written by the Rev. F.A. Mood during a stay in Paris. His subject is crinolin; and after some introductory words, continued: "As I have presumed to touch upon a subject about which I confess I know nothing except what I see and read, let me add that it is an entire mistake what some deluded European correspondent has recently had inserted in the American papers. He says that the fashion is about to be abandoned, and has already in Paris greatly diminished. Where his eyes were when he penned such a statement, anyone now in Paris must be at an utter loss to imagine. Never were its demands more exorbitant or extensive. Broad as are the Boulevards, it requires their nice observation to navigate smoothly. But let me give a bit of experience in proof. Do not suspect that this now is an effort to make out a case for a special subject, or that there is a bit of exaggeration about it – or that it is a malicious fabrication; because your correspondent has no particular opinion on the subject, and has but one quarrel with it as he will state. Last Sabbath at the church, comfortably seated, a fashionably dressed lady – I need specify no further – undertook to go out. We were all seated in chairs, as is usual here, and they were crowded very close together; in forcing her passage, after several ineffectual attempts, she made a determined push and pull which actually knocked me down, and a young lady alongside of me, and she reached the aisle, dragging several – at least two – chairs after her, which were wrapped in the folds of her dress. You can imagine what a sensation was produced by such a proceeding. I felt much more for the young lady next to me than myself, for a gentleman kindly caught me, but the young lady had a regular scramble among the chairs to recover her footing . . . "

Even a health hint from "Hall's Journal of Health" is found in the scrapbook. These suggestions have long since been laid on the shelf, but at that time no doubt most of them, at least, were considered all-important for good health.

"Once a week is often enough for a decent white man to wash himself all over; and whether in summer or winter that ought to be done with soap, warm water and a hog's hair brush, in a room showing at least seventy degrees Farenheit.

"Baths should be taken early in the morning, for it is then that the system possesses the power of reaction in the highest degree. Any kind of bath is dangerous soon after a meal, or soon after fatiguing exercise. No man or woman should take a bath at the close of the day, unless by the advice of the family physician. Many a man, in attempting to cheat his doctor out of a fee, has cheated himself out of his life; aye, it is done every day . . . "

Some helpful hints preserved by the keeper of the scrapbook may be passed on:

"According to the 'American Chemist,' a solution of three parts of borax and two-and-a-half parts of sulphate or magnesia will render dress fabrics fireproof."

"Kerosene oil is the best furniture oil; it cleanses, adds a polish, and preserves from the ravages of insects."

"To get rid of moths and roaches from closets and bureau drawers, sprinkle powdered borax over and around the shelves, and cover with clean paper."

A recipe for Corn Oysters sounds tasty: "Grate six ears of sweet corn – add a half pint of rich milk, a scant teaspoon of pepper, half as much salt and half a tea-cupful of flour. Mix well together, and fry in hot butter."

As seen from quotations given, scrapbook browsing can be very rewarding for one who is really interested in learning of the life of people more than 100 years ago.

1920 Manuscript Recalls Sumter Of Another Era

From the manuscript of a speech delivered before the Fortnightly Club on March 6, 1920, by the late Judge Robert O. Purdy, one may obtain a vivid picture of Sumter in the mid-1880's. The paper was obtained through the courtesy of Judge L.E. Purdy, a son of the writer.

This paper, treating almost every aspect of life in the country as it was lived more than three-quarters of a century ago, is not only a record of the past in Sumter, but between the lines one can get glimpses of the power of observation, the friendly, understanding personality and the kindly humor of this man who was much loved and highly respected in Sumter.

First, he speaks of the physical appearance of the town which claimed a population of 3,000 at that time, though he doubted the accuracy of the claim. The limits extended only as far as the J.B. Roach house (which once stood on a corner of Main and Charlotte), but there was "much vacant space between lots." There were a few homes on the northwestern part of the town with the corner of Church and Broad as the limit in this direction.

There were few buildings beyond the Convent (Raffield Arms location) on the east. Most of the land below the A.C.L. Railroad was "farming property," owned by Ferriter, Tuomey and Hoyt.

Harby Avenue was the limit on the west. Mr. C.M. Hurst, sheriff of Sumter County for a long time, built on the corner nearest what was later McLaurin Junior High and opened up Harby Avenue, planting trees in the area. Beyond Liberty Street were the Edwards farm lands.

Apparently Sumter was built in a pond, for it seems that after every heavy rain, the area was flooded. The drains were open ditches wholly inadequate for draining the land. One of the "open drains came up from Turkey Creek to Church Street, being very shallow, of course, as it led off from that street, going to a greater depth as it crossed Main Street near the Grier Bakery (between Calhoun and Warren Streets)."

Judge Purdy told of an incident that happened in '93 or '94 when he was "dining" at the home of "Mr. Ingram" on the corner of Washington and Canal. A heavy rain fell while he was there and the water ran over the sidewalks and through the yard.

The streets could hardly be called streets; they were little more than continuations of the country roads with deep sand beds in places. So rough were the roads that a farmer could bring only two bales of cotton on a two-horse wagon.

The system, used in buying and selling cotton in those days, was quite simple: "Cotton was brought to market and the wagons stopped along the streets and the bales were sampled and bought. Cotton was weighed on the scales of the person who bought it, and was dumped along the sidewalks. I have seen cotton bales piled along the streets in such heaps as to make traveling difficult."

Late each day a team belonging to Mr. George Cooper Epperson would haul the cotton to the Atlantic Coastline Depot, which was at that time a very small building with one man doing all the work.

Much of the cotton went to the merchants who did a lien business, providing the farmers money for making their crops. After they deducted the amount due them, they turned the rest over to the farmers. For a long time, there was only one cotton buyer in town, Mr. C.E. Stubbs. Of him the speaker said: "Such was his sterling honesty and such was the faith the country people had in him, that I never heard during the years in which he was a cotton buyer, a single complaint made against him."

According to the paper, the first bank was established in 1883, but "how people got along in commercial life prior to that time, I have no accurate recollection," said Judge Purdy, "except that I recall that Mr. John W. Dargan cashed drafts on out-of-town people and banks. He lived on the site of the present Post Office (now the Federal Building) and it was currently believed that he kept his money in a shot pouch, and this belief doubtless arose from the fact that in cashing drafts, he generally got the money from such a receptacle."

Continuing his discussion of the financial situation in Sumter, the speaker said: "The coming of a Bank to Sumter was the commencement of the revolution of its commercial history. Prior to that time, it was in the grip of Charleston, and no commercial enterprise was thought of being entered into until the money power of that city had been consulted. The money power then was its cotton and naval stores factors, and they exacted in one form or another a rate of interest which ranged all the way from seven to seventeen and twenty per cent. There was a short time during the period in which it was lawful to exact ten percent as interest."

The speaker recalled that before the turn of the century, there was only one place of amusement, the Academy of Music. He spoke, too, of the place of marketing behind the Academy. Purchasers, he said, took their own packages home. "I can well remember," he said, "the day that the first delivery wagon came upon the streets and what interest it created. Mr. Curtis, from Charleston, came up and opened a grocery store and brought up a delivery wagon and put bells on his horse."

It was Judge Purdy's opinion that this was the beginning of the increased cost of living in Sumter, for from that time, people began to require luxuries and prices began to go up. "Of course, everybody else in a commercial business had to add a delivery system to their business and naturally had to add to the cost of doing business. I might add that the originator of the business soon failed."

Back in the 1880's communication with the outside world was very slow. In those days "the Telegraph operator, one of the Brand boys, later high up in railroad circles – had a little wooden office and was operator and messenger all in one. . . . While he was delivering the message, the office took care of itself. I remember once he told me, with a great deal of pride, that he got half of the receipts of the office and that his share was twenty-five dollars a month."

In a further discussion of the communications systems of the time, the Judge said, "Although Mr. Bell, as early as 1876, was trying to get the public to believe that he had a means of communication by telephone, it was a long, long time, accompanied with a hard struggle on his part, before he could make people believe that one person could so communicate with another, and that the sound of the human voice could be transmitted over a wire."

Finally, four citizens – Dr. C.C. Brown, Col. J.D. Graham, A.S. Brown and Judge Purdy – decided it was time to try for some system in Sumter. They heard of the Stronger System in Chicago and bargained with that company to put a number of phones in Sumter. It was the speaker's recollection that only four telephones were installed, but the town paid the price according to the contract. And those four were soon out of order.

It was then that C.J. Mason was called in, remembered Judge Purdy, to see what was wrong with the phones. He took one to his shop and invented a part that was different from Bell's and thus began the Sumter Telephone Co.

Not only was communication poor at the time of which Judge Purdy was speaking, but transportation was equally slow.

"Thirty-five years ago," he said, "you could count on the fingers of one hand, the number of people living in town who kept horses and buggies. . . . Practically no one kept a horse for his private use. A man who kept a horse and buggy was looked upon as wealthy or extravagant.

"I remember when the first bicycle was talked about.

"The first 'wheel' that I recall was an old Rambler. Mr. Wiley McKain kept a livery stable . . . He had this wheel, which he kept for hire at ten cents an hour, and it was used for beginners. The writer learned to ride upon it, as did many others."

Before 1883, one could reach Charleston only by way of Florence or Columbia, but in that year the Central Railroad was built. Later the C.S.N. was completed, and later still the road from Sumter to Augusta. Then the Wilson and Summerton road was extended from Summerton to Sumter. These roads were followed by the Southern from the Wateree Junction to Sumter and the Seaboard to McBee. After these roads were built, Judge Purdy believed that Sumter had "one of the best railroad positions in the State."

The next topic discussed by the speaker was the fire protection which "consisted of a reel with a pump worked by hand. We had circular wells in the middle of the streets in the business part of the town, and when a fire broke out, the top was taken off the well, the pump dropped in and the boys pumped water by hand. Sometimes a fire was extinguished and sometimes the building burned. There was practically no protection against fire in the residential part of the town.

The following paragraph will give an idea of the crude method of lighting the town: "Prior to 1888 or 1889, the lights afforded to the town were procured from kerosene lamps fastened to the top of posts. Mose Harrison, an octoroon, the father-in-law of Dr. Birnie, was in charge of the lights. It was popularly believed . . . that old Mose cleaned the lamp shades as far down as his fingers would reach, and then cleaned his fingers on his face. . . .

"When one left the vicinity of the main square, he soon went into darkness. If one wished to have light on his way home, he had to carry his lantern. About 1888 or 1889 the electric light system was installed."

The speaker went on to say that the contract for the waterworks system was signed in 1890.

"Thirty-five years ago," remembered Judge Purdy, "Sumter had the most popular hotel in Eastern Carolina, kept by Mr. Jim Jervey . . . the building was owned by Gen. Moise, and was originally a large wooden structure, afterwards enlarged on one side. Travelers from every direction from which Sumter could be reached, within a radius of a great many miles, came in to spend the weekends. The reputation of this hotel continued for a good many years."

He added that there were only two other places where travelers could be accommodated at that time – Mrs. Brunson's, which was located where Courtright Chevrolet was a few years ago, and the Curtis House, near the overhead bridge on South Main Street.

In discussing the schools of this period, the Judge said that facilities were very poor for black and white.

He stated further that about 1890, "we agitated the question of building a public school, and the authority to do so was obtained with some difficulty." After the permission was granted, the first school for whites was built on the corner of Washington and Hampton.

He went on to pay tribute to Dr. S.H. Edmunds, "whose reputation as an educator is coextensive with the reputation of the schools which had been made under his management."

In connection with the growth of the public school system, he said that in 1890, "we undertook to put the colored graded schools under the management of the superintendent of our white schools, and it would not be amiss also to say that we have in the colored schools perhaps one of the best Negro teachers in the South, Martha Savage, who has been a teacher for perhaps thirty-five years."

In his recollections concerning the churches, Judge Purdy said that the churches were made of wood. The Catholic Church, he said, was on Liberty Street in front of "the residence of Mrs. Barrett." That would be across from Dr. Eddie Durant's office. The Episcopal Church was on the corner of Main and Bartlette where the Claremont Hotel stood until a few years ago. "The Baptist, Presbyterian and Methodist churches occupied their present sites, save that the churches have been supplanted by modern buildings."

Judge Purdy next gave some revealing information as to office management in the earlier days of his practice as a lawyer. "I can recall," he said, "the coming of the typewriter into active use and the bringing of the stenographer into the business life. They were adopted slowly in Sumter, and were received with a feeling of resentment and almost of scorn by the then most active member of the bar, Colonel Lee, who was a man of the greatest diligence and industry, never abating his energies in the discharge of his duties to his clients. For a long time after some members of his firm were availing themselves of the use of a stenographer, he insisted on writing out everything on his side of the office with his hand. He followed the custom that had prevailed prior to that time, of having two boards a little longer than the legal cap paper, with hinges to the board, and with cardboards and blotters. Copying ink was used on the papers, and for keeping records of letters tissue paper books were used, a blotter slipped between the leaves, which were moistened, and then one or more letters, usually the number that you wished to copy was inserted and the book was slipped in a big iron press and the handle turned on the book. Col. Lee insisted on following this practice not many years before he retired."

In speaking of the lawyers who practiced in Sumter and the state in the late 1800's and up to the time of his speech, he said, "I think I may, without disparaging any, say that for real oratory Gen. Moise had no peer at the bar, and he had few equals in the State, perhaps one other, in the person of Gen. Youmens.

"One of the most progressive citizens that Sumter ever had was Maj. Marion Moise, who was not only a successful lawyer, but the development of Sumter was largely due to his optimism. There was no enterprise that had any reasonable foundation that was presented to him by any man of character that was not financed by him. I asked him once what his financial rule was, and he said it was never to hesitate to finance any enterprise or to handle any paper if he believed in it. I have heard it said that after the day's work was over, he turned a crank at night, in order to provide money for the next day's promotions. It really looked as if this was so."

Sumter had no manufacturing enterprises even up to the time of Judge Purdy's address. He noted that there had been a small cotton mill once in the area, "which after several futile attempts at going, utterly failed, . . . We have a singular class of citizenship . . . and most of our citizens have an abiding faith in Sumter."

As always the financial needs of the town were met by taxes, but the speaker recalled that for the most part taxes in the late 1800's were almost nominal.

"The offenders against municipal ordinances," remembered Judge Purdy, "were summarily tried by the mayor, and there were many cases almost daily brought before him. The weekend usually brought into the Monday morning Court an array of soreheads and recent drunks.

In naming some of the leaders of that time, the speaker said that W.H. Cuttino was Clerk of Court. "He was an uncompromising prohibitionist, believing the day would come when prohibition would prevail in Sumter. He passed away fighting for it."

He mentioned Mr. C.M. Hurst, Clerk and Treasurer for many years, as a "man of very rare faithfulness in the discharge of his duties, looking after every detail affecting the financial interests of the town. While not required to do so, he kept in his drawer a bag of silver and took the trouble to relieve the wants of the employees of the town during the months as their needs required."

There was a time when Sunday was very quiet in Sumter. Few people were seen on the streets except at church-going time. Stores closed and no vehicles were in use, "horses were not hired at the livery stable."

With the coming of the bicycle, however, young people could be seen riding in "parties of two or three or more, winding their way out into the suburbs or into the country, and bye and bye, they commenced to ride around town. Then such vehicles as were available gradually came into use, and Sunday recreation, particularly on Sunday afternoon, increased. Since the coming of the automobile, such recreation as we all know, greatly increased."

"Social visiting from house to house has never prevailed to any extent, and there has been less change in this than in any other respect, and in this we have been a selfish people. Social intercourse has been carried on largely through meetings of organizations of different kinds."

Judge Purdy's speech ends on a philosophical note, as he contemplates a future for his beloved home town that would be an outgrowth of what had taken place before and during his time.

"It is needless to recite to those here the progress that has been made in the affairs of Sumter. They are everywhere manifest. This is due largely to the spirit of the men who make up Sumter, and not to any great financial advantages from outside influence, for we are supported largely by the good will of the agricultural communities reaching out for some distance from Sumter.

"The new generation has inherited the spirit of the older generation, with intensified optimism. How far this optimism can reach with safety, I do not dare to predict, because my vision is not sufficiently large to foresee what may be done, or what may happen.

"There are so few people, my contemporaries in age, who were here thirty-five years ago, that it makes me pause and consider. New opportunities for usefulness with an enlarged vision entails new and greater responsibilities than ever, and the recital of the things that have happened would be without avail if we do not look forward to the future and profit by the experiences that are behind us. It takes strenuous thought and strenuous action now to meet the demands of this age. How much further we may be called upon to enlarge our vision, I cannot conjecture, but we cannot stand still.

"There have been crowded into the past thirty-five years more and greater events than have been recorded for perhaps a hundred years prior to that time. If the human mind can grasp it, and human ingenuity can encompass it, and the same progress made in the next thirty-five years, it would not be an idle dream to imagine one traveling from one point to another in this country in almost a moment of time through a frictionless atmosphere by a means not yet in existence."

Life In Sumter County: 1900-1922

Some six months ago in these columns a "look-back" was taken on the governmental, business, educational and social life of the city of Sumter during the first quarter of the 20th Century. It may be of interest to follow up this brief view of the city with a look at some of the trends in the rural areas of the county during approximately the same period.

According to the United States census, an urban center must have a population of at least 2,500 inhabitants. Therefore, Sumter is the only true urban center in the county, the smaller towns such as Mayesville, Pinewood, Wedgefield and others being classified as rural areas.

Sumter County, a geographical unit of 574 square miles or 367,360 acres, had in 1920 a total population of 43,040,[3] an increase of 4,568 since 1910. The average density of population was 75 per square mile, the figure a decade before reading at 67 each square mile.

When the population of the city of Sumter, 9,508, was subtracted from the total, the rural areas were left with 33,532 people or 78.9% of the entire number of the county. Significantly the population of the urban area showed a greater increase from 1910 to 1920 than did the rural.

According to figures from the 1920 census there were three times as many Negroes as whites in the county. Since 1910 the white population had increased two per cent, however, and the Negro had decreased two and one-tenth per cent. In 1910 white males outnumbered white females by 212; but in 1920 the order was reversed, with females outnumbering males by 151.

Basis of economy in the county was agriculture with at least 75% of the population being engaged directly with farming. In 1920 the value of the leading crops was $14,200,441 and returns from industry amounted to $2,622,819. This tabulation referred only to crops, without consideration of livestock products.

The soils found in the county were suited to the growing of crops, though they varied in types from one part of the county to another. There were three principal kinds of soil, very different in origin. In the High Hills of Santee the types were sand gravel and sandy clay, ranging in color from brick red to pink, purple, yellow or white. These types of soils are known as Orangeburg sand loam, Orangeburg and Orangeburg sand and Orangeburg coarse sandy loam.

The level country, beginning just east of Wedgefield was composed of yellow sandy clay, with here and there iron stains. Those types were called Norfolk sand loam, Norfolk fine sandy loam, Norfolk coarse sand, Portsmouth sandy loam and Portsmouth fine sandy loam.

Along the Wateree River was a soil brought down from the Piedmont section. On other streams – Pocotaligo Swamp, Black River and Lynches River – were also found overflow soil deposits, mostly Norfolk fine sandy loam. This dark soil was very fertile and was easily cultivated.

As to minerals found in the county, so far as the commercial value was concerned, there were very few worthy of note. Sand, Fuller's earth, marls and clays usable for making brick were the only ones.

Forest lands in Sumter County at that time comprised a total of 187,194 acres, 101,000 acres of this being swamp lands. Growing in the wooded areas were trees of practically every variety native to the state. Pines in great numbers and various types grew in the hills section as well as in the lower lands. Some of the more numerous specimens of the pine family included the long leaf, found especially in the hills, the short leaf and the loblolly. In the swamps were hardwoods, oak, ash, poplar, gum and cypress. These timberlands constituted the country's chief "potential sources of wealth."

It was said later that in that period several million feet of timber was cut every month, and there was a legitimate fear that at such a rate the supply would be depleted in a few years unless some steps were taken to preserve or replenish this valuable natural resource.

In 1920 the assessed value of taxable property in the county was $11,202,891; while in 1910 it was $7,487,817. There was, therefore, an increase in 10 years of 51%. The per capita wealth in 1920 was $891.22. In 1910 it was $343, showing an increase in that decade of 170%.

The 265,759 acres composing the farmlands, according to the 1920 census, were divided into 4,897 farms, 19 of which contained under three acres; and 13, over 1,000 acres, the average being 54.3 acres with 24.2 acres improved for tillage. Thirty-seven per cent of the farming land at that time was lying idle.

It was hardly possible for a family to maintain a desirable standard of living on such a small acreage. Small farmers were unable to afford expensive machinery and fertilizers to improve their land. Most of the money for running their farms was obtained on the time-credit plan; thus the cost of growing and harvesting a crop was sometimes much more than if the farmer could have bought his necessary supplies on a cash basis. A look into the future caused Ralph Ramsey, Jr., author of an article in the bulletin entitled "Sumter County – Economic and Social" published in 1922, to say: "It is possible that the next few years will see a decrease in the number of farms, many small farm owners and tenants finding it more profitable under boll weevil conditions to give up their farms and work for wages."

The practice of depending on cotton as the basis of income for the farmers was one reason for the failure of the farms to afford an adequate living. In the first decade of the century cotton was the only non-food crop planted, but by 1920 tobacco had gained an important place in the agricultural economy. But not until the farmers began to realize that a cooperative effort in the sale of their products, was an essential to receiving a just price for their money crops, did they make their efforts bring in the best results.

In 1921 steps were taken to organize the first Cotton Growers Cooperative Association and tobacco growers began joining the Tri-State Tobacco Growers Cooperative Association.

It was during these years that farmers began to realize that corn, wheat, velvet beans, sweet potatoes, oats, in addition to being food crops, had a definite commercial value as well. In the decade, 1910-20, farmers became convinced that money could also come from livestock products. During those years every species of livestock except sheep increased. These changes in farming procedure were due for the most part to the County Agent and the Extension Department of Clemson.

Growing out of the increased importance placed by farmers on livestock products and the cultivation of food crops was the establishment in the city of Sumter of two industries. The Sumter Creamery, organized in April, 1922, with a capital stock of $30,000, was built to accommodate farmers not only of Sumter County but of the entire state. With L.D. Jennings as president and C.W. Smolke as general manager, this industry was designed to handle cream, milk, butter and ice cream. Its capacity was 20,000 gallons of milk, 10,000 gallons of ice cream and 100,000 pounds of butter each month.

The other new plant, begun in the spring of 1922, was the Sumter Canning Factory. The significance of this movement was that farmers could profitably grow all kinds of truck and have a market near at hand ready to receive and utilize their products.

Spinach, beans, tomatoes and sweet potatoes were the first products canned, at a rate of 20,000 cans per day. In addition to preserving the food stuffs grown in the county, the cannery added to the economy of the area by providing employment for 175 men and women.

In 1921 a group of farmers and businessmen organized the Wedgefield Peach Corp. With a capital stock of $10,000, the company was ready to begin operations. Serving as president was Hugh McLaurin, and J.P. Booth was vice president. As a beginning, about 100 acres of land in the hills around Wedgefield were planted in peach trees. The expectation was the harvesting of a full crop in four years.

The area in the High Hills of Santee was considered especially suitable for growing peaches. In addition to the acreage planted by the corporation, approximately 100 acres were planted by individual farmers. It was believed that Sumter County could become the leading peach-growing county in the state.

Some interesting facts concerning education in the county in those first years of the present century may be cited; however, there is no distinction made here between urban and rural areas.

A.H. Green, in an article found in the bulletin mentioned above, made the following comment: "Sumter County stands as a leader among the counties of the state in the efficiency of the teachers in the public schools. This fact is due to the high salaries paid. Those at the head of our educational system have realized that to secure efficient teachers they must be paid higher salaries."

This article then stated that only two other counties paid white men teachers more than did Sumter, the average being $1,931.40. White women teachers received an average of $754.78, the county coming second in this category. Negro teachers, however, received lower salaries, the county's rank being 10th in the state. Thus the total average was low.

There was also another side to the educational picture that was not so complimentary. Of the 126 schools in the county, both Negro and white, 95 were one-teacher schools – 30 white and 65 Negro. There were only 14 that had as many as three teachers.

Resolving in 1920 to improve roads in Sumter County, citizens voted a $2,500,000 bond issue to raise funds for this purpose. Their plans were at the time to build approximately 100 miles of asphalt – concrete roads leading into the city from all directions. One-half the cost of all bridges was met by federal funds. Federal aid also paid half the cost of the Sumter-Columbia highway through Wateree Swamp.

Sumter County had much to be proud of in those years after the turn of the century. Though many changes and marked improvements in countless ways have come in the intervening years, much groundwork was laid then for the progressive county that citizens, both urban and rural, enjoy and take pride in today.

A MODERN LOOK AT FARMING

Corn, soybeans, peanuts, onions, Jerusalem artichokes, muscadines and dozens more vegetables and fruits are found on the 300 or more acres of the Sumter Area Agricultural Development Project located near the Sumter Airport. Insect control methods, irrigation devices and demonstrations, Nematode control, and many other agricultural activities are carried on throughout the year.

The project was begun in 1970 on a 50-acre plot by agricultural leaders in the county, officials of the Sumter County Commission, Clemson University and Sumter Area TEC for the purpose of pointing up the importance of agriculture and the many complex problems of production and marketing of crops.

The program is funded by many volunteer participating units, agencies, commissions, private and public organizations and individuals.

In charge of all test plots, studies and demonstrations are Clemson University Cooperative Extension Service specialists.

In addition to the tests and demonstrations done by SAADP for the improvement of crop production, it serves as a learning laboratory for Sumter Area TEC agricultural mechanization students who do most of the construction work in addition to classroom study.

Director of the project is Agronomist Harvey W. Tiller, Jr., a graduate of Clemson University. He instructs these students in the classroom as well as directing them in the actual work on the project such as constructing buildings, laying pipe, wiring, etc. The classroom and agriculture mechanization laboratory was completed in 1973. This building improves teaching facilities for the course offered by TEC and provides a place for agricultural meetings and demonstrations on equipment use.

Tiller is well qualified for his position as instructor and director. He has been honored with a merit award by the National Conservation Society. He is a member of the Sumter County Development Board and the Beautification Advisory Board.

One of the objects of the project is to show the use of irrigation as a tool in the successful growing of crops. In 1973 the installation of underground mainlines for the irrigation system was completed.

With the idea of adding to the list of truck crops, commercially grown in this area, experiments were carried out in the growing of grapes, Irish potatoes, fall sweet corn, onions and other such crops.

Lawn grass and ornamental shrubs are grown and these plots serve as a site for teaching the development of nurseries and landscaping.

One of the interesting parts of the project is the nature trail used by preschoolers, Boy Scouts, Girl Scouts, Garden Clubs, Salvation Army, Boys Clubs of America and many other groups.

To encourage local people to engage in public gardening, the authorities lease each year 100 garden plots plus water for a fee of $20.00.

Visitors come from 14 states and 25 foreign countries, including Argentina, Mexico, Sweden, Australia, Indonesia, Malaysia, West Africa, Holland, Taiwan, England, Thailand.

Organized tours are conducted during the summer and fall each year with sometimes as many as 400 in a group. There are two tour "cars" designed and built by boys under the direction of Tiller. This year a high school field day was held with agriculture students from a number of schools taking part.

One of the interesting side projects enjoyed by both boys and instructor is the building and erecting of blue bird nesting boxes. The blue bird, one of the loveliest species, has practically disappeared from this area because it has nowhere to build a nest, with so many of the old trees gone; so the boys have furnished 10 "homes" and so far a few birds have made use of them. Tiller says he gets phone calls from far and near to ask questions and report results.

During the first two years of the project, 23 different crops with 241 varieties were planted with an estimated 200 treatments. Since that time much progress has been made with more and more experiments completed. The future of the Sumter Agricultural Development Project seems promising as an opportunity for farmers to use modern technology to overcome the majority of their production problems. It seems to be in reality "Solving Today's Problems for Tomorrow's Progress."

A Look At Sumter 1900-1925

During the first 25 years of the 20th century, Sumter experienced much activity along many lines. A few brief glimpses into the business, governmental, educational and social life of this quarter century will serve to show that as the second century of local history began, public-minded citizens were alert to opportunities for growth and improvement.

First we look at the business and industrial picture of downtown Sumter. As the new century began, streets were unpaved, as a picture that is familiar to all shows the wagons piled high with bales of cotton crowded together on a rough, muddy or sandy street. This photograph was no longer relevant, however, after 1908 when the paving of Main Street was begun. Brick was used for the first improvement project, which extended between Bartlette and Canal. This stretch of the main thoroughfare was completed in 1910, during the mayoralty of W.B. Boyle.

Conducting retail business in 1900 were merchants of varied types. V.H. Phelps opened a store for selling "Groceries and Fresh Meats" at 20 N. Main Street, and at the same time Levy and Moses were advertising Health Foods, such as Granose Flakes, Wheatlet, Parched Farinose, all of which were to banish medicines from the homes. Situated on the "Tuomey Block" was, in this same year, the Palace Shaving Parlor – a rather sophisticated name for a barber shop one might say. The Cash Dry Goods Co. was being operated at 7 South Main.

Four years later the J.D. Craig Furniture Store was doing business in the downtown area and W.S. Reynolds was running the

Headquarters for Sporting Goods at 108 S. Main. Plying his trade as a photographer, J.H. Winburn was located at 108½ South Main.

In 1906 DuRant Hardware was advertising a full line of hardware. That same year E.L. Bogel set up shop at 116 S. Main for selling bicycles and accessories. A very popular men's store was the D.J. Chandler Clothing Co., and Cuttino and Chandler were advertising as "Clothiers and Hatters" at 24 S. Main.

The Sumter Pressing Club was at 118 S. Main in 1906, and the Railway and Supply Co. was on Harvin Street. On North Main, No. 37, T.B. Jenkins was advertising the Reo as being "Just Right."

There was a music store in 1904 run by Prof. Schumacher. At No. 10 East Liberty he was selling music rolls, violins, mandolins, guitars, banjos, harps, Columbia zithers, "talking machines."

Hearon's Pharmacy opened for business in 1907 and remained for many years one of the most popular drug stores on Main Street.

There were many changes in 1911. A retail lumber yard known as the Central Lumber Co. was established at the "Foot of Calhoun Street." Witherspoon Bros. Furniture apparently opened in the same year.

The Sumter Marble and Granite Works was founded also in 1911, with Joseph Palmer Commander as "sole owner and manager." The first location was on Manning Avenue, but the business later moved to the corner of Magnolia and Hampton. The New York Bakery was making "Mother's Bread," and the Star Restaurant invited "Ladies and Gents" to come in to eat.

W.G. Stubbs was the "Tailor and Haberdasher" at 14 S. Main. Through many of these 25 years, O'Donnell and Co. operated what might have been called a department store, selling dry goods, household furnishings as well as "Staple and Fancy Groceries."

Dry cleaning establishments came to be lucrative businesses in this period. Both the Bee and Dee Cleaners at 28 W. Liberty and Kirkland Cleaners, 25 W. Liberty, opened in 1925.

A.J. Hatfield opened his auto and truck parts business at 140 N. Main in 1919, and in 1920 Tom Evans began operating a garage at 142-144 N. Main. In 1921 the Nu-Idea School Supply Co. was begun by R.H. Tucker.

There were several banks in these early years: The Farmers Bank and Trust Co. was organized with C.G. Rowland as president; R.F. Haynsworth, vice president; R.L. Edmunds, cashier. Also the Bank of Sumter was operated by Richard I. Manning, president; Marion Moise, vice president; W.F. Rhame, cashier.

Neill O'Donnell was president of the First National Bank and O.L. Yates was cashier.

Sumter's economy was aided by several manufacturing firms. Two of these were the Machinery and Manufacturing Co. run by Davis D. Moise, president, and E.W. Moise, Jr., secretary and treasurer; the Sumter Machinery Co., a firm known for its high standard electric and mill supplies.

The real estate business seemed to reach a high spot during this period. James R. Ligon was a realtor and insurance agent with his office at 106 S. Main. White and McCallum were advertising the following properties among several for sale: 7-room, 2-story house on the northwest corner of Calhoun and Washington and an 8-room, 2-story structure on the Southeast corner of Canal and Washington. One interesting real estate transfer was given as follows: Bishop of Charleston to R.D. Lee, Neill O'Donnell and S.C. Baker, executors, lot on Liberty Street, $3000.

These few miscellaneous items are an indication that business was booming as the new century began.

Farming, too, had an important place in the economic picture of city and county. An item in **The State** in 1923 mentioned the specialization trend in Sumter County in the breeding of Guernsey, Duroc Jersey and Rhode Island Reds strains of cattle, swine, and poultry.

A very active Farmers Union was in operation with E.W. Dabbs as president. In 1910 the Union organized the Union Brokerage Co. as an enterprise for the benefit of farmers.

Encouragement was given to young people on the farms. The Union was offering prizes to members of the Boys' Corn Club in the same year. A little later (1913) Miss Mary Lemmon began tomato club work.

As to the population of the town in 1911, dissatisfaction was expressed concerning results of the 1910 census. Although authorities were convinced that the Federal count would not be changed, 20 loyal citizens volunteered to take a new census. It seems that Sumter's count is given to inaccuracies, since there was a similar complaint in 1970.

In 1912 Sumter set an example in city government that has been followed by more than 1,000 cities and towns in the country. Feeling the need for a more business-like form of government, Dr. S.C. Baker directed the Chamber of Commerce, of which he was the very strong president, into a place of leadership in seeking a change.

After much study and discussion, the Council-Manager plan was favored by a referendum. L.D. Jennings was re-elected mayor; C.G. Rowland and J.P. Booth were chosen as councilmen. This was a happy choice since diverse interests were represented. Jennings was described as an "aggressive progressive"; Rowland, a "hard-headed conservative economist and banker"; Booth, "a successful businessman experienced in several lines" and considered a "balance between Jennings and Rowland."

The first duty of the Council was the choice of a city manager, a choice which seemed to have been made by the trial and error method. The first man, an engineer who had no business or administrative background, was completely overshadowed by the dominance of a strong council. He lasted only a year. The next man chosen was no more successful, resigning in less than a year.

There followed several other men but none "filled the bill" until Robert L. McLeod, who had the advantage of having served on the Council previously, took the position and made his weight felt. He remained as the very successful manager until he accepted a position with the South Carolina National Bank.

Other efficient managers followed McLeod, proving that the Manager-Council form of city government, the first such experiment in the world, can and does succeed.

In the educational picture much progress was made, though most schools had their beginnings in the preceding century. However, there were a few public schools built in the county in Pinewood in 1908 and in Mayesville in 1909.

In 1915 the Carnegie Foundation granted $10,000 for a free library in Sumter and promised to provide $1,000 annually for the upkeep. The building behind Washington School and Academy Square was completed in 1917. The importance of this library to the intellectual growth of young and old can scarcely be described.

However interested Sumter citizens have been in good books and literature, the community has comparatively few literary figures of note. There were some magazine and newspaper articles, pamphlets, and books published in the 1900-25 period. Just after the turn of the century Miss Kate Furman, of the Privateer section, using old papers and account books of her ancestor, William Murrell, wrote "An Old-Time Merchant of South Carolina." She also wrote "General Sumter and His Neighbors." Both of these were published in "Publications of the Southern History Association."

Mrs. Octavia Harby Moses' verses for children were collected under the title "A Mother's Poems" and published in 1915.

Thomas Childs authored a unique volume, titled "Wooden Works of Thomas Anonymous," in 1904. This book contained 30 wooden pages held between walnut covers with brass rings.

Life on the "Old Plantation in Ante-Bellum Days" or "A Story Based on Facts" by Rev. I.E. Lowery, son of slave parents who lived on Puddin' Swamp near Mayesville, was published in 1911.

An example of local humor is a record of children's "boners" kept by Mary Hughes Girardeau, a teacher in Sumter for many years. This pamphlet, "Pupils' Potpourri," was printed in 1902.

Another book of reminiscences was "A Genealogical Record With Reminiscences of the Richardson and Buford Families," written by Elizabeth Buford Richardson and printed in 1906. "The Singletons of South Carolina," another genealogical endeavor was written by Virginia Eliza Green Singleton and published in 1914.

Two textbooks – "School History of South Carolina" by John J. Dargan, and "Little Clusters: A Mixed Method for Beginners" by Lucie Bragg Anthony, M.D., were published in 1906 and 1925, respectively. The "Foreword" for the latter was written by the Rev. J. Bentham Walker.

Though in the period under consideration in Sumter history there were no outstanding composers, the city had a fair share of musicians and music lovers. A recital given in 1904 by the pupils of Miss Ammie Teicher and Professor Schumacher was received with great interest and praise.

On the social scene there was a variety of "doings." The town turned out for a great affair planned for the returned soldiers on Armistice Day in 1919. (Much against the desires of some veterans of World War I, the name has been changed to Veterans Day.)

The Kiwanis Club observed Ladies Night with a Halloween Party in 1925. Witches, goblins and all personalities of the day were used in favors and decorations. The committee, consisting of W.R. Plowden, W.B. Burns, Jr., S. O'Quinn, A.M. Broughton and L.A. Corning, went all out to make it a perfect occasion.

Dances were enjoyed in those days. One was announced for Providence Springs (near Dalzell). The train arranged a schedule to transport the revelers to and from the dance.

Another dance was held at Second Mill in 1925.

These occasions were only typical of the many social functions planned for the young folk, and the older ones, too.

The present version of the Y.M.C.A. was begun in 1910. This institution, known for its physical and spiritual training, has had a wholesome influence on the youth of Sumter, "graduating" many of Sumter's finest leaders. At first its quarters were at Liberty and Sumter Streets.

The football hero of the era was Allen Ralph (Buck) Flowers (in Football Hall of Fame), who was named the "greatest player" on the 1920 Georgia Tech team and was called the "All-American" player.

Older citizens, in looking back, may note that much of Sumter's current life harks back to the early years of this century, and trends begun then influence significantly the high standard of living enjoyed in city and county today.

Early Transportation Problem Here

In South Carolina's early days, transportation must have been a very serious problem.

The Gaillard-Cook map of 1770 shows only two roads in what became Sumter District – The Great Road or King's Highway and the Black River Road. On Finley's map of 1827 is shown also a main road, going north from Nelson's Ferry through Sumterville and dividing at Scape Hore (O'er) Swamp.

By an act of the legislature in 1795, Commissioners of Roads and Bridges were appointed. One of the improvements made by these men was the chartering of DuBose's Ferry over Lynches Creek in 1798. This ferry was located on what is now the highway between Bishopville and Darlington.

Another act that had to do with transportation was passed in 1806 authorizing the "laying out and keeping in repair" of a road that would connect Stateburg with Sumter's Landing in the Wateree, a distance of six or seven miles.

In 1798 a law was passed to provide for a road to run to the Santee Canal through Salem, Claremont and Clarendon Counties, thus making progress toward opening up a nearer way to Charleston from this area at the completion of the canal.

The problem of transportation was still existent in Sumter in 1894, as seen from a letter appearing in **The Daily Item** of October 25 of that year from "A Lady Reader."

"Dear Item: I notice that Mr. Julian Fishburne is about to build an electric steel railroad in Charleston, S.C. Could you not agitate the subject so that a Julian Fishburne would do the same for our city? We have lights and water and now want street cars badly."

Edwin Scott in his **Random Recollections** tells of the condition of at least one road traveled by the settlers in the eastern part of the District.

His father kept a tavern in Sumterville around 1806, and during court week all the rooms were filled. In order to get young Edwin out of the way, he would send him to his grandfather, William Anderson, who lived beyond Black River near Brick Church. He recalls that the road he had to travel was narrow and crooked. There was swamp water on each side and he describes the way as "gloomy, hazardous, and sometimes impassable."

This road was later improved, according to Scott, by Matthew

Muldrow, former Commissioner of Roads.

(It may be mentioned here that there were two kinds of taverns in that day – the one with a questionable reputation where men gathered to buy and drink liquor ("groggeries"), the other in reputable standing, similar to inns, hotels, or motels today, where travelers could obtain food and lodging).

From **The Sunday News** of Charleston, May 20, 1923, is a news story relating to highway construction in the state at that time. One paragraph reads: "Motorists going between Columbia and Sumter over Wateree bridge which has just been opened to traffic are advised to go by Eastover on the Richland County side of the bridge in order to avoid construction work."

Commutor Accommodations Available

In the early days of Sumter County, travel was slow and tedious because roads were inferior and round-about; in spite of the handicaps, however, many found it necessary to travel long distances. Because of the inconveniences suffered by those who were forced to make long trips in wagons and buggies or on horseback, hospitality houses sprang up along the more traveled routes. In Sumter County there were many of these. At first they were called taverns.

One of the earliest of these stopping places was that of Sherwood James, one of the first settlers in the area known as the "High Hills of Santee" (Sante'). This tavern was a popular resting place for soldiers during the Revolutionary War and is believed to have existed until the 1790's."

No doubt the earliest one in the town of Sumterville was Scott's Tavern, which was operated from 1806 until 1811 by his father as told by Edwin Scott in his **Random Recollections of a Long Life**.[4] It was especially popular during "court week" when many out-of-town people were on hand to attend the sessions of the court.

Because of some unsavory activities at some of these places, the word "tavern" was less often used in referring to rooming houses.

As related by Dr. Gregorie in her **History of Sumter County**, there stood on the west side of Main Street at Liberty, Werner Macon's Hotel[5] and it was taken over by James Watson in 1832 and sometime later by D.B. McLaurin. In 1841 Alfred China was running the business and he was followed by John China, who refitted and enlarged the hotel and provided stables for 52 horses; but in 1856 it was in the hands of the sheriff for debt.

W.K. Bell purchased the property at that time and two years

later it was bought by Noah Graham and Son.

Across the street on East Main, the Agur T. Morse tavern was open for customers. Morse later sold the property to Archibald R. Ruffin and two years later he sold it to Tyre J. Dinkins. It was in this hotel during the 1840's that a drum was beaten every night to mark the beginning and end of the town watchmen's duties.

Somewhat later a bell was used instead of the drum. During this time the business was known as Windham's Hotel. It was later kept by Fed Meyers and called the Sumter House, with the name being later changed to Meyers' Hotel.

In 1862 Mrs. M.C. Clark was advertising the Confederate House, which occupied the place of the Pool House. She was inviting her old customers and the traveling public to patronize her new establishment. Her advertisement appeared in the **Tri-Weekly Watchman.**

Another popular stopping place in Sumterville was the Jervey House, the owner of which had an interesting history as told in the **Review of the State of South Carolina.** Vol. III published in Charleston in 1884.

Coming to his home in Charleston after the Civil War in which his father and two brothers were killed, Col. J.E. Jervey, S.C. Rangers, Company D. 5th South Carolina Cavalry, Hampton Legion, found his mother, seven sisters and one brother refugees in Manning. He worked for a while around Manning, but in 1869 he moved to Sumter and soon began his hotel in a little brick house near the depot, doing most of the work himself.

He catered to the first-class trade of transients and soon found it necessary to enlarge. He erected a large building on Main Street near the business houses. It was the largest frame building in town at that time, having three stories. He furnished the 23 sleeping rooms with good beds, and whoever stopped at the Jervey House had a good word for it.

In 1934 a large hotel was built at 132 South Harvin and was advertised as a place where the "needs of tourists received attention." It specialized in "good food, comfortable rooms and excellent service."

This was known as the Imperial Hotel. It was in an excellent location near the depot since in those days many "drummers" or traveling salesmen rode the trains.

As roads were improved and people began using their automobiles, more, the hotel lost its customers. The same was true of a number of other "hostels" in Sumter.

One of the finer hotels that prospered in Sumter was the Claremont, built in 1914 by Wise Granite Company, and was said to have been a haven for traveling salesmen, who often found it convenient to spend more than one day in a town.

Claremont provided six "sample rooms" for these salesmen where they might show samples of their wares to the merchants who came to see what the salesmen had to offer and to place orders for merchandise with which to stock their shelves.

As mentioned above, business for a while became slow for hotels as traveling conditions improved. However, after World War II there was a marked increase of business. Claremont was encouraged to remodel in 1955. An automatic elevator and 40 air conditioning units were installed. A bus station was constructed next to the hotel.

Then in 1965 this fine, up-to-date hotel burned and was never replaced.

Another large hotel was the Fladger which was owned by John and Florence Fladger. He had been in the hotel business for 18 years. The entrance to this hotel was on Highway 15, one half block from the overhead bridge. Though popular for a while it, too, lost its usefulness.

Others such as the Calhoun House, the Curtis House, Central Hotel may be remembered by an older generation.

Now in the time of good roads and faster means of transportation, motels prove more convenient for travelers, but no doubt some type of accommodations for travelers will always be needed.

Reminiscences of Sumter's Beauty

In **Carolina Gardens,** E.P.H. Shaffer states that according to the official report of the Commissioner of Agriculture, Commerce and Industries, Sumter had "eleven acres of municipally owned and maintained parks; many miles of tree-shaded streets, that the trees are provided for in the annual city budget."[6]Shaffer learned also that the city at that time was noted for its public and private gardens.

One of the moving spirits for the beautification of Sumter at that time was Julia Lester Dillon. Not only did she grow beautiful flowers, she inspired others to do the same. She helped plan Memorial Park and was instrumental in carrying out every detail in making it a place of beauty in the heart of Sumter and was responsible for its upkeep.

Mrs. Dillon, an accomplished writer, pictured the beauty of her town in articles that she might attract others to see the importance of growing flowers and trees for the beautification of the city and to have a part in making the city a place to be appreciated by residents and guests.

In an article published in **The Sumter Daily Item** in 1938, she told of several other park areas in and around the city. One covering 33 acres, found at the Water Works and Pumping Station was a real spot of beauty with lovely old oak trees in spacious green lawns.

In the same article she described a woodland tract of 45 acres on Liberty Street near the industrial section of the city. There one could see long leaf pines, sweet gums, sycamores, chestnut trees, various kinds of oaks, hollies, magnolias, crab apples, sourwoods, hawthornes, myrtles. She mentions, too, rustic bridges over the drainage ditches, a house for picnics with table and benches, a rustic spring house, "covering a flowing well." This lovely spot, she said, was enjoyed by tourists on Highways 76 and 54.

Mrs. Dillon noted with praise every citizen who made an effort to beautify his or her home. She mentioned in other writings a number of men who were enthusiastic gardeners. Among these was Mr. T.H. Siddall, Sr., who grew fine chrysanthemums and dahlias as well as roses. She cited Mr. Hubert Osteen for his prize-winning dahlias. He was praised, too, for his camellias, azaleas, iris, lilies, gladioli. Other growers of dahlias on her roll of honor were Mr. Clarence Haynsworth, Mrs. Brooks Bultman, Mr. H.C. Bland, who was widely known for his Japanese Iris. Dunndell was also mentioned where Dr. J.R. Dunn has hundreds of lovely plants of many kinds. Among the men specializing in roses, she spoke of Dr. Robert Bultman, Mr. Martin Rosefield and Mr. Eugene Moses, Sr.

Many women, in addition to Mrs. Dillon herself, took great pride in their gardens. These included: Miss Ellen Siddall, Misses Polly and Julia Obenschain (the latter growing medicinal flowers at the hospital), Mrs. T.M. Brice, Mrs. Ramon Schwartz, Miss Janie Mikell, Mrs. E.K. Friar, Mrs. R.C. Williams, Mrs. K.K. Skinner, Miss Emily Spann.

Shaffer, in his book, wrote especially of the beauty of Sumter's streets. He spoke of the residential streets as being "green Gothic aisles between their bordering lines of trees." On his visit he was especially impressed by the "cared for, vigorous appearance" of all the trees. Of peculiar interest were "many notable old willow oaks along the streets, some measuring five feet in diameter, six feet above ground." He estimated more than 300 trees on the parkways, and he praised the "Sumter plan of long street parkways planted with trees and ornamental shrubs."

Years have gone by since these observations were made and Sumter is still a beautiful town. Many garden clubs are enthusiastic in planting trees, shrubbery and flowers for the beautification of streets and parks. In most yards azaleas, camellias, dogwood and other flowering shrubs make the town a place of great beauty most of the year. Men and women still take pride in growing their favorite flowers.

But few streets now have the magnificent old trees for which Sumter was widely known at one time. Mrs. Dillon, Mr. Shaffer and many others must have felt about trees as did Lucy Larcom when she wrote:

"He who plants a tree
He plants love.
Tents of coolness,
spreading out above
Wayfarers he may not see."

In 1920 white citizens of Sumter, with a sincere desire to honor those men from the county who had given their lives in World War I, bought six and a half acres in a residential section of the city at Hampton and Park Avenue and gave it to the City Council, requesting that a park be developed in memory of those brave men. What a wonderful thought! For is not the beauty of flowers and trees symbolic of the spirit of those who were willing to make the supreme sacrifice!

The spot selected was indeed a happy choice. Here once stood the spacious home of the Blandings and later of the Bowmans, two of Sumter County's leading families. Already many stately trees, planted by those who had loved these grounds, stood in majestic beauty.

And how fortunate were those who had dreams of a place of great beauty that they were able to secure the services of Mrs. Julia Dillon to plan the park and direct the work to be done. Given two men, Bob and Poss (as they were called), to help with the work, she soon began to attract visitors to the new park. Skilled in the science of horticulture, gifted with a "green thumb," and inspired by a love of beauty, she made the park into a dreamland of loveliness, and a place where all could come and find enjoyment. Each day she could be seen headed for the park in her little one-seated car with her little dog beside her, and for each day she had many definite plans. There were no idle hours and soon results began to show.

For the backgrounds, she planted trees and thick shrubbery of many varieties, some unknown in Sumter. There were borders of magnolias, hollies, Photinias, Ligustrum, Japonicas, Carolina cherries and Japanese oaks. Here and there were stately Himalayan cedars, Italian cypresses, junipers and spruce.

For color there were pyracanthas, which in spring were white with blooms and in fall and winter loaded with orange and scarlet berries. Nandinas with their rich red berries made bright spots in winter.

The park was a haven for all kinds of birds for they could find food there in abundance. And an attractive bird bath gave them water and a place where they could refresh themselves.

And flowers were everywhere – each month having special favorites. Flowering shrubs and flowers were planted so that colors would harmonize. There were pink and white dogwoods, spireas, red bud trees, philadelphus and pearl bushes. Daffodils, in different shades of yellow and pansies furnished color beneath the taller shrubbery. Pink crab apples were grouped with Chinese forget-me-nots; while beneath white flowering almonds were daffodils and dark blue larkspurs. There were plantings of white flowering peaches complemented by golden forsythia and yellow jasmine. In summer there were crepe myrtles and altheas.

On another side was a border of ferns, azaleas, Japanese iris, mountain laurel and myrtles with a background of tall evergreens. To give color at different seasons were beds of gladioli, larkspur and phlox. There was a border of iris of varied shades 250 feet long with here and there dogwoods and flowering crab apple trees.

Blooming at different seasons were patches of cornflowers, stokesias, candytuft, poppies, columbines, sweet Williams, snap-dragons, delphiniums, zinnias, marigolds, daisies.

Near the main entrance on Hampton Avenue stood a pergola with climbing roses covering the columns and lattice work. Here the May Queen was crowned each year and the Maypole dance was one of the exciting forms of entertainment.

Swings to suit every size were hanging in one area for the children's enjoyment. In another spot was a giant swing for the older and more daring ones. See-saws were also placed conveniently for those wishing a quieter form of pleasure.

Another source of delight was the wading pool, shallow enough at one end for the smallest tots and a little deeper farther on for the larger ones.

Protected by shrubbery near one side of the park was a small fish pond containing many pretty goldfish, which the children enjoyed watching.

Comfortable green benches were placed here and there and used by the nurses as their charges were playing.

Most joined in the active games such as "Farmers in the Dell," "Blind Man's Bluff," and other children's games. There were acrobatic stunts with prizes, and each year the Trolley Car parade claimed the attention of the whole town.

Near the back of the park at the end of the shrubbery and flower-lined walk from the main entrance was the band stand. On Friday nights there were band concerts conducted by L.C. Moise or Mr. Girard. During the daytime hours Mrs. Dillon taught here those who were interested how to knit, crochet, embroider, make dinner napkins, potholders and other articles. She was an expert in all kinds of hand work.

Susan Moore (now Mrs. Ray Hamilton), who as a little girl lived on Calhoun Street, recalls that her backyard joined the park and that she spent much of her time with the many other children who came to the park every day to play. She remembers the Rowlands, Eppersons, Boneys, Beamans, R.T. Browns, Palmers, Burnses, Brogdons, Nesses, Blandings, Bulls, Roaches, Cockerills and others who frequented the play areas all during the summer months in good weather.

Her father, Mr. Moses Moore, Sr., kept an eye on the park at night to guard against vandalism.

There was something in this lovely place for everyone. For the older young people – high school and college age, three excellent tennis courts were kept up. These were in constant use, for at intervals there were tournaments that encouraged much practice.

Older people, too, found the benches, nestled in the midst of flowers and shaded by lovely trees, a place for relaxation. Miss Julia Reynolds tells of three who found enjoyment there in pleasant weather. Her two aunts, Mrs. Benjamin Hodges and Miss Margaret Reynolds, and a friend, Mrs. Beattie, sought out a desirable spot in the park for hours of friendly companionship. While two did fancy work, the other read aloud.

Because of her love for children, Mrs. Dillon planned for their pleasure; they loved her dearly and followed her rules to the letter, even counting carefully the number of pansies they were allowed to pick.

Her influence is still felt in Sumter, for her love of natural beauty was contagious; and because of her, many of the beautiful gardens in the city were begun. It is said that many came to the park to ask questions about the growing of plants that were unknown in this area before Mrs. Dillon introduced them. She said, "Memorial Park represents the development of an ideal," and this ideal was truly an inspiration to the people of Sumter.

The Park is no longer the center of relaxation and recreation it once was. Though the tennis courts have been improved and are still in use, the park has lost much of its attraction. However, it is a reminder to older citizens of its former beauty and the purpose for which it was developed.

Sumter's Iris Festival

The 1980 Iris Festival was the "best ever" with a full week of activities with something exciting for every age group.

With lapses during World War II, 1941-1947, and from 1956 to 1960, this Festival has been a highlight in the life of Sumter. It centers around Iris Gardens during the last week in May and attracts crowds from "all over" to Sumter.

The first Iris Festival, planned by the late J.J. Brennan, was sponsored by the Kiwanis Club, May 24, 1940.[7] Thousands of people from all parts of the state came to Sumter to enjoy the beauty of Iris Gardens, developed by the perseverance and skill of Sumter's own lover of natural beauty and philanthropist H.C. Bland. Completing plans for this festive occasion was J. Cliff Brown after Mr. Brennan became critically ill.

Events of this first Iris Festival included a swimming contest at Pocalla Springs, a parade, a May Day party, sponsored by the ladies of the YWCA, and a formal ball at the armory as a climax. Iris Queen chosen that year was Sara Harvin, and Jim Singleton was King.

The 1941 Festival was under the auspices of the Sumter Chamber of Commerce, assisted by business organizations of the city. It proved equally successful.

Because of the deep involvement of Sumter during the years of World War II, the idea of a Festival was abandoned temporarily.

The colorful affair was revived with the addition of several attractions in 1947. Again the Chamber of Commerce was the sponsor, and chairman of the program committee was H.D. Osteen, with Horace Harby as the Parade Marshal. This festival began with an outstanding air show at Shaw AFB and ended with a ball game at Riley Park. Chosen Queen that year was Lou Ann Baumann and Frank Singleton was King.

In 1948 the Festival was known in many parts of America as "the South's most colorful floral festival." Head of the steering committee was T. Doug Youngblood, manager of Radio Station WFIG (World Famous Iris Gardens).

Eighteen young ladies from various parts of the state came to Sumter to enter the "Queen Iris – 1948" Contest, and a number of distinguished guests, among whom were Governor and Mrs. Strom Thurmond, were on hand for the festivities. The biggest parade ever – a mile long – was viewed by some 50 thousand men, women and children from different parts of the nation.

As the time approached for the ninth Festival, it was decided that since the event had grown so much, a steering committee was needed to take care of all the numerous details involved. The committee with officers and directors was elected and that procedure has been followed since that time. First president was T. Doug Youngblood, and he was supported by other officers and 14 directors.

During the 1949 Festival, a number of events were added;

namely, another evening ball, a water carnival with the choosing of a "Bathing Queen" from the Queens visiting from other cities in the state; an Historic Pageant, tours of Swan Lake and Dundell Gardens, a band contest, field day events and possibly others. The Festival now lasted six days instead of the original one day. And it continued to grow.

In 1956, however, the lack of funds forced the city to abandon the Festival temporarily. But four years later Sumter's famous Iris Festival was revived and it has continued as an annual event since that time. From year to year, new attractions such as athletic events, activities for children and for senior citizens, contests, etc., are added.

The Iris Festival committee for 1980 consisted of: John Edens, 1979 ch.; Burke Watson, Jr., 1980 ch.; Ken Holt, co-ch.; Danny Chandler, special events; Margaret Harris, exec. sec.; Jim White, treas.; Cecil McCaskill, "Queens" ch.; Andy Purvis, parade ch.; Jim Stubbs, Jaycee pres.

Firemen Deserving Of Gratitude

Firemen, those men who risk their lives day or night, summer or winter, merit the admiration and gratitude of all citizens in every community.

Fire is a ruthless force, leaving death and destruction in its wake; and if its ravages are to be halted, it must be met by courage and strength. Those valiant men who fight this merciless enemy are the members of the fire department in any town, city, or country community.

In the beginning years of America, the only fire-fighting groups were those sponsored by insurance companies for the purpose of protecting property insured by the companies. As time passed, however, local groups formed "bucket brigades" and those with a neighborly spirit were ready to lend a hand when someone had a fire.

When Sumter was only a village composed mostly of wooden buildings, the danger of wholesale destruction was voiced editorially in **The Banner**: "Let not our village smoulder in ashes as soon as it has awoke (sic) to enterprise." Not much interest was aroused, however, until a fire in the jail yard burned to death a slave woman and her three children. It was said that the only thing that saved the village was the fact that there was no wind.

Awakened to the danger, men organized the Sumter Volunteer Fire Department. This outfit owned an old hand pump which was dragged by hand through sand or mud (streets were not paved) to the well nearest the fire. A suction hose was dropped into the well and the fire fighters began to pump by hand, thus throwing a stream of water on the burning building. Since pumping was very tiring, other men relieved the pumpers at intervals. If the fire was extensive, often the water in the well dropped below the reach of the suction-pipe; and then the blaze could easily get out of control while the fighters were waiting for the water to rise again.

The largest "downtown" well was at the corner of Main and Liberty Streets; smaller ones were located at other intersections. If the fire was in a residential section, the well in a neighbor's yard was used.

This first fire department was composed of volunteers from the businessmen of the town, who gave much of their extra time to this cause.

The next step in the development of fire prevention was the "steamer." This machine was also hand-drawn at first, but it eliminated the work of pumping by hand. The steamer was used until the completion of a waterworks system.

At this time four hand-reel squads were organized. Of these four, the "Delgar Number 3" and the "Monaghan Number 2" not only survived, but increased in numbers and interest. These squads pulled the reels to the fire and attached the hose to the source of the water supply, the pressure of which was so strong that two men were needed to hold the nozzle.

The two squads kept up a friendly rivalry; thus their strength and skill were increased steadily. There was always a race to see which would arrive first at the scene of action. It is said that growing out of this rivalry was the "most efficient fire department in the South."

Finally the Delgar squad decided to purchase a horse to draw its reel. A one-horse wagon with a step at the rear and a set of "quickhitch standard fire-department harness" completed the outfit.

To meet competition the Monaghan squad bought a pair of horses, known throughout the state as Billy and Barney. Immediately the "Delgarites" bought a second horse to complete a team. Both groups then bought regular fire department wagons and the improvement continued. Money for most of this equipment was raised by the men themselves (with the help of the ladies) through annual bazaars that sometimes lasted two days and two nights. Many donations were made by able citizens of the town and by those who had been helped and who wanted to show their gratitude.

It was necessary for members of these squads to meet strict qualifications and new members were taken in by the vote of the group. It was considered an honor and privilege to belong to one of the squads. Members were closely bound by a strong sense of devotion to duty, and as a result, the department was very efficient in its service to the town. Their enthusiasm was boundless and all derived much pleasure from the social occasions sponsored by the squads.

Some of these early firemen were H.B. Bloom (chief), Capt. Willie Graham (who was killed fighting a fire on South Harvin Street),[8] Allen Filbert Flowers, John B. Miller, H.W. Hood, E.S. Miller, Ebb Wells, Sol J. Ryttenberg, H.G. Hill, C.B. Yeadon, W.R. Phillips, I.A. Ryttenberg, Douglas China, and H.T. Folsom.

Serving as chief of the department for several years was R.S. Hood, who was followed by E.H. Lynam. Upon Lynam's retirement, C.V. Wilder became the chief and served until his retirement on June 30, 1971. Robert White then became chief, but served only two months. From September 1, 1971, till January 1973, the Fire Department was operated under Public Safety Director L.W. Griffin. At the end of this period, T.A. Green became chief and is still serving.

The department is examined every 10 years by Southeastern Insurance Engineers in Atlanta, Georgia, for the purpose of classification. Many things enter into the judging: city water supply and pressure, alarm system, age and condition of fire fighting equipment, the manner in which records are kept, etc.

As of January 1980, the Sumter Fire Department became Class III, one of only five in South Carolina to receive this rating.

The city department is now housed in three stations, one main headquarters building, located in the Civic Center, on the corner of Hampton Avenue and Magnolia Street, and two substations. The first substation completed in October of 1973 is on Alice Drive. It is called the Lynam Station in memory of the former fire chief. The other substation is in the lower section of the city on Highway 521. It was completed in February 1977.

In addition to their duties in fighting fires, members of the department have regular drills and instructional programs. They are skilled in first aid and resuscitation procedures.

They must know all changes in city safety laws, all streets, building codes, location and condition of all hydrants; in fact, they must be familiar with every phase of city government.

All volunteers must have completed the minimum of basic fire fighting training.

The City Fire Department now operates seven pumpers, ranging from 750 to 1000 GPM pumping capacity, two mini-pumpers, one of which was built by the men of the department for approximately one-half the cost of a factory-built unit. The equipment also includes two tankers and two rescue trucks having "Jaws of Life." (Shaw Air Force Base has the only other such unit in the county.) These units are called to the scene of an automobile accident or a drowning. Aerials of 65 and 100 feet are also a part of the City Fire Department equipment.

The department still has the "steamer," for which they have built a trailer. It is displayed in parades.

There are 60 full-time members of the department who work 24 hours and have 24 hours off. And there are 300 volunteers.

The Sumter Fire Department has a close connection with the State Fire Marshal's office in Columbia.

With all the improvements made in the Fire Department of the City of Sumter, the county for a long time had little protection against destructive fires. But as time went on, the people realized that something should be done to relieve the need in the county. In 1956, therefore, concerned citizens were able to approve a referendum that required a rural fire department for the entire county.

At first only eight stations were established, but the number increased until by 1973 there were fourteen.

There were still many glaring needs. The volunteers lacked protective clothing and formal training. Maintenance of the apparatus was far from adequate. Then in 1973, the city and county agreed that the County Fire Department would come under the direction of Fire Chief Green, who from that time has been responsible for rural, as well as urban fire protection.

The rural fire department has now 15 stations located at strategic points to make available fire protection for a five-mile radius from each. Each station has a pumper, while four also have tankers. Others will receive tankers as finances permit.

The entire system is so organized that fire calls or other alarm calls come to the city department by means of the "911" emergency dialing number. The dispatchers in the city, after determining the nearest station to the emergency, alert that station. At the same time he alerts volunteers through monitors installed in the homes of the volunteers. If the emergency requires, other stations are alerted.

There are many problems facing rural fire protection, but the greatest is the lack of water for battling large fires. Though some communities have water systems, most do not.

The hazards that face all members of the Fire Department are many and great. Suffocation from lethal smoke, especially since synthetic materials are so widely used in home furnishings, is a grave danger that these men face when entering buildings to rescue occupants. Falling walls always pose a threat. In short, the life of a fireman is under tremendous pressure at all times and it is found that the lifespan of a fireman is 10 years shorter because of his chosen career. Therefore, citizens owe a great debt of gratitude to these servants of their fellowman.

Old County Post Office Had Two Unusual Names

Usually there is some reason for a name; families often derived their surnames from the occupation of the first male in the line of descent. Places have been called by the name of the first settlers or from some characteristic of the area in which they are found or perhaps in honor of some illustrious citizen.

At the turn of the century, however, there existed a Post Office of seven years' duration that was called by two names, no reason for either of which has been found so far.

Former Postmaster W. Loring Lee, Jr. learned that there was a Post Office established in Privateer Township, Sumter County, by the name of Soeven. Intrigued by the find, Mr. Lee wrote the Historical Section of the United Postal Service in Washington to get any available facts concerning this old Post Office.

In answer to his inquiry, he received in brief the date of establishment of Neason and the discontinuance, of the name Soeven, as well as names of the postmasters, along with a note stating that for the payment of a dollar an electrostat of the "site location report relating to the Soeven Post Office" could be had.

The dollar was sent and the additional information was received. Since that time other research has been made by several interested persons in order to locate additional information concerning the name.

This Post Office was situated on what was known as Cane Savannah Creek, ten miles east of Wateree River and seven miles southwest of Sumter.

It was established on November 26, 1898, as Neason, with the name changing on October 1, 1900, to Soeven.

The first postmaster was Miss Susie Jackson, who later married a Mr. Miller and moved to Richmond, Virginia. Her brother, Willis Jackson, took her place as Postmaster on October 1, 1900. According to the information received from Washington, the office was discontinued on April 16, 1906.

From another source came the information that Rural Free Delivery from Sumter began with Route 2, which served this section in 1903, with J. Brogdon Jones as the first carrier. (Incidentally, he remained in this position until 1915.) Since Soeven remained open until 1906, there must have been a duplication of services for three years.

It has been determined that the office, first named Neason and later Soeven, was kept in a large room made of logs built onto the home of Willis Jackson and his three sisters – Misses Susie, Ida and Iola – and his brother, Mack, for a while. The old home is now occupied by John E. Follin, a rural carrier and local representative of the National Letter Carriers Association, and his family. Since moving into this old home several years ago, the Follins have done considerable remodeling, covering the original log portion with siding. Still seen in the eight-inch wall in the door opening in that part of the house are the wooden pegs used in securing the logs. The large room has been divided into two smaller rooms, the inside walls being covered with paneling. The original ceiling, made of wide and narrow boards, has been kept.

A number of old letters addressed to Neason and Soeven are in the possession of Mr. and Mrs. Fallow Jackson. Some of these carry the postmark on the back. Brother of the two Postmasters, Thomas J. Jackson, was the "star route" carrier, taking mail to and bringing mail from Sumter for Neason or Soeven two or three times a week. His mode of travel was a road cart drawn by a mule. Thomas J. Jackson was the father of Fallow, who recalls hearing his father tell of the hardship connected with the job. He told of occasions when in cold weather his breath or the rain (when it was raining) would freeze on his moustache as he rode along in the open cart.

Surely in those days could be applied to the mail carriers the slogan of the Persian postal system, credited to Herodotus, the Greek historian, who lived around 425 B.C.:

"Neither snow nor rain nor heat nor gloom of night stays these couriers from the swift completion of their appointed rounds."

Some Of Sumter's Street Names

Most names of people and places have significance related to other persons, places or occupations. There are, of course, exceptions to this custom.

When the little town of Sumterville was laid out, there were only eight named streets. The chief street, running north and south, was known as Broad; but the reason for this choice of a name is not known. Sometime later the name was changed to Main.

From the beginning Harvin Street, named for either William R. Harvin or the Harvin family, ran parallel to Main from Republican Street to Marion, named no doubt for Francis Marion, (now Calhoun).

By vote of the City Council on Sept. 24, 1902, the name of

Republican Street was changed to Hampton Avenue probably in honor of Gen. Wade Hampton. It was possibly named in the beginning from the regime of the four presidents, who were known as Jeffersonian Democrats and sometimes Republicans (1801-1828).[9]

These are four of the only named streets on the original map. Two others running north and south were Sumter and Washington. The reason for their names is obvious.

Liberty was shown on the map a block below Republican but Main and Harvin did not intersect this street. At the places of the present intersection was shown a pond.

The street now known as Canal was on the map as Decatur so named probably for Stephen Decatur, a naval hero.

Warren Street was possibly named for Gen. Warren Moise, who owned land in that section of the town as early as the 1860's.

Dugan Street, only two blocks long, was named for Thomas Dugan, who came to Sumter from old Mt. Hope Plantation a few miles from Sumter on Highway 15. He served as a state representative and senator from Sumter (1830-1838). His home was on the northwest corner of Main and Dugan Streets.

Other streets named for specific reasons include: Alice Drive, formerly Camp Alice Road for the camp built for tuberculosis patients, which was on that road and named for Alice Harby, a victim of the disease; Caldwell Street named for a teacher in Sumter around the turn of the century.

Salem Avenue, originally known as New Street, is said to have been given its present name by George D. Shore, Sr., who came to Sumter from the old town of Salem in North Carolina. However, some think its name came from two divisions of Sumter District Upper and Lower Salem Counties.[10]

The present Trinity United Methodist Church once stood at the intersection of Liberty and what is now Church Street, which took its name from the church.

Charlotte Avenue was named for Charlotte Anna Brunson Roach, whose home was on the southeast corner of Main and the present Charlotte Avenue. The home was built for her by her father, W.L. Brunson, who owned much of that part of Sumter, his holdings extending as far out as the location of the Eastern Star Home. The Roach home was said to be the oldest home in Sumter at the time when it was demolished.

The names of two other streets were connected with the same family. Loring Place was named for Capt. Lucius Pitts Loring, son-in-law of W.L. Brunson, and Anne Park for Mr. Brunson's granddaughter.

Mason Croft Drive is on property that was formerly owned

by C.T. Mason, Sumter's well known inventor.

Guignard Drive received its name from Guignard Richardson, a wealthy landowner in that part of the city.

Bartlette Street was named for a minister, Rev. J. Lyman Bartlette.

The Lafayette Highway Association, an organization involving cities from Raleigh, N.C. to Savannah, Ga., was instrumental in completing a paved highway between those two cities some years ago. The highway, which goes through Sumter, is known as Lafayette Boulevard from the name of the group that made it possible.

Through the years Sumter has extended its limits in all directions and many additional streets have been laid out and named for various reasons. Many are named for flowers, such as Buttercup, Wisteria, Periwinkle, etc. Others bear family names – Cuttino, Hunter, Martin, Porter and many others.

There are a number with unusual names. Some of these are Gordonia, Docel, and Mineola.

A further study of the origin of names of streets might be of interest; but whatever the names, though in some cases they have lost their significance, there was some reason for the naming; and the names tell something of the city and its citizens.

A Venture Into Storybook Living

How tastes in reading have changed in the past 50 years or more!

And the oldtimers who delighted in those books, written in the early 1900's, will agree that literary tastes of today show no marked improvement.

Louisa M. Alcott's "Little Women," "Little Men" and "Jo's Boys" are real classics that are seldom read in this sophisticated age. "Anne of Green Gables" and other "Anne" books by L.M. Montgomery were choice reading for the young folk of another generation.

Perhaps one of the most popular series written around the turn of the century was "The Little Colonel" stories. These books followed Lloyd Sherman, a petite Kentucky girl, from her fifth year till the time when she married her Prince Charming and "lived happy ever after."

She was called the "Little Colonel" because she was so very much like her grandfather, Colonel Lloyd, who lived on a beautiful Southern plantation. He pined for the days when his beloved wife Amanthis was living, before his only son had been killed in the War Between the States, where he himself had lost an arm, and before he had disowned his only daughter, the "Little Colonel's" mother, because she had married a Yankee; but he received no sympathy because his temper was explosive and his tongue was sharp.

The little namesake wandered into forbidden territory one day and stopped to eat strawberries in her grandfather's prized garden. Never having seen his little granddaughter, Colonel Lloyd did not know who she was. He scolded her soundly for having the audacity to help herself to his berries and even to feed them to her little dog. Then when he asked her name, she replied, "They calls me the 'Little Cun'l,' 'cause I'm so much like you . . . I'm got such a vile tempah, an' I stamps my foot when I gets mad, an' gets all red in the face . . . "

Thus she pictured herself at five, but those temper tantrums were short-lived. She was lovable, sensitive to beauty, kind-hearted, mischievous at times but never with an unkind intent. And as she grew older, her disposition became more even and her unselfish impulses endeared her to all who knew her.

Is it any wonder that such an attractive and unusual girl should captivate the imaginations of a group of little girls and make them want to be like this charming Southern miss?

When a sixth grade teacher in Sumter, Miss Lydia Richardson, read one of the books in the series to her class of girls, the other stories became a must in their reading. As they lived out the stories, identifying with the characters, they decided to form a "Little Colonel's Club." Enthusiasm was great as 10 little girls made plans for their organization which began in 1911. The insignia of membership was a diamond-shaped pin inscribed with the letters LCC in gold on a black background and bearing the date of the club's beginning (1911).

Dorita Moise (now Mrs. August Kohn of Columbia) spoke to be the "Little Colonel," while each of the others selected one of Lloyd's friends with whom to identify. Kittie Stubbs (now Mrs. LeRoy Davis) remembers that she was Rob Moore, the one whom the "Little Colonel" married. Phil, an earlier sweetheart, was the part taken by Frances DeLorme (Mrs. J.J. Roche). There were many other attractive characters "played" by the others in the club.

Officers such as any organization would have were duly elected. Caroline Dick (Mrs. Irvin Belser of Columbia) was the first president. Kittie Stubbs served as vice president and Dorita Moise as secretary. Since there were no dues, the group did not need a treasurer.

Regular meetings were held every two weeks at the homes of the different members, and Dorita's father, Harmon Moise, by common consent, was honorary publicity chairman, publishing in the local paper a colorful account of each meeting. Only a few of these graphic reports have been kept these 50 and more years, complete dates for which are missing but most seem to have been written between 1914 and 1916. Those of earlier and later years have been lost in one way or another.

The account of one meeting, which was held at the home of Elizabeth China, began thus: "Recitations on the piano forte occupied the first period . . . " After a business session was held and the girls had enjoyed sewing for awhile, "the doors opened on the dining room and all the 'Little Colonels' joined in leading the charge through them to the most beautiful table of royal viands spread bounteously for them in lovely fashion. Apple seeds contained in the fruit on the table were consulted from which their number were to determine interesting questions hitherto veiled in mystery – as to future alliances – the results, however, will be deleted by the censor, so they may as well be omitted." The report continued with the announcement that the next meeting would be held at the home of Frances DeLorme, "where next the assemblage may renew the happy hours of the meetings of this club, which seems to grow and flourish like the rose."

At the meeting just before Christmas, the girls subscribed to a fund to be turned over to the associated charities for the needy.

As an indication that these girls were diligent as well as fun-loving was the fact that a part of each meeting was given over to needlework. In fact, some of the members were so industrious that they sewed while business matters were being discussed.

Some of Mr. Moise's most vivid reports concerned the refreshments served at each meeting. Of one occasion he wrote: "An alluring and bountiful collection of dainties so seductive was arranged over this long to be remembered table that no urging was required to insure a full attendance and the attendance became rapidly fuller and fuller."

One meeting took the form of a planned program with the following members taking part:

"A paper on 'The Origin of the Little Colonel Club' was very entertainingly read by its author, Miss Dorita Moise.

"Miss Caroline Dick set all a-laughing with a great collection of jokes selected and read by her in her own inimitable manner." (Like father, like daughter those may think who remember Dr. Dick's vast store of anecdotes.)

"Miss Kittie Stubbs convulsed everyone with her characteristic musical act, imitation of violin and other instruments.

"A solo by Miss Grace Reynolds and a poem by Miss Elizabeth China from a classic author were followed by a word forming contest in which the prize was a delicious bottle of toilet water, won by Miss Sadie Herbert.

"Miss Margaret Blanding on the piano rendered some stirring music to the great delight of the attentive audience.

" . . . and last of all the charming numbers came the mock marriage, long to be remembered, as indeed was every part of that pleasant session, by all who were so fortunate as to have been one of the number."

Another club, "Aunt Jane's Nieces," one year entertained the "Little Colonel Club" with a Halloween party at the home of Mary Knight. And a party it was to surpass all parties!

The setting was described in these expressive words: "The walls all hung with grinning lanterns around, and black cats coiled to spring, and owls with wide-stretched eyes glowed from the deathly shrouds from window, wall and frame."

Girls in both clubs were dressed in costumes representing Halloween, historic, and fairyland characters. Hilarity reigned as they discovered who was who.

After games and refreshments, weird ghost stories were told and "Ever more and more tense the interest grew . . . "

The happy occasion could be summed up by one sentence from the pen of Mr. Moise: "Oh joy is unconfined when youth and pleasure meet to chase the flying hours with dancing feet."

Though the meetings of the club were important to the girls, as well as entertaining and enjoyable, they were only a part of the interest in the organization. Much of their time these ten girls spent together embarking on many adventures.

Dorita was the proud and envied owner of a black and white pony, a carriage, a goat and a goat cart. Naturally her home was the popular place for all to meet. Sometimes they rode in the carriage or cart. At other times they rode the pony, and at least once some had "a spill" from his back.

A popular pastime was a picnic, the favorite place being the school yard, then popularly known as "the green." The bandstand was the perfect place for spreading their sandwiches, cookies and other goodies wheedled from their mothers for the occasion. The ten were usually seen together at school and groups of them "divided" lunch with one another.

It was their desire to make the club permanent; but when they separated at the end of high school, meetings were impossible except on holidays and during vacation.

Finally these friends, now grown into young ladies, found that it was necessary to give up their venture into "storybook living."

Trolley Parade A Charming Tradition

Mary had a little trolley
She built its frame with care,
And up and down the street she went
Showing her trolley fair.

Yes, scores of Marys, Johns, Dicks and Janes in each generation for more than 60 years have built their "trolleys" in Sumter and shown them with pride.

An additional entertainment for the kiddies this activity has been and – so far as is known – has belonged to Sumter alone. Who was responsible for the idea in the beginning is not known. (Could it be that someone living in Sumter today was the "inventor" who brought so much joy to so many?) Nor is it known definitely just when the first "trolley" was built. Beyond a doubt, it was as early as 1904 or 1905, and 1901 has been mentioned as the possible beginning of the "business."

At any rate, many years ago some ingenious boy (or was it a girl?) heard somehow that trolleys were vehicles of transportation (Sumter has never used this form of conveyance) and decided to "invent" one. Little did he know that he was starting a tradition that would become a real part of Sumter's juvenile population and would gain momentum as the years passed by.

So successful was his "model" and such a winsome salesman did he prove to be, that the idea immediately "caught on." The friends of this first "genius" began to use their imaginations in designing and constructing their trolleys. Soon all the little heads in the neighborhood were buzzing with unique ideas. Parents, too, were caught up in the enthusiasm of their children and began lending their aid in the building boom.

In order to show off their handiwork, the owners of the trolleys planned a parade in which each proud owner would draw his trolley by a string attached to the front. All the neighbors would come out to view these "marvels" of invention and construction. Parents beamed with pride on the accomplishments of their off-spring. It is thought that the first parade ground was "The School Green" on the corner of Washington Street and Hampton Avenue. "It was a beautiful, gay parade," said one who was a witness many times and perhaps a participant in some of the shows.

At first the materials needed for the construction of these masterpieces of ingenuity were few indeed: one or more cardboard boxes (any size or shape), thin, brightly colored paper, flour paste, candles and a piece of cord (just the right length).

Sounds simple, doesn't it? But, oh the thought and skill and patience that went into the making of these little vehicles!

Cut in the sides of the boxes were "windows" of various shapes – square, oblong, round, cathedral. These were covered with brightly colored paper through which light from the candles that were placed inside would shine.

If a second "deck" was desired, a smaller box was attached to the top of the first with similar openings in the sides. Sometimes even a third "story" was added. Decorations were placed on the sides and top to carry out different themes; such as, nursery rhymes, famous buildings, modern scientific ideas, comic strips and countless other ideas that may take form in the active brain of youngsters.

For many years the tradition continued solely as fascinating entertainment for the children (and grown-ups, too).

In 1916 or 1917 the parade became a part of the city recreation program and was the big event of the year, taking place each August. The parade ground was later transferred to Memorial Park. Each year designs for the trolleys became more intricate and skills necessary for construction more complicated. More materials were needed for the more elaborate patterns. Little wagons were sometimes used instead of boxes, and after one or two trolleys overturned and caught fire from the candles, flashlights were substituted.

Gradually as the classic event became increasingly important, involving greater numbers of children, some of the stores in Sumter offered prizes; such as, comic books, balloons and lollipops, for the winners selected by chosen judges. The more formal contests necessitated the formulation of rules and regulations. No child over 12 could participate; different categories were set up. In one, those who worked alone submitted their trolleys; in another adult help was permitted. At one time a group working together could enter a group project.

In 1948 the parade received newspaper publicity for the first time. Advance articles were published and the results were listed. That year music was provided by the Sumter Municipal Band. There were 72 entries and 800 turned out for this unusual "spectator sport."

As always in such affairs, many young hearts beat high with happiness; while many boys and girls went home disappointed because their "trolleys" didn't perform properly or for some reason their efforts were not rewarded.

In the most beautiful category that year the trolley receiving first prize was the one entitled "Wedding Party" made by Edna Suber. The second most beautiful was "Merry-Go-Round" by Marty Upshur, and Virginia Ann Harvin was in third place with

"Mistress Mary Quite Contrary."

Sidney Stubbs, with his large "Steamboat," walked away with first prize in the "Most Original" classification. Ricky Compton's "Circus Wagon" was in second place and Lynn Johnson won third prize for "The Old Woman Who Lived in a Shoe."

Prizes for most artistic were given to Patsy Wells for her "Lighthouse," Helen Edmunds for her church, and Sammy Pringle for "An Army Hangar."

In some years records of contests were not kept in detail. Sometimes only the winners were named with no mention of themes; while results of contests in other years were not recorded.

Among the 44 entrants in 1955, winners included: Betsy Clark with "Little Miss Muffett"; Jeannine Rogers, "Mary, Mary, Quite Contrary"; Chip DuRant, "Davy Crockett"; Jane Strother, another interpretation of "Mistress Mary –"; Arlene Edwards, "Sweetheart." All of these were done with adult help.

Blue ribbons won by those who did their projects without help went to Jane Jenkins (Hill), Frances Jenkins, Howard Jennings, Randy Tisdale and Angus McDuffie. Jane recalls that her theme was "Life in Iran." She used a little wagon on which she arranged authentic Iranian dolls dressed in the costumes of the country. The peasant wore a full draped garment made of a dark material splashed with large brightly colored figures. Her head was covered in similar material. Strapped to her back in a pouch was a native baby. The dress of the noble lady was made of the finest material in shades of blue and red. It was beautifully embroidered with beads and jewels. Her headdress was a long flowing scarf of very lovely material. Center of interest in the scene was a camel with a double pack. It seems that in that country the camel is an important animal and wears sweet-toned bells that enchant the ones who hear (especially Americans in Iran) as it walks down the main street of a village.

Frances Jenkins recalls her search for materials to portray the First Presbyterian Church, with its lovely colored windows, showing Bible characters.

In the same contest Martha Jenkins, with help from her mother, won a second place for her "Statue of Liberty." She used a doll to represent the "Lady" and somehow attached the torch to give the right effect. Martha remembers that her choice was very difficult to perfect.

These examples give some idea of the amount of thoughtful effort that went into these undertakings. However, the tradition has never lost its charm, and each year there is the same enthusiastic participation.

The 1970 show was held at the Fairgrounds and competition was among the recreation centers with three categories judged.

In the "most beautiful" classification, first place was won by Memorial Park; Jenkins Center was first in the "most original"; Crosswell won in the "most artistic" category. The "best in the show" honor went to Mt. Pisgah.

Imagination, extending into an exciting and delightful form of entertainment for little friends in a small neighborhood, has grown from year to year until it has become a major project of the City Parks and Recreation Dept. Although it may involve more children and draw attention from a greater number of people, it brings no more joy than did those first creative efforts in the long ago.

Family Christmas

Some folks inherit money
Which really isn't bad.
But I wouldn't trade with anyone
The heritage I've had . . .
The art of gracious living
A thrill from simple things
And Joy and Peace – the true import
The Christmas season brings.

This little verse was penned by the late Irene Bryan. Some years ago she recorded in her memory book her recollections of Christmas celebrations that she and her close-knit family enjoyed when she was a child. In her telling she carries the reader back and helps him or her to feel the excitement that filled the old country home for days before Christmas. Sisters and brothers detected an air of secrecy as "Mother" and "Aunt Mary" worked feverishly on gifts while the children were out playing. When one came into the house under the pretext of getting a drink of water or a toy, objects were quickly hidden under the folds of the long full shirts or aprons – the fashion in those days.

Irene's sister Abbie added some details at this point in the narrative that somehow Irene omitted. The house was decorated, says "Miss Abbie," with holly leaves and berries, sprays being placed on the mantel, the table, over the pictures – anywhere it was possible to attach a twig. Thus the home took on an air of festivity and the children had a share in the preparations.

Long before Christmas the brothers and sisters pored over a well-worn J. Lynn & Company Catalog to select their choices. The two music lovers in the family ordered pink song sheets and enjoyed singing the songs they knew and making up tunes for those they didn't know. The boys usually wanted pocket knives and the girls chose pretty little rosebud stick pins which cost a penny each. Sometimes one ordered a ring with "Dear" or "Darling" on it at a cost of seven or nine cents. These could not be worn long at a time, remembered Irene, because they "would 'blue' one's fingers."

One day just before Christmas they were all packed into the surrey for the exciting nine-mile ride to Sumter to spend the 25 or 50 cents they had made picking cotton or had saved up through the year. They had dinner with "Aunt Eva" and "shopped" at Scaffe's Racket Store.

After seemingly endless waiting Christmas Eve would finally come. After "Mother" read the Christmas story from Luke 2 and had prayers, and a glass of milk and a slice of cake were placed near the fireplace for Santa, the children were sent off to bed. Long before daylight, however, they were awake, ready to examine those long stockings borrowed from "Mother" for the occasion.

Someone would build a fire and the great moment was at hand. One of the "prizes" was an orange in the toe of the stocking. This orange was precious because it was possibly the only one the children would see for a whole year. Then there were raisins, nuts, and homemade cocoanut candy. Each child received some special gifts such as a scarf, cap, mittens, a pin cushion, pen wiper or other treasure which had been made by the loving mother and aunt as Santa's helpers. Each girl also received a handmade doll and the boys, a knife and package of firecrackers. How thrilled each one was! And Sister Abbie added her remembrance of their shouting up the chimney, "Thank you, Santa!"

After the stockings were emptied and each gift was admired, all were ready to meet their father who was just arriving home from St. Charles where he had worked late on Christmas Eve night. He had to travel the 25 miles by wagon, reaching home just in time for a wonderful breakfast of country sausage, hominy, batter cakes and molasses.

One of the most reassured recollections of those Christmases back in the late 1800's was the traditional dinner and Christmas tree at the three-story home of "Grandma Carson" at "Homefield" plantation near Dalzell, then called Scarborough.

Early after breakfast the whole family would start out to spend the day, some riding and some taking the half-mile short cut through the woods and over the board footbridge across the branch.

The parlor doors remained closed all morning, but the children were ever on the alert to catch a glimpse inside as the adults went in and out to tend the fire in the large open fireplace or add something to the tree.

Finally the hour for dinner arrived and all were seated – the grownups and older grandchildren at a long mahogany banquet table and the younger ones at a smaller round table all using the best china and silver. All held hands as grace was said. Then food was brought in by "Ma'um Lizzie," "Aunt Kate," and "Munchie" and perhaps other servants. And what a feast to delight the eyes and appetites! All the essentials of a Christmas dinner were there – turkey with "stuffing," rice, ham, macaroni, etc., etc. For dessert there were cocoanut and mince meat pies.

After dinner the parlor doors were thrown open and there it stood – an immense Christmas tree reaching to the ceiling and the ceilings were high in those days. What a magnificent sight it was with colored paper decorations and many many twinkling wax candles. And best of all a gift for each one. Again the gifts were homemade in most cases, but young hearts were thrilled. And the servants were not forgotten. Each one received something useful.

After the excitement of the tree subsided, the grandmother sat at the upright piano and played while all joined lustily in the singing of Christmas carols.

As darkness came on, all went out to look on as the boys shot their fireworks. When the supply was exhausted, they shouted "Merry Christmas" and reluctantly departed for home.

Other old folk have spoken of the close family ties of those early days, the use of decorations from nature, the emphasis on the spiritual meaning of the day, the enjoyment derived from simple things. Many of these believe that today with all the elaborate "store-bought" decorations, the gala celebrations, the breathless activity in preparation for the holidays, expensive gifts, young people are missing too often the vital part of Christmas – the love, joy, peace that came to the world that first Christmas more than 2000 years ago when the angel announced to the shepherds " . . . unto you is born this day in the City of David, a Savior which is Christ the Lord." (Luke 2:11)

Fall Festival Once A Colorful Event Here

Around the turn of the century, Sumter was not lacking in entertainment and festivities of various kinds.

One such occasion, as reported in **The Evening News** of December 1, 1904, was "Sumter's Great 'Fall Festival,' " in which there were two colorful events: the Floral Parade and the Tournament.

The Parade was described as "truly a thing of beauty" with "the many carriages, buggies, and motor cars decorated most elaborately." Heading the parade, which formed on South Main and moved up to Liberty, on to Warren, and back to Liberty, were Chief Bradford and "a cordon of police mounted on horses." Following these was the Second Regiment Band. Chairman Levy came next "driven by Mr. Abe Ryttenberg." "Marshals" W.S. Jones, J.M. Knight, C.S. McFaddin, Douglas China and C.L. Stubbs were next.

Then came the "magnificent chariot, all in white, drawn by four white horses, and driven by Mr. Harry Reid. In this sat the stately Queen, Miss Burdell, and her maids of honor, all beautiful with youth and joyousness." Miss Rosalie Moses and Miss Marie Moise were the maids. Looking like "heralds of old" were the "outriders to the throne carriage, Masters Waverly Levy and Marion Pauling."

Following the Queen's carriage was Mrs. J.A. Mood (winner of first prize) "driving a magnificent pair," and "her carriage was a mass of roses."

Some others in "elaborately decorated" vehicles included: Mr. Davis Moise, in a "solid white victoria," accompanied by Mrs. Moise, Mrs. Bogin, and Mr. I.H. Moses, all in "complete white"; Mrs. George Epperson, in purple, driving a double team; Judge Horace Harby in a trap of green "covered with thick clusters of red oak leaves"; Dr. Archie China, whose vehicle was decorated with holly; Miss Nina Solomons (second-place winner) in a Japanese trap; Monaghan Hose Wagon, "dressed in its colors with a large fire bell of gold and black." There were two "autos" in the parade, one driven by "Mr. McKeown" and one by Harry Hood.

At Warren St. the parade was joined by the "graded school children" in costume with Superintendent Edmunds heading the procession on horseback.

When the parade drew up in front of the courthouse, Mayor George W. Dick "made a short address of welcome to the queen and her subjects."

In the contest for the best lady driver, the judges – "Messrs. Graham, Harby and Booth" – stood in front of the courthouse while the contestants drove up and down the block, "two vehicles at the time." First prize winner in doubles was Miss Lola Brown and second prize went to Miss Emma Boyle. Mrs. I.C. Strauss won first prize in the singles event, and Mrs. H.M. Stuckey was second place winner.

Prizes for the Floral Parade were $15 for the first double and $10 for the first single. Second prize in each was $5.

In the contest for best lady driver, first place winners received "handsome lace collars," and second place winners, two lace handkerchiefs.

Judges for the Floral Parade were Mrs. Adrena Moses, Mrs. J.M. Knight, and Mrs. A.D. Harby.

The second event of the Festival was the Tournament, the course being on Dingle St. between Washington and Council. Witnessing this exciting spectacle were approximately 1,700 people.

Knights taking part were Blanding Durant, Charlie Durant, R.E. Durant, T.O. Sanders, A.L. Ardis, Warren Moise, R.H. Ervin, J.D. Shirer, J.D. Truluck, J.E. Truluck, J.W. Boykin, E.E. Spann, H.P. Brown, J.M. Brown, M.B. Wilson, S.P. Oliver. There were also five "Burlesque Knights" – Peter May, Jr., Walter Folsom, H.W. Cummings, Weslie Burkett, W.V. Wilson.

Winner in the Tournament was R.E. Durant, having taken eight rings. His prize was $50 and a suit or overcoat donated by the D.J. Chandler Clothing Co. In the Burlesque Category the prize was won by Mr. Peter May, Jr., riding an ox.

The most successful unmarried contestant, Mr. J.W. Boykin, according to the rules, was permitted to choose a queen. His choice was Miss Louise Durant, who received a "handsome coronet" and a silk coat "contributed" by Sumter Dry Goods Co.

Review Of Past Presents Challenge To Future

"Study the past if you would divine the future." – Confucius.

The first month of the year was named January from the Roman god Janus, pictured by the ancients as having two faces. Thus January looks back on the old and forward to the new.

As a new year in this 20th Century is begun, Sumter citizens may profit by a backward look to the time when the first settlers of this area struggled against tremendous odds in order to produce a good life for their descendants to enjoy.

The Land East of the Wateree, as this section was first called, was full of promise. The acres of fine timber and the rich soil lured many hardy souls from other parts of the country to come here, seeking greater opportunities. In the western part, known as the High Hills of Santee (Sante') many land grants were secured from the King of England. The first, according to Dr. Gregorie in her **History of Sumter County**, was Isaac Brunson, who settled on his land around 1740. Claiming grants a little later were Matthew Singleton, Sherwood James, Wood Furman and others too numerous to name.

From the same source is the information that David Anderson lived on Black River in the eastern part of the area in 1842, but he did not claim a grant until much later. Many others – Henry Cassels, James and Samuel Bradley, William Wilson, to name only a few – soon made their claims and settled in that section. From time to time other families, hearing of the promising features available moved into the area which later became known as Sumter District. (Later still Sumter County was formed and Sumterville, the village, grew into Sumter the city.)

But growth didn't come overnight. Life was hard for these early planters. The men worked tirelessly, cutting timbers to build homes that in the beginning offered few comforts. Cultivation of the land was very difficult with the few farm implements available.

Finally, however, by hard work and much sacrifice, they began to succeed with their efforts. Cotton was the chief money crop, but at first the lint had to be separated from the seeds by hand. Then with great difficulty, the cotton was transported by wagons over well-nigh-impassable roads to Charleston to market. Most of the supplies also came from Charleston.

Country children had few educational opportunities in those early times in this area. Parents sacrificed much to secure teachers for short term schools or for home tutoring.

Bringing with them the faith of their fathers, these early settlers, as soon as possible, established places of worship. The earliest churches were St. Mark's Episcopal and High Hills Baptist on the east and Salem Black River (Brick) Presbyterian on the east. Because of poor travel facilities, it was difficult for families to attend services in very severe weather, but they were faithful. Then one by one other churches were begun and today there is a church within easy reach of every person in the county.

There were no conveniences in those days. The telephone nor telegraph had been invented; therefore, news from other parts of the country or world took several weeks to reach this area, according to Edwin Scott in his **Random Recollections of a Long Life**. He also reminds the reader that there were no matches. One either kept a candle or fire burning or used flint and steel to start a blaze. Quills were used for pens and it cost 25 cents to take a letter to a distant destination. Scott noted that as late as the 1820's water was supplied to those living on the surrounding squares from a pump on the Court House corner in Columbia and from this pump buckets were filled by the firemen when there was a fire. If this was true in the capital city, what must have been the conditions in the country communities?

Much of the Revolutionary War involved Sumter District, which was the camping ground for the Red Coats on many occasions. Women and children were kept in constant terror since most of the men were with the troops. Crops were necessarily neglected and food was scarce.

During the Civil War, similar privations and dangers were faced.

After this war the so-called Reconstruction was, in some respects, harder to bear than the war itself. The whole state was poverty-stricken. Public buildings and some homes were burned by Sherman and Potter and there was no money to replace them. Railroads were destroyed, countless bales of cotton were burned, and animals, so necessary for tilling the soil, were confiscated. It was difficult to restore good government and there was much crime. However, wise heads were at last able to restore order and conditions began to improve. But it took many years to regain what had been lost by war and its aftermath.

Through the years, from the first settlement of Sumter District to the forming of Sumter County, to the beginning of Sumterville, to the present, each generation has made its contribution to what is now a relatively stable and prosperous community.

Alfred, Lord Tennyson in his poem, "Ulysses," after telling of the tragic experiences of hardship and danger faced by the Greek hero, has him say, "I am a part of all I have met." So life today is a composite of all the pioneers' ingenuity in meeting the almost overwhelming problems they had to face, the tragedies of war and privation, the struggles to establish law and order, the conquering faith in God that sustained them through it all.

Though it must be recognized that there are still many unmet needs in the community, as in all of America, such as in some cases lack of food, clothing, comfortable homes, the people as a whole enjoy a good life. The standard of living is such that things that were once luxuries are now considered as necessities.

Now what of the other face of Janus? What of the future?

Just here some lines from Kipling's "Recessional," which is essentially a prayer, may be appropriate:

"God of our Fathers, known of old
Lord of our far-flung battle line,
Beneath whose awful Hand we hold
Dominion over palm and pine –
Lord God of Hosts, be with us yet,
Lest we forget – lest we forget.

" . . . For frantic boast and foolish word –
Thy Mercy on Thy People, Lord."

The "good life" that is enjoyed today brings with it a responsibility – the responsibility to pass on to the coming generations, the heritage of ingenuity, endurance, sacrifice, faith that have brought the land to its present state of prosperity. There are problems to be faced – problems that may not be the same as those faced by the ancestors of present-day citizens, but problems of even greater magnitude. Threats of destruction from within and without are realities that must be dealt with now, or else the future will be dark indeed.

An unknown author has expressed so well the challenge of the present and of the years that follow:

"We pledge ourselves
To follow through the coming year
The light which God gives us:
The light of Truth, wherever it may lead;
The light of Freedom, revealing new opportunities for individual development and social service;
The light of Faith, opening new visions of a better world to be,
The light of Love, daily binding brother to brother and man to God in ever closer bonds of friendship and affection
Guided by this light.

"We shall go forward to the work of another year with steadfastness and confidence."

Sumter's City Government Plan

In 1911 some of the early leaders of Sumter, including Richard I. Manning, L.D. Jennings, Neill O'Donnell, Hubert G. Osteen, met together to seek a way to improve the government of the city.

From 1845 when the town was chartered, the government of Sumterville was under the direction of an intendant and four wardens. In January 1888 the town became a city with a mayor and four aldermen. Then there was another change in 1894 when the number of aldermen was increased to eight.

This form of government had its drawbacks, which led to a desire for change. A plan in Staunton, Va. aroused the interest of these men. There the government proved cumbersome and they hired a business administrator to manage the town's affairs, carrying out the desires of the mayor and twin chambers of the council. After studying the plan of Staunton, they liked only the idea of a business manager. Therefore this group decided to try to sell a similar plan to the city.

A committee, consisting of Dr. S.C. Baker, dynamic president of the Chamber of Commerce, Mayor L.D. Jennings, (both ex-officio); Arthur V. Snell, executive director of the Chamber of Commerce; C.M. Hurst, city clerk and treasurer; Davis D. Moise, H.G. Osteen, was appointed to draw up a bill to be presented to the General Assembly for an enabling act, which was eventually granted.

A referendum was held and the plan was adopted in 1912.[11] L.D. Jennings continued as mayor; C.G. Rowland and J.P. Booth were chosen as councilmen.

The news of the adoption of the first "Council-Manager

Plan" was sent to papers all over the United States with the result that the idea spread "like wild fire." Dayton, Ohio, a much larger city than Sumter, adopted the Sumter "Plan" in 1914. In the next two years 31 cities across the country inaugurated this form of government and the list of communities adopting the "Plan" continued to grow.

The Council-Manager Plan is very simple. It provides for the election of a small council or commission and a mayor. The council employs a person with marked business ability and good judgement as manager to attend to the business of the city government, reserving the right to dismiss him when he fails to measure up to the requirements of the position.

The first manager employed for the office was W.M. Worthington, who was connected with the Coastline Railroad. He was very competent, but his ideas did not always agree with those of the council members or mayor. Therefore his stay was short.

The next one to hold the position was W.F. Robertson, who had a number of years' experience as a construction engineer. He was successful in systematizing to some extent the affairs of the city, but because of some friction he too resigned in less than a year.

Then there came a number of men to the position, each remaining only a short time. These were L.E. White, E.S. Shuler, W.T. Brown, Howard Stillwell, and S.O'Quinn. Each, however, was known for some accomplishment.

Then in 1928 came Robert L. McLeod, who had the advantage of having served for four years on the council. His term, in cooperation with the council, was marked by success. However, he was offered a position with the South Carolina National Bank which he accepted after four years as city manager.

S.K. Rowland was the next city manager but was two years later elected city clerk and treasurer.

It was then that J.A. Raffield was elected as city manager, after having served as city councilman and as mayor.

Raffield continued in office for approximately 18 years, developing in Sumter a program that brought improvement to all city departments and working well with several councils through the years.

During his term of office (1944) the number of councilmen was raised to five.

Suceeding Raffield was Wade S. Kolb who took office Aug. 1, 1952 and served well until Sept. 30, 1973. On Oct. 1, 1973 R. Powell Black became city manager, and his term expired Oct. 31, 1976.

Horace B. Curtis was acting city manager from Aug. 31,

1976 until Nov. 1 of the same year when he became city manager and since that time has served his fellow citizens successfully, using good judgement in planning for the city's growth and improvement.

The Council - City Manager Plan for conducting the government of a city which was planned and put into effect 1911-1912 has proved the best plan for governing the affairs of a metropolitan area conceived so far. Thousands of other cities have followed Sumter in adopting this plan.

A speaker from Staunton, Va., said in a speech delivered in Columbia some years ago that " . . . some Sumter citizens showed vision and courage . . . " in conceiving this plan and putting it into effect.

Sumter Chamber Of Commerce Helped To Build City Of Note

The Greater Sumter Chamber of Commerce has to its credit many years of concerted effort in helping Sumter to grow into a city of note. Numerous citizens widely known for their business ability have through the various divisions of this organization dedicated their best efforts to the success of its undertakings toward the industrial, educational, business, cultural and religious growth of the community.

It was around 1909 that Sumter citizens realized the necessity of an organization through which to concentrate their endeavors. Therefore the first Chamber of Commerce was formed. Though somewhat later the organization was known as the Board of Trade, the purposes were the same.

Records of the early years of Sumter Chamber of Commerce – Board of Trade are sketchy. The only facts are shown in a quotation from a letter written July 17, 1974 by Manager Eaves in his search for information.

"The following are the only facts that I have come across to date:

"President in 1932: John J. Riley with R. Brice Waters as Secretary.

"President, year unknown, J.A. McKnight with Waters still Secretary.

"President, 1939, just before the change: H.A. Davis with R.H. Tucker as Vice President.

"I.M. Richardson, Secretary in 1939; Warren T. King in 1942; C.P. Gable and W.A. Thompson in 1941.

"President in 1931 Fulton B. Creech, Sr.

"First President under new name: W.E. Covington, 1939-1940.

"I have the minutes of the 1939 program but no others. Other names mentioned at that date are Dr. G.F. Bultman, M.S. Boykin, M.B. Cox, W.E. Pratt, Henry P. Moses, T.V. Walsh, Jr. and Dr. S.H. Edmunds."

In 1939 the organization was revitalized under the name the Greater Sumter Chamber of Commerce with the goal of producing a city that was "greater" in every respect.

Presidents after W.E. Covington are listed as follows: 1940-42 W.E. Bynum; 1942-43 E.W. Hartin; 1943-44 L.H. Harvin; 1944-46 F.B. Creech; 1946-47 W.C. Eldridge; 1947-48 E.C. Stroman, Sr.; 1948-49 H.D. Osteen, Sr.; 1949-50 E.L. Freeman; 1950-52 A.T. Heath, Jr.; 1952-53 J.J. Blum; 1953-54 G. Werber Bryan; 1954-55 C.C. Goodwin; 1955-56 W.T. McCracken; 1956-57 J.E. Eldridge, Sr.; 1957-58 D.B. James; 1958-59 William B. Boyle; 1959-60 J. Clarke Hughes; 1960-61 J. Clint Brogdon, 1961-62 Julian T. Buxton; 1962-63 Ramon Schwartz; 1963-64 R.E. Graham; 1964-65 John S. Wilson; 1965-66 I.H. Moses; 1966-67 Henry G. Martin, Jr.; 1967-68 S.L. Roddey, Jr.; 1968-69 Ross S. McKenzie; 1969-70 J.C. McDuffie; 1970-71 Richard P. Moses; 1971-72 R.B. Dean, Jr.; 1972-74 E.C. Stroman, Jr.; 1974-75 Doug Purdy; 1975-76 W.S. Heath; 1976-77 W.C. Bochman; 1977-78 Marvin D. Trapp; 1978-79 Charles R. McCreight; 1979-80 George B. Moseley, Jr.; 1980-81 W. Andrew Dowling.

Since 1939 the accomplishments of the Chamber have been so numerous and the results so great that it would not be possible to pinpoint every achievement but some will be mentioned.

One of the most notable achievements was the significant part it had in bringing Shaw Air Force Base to Sumter and its continued interest in forming strong ties between the military and civilian communities.

The Chamber since its beginning has dedicated itself to the improvement of every phase of the economic base of the community and the result has been a continued expansion of Sumter's economy.

It has been instrumental in bringing many excellent businesses and industries to the city and county. Citizens have received great benefits from such educational facilities as USC-S and the Technical Education Center. Improvements in transportation, better cooperation with agricultural interests and many other beneficial contributions may be credited to the Chamber of Commerce.

Many of the industries have continued to expand, thus increasing payrolls. During one year (1963) the five major industries practically doubled in size, greatly increasing the buying power of Sumter County citizens.

On May 15, 1960 James M. Eaves became Manager of the

Chamber. The election of this very efficient person for this position was indeed a wise and happy choice. He, with presidents and other officers, has made much progress in expanding the work of the organization and in improving life in Sumter.

In the 21 years as manager he has proved an asset to the community taking an active part in the Sumter County Historical Society, the Sumter Little Theater and other organizations.

In 1961 the Chamber moved into its new quarters on Washington Street. The building includes conference rooms, a research center and work areas. More than 75 per cent of the building materials were produced locally.

The Sumter Chamber program and building have been used as models for many Chambers throughout the Southeast.

The Greater Sumter Chamber of Commerce was accredited by the U.S. Chamber of Commerce in December 1980. It is one of the 350 out of more than 5,000 in the United States to achieve this recognition.

During 1978-79 the Chamber held Workshop Retreats with some notable results, among which are the following:

W. Bernard Jones conducted a Leadership Seminar with 48 participants. Leonard E. Bloomquist, Plant Manager for Crescent Tools, directed a very successful Clean-up Drive. The Business Ethics-Consumer Interest Committee with W. Avery Frick as chairman conducted successful educational seminars alerting the public concerning fraudulent schemes and helping consumers and businesses with their problems. Miss Helen Sprott with the Health Needs Committee worked out programs for informing the public as to various health services available.

The Business and Professional Executive Committee under the leadership of Robert F. Marye and Charles Riley is entering upon a new plan for meeting needs of the community.

The Chamber has also sponsored the Sumter County Restoration and Preservation Foundation, Inc. and the Freddie Solomon Foundation, the latter for the purpose of bringing Annual Track Events to Sumter.

W. Andrew Dowling, 1980-81 president, says that with the Greater Sumter Chamber of Commerce, "There is no status quo. Sumter is constantly changing."[12] And he urges all members to work together to make these changes worthwhile for the good of all citizens.

Early Sumter Businesses

"It is in exchanging the gifts of the earth that you shall find abundance and be satisfied." – Gibran

So it has been from time immemorial. By bartering, trading, buying and selling, man has found those things needed and wanted for his existence and happiness. And it was no different for the pioneers of Carolina before merchandising became a vocation and establishments for the buying and selling of products became a reality.

The first large merchants in South Carolina were in Charleston, and for many years the inland settlers, including those in Sumter District, sent their produce there and brought back large quantities of foods, not grown in the area, clothing, furniture and other commodities. This trade was carried on by wagons, drawn usually by four horses. Those in the western sector of the District used the old Catawba Trail, which in 1753 became a public road known by several names – "Broad Road," "Great Road," "Charleston Road," and later the "King's Highway." Those on the east of Black River had no public road until 1762 when one was built in response to a petition. Before that time the trip was said to have taken four weeks, or more if the river was flooded and swamps were muddy. These wagons, heavily loaded, traveling in "trains," crossed the rivers by ferry. Even those on the west, who had a good road, sometimes had to wait for the flood waters to subside before the ferry could operate.

When the wares were brought back from Charleston, they were stored in commissaries and meted out to slaves by the plantation owners and after the Civil War sold to sharecroppers and others who had no means of obtaining the "stuffs" from the seaport city.

Thus country (general) stores came into being and answered the needs of those living in a country community or neighborhood. As towns began to develop, merchants set up small stores from which they drew a livelihood; and, as the population increased, larger mercantile businesses were established.

In what may be classed as department stores were one owned by H. Baruch and another by McKinney and Corbett. Both of these advertised dry goods, groceries, hardware, boots and shoes, notions, etc., and both claimed the doubtful honor of being "cheap stores."

A.A. Solomons ran a very popular store of "Staple and Fancy Dry Goods" in the 1880's and possibly longer. A few of the items in a bill of sale made to C.I. Hoyt were as follows:

1 yd. silk velvet	$2.25
1 spool of silk	$ .10
1 spool of cotton	$ .05, $.15
1 card of hooks and eyes	$ .05
1 yd. Cream Bunting	$ .50
2 yds. crinoline	$ .20

2 pr. Black Hose, 33 1/3	$ .67
2 pr. Red Stockings	$ .15
1 pr. Black Bordered Handkerchiefs	$ .40
1 Handk.	$ .50
Total:	$ .90

Billheads for Bultman's, a well-known shoe store in the '80's read: "Manufacturers and Dealers in Boots and Shoes, Leather, Lacing, Shoe Findings, Trunks and Valises." [13]

A bill of sale from this company to C.I. Hoyt, "Exor," shows quite a number of items. The names in parentheses were evidently ladies for whom he was making the purchases in his role as "Exor." A few items will be listed to show prices in those days (1888).

1 pair shoes (Miss O)	$2.50
1 pair Butt Boots (Miss L.)	$3.50
1 pair Slippers (Miss O.)	$1.40
1 Oxford Ties (Miss O.)	$1.70

There were jewelry stores doing a thriving business apparently in those long ago times. The record states that Freeman Hoyt, "a young journeyman watchmaker from New Hampshire," came to Sumterville by horseback in 1831 and opened a jewelry shop and "prospered."[14] Somewhere through the years for some reason he evidently closed his shop, for it is recorded in a letter to Mary French Hoyt that in 1865 he "reopened his Main Street shop and with the help of his young son, Oliver, did a good business repairing the watches of the soldiers."

In 1889 C.I. Hoyt and Bro. advertised "Gold and Silver Watches, Clocks, Jewelry, Spectacles, Meriden Britania Silverware." Information is not available as to the final closing of this business, but it had a long and successful life.

Another jewelry store existed in Sumter for many years, having closed only a few years ago. It was established in 1868 by F.H. Folsom and Bro. and in 1889 it was advertised by L.W. Folsom. Through the years this firm stood for the best in jewelry, clocks, watches, etc. At one time the company sold fishing tackle, sewing machines and razors. Many adults in this area remember the closing of this popular store, which for a lifetime "had the patronage of those identified with the social life of this city and country."

One of the oldest drug stores was that run by George P. McKagen, who was advertising "Drugs, Medicines, and Chemicals, Fancy Articles, Perfumery, etc., etc." in 1867.

China's Drug Store was another "first" in this category. In 1904 the advertisement of this store began: "A Good Name is rather to be chosen than great riches. We Have It." There is evidence that this business was enjoying prosperity as far back as 1896 and it likely was even older.

Still another pharmaceutical establishment that ran for a long time, being discontinued in very recent years, was DeLorme's Pharmacy. In 1896 the proprietor was J.F.W. DeLorme and it passed down to other members of the family.

A little 18' x 20' building was the millinery shop of Annette Hulburt, wife of O.C. Hulburt, who owned the brick business on the outskirts of the village.

One type of store that is no longer in demand, but did quite a lucrative business in those early years in Sumter County was the livery stable where horses and mules were bought and sold. These animals were used exclusively in transportation and farming in this area in the 19th century and even into the early part of the 20th. H. Harby, in 1889, was advertising first-class animals from Kentucky. He also dealt in harness, buggies, carriages and wagons. In the same year, William M. Graham advertised mules suited for plantation and timber purposes and horses for driving and saddle purposes. George F. Epperson was in the same business in 1896 and probably before.

People were music-minded then as they are today. The Sumter Music House seemed a prosperous business establishment. In 1896 M.B. Randle, manager of this store, was selling pianos and organs, as well as exchanging new instruments for old.

There were shops established to provide men with the latest fashions. The Sumter Clothing Company, No. 5 South Main Street, had "The Most Stylish Clothing . . . ever displayed in our city . . . Every garment possesses the essence of Style, Smartness, and Quality necessary to distinctive garments that will retain Their Shape, Wear Well, Look Well, and fit Perfectly." This company seemed to be doing a good business in 1904.

As far back as 1896 there was at least one "gift shop" in town, known as "The Sumter China Hall," with Freeland and Hogan as proprietors, which offered for sale fine Haviland china and Austrian ware, as well as many other expensive and cheaper items.

All of these businesses and many others prospered for a time, but have all become a part of the past history of Sumter. Only three stores begun in the 1800's are still "doing any business" today. Sketches of these will follow. They are Schwartz', Burns' Hardware and Gift Shop, and Sumter Dry Goods. The oldest of these is Schwartz', which was organized in 1887 by Isaac, Charles D. and Miss Emma Schwartz. It was first located on what is now the W.B. Burns and Sons Hardware site. Somewhat later it moved across the street to the site where it stood for many years on the west side of Main. The original business at this location occupied two floors and was well known all over the state as a first-class department store for women, carrying the very finest lines of merchandise. Later the firm was reorganized as a dress shop, advertising exclusive lines of dresses, suits, coats, hats and accessories. Some of the "best" in those days included Ken Classics, Izod of London, Knox Hats.

In 1929 just before the death of his father (Isaac), Julian Schwartz took over the business, continuing for 40 years to uphold the high standards upon which the reputation of the store was established.

Upon the death of Julian Schwartz on October 30, 1969, the business was sold. However, it is still being run under the same name, with the same policy of offering only the best in ladies' ready-to-wear, but is now located in Palmetto Plaza.

BURNS HARDWARE

In 1892 Burns Hardware Company was organized and began business on Main Street below the City Hall. This first building was burned in the same year in a fire originating in the old Opera House. Property was immediately purchased on which the present building was erected.

For a while J.H. Burns was associated with his brother in the business, but later organized a hardware store in Camden under the name, Burns and Barrett. In 1906 or '07, W.B. Burns, Sr., retired, selling his store to J.J. Wescott and Bill Moran, granting them permission to run the business under the same name. W.B. Burns, Jr., began working for this firm in 1909, but later formed a company known as Burns and Lowry, occupying a building across Main Street, next to China's Drug Store.

When Wescott and Moran went into bankruptcy, W.B. Burns, Sr., came from retirement and took over the business. At this time, W.B. Burns, Jr., became associated with his father, and the firm became W.B. Burns and Son. Later A.C. joined his father and brother and the name then became W.B. Burns and Sons Hardware Company.

In 1953 W.B. Burns, Sr., one of Sumter's pioneer businessmen, loved and respected by his fellow citizens, died at the age of 83, but the business continued until recently under the same name.

From time to time the business was enlarged and improved. An excellent gift department was added, at the time said to be the largest in the state.

After many years of serving Sumter, this hardware business has closed its doors. The gift shop, which has been moved to Hampton Avenue, is still in operation, however.

KEITHS OF SUMTER DRY GOODS

Located on the southeast corner of Main and Liberty Streets in the old A.A. Solomons building, in which a ready-to-wear and general merchandise establishment was flourishing in 1880, is The Sumter Dry Goods, one of Sumter's oldest stores.

Published in the **Evening News**, a daily paper in Sumter, on June 13 and 14, 1895, was the notice of the opening of "Books of Subscription to the Capital Stock of The Sumter Dry Goods Company."

On June 15, 1895, the first subscribers met at 12 noon in the office of Purdy and Reynolds.

The names of the subscribers with the number of shares and amount were as follows:

Jas. H. Burns, Ten Shares, One Thousand Dollars
W.B. Burns, Ten Shares, One Thousand Dollars
Robert O. Purdy, Ten Shares, One Thousand Dollars
Campbell L. Stubbs, Ten Shares, One Thousand Dollars

After each amount were the words, "payable in money."

The first meeting of the Stockholders, held July 16, 1895, was for the purpose of electing officers and directors. W.B. Burns was elected president and the other four were the first directors.

It was also decided that a charter should be applied for. Mr. Purdy prepared a certificate of request to be sent to Secretary of State. These minutes were written by G.A. Lemmon, then serving as secretary.

On August 1, 1898, G.A. Lemmon was elected president and in the meantime two more stockholders had joined the company; namely, James L. Haynsworth and T.H. Clarke.

In 1902 it was decided to increase the stock from $6,000 to $12,000. And so the assets of the company grew through the years.

In 1905 Mr. T.H. Clarke was elected manager of the store upon the resignation of Mr. Lemmon, who remained president of the corporation.

In 1937 it was stated in the minutes that Miss Daisy Yeadon, Mrs. G.A. Lemmon, administratrix of the estate of her deceased husband, and Mr. Clarke, "the owners of all of the shares of stock of The Sumter Dry Goods Company, were present."

On March 9, 1953, a call meeting of the shareholders was held and at this time Mrs. Lemmon, Mr. Clarke and H.H. Keith, "representing the majority of the shareholders," were present. Officers elected were T.H. Clarke, president; H.H. Keith, vice president; Mrs. Lemmon, secretary. It was also stated that Mr.

Keith would be general manager.

Later, after Mr. Clarke's death, Mr. Keith bought the stock from other shareholders and became sole owner of the business.

In the early years, Sumter Dry Goods Company sold draperies, linens, shoes, with piece goods claiming three-fourths of the stock. Everything in the store was of very high quality. It was the number one center where the well-dressed women of the city gathered, knowing they would find the best materials and would meet their friends to exchange pleasantries. Many came also from nearby towns to shop. Miss Ruby Beatty, in charge of draperies, was well able to advise homemakers as to the best buys to suit the decor of their homes.

Mr. Keith discontinued the sale of piece goods, and, after Miss Beatty retired, no longer carried draperies. He departmentalized the store with 18 departments. A few years ago the shoe department was discontinued. Fine linens were kept until the fire on November 7, 1974.

He made the building more comfortable for workers and shoppers by insulating, improving the lighting and installing air conditioning.

The second floor is now used for office space, and on the first floor may be found ladies ready-to-wear, fine lingerie and accessories.

Having succeeded so well on Main Street, Mr. Keith opened a small store in Wesmark Plaza. That store was later moved to Bultman Drive, where, in addition to ladies' ready-to-wear and accessories a small men's department has been added. But for the success of the downtown store this expansion would not have been possible.

Employed by Keiths of Sumter Dry Goods, as it is now called, are a number of well-trained and efficient personnel. With the company when Keith joined the business were Mrs. Lillie Hudnal, who has charge of the office; Mrs. Alice Rappe (now deceased); Mrs. Margaret Beatson and Mrs. Ethel Gathings.

Another group has also been employed for a number of years. Included are Mrs. Evelyn Rembert, Mrs. Ruth Tisdale, Mrs. Syrena Ferguson, Mrs. Martha Saunders, Miss Shirley Geddings (in office), Mrs. Beulah Wheatley, Mrs. Marie Russell and Mrs. Kizzie Amos.

Some who have come to the business more recently are Mrs. Maude Compton and Mrs. Myrtle Spencer (both on Bultman Drive), Mary Bailes (assistant in office), Mrs. Eddie Brunson, and John Donald.

In the alteration department are Mrs. Margaret Marshall (at Bultman Drive), Mrs. Elsie Suiters and Mrs. Florence Burkett (downtown).

Hunt Keith, upon graduation from the University of South Carolina, joined his father in the business in 1973, and is presently the manager of the Bultman Drive store.

Active in religious, cultural and business aspects of life in Sumter, Mr. Keith has wholeheartedly supported every endeavor for improvement of the city and all its citizens. He is amazed, he says, by the influx of newcomers to the community. Many are brought by Shaw Air Force Base and a large number of these elect to retire here. Others come with the large industrial companies that have been setting up plants in and near the city. "I continue to be more than pleased with the success and growth which we have enjoyed in downtown Sumter," he stresses.

General Store Operates After Century Of Service

Old timers look back with nostalgia to the "good ole days" when the general store was not only the place where all the family necessities could be purchased, often "on time," but was also a meeting place where neighbors could sit around the "potbelly" stove and discuss politics, air grievances or tell jokes.

Those days have practically vanished as well as those stores where anything from food stuffs to garden tools, as well as articles of clothing etc., could be purchased.

But Sumter still has one such store. Though there is little room for social gatherings, almost anything can be found there. This unique little store is B.J. Barnett, Inc. on East Liberty Street. On the outside may be displayed bags of fertilizer, boxes of potatoes or other vegetables. In the windows are brooms or tools hanging in view of the passer-by.

There is no name plate on the front and if one is not careful, he may miss the narrow entrance. Though modest in appearance, this store holds much for the buyer and is well worth visiting.

In the back of the store is a large space set apart and equipped as an office with desk, chairs, telephones, files etc. On the sides merchandise is displayed on shelves.

The original owner, B.J. Barnett, came in 1880 to Sumter from Manville in what is now Lee County, where he had a farm and store. By 1881 he had a lucrative business established on Main Street "in the Bend," where the Army and Navy Store is now located. The company did a very large lien business, furnishing the farmers in the area everything for family or farm use. Debts were paid by the farmers in the fall when crops were gathered.

A bill of sale dated in 1889 showing items purchased by Mr. James E. Herriot (sic) will give an idea of the variety of merchandise found in the store and the prices in that era. (This bill was published in **The Lake City News,** Sept. 20, 1971 having been given that paper by J.S. Dixon, Jr.)

20 pounds of rice	$4.20
20 pounds of coffee	5.00
1 gal. K. oil	.25
1 pr. plow lines	.25
3 gals. N.O. Molasses	2.40
Eagle Plow	1.00
1 pr. ladies shoes	1.50
1½ in. augur	.40
1 pk. potatoes	.50
Hand Saw	1.50
10 pds. Gr. sugar	1.10
9½ yds. calico	.90
10 yds. shirting	3.50
5 yds. pants cloth	1.50
4 cans salmon	.80
can potted ham	.10
1 coffee pot	.20

Someone in the business went on buying trips to Charleston and Baltimore. Purchases made would be sent by freight car to Sumter and were hauled to the store by horse and wagon, which were kept behind Mr. Barnett's home.

The store was opened at 6 o'clock in the morning for the convenience of the farmers. Later the store keepers would go home for breakfast and return later for the remainder of the day.

B.J. Barnett was married to Zelda Loyea and they had four sons and three daughters – Lena, Janie and Rosa. They brought with them to Sumter the three daughters and two sons, (one of whom died young in Charleston). The other was H.D.

The family home was on the southeast corner of Washington and Warren Streets, where a Gulf service station now stands. H.D., son, and the three daughters later had homes on Warren Street.

H.D. was in business with his father in the large store on Main Street. On the wall in the present store is a picture of the original store with B.J. and H.D. on one side of the door and three men who were assistants in the store at that time – B.C. Wallace, Allen Flowers and H.D. Gardner – on the other.

After B.J. Barnett's death H.D. Barnett continued to operate the business until his death at the age of 87. He left one son, H.D., and three daughters – Ruth B. Kaye in Chevy Chase, Md.; Lucile Merman, Akron, Ohio; Zelda Morrison, Savannah, Ga.

When chain stores began opening in Sumter, there was not as

much business for the general stores. Then when Federal Land Bank and the Production Credit Association began operating, the farmers received loans from these and the lien business was no longer needed. It was then that Barnett moved the business to the small store, which was formerly the warehouse for the large store. Though small, the store has numerous customers with good business.

This little store has a storage room at the back where are kept stacks and stacks of files containing records of the business for many, many years.

The Barnetts have not only run a successful merchandising business but they have been prosperous farmers as well; and for some years the general office of the Barnett's business interests was in this store, but it is now located at one of the farms.

H.D. Barnett is married to the former Patricia Levi and they have two sons – H.D. and Wendell – and one daughter. H.D. is married to Carol Riner. The daughter is Patricia Greenberg of Florence.

The two sons work with their father in running the extensive Barnett business. They own approximately 5,000 acres in Lee, Sumter and Clarendon Counties. This acreage includes farms near Bishopville, at Britton's Siding and Elliott, between Manning and Paxville, near Bethel Baptist Church, and three in the vicinity of Dalzell.

They have a very large peach orchard on some of their land. Since 1956 when the older H.D., on the day that his son H.D. was born planted the first tree, the orchard has grown till it is now one of the top six producers of peaches in South Carolina. They grow between 15 and 18 different varieties of peaches each year.

Barnett explains that growing peaches is a year-long process. There is always work to be done. This year they are beginning a new orchard containing 10,000 trees.

In October 1980 H.D. Barnett, grandson of B.J. Barnett, received a signal honor when he was awarded the Outstanding Conservation Award from the Pee Dee Soil and Water Conservation District.

In charge of the store on East Liberty is Henry Wenzell Mathis, who has been with the company since 1926. He is assisted by his wife, Mrs. Mary B. Mathis, T.W. Stone and George H. Dantzler on a rotating basis.

Mathis is called on frequently to help with tax returns, questionnaires concerning food stamps and other business correspondence. He has many friends among those who come in "to trade" in the store.

Through the years others have made worthwhile contributions toward the success of the business. These include: J.H. Darr, Moses Moore, Wade Reynolds, Arthur Smith, Jim McClary, Wallace Turner, Allen Davis, Bernard Davis and a Mr. Wilder.

Sumter Laundry And Cleaners

"If you want a thing done, do it yourself." This proved a worthwhile motto for the late Leland Moore, a prosperous businessman of Sumter in the early 1900's. He ran a successful lumber business and in 1920 he was proprietor of the old Imperial Hotel that stood on Harvin Street across from the Atlantic Coastline depot and was a convenient stopping place for the many who traveled by train in those days.

However, Mr. Moore was faced with a problem. It was difficult to get the laundry done for use in the hotel.

What did this ingenious owner do? He started his own laundry in a converted mule stable on Sumter Street. Behind the laundry there was a smaller stable where he kept the three horses needed to draw the three delivery wagons which were used in those days. On the lot used by Edwards' as a parking lot today was a blacksmith shop, which was convenient for keeping his horses shod and his wagons repaired.

Thus began the Sumter Laundry and Cleaners, one of the largest and most modern in South Carolina today, with six offices operating on regular schedules, the largest having recently been completed on Sumter Street across from the original plant in the downtown area of the city.

After Mr. Moore's death in 1957, his wife, Mrs. Aline Moore, took over as president, a position she holds today.

James D. Harrelson, secretary-treasurer, joined the firm in 1946 after having served as a fighter pilot in World War II. James D. Harrelson, Jr., grandson of Mrs. Moore, has been in the business since 1974 and is presently general manager.

Harrelson, Sr., is a graduate of the University of South Carolina and James, Jr., received a degree in business administration from Emory University. Both have graduated from American Institute of Laundering in Joliet, Ill., and the National Institute of Dry Cleaning in Silver Springs, Md.

Their education is a continuous process – visiting outstanding plants, studying books, booklets, magazines and anything available on the newest methods, machinery and materials for cleaning or laundering all kinds of fabrics, both new and old.

The business has had in its employ from the beginning careful and reliable workers, whose abilities are time tested. The late Ed

Geddings was with the firm from its beginning until his illness and death in recent years. So faithfully and skillfully had he given himself to the good of the business that the company wished to have him cut the ribbon for the new facility, but he was ill at the time.

Kate C. Pate, another faithful employee, has been secretary for many years and considered by all to be a very permanent and much-loved part of the organization. Others that must be mentioned are Raymond Hodge, Buddy Hatfield, Coy Collins, Lillian Benton and Wesley Moore, all with over thirty years service.

There are altogether 85 full or part-time employees who are very well trained and dependable. Mr. Harrelson says that with all the changes in method and mechanization and the testing of these, the business still relies on skilled and conscientious personnel.

The company refers some problems to the Institute for solving. In fact, there is no stone unturned in insuring satisfaction for the customers because repeat business is essential for the success of any undertaking. They take time to advise customers on the care of garments.

A novice taking a tour through the plant will find the machinery complicated and intriguing. There is a special kind of machine for washing, another for dry cleaning, another for drying, another for removing wrinkles; and there are many more. Most amazing is one for folding contour sheets. The number of soaps and dry-cleaning fluids is interesting, but confusing to one who doesn't know all the elements found in these materials that will clean some fabrics and spoil others.

Fabrics that give trouble in cleaning are leathers, since some suedes come from countries where they are not prepared properly. Those coming from Spain are usually of excellent quality, but those from Southeast Asia are often faulty. One should inquire as to the sources of these garments before purchases are made.

The company has a large fur vault where customers may have their furs cared for during the summer. The temperature in this vault must be kept between 60 and 70, but the humidity, which demands the greatest consideration in proper storage, must be below 50.

Having a vital interest in community life, Mr. Harrelson has been involved for years in organizations working for civic improvement. For two terms he was a member of City Council. He has served on the board of directors of the Chamber of Commerce, as president of the Merchants Association for two terms, president of the board of directors of the YMCA, member of board of directors of Tuomey Hospital.

The company moved into its new facility in 1977. Here there is considerably more space for the increasing amount of business that the downtown firm has attracted. There is ample room for customer parking and delivery trucks that the company owns and operates daily. Harrelson feels that this location is definitely favorable for attracting customers. It is near other popular businesses on Main Street and its drive-in entrances give it an additional advantage for the convenience of customers.

Sibert's Rexall Drugs

The Sibert name has held for many years a highly respected place in the pharmaceutical business in Sumter, W.W. and George M. having come to this area from McCormick (at that time Abbeville) County around the turn of the century.

The family line, as traced in this country, goes back to the time when South Carolina was first settled, their ancestor, David Sibert, having come to Charleston as a Lutheran minister delivering his sermons in German. A member of a later generation was said to have made a heroic record in the Revolutionary War. George M. Sibert, father of the two who came to Sumter, was a large landowner.

Upon first coming to Sumter, W.W. Sibert was a salesman for Geer Drug Co., but in 1903 he decided to begin a business of his own. The place selected for his pharmacy was No. 8 South Main St. For a while his brother George M. worked with him, but later decided to open a store in Florence.

As soon as young George was old enough, he began working for his uncle. He felt very close to W.W. Sibert, for not only was he his father's brother but he had married his mother's sister, the former Miss Bonnie Brown, who had helped take care of him as a child.

Sibert's Drug Store from the beginning was numbered with the most enterprising businesses in Sumter. In 1907 Sibert contracted with Lewis K. Leggett of Boston for the Rexall Agency in Sumter, and from that time to the present this store has handled Rexall products. This was one of the earliest drug stores in South Carolina to have the agency, there being only three others in the state at that time.

No. 8 South Main was a popular gathering place for young and old in those early days. The store maintained a soda fountain until 1948 and that was a drawing card. Another special attraction came at election time. A part of the street was roped off in front of the store where crowds could gather to see the returns flashed on a large screen visible to all.

Men, especially, were lured at another season of the year. The results of World Series games received by telegraph were posted outside the store. When radio and television came, however, there was no longer any need for these services to the public.

When W.W. Sibert died in 1944, the responsibility for the business was taken on by his capable and well-trained nephew. Since that time the business has continued to prosper.

In 1952 it became necessary to move the store from Main Street, and the management found a suitable building at 35 W. Liberty Street, where the business now operates.

Sibert's, having a very extensive prescription clientele, employed in addition two other helpers, Dr. David M. Eason of Charleston and Dr. J.C. Orvin of Manning.

Dr. Eason returned to Charleston in February of 1974, and Dr. Glen Coker of Turbeville worked with Dr. George Sibert until January 1, 1975, at which time he purchased the business from Dr. Sibert, who was retiring.

Dr. Coker is continuing the firm under the former name Sibert's Rexall Drugs.

Berger's

This business, located on North Main Street for more than a half-century, is Berger's Men's Clothing and Shoe Store. It was in 1912 that the founder of this store, Abraham Isaac Mazursky, born in Russia in 1892, came to South Carolina and the following year to Sumter County.[15] He began business with Henry Weinberg in Mayesville, establishing a general merchandising store there. He, with his wife, daughter Helen and son Morris, continued to live in that town for a number of years.

In 1923 he established a business of his own, a department store on the east side of North Main Street in Sumter. This store, known as "The Hub," drew much trade. "Mr. Abe" or "Mr. Hub," as he was frequently called by his friends, of whom he had many, knew the merchantile business and was a "born" salesman. Being in a strategic location, he attracted those who came in from the country to sell their produce and/or to make necessary purchases, as well as city dwellers.

His daughter, having inherited the business acumen and personality of her father, in the meantime was married to Harry Berger, who was also interested in the merchantile business. In 1951 they became partners with her father, and the name of the store was changed to Berger's.

Then the store was moved to the west side of Main Street to

a location that in the early years of Sumter's history had been occupied at different times by Theodore Solomons and Co., J. Ryttenberg and Sons and Levi Bros.

The image of the store, as well as the name, was changed. Instead of a department store carrying wearing apparel for men, women and children, as well as other merchandise in the dry goods category, it became what it is today – a store for **Men's Apparel.** It carries excellent makes of suits, such as Campus, Cotler, Normano. It specializes in fashion men's shoes – Padrino, Harbor and others.

In addition, all accessories such as shirts, hats, sweaters, scarfs, belts, ties, etc., may be purchased by the well-dressed man. There is a satisfactory choice for every man at prices that will please.

Recently Stephen Berger, son of Mr. and Mrs. Harry Berger, became a partner in the firm. Thus Berger's is a business of continuous family interest and ownership, guaranteeing to the public the services of a partnership built on a foundation of thrift, integrity and an interest in the growth of Sumter.

It was the desire of the founder, "Mr. Abe" Mazursky, to establish such a business, that he might leave behind the heritage of a good name. He loved America and wanted to be a good citizen of his adopted country. He loved Sumter and made his contribution toward its growth. In the same spirit his descendants are carrying on this great tradition.

Four full-time salesladies are employed. Three of these – Mrs. Ethel Scurry, Mrs. Ruby Robbs and Mrs. Martha Hancock – have been with the firm more than 25 years. Mrs. Addie Hinson has been an employee for 15 years.

These ladies have a thorough knowledge of the stock of goods as well as the latest trends in men's wear. They are cordial and friendly, knowing how to meet the public and assist the customers.

The fact that they have been with the company so many years shows their ability and loyalty as well as the successful growth of Berger's.

Clinton Caesar, another full-time employee, has been with the business approximately a year. He is responsible for window and inside displays, as well as being a salesman.

One part-time employee, Harold Brogdon, is a full-time student at the University of South Carolina-Sumter.

Hapco Founded In 1919

Success stories are always of interest and very often prove inspirational as is true in the case of the late A.J. Hatfield, one of Sumter's well-known and highly respected citizens.

He was a man who began the hard way, working early and late to build his business for which he borrowed $500 for a start. His first venture was a modest little bicycle shop located on Liberty Street. Later as his business grew, he moved to a better location on the same street. His next move was to a place on North Main Street now occupied by SEACO. Having outgrown this location, he built a shop on Canal Street.

At first he had two helpers – Jim Shirer and Jim Richardson – who worked with him in the bicycle business for many years.

In those early days bicycles were used extensively as a means of transportation, especially in cities and towns. Mrs. Hatfield relates that she rode a bicycle and that Mr. Hatfield would take their first child to Sunday School on his bicycle each Sunday.

As automobiles came into use, this astute businessman began to stock parts for cars and to buy fewer bicycles, until he replaced the bicycle shop with a shop handling automobile parts entirely. Thus the name HAPCO was adopted – Hatfield Automobile Parts Company – which was operated on Canal Street for many years. In 1960 a second store was built on Broad Street. With this addition the floor space occupied by the business was increased from 4,000 to 8,000 square feet. In 1969 the Hatfield business celebrated its 50th anniversary, having shown phenomenal growth since its small beginning on April 9, 1919.

After the death of A.J. Hatfield in 1965, his son Aubrey, who had been with his father since 1946, took over the management of HAPCO and is carrying on in the tradition of a businessman of the highest caliber. A look into his establishment gives every indication of the expert manner in which he conducts every phase of the business.

Having graduated from Boys' High School, he attended Clemson College for one year, and spent 30 months in the Army Air Force; he then joined his father and had the privilege of learning the business "from the ground up" from a wise and talented manager. He says now that he doesn't really know why he became a part of the company except that somehow it presented a challenging venture for him with a desire for success as an impetus.

In addition to dealing in automobile parts, HAPCO runs machine shops to do specialized jobs for filling stations and garages, and for wholesale customers who do not have equipment for installation of parts.

The establishment serves Sumter County and surrounding areas and is open each day except Sunday from 8 a.m. to 6 p.m. Employees include: outside and inside salesmen, office workers, stock clerks, delivery men, machine shop personnel. There are five delivery trucks, making from 80 to 100 miles each day.

Much business is transacted by telephone. The main warehouse in Charlotte, N.C., is called every day for ordering parts which are delivered the following morning. On the shelves are kept 40,000 items with 40,000 more in the warehouse ready for delivery. As each article is sold, an entry is made in the files so that there is kept at all times an accurate record of all articles on hand. As parts are sold, they are replaced immediately so that an adequate supply is always ready for sale. All items on the shelves are kept in labeled pigeon holes; therefore, there is never any delay in finding a desired article. According to Mr. Hatfield, his motto is "A place for everything and everything in its place."

The success of the business and the standards upheld by the owners reflect the ability and integrity of the founder, who, 50 years ago, established his store on the highest business principles with the willingness to spare no effort to maintain these principles.

A.J. Hatfield was not only a successful businessman but a civic leader and a dedicated churchman as well. He aided his town and community by serving on the Advisory Board of the Salvation Army. As a member of the Sumter Cemetery Assn., he helped this group to develop financial strength. His service to the state included one term in the General Assembly and 20 years as a member of the South Carolina Unemployment Commission, being a charter member of the commission.

For many years he was a member of the Grace Baptist Church and was instrumental in establishing Northside Memorial Baptist Church, donating the land for the first building. His devoted Christian influence was felt throughout the activities of this church and as recognition for his services a Sunday School class was given the name Hatfield Bible Class.

After living on Broad Street for many years the Hatfields built a beautiful home on the corner of Wise and Alice Drive. They then moved their membership to Alice Drive Baptist Church, where he continued his Christian witness. He served as deacon in all of the churches of which he was a part; and when his health failed so that he was no longer able to serve actively, he was made an honorary deacon at Alice Drive.

Mr. and Mrs. Hatfield (the former Addie Cato) reared five children who are carrying on the good name of their parents in their respective communities.

Some years ago Mr. Hatfield established a business in Bishopville which is being managed by his son-in-law, Ned Muldrow. Another son-in-law, Charles Windham, is in charge of a similar business, also begun by Mr. Hatfield, in St. George.

Paying tribute to the memory of his father, Aubrey Hatfield

said, "He never smoked, never drank, never lost his temper." What a heritage for a father to leave for his children!

Though beginning in a small way, HAPCO now, as voiced by a salesman, is the largest store of its kind in the state. Thanks are due from the citizens of Sumter for this establishment which has always stood for the best in business methods and congratulations are in order on this, its golden anniversary. (Note: Written April 10, 1969.)

Tuomey Hospital

Sumter is justly proud of Tuomey Hospital.

It has comfortable rooms; equipment for diagnostic tests is up to date; there is a maternity ward with an ample number of bassinets for the babies; sufficient space for surgical operations. The emergency department is modern and well equipped; the laboratory is up to date in every way. A lovely chapel was added some time ago and there is ample office space for the convenient handling of business affairs.

Staffing the hospital are highly competent doctors, including skillful surgeons and specialists in many fields of medicine. There are nurses and nurses' aids to attend to the needs of the patients. Trained administrators and assistants operate the hospital in a business-like and expert manner.

Tuomey Hospital is approved by the American Hospital Association and the Joint Accreditation Committee, and holds a license from the state.

But a look into the past will show that Sumter did not always have the medical facilities available today. The first venture in hospitalization in the county was a small 10-bed clinic or private hospital built in 1894 on Hampton Avenue (then Republican Street), between Sumter and Washington Streets, by Dr. S.C. Baker, father of Dr. C.R.F. Baker, and Dr. A.C. Dick. Later in the same year, Dr. J.A. Mood constructed a private hospital, also with a 10-bed capacity, on Washington Street. These clinics were known as the Baker-Dick Infirmary and the Mood Infirmary, the doctors in each administering the business aspects, as well as treating the patients. They were designated as "private" because they were financed by the doctors themselves and by whatever fees were collected from patients. Any and all who were ill were admitted and treated by those doctors who were possessed with a compassionate heart and a desire to relieve suffering.

Nurses were trained in these infirmaries, with the doctors teaching and directing the practice. In 1897 Doctor Mood had as his first superintendent of nurses Miss Anna Simpson.

Soon after 1900, Doctor Mood was joined by Dr. C.P. Osteen, who remained in the partnership until 1911. In the meantime, Dr. H.A. Mood began practice with his father.

In 1904 Doctors Baker and Dick were joined by Doctors H.M. Stucky, Walter Cheyne and Archie China in the building of what was known as Sumter Hospital, which operated as a private institution with 30 beds.

In the **Evening News** of December 1, 1904, there was an article concerning the construction of this hospital:

"Those who have looked at the walls going up on West Calhoun Street will see that they are not of wood or brick, but they appear to be of a dull colored stone. But they are not of stone; they are dirt. The Sumter Hospital will be a house built of sand. However, this sand house has been worked by a process whereby it has the hardness of granite, and the longer it stands, the harder and more compact it becomes."

The article goes on to point out the advantages of this material, stating that it would be more economical, it would require less foundation than stone since it is lighter, the insurance would be less, there would be no need of paint, and the walls would be free of rats and mice.

This early structure has since been replaced by a brick building, though it remained a part of Tuomey for many years.

Somewhat earlier (in 1901), the Sumter Training School for Nurses was chartered, with Robert O. Purdy as president and Van Talbery Hofman, secretary. From 1902 to 1905, there were seven graduates: Misses Antonia Gibson, Josie Weatherly, Lila Davis, Rean Alexander, Sudie Furman, May Harvin, and Mollie Kennedy.

Soon after the Sumter Hospital was chartered, the Mood Infirmary was consolidated with the new institution, the Doctors Mood receiving shares of stock in exchange for their equipment.

In 1897 Timothy J. Tuomey, a public-spirited citizen and leading businessman of Sumter, who had considerable holdings, died, providing in his will for the erection of a hospital to be known as Tuomey Hospital. After the death of his wife, the bulk of his estate was to be used as a perpetual endowment for the institution.

His will also stated that the hospital was to be managed by a Board of Trustees, three of whom were named as life members with perpetual succession. The mayor and two councilmen were to be named to the board, these six electing a seventh from the county. The original life members mentioned in the will were Col. R.D. Lee, Neill O'Donnell and Dr. S.C. Baker. The wishes of this benefactor have been honored and the hospital continues to be thus administered.

At Mrs. Tuomey's death in 1909, not only the property left by Tuomey but by her will (an additional bequest of $35,000) came to the hospital.

In 1913 the Board of Trustees purchased the Sumter Hospital, which was chartered in 1914[16] as Tuomey Hospital, and the doctors who owned the original institution became the first members of the medical staff.

The following year the Tuomey Hospital School of Nursing was established as a part of the hospital, and for many years a class was graduated each year. Only recently has the school ceased to operate.

From the estate of Neill O'Donnell another gift was received in 1937 to be used as an endowment fund. In memory of O'Donnell, who had served as trustee for more than 25 years, the new nurses' home was named The Neil O'Donnell Memorial Residence for Nurses.

The hospital has made continuous progress from year to year, adding more rooms and increasing the facilities through grants from the federal government, endowment funds, contributions from city and county and gifts from individual citizens.

Patients who have received professional treatment and attentive care in this hospital are always ready to express gratitude for the excellent service this institution is equipped to render the sick and injured.

But while rejoicing in the present, one must not forget the past and the pioneers who, with limited resources, laid the groundwork for what the community proudly possesses today. Those small infirmaries, begun in the last century, and the dedicated doctors who founded them, were an inspiration for Tuomey, which stands as a memorial to their loving concern for the suffering and their sacrificial effort. It is a monument, also, to others who, through the years, have made worthwhile contributions by financial backing and unselfish service in order that the dream of a creditable hospital for Sumter and surrounding areas might become a reality and plans are now going forward for additional improvements.

The National Bank Of South Carolina

NBSC has really had "A Good Thing Goin' " since a business genius from the Tar Heel State started it 75 years ago and the "Good Thing" is promised for the future.[17]

Charles G. Rowland left his home in Henderson, N.C., to seek his fortune; and he not only succeeded in finding his own niche in life, but he opened a road to success for numerous others and made Sumter a center of banking interests.

Mr. Rowland came to Sumter County in 1887, stopping first in Mayesville, where he became station agent and telegrapher for the Atlantic Coastline Railroad Company. Not altogether satisfied with this work, he left for South Georgia, where he worked in the turpentine manufacturing business. Several years later, he returned to Sumter and became station agent for the same railroad company with which he began his career.

In 1905, prompted by the fact that so many farmers brought him their money for safekeeping, he organized the Farmers Bank and Trust Company.

Not only were the assets small at the beginning, but the quarters used for the institution were very modest. The site for this little bank was a "partitioned-off corner" of the Cash Grocery Store on the northeast corner of Main and Liberty Streets. But though its home was small, it had the advantage of being in the heart of the business district of the town – a location that proved strategic. In 18 months the assets had doubled.

Prior to this, plans were made to acquire more permanent quarters. Since a new county courthouse was to be built, the bank management arranged to purchase the building that the old courthouse was occupying on the west side of Main Street where Edwards Department Store now stands. This was a fireproof structure designed by Robert Mills in 1820, with curving front steps reaching to the second floor. By an Act of the General Assembly of February 2, 1906, this site was purchased for $15,000. It had a frontage of 50 feet and a depth of 200 feet. This was an important location since its prestige had been fixed in the minds of the citizens for many years. It was the place where people had attended many political and patriotic meetings. During the War Between the States it had been used as a convalescent hospital for Southern soldiers.

Soon after the bank moved to its new quarters, a renovation plan was undertaken. The steps were removed and a little later the columns and arches were replaced with a more modern front of stone with bronze doors.

The Farmers Bank and Trust Company was nationalized in 1914 and soon afterwards the name was changed to The National Bank of South Carolina.

The application for a charter for the bank in 1905 was signed by C.G. Rowland, R.F. Haynsworth, R.J. Bland, L.B. DuRant, Isaac Schwartz and Mark Reynolds. The first board of directors included Rowland, Haynsworth, Schwartz, Bland, George F. Epperson, W.B. Burns, J.K. Crosswell, G.A. Lemmon and George D. Shore. Rowland was elected president; Haynsworth, vice president; R.L. Edmunds, cashier.

With an inborn gift for financial affairs and with tireless energy, Mr. Rowland led the way in increasing the capital stock from $200,000 to $300,000 in shares of the par value of $100 as early as 1921.

So sound was this bank that it was able to withstand the depression that caused many banks all over the United States to close their doors in 1932 and 1933. But because all banks of the nation were ordered by the Comptroller of the Currency in a "Bank Moratorium" in March of 1933, its doors were closed. However, it remained closed only five days, and after the crisis it was stronger than before.

Earle Rowland became president of the bank in 1944 and his father became chairman of the board. The younger man had started as a collection clerk and came to his position as president step by step. Endowed with his father's business ability and his ambition to succeed, he was successful in all the positions he held. At one time he was serving as vice president and cashier. While he was president, the resources of the bank soared to $15,000,000.

The year 1951 brought severe blows to the bank. President Earle Rowland died on June 13; and his father, on September 30.

Ramon Schwartz became the interim president, serving until November, when an election was held. At that time, S.L. Roddey was elected. In 1955 he became chairman of the board and the late Harry E. Wilkinson, Jr., was made president. He was succeeded in 1973 by Marvin D. Trapp.

In 1957 the bank moved to its new location on the east side of North Main Street in a handsome headquarters building, with spacious rooms for transacting different phases of its expanding operation.

In 1963 NBSC opened a branch bank at Palmetto Plaza and in the same year it organized a branch in Manning. Within two years branches were opened in Columbia and Bishopville. Thus a small, independent bank was stepping into competition with larger banking systems and winning success.

As the home base expanded into other areas, it found itself in need of additional space for the ever-expanding growth on Main Street in Sumter. Plans were laid for a new three-story Operations Center, just back of the Main Office building, which was completed in the late fall of 1974.

In this building are located the following departments: The Sumter Installment Loan, the Accounting, the Audit, Central Operations, which includes Bookkeeping, Proof, Data Processing; the Credit Administration; and the NBSC Bank Card Center.

On June 10, 1974, the National Bank of South Carolina completed a merger with the Farmers Bank of Loris. This merger brought two branches in Loris and two in North Myrtle Beach to the NBSC system.

The Dutch Square office, which opened for business Dec. 8, 1975, made a total of five branches of NBSC in Columbia.

At the end of 1978, NBSC had 15 branches: four in Sumter, five in Columbia, one in Manning, one in Bishopville, two in Loris and two in North Myrtle Beach. Three new branches have been approved by the Comptroller of the Currency. These, scheduled to open for business in mid-year 1979, will be located in Sumter, Columbia and Summerville.

The Farmers Bank and Trust Company began with a capital stock of $60,000 and at the end of Nov. 1978 total assets of NBSC amounted to $147,653,350, a gain over 1977 of more than $16 million. Last year this bank had the highest percentage of agricultural loans to total assets of any bank in the state.

Founder of the bank, C.G. Rowland, was possessed with a vision that led him to see ahead to the possibilities of a banking institution in Sumter and he had the ability to lead others along the path that he blazed. Even after his death, his influence continues to live. A road marker erected by Rowland more than 50 years ago on the Wedgefield Road was brought to the bank by employees and dedicated in his memory in October 1978. But it must be said for those who followed that they, too, had financial expertise. Into the success of NBSC have gone the talent and capability of many strong men and dedicated women, too numerous to name.

Presently serving as president and chief executive officer is Marvin D. Trapp; Robert R. Anderson is executive vice president and chief administrative officer — Banking Division; senior vice president and cashier is James C. Mixon, Jr.; Harold Amick is vice president and acting Sumter city executive. These are aided in the tremendous task of running such an institution successfully by numerous other faithful officers, directors and workers.

The growth of this institution is due in great extent to its location through these three score and fifteen years in the center of the city, as well as the large number of outstanding businessmen who have been associated with the institution. (Written March 28, 1978.)

First Federal Savings And Loan

This institution was chartered on Nov. 23, 1923, with the following directors: J.P. Commander, S.L. Roddey, Perry Moses, Sr., John D. Lee, Sr., George D. Levy, R.L. McLeod, F.M. Moise,

John J. Riley. On the advisory board was F.B. Creech.

Though the association has made two moves since its beginning, it has always been located on Main Street. The main office is now on the corner of Main and Calhoun Streets. A few years ago a branch office was built at the intersection of Miller Road and Guignard Drive.

In the first year the amount loaned was $19,000 and $100 was spent for advertising. At the end of five years the assets amounted to $122,000.

At the end of 1980 the association had made a total of 3,039 loans amounting to $71,155,414. At this date there were 15,475 depositors with total assets of $81,708,853. Amount on Savings was $74,357,449.[18]

Money deposited in First Federal is insured, the rate having been raised by the Federal Savings and Loan Insurance Corporation of **$100,000** for each depositor.

First Federal, along with other Savings and Loan Associations, offers a great opportunity for parents who expect to have children in college, expenses for which are rising all the time. Today a college education costs $30,000 or more.

The Savings and Loan Foundation College Savings Plan "cushions the future shock of skyrocketing college costs by offering parents a new and more profitable way to save for their youngsters' educational future."

Its principle is very simple. It is made possible through the Uniform Gifts to Minors Act and under Federal and State Income Tax statues. Each state has its own provisions and the information concerning the South Carolina law may easily be obtained by inquiring at First Federal in Sumter.

One of the most popular plans for saving used at First Federal is the "It's the Nuts" Plan, or The Squirrels Club. This special club is designed to teach children how to save. Make a deposit for a child under 13 and this boy or girl is on his or her way to a new and exciting experience.

All the Squirrels receive on the first deposit the official New Member Squirrels Kit, which contains all kinds of "nutty" things. And all members receive official messages, birthday greetings and the "Nutty News," which comes each quarter. Depositors are also given the opportunity to participate in the Flying Squirrels Squad and other "Squirrelly" activities.

These memberships make excellent birthday, Christmas or other occasion gifts from mothers, fathers, grandparents, aunts, uncles, friends. A boy or girl living anywhere may be enrolled in Sumter.

Another convenience offered by First Federal to each depositor is that of having Social Security checks deposited directly to his account. This method is quick and safe.

President and Managing Officer of First Federal is Henry G. Martin, Jr., a native of Columbia. A graduate of Columbia High School, he attended Clemson and the University of South Carolina. Before coming to Sumter, he was employed by the Peoples Bank of Bishopville.

He is an active member of St. James Lutheran Church, serving currently as organist. A talented musician, he is involved in the cultural organizations of the community. He has served as director of the Sumter-Shaw Community Concert Association. The Sumter Little Theater claims much of his leisure time. He has also taken a personal interest in the high school bands.

Interested in promoting such activities in the community, First Federal gives help to Little League baseball and sponsors ladies softball and bowling teams.

A citation was given Martin for Community Services by the United Fund.

He is a member of the Greater Sumter Chamber of Commerce. On the state level he was on the board of directors of the South Carolina Chamber of Commerce 1969-72, is a member of the South Carolina Savings and Loan League.

As a member of the Downtown Sumter Improvement Association, he has used his influence in every way to live up to his motto "Help Sumter Grow." Through all of his contacts his sincere and friendly personality wins friends for himself and his business. Says President Martin, "First Federal is owned by the people of the community and is a service organization."

Other officers of the Association are as follows: F.B. Creech (recently deceased), vice president; R.E. Graham, board chairman; John M. Graham, senior vice president; Evelyn M. Mitchell, secretary-treasurer; Thomas A. Johnston, Jr., vice president and loan officer; Larry C. Graybill, assistant vice president; Robert S. Wilson, assistant vice president and assistant loan officer; Doris H. Gaillard, assistant secretary-treasurer; Betty B. Barger, manager, Westside Branch. S.K. Nash, a long-time officer, is recently deceased.

Directors not serving as officers include: S.A. Benson, certified public accountant; W.T. Fort, Jr., Fort Roofing and Sheet Metal Works; John D. Lee, attorney; and Robert B. Moise, insurance and real estate.

All connected with this Association have worked and are working in the interest of all depositors, ever seeking additional ways of serving the people of Sumter. They believe with President Martin that the depositors deserve the best financial assistance possible.

PART II. EARLY FAMILIES

Papers Shed Light On Broüns

The Sumter County Historical Society recently received a very valuable collection of historic papers that reflect interesting data concerning the settling of a part of Sumter District which included what is now Sumter County. Included in this collection are early land grant records, indentures, plats and other material descriptive of lands located for the most part in the western part of the county.

Instrumental in procuring these papers is Mr. Sherman Smith. The donors were Mrs. T.D. Broün and Matthew Singleton Broün in memory of his brother and her husband, Thomas Day Broün.

Since none of the documents bear the name Broün and since few of this name ever lived in the area, it will be of interest to know just where this family fits into the picture.

The background of the family is a fascinating and intriguing one. Coming to England from Normandie in 1066 with William the Conqueror was a family with the French name le Brun that settled in Scotland. Seemingly the name was changed to Broün with a macron (indicating a long vowel) over the **u** to indicate that it was pronounced like **Broon.** Some members of the family originally spelled the name **Brohun** and it was said that when the **h** was dropped, the macron was used to denote the omission of a letter; however, Webster says that the mark indicates a long vowel. The **Brohun** spelling is used in the record in the auditor's office in the Sumter courthouse. One member of the family said that 75 percent of the people pronounced the **ou** correctly; while the others pronounced the **ou** as a diphthong as in **out,** making the name like **Brown.**

In 1480 William Broün "was flourishing" according to the record and in 1596 his son Patrick became Laird (Scottish for Lord) of Colstoun and was succeeded by his son George, who in turn was succeeded by James. When James died in 1669, his son Patrick became Sir Patrick of Colstoun and Nova Scotia by a decree of King James, II. At Patrick's death in 1688, he was succeeded by his son George, who fell heir to a large fortune; but since he was a compulsive gambler, he had to sell his estate to his younger brother Robert to get money to pay his gambling debts. Mother of Robert was Lady Elizabeth McKenzie, daughter of an earl.

Robert and both his sons were drowned in a flash flood, and the property fell to his sister, Jean, who married a cousin, Charles Broün.

Though there is no documentation showing that the Broüns who came to South Carolina were from the Colstoun clan, there are indications that they were of this line. These will be mentioned later.

George and Margaret Broün came to South Carolina from the north of England with their two sons – Robert and William – in 1735, landing in Charlestown. Later they moved with son William to Virginia. Robert, however, became a doctor and settled at Goose Creek sometime after 1737. In 1738, he married Elisabeth Thomas.

Archibald, son of Dr. Robert and Elisabeth Thomas Broün, served as a captain in the Revolutionary War. There is a story told in the family that he was sent during the war to France on an important mission to negotiate for supplies. On the way back to America the ship was wrecked and supplies were lost at sea. Capt. Archibald was taken to Boston, whence he rode horseback to his home in South Carolina.

Archibald was married to Elizabeth Deas. Their son, Robert, born in 1781, somehow came to the High Hills of Santee and married Harriet Richardson Singleton, daughter of Capt. John Singleton, granddaughter of Col. Matthew Singleton.

Robert Broün died in 1809, leaving his wife and three sons – John Peter, Charles Deas and Robert Henry. Harriet was later married to John Russell Spann. She died in 1817.

According to Capt. John Singleton's will, recorded in 1820 (after the death of his daughter), John Peter Broün, his grandson, received the plantation known as Deer Pond; to Charles Deas he left another plantation and $30,000. Before he died, he devised to Robert Henry 2,000 acres. There seems to be no record of what became of that land. Robert Henry went to New Orleans and died of yellow fever at the age of 26.

John Peter Broün married Abigail Hinman Day and they were the parents of several children, three of whom are of special interest in this paper. One daughter, Harriet, married John Coles Singleton, Sr., and Annie Hinman married Richard Richardson Singleton in a double wedding ceremony. Both young men were direct descendants of Matthew Singleton.

Robert Broün, son of John Peter and Abigail Broün, married Caroline Belser. Their son, Thomas Day, known as "T.D.," was the one who had in his possession the collection of documents given the Historical Society. He was born in 1886 and died in 1970. He was twice married, first to Harriet Lee Moore and next to Gladys Stallworth, who survives him. There were no children from this marriage.

The other son of Robert and Caroline Belser Broün, Matthew Singleton, was born in 1892 and died recently in Washington, D.C., where he had been living. His wife was the former Fannie Underhill.

Thus the Broüns were connected with the Singletons, who at one time owned much of the land in the Manchester and Wedgefield section of Sumter County, and names are found in most of the papers in the collection now owned by the Society.

As one proof that the Sumter County Broüns came originally from the royal family in Scotland, three heirlooms came down through the family. John Peter had in his possession for many years a watch fob of topaz and a hand seal and signet ring, upon both of which were engraved the arms of Sir Patrick. Somehow the fob and hand seal were lost, but the ring was handed down to Thomas Day, who lost it in recent years in a field near his home in the vicinity of Wedgefield.

Documents in the collection now in the possession of the Society may be seen at the Museum-Archives, 122 N. Washington, when the room is open, and will be of interest for various reasons. Some of these original land grant records were authorized by King George III, himself, and have the mark where his seal was once attached.

Many Doctors In Dick Family

In the generations past, especially, the family doctor held a unified place in the life of a community. As he traveled from place to place, by horse and buggy mostly, he was known, loved, and honored by all whom he served so faithfully, bringing relief from pain, advice on many problems, encouragement and comfort.

Sumter had many such ministers of mercy in the past and is most fortunate today in having many skilled physicians to treat the multiplied number of illnesses and accidents. Doctors are a blessing to any community in any age.

Special tribute is here paid to the Dick family in which there have been five generations of medical men, beginning in the early

1800's, spanning the intervening decades and continuing into the future.

Dr. Alexander Colclough Dick, upon whom this sketch will focus, was of the third generation of an unbroken line of physicians. His grandfather, Dr. Thomas Morritt Dick, was born in Georgetown County in 1804. On his mother's side he was descended from Col. Anthony White, one of the "foremost commanders in the partisan forces of Gen. Francis Marion" during the Revolutionary War. Dr. Thomas Morritt Dick received his training in Jefferson Medical College of Philadelphia, Pa., finishing there in the 1820's. He was one of those early "horse and buggy" doctors practicing from an office on his plantation, Glenwood, a few miles from the town of Sumterville.

One of his sons, Leonard White Dick, born in 1834, was second in the line of doctors in this family. He completed his training at the University of Pennsylvania Medical College in Philadelphia just before the outbreak of the Civil War. He volunteered for military duty and served in the Army of Northern Virginia until wounded; and as soon as he recovered sufficiently, he became a surgeon in the Southern Army.

Taking up private practice after the war, he had an office both at Pineville plantation, 12 miles from Sumter, and at his ancestral home on the Glenwood plantation, where he practiced until his death in the 1870's. He was married to the daughter of John Ashby Colclough.

Thus Dr. Alexander Colclough Dick, having a noteworthy legacy of interest in medicine, became one of Sumter's outstanding physicians, making great contributions to the entire area.

He was born in 1861 at Pineville, the home of his grandmother, Mrs. Eliza Macdonald Colclough, widow of John Ashby Colclough.

He first attended Fort Mill Academy, going from there to Davidson College where he was graduated.

For a while he and his brother, Leonard White Dick, Jr., conducted a school for boys in Sumter. Samuel Henry Edmunds, who later was superintendent of the city schools of Sumter for many years and was known to later generations as the beloved "Doctor Edmunds," attended their school.

So ingrained in young A.C. Dick, however, was the love for the practice of medicine and so urgent was his call into this profession that he gave up teaching and entered the Virginia Medical School of Charlottesville, Va., but later withdrew. He then received his degree in medicine at the Medical College of Charleston.

At Davidson and in medical school in Virginia he became fast friends with another young medical student from Sumter, Samuel Chandler Baker, who proved to be one of Sumter's great doctors of the past. He, too, came from a family that followed the medical tradition.

Upon graduation these two young men were taken into partnership with Dr. John J. Bossard, a kinsmen of A.C. Dick, and one who was honored in many ways by his fellow citizens not only for his medical skills but for his contributions as a civic leader.

The three established in 1894 on Republican Street (now Hampton Ave.) what was first known as the Bossard-Baker-Dick Infirmary which had ten beds.

Soon, convinced of the need for trained nurses, the doctors agreed to begin a school of nursing in connection with the Infirmary, and the question arose as to where to find the right person to serve as superintendent of the training program.

Through two from the Sumter area, Miss Margaret Reynolds and Mrs. Ferd Levi, who had been patients at Johns Hopkins Hospital in Baltimore, Md., they were given a lead in their search. These ladies were so impressed with a young student nurse in the hospital that they recommended her for this newly established position.

The young nurse was Miss Clara Peale Russell. A member, on her mother's side, of the well-known Peale family, noted as portrait painters, she was born in Baltimore and reared at Queenstown in Queen Anne County on the Eastern Shore of Maryland. Under strong protest from friends and relatives, since nursing was a rather new vocation and somewhat frowned upon, she entered training in the first class of nursing at Johns Hopkins, receiving her training from Miss Nutting, a former pupil of Florence Nightingale and a nurse who had gained prestige on her own merit.

Because of the favorable recommendations the doctors had received, Miss Russell was contacted and offered the position with the then Baker-Dick Infirmary, Dr. Bossard having retired, and she accepted the offer in 1896.

Among the nurses whom she trained were Mrs. Pauline Cordes and Miss Lila Davis, the latter becoming superintendent of nurses later.

Soon Cupid began throwing his darts in two directions and Doctor Dick was able to win the hand and heart of his chief nurse. The wedding took place on September 15, 1897, at the Church of the Holy Comforter (at that time on the corner of Main and Bartlette Streets). Emma Baker, daughter of Dr. S.C. Baker, was the flower girl and Sam Cordes, son of Mrs. Pauline Cordes, was ringbearer. They spent their honeymoon at Blowing Rock, N.C.

Though Mrs. Dick gave up outside nursing to care for her own children, two of whom, Russell and Macdonald, were very ill at one time with diphtheria, she kept up her interest in the hospital and school of nursing. She was ever showing kindness and hospitality to the nurses and doing volunteer work when possible. She formed lasting friendships with some of the nurses. Among these were Miss Astred Hofseth, Miss Hume, who married first Dr. Walter Cheyne and after his death, Mr. R.L. Edmunds, and Miss McAllister. It was Miss McAllister, superintendent of nurses at the time, who called Mrs. Dick "Mrs. Willing Feet" because of her many deeds of mercy. During the flu epidemic of 1918, she rendered valuable assistance as a volunteer.

With the help of Dr. H.M. Stuckey, Dr. Archie China and Dr. Walter Cheyne, Dr. Baker and Dr. Dick formed the Sumter Hospital. After a generous bequest the name was changed to Tuomey in honor of Mr. and Mrs. Timothy Tuomey, loyal citizens of Sumter. Earlier the Mood Infirmary had been merged with the Sumter Hospital.

Dr. A.C. Dick, though never specializing in surgery, was said to have been deft and skillful with surgical instruments. He was especially interested in neurology and during his years of practice treated many emotionally disturbed patients, often taking them into his home and after treating them for some time was able to dismiss them in a greatly improved condition. So interested was he in mental disorders that he was asked to be a member of the board of the State Hospital. During his service in this capacity he was instrumental in securing as director the late Doctor Williams, who was greatly esteemed for his work with this institution.

Afflicted with a congenital heart ailment, he was forced to rest at intervals; and as his heart continued to enlarge, these periods of rest became longer and more frequent. More and more time was spent at "Goshen" and at his home at Bradford Springs.

In 1906 he went to Johns Hopkins Hospital for treatment but received little encouragement from doctors, who said they had never seen a heart in the condition of his. Nevertheless, he continued to practice whenever he was able until the end came in 1917 when he was only 56.

His life was comparatively short but it was full and useful. Dedicated to his profession, he brought healing and comfort to his countless patients through his work in the hospital and his private practice.

His beloved wife lived on after him until 1957, having almost reached the age of 90. Husband and wife are buried in the same grave in the historic old church yard of St. Philip's Church at Bradford Springs.

Keeping the three-generation family tradition, two sons of Dr. A.C. Dick became physicians. Dr. Macdonald Dick, a graduate of the Medical School of Johns Hopkins University in Baltimore, Md., served on the faculty of Duke University Medical School for many years. Retiring from this position at the age of 70, he still practices medicine in Durham, N.C.

Dr. A.C. Dick, Jr., is a graduate of the Medical School of the University of Pennsylvania and is now chief surgeon and director in the Queen Anne's County Chester County Hospital in Chestertown, Md. His son, Dr. Macdonald Dick, II, named for his uncle, is on the staff of the Harvard University Medical Center in Boston, Mass., having received his degree from the Medical College of the Univeristy of Virginia.

There are three other members of the Dr. Alexander Colclough Dick family who, though not following a career in medicine, have made very worthwhile contributions in other areas.

The eldest of the family, Russell, after receiving a B.A. degree from the University of Virginia, as well as masters and doctorate degrees from the University of Chicago, taught first in Wyoming and later spent a number of years in the romance languages department in Northwestern University.

Bossard chose business as his vocation and has spent most of his life in Sumter.

The only daughter in the family, Ida (Mrs. Princeton Dauer), after graduation from Northwestern University, taught in the schools of Sumter until her recent retirement. These five physicians of the same lineal descent are not the only descendants of Dr. Thomas Morritt Dick who have excelled and are continuing to serve their fellowman. For instance, Dr. McFaddin Dick, of Salisbury, Md., is the son of Capt. Thomas Hasell Dick and grandson of Dr. Thomas Morritt Dick.

In the field of dentistry, Dr. George W. Dick, another descendant of the famous Dick ancestor, is remembered by many in the Sumter area, where he had a most successful practice of long standing. His son, Dr. Noble Dick, carried the family tradition all the way to California and Alaska.

Dr. Frank Holman was the great-grandson of Dr. Thomas Morritt Dick. Stationed in Bethesda, Md., as a Navy doctor is Dr. Glenn Davis, great-grandson of Dr. Leonard White Dick. His mother was Emma Dick, daughter of Leonard White Dick, Jr. Still another descendant of Dr. Thomas Morritt Dick is Dr. Erskin Fraser of Chapel Hill, N.C.

A great-granddaughter of Dr. George W. Dick is a graduate in pharmacy and is married to a doctor in Lexington, S.C. They are running a clinic there.

What contributions for one family to make toward the good

of mankind! And doubtless as the years pass, other descendants will be added to the roll of honor which had its beginning in another century.

The Dinkins Family

Half hidden from the eye, at the end of a long avenue on each side of which ancient cedars still stand, is the historic home of Mr. and Mrs. Willie Dinkins. Dating back to around 1810, it was built on land that is thought to have been a part of a grant to John Barden.

Walter James, who came from Virginia selling horses, met Esther Barden, married her and built his home either on Barden land or on a neighboring plantation which he bought.

The daughter of Walter and Esther Barden James, Frances married Langdon Hastings Dinkins, who at the death of Mrs. James, bought the 250 acres in the home place. Thus Frances James Dinkins was born and died in this old home.

When Langdon Dinkins came into possession of the home, he began making changes. In the 1870's he pushed the kitchen up to the house, which had two main rooms downstairs and two upstairs. Two shed rooms, 9 x 15 feet, were built on the back.

At the death of Langdon Dinkins the home was inherited by his unmarried daughter, Elevena Williametta; and at her death it came to the present owner, who was named William for this aunt.

Other changes were then made. The kitchen and the shed rooms were torn away and other rooms were built on the still solid foundation of these. All that now remains of the home built by the owners of the past are the two large downstairs rooms and the two on the second floor, with an attic.

In olden days the house, of course, was heated from fireplaces. Therefore there was a chimney on each end of the house with a large fireplace in each room. Though the home is now heated from a central heating plant, at least one of the fireplaces, the one in the living room, is still used to bring cheer to the family. The original mantels are still in place.

The walls were originally of red plaster. The chair boards are a yard wide, one board for each section of wall.

As in most old homes the sills and other timbers are of heart pine and pegs were used instead of nails.

The family cherishes many heirlooms that have come down through the years with the house. One of these is the beautiful drop-leaf dining table.

Another unusual possession is an old razor made in England

for which Grandfather Langdon was offered $25, but it was not for sale. There is also the quaint old shaving stand that the grandfather used. His sword and musket, relics of the War Between the States, are cherished by all the family. There is also the original commission granted to Langdon H. Dinkins. It reads in part: "We, reposing special trust and confidence in your courage and good conduct, in your fidelity to the State of South Carolina and attachment to the United States of America, have commissioned and appointed, and by these presents do Commission and Appoint you, the said Langdon H. Dinkins Ensign of Beat No. 1 – Upper Battery – 44th Regiment S.C. Militia, to take rank from the 27th July 1839 which said company you are to Lead, Train, Muster and Exercise, according to Military Discipline. And you are to follow and observe all such orders and instructions as you shall, from time to time, receive from the Governor, the Commander-in-Chief for the time being, or any of your superior Officers, according to the Rules and Discipline of War, pursuant of the Laws of this State, and of the United States."

It was signed by Patrick Noble and John Ballard and was dated April 2, 1840.

The front of the house has also been changed with a more modern porch added. On the porch is an old joggling board said by the present owner to have been made by his grandfather more than 100 years ago.

The front yard has presented an inviting play area for the children of more than one generation. The shade of the ancient oaks and other trees is tempting to anyone to stop for a rest. Drawing the attention of visitors is an old tree thought to be a catalpa, which has been dead for many years. Part of it was blown to the ground years ago, but the whole trunk is still there, never having suffered decay.

This old home has experienced much happiness as well as some sorrow. Music has always resounded through the rooms as the families that have lived here have been great lovers of music. Langdon H. Dinkins played the violin and loved it. It is said that once when he was in Florida, he visited a home in which the family was much disturbed because of a report that Indians were on the warpath and were coming their way.

He was invited in, however, and he began playing his violin. Soon the Indians did come, but so charmed were they with the music that after listening a while they went away very quietly without causing any trouble.

And the tradition goes on and music still echoes through the home. The father plays the violin, the mother sings, the children sing and some play the piano. Though all the children are married now and have families of their own, those living near come often and join their parents in an evening of music. . . . An interesting house usually indicates an interesting family with an interesting history. Facts on the Dinkins family have been compiled by Capt. James Dinkins of New Orleans, La., who states that he was told by a Mr. DeCourcy that the family has been traced back to around 1500 in Wales.

Members of the Dinkins family are thought to have moved into the lowlands of Scotland in the 16th century and from there they migrated to Londonderry in the North of Ireland. But through all the moves they retained their Welsh name which means "The Devil in the Bush," for they were great fighters.

In 1717, according to Capt. James Dinkins, three brothers – James, John and Samuel – together with cousins – Thomas and Joshua – came to the New World. According to another record one cousin was named Henry, and this record states that the following year Henry and Thomas returned to Londonderry to bring Henry's wife "Sussie" and his brothers Paul and Samuel.

John and James moved on to Mecklenburg County in North Carolina, settling in the Steele Creek Settlement. Thomas went to Georgia near Gainesville. Henry, Paul and Samuel are supposed to have remained in South Carolina. During the Revolutionary War, descendants of James and John fought with a company known as the "Hornets," commanded by Capt. Richard Springs who later moved to Lancaster District, S.C., and was the ancestor of the noted Col. LeRoy Springs of Lancaster County.

Some of the descendants of the Dinkins immigrants who remained in South Carolina fought under Gen. Francis Marion.

From the late Leonardo Andrea, a noted genealogist who lived in Columbia and who did much research on the Dinkins family, comes the information that some of the Dinkins Clan came from Ireland in 1732 to the present Anson County in North Carolina. One branch, he said, went to Virginia and two came into South Carolina. Some of these went on to Mississippi and Louisiana and thence to Texas and other Western states.

However, wherever and whenever they arrived in South Carolina, the family has made a name for itself. From the beginning, wherever they settled, whether in this state or some other, they made worthwhile contributions. It is said that they took an interest in anything that led to the welfare of their neighbors.

They assisted worthy young people in getting an education and gaining a good start in life. Many children were named for a member of the family it is said. With the help of their numerous slaves, they raised food crops of which they gave freely during the War Between the States. More than one person was heard to say, "We do not know how we could have lived through the war without the bounties we received from Mr. and Mrs. A.H. Dinkins." These two apparently lived in North Carolina and were the parents of Capt. James Dinkins.

It is believed that William Dinkins, who married Sarah Tompkins, was the ancestor of those of the Dinkins name living in Sumter County. In the Prince Frederick Parish record is the notation: "February ye 12th 1738 William Dinkins and Sarah Tompkins marryed." He took his bride to Chesterfield, where they were members of the famed old St. David Episcopal Church in Cheraw. They are likely buried there.

However, it is recorded in the family Bible that William Dinkins, Jr., was born in Craven County May 18, 1746. In 1768 he was married to Sarah Wright, daughter of William and Sarah Patterson Wright. She, too, was born in Craven County.

The Wright family dates back to Colonial times. It was a very wealthy family, owning much property in the Stateburg area. William Wright and Sarah Patterson were married December 26, 1745. They were members of St. Marks Episcopal Church and later the Church of the Holy Cross.

After the death of William Wright, Sarah was married to Dr. Joseph Howard of Stateburg.

William Dinkins, along with other patriots of the District Eastward of Wateree, signed the South Carolina Revolutionary Association for Public Defense in 1776. On August 11, 1777, he enlisted as a private in the 5th South Carolina Continental Regt. and was a member of this unit when it disbanded in 1779. In addition to his service as a soldier, he furnished supplies from his plantation for the State Militia and the Continental Troops.

After the death of Sarah, he married Nancy Smart and moved to Georgia. However, when he died February 26, 1818, he was buried in the Wright-Dinkins-Atkinson Cemetery beside his first wife who died in 1791.

William and Sarah Wright Dinkins had five children – Samuel, Asa, William, Wright P., and Sarah.

Samuel was born March 17, 1769, and died unmarried September 12, 1825. As a lad, along with Christopher Gayle, he took some potshots at British soldiers as they were marching near his home. They were arrested and Gayle was hanged, but being the smaller of the two, Samuel was put in chains in the Camden jail. Somehow with the help of friends he managed to escape.

The Dinkins Mill Tract was willed to Samuel by his Uncle William Wright. Since he died unmarried, the vast estate containing hundreds of acres was inherited by his brother Asa.

Two other sons of William and Sarah Wright Dinkins – William and Wright P. – died in infancy, and only daughter Sarah died unmarried at the age of 20.

Dinkins families, as well as some other families in the Sumter area, trace their lineage to Asa, the second son of William and Sarah Dinkins. He was born March 1, 1771, and was married on June 6, 1792, to Mary Anne Jennings (1775-1836), daughter of John and Jerusha Tynes Jennings. (There are two Tynes signatures – Samuel and William – on the South Carolina Association of Defense.) Asa and Mary Anne were the parents of 11 children:

Eldest, Marie Ann (b. 1795), married Manson Sylvester. They had eight sons and daughters.

Laurel Jennings Dinkins (1798-1859), oldest son of Asa and Mary Anne, married Camilla Holmes and was the father of eight – Charles C., Lewis M., Emmal., Percival, Bradley, Laurella, Moultrie, Mary Caroline.

Second daughter of Asa was Emily (b. 1802). She married James R. Spann and from this union came many of Sumter's well-known citizens. They were the parents of nine: James Videau E. Tyre (b. 1832, married R.L. Jones), Henry M. (1835-1923), Lucian (b. 1837), Sarah (b. 1839), Mariah (b. 1841), Langdon (b. 1843, married Rosa Jennings), and Danna.

Henry M. Spann married Caroline Virginia Dinkins and they were the parents of Frances (married to Wes Burkett), Mannie (married to Willie Buckester), Dinkins, Laurel (married to Stella Atkinson), and Virginia.

Second son of Asa and Mary Anne Dinkins was Larkin Tyre (1805-1854). He married Frances Margaret McLaughlin of Richland County in 1833. She was the daughter of John and Mary Atkinson McLaughlin. Mary Atkinson was the daughter of Fred and Mary Atkinson. Frederick's name is also on the South Carolina Association of Defense document, showing that he was living in the District Eastward of the Wateree. His father James and mother Elizabeth were living in Tarboro, N.C., in 1734, having come from Virginia.

Larkin and Frances Margaret were the parents of six: John (b. 1836), Mary Elizabeth (1838-1888, married to Rev. James Russell), Leonora (b. 1840, married first to Thomas Wright Lenoir and second to John J. Neason). Leonora and Thomas Wright Lenoir had three children – William Eugene, George Hodge and Mary Edisto, who married Harris Covington Bethea.

The two youngest children of Larkin and Frances Margaret were twins – Sumter and Frances Caroline. The story has come down through the family that Frances Caroline spent the night in the ditch with a cow that had fallen and couldn't get up, feeding the poor animal hominy.

Cornelia Beattie Dinkins, fourth child of Larkin and Frances Margaret, was born May 14, 1843. She married Robert Ellerbe Atkinson, son of James Atkinson (1810-1891) and Courtney

Sanders, daughter of John Sanders and Elizabeth Ballard. James Atkinson was the son of John, the son of Fred Atkinson.

Robert Ellerbe Atkinson and Cornelia Dinkins Atkinson had three children – Mary Courtney (1882-1961), Robert Eugene (1879-1931), and John Russell (1877-1943).

John Russell married Lalla Rosser Hix (1886-1947) in 1907. They had six sons and daughters.

1. Robert Hix married Doris Franklin and had one son, Robert Irvin.

2. John Russell, Jr., married Willie Mae Andrea.

3. Cornelia Louisa was never married.

4. Mary Courtney married William J. Valentine and had two – Louise and Courtney.

5. Edward Vandiver Atkinson is the third son in the family. He married Margaret (Possie) Delp, daughter of John Edward, Jr., and Agnes Moore Rodgers Delp of Philadelphia, Penna. Edward is a well-known and successful lawyer in Sumter. He and Possie have three daughters: Suzanne Rodgers Hiott, wife of Dr. J. Capers Hiott, son of Joseph Capers and Annette Golson Hiott. They have two sons – Edward Capers and Brenton Rodgers. They live in Sumter.

The second daughter is Courtney Lucinda, who married Gary J. Vechnak, and lives in Tampa, Fla. They have one son, Peter Bennett.

Stephanie Bennett is the youngest daughter of Edward and Possie Atkinson. She and her husband, Silas Jerrell Wilson, live in Sumter. They have one son, Grover Clark.

6. Sixth and youngest child of John Russell and Lalla Hix Atkinson was Francis Harrison, who was never married.

Fifth child of Asa and Mary Anne Dinkins was William Wright, who married first Amanda Lenoir; second Frances Collins.

The sixth in this family of Asa Dinkins was Lucian Asa and seventh was Wiley H., who married Rosanna A. Timmons in 1843. James Wright, the next son, married Mary ____ . Sarah Wright, the next daughter, married John W. Sylvester.

The tenth child and seventh son was Tyre Jennings Dinkins. He married Esther Amanthis James, daughter of Walter James and Easter (Esther?) Barden James, 1833. They were the parents of a large family:

1. Joseph Hemphill

2. Thomas Waties (d. 1868). One son, Tyre Jefferson.

3. Samuel Mayrant (born October 29, 1844, and died May 28, 1888). He married first Alice J. ____ (d. 1872) and second Harriet Crosswell (1848-1937).

4. John Scriven Dinkins married (1) ____ Wright, (2) Susan M. Jones.

5. Ulrika Dinkins (single)

6. Louisa Elizabeth Dinkins married Claudius Pritchard Steinmeyer and had one daughter Claudius Dinkins Steinmeyer.

According to Dr. Anne King Gregorie, Thomas Waties, second son in the family given above, was a lawyer and for a short while, editor of **The Dispatch**, a short-lived newspaper in Sumter. His wife, Ann Moise Dinkins, was also a talented writer for that paper.

7. Jane Moses Dinkins (1857-1951) married William Harry Pate (1851-1935).

Youngest in the family of Asa and Mary Anne Jennings Dinkins was Langdon Hastings (mentioned earlier). He was born in 1812 and died in 1879. He married Frances Louise James in 1839, daughter of Walter and Easter (Esther?) Barden James. She was born April 25, 1818, and died February or March 1898.

Langdon Dinkins was an outstanding member of his community. He is said to have been the first commissioner in Sumter and was also tax collector. He had wide farming interests. An interesting coincidence is connected with his cotton business. In 1840 he sold cotton to Elisha Carson in Charleston and his grandson, William, who still has the bill of sale, sold cotton to the same firm 100 years later.

Langdon and Frances Dinkins reared a large family of six daughters and four sons. Many of this family remained in Sumter and have descendants who are prominent citizens of this area today.

Oldest in this family was Mary Esther, who was born September 24, 1839, and died August 18, 1912. She married William Hamilton Jennings.

Caroline Virginia, second daughter, married Henry M. Spann. (This line was given earlier.)

The oldest son of Langdon and Frances Dinkins was Walter James, born January 17, 1846, and died unmarried.

Next in line was Tyre J. Dinkins who also died single. He was born July 15, 1848.

Winfield Scott Dinkins was third son. The story has come down through the family that Langdon admired Gen. Winfield Scott, as he knew him in the mid-1800's – during the trouble with Mexico – and thought so highly of him that he named his son for him. Later when Scott joined the Union Army during the Confederate War, he regretted having given his son that name.

Winfield Scott married first Nora Osteen and after her death he married Florence Spann. Nora was the mother of Esther Annie Dinkins, who married Langdon Dinkins ("Lang") Jennings, who was a political leader in Sumter. He served as mayor of the city for 12 years and was a State Senator.

Elevena Williametta Dinkins (1853-1899) was mentioned earlier.

Next in line was Sarah Rebecca Dinkins. She was born March 15, 1856, and died December 7, 1943. She married B. Frank Burkett (1844-1913).

Eighth child of Langdon Dinkins was Robert Brownfield, who was born August 28, 1858, and died April 9, 1938. He married first Mattie Doby. She was born February 20, 1871, and died May 18, 1908. After her death he married Anna L. Jennings (1866-1931).

Robert Brownfield and Mattie Doby Dinkins were the parents of five sons and daughters, the oldest being Langdon (1894-1900), named for his grandfather.

Leila Dinkins, the second child, married Carl Douglas. She was born September 1, 1896, and died December 23, 1969.

Second son of Robert Brownfield was James D. Dinkins, born November 8, 1900, deceased August of 1969. He married Annie Ross, a well-known nurse in Sumter. They were the parents of one son, Robert Ross Dinkins, a real estate dealer in Sumter. He married Mae Lee Haston, daughter of Mr. and Mrs. Ivory Haston, Dardanelle, Ark. They have two children – James Nathan and Matthew Colin.

William Dinkins, who lives in the historic home described earlier, was born September 26, 1902. He married Annie Webb of Columbia, whose parents were T.L.L. Webb and Emily J. McClure.

In this family are five sons and daughters. The oldest is William, Jr., who married Joan Marshall of Columbia, daughter of Mr. and Mrs. John Lewis Marshall. They live in Kansas City, Missouri, and their three boys are Bill, Rick and Ken.

Emily Dinkins married Laurance Kannon and is the mother of three – Dayton, William and Laurance. This family lives in New Orleans, Louisiana.

Next in the William Dinkins family is Mattie, who married Maj. John Roscoe, son of Mr. and Mrs. Lloyd Vincent Roscoe. Their children are Annie, Lloyd, Rett, Lang and Rachel, and they live in Morgan, Utah.

Frances Leila is the youngest daughter. She married Jimmy H. Strong, son of Mr. and Mrs. J.H. Strong of Sumter. They have a boy and a girl – Jimmy and Ruth – and they live in Sumter.

Second son and youngest child of William and Annie Webb Dinkins is Langdon Hastings. He married Barbara Cook. Their two children are Traci and Lang. They live in Sumter.

Next in the Robert Brownfield family is Robert B. Dinkins, born August 21, 1906. He was general manager of Black River

Electric Cooperative before his retirement. He also has large farming interests. He married Loretta Phifer of Yadkin County, N.C.

Their eldest son is Robert, Jr., a contractor in Sumter. He married Beverly Jones, daughter of Robert C. and Bertha Lawrence Jones. Their children are Robert, III, Lauri, Brian Phifer, and Philip Carson.

Charles William is the second son of Robert and Loretta Dinkins. He married Nancy Culler, daughter of Reese M. and Mary Inabinet Culler of Orangeburg. They have three children – Monica Christine, Michael David and Rob – and they live in Sumter.

David Hastings, third son in the Robert Dinkins family, is now studying for the ministry at Southwestern Southern Baptist Seminary in Houston, Texas. His engagement to Susan Pamela Holladay, of Summerton, has been announced; the wedding to take place in June.

Youngest son in the family is Stephen Lillington, who married Celeste Gordon, daughter of W.M. and Meda Dycus Gordon. Their children are Meda Loretto and Stephen, Jr.

Ninth in the Langdon Hastings Dinkins family was Florence Viola (b. 1860), who married William Hamilton Jennings. The tenth and youngest in the family was Ida Valentine (1862-1939), who married Robert Ives, and they had five children. Robert Francis married Christine Williamson; Walter Langdon; Ida Elizabeth, who married Ira Calhoun; Mary Kathleen married to Frank McCarthy; Virginia Dinkins Ives, who married Morgan Timmons.

Another line in the Tyre Jennings Dinkins genealogy has been made available and will be inserted here. Though it is not in the logical place, it can easily be connected.

John Scriven Dinkins married (1) Miss Wright, who was the mother of one daughter, Charlotte Essie. She married Francis Ollie Jennings and there were three in this family – Ulric Scriven (1891-1916), Louise Vermelle (1900-1901), Wilhelmina, who married Carol Burkett. There were two children: Helen, who married Haynsworth Pitts, and Clinton.

John Scriven then married Sue Jones and they had three: Rosa Amanthis (1879-1949), Vernon Robert (1887-1961), and Claude.

Vernon Robert married Frances James Mellette (b. 1893). They had four: Francis Mellette (1919-1921), Mary Esther (b. 1922), Vernon Robert, Jr. (1924-1942), and Laura Katharine (b. 1928).

Mary Esther married Arthur Whiteford James, son of Charles Sebastian and Leila Thompson James. They were the parents of three — Arthur Whiteford, Jr. (b. 1946), Robert Hastings (b. 1951), and William Hamilton (b. 1957).

Laura Katharine married Manning Roddey Rappe, Jr., son of Manning Roddey Rappe, Sr., and Alice Brogdon Rappe. Their children are Katharine Brogdon (b. 1952) and Manning Roddey Rappe, III (b. 1956). Katharine Brogdon married Richard Willis.

Claude Dinkins (1889-1968), son of John Scriven and Sue Jones Dinkins, married Sarah Ann Mellette (1891-1958). Their children were Claude, Jr. (1917-1929), Sarah (b. 1919), Edward (1922-1965), and Eugene Mellette (b. 1924).

Sarah Dinkins married (1) Clarence Blume (1918-1943) and they had one son, Clarence, Jr., who married Betty Cappell and their children are Tina Lorraine (b. 1965) and Donald.

Sarah married (2) Donald Picker and their children are Donald, Jr. (b. 1946), who married Glenda Rae Swearingen and had one daughter, Nerissa Mae, and Susan Pickler (b. 1952), who married Joseph McLeod and is the mother of Joseph McLeod, Jr.

Edward A. Dinkins, second son of Claude and Sarah Anne Mellette Dinkins, married Betty Nash, daughter of Annie Mae Mahoney Nash and Homer Dickson Nash. Their children are Edward A., Jr. (1945-1946), Edward A., Jr. (b. 1946), and Claude Nash (b. 1949). Edward A. Dinkins, Jr., married Dianne Virginia Huskins and they have one child, Kristin Leigh (b. 1973).

Claude Nash Dinkins married Mary Catherine Walker (b. 1949), daughter of Dr. R. Murdoch and Gussie Williams Walker. They have one son, Claude Nash, Jr. (b. 1973).

Youngest son of Claude and Sarah Ann Mellette Dinkins is Eugene Mellette (b. 1924). He married Mary Jane Rembert and they are the parents of eight: Sarah Janelle (1946), Sherrie Jean (b. 1949), Richard Rembert, Daniel Hoyt, and Eugene Mellette, Jr. (triplets, b. 1953), Juanita Hoyt (b. 1956), Daniel Eugene (b. 1958), William Richardson (b. 1961).

Sarah Janelle married Jerry Lucas and had one daughter, Ingrid. Sherrie Jean married Michael Parker.

Though Capt. James Dinkins is not in the direct line from William and Sarah Wright Dinkins, another word may be said for him since it is to him that the family owes gratitude for the research he did.

Tyre Jefferson Dinkins, son of Thomas Waties, who was the son of Tyre Jennings and Esther Amanthis James Dinkins, gives some information concerning this distant cousin in some old letters that have been kept in the family.

While living in New York, "Jeff" as he signed himself, went to New Orleans and met "Captain James." Later Capt. and Mrs. James Dinkins went to New York and a second interview was arranged. "Jeff" reported him to be a "most wonderful old gentleman, active, spry, entertaining and a typical Dinkins."

In addition to all the other good traits found in members of the Dinkins family through the years, it can be said that they appreciate their great heritage. To show their gratitude, those in Sumter County, together with some from other places, held a memorial service on July 4, 1959, at the old Dinkins Mill Cemetery, the last resting place of many of their ancestors.

Markers to William and Asa Dinkins were unveiled and decorated and an appropriate program including speeches and music was presented by descendants of the two especially honored.

At the end of the printed program appeared the very appropriate quotation: "The children of the Righteous shall rise up and call them Blessed from Generation to Generation."

(Written June 1976)

The Montgomery Family, Part I

A well-known name in lower South Carolina, a name with an ancestry that stands tall in history, is that of Montgomery. According to one researcher, Laurence Scott Barringer, the name at first was Mundgumbri, meaning "gloomy mountain" from the section where the family lived in Italy.

It is believed that Sieur Roger de Mundgumbri arrived in England in 1066 along with William the Conqueror and was made First High Steward of Scotland as a reward for his part in the Battle of Hastings. Later he received other titles before leaving England for Scotland.

At the invasion of Ireland by King William III of England, Hugh Montgomery was one of his officers, who later settled in Ireland, in County Cork. There he married the "heiress of Killee." They were the parents of one son, George.

One record states that George came to South Carolina sometime before 1742 since in that year he signed a Petition to the Royal Governor. It is not known who his wife was. According to the "family tree," however, researched by Joseph H. Montgomery, Hugh Montgomery, George's son, born in 1738, came to Williamsburg, South Carolina, in his "early manhood."

Whenever he came, he became an outstanding citizen of the Williamsburg area. He served in the American Revolution as a member of General Marion's Brigade and was paid 23 pounds and five shillings for his services. At the time of the 1790 census he was living on a large plantation on Black River and apparently was quite wealthy.

Hugh Montgomery was married to Janet (Jennet) Daniel. He died in 1793 at the age of 55, and she lived till 1814 and was 65 at the time of her death. Dr. James Cousar, in his **Physician Turned Planter**, tells of visiting their graves in the old Orr's Field Graveyard or Montgomery Cemetery off Highway 261 in Williamsburg County.

From this marriage are many descendants in Sumter, Lee, Clarendon, Williamsburg Counties and many are living in more distant places, but only the descendants of son John will be treated in this sketch.

Connecting two distinguished families of South Carolina was the marriage of John Montgomery and Eliza Witherspoon, great granddaughter of John Witherspoon, the immigrant, and a descendant of Rev. John Knox and Lady Margaret Stewart.

From this union there were four daughters and two sons. The eldest daughter was Thermuthis Ann, who married George Cooper, a planter of Williamsburg County. Next was Jennet Parthenia, who died at age 14. Margaret Leonora married John Allen Burgess, and the youngest, Mary Eugenia, died at 10 months. The younger son, William Reese, lived only one year.

It is John Witherspoon Montgomery, elder son, whose descendants will now be given. He was born in Williamsburg in 1816 and died in Sumter in 1877.

He married Margaret Emily Wilson, daughter of Hugh Wilson. She was born in Sumter in 1819 and died in 1866. Their children were Hugh Wilson (1839-1861); John (1841-1905); Elizabeth H. (1843-18??); Susanna Thermuthis (1845-1866); Mary E. Almira (1848(?)-1861), killed accidentally at age 13; Elizabeth Parthenia ("Tenie," 1856-1860), married to Archibald Alexander Brearley; infant son, unnamed.

The home of the John Witherspoon Montgomery family was known as "Mineral Springs." It was located in old Sumter County according to a map compiled by M.H. McLaurin in 1878.

They later built a home nearer Swimming Pens and the old place was then occupied by "Tenie" Montgomery and her husband A.A. Brearley.

Hugh Wilson Montgomery, along with Thomas Goulding Reid, William Moultrie Reid, Jr., Robert English, Eli Cooper, Roy Shaw and Dr. Munson Shaw, all "boys" of the same community, left Mayesville on July 4, 1861, to go to training camp for the Confederate Army and were sent on to Virginia just before the first Battle of Manassas.

On August 30 word was received that Hugh and John, who was also in the service, were seriously ill in Virginia and soon Hugh died. John was brought home to recuperate.

The Civil War brought misery and heartache to most in South Carolina; even the elderly were forced to serve in some way. In 1863 John Montgomery and others, though too old to fight, were ordered to Charleston to direct the work of their slaves in building fortifications along the coast and possibly in giving relief for the needy.

Susanna Thermuthis, second daughter of John and Margaret Emily Wilson Montgomery, was married to Moultrie Reid Wilson in 1865, but died in less than a year. (Her name Thermuthis was by tradition the name of the Egyptian princess who took the baby Moses into her care.)

These young people carried on a correspondence during the war days that has preserved for posterity a vivid picture of life in the army and in the homes in those days of deprivation and suffering. These letters, with additional information concerning the central figures, their families and others in the community, served for the most part by old Mt. Zion Presbyterian Church in Lee County, have been published by Mrs. Lucile Wilson Trout and Mrs. Gertrude McLaurin Shaw, grandchildren of Moultrie Reid Wilson, under the name **Memory's Golden Chain** from which some facts in this article came.

John Montgomery, second son of John Witherspoon and Emily Montgomery, married first Evie (Evelyn) Irene Fraser (1848-1883) and they were the parents of three: John W., Ladson Fraser, and Tenie Evelyn.

Second wife of John Montgomery was Genie Law. They had one daughter, Mary Hart.

John W. married Madge Fraser, daughter of Dr. W.W. Fraser, and Martha McCutchen Fraser. Their eldest child was Martha, who died during the 1918 influenza epidemic. She was a student at Coker College at the time of her death.

The next daughter, Genie, is well known in Sumter, where for some years she was a milliner and a connoisseur in Ladies' Fashions. She is now retired and making her home at the Presbyterian Home in Clinton. (Now deceased.)

Willie, the first son, was never married.

The next son, Henry, married Mary Wells, of Sumter.

Madge taught in Sumter before marrying Benton C. Shafer. She lives in Winter Haven, Fla., and Guntersville, Ala.

The youngest son, John, married Carolyn Plowden, of Manning. They live in Statesville, N.C., where he was for a time president of Mitchell College.

Youngest in the family is Genoese. She is married to Charles Batts and they live in Hampton, Va., where he is serving as a Captain in the U.S. Army.

Ladson Fraser Montgomery married Martha Jane McCutchen

and they were the parents of a large family.

The latch string was always on the outside at this home. As one of the daughters says, "My home . . . was 'open house' at all times for the young as well as the old." She also said, "My parents had hearts of gold and loved everyone . . . "

Eldest in the family was Evelyn Irene, who married Dr. Cecil DuBose Brearley. Before his retirement, Dr. Brearley held pastorates in several of South Carolina's Presbyterian churches and has held a leading position in his denomination. The Brearleys now live in the Presbyterian Home in Summerville.

Hannah, next in the family, married William Ewart Easterling and they live in North Carolina.

Vermelle McCutchen, next daughter, married Thomas Alexander DuBose, member of a fine old Lee County family. He is now deceased. Vermelle continued to live in their home on Highway 15 and was engaged in a number of outside activities, especially those of her church where she was the pianist for a long while. She now is a resident at the Presbyterian Home in Summerville.

Oldest of the six sons in the family of Ladson Fraser Montgomery was Ladson Fraser, Jr., who is now deceased. He first married Roberta Shaw of the same community. His second marriage was to Olive Brodie of the Orangeburg area.

Robert White (deceased) married Elizabeth Montgomery of Kingstree.

Yancy Alford (deceased) married Dixie Robertson.

Augustus Cooper died at six months.

George Hugh (deceased) married Anna Merritt.

Henry Junius (deceased) married Ruth Green.

All of these young men who grew to maturity were successful businessmen and filled an important place in their community.

Youngest child of John Montgomery and Evie Fraser Montgomery was Tenie Evelyn (1876-1914). She married George Henley McCutchen and there were seven children in this family: John Montgomery McCutchen, born June 10, 1901; Elma McCutchen, born Nov. 15, 1903; George Henley McCutchen, Jr., born July 19, 1905; William O'Thello McCutchen (Nov. 17, 1907-Jan. 14, 1927); Ladson Fraser McCutchen, born Nov. 8, 1910; Atwood McCoty McCutchen (Oct. 24, 1912-Jan. 2, 1913); Tenie Evelyn McCutchen, born and died April 10, 1914.

Through the years Montgomerys and their connections have proved worthy of their noble ancestry, making a lasting imprint on the communities in which they have lived and taking a leading role in various fields of endeavor.

(A sketch of the family of Joseph Montgomery, son of Hugh and brother of John, will be given in Part II. Both parts were written in 1977.)

The Montgomery Family, Part II

Born in Ireland in 1738, Hugh Montgomery, son of George, came to Williamsburg District while still a young man. There he met and married Janet Daniels. Both are buried in the old Montgomery Cemetery off Highway 261.

There were at least two sons from this marriage. The descendants of John were treated in an earlier article. This sketch will tell something of son Joseph and his descendants.

According to Dr. James Cousar in his latest book, **Physician Turned Planter**, Joseph must have been a very interesting man. His personality is revealed in a diary which he kept from his wedding day, February 20, 1817, to December 27 of the same year.

He married Elizabeth McFaddin when she was only 15 years of age. She was the daughter of Robert McFaddin and his second wife, Leah Lenoir Dickey McFaddin, better known as "Aunt Leah." Many legends which have lived through the years are still being told and retold of the activities of this remarkable and colorful person. She was a business woman without equal; she knew well how to manage the workers on her plantation; she held deservedly the admiration of all who knew her. A contribution of far-reaching influence was her organization of a Sunday School at Concord Presbyterian Church, as early as 1837, for the benefit of many who had never enjoyed such a privilege. She was on hand each Sunday, though for many years she came by buggy for eight miles over poor country roads.

No doubt, Elizabeth gained many fine qualities from her unusual mother, for she made Joseph a good wife.

In that first year of marriage, Joseph went on one occasion to visit his wife's family and liked the place so well that he wanted to settle there. Whether his father-in-law heard his wish or not, he received a grant from the wealthy Robert McFaddin for over 902 acres of land in the "forks of Black River."

Here he built his house known as "Victory Plain." It has been described as "a spacious two-story dwelling with two large chimneys at each end, the whole built upon brick pillars about six feet high."

Joseph was a successful farmer, but he expressed an active interest in politics of his county and state. However, he was never elected to public office.

Though the life of this Montgomery family was the usual well-ordered life of a large planter of that era, there were some sorrows mingled with the joys.

One near tragedy might be mentioned. Two slaves wished to marry, but for some reason they were not allowed to do so. To get revenge they ground seeds of the Jimson weed (member of the deadly nightshade family) and mixed the substance with the coffee that the family of father and mother and six children drank. They became violently ill, but under the treatment of a new doctor in the community, Dr. Robert R. DuRant, all recovered. The culprits were found out and hanged. Perhaps it was a severe penalty since no one died; but there was plenty of Jimson weed and there could have been a second attempt on the lives of this family or another.

One interesting related incident was the marriage of Elizabeth's sister, Mary McFaddin, to the new doctor.

Elizabeth Montgomery died on July 18, 1837, leaving a grieving husband and a large family of sons and daughters, ranging in age from nine to nineteen.

1. Margaret married Hugh McFaddin. From this marriage came the family of Dr. H.J. McLaurin – those wonderful sisters who contributed so much to the educational and religious life of Sumter.
2. Leonora, who became the wife of Robert Boyd Muldrow.
3. James Hugh married to Miss Mary M. Robinson.
4. Robert McFaddin, who married Laura Pugh.
5. Mary Elizabeth, wife of William James Wilson Muldrow.
6. Joseph Hayne, who married Lou Langham and moved to Texas.
7. Susan, who died unmarried.

Families of some of these will be traced in detail later.

Joseph never remarried; and to the great surprise of family and friends, he moved to Alabama in 1848. The plantation on which he had lived during his married life remained in his possession, but in Alabama he purchased 1600 acres and built a home. He divided his slaves, leaving some to farm his land in Sumter District and taking some with him to Alabama. Two of his sons, Joseph Hayne and James Hugh, accompanied him to his new home.

His life in his adopted state apparently was successful and relatively happy. He returned home in 1861 and died later that same year.

The family is in possession of two of his letters – one written in 1858 to Robert McFaddin Montgomery from Appleton Mills, Ala. He tells of a spell of "chill and fever" that he had had. His description gives a touch of his old-time humor: "It has brought more debility and crooked deformity over me than all the years that have rolled over my head, the eyes grow faint and dim, that voice which was at one time melody itself, now sends forth words with a Splitteration, hard to be understood:—"

He spoke of his son James Hugh and described him as happy, though he was far away from his old home in South Carolina. And one letter from James Hugh to his sister Susan, written October 27, 1859, shows some reason for his happiness. He wrote: "On the morning of the 20th inst. between the hours of twelve and one o'clock Mollie presented to me and the world a fine Daughter. Oh, how I wish you could see it, everyone says it is the image of you, a Montgomery all over."

He also tells in this letter of his being sick and the illness of several of his slaves. His letter ends on a rather despondent note, though he is evidently able to show a cheerful face in the presence of his father.

Janet Leonora, believed to have been the eldest daughter of Joseph and Elizabeth McFaddin Montgomery, was born December 5, 1820. She married Robert Boyd Muldrow February 19, 1839. She died November 23, 1899. He died November 5, 1857. They reared a large family.

1. Margaret Elizabeth ("Betsy"), born February 14, 1840, was married January 13, 1864, to Joseph Sidney DuRant. She died November 14, 1919, and is buried in the DuRant Cemetery.

2. Susan Louiza ("Big Auntie"), born July 15, 1842. On October 10, 1871, she became the second wife of J. Anderson Mills. She died June 30, 1928, and is buried at Brick Church.

3. Jane Cooper, born May 7, 1844, became the first wife of J. Anderson Mills June 8, 1864. She died September 30, 1869.

4. Robert, born December 21, 1848, joined the Confederate Army March 10, 1865, and died of typhoid fever April 7, 1865.

5. Joseph, twin brother of Robert, died October 23, 1918. He was never married.

6. A daughter lived only 20 days.

7. Albert Boyd (1850-1851).

8. James D. McFaddin Muldrow (1851-1865).

9. Edward Boyd, born May 7, 1853, married Elizabeth Henrietta Mayes November 27, 1873. He died August 30, 1911.

Children of Margaret Elizabeth Muldrow (daughter of Janet Leonora Montgomery and Robert Boyd Muldrow) and Joseph Sidney DuRant were as follows:

a. Joseph Sidney DuRant, Jr. (1864-1935) b. Mary Leonora ("Aunt Darling"), born February 11, 1866, and died November 14, 1929. c. Maggie Muldrow DuRant became second wife of William Evander Daniels on July 24, 1907. She was born April 28, 1867, and died May 19, 1948. She is buried in the Manning Cemetery. d. Infant daughter (1868). e. Eliza Gertrude, born May 26, 1869, died December 8, 1957, never married.

f. Infant daughter (1870).

g. Robert Rees (1871-1956) married Maggie E. Keller.

h. Jane Cooper, born August 16, 1873, died April 19, 1940, buried in Manning Cemetery. On May 12, 1897, she married Warren Burgess Dickson.

i. Henley Thornwell (1876-1880). Buried in DuRant Cemetery.

j. Virginia Irene (1815-1911), never married. She is buried in the DuRant Cemetery.

k. Bessie, born January 25, 1878, died June 5, 1949. She married Robert Early Thompson on November 28, 1905. They were the parents of five.

1. Virginia Lois Thompson married Nicholas Doscher.
2. Robert Dick Thompson.
3. Joseph DuRant Thompson.
4. William Early Thompson.
5. Edward Archer Thompson.

Children of Edward Boyd Muldrow, ninth child of Janet Leonora Montgomery and Robert Boyd Muldrow, and Elizabeth Henrietta Mayes were as follows:

1. Isabelle, who married Rev. John Gray. Issue: Jane and John.
2. Mary, who married James McKay Shaw. Issue (adopted): Billy, Mary Frances, and Sonny.
3. Janie (Jennie). Unmarried.
4. Edward Boyd, Jr., who married Margaret Montgomery. Children named in a later connection.
5. Robert married Mary Scott Witherspoon. Issue: Joseph Edward, Margaret, Hugh Gray, and Robert (died in infancy).
6. Willie James married Bess Tolly. Issue: Willie, Georgia (married Gilmer), and Elizabeth.

Margaret Scott Montgomery married Hugh McFaddin, and their descendants were mentioned earlier.

James Hugh Montgomery married Mary M. Robinson in 1855 — one daughter, Leonora. He died June 28, 1860.

Robert McFaddin, son of Joseph and Elizabeth Montgomery, married Laura Ann Pugh on November 26, 1850. They have many descendants who have been and are outstanding citizens of this area.

Their eldest daughter was Elizabeth, born November 14, 1851. She married Samuel McBride Witherspoon, and in this family were many sons and daughters who have been leaders in their respective communities. These were the following:

a. Hugh (1878-1977)
b. Mary (Mrs. Robert Muldrow)
c. Robert
d. William Judson (who moved to Wyoming)
e. Samuel McBride (living at Myrtle Beach)

f. James (who lived in the West)

g. Joseph Theodore (living at Gable); Annie Laurie (Mrs. David Wilson)

Second in the Robert McFaddin-Laura Pugh Montgomery family was Margaret McFaddin (1853-1885), not married.

William Pugh was eldest son, born 1855. He married Lillie Witherspoon. No children. He was a successful farmer.

James McFaddin, second son, was born in 1857. He married first Maria Burgess Plowden, November 18, 1880. Their children were: 1. Sam Edgar, born October 20, 1881, and died at age 26. 2. Richard Carroll, born December 18, 1884, and died at age 23. James was also a large planter.

After the death of his first wife, James McFaddin Montgomery married on December 17, 1890, Sara Eliza (Lila) Plowden. Their children were as follows:

1. Margaret McFaddin, who married Edward Boyd Muldrow, Jr. Their children are: a. James Montgomery (living in Greenville); b. Lila Elizabeth (Mrs. Roscoe Riggins); c. Edward Boyd, Jr. (Ned), living in Bishopville; d. William Pugh (Will); e. Robert Warren; f. Leonora Janet (Jean).

2. James Hargrove married Mary Poag. He lives near the old home on the Brewington Road (in early days a direct route from Camden to Charleston). His son, James Hargrove, Jr., farms his father's place.

Other children of James Hargrove and Mary Poag are (1) Nevada Stultz (Follin), (2) Mary Reid, (3) Margaret.

3. Irvin Plowden was the second son of James McFaddin and Lila Plowden Montgomery. He married Margaret Griggs, and their children are Marjorie Ann, Mary Elizabeth, Irwin Plowden, Jr., and Clara Eloise. Irvin Plowden taught until his death in 1951.

4. Younger daughter of James and Lila Montgomery is Ada Elizabeth, who is married to Forest Lanor Jordan. She was a teacher in Camden for a number of years. She lives at the site of the old Robert Montgomery home. The attractive country home where the Jordans live was built after the old home burned in 1911. There are no children in this family.

The fifth child of Robert and Laura Ann Pugh Montgomery was Hugh (born 1860), who married Nannie Scott in Paris, Ky. There were no children. He was a "drummer" who sold shoes.

Joseph McFaddin Montgomery, sixth in the Robert McFaddin Montgomery family, was born on June 28, 1862. He married Mamie ___, but there were no children. He lived in Montgomery, Ala., and practiced law until his health failed. He then became postmaster. However, when a friend became involved in a law suit, he undertook to defend him and died in the courtroom.

Seventh in the family was Robert Muldrow (born 1865). He was married three times: (1) Ruby Wilcox, (2) Mamie ___, (3) Carrie ___. He was a doctor in Hazlehurst, Ga. He has one surviving daughter, Evelyn ("Doodle") Montgomery Brannon, living in Darien, Ga. She occasionally passes through the Sumter area and stops for a visit with relatives.

Mary Susan, youngest daughter of the Robert and Laura Montgomery family, was born October 8, 1867, and died February 2, 1869.

Youngest son was Charles (born 1869), who married Della C. McRae. He was a Presbyterian minister in Mt. Vernon, Ga., for about 25 years before moving to Virginia, where he died. One daughter, Marguerite Jervey, and two sons – Robert and Elijah Paul – survive him. All live in Virginia. The daughter, known as "Cricket," visits relatives in the Sumter area occasionally.

Mary Elizabeth, fifth child of Joseph and Elizabeth McFaddin Montgomery, was born about 1830 and died November 24, 1918. She married William James Wilson Muldrow, who died January 20, 1903.

One of their daughters married James English Cousar, Sr. They were the parents of Dr. James English Cousar, Jr., well-known and beloved Presbyterian minister and author of several books. In his latest book, **Physician Turned Planter**, he tells much of his grandmother. He says that she "knitted socks for soldiers in four wars – the Mexican, the Confederate, Spanish-American and World War I."

Other children of Joseph and Elizabeth McFaddin Montgomery include Joseph Hayne Montgomery, who married Lou Langham and moved to Fisher County, Tex., and died there.

There was also a Robert McFaddin, who died as a child. Then the Robert McFaddin, who was listed earlier, was born later.

Some additional excerpts from old letters that were written more than a century ago and still treasured will throw some light on a few of the members of this remarkable family, a family that played an important role in laying the foundation for the economic, educational, and religious culture found in this area today.

Some lines from a letter written to Robert McFaddin Montgomery by R.C. McFaddin in 1861: "We are here as you know in the 'Old Dominion' but whereabouts in it is hard to say. I think when the Maps and Atls (sic) were made, these parts were overlooked entirely. We were put off the cars at a place called Manassa (sic), near where they had the big fight, but there was nothing to be seen at the place except Batteries on every hill filled with Cannon ready for shooting, which would have given me buck ague instantly if I had not been so hungry. After satisfying my appetite and quieting my nerves I walked out to the battle field six miles and you may say to Buck that when I searched it there was only one thing that kept me from taking a bee line for Black River, and that was, I did not know which way to run."

A letter from Joseph Montgomery from Tumbull P.O., Monroe County, Ala., to his son, Capt. Robert M. Montgomery, Plowden's Mill P.O., Sumter District, S.C., shows something of the political situation in the 1850's when the letter was likely written.

" . . . this is the first triumph that the Southern Rights party have ever gain'd over the Northern party; Maj. Andrews beat McCaskill at Monroe Springs and at Tumbull . . . Langdon was proven to be Northern all over, had taken the benefit of the Bankrupt Laws and was indebted as principal to 1 Bank in Mobile in the sum of 32,000$ and as security for 68,000$ . . .

"I voted at Germany there was one lawyer Roberts from Monroeville got up to enlighten the Germany voters and show that C.C Langdon was all right. . . . The Honorable the Reverend Mr. Sessions rose and thank'd the learned gentleman for his goodness in coming so far to enlighten him and his poor ignorant German voters but . . . C.C Langdon was a Bankrupt. . . . He then set forth rights of the South and pointed to Northern oppression and upon the whole he advanced the best doctrine that I have heard in Alabama. . . . Two days afterward at Pinevill I heard . . . Mr. Riley resolved never to pay Mr. Sessions anything more for preaching. I sent them word that I would see that Mr. Sessions pot should boil as long and as strong as ever it did, and call'd the patch behind the corn house 'Mr. Session's Cotton.' "

(Written in 1977.)

Rhodes Family Has Rich Heritage In County

Descended from Gerard de Rodes of Horn Castle, Lincoln Co., England, during the reign of King Henry II is one of Sumter County's oldest and most respected families. Sir Francis Rhodes was created a Baronet in 1641. The coat of arms featured a lion, a charge adopted by all the emperors of that time and signified strength and fortitude. The oak and acorns in the arms were symbols of dependability and strength. The colors of argent (silver), gules (red), and azure (blue) signified purity and constancy, military fortitude, truth and sincerity.

Zachariah Rhodes (1603-1665) is believed to be one of the first settlers of Pawtucket, Rhode Island. He, with Roger Williams, established the Baptist belief in America.

Another early settler in America was Thomas Rhodes, who aboard **The Amities**, was bound for St. Christopher's in 1635.

The Darlington County Rhodes families, who have descendants in many parts of the state, trace their ancestry to Joseph Edward Rhodes, who came there from Sampson County, N.C. Those in Sumter County are not connected with these so far as can be determined.

The Sumter County line seems to have come from Thomas Rhodes, who is thought to have been listed as a male between 10 and 16 in the 1800 census in Moore County, N.C., in the family of William Rhodes in that county. Thomas married Margaret McPherson, daughter of Alexander McPherson, Jr., who was born ca. 1754 on "The Isle of Jura" in Scotland, and his wife, born ca. 1760 in Cantrye, Scotland, was Elizabeth Murrary. Alexander died Jan. 21, 1821, and Elizabeth, March 29, 1841, in Cumberland County, N.C.

Thomas and Margaret McPherson Rhodes are buried in Union Presbyterian Church cemetery near Carthage in Moore County, N.C.

The children of these two were as follows:

1. Nancy, b. Dec. 23, 1810; m. ____ McNeil. They had children.
2. Lucretia, b. April 1, 1813; d. Dec. 7, 1900.
3. David, b. July 5, 1815, d. Sept. 6, 1881.
4. Martin, b. Sept. 12, 1817; d. Nov. 5, 1910.
5. Thomas, b. Nov. 7, 1819; d. Apr. 4, 1870.
6. Mary Ann, b. Oct. 15, 1822; d. Mar. 2, 1902.
7. Elizabeth, b. Oct. 25, 1825; d. Oct. 20, 1878.
8. William, b. July 4, 1828; d. Sept. 8, 1855.

Most of the early Rhodes family were buried in Union Presbyterian Church cemetery near Fayetteville, N.C.

From this point the family of Martin Rhodes, second son of Thomas and Margaret Rhodes, who came to South Carolina, will be traced.

On Dec. 31, 1844, he married Elizabeth Shaw, daughter of David and Rebecca McBride (sister of Samuel McBride) Shaw, either in Sumter or Williamsburg District. She was born Oct. 20, 1821, and died Mar. 21, 1848.

Martin and Elizabeth Shaw Rhodes were the parents of a son and a daughter – William David (b. Sept. 29, 1845) and Mary Elizabeth (b. Mar. 7, 1848). On Mar. 21, 1848, Elizabeth died and the two children were reared by their mother's sister, Henrietta Shaw Mayes, wife of Squire Matthew Peterson Mayes, founder of Mayesville.

On Dec. 7, 1848, Martin Rhodes was married to Sarah Elizabeth Whitworth (b. Oct. 30, 1826; d. Feb. 10, 1892), daughter of Isaac DuBose Whitworth and Sarah Elvira Shaw, oldest daughter of John and Lillis Mitchell Shaw.

From this marriage there were ten children:

1. Lillis Shaw Rhodes (b. Dec. 12, 1850; d. Feb. 23, 1862).

2. Sarah Elvira Rhodes (b. Oct. 20, 1852; d. Dec. 16, 1929). She is buried in Salem Black River Cemetery. She was known lovingly by the family as "Aunt Tump." She was never married.

3. Margaret Rhodes (b. Mar. 28, 1855; d. Mar. 21, 1943). She married a Mr. Chapman and lived in Cheraw. She is buried at St. David's Church in Cheraw. She was known as "Aunt Maggie."

4. Lucretia Rhodes (b. June 4, 1857). She married Ervin Wilson in Mayesville and is buried in the Mayesville cemetery.

5. Martin Luther Rhodes (b. July 26, 1859). He was known in the family as "Uncle Luther." He married Julia Douglas of Florence and is buried in that town. There were no children.

6. Mary Mae Rhodes (b. May 30, 1861; d. June 2, ____). She married Edwin Wilson of St. Charles. They were called "Uncle Ned and Aunt Mae" by the family. She is buried in Mt. Zion Cemetery near St. Charles.

7. Jane Whitworth Rhodes (b. Aug. 26, 1863; d. Oct. 27, 1934). She married Mr. Funderburke. There were no children.

8. John Whitworth Rhodes (b. Dec. 29, 1865; d. Sept. 23, 1880).

9. Thomas Dow Rhodes, "Uncle Dow," (b. Oct. 31, 1868; d. May 30, 1906). He is buried in Salem Black River Cemetery.

10. Eula Lee Rhodes (b. Feb. 20, 1871). She married La Coaste Evens, Cheraw, S.C. She is buried in St. David's Cemetery.

Martin Rhodes lived to be 93 and the story in the family is that he still had all his teeth.

Elizabeth Rhodes, daughter of Martin Rhodes, and his first wife, married Isaac Whitworth Bradley and her family is traced in **Historical Sketches of Sumter County** by Nicholes and **The Bradleys and Allied Families of S.C.** by Ensworth.

Since the descendants of William David Rhodes, son of Martin and Elizabeth Shaw Rhodes, carry on the Rhodes name in this area, this line will now be traced.

William David Rhodes (b. Sept. 29 (?), 1845) married Mary Whitworth (b. Oct. 2, 1851).

It had been a tradition it seems in the early Rhodes name only one son in a family married. However, the "spell" was broken when both William David and his half-brother, Martin Luther, were wed.

At the age of 16, William David volunteered to serve in the Confederate Army. In 1892 he was elected to the state legislature on the "Straightout" ticket. He was a lifelong member of Salem Black River (Brick) Presbyterian Church, serving as deacon, librarian and ruling elder. At his death, which came May 24, 1924, his obituary stated that he was "a very prominent farmer and widely known." The obituary closed with this tribute: "He was devoted to his family, his church, his state and community. His death is a severe loss to Salem Black River and vicinity."

Upon the death of his wife, Feb. 24, 1927, a neighbor wrote a beautiful tribute to her, speaking of her beautiful formal garden, one of the last of its kind in the Salem community. Lining the walkways in the garden were lovely specimens of boxwood and inside the borders of boxwood perennial and annual flowers bloomed. Scattered throughout the garden were azaleas, magnolias and sweet olives. As years passed, the descendants spent less and less time keeping up the garden and no trace of it is left today.

William David and Mary Whitworth saw to it that their children had the best educational advantages, though at times with five-cents cotton they found the going difficult. All the daughters were graduates of Converse College; and the sons also attended college, one at the University of South Carolina, one at Kings Mountain Military Academy in York, S.C., and one at Bailey Academy in Oxford.

In this happy family there were nine children:

1. Infant son (b. Jan. 9, 1869; d. Jan. 10, 1869).

2. John Whitworth Rhodes (b. Dec. 29, 1869; d. Aug. 10, 1933). On Dec. 11, 1902, he married Ada I. Mayes, daughter of James Edgar and Sarah Lynda Chandler Mayes.

From this marriage there were six children:

a. Mary L. (b. Sept. 30, 1904; d. 1911). She is buried in the cemetery at Salem Black River.

b. Sarah Elizabeth Rhodes is unmarried. She lives in Mayesville in her ancestral home.

c. Lynda Rhodes married Everette Wysong and has two daughters: (1) Letitia, who married James Baker and they have one son and three daughters. (2) Ada Lyn married Fred Collins. They have four sons and one daughter and live in Sumter.

d. John Whitworth Rhodes, Jr. He is unmarried and lives in Columbia.

e. William David Rhodes, II, married Henrietta Sydnor. They live in Mayesville and have a son and a daughter: (1) Charles William Rhodes, unmarried, living in Mayesville and (2) Rebecca Sydnor Rhodes married Wade Parks Stowe, III. They live in Columbia.

f. James Edgar Rhodes (deceased May 26, 1948). He is buried in the Salem Black River Church Cemetery.

3. Elizabeth Shaw Rhodes (b. May 9, 1874; d. Nov. 13, 1957). She married (1) Harry H. Cooper on Dec. 15, 1898, and (2) M.

Bradley Wilson, Dec., 1922. She is buried in Mayesville Cemetery.

4. Lillis Jane Rhodes (b. Mar. 1, 1877; d. Aug., 1956). She married Eugene Linwood Cooper on Dec. 9, 1903. She is buried in Mayesville Cemetery.

Children:

a. Mary Whitworth Cooper. She married James Thomas Clark (d. Dec. 25, 1977) in Chatham, Va. They had four daughters:

(1) Mary Jane Clark married John Pickens Reeder, Jr. They have one daughter and one son. They live in Providence, R.I.

(2) Gene Pat Clark (d. Sept., 1970). She married Marc J. Gurwith. No children.

(3) Nancy Lee Clark (twin) married William Orrin Tune. They have a son and a daughter and live in Roanoke, Va.

(4) Sarah Ann Clark (twin) married Creig Langager. They live in New York City. No children.

b. Louise Linwood Cooper married Frank Allen Terry, Chatham, Va. They have one son and one daughter.

(1) Frank Allen Terry, Jr., married Virginia King. They live in High Point, N.C., and have one daughter.

(2) Elizabeth Cooper Terry married Alfred Tyler. They have a son and a daughter. They live in Los Angeles, California.

c. Ethel (Dicki) Cooper married Harold Theodore Turner and they live in Mayesville. They have two daughters and a son: (1) Theo Louise Turner married Eugene Woods, Beaufort, and they have one son. (2) Harold Linwood Turner married Mary Dozier Thompson. They have one son and one daughter and live in Mayesville. (3) Lillis Frost Turner married William T. Brogdon, Jr. They have two sons and live in the Brogdon section of Sumter County.

5. Carrie Lee Rhodes (b. April 2, 1880; d. Oct. 25, 1921). She married on Nov. 22, 1899, Milner Bradley Wilson. She is buried in Mayesville Cemetery.

Children:

a. Henry Franklin Wilson (b. April 17, 1900; d. Sept. 18, 1915).

b. Milner Bradley Wilson, Jr., married Margaret Nash and they live in Clemson.

Children:

(1) Milner Bradley Wilson, III, married Nancy Brook. They live in Columbia and have one son and two daughters.

(2) Douglas Nash Wilson married Ann Kelbough. They have one son and one daughter and they live in Charlotte, N.C.

c. William Rhodes Wilson (b. April 13, 1906; d. Sept. 11, 1915).

d. Elizabeth Lee Wilson married Thomas Everett Cox (deceased July 25, 1954). She lives in Miami Springs, Fla. There is one daughter.

(1) Betty Cox married Vernel Champeaux. They live in Chelmsford, Mass., and have two sons.

e. Harry Cooper Wilson married Billie Marie Cole. They live near Mayesville and have one son.

(1) Harry Cooper Wilson, Jr., married Lucy Sanders. They have two daughters and live in Sumter.

6. Mary Louise Rhodes (b. March 13, 1882; d. Dec. 10, 1942). She is buried in Salem Black River Church Cemetery.

7. Samuel McBride Rhodes (b. Oct. 26, 1884; d. Oct. 8, 1964). He married (1) Lucy Wade Pugh Sept. 23, 1915; (2) Alice Douglas Pugh April 2, 1942.

Children from first marriage:

a. Lucile McBride Rhodes married Joseph Edward Muldrow (deceased April 18, 1968). She continues to live near Mayesville.

Children:

(1) Joseph Edward Muldrow, Jr., married Cynthia Farr. They live in Taylors and have three sons.

(2) Lucy Pugh Muldrow married Wattie Myles Brunson. They have two daughters and live near Mayesville.

(3) Robert McBride Muldrow married Patricia Ann Brunson. They have two sons and one daughter and live near Mayesville.

(4) Mary Alice Muldrow teaches at the Clarendon County Vocational School and lives with her mother.

b. Samuel McBride Rhodes, Jr., married Harriet Sumter Tisdale. They live at the "Old Rhodes Place" near Mayesville. They have one son and three daughters.

(1) Samuel Francis Rhodes married Ruth Davis. They live in Sumter and have a son, Samuel McBride Rhodes, II.

(2) Katherine McBride Rhodes lives near Mayesville.

(3) Harriet Lucile Rhodes married Allen Watts. They live near Mayesville and have two daughters.

(4) Elizabeth Wade Rhodes married Wayne Bryan. They live in Mayesville.

c. William Thomas Rhodes (d. Oct. 29, 1973). He was married to Mildred Lee. She lives in Charlotte, N.C. There were two children from this marriage — a son and a daughter:

(1) William Thomas Rhodes, Jr., married Suzanne Locke. They live in Irmo and have a daughter and a son.

(2) Jane Lee Rhodes married Tobi Edward Tyler. They also live in Irmo.

8. Jane Bradley Rhodes (b. Jan. 24, 1887; d. June 1, 1968). She married Robert James Mayes on Nov. 3, 1909. They lived in Mayesville. Both are buried in Mayesville Cemetery.

Children:

a. Janie Louise Mayes married Charles Madison Ferguson. They live in Winston-Salem, N.C., and have one daughter.

(1) Jane Rhodes Ferguson married David Stuckey Watson. They live in Summit, N.J., and have two sons.

b. James Edgar Mayes married Margaret James Beaty (Katie). They live in Mayesville and have two daughters and one son.

(1) Kathleen Beaty Mayes (Kathie) married Dr. Edward McDonald DuBose. They live in Mayesville and have two sons.

(2) Patricia Rhodes Mayes (Pat) married Richard Hines. They live in Spartanburg.

(3) James Edgar Mayes, Jr., married Lisa Jackson. They live in Mayesville.

c. Mary Elizabeth Mayes (Mamie) married William James Cooper, of Kingstree, where they now live. They have four sons.

(1) William James Cooper, Jr., married Patricia Holms. They live in Baton Rouge, La., and have two sons.

(2) James Mayes Cooper married Frances Kean. They live in Los Alamos, New Mexico.

(3) Hugh McCutchen Cooper. He lives in Kingstree and is attending law school at the University of South Carolina in Columbia.

(4) David Saunders Cooper married Catherine Cameron. They live in Atlanta, Ga.

d. William Rhodes Mayes married Jane Chappell. They live in Mayesville and have one son and two daughters.

(1) William Rhodes Mayes, Jr., lives with his parents.

(2) Jane Whitworth Mayes married Thomas Cubbage. They live in Columbia.

(3) Maria Chappell Mayes is married to Douglas Benton Watson. They live in Taylors, S.C.

9. William David Rhodes, Jr. (b. July 3, 1891; d. April, 1950). He married on April 25, 1923, Marie Antoinette (Nettie) Mayes. Both are buried in Mayesville Cemetery. They had two sons.

a. William David Rhodes, III, married Jennie Richards Moore. They live in Summerville. They are the parents of four sons.

(1) William David Rhodes, IV, married Judith Morse. They live in Columbia and have one son.

(2) Richards Rhodes died in an accident Sept. 28, 1970, while attending the University of South Carolina.

(3) Steven Mayes Rhodes is now attending the University of South Carolina.

(4) Robert La Teague Rhodes. He lives in Summerville.

b. Robert James Rhodes (d. Sept. 8, 1974).

The family of William David Rhodes and Mary E. Whitworth Rhodes lived a very interesting and happy life. The old home still stands and can be seen from Highway 76 between Mayesville and Lynchburg. It was originally a Bradley home, having been built by Roger Bradley in the late 1700's or early 1800's. It was inherited by Isaac Whitworth Bradley, brother-in-law of William David Rhodes, Sr., who lived not too far away in a country home. The two, around 1877, decided to exchange homes. This pleased Mary Whitworth Rhodes, since this was the homeplace of her grandfather, William Wilson Bradley, where her mother had grown up.

This old home has seen "a lot of happy living." Many fond memories are recalled by the grandchildren of William David Rhodes and his devoted wife. They recall the Sunday afternoons when children and grandchildren visited at the old home. The grownups would sit on the front piazza; while the children gathered on the back porch, taking turns on the joggling board or playing games.

There were always teacakes in abundance and other goodies to be enjoyed. Sometimes they took turns spending the night, and they well remember the time of family prayers. All gathered in the living room and listened while "Grandfather" read from the large family Bible. Then during prayers each one knew to get on his knees and put his head in the chair where he had been sitting.

There were some amusing incidents, too, that still bring chuckles to the grandchildren and the "great grands" as these stories are told over and over through the years.

One such incident occurred when a young man of the neighborhood dressed up in a stylish new suit – white coat and white pants – came to call on one of the young ladies in the family. "Old Joe" met him, as the custom was, and took his horse to the hitching post. When the young man, "proud as a peacock" in his new outfit started toward the steps, "Old Joe" called to him, as the story goes, and said: "Boss, Boss, I don't think you had better go in. I don't think Cap'n would like ye callin' on his daughter in yer night clothes!"

All the children of William David and Mary W. Rhodes have passed on, but most of the grandchildren remain.

As the years have passed, they in turn have become grandparents. And it is their sincere hope and earnest prayer that they can pass on the wonderful Christian heritage to their children and grandchildren that they have enjoyed.

(Information for this genealogy was furnished by Lucile Rhodes (Mrs. J.E.) Muldrow. She gathered the facts from the Mary E. Whitworth Rhodes and Martin L. Rhodes Bibles, the former being in her possession; from tombstones at Salem Black River and Mayesville Cemeteries; from the William David Rhodes, Sr., Bible, which is in the possession of W.D. Rhodes, 107 Presidents Circle, Summerville, S.C. 29483; letters John S. Whitworth wrote to his wife, Jane Bradley Whitworth, while on the battlefields during the Civil War, in the possession of Louise Cooper Terry (Mrs. Frank), Box 218, Chatham, Va. 24531. The early history comes from N.C. Bible records, tombstones, deeds and wills.

Books used include: **Immigrant Ancestors, A Registry of American Families,** Hotten's **Original Lists of Persons of Quality (Who Went From Great Britain to the American Plantations).**

The Bloom Hill Richardsons

(Most of the information for this series on the Richardsons of Bloom Hill came from a paper written by Elizabeth Buford Richardson in 1906.)

Sumter County is rich indeed with historic lore and no name of the past is more intriguing than Bloom Hill. The name suggests that it was always a place of natural beauty.

"Milford," that magnificent estate once owned and occupied by former Gov. John Laurence Manning, is now a part of the vast acres of Bloom Hill Plantation.

Land here is said to have been bought by John Owen, who came from England with five sons – John, Robert, Luke, Tom, and Alfred. These sons married and built homes on different parts of the land. Later, however, they moved away. Luke, it is said by one of the descendants in the family, Mrs. Eloise Adcock, of Columbia, is buried in the old Richardson graveyard, which is still accessible to members of the Richardson family, though the estate belongs to the Clark family, formerly of Detroit, Mich.

William Richardson, in some point in history (1773, date given by Gregorie in **History of Sumter County**), bought much (if not all) of the original plantation (8,000 acres) and built his home there.

Bloom Hill played an important role in the Revolutionary War. William Richardson, too, was an important figure during those years of young America's struggle for independence. And it is the Richardson family that will be traced in this series. Linked with the Richardsons are many families of note in this area. These may be traced later.

This Richardson family, according to family records, goes back to Sea Capt. Edward Richardson, who ran away from his home in England to engage in seafaring ventures. He became captain of a vessel and spent much of his life at sea.

Somewhere, possibly in Virginia, he met and married Elizabeth Poinsett and they had a large family. Though the records in Charleston state that Edward Richardson, master of a vessel,

Elizabeth, entered the Charleston port about 1740, he never lived in South Carolina; therefore, little is known of him.

William, seventh son of Edward and Elizabeth Poinsett Richardson, is the head of the branch of the family in South Carolina that is being treated here. He, with his younger sister, Susannah, left his father's home in Virginia (likely after the death of his mother) and came to Charleston.

Susannah later married John Smythe in Charleston and continued to live in that city, but they are both buried in the Richardson graveyard at Bloom Hill. They left no descendants.

It seems that Edward never forgave his son and daughter for running away. However, when he died, mourning rings bearing his name, date of death, etc., were sent to William and Susannah. The rings were lost at some time.

William, head of the South Carolina clan, married Ann Magdalen Guignard on Oct. 17, 1768. A notice in the **South Carolina Gazette** and **County Journal** reads: "Married Mr. William Richardson, merchant, to Miss Ann Guignard, daughter of the late Mr. Gabriel Guignard."

Having greatness of character, William was able to cope with adverse circumstances when he found himself on his own in a strange city at an early age. He soon established a lucrative mercantile business and won a wife from one of the distinguished families of early America. It seems that he won the admiration and respect of all who knew him.

From records it has been found that he was elected a member of the first Provincial Congress of South Carolina. He was also appointed to the Committee to carry into effect the Continental Association.

In 1776 he was made a captain in the Regiment of Riflemen, and during much of the Revolution he was Commissary General; therefore, there was always activity at his home.

His ingenuity in hiding supplies was unbelievable. For many years, people wondered how he could conceal these much-needed provisions so well. He seemed always able to supply food and ammunition when needed; and though the British made raids, there is no record that they found anything. Many of the supplies for the patriots were paid for by his own wealth.

Soon after marriage, he, leaving Charleston, purchased pew No. 30 in St. Michael's church for the price of 350 pounds sterling. It seems that the deed is still in existence, showing that the purchase was made on May 30, 1769.

Magdalen was reared in an atmosphere of culture and refinement, and it is quite understandable that she did not share her husband's enthusiasm for moving to his estate in the High Hills of Santee (Sante). Such a move must have seemed to her like leaving civilization for a wilderness.

Being an understanding and loving husband, William made every effort to render the change less traumatic for her. The place he prepared was a beautiful home named characteristically "Bel-Air," since it was situated on a high bluff where breezes brought comfort on hot summer days.

According to Dr. Anne King Gregorie in **History of Sumter County**, he planted beautiful gardens, hiring an Irish gardener to grow flowers for his wife's pleasure. In his letters to his wife, still in Charleston, he described the pinks and "rosaries" (an old name for rose bushes).

He also ordered for her enjoyment a fine, sweet-toned organ from England and a collection of English-bound books with the Richardson coat of arms stamped on each cover. In fact, he left "no stone unturned" to make "Bel-Air" the most beautiful home possible. And his efforts were not in vain, for his became a happy home for the family and an attraction for visitors who were always welcomed with generous hospitality.

William Richardson counted the great of his day among his close friends. He was a valued confidant of Gen. Francis Marion during the Revolution. And when it became necessary for Gov. John Rutledge to leave Charleston for his safety, he found a ready welcome at Bloom Hill. Gen. Nathaniel Green sought and found rest and comfort at the home of Captain Richardson; Charles Cotesworth Pinckney was also a treasured friend.

According to family tradition there was a large hollow tree near the home where patriots deposited bits of information concerning war tactics to be picked up by their friends.

Once the British entered "Bel-Air" looking for Richardson. When they didn't find the object of their search, one of the soldiers thrust his bayonet through the eye of a portrait of Richardson hanging on the wall. The tear was repaired by an artist and the portrait now shows no defect.

Captain Richardson was blessed with a faithful servant by the name of Davy. He was ever ready to protect his master and family from any threat of danger.

Davy was buried in the west end of the Richardson graveyard. His marble tombstone bears the inscription: "Faithful Davy."

As the years passed, the cool breezes brought in mosquitoes from the swamps and malaria became a dangerous enemy to the family living at "Bel-Air." Captain Richardson decided around 1784 to move farther away from the river. He selected another beautiful site and was building a handsome home when he died. His widow completed it, but she changed the plans, modeling it after her grandfather's home in France. The first story was built of stone, while the second and third stories were of cypress. But this beautiful home was burned in 1865.

Capt. William Richardson died of fever on Feb. 17, 1786, at the early age of 42. In the **Charleston Morning Post** and **Daily Adventurer** was the following notice: "Died at the High Hills of Santee, William Richardson, Esq., of that place."

In the Richardson burial ground on the Bloom Hill plantation his tomb bears this tribute: "He was a most affectionate husband, tender parent, indulgent master and valued friend."

This Scripture verse also reflects something of the Christian he must have been: "Behold God is my salvation, I will trust and not be afraid, for the Lord Jehovah is my strength and my song."

Captain Richardson made his will on Dec. 1, 1785. It is not a long document, but he remembered his wife and children (though not by name). This excerpt from his will expresses an unusual wish: "As I (sic) always have had an aversion to the name of Richardson, I desire and request that my children would change it for Rich, which is a short easy wrote (sic) name and the first Syllable of my name and if they love me or respect my memory they will acknowledge no other name."

(Only one son followed the request. That line will be traced in a later installment.)

Mrs. Richardson died in 1810 in Columbia at the home of her daughter, Mrs. James Sanders Guignard. She was buried beside her husband at Bloom Hill.

Captain William and Magdalen Guignard Richardson had four daughters and four sons. The eldest of these was Ann, born May 22, 1771, in Charleston and was baptized the same day by Rev. Samuel Hart. She grew up on the Bloom Hill Plantation.

On May 17, 1787, she married Col. William Mayrant, attorney at law. For the young couple her grandfather, John Gabriel Guignard, built a lovely home near Stateburg, known for many years as "Ararat," meaning "Here I rest."

The Mayrants were among the first settlers in South Carolina. Nicholas Mayrant was one of a group of French refugees that was granted citizenship in Charleston by an Act of the Assembly about the year 1689.

William's father, John Mayrant, was the son of Mrs. Susannah Mayrant (widow) of St. James, Santee. Hon. William Mayrant was a member of Congress about 1813.

Mrs. Mayrant was very beautiful and a portrait of her hung in her brother's home at Bloom Hill for many years. She and her brother were very close.

William died in 1840 and Ann about 10 years later. Theirs had been a very happy home with 13 children born to this devoted couple.

The children were as follows: a son and daughter who died at birth; William and Charles (twins), Ann, Frances, Placidia, John W., Woodruff, Emily, Samuel, Robert Pringle, and Charlotte.

William Mayrant, Jr., attorney, married Sarah Hall Horry Ray. He was born May 18, 1792. He was a graduate of South Carolina College. He died March 22, 1840, at the age of 48. Four children were born to them:

1. Sarah Ann married William E. Richardson, a cousin. This line will be traced later.

2. William H. Mayrant married Katherine Drayton. They left two children: Katherine Drayton, who married S. Lewis Simons. (Their daughter, Drayton Mayrant Simons, was a well-known writer.)

3. John Richard died young.

4. Mary Charlotte married R.H. Clarkson.

Charles Mayrant, son of Col. William and Ann Richardson Mayrant, married Caroline Kinloch, daughter of Francis and Martha Rutledge Kinloch.

Charles and Caroline Mayrant left four children: 1. Francis Kinloch Mayrant married Ann Waties. 2. Ann Mayrant married Edward Simons of Charleston. 3. Frances Caroline Mayrant married William Waties Rees, of Stateburg, and they were the parents of six: 1. William James married Annie C. Childs. 2. Katherine Waties married Thomas S. Sumter. 3. Wilson Waties married Julia Frierson. 4. Caroline Kinloch married de Saussure Bull. 5. Charles Mayrant married (1) Julia Hayden, (2) Miss Witrell. 6. Mary Waties married John Rutledge Sumter.

Charles W. Mayrant, son of Charles and Caroline Kinloch Mayrant, never married.

Ann Mayrant, next in the family of Col. William and Ann Richardson Mayrant, was born May 15, 1794, and died the following November.

Frances Mayrant married Robert Bentham, Esq., of Charleston. She was born October 10, 1795. They lived in a beautiful home in Charleston and had two children, Charles and Mary Ann.

Placidia, seventh child of Col. William and Ann Mayrant, married J. Jasper Adams.

Next in the Col. William Mayrant family was John W., born October 10, 1799. He moved to Mississippi.

Woodruff lived approximately a year.

Emily, 10th in the family, lived only three years.

Samuel was next. He was a lawyer and was born on Sullivan's Island. He lived in Sumter most of his life and died in 1872.

Robert Pringle Mayrant married Frances A.M.H. Guignard, a first cousin. He was born October 23, 1808. In 1828 he was appointed a midshipman in the United States Navy by John Quincy Adams. There were seven children: Ann Caroline, James Sanders Guignard (who married Emma Buford Richardson), Robert Pringle, William Richardson, John Gabriel, Frances Heyward, and Laura.

Youngest in the Col. William Mayrant's family was Charlotte, born November 27, 1813, and died August 30, 1814.

William Guignard Richardson, second son of Capt. William and Ann Magdalen Guignard Richardson, was born May 22, 1773. He married first Harriet Eveleigh on February 26, 1798, the Rev. Gabriel Gerald officiating. She was the mother of four before her death. Her husband's record of her death reads: "Harriet R., wife of W.G.R., died February 25, 1804, in the 26th year of her age. Bow down thine head O Man, and submit with reverence to the will of the Maker."

After five years, William married (2) Emma Corbett Buford. The wedding took place on March 5, 1809, with the Rev. Hugh Fraser officiating.

William G. was a cultured and scholarly gentleman. He finished his education under the foremost masters of Europe. At one time he served as state senator. He inherited Bloom Hill and lived there many years, loving his home very dearly. But because of his generosity and faithfulness to his friends, he lost everything. He stood security for a friend, and when the time came for payment, the friend failed to meet his obligation. Because of the strictness of the laws in those days his home, slaves and other possessions were sold by the sheriff to pay the debt. It was indeed a sad day for this noble man. To ease the blow, however, his brother, Judge John S. Richardson, bought the home to keep it from falling into the hands of strangers and lived there the rest of his life.

William was elected sheriff of the district and moved to Sumter and lived there until after the death of his second wife. He then moved to Bloom Hill on one of the subdivisions. He died there September 8, 1849, in his 77th year. He was buried in the Richardson burial ground between his two wives.

Children of William G. and Harriet Eveleigh Richardson were Evelina Ann, William Eveleigh, Laura, and Harriet.

Children of William G. and Emma Buford Richardson were Julian, Joseph Johnson, Elinor Frances, James Sanders Guignard, Elizabeth Ann, Hugh Fraser, Mary Caroline, Lydia Clegg Chovine, Samuel Clegg Chovine, and John Manly.

1. Evelina Ann married William Ballard, M.D., of Providence, Sumter District. Their children were Harriet, William and Magdalen.

2. William Eveleigh, lawyer, first son of William G. and Har-

riet, was born October 14, 1800. They lived at Stateburg and he died there April 8, 1888. Children in this family were William, Thomas, Margaret, Alister, and Mary Ellen.

3. Laura, born August 18, 1802, was never married. She was very intelligent, a devoted Christian and greatly loved by all who knew her. Her home was in Sumter until her later years, when she went to live with her sister, and after her death went to Columbia. She is buried at Bloom Hill.

4. Harriet, youngest child of W.G. and Harriet Eveleigh Richardson, was born February 15, 1804, and died March 6, 1805.

5. Eldest child of W.G. and Emma Corbett Buford Richardson was Julian. He was born December 31, 1809, and died February 3, 1810.

6. Joseph Johnson, second child of Emma Corbett Richardson and sixth of William G., was born May 6, 1811. His home was on Weetee Lake and he married first Caroline Stark. After her death he married Miss Pipkin. When the Civil War was over, the family moved to a home near Camden.

Children of Joseph J. and Caroline Stark Richardson were as follows:

1. William Guignard married Mary Cooper and their home was in Savannah, Ga., and their children were Mary, Guignard, Allen, and Alice.
2. Emma married Alexander Smith. He died about 1890.
3. Joseph Johnson married Charlotte Nesmith.
4. Buford married Marie Headleson. They lived in Williamsburg County. It is said that he was a "true, noble Christian man. He died in 1905.
5. Anna Roberson died in 1892.
6. Elizabeth died in infancy.
7. Laura Ellen married John G. Bearden from Milledgeville, Ga.

Children of Joseph Johnson Richardson and Pipkin Richardson are as follows:

1. Martha Jane married Thomas Smith.
2. Adrianna died in childhood.
3. Mary Davis married Charles Montgomery.
4. Samuel Chovine
5. Kershaw
6. Edward
7. Frances Heyward died in childhood.
8. Elizabeth Gordon.
9. John Smythe married Elizabeth Wedamen.

Elinor Frances Richardson, third child of William Guignard and Emma Corbett Richardson, was born February 9, 1813, and died April 4, 1814.

Next in the William Guignard Richardson family, James Sanders Guignard Richardson, born April 12, 1815, gained fame as a lawyer in Sumter where he made his home. He was married to Mary C. Wilder and their children were Emma Buford, James Sanders Guignard, Eliza and Samuel Mayrant, the last two dying in early childhood.

Emma Buford (born July 30, 1841) married Franklin J. Moses, Jr., only son of Chief Justice Franklin J. Moses. When her husband became governor, the family moved from Sumter to Columbia. They had four children: Franklin J., III, Mary Richardson, Jane McLelland, and Emma Buford.

Franklin, born in 1860, married Marie Raum of Chicago, Ill. He was an officer in the U.S. Navy.

Mary Richardson married (2) Gen. William N. Taft and (3) Dr. H.D. Geddings of the U.S. Marine Hospital Service.

Jane McLelland married Dr. S. Chandler Baker, a beloved physician of Sumter. They had two children – Emma Richardson and C. Richard Furman, also an outstanding Sumter physician.

Emma Buford married Charles H. Price and lived in Washington, D.C.

James Sanders Guignard Richardson, Jr., a lawyer, served as a Confederate soldier during the War Between the States. He first married Julia A. Colclough.

His second marriage was to Gertrude Dick, daughter of Edward and Posthuma (Colclough) Dick. He died circa 1800, leaving three children.

Fifth child of William Guignard and Emma Corbett Richardson was Elizabeth Ann, born February 8, 1817. She married Alister Garden, a lawyer in Sumter. He had distinguished ancestors, two of whom were Chancellor DeSaussure and Chief Justice Gibbes.

Garden died in his 33rd year (1843) and was buried at Bloom Hill. Mrs. Garden survived her husband many years, dying in Warrenton, Va., at the home of her son, Hugh, in 1874.

Hugh Garden brought honor to himself and family; he was graduated with distinction from the South Carolina College in 1860. In the following year he joined his Southern comrades in the service of the Confederate Army. At the capture of Fort Sumter, he was a private; at the first Battle of Manassas he was color bearer for Kershaw's regiment, and later commander of the Palmetto Battery.

After the war he continued his education by taking a course in the law at the University of Virginia. He practiced for a few years with his great uncle, Hon. W.F. DeSaussure, in Columbia, before moving to Warrenton, Va., where he continued the practice of law.

He was honored in 1892 when the University of the South conferred on him the honorary degree of Doctor of Civil Law.

Frances Emma, daughter of Alister and Elizabeth Ann Garden, was widely known as "the beautiful Miss Garden." She married Charles Manning Furman, son of Dr. James C. Furman, member of a distinguished South Carolina family. Frances died young, leaving six children: Constance, wife of Rev. W.I. Herbert of the South Carolina Methodist Conference; Harriet Elizabeth, deceased in childhood; Alister, married to Elinor Hoyt; Annie Elizabeth, wife of Rev. E.R. Pendleton; Charles Manning; Hugh DeSaussure, deceased in infancy.

Alister, youngest child of Col. Alister and Elizabeth Ann Garden, died in the Confederate service during the Civil War.

Hugh Fraser, sixth child of William Guignard and Emma Buford Richardson, was born April 11, 1819. A very talented young man, he was graduated in medicine and planned a useful practice, but at the age of 21, he contracted that dreaded fever that brought death to so many in the low country and died at the home of Willis Cantey of Santee.

Born September 26, 1821, Mary Caroline was the seventh in the William Guignard Richardson family. She married William Mazych of Clarendon County. They lived for sometime in his ancestral home, "The White House," on Santee River, but in 1850 they moved to Houston County, Ga., where they built a handsome plantation home known as "Moss Hill."

He was a true "gentleman of the Old South."

During the Confederate War he received a wound that brought on his death in 1870.

He was survived by his wife and a large family of children and grandchildren, all of whom remained in Georgia. The children were John Gamble, William Richardson, Ella B., Buford McDonald, Edward Bertrand, Willielma Lodoiska, Henry Colclough, Minnie, Richard Manning, James Manly, Willis Cantey, Mary Caroline, Chovine Richardson.

Lydia Clegg, next in the William Guignard-Emma Corbett family, was born November 12, 1824. She married Dr. John Smythe Rich, a cousin. He was the son of Charles Poinsett Richardson, who changed his name to Rich. The line will be traced later.

Ninth child of William Guignard and Emma Corbett Richardson was Susan Emma, born August 29, 1827. She married James Henry Colclough in 1848. They lived on the Santee until after the Civil War and then moved to the Bradford Springs area of Sumter District, where they lived in a country home known as "Bleak House."

Mrs. Colclough died suddenly on November 13, 1890, at the

home of her brother, Dr. Samuel Clegg Chovine Richardson, in Manning. Mr. Colclough died in 1899. They left 12 children: John Ashby, Julian Richardson, Charles Axam, James Henry, William Davis, Emma Buford, Alexander Guignard, Edward Bertram, Samuel Mayrant, Leonie Davis, Chovine Richardson, and Benjamin Davis.

Samuel Clegg Chovine was the tenth child of William Guignard and Emma Corbett Richardson. He was born May 5, 1829, on one of the subdivisions of Bloom Hill. Having graduated from medical school in 1852, he began the practice of medicine in Clarendon County, where he continued as a beloved physician and successful businessman all his life. He was confirmed in the Episcopal church July 31, 1889.

Dr. Richardson was said to have looked like the portrait of his grandfather, Capt. William Richardson. Though a very handsome man, he was never married. He died in his 67th year and is buried in the cemetery in Manning.

Last in the large family of William G. and Emma C. Richardson was John Manly, who was also born on a subdivision of Bloom Hill. His birthdate was March 13, 1831. He studied at the Military Academy in Charleston and was appointed assistant instructor in mathematics. He then went to the University of Virginia, where he won distinction in mathematics, chemistry and philosophy.

After leaving Virginia, he went on to Harvard, where he received a B.S. degree. While at Harvard he was an assistant in mathematics in Lawrence Scientific School.

After graduation he, with Rev. C.A. McDaniel, founded Bowen Collegiate Institute in 1856 in Georgia. His next work was mathematics professor in the North Carolina Military Academy.

When the Civil War began, he enlisted and became a major. However, he later was forced to resign his commission and leave the service because of a severe attack of rheumatism. When partially recovered, he taught for a while at the Military Institute in Marietta, Ga., but when his health was sufficiently restored, he received an appointment as an officer on the general staff of the Confederate Army.

Near the end of the war a severe battle wound cost him the loss of one leg. The rest of his life was given to teaching.

While recovering from a spell of rheumatism, he studied law and was admitted to the bar. He was also a writer of note on legal, social, political, scientific and literary subjects.

He was described as a "zealous Democrat, a public spirited citizen, a true man and a faithful friend." Another said of him, "His was a pure, noble spirit, a fitting exponent of what a long line of pure, noble ancestry can produce."

A member of the Methodist Church South for 40 years, "his Christian character was beautiful . . . "

John Manly Richardson married (1) Lavinia Eugenia King of Perry, Ga. She died May 31, 1887. After six years he married Elizabeth Buford (Richardson) Godbey, a cousin.

He died February 4, 1898, leaving a large family. His children were from the first marriage. They are listed as follows: Emma Buford, Carrie Louise, Anna Elizabeth, Brisbane King, William Chovine, John Manly, Gabriella Guignard, Mary Laura, Hugh Davis, Alister Clegg, Lavinia Eugenia. Three of these died in childhood and the others lived in other states than South Carolina.

Third child of Capt. William and Magdalen Guignard Richardson was Charles Poinsett Richardson, who changed his surname to Rich in accord with his father's wish as expressed in his last will and testament.

He married Elizabeth Lynum and they lived in Williamsburg District, S.C. Their children were Charles Augustus, Napoleon Gustavus, John Smythe, Caroline and Mary Marcia.

The eldest, Charles Augustus Rich, married Video Ann Jennings and they lived in Sumter District until his untimely death at the age of 23, three days before the birth of his only child, Charles Augustus Rich, Jr.

On December 24, 1849, Charles, Jr., married Mary Charlotte Brumby and they made their home in Clarendon County. They had a long and happy life together (more than 50 years) and were the parents of 11 sons and daughters.

1. Ann Elizabeth married Joseph E. Touchberry; 2. Mary Sumter married Noah Graham Broadway; 3. Henrietta Buford married William Touchberry; 4. Video Harreltine married Henry Broadway; 5. Frances Emily married Riley Bradham; 6. Margaret Ann married John Touchberry; 7. Joseph Augustus married Eunice Bertram; 8. Espy Ann married Grier Frierson; 9. Charlotte Judson married Joseph Singleton; 10. Charles James; 11. Thomas Brumby.

The second son of Charles Poinsett and Elizabeth Lynum Rich, Napoleon Gustavus, married Magdalen Singleton, who died soon after their marriage.

John Smythe Rich, M.D., third child of Charles Poinsett and Elizabeth Rich, married a first cousin, Lydia Clegg Buford Richardson. Their home was in Clarendon County. They were the parents of two daughters and four sons: 1. Egeria Rich married Needham T. Pittman and was the mother of two: Elizabeth (married to G.M. Beasley) and Robert. She died young.

2. Emma Buford married W. Pittman, brother of Needham Pittman. Her husband died young, leaving one son, Troy, who

died in childhood. After the death of her husband, Emma married her brother-in-law, Needham Pittman.

3. William Davis Rich, M.D., married Alice McIntosh.

4. William Guignard Rich

5. Samuel Davis Rich and 6. Charles Poinsett Rich died young.

Fourth child of Charles Poinsett and Elizabeth Rich, Caroline, married James L. Jones and lived in Clarendon County. Their five children were Charles R., Susan, Hallum, Mary and Eliza.

Marcia, youngest daughter of Charles Poinsett and Elizabeth Rich, never married.

Among the outstanding members of the Richardson family was John Smythe, the fourth child of Captain William and Magdalen Guignard Richardson. He was born April 11, 1777. Educated in Charleston, he studied law under Col. John J. Pringle and was admitted to the bar in 1799.

He was married in 1802 to the widow of Thomas Couturier, the former Elizabeth Lucretia Buford. The Couturiers were French Huguenots, who were among the first settlers of South Carolina.

Mrs. Richardson, daughter of William and Frances June Buford, who emigrated from Brunswick County, Virginia, in the 1700's, and lived near Gourdin in Williamsburg District, was born in Virginia around 1775.

She was a charming person, having "many social virtues." Her Christian spirit and innate kindness of heart made for her many friends. The slaves in the family loved her devotedly. Indeed, she was the perfect helpmeet for John Smythe Richardson, who was outstanding in every respect.

He practiced law in Charleston for a few years before moving to Stateburg in Sumter District. Soon he was elected to the state legislature and was serving as speaker of the house, when in 1810 he was elected attorney general.

Then in December of 1818, he was elected a law judge and resigned his position as attorney general. Two years later he was asked to represent the Republican Party in Congress, but he declined.

From 1841 till 1846, he was president of the Court of Appeals of South Carolina and of the Court of Errors from 1846 till 1850. He was respected and loved by family and friends. Most considerate of his slaves, he built them a church and named it "Elizabeth Chapel" in honor of his wife.

During the latter part of his life, it was necessary for him to travel all over the state from one court to another. But there were no planes, automobiles or trains in those days. He traveled in a carriage drawn by beautiful horses and driven by an expert driver who was also his faithful and trusted valet.

While still presiding judge, he died in Charleston, May 8, 1850. In making remarks to the court on the day of the death of Judge Richardson, Judge O'Neil said in part, "... In his seventy-fourth year he has been called from us. He died in the full triumph of a Christian faith, and we are justified in believing that he is in the place of glorious rest prepared for him. He has died full of years and full of glory, and we can only say, 'It is God's will.' "

He was buried in the family burying ground on Bloom Hill Plantation. He had come into possession of his ancestral home there and had continued to make that his home.

His widow died in 1859 in her 84th year and is buried by his side, leaving behind loving grandchildren, who were ever attentive to her desires. In spite of suffering in her last years, she was always cheerful and her sweet Christian character was a great inspiration; she left a lasting influence on those who knew her.

Their children were Thomas Couturier, John Smythe, Elizabeth Frances, Susan William Ann, David Evans, Maynard Davis, Eleanor Lucretia, William Buford, Langdon Cheves, and Francis DeLessiline.

The eldest, Thomas Couturier, died at the age of five.

John Smythe, second son, was born August 31, 1805, and on April 9, 1827, married Sophia Hyatt in Providence, R.I.

Leaving the junior class at the South Carolina College in Columbia, John Smythe went on to Brown University, where he was graduated in 1827. He began practicing law there, but soon came to Sumter. With the help of overseers he ran a farm of 800 acres in the county.

The change from a northern climate to the South was a tonic for his wife, who was very frail. But after 12 years she developed a bronchial infection and was taken to Cuba where it was thought the climate would bring a cure to her trouble. However, she grew worse and died in 1840. She was buried at sea. There were eight children from this marriage, three dying in childhood.

After her death, Colonel Richardson married Adrianna L.C. McDonald of Sumter County, but there were no children from this marriage. The couple adopted one daughter, Laura Ellen, a niece of Colonel Richardson.

About 1843 John Smythe Richardson became a minister in the Methodist Church. He was an eloquent speaker and a dedicated minister, though he did not join the conference or preach for pay. After the war he, with his wife and adopted daughter, moved to Georgia, where he died in 1871, his wife surviving him by seven years.

The children of his first marriage were John Smythe, Charles

Hyatt, Anna Elizabeth, Maynard Davis, Mary Sophia, William Buford, Elizabeth Buford, and Samuel Mayrant.

The eldest, John Smythe, was born at Bloom Hill in 1828. He studied under a tutor before entering the famous Cokesbury School in Abbeville, S.C. Upon completion of work there, he entered South Carolina College, where he was graduated in 1850. He was married to Agnes Davidson.

He studied law in the firm of Richardson and Mayrant in Sumter and was admitted to the bar in 1852. He began immediately to practice law. He also edited **The Sumter Banner** and **The Sumter Watchman** for a while.

In 1855 he became a law partner with Col. James D. Blanding and remained with him until he went into politics. In 1861 he entered the Confederate Army and was made captain of the "Sumter Volunteers." He saw much service during the war and was wounded once.

After the war he continued the practice of law and was elected to the legislature. He also farmed extensively. He was instrumental in forming the Grange Movement in the Sumter area and took an active part in the State Agricultural Society.

He was elected to Congress and served for two full terms, but declined to run for the third. In 1884 he became master in equity for Sumter County, which office he held till 1893, one year before his death.

He was respected and admired in Sumter and elsewhere. According to an article in **The Sumter Advance**: "He was true in all relations of life; a staunch friend, a kind, loving brother, an affectionate son, and a devoted husband and father . . ."

His wife died February 23, 1893. Both are buried in the Sumter Cemetery. They had four children:

1. John Smythe, born September 11, 1851, married Mary Baker and was the father of nine.

2. Davison McDowell, born March 5, 1853, married Lena Cordes and lived at Shady Side near Sumter. They had four children. He married (2) Jennie Simons of Charleston and they had three.

3. Katherine McDowell, born February 16, 1855, married D'Arcy Paul Duncan and was the mother of five.

4. James McDowell died in infancy.

Charles Hyatt Richardson, M.D., second son of Rev. John Smythe and Sophia Hyatt Richardson, was born January 30, 1830.

He was graduated in medicine from South Carolina Medical College in Charleston in 1852 and began practice in the Privateer section of Sumter County. In 1854 he married Margaret Elizabeth Nettles of that community. She was the daughter of John and Elizabeth Miller Nettles and granddaughter of Col. John Blount Miller, one of Sumter's leading citizens in early days, and Mary E. Miller.

In 1858 Dr. Charles Richardson moved with his family to Fort Valley, Georgia, where he continued the practice of medicine and was a successful farmer.

He fought in the Civil War, was in politics and served faithfully in the work of the churches in his area. He died in 1886.

The four children of Dr. Charles and Elizabeth Nettles Richardson and their families remained in Georgia.

The next three children of Rev. John Smythe and Sophia Hyatt Richardson died in childhood.

The sixth child, William Buford, M.D., born in 1835, married Sarah Dargan of Sumter District. After graduating in medicine in Charleston, he, too, with his family moved to Georgia. He died in 1869. Their five children continued to live in Georgia.

Elizabeth Buford Richardson, daughter of Rev. John Smythe and Sophia Hyatt Richardson, was born March 27, 1837. She married Dr. John T. Gaddy, a dentist, and lived in Milledgeville, Georgia.

After the death of Dr. Gaddy, she married a cousin, Major John Manly Richardson, and lived in Texas.

After his death on February 4, 1898, Mrs. Richardson returned to her home in Milledgeville. (She was the author of the record which was the basis for this series.)

Rev. Samual Mayrant Richardson, youngest child of Rev. John Smythe and Sophia Hyatt Richardson, was born May 16, 1839. He was twice married – first to Ruth Wood and second to Celia Hatcher.

Upon graduation from South Carolina College he entered the Confederate Army and served through the duration of the Civil War.

He joined the First Baptist Church in Sumter and began studying for the ministry. While still in the seminary, he received a call from this church. He was ordained and began the pastorate on November 22, 1868, and remained until July 30, 1871.

From Sumter he went to Timmonsville and became a faithful member of Welsh Neck Association, doing missionary work in Darlington, Florence, Williamsburg and Georgetown Counties. He exercised his missionary spirit in preaching to the poor and weak churches and organizing others. He continued to preach at Timmonsville Baptist for 13 years, until the church was able to support a regular pastor. He baptized 756 persons, married 121 couples, and in the last 18 years of his life averaged preaching four sermons each week. From church to church he traveled many miles on bad roads, in heat and cold, by day and night, traveling by means of horse and buggy.

A brother minister wrote of him: "He was an ardent and untiring friend in the temperance cause. He saw the evils of the whiskey traffic and buckled on his armor to wage war against it. . . . May it be the will of Heaven to raise up a man to wear with honor the mantle that fell from Richardson's shoulders . . ."

Col. W.F.B. Haynsworth, one of Sumter's foremost citizens of that era, said of him, "He was very gentle, but of great decision of character; as true and conscientious as any man I ever knew, and had the courage to endure martyrdom if following the right should lead to that."

This great and useful man died May 30, 1893, and was buried in Timmonsville. His second wife, Celia Hatcher Richardson, survived him and served for some years as Mother in the Margaret Home for missionaries' children in Greenville. She was the mother of one daughter, Ruth Wood Richardson.

Rev. Samuel Mayrant and his first wife, Ruth Wood Richardson, were the parents of three: Samuel Howard, who died in his 13th year; Jessie Ruth, who married David R. Coker, son of Major James Lide Coker of Hartsville, founder of Coker College; Elizabeth, who died as an infant.

Susan William Ann was the only daughter of Judge John Smythe and Elizabeth Lucretia Richardson. She married Dr. Thomas Muldrow Logan. Their children were as follows: John Richardson, Margaret Muldrow, Thomas Muldrow (moved West), Elizabeth Lucretia (died as an infant), Susan Richardson (married Rev. Asbury Mood, well-known and beloved minister in the South Carolina Methodist Conference).

Fifth child of Judge John Smythe Richardson, David Evans, died at the age of two years.

Elinor Lucretia, William Buford and Langdon Chevis, seventh, eighth and ninth children of Judge John Smythe, all died young.

Francis de Lessiline, youngest in the Judge John Smythe Richardson family, married Agnes Fraser and practiced law in Charleston. There were four children in this family; the oldest, Maynard Davis, and the youngest, Peter Fraser, died in infancy. Agnes Fraser died unmarried and Emma Buford married James Sanders Guignard Mayrant, a cousin. They had two children: Frances de Lessiline, who married Alfred Wallace, and Agnes Fraser, who married Arthur Daniel Morgan, M.D.

Caroline Richardson, fifth child of Capt. William and Ann Magdalen Richardson, was born February 7, 1779. She married James Sanders Guignard, a first cousin. It was in their home in Columbia that Mrs. William Richardson died May 23, 1810.

Children of James Sanders and Caroline Richardson Guignard were as follows:

John Gabriel, born in 1801, was a member of the South Carolina legislature. He was a planter and successful businessman. He died in 1857, in his 56th year.

James Sanders, Jr., born in 1803, married (1) Elizabeth Richardson (apparently not related) and (2) Mrs. Anna M. Edwards. He died in Columbia in his father's mansion on Senate Street, which he had inherited.

Children of James Sanders, Jr., and Elizabeth Richardson Guignard were James Sanders, III, John Gabriel, Caroline Frances, Sarah Slaun, Laura, Susan, Emma Slaun, William, and Benjamin.

James Sanders, III, moved to North Carolina and Elizabeth married Greg Maxey and moved to Florida.

John Gabriel (born in 1832) married Jane Bruce Salley from one of the respected old families of Orangeburg. Their nine children were as follows: Gabriel Alex, Mary, Rev. Sanders Richardson, Carolina, Susan Richardson, William Slaun, Christopher Gadsden, Jane Bruce, and Elizabeth.

Susan married Rev. Paul G. Jenkins and left five children – Emma, Caroline, Estelle, James Sanders, and Mary.

Caroline Elizabeth, fifth child of James Sanders and Caroline Richardson Guignard, married Robert W. Gibbes, M.D., of Columbia. They had 12 children as follows: James Guignard, Robert Wilson, Samuel G., Mary Caroline, Wade Hampton, William Moultrie, Washington Alston, Deveaux, Benjamin, Harriet, Thomas Hazel, and Alice.

Sarah Slaun, daughter of James Sanders and Caroline Richardson Guignard, married John Alex Scott of Mississippi.

Frances Ann Margaret Horry, seventh in the James Sanders-Caroline Richardson Guignard family, married Robert Pringle Mayrant, a first cousin. She was born Jan. 5, 1815.

They had seven children, one of whom, Frances Heyward, married Newman Kershaw Perry. Their daughter, Laura Perry, married Lueco J. Gumter, and their son, Lueco J. Gunter, born in 1908, married Mary Byrd Fant. One of the daughters of this marriage was Margaret Anne, born in 1943. She is now Mrs. Joseph B. Riddle, III, of McLean, Va. She visits in Columbia and recently paid a short visit to Sumter searching for relatives.

Youngest in the James Sanders Guignard family was Mary Susan Poinsett, who married James Wilson Gibbes of Charleston and was the mother of three.

Sixth child of Captain William and Ann Magdalen Richardson was Manly, born at Bel Air, February 4, 1781.

His mind was impaired and it was necessary for him to spend most of his life in a sanitarium, where he died on October 2, 1829.

Emily Richardson, born in 1782, was the seventh in the Capt. William Richardson family. She married a cousin, Gen. John Ioor.

It is said in the family that she was very beautiful and "lovely in heart and life." She was a favorite with all relatives and family friends. She paid long visits in the homes of Gen. Francis Marion and Mrs. Marion and Gen. and Mrs. Peter Horry.

John and Emily lived near Stateburg until 1810. They then moved with their three children — Peter Horry, George and Ann Fley — to the Mississippi Territory. They established a plantation, worked by the slaves they took with them, and named their home "The Hills," in memory, no doubt, of the High Hills of Santee in Carolina, which they always loved.

General and Mrs. Ioor had 12 children of their own and reared four motherless nieces and nephews.

This highly respected gentleman was killed one night on the way to a lecture by a neighbor with whom there had been a line dispute. He was only 56. His wife continued living at "The Hills" until her death in 1864. She was in her 81st year.

Most of the children lived away from South Carolina.

Youngest daughter of Capt. William and Ann Magdalen Richardson, Bethia Frances, accompanied her sister, Mrs. Ioor, to Mississippi. She married Moses Liddell, and after her death the Ioors reared her four children.

Thus ends a sketchy account of the early history of a family that has played a major role in the life of Sumter and Clarendon Counties. There are many outstanding people in this area descended from Capt. William Richardson and the families into which his descendants married, and they can enjoy genuine pride in their ancestry.

The Shaw Family

Schaghe, Schgh, Schaw, Sha are thought to have been some of the original spellings of the name Shaw. The name probably originated from the middle English "schawe" coming from the Anglo-Saxon "seagn," meaning a thicket, and eventually it became the surname of one living in a small wooded spot.

Another theory is that it came from the old Gaelic "Seach," a name inferring pride. The name was also spelled "Sha." Other old spellings are de Schau, de Schaw, de Shaw.

According to "Historical Memoirs of the House and Clan MacIntosh and of the Clan Chattan" by Alexander MacIntosh Shaw which is on file in the library of Inverness, Scotland, in 1161-63 in an expedition by King Malcolm, he was attended by

Shaw or Seach, second son of Duncan McDuff, fifth earl of Fife. He was designated as "son of the foremost man-Mac-an-Toiseach." Clan Shaw was the most ancient of the MacIntoshes.

The founder of the Shaw Clan received, because of his bravery, Rothemurcus; but his son Alan after his death sold the land and the Clan was broken and became unknown, for a while at least.

Then appeared a James Shaw whose ancestry is not known. In Invernesshire there is an old cemetery where Shaws have been buried for a thousand years.

Many genealogists in America are firm in their belief that the Shaws came from McDuff, Thane of Fife found in Shakespeare's **MacBeth**. However, many of the name hold to the tradition that their ancestors originally came from the Highlands of Scotland, where many of the name found refuge during the reign of Charles I of England (1625-1649) because of religious persecution.

Those who are convinced that the family came from the Mac-Intosh Clan can point with pride to the prowess of their ancestors. Ruins of old castles owned and occupied in times of danger are a mute testimony to the wealth and bravery of these Scottish chieftains as they sought to protect themselves and their possessions from rival clans.

One example of these strong towers is Sauchie on the barony which was granted by Robert Bruce in 1324 to Henry de Annand, one of whose descendants was married to James Schaw, who may have built the tower. Over a window is the motto of the Schaw family in French, the English translation being, "In well doing I satisfy myself."

Those who believe their ancestry came from the Scottish Highlands have cause for pride in the picturesque life of the Highlanders. They, too, had their stone castles. They had their music as well, and their colorful dance, which give pleasure to many people today.

Many immigrants found their way to America in the 17th and 18th centuries and among these were numbers of Shaws. It is said that this is the 127th most common name in America. Many came to South Carolina. As listed in "A Dictionary of Scottish Emigrants to the U.S.A.," compiled and edited by Donald Whyte, nine came to South Carolina in 1716 alone and of the nine there were three bearing the name "John," who arrived in Charleston, two on the same boat.

None of these, however, seems to have been the ancestor of the numerous bearers of the name in Sumter and Lee Counties.

The John Shaw, whom most believe to be the forebear of those living in this area is the one who came on the good ship **Hopewell**. This was one of the five ships on which Rev. William Martin brought his congregation, and some from other congregations -- some 467 families altogether. They set sail from Belfast, Ireland, 19 October, 1772, after many delays. They arrived in Charlestown on 6 January, 1773, after a trying voyage, with a loss of life from smallpox.

Many of them were able to get lands in the Rocky Creek area where Reverend Martin settled, but some received their grants elsewhere. Among these was John Shaw, Sr., who, after a wait of approximately a year, was able to get a grant of 100 acres in Craven County on Hope Swamp. He received his survey map on 20 June, 1774. His grant was bounded on one side by land of William Cassel and on the other sides by vacant land.

"There is a pre-Revolutionary grant for 100 acres on Hope Swamp, Volume 32, Page 139, which exactly matches (in my opinion) the same 100-acre portion of land listed in a January 5, 1807, deed of gift to David Shaw, unquestioned son of John Shaw, the immigrant. The pre-revolutionary plat folder, number 1697, shows the matching plat with a precept date of 6 January, 1773. The lapse between the precept date and the grant date is due to the fact that the South Carolina Land office was closed during most of this interval (I am told). As Dr. Stevenson's book had noted, the **Hopewell** arrived from Belfast, after a two-month voyage, on either December 22 or 24, 1772."

Another theory that has been advanced, though no proof has been found, is that John Shaw, Sr., came down from Pennsylvania. Williamsburg Township was laid out especially, it is said, for Scotch-Irish immigrants in 1732 and many early settlers came directly to Charleston from Ireland. One genealogist has made the statement that some of those planning to come to South Carolina had to leave on a later ship which took them to New England. From there they came down to Pennsylvania and then to South Carolina on the Old Wagon Trail. Salem Black River Presbyterian Church, in Sumter County, was formed by Scotch-Irish settlers and John Shaw, Sr., was an Elder in this church from 1797 until his death in 1810.

Elizabeth McKee, sister of John Shaw, mentions his children in her will in 1810. Nothing more is known of her.

John Shaw was buried on or near his plantation, but in 1970 his gravestone was moved to the cemetery at Brick Church and placed beside the grave of his second wife. This cemetery is on land given to Brick Church by Robert Witherspoon in 1830, approximately 20 years after the death of John.

At his death, 1,344 acres of land were left to be divided among his heirs. Because of this vast amount of property apparently accumulated in a relatively short time, some wonder, if this one could possibly be the John Shaw who received 100 acres in 1774. Be that as it may, most of those in the area who have done extensive research firmly believe this one to be their ancestor.

It is not known who his first wife was, though some think that she may have been a Frierson. No records have been found to tell of his Revolutionary War activities. This fact is mystifying since most participated in this struggle either by serving on the battlefield or furnishing supplies. Could it be possible that he returned to Ireland during this time to bring his family to America? Of course, this is only a conjecture. The fact that he received only 100 acres of land pointed to the fact that he came alone to South Carolina.

From his first marriage, there was one son, David, born about 1780. He was an Elder in Salem Black River (Brick) Presbyterian Church, as well as a "staunch supporter" of Concord Presbyterian.

The Shaws of Sumter County are descendants of David Shaw, son of the first wife of John Shaw, Sr., and also of his second wife, Lillis Mitchell, whose daughter Sarah Elvira married Isaac DuBose Whitworth. The names Lillis and Whitworth continue to be used in the various families.

The Lee County Shaws, for the most part, are descendants of John's second marriage.

David was married to Rebecca McBride, daughter of John and Frances Moore McBride, 20 December, 1804. She died in 1826 between the ages of 32 and 42.

David and Rebecca McBride Shaw had at least eight children, eldest of whom was Henrietta Warner Shaw, born 23 April, 1806. She married 1 April, 1821, Squire Matthew Peterson Mayes, founder of the town of Mayesville. They were the parents of a large family, including Algaeus, a doctor in Mayesville, William David, Thomas Alexander, Mary Henrietta, Margaret Elizabeth, Sarah Jane, Robert Peterson, Frances Anne, and Matthew Peterson, III.

The second daughter of David and Rebecca McBride Shaw was Frances Moore, who married John Bethune 27 May, 1830. She was born 15 July, 1814, and died sometime prior to 1843. The only children known of this family were Rebecca McBride Bethune, Roderick Bethune, Samuel Bethune, and David Shaw Bethune.

There is nothing known of the next child, Esther Selina Shaw, except that she was born 15 July, 1814, apparently a twin to Frances Moore.

The eldest son was James McBride, born in 1817. No other information is available.

John Gadson Shaw was born 18 October, 1819, and left Sumter to settle in Harrison County, Mississippi. He taught in the first school in Harrison County and operated a grist and sawmill. He and his wife, the former Anna L. Adner, were the parents of 15 children: David, Rebecca, Carlos, Samuel, Ervin, Junius, Henrietta, Harriett, John Bethune, Calvin, Lillis, Emily, Aline, Edgar, and Joseph. Still prized by the family is the trunk John Gadson used on his first trip to Harrison.

Elizabeth M. Shaw, sixth child of David and Rebecca Shaw, was born 20 October, 1821. She married Martin L. Rhodes and was the mother of two — William David Rhodes and Elizabeth Shaw Rhodes.

Rebecca McBride Shaw, daughter of David and Rebecca Shaw, was born 11 February, 1824, and died 5 February, 1825.

On 19 March, 1826, another girl was born and named Rebecca MacBride for her little sister who had died a year earlier. This second Rebecca died unmarried 20 July, 1845.

After Rebecca's death, David married Sarah Douglass in 1827 and they had seven children.

Ann Matthews Shaw, the eldest of David's second marriage, was born on 17 September, 1828. Her grave is in the Chandler Cemetery on Rocky Bluff Swamp. She was married 17 January, 1850, to Joseph Chandler and their children were William Shaw Chandler, Elizabeth Adriana ("Addie") Chandler, who married William Turner Brogdon, I, member of one of Sumter County's respected families, Joseph David Chandler, and Sarah Ann Chandler.

Second daughter of David and Sarah Douglass Shaw was Mary Jane, born 10 November, 1829. In March of 1852 she was married to John McEwen Plowden to which marriage there was no issue.

William, oldest son in this line, was born in 1830 and died at the age of five.

The next daughter, Lillis M., was born about 1831. She became on 17 January, 1850, the second wife of a prominent citizen of the area, Edgar Nelson Plowden, the grandson of the Irish Immigrant, Edward Plowden. Their children were Isabella, Clara, Vera, Edgar Shaw, Lillie, David Calvin, Eloise, Lila, Annie and four others whose names are not known.

The second son of David and Sarah Shaw was Ervin James, whose line will be followed in detail later.

Cynthia C. Shaw, child of David and Sarah, was born about 1838 and married John E. Muldrow, thus becoming connected with another prominent Sumter District family.

The youngest son was David Calvin, born 10 April, 1836. He married 26 November, 1860, Anna Jane McFaddin, granddaughter of Robert and Leah Lenoir Dickey McFaddin, outstanding citizen of Sumter District.

In 1869 David Calvin moved with his family to Florida where he died in 1895 and his wife, in 1927. They are buried in Apopka, Florida. Their children were Frances Ellen, David Arthur, Mary Alice, Pauline Grimball, Theodore McFaddin, and Robert Charles. According to one source, T.M. (Theodore McFaddin) moved to Texas, where he married Josephine Hortense Howell in 1893. Their children were Lela Mae (married Otto Watts of Abilene, Texas), David Arthur, Norman Perry, Willard Henry, Helen Bernice, James Milton and Robert Charles.

David Shaw (son of John Shaw, Sr.) died July 1843 intestate, leaving no widow (according to information from Collection of Wilhelm Von Hacke), but his burial place has never been found. The Von Hacke records show many land transactions – sales and purchases – on Rocky Bluff, Alligator Branch in Salem, Puddin' Swamp, Newman Branch and Woodbury Bay and other locations. Recorded also are transfers of extensive land holdings to his various children. Among tracts mentioned is the original tract granted to John Shaw, Sr., in 1774.

Fourth son of David and Sarah Douglass Shaw, Ervin James, from whom many of the Sumter Shaws were descended, was born 8 December, 1834. At the approximate age of 20, he married Lillis Hester Jane Whitworth, daughter of Isaac DuBose Whitworth.

At the beginning of the Civil War, he was mustered into Capt. T.B. Walsh's company, "Claremont Cavalry," Holcombe Legion, South Carolina Volunteers, C.S.A. He was a member of Claremont Masonic Lodge No. 64 and when he left home for the battlefield, he placed the Masonic emblem in his wife's hand and told her it might save her and the family should the enemy invade the district. (The highly prized emblem is still in the possession of one of his descendants.)

He returned home from the war, but died of a heart ailment (no doubt a result of the rigors of war) on 18 May, 1879, when only 45 years of age. Lillis survived her husband by approximately 18 years.

Their children were Mary Lou, Sarah Ann, Ervin Bartow, Lula Jane, Willie, David Charles, Etta Lee, and John Whitworth.

Etta Lee, youngest child, was the only daughter to marry. Born about 1878, she was married to Hugh McCollum and they were the parents of two daughters.

The older, Lillis Josephine McCollum, born 19 October, 1903, married Joe N. Allston of Hartsville in 1923. Their children were Joseph Hugh, who married Jane Reynolds, and was the father of three – Joseph Herbert, Stephen and Alline Reynolds; Lillis Adele Allston who married Dr. William Wyman King, Jr., of Newberry. Their children were William Wyman, III, Luke Allston King and Lillis Janice King.

The other daughter of Hugh and Etta Lee Shaw McCollum is Hughla Lee, born 18 October, 1913. She married on 11 September, 1934, Francis K. Hollman. They are residents of Sumter.

The Holmans have two daughters – Elizabeth Lee and Lillis McCollum – and one son, Frank Kennedy, III. Elizabeth Lee, born 5 December, 1935, married on 26 December, 1956, Dr. Welbourne Andrews White. Their children are Welbourne Andrews, Jr., Edward Kennedy, Christopher Mark and Elizabeth Holman.

Lillis McCollum Holman was born 6 September, 1937. She married William Martin McCormick on 26 November, 1956. Their children are Cecelia Lee (born 26 December, 1961) and William Martin (born 1 October, 1967).

Frank Kennedy Holman was born 18 August, 1947, and was married 23 December, 1969, to Mary Ellen Knight.

Ervin Bartow Shaw, eldest son of Ervin James and Lillis Whitworth Shaw, was born 24 March, 1861, just before his father left for war.

In 1890 he married Annie Hickson Pringle, who was born in January of 1861, the daughter of Dr. William Judson Pringle and Victoria Hickson Pringle. The Pringles were leading citizens of the Concord section of Sumter County.

Ervin Bartow Shaw was a successful planter and merchant of Sumter County, where he lived until his death of typhoid fever in 1909. His wife preceded him to the grave by eight years.

Their eldest son, William Judson Shaw, Sr., was born 5 May, 1891. His first marriage was to Lucia Rogers Williamson, daughter of Charles Lucius and Sarah Ada Rembert Williamson of Dalzell, in 1910. She was born 30 April, 1892, and died on 1 May, 1921, leaving two small boys – Ervin Bartow Shaw and William Judson Shaw, Jr.

Ervin Bartow Shaw, born 3 October, 1911, was married on 28 June, 1941, to Mildred Elnora Brown, daughter of Robert Tilman Brown, Sr., one of Sumter's outstanding civic leaders, and Mildred Lee Hall Brown of Sumter. Their residence is on Frank Clarke Street in Sumter.

They have a son, Ervin Bartow, Jr., who is a very successful pathologist practicing in the Lexington County Hospital. He is a graduate of The Citadel and the South Carolina Medical College in Charleston. He is interested in genealogy and much of the information for this history of the Shaw family was collected by his efforts.

He was born 5 December, 1943, and on 12 July, 1969, married Dixie Lee Brown whom he met in the Columbia Hospital where she was practicing as a radiology technician. She is the daughter of Jones William and Ruth Doris Verney Brown of Cayce.

They have one daughter, Jennifer Lee, born 30 July, 1971, and a son, Ervin David, born 22 June, 1974.

Mildred Hall Shaw, daughter of Ervin Bartow Shaw, Sr., and Mildred Brown Shaw, was born 1 February, 1945. She is married to George Gerhardt Berg, son of a Lutheran minister of Porterfield, Wisconsin. He is a captain in the U.S. Marine Corps and at present is stationed at Cherry Point, North Carolina. They have one child, Amanda Lee, born 17 August, 1974.

William Judson Shaw, Jr., second son of William Judson Shaw, Sr., and Lucia Williamson Shaw, was born 25 August, 1913. He married on 15 June, 1935, Thelma Odessa Jenkins (born 30 July, 1915), daughter of Charles Burgess and Martha Odessa Brockington Jenkins. They live on Mood Avenue in Sumter. They have one daughter, Lucia Madge, born 6 August, 1936. She married M.O. Gillett of Salt Lake City, Utah, on 8 November, 1958. They now live in Bartow, Florida, and have two daughters – Karen Lynn (born 1 March, 1961) and Marcia Ann (born 27 October, 1963).

W.J. Shaw, Sr., married on 14 January, 1922, Bertha Madge Griffin, R.N. (born 22 November, 1890), daughter of Samuel Graham and Annie Eliza Barwick Griffin of Pinewood. She died 5 November, 1969.

W.J. (Will) Shaw served as auditor of Sumter County. He was at one time a trustee of the Sumter County Schools. His health failed and he was a patient at Hopewell Nursing Home at the time of his death in April of 1973.

The children of W.J. Shaw, Sr., and Bertha Madge Griffin Shaw are Annie May (born 5 March, 1923) and Betty Carol (born 30 December, 1930), adopted. Annie May married first George Taylor Eaddy of Hemmingway and they were the parents of Elizabeth Madge (born 11 October, 1947), Carol Ann (born 1 November, 1949), Barbara Dale (born 7 January, 1954).

Annie May was married second to James S. Prevatt of Hemmingway on 21 January, 1967.

Betty Carol Shaw married William J. Carter of Sumter and they live on Paisley Park. Their four children are Betty Carol (born 12 July, 1952), Vickie Louise (born 17 August, 1955), William J., Jr. (born 26 April, 1957), Cynthia Ann (born 15 March, 1962).

Ervin James Shaw, second son of Ervin Bartow Shaw, was born 28 April, 1895. He married Kathleen Walsh, descendant of Col. Thomas V. Walsh, who was commander of a unit in the Civil War. They have no children and are now living in the Bethea Baptist Home near Darlington.

Only daughter of Ervin Bartow and Annie Pringle Shaw was Annie, who was born 28 June, 1897. She died at the age of four months and was buried at Concord Presbyterian Church.

Willie Shaw, son of Ervin James and Lillis Whitworth Shaw, was born 13 November, 1868. He married on 8 November, 1893. Susan Henrietta (Nettie) Pringle (born 28 February, 1870), daughter of Dr. William Judson Pringle and Annie Prothroe Hickson Pringle of Sumter County. She died 31 October, 1925, and he died 26 May, 1931. Both are buried at Concord Presbyterian Church. After her death he married Martha Hix. There were two children from the first marriage and none from the second.

Daughter of Willie and Nettie Pringle Shaw is Florence Pringle, who was born 4 May, 1895. She was married 15 November, 1923, to Halbert Dantzler Shuler of Holly Hill. He was the son of P.W. Shuler.

Florence Shaw Shuler lived in her ancestral home at Shaw's Crossroads in Sumter County until her death. Part of this home was built by a Chandler more than 100 years ago.

Her son, William Shaw Shuler (born 28 November, 1929), lives nearby with his family. He married Bunnie Brogdon and they have four children: Rebecca Keels (born 27 September, 1957), William Hal (born 12 November, 1958), Thomas Gilmore (born 26 November, 1960), and Patricia Leigh (born 21 August, 1969).

Only son of Willie Shaw was William Henry Shaw, born 16 April, 1897. He died unmarried 8 December, 1923.

David Charles Shaw, son of Ervin James and Lillis Whitworth Shaw, was born 27 June, 1891. He first married Lula Alderman, daughter of D.W. Alderman, who was one of Sumter District's leading businessmen. He was the "father" of the little town of Alcolu.

David Charles and Lula Alderman Shaw were the parents of five sons and two daughters. Their first son, Ervin David, was born 13 September, 1894. He enlisted in the U.S. Army in September 1917 and was first sent to Ohio State University, where he studied aviation, before joining the American Expeditionary Force in Britain. There he was attached to the R.A.F. and received Air Corps training at Oxford University and in Scotland. He was then sent to France for active duty. Fellow aviators called Lieutenant Shaw "the most daring and skillful pilot among us." He never hesitated to go on dangerous missions, always responding beyond the call of duty.

Then on 9 July, 1918, in an air encounter with three enemy planes, his ship was blown to pieces. To honor this brave airman, the government named the basic flying school at Sumter, Shaw

Field, which is now Shaw Air Force Base.

Gifford W. Shaw (born 5 February, 1898) was the second son of David Charles and Lula Alderman Shaw. He married Dorothy Burns, who was born on 7 March, 1900. He died 7 April, 1963.

Children of Gifford W. and Dorothy Burns Shaw are Marylu Shaw (born 16 February, 1931), who married 20 November, 1954, O. Lee Taylor, Jr. Their children are Joe (born 13 March, 1956) and Elaine (born 15 October, 1957).

Second daughter of Gifford W. and Dorothy Burns Shaw is Martha Priscilla (born 20 June, 1935) who lives with her mother in Sumter.

Son of the Gifford W. Shaws is Ervin Burns Shaw (born 31 August, 1932). He married 22 December, 1953, Anne Murrel (born 13 October, 1933). They have four children: Gifford Murrel (born 11 September, 1955), Dorothy Ann (born 22 October, 1956), Alfred Ervin (born 24 May, 1958), and Martha Louise (born 19 July, 1970).

Gifford W. Shaw was a successful and prominent business and public-spirited citizen of Sumter. He, with his son, Ervin Burns, operated the Shaw Manufacturing Company, and since his death his son has continued the business.

Paul Whitworth is the third son of David Charles Shaw. He was born 29 July, 1899, and on 9 May, 1923, he married Lillie Bell Lemmon, who was born 17 January, 1900. They live in Sumter and have one child, Charles Lemmon, who was born April 4, 1924. He married Mary Derrick Brown and their children are Mary Brown Shaw (born 27 December, 1948) and Paul Whitworth (born 22 July, 1952).

Paul Whitworth Shaw is also a successful lumber man in Sumter. He, with his son, operates the Shaw Lumber Company. He is one of Sumter's outstanding civic and church leaders.

David Charles Shaw, Jr., married Betty Cole and they live in Florence. Their children are David Charles Shaw, III (born 30 September, 1944), who married Joyce Evelyn Floyd; Margaret Elizabeth Shaw (born 5 December, 1946), who married Frederick Mishoe Dargan; Susan Boynton Shaw (born 27 August, 1948).

The first girl in the family of David Charles Shaw is Martha Priscilla, born 29 August, 1904, and she has laid claim to other "firsts" during her very active and successful life. In 1955 she was elected mayor of Sumter, a first woman mayor for the city and for the state, as well.

She served on the legislative committee to the American Municipal Association. She received national attention on ABC Television's "Woman's World."

She taught for 15 years and directed her own camp at Roaring Gap, North Carolina, for 25 years. She is now connected with the Alderman-Shaw business corporation in Sumter and she always finds time to serve in her church and in several civic groups.

Youngest son of David Charles and Lula Alderman Shaw was Bartow Solomon Shaw, born 4 June, 1907. On 31, 1931, he married Esther Boney, member of a prominent Sumter family. Their children are Bartow Solomon Shaw, Jr., and Marian.

Bartow ("Bow") Solomon Shaw, Jr. (born 23 May, 1941), married Victoria Livingston, daughter of C.E. Livingston of Hendersonville, North Carolina, on 19 November, 1966.

"Bow" is a graduate of Clemson University and is now engaged in business in Sumter. He is manager of Alderman-Shaw Company.

They have three children – Bartow Livingston (born 10 August, 1971), Marianne David (born 23 November, 1973), and Martha Rutledge (born 22 October, 1976).

Marian was born on 11 July, 1936. She married Paul Lamb, III, on 27 April, 1957. Paul Lamb, IV, born 25 August, 1963, is their only child.

The other daughter of the David Charles Shaw line is Lula Mae, who married Fred Graef and lives in New Jersey. They have two children, Fred and Priscilla.

Fred is an officer in a New York bank and Priscilla is manager of computer programming for **Newsweek**.

After the death of his first wife, David Charles Shaw married Mrs. Lutie Patton Pryor of Decatur, Alabama. As a young man he was engaged in the mercantile business in Alcolu, but came to Sumter in 1904 and became engaged in the automobile business and other interests in Sumter and Columbia. He lived in Decatur, Alabama, for the last 12 years of his life. He died there in 1942 of an unexpected heart attack at the age of 70.

Another son of Ervin James and Lillis Whitworth Shaw was John Whitworth. He was born 28 June, 1873. He married first Mamie Wells Alderman, who was born 8 March, 1876, and died 23 July, 1890.

On 6 December, 1899, he married Eva Pierson, a descendant of the esteemed Burgess family of Williamsburg County. She was descended also from William Frierson, immigrant to Williamsburg County in the 1830's, from Lt. Joseph Scott of Revolutionary War fame, and from Alex McCrea, an early settler in Williamsburg County. Her father, Gaither Pierson, was a very successful businessman in Sumter, owning much property in the city. The wedding ceremony was performed by the beloved Dr. Wilson James McKay.

Elder son of John Whitworth and Eva Pierson Shaw is John W. Shaw, Jr., born 24 February, 1901. He was a successful businessman of Sumter, having several interests, and he is now retired.

He married Mary Frances Bass, whose father, Fleetwood Jennings Bass, was a leading merchant in Mayesville for several years, having come there as a buyer for the American Tobacco Company. He was descended from Nathaniel Bass, who came to Jamestown, Virginia, in 1619. Her mother, Lois Terry Bass, was a descendant of several old Virginia and North Carolina lines including the Barnett, Winstead and Adams families, her father being a Confederate veteran, later studying at Davidson College and practicing law in Roxboro, North Carolina.

Daughter of John W. and Mary Frances Shaw, Mary Catharine, was born 13 June, 1940. In 1963 she married Barney Levy Williams, M.D., son of Barney L. and Christine Kolb Williams. Barney is a popular young obstetrician and gynecologist and is chief of staff at Tuomey Hospital in Sumter. Their children are Barney Whitworth (born 24 May, 1964), Scott McCrea (born 27 March, 1969), Catharine Adams (born 22 April, 1970).

Son of John W. Shaw and Mary Frances Shaw, John W., III, D.V.M., was born 18 May, 1943. He owns and operates a veterinary hospital in Sumter. His marriage to Brenda Outlaw was on 16 July, 1966. Their children are Elizabeth Allen (born 7 September, 1970), John Whitworth, IV (born 21 February, 1972), the youngest of the Shaws bearing the name of John, the immigrant; Allen Bass (born 2 July, 1974).

Eva Pierson, the only daughter of John Whitworth and Eva Pierson Shaw, was born 28 October, 1907, and died 9 August, 1909.

Younger son of John Whitworth Shaw is Burgess Gaither Shaw, born 26 September, 1916. He married on 13 January, 1943. Elizabeth Susan Burns, born 14 August, 1922. She died 22 April, 1970.

Their children are as follows:

1. Burgess Gaither Shaw, Jr., who was born 12 June, 1944. He married Pamela Ann Hall, Bethesda, Maryland.

2. James Crawford, who was born 25 January, 1949, and married Virginia Howell Smith from Oklahoma City, Oklahoma.

3. Elizabeth Parker was born 18 January, 1952, and married Dwight Lowrance Crowell, III, of Salisbury, North Carolina.

4. Susan Pierson was born 5 November, 1954. She married Roy Boykin of Camden, South Carolina.

Additional information has been received on Etta Lee Shaw's line.

Lillis McCollum Holman McCormick's daughter, Frances Harley McCormick, was born 6 December, 1964. The family lives in Greenville.

Frank Kennedy Holman, III, has one son, Nathan Kennedy Holman, born 10 September, 1973.

After the death of the first wife of John Shaw, Sr., he married Lillis Mitchell, daughter of John and Jean Mitchell, and their oldest son was John Shaw, Jr., who was born in 1788 and was an 1809 graduate of the University of South Carolina. He married Maj. John Gamble's daughter, Susannah Cooper Gamble, born in 1796.

The tradition is that he was a captain in the War of 1812, but there seems to be no war records to substantiate the fact. However, it is mentioned also in the Von Hacke collection in the possession of Maynard Davis of Summerton.

After serving for 12 years as an elder in Salem Black River Presbyterian Church, he died 27 or 29 October, 1831. Susannah had died a year before. Both are buried in the Salem Church Cemetery.

John Shaw, Jr., and Susannah Cooper Gamble had five daughters: Sarah W., who married David Kennedy; Isabella B., who married John G. Schull, M.D.; Eliza Agness (born 1827); Susannah G. (born 1830) married Robert Manton English as his first wife; and Lillis Susannah (1825-1826).

The only son of John, Jr., and Susannah Cooper Gamble was John Calvin, who was born a twin to Susannah G., 19 February, 1830, one month before his mother's death. He married Anna Elizabeth English (born 1832), daughter of James Wilson and Mary Jane Bradley English. They lived in Lee County in the old English home, which was most unusual in structure. The first story was all brick and the second story was of wood. It was built in the form of three cubes. The front cube was the parlor and behind that were two cubes. The bedrooms were upstairs. The family later moved to Bishopville.

There are many interesting stories connected with John Calvin Shaw. He enlisted in the Confederate Army in 1861 and became a lieutenant of Company E, 19th South Carolina Regiment on 23 May, 1862. Taken ill on 28 May, he was on leave into June, and it seems he was off duty at intervals the remainder of the year. Part of November and December of that year he was on furlough.

The muster roll shows that he was on recruiting duty 26 January, 1863, and apparently this was his assignment for all of that year under orders of Generals Polk, Bragg and Pillow.

In 1864 he was back on active duty with his regiment, and on 22 July of that year he was captured near Decatur, Georgia, taken to Marietta, Georgia, and on to military prison in Louisville, Kentucky. From there he was sent to officers' prison at Johnson's Island, Ohio, arriving there 1 August, 1864, and remaining for the duration of the war.

He was released 15 June, 1865. The family tradition is that, walking all the way, he reached home eleven months later, broken in health. He was never well again and he died 15 December, 1872, at the age of 42.

The story is told in the family that when the Yankees came through Bishopville, his little daughter, Mary Susan, 11 years old, playing in the yard, was asked where her father was. She sent them to her mother, whose reply to the query was, "In Virginia, fighting with Lee. Where else?" Not liking her answer, they ransacked the house, taking all the valuables; but when they found a Masonic emblem, they returned everything they had taken.

John Calvin and Anna English Shaw were the parents of five children. Mary Susan (mentioned above), who was born in 1851, married Robert A. Carnes of Bishopville. As a lad, he took potshots at the enemy when they came near Mary Susan's home. She died in 1906 and he in 1910.

Second daughter in John Calvin's family was Sarah W.R. Shaw (born 1855) who married Robert Carter McCutchen, Jr. She died in 1916. Both are buried in the Bishopville Presbyterian Church Cemetery.

Anna English Shaw, third daughter, was born in 1858. She married Lucien Bethea. She died in 1886 and is buried in the cemetery at Bishopville Presbyterian Church.

The older son of John Calvin Shaw was Samuel Rutherford, who was born in 1860. He married in 1884, Minnie Thompson Green, daughter of Major Green. After his death in 1890, she married W.W. Hearon of Bishopville. She and her first husband are buried in the Bishopville Presbyterian Cemetery.

Son of Samuel Rutherford and Minnie Green Shaw was Samuel Loraine (born 1885). He married Marcia Marvin Wolling, daughter of Rev. J.W. and Elizabeth M. Rice Wolling. They lived in Bishopville and Orangeburg. He died in 1958 and she, in 1966. They are buried at Bethlehem Methodist Church in Bishopville.

Children of Samuel Loraine and Marcia Wolling Shaw:

1. Spencer Loraine (born 1911) married Margaret Ruth Schofield and they moved to Los Angeles, California. He died in 1968. Their children are Susan Lee (born 1941) and Spencer Loraine, Jr. (born 1935), who married in 1957. His children are Laura, Diana and Andrew.

2. Dorothy Marcia (born 1915) married Dan Autrey Taylor in 1941 and they live in Moultrie, Georgia. Their children:

a. Marcia (born 1944) is the wife of James Malcolm McHargue and they live in Tallahassee, Florida.

b. Rebecca Lee (born 1948) married Larry DeMott and lives in Moultrie, Georgia.

c. Jan Dorothy (born 1952).

3. Meredith Carlisle (born 1919) married Dorothy Walker in 1947. They live in Fort Lauderdale, Florida. They have three children: Patricia Diane (born 1948) married to John La Rosa; Michael Carlisle (born 1950); Stephanie Irene (born 1955).

Anna Lee, only daughter of Samuel Rutherford Shaw, was born in 1887 and married Henry Porter Moore in 1915. She died in 1960 and is buried at the Presbyterian church in Bishopville.

Her children are:

1. Minnie Green (born 1915), who married Thomas K. Johnstone. They live in Greenville and their children are Nan; T.K., Jr.; Alban.

2. Henry Porter Moore, Jr.

John Thompson Shaw, second son of Samuel Rutherford and Minnie Green Shaw, was born in 1889. He married Josephine Wagner in 1915 and died in 1925. His widow lived until 1965. They had two children:

1. Barbara Lee (born in 1916), who married a Lehman, and they live in Bainbridge, Maryland.

2. John Thompson Shaw, Jr. (born 1919), married Mickey Tallon.

John Calvin Shaw, Jr., son of John Calvin and Anna English Shaw, was born in 1865. He married in 1886 Selina Abigail DuRant and they lived in Bishopville. She died in 1934 and he died four years later.

Eldest son of John Calvin Shaw, Jr., was Russell Ramon, born 10 October, 1887. He married first Rosa Boyd. There were apparently no children from this marriage.

On October 20, 1920, he was married to Marion Louise Baskin, who was born 2 June, 1883, with the Rev. W.V. Dibble performing the ceremony in Bishopville. He died 3 February, 1940, and she lived till 19 October, 1969.

Cora Elizabeth Shaw was the eldest daughter of John Calvin Shaw, Jr., and Selina A. DuRant Shaw. She was born 11 October, 1889, and married 10 July, 1910, Baxter Adams Fletcher (1878-1918). She died 7 March, 1967.

The next son was John Calvin, III, who was born 13 October, 1891, at his uncle J. O. DuRant's home near Society Hill. He married first Lucia Fogle and his second wife was Marie Hammett. He died in 1971.

Another son of John Calvin, Jr., was Leonard Lewellen, who was also born at his uncle's home, and the date of his birth was 29 October, 1893. He, too, married twice – first to Kathleen

Tisdale and second to Vida Hope Kelly.

Eulalie, second daughter of John Calvin, Jr., was born near Bishopville on 8 December, 1895. She married Tom McLendon.

Another daughter of John Calvin Shaw, Jr., and Selina Abigail was Clelia Florence, born 23 October, 1905. She died at the D.E. DuRant home near Bishopville, 1 January, 1975. She was the wife of James Asbury DuRant, who also died in 1975.

Youngest son in the family was Marion DuRant Shaw, who was born 27 July, 1900, and died 2 June, 1901.

Eldest child of John C. Shaw, Jr., and Selina A. Shaw was Russell Ramon (mentioned above). He was born 10 October, 1887. He and his second wife, Marion Louise Baskin, who was born 2 June, 1883, and died 19 October, 1969, were the parents of four children: Maria Baskin Shaw was born 30 May, 1921, and died the same day; English Baskin Shaw was born and died 29 August, 1922; an unnamed son was also born and died on the same day, 29 November, 1923.

Russell Ramon (born 28 March, 1926) married on 14 August, 1954, Renata Elizabeth Helene Vitzthum von Eckstadt, with Rev. Richard Hjelt-Helaseppa performing the ceremony in Manta, Finland. They live in Chevy Chase, Maryland, and have two children: Rembert Baskin Vitzthum Shaw (born 5 May, 1961) and Lori Renata Harrach Shaw (born 30 October, 1962).

Russell attended school in Bishopville and was graduated from the University of South Carolina with a major in Political History and Fine Arts. He then attended the University of Chicago where he studied Byzantine History and Art.

He met his wife at the University of Chicago where she received a double major in English Literature and Art History. After his graduation he worked in Helsinki, where he was near enough to his future wife's home to see her often. As he said he kept proposing and she kept refusing, but finally she said "yes." She relinquished the title which she had in Finland and returned to the United States, where they are happy in their very worthwhile pursuits.

Russell recalls many interesting stories about his father and grandfather. He tells of experiences his father had while living on his grandfather's farm: He remembers going, as a boy to his grandfather's home in town and marveling at the hundreds of books in that gentleman's library. There were learned tomes in Greek and Latin and Cowboy stories as well.

His father, Russell Ramon Shaw, was a mail carrier as well as a farmer. His daily routine seldom varied – up early and to the Dixie Cafe in Bishopville for coffee – back home to tell hands on the farm what to do for the day – on to his mail route.

He was very fond of hunting and always kept on the farm

from 15 to 30 dogs. He was one of the founders of the South Carolina Fox Hunters Association and held various offices. He also enjoyed writing stories.

John Shaw, Sr., and Lillis Mitchell were the parents of another son, William Alexander, who was born 3 November, 1794. He married Elizabeth Emmaline Bradley, daughter of Samuel, Jr., and Mary Bradley. She was born in 1800 and died in 1886. He died in 1864. He was one of the two Elders of New Hope, a church organized in 1831 of members of Mt. Zion Presbyterian who had withdrawn. William Shaw later returned to Mt. Zion where he was a dedicated worker until his death.

The oldest child in this family was Mary Elvira, who was born in 1820, died in 1822 and is buried in the old Shaw cemetery.

The eldest son, John James Shaw, Sr., was born 24 August, 1822. He married, in 1843, Caroline Cynthia Wilson (born in 1825), daughter of James Harvey and Elizabeth Wilson. They lived in Lee County. He was a deacon from 1848 until his death in 1879. He was very active in the affairs of old Mt. Zion Presbyterian Church.

From a letter written by John James to a relative in Alabama on December 15, 1855, it is learned that he was engaged in turpentine "farming." Since it was a new industry, the writer said that he was having much difficulty in proceeding correctly. However, he had hopes of making money on the venture. According to this letter, crops were poor that year. His philosophic conclusion, however, was "while we can get enough of 'hog and hominy' there is no danger of starving."

Another letter, written January 1856, spoke of the bitterly cold winter. There had been two snows and a very heavy sleet storm. He said that "Cousin Lizzie English" had prophesied that there would be three snows during the month.

John James and Caroline Wilson Shaw were the parents of six, the oldest of whom (according to one record) was Mary Stuart Shaw (born 1845). She married William Othello McCutchen in 1857 and died in 1868. She is buried in Mt. Zion cemetery. They had one daughter, Mary Shaw McCutchen.

The next three daughters were apparently unmarried. They are Elizabeth E. (1848-1879), Margaret Jane (1857-1928), Adelle Louise (1853-1943). All are buried in the Mt. Zion cemetery.

The older son of this family was John James Shaw, Jr. (born in 1859). He married Vara Jane DuBose, daughter of J. Harvey and Elizabeth Shaw DuBose. She was born in 1855.

He had large farming interests in Lee County. He was a deacon in Mt. Zion Presbyterian Church from 1887 till 1904 and an Elder from 1904 till 1941. He was very active in all church affairs, serving on the building committee for the present sanctuary, built in 1912, and the old parsonage built in 1914.

She died in 1940 and he, in 1941. Both are buried at Mt. Zion.

John James Shaw, III, son of John James Shaw, Jr., and Vara DuBose Shaw, was born in 1885. In 1913 he married Jessie May Owen (a Shaw genealogist from whom much information came). Their daughter, Caroline Elizabeth married Hubert J. Privette in 1942 and they live in Canover, North Carolina.

Second son of John J. Shaw, Jr., was Harvey Wilton, born 1889. He married Ethel Vaughan of Van Wyck in 1920. They lived in Lee County on part of his ancestral plantation, where he was successful in farming and in other interests.

He was a dedicated member of Mt. Zion Presbyterian Church, serving as a deacon from 1920 to 1929 and an Elder for 44 years. From 1929 till 1946 he was Clerk of the Session. He died in 1973.

Mrs. Shaw is a faithful worker in Mt. Zion.

Their son, Harvey Wilton Shaw, Jr., was born in 1926. On 1 July, 1950, he married Mamie Spann Dowe (born in 1927) from Alabama. He moved his grandfather's house and they lived there until it burned some years ago. They then built a lovely modern home on the same spot.

He is a graduate of the University of South Carolina and is a community leader. He has extensive farming and other business interests. As was his father, he is a leader in Mt. Zion Presbyterian Church. He is an Elder and Clerk of the Session.

Mrs. Shaw is also devoted to the work of the church. She has served as president of the Women of the Church and was chairman of the committee in charge of renovating the interior of the old Session House when it was returned recently to Mt. Zion.

They have two children — Harvey Wilton, III (born 14 August, 1955) and Mamie Vaughn (born 31 January, 1960).

The next son, William Edgar, was born in 1892 and died in 1961.

There were two girls in the family — Alice Carolyn (1887-1888) and Mary Caroline (1894-1898). These were followed by three unnamed infant sons who died in 1893, 1896, and 1897.

The next son of John James Shaw, Sr., was Andrew Flynn (born 1861). He married Anna Elizabeth English Law (born 1869), daughter of Robert and Margaret Shaw English. They lived in St. Charles. He died in 1936 and she in 1944. Both are buried in Mt. Zion Cemetery.

Eldest son of Andrew Flynn and Anna English Shaw was Wilson Flynn (born 1900). He married Mary Haynsworth Ellerbe, daughter of E.B. and Mary J. McCall Ellerbe. They lived in King's

Mountain, North Carolina. He died in 1961 and is buried in Grove Hill Cemetery, Darlington.

Franklin English Shaw (born 1904), the next son of Andrew Flynn, married Irene Ellen Potter. They live in Ridgefield, Connecticut. Their children are Franklin English, Jr., and Elizabeth Ann. They were born in 1935 and 1938, respectively. He married Patricia Ann Brady and her husband was A.N. Morelli.

Robert James Shaw, the next son of Andrew Flynn, was born in 1906 and married Gertrude McLaurin, daughter of Daniel B. and Sue Wilson McLaurin. They lived in Charleston for a number of years, but they have now retired and live in Sumter. She is a genealogist and has collected valuable information on several Sumter District families, with which she and Robert J. are connected.

Fourth child of Andrew Flynn Shaw was Caroline Elizabeth (Beth). She married Robert Archibald Cousar, son of John Richard and Martha J. English Cousar. Both are deceased.

They had two adopted sons: William James (born 1944) and Richard Flynn (born 1945).

Mary Adele (born in 1909) is the fifth in the Andrew Flynn Shaw family. She married Eulah Miles Knight.

Margaret Law, daughter of Anna Elizabeth English and John Law, II (her first husband), married Clinton B. Walsh.

Margaret B. Shaw, daughter of William A. and Elizabeth E. Bradley Shaw, was born in 1824. She became the second wife of Robert Manton English. They lived in Lee County until his death in 1885 and hers in 1904. Both are buried at the Presbyterian Church in Bishopville.

Their children are:

a. Margaret, who married George Muldrow.

b. Adeline, the second wife of John Law, Sr., later marrying John DesChamps.

c. Martha Jane (born 1867), wife of John Richard Cousar, son of Rev. John and Lillis Shaw Cousar. She was the mother of Mary, Mattie and Robert Cousar. She died in 1909.

d. Anna Elizabeth (born 1869) married first John Law, II, and second Andrew Flynn Shaw.

Samuel LeRoy, fourth child of William A. Shaw, was born in 1826. He first married Jane Cooper. They lived at Carter's Crossing Township. She died in 1880 and he later married Mary Flynn Cooper Harrington, daughter of Samuel and Margaret English Cooper. Their children were:

a. Samuel E. Shaw (born 1855). He married Agnes Chandler, daughter of Capt. Isaac James Chandler. Both died in 1927 in St. Charles.

b. E. Margaret Shaw (born 1862). She married Bertrand Colclough and they were the parents of six: Mary, Henry, LeRoy, Hugh, Jennie (married to Porcher Gaillard), and Waring.

d. William Flynn Shaw (born 1860). He married Madge McLaurin, daughter of Dr. Henry McLaurin. Their children were Wilfred Shaw, M.D., and William (Bub) Shaw.

e. Dwight LeRoy Shaw (born 1869). He married Florence Cooper. They lived in St. Charles. She died in 1932 and he in 1944. Their children: Dwight LeRoy, Jr., married Dora Mae Forest; Mary Flynn married Marion DuRant; Roberta married Ladson Montgomery; Robert Cooper (1911-1913).

f. Ida C. Shaw (born 1857).

g. Son died as an infant.

William A. Shaw's next son, William Reese, was born in 1828 and married Mary M. Carnes. They lived in Bishopville. After his death in 1864 she married Henry C. Miller.

Children of William Reese Shaw:

1. William Reese Shaw, Jr. (born 1861), married Olive Sumter DuRant. Both died in 1941 and are buried at Bishopville Presbyterian Church.

2. Mary E. (Mattie) Shaw died an infant in 1865.

3. James A. Shaw (1860-1861)

4. James A. Shaw (probably named for the one who died)

5. Elizabeth M. Shaw

Augustus Leander Shaw was the next son of William A. Shaw. He was born in 1834 and married in 1864, Margaret English. They lived in Mayesville. He died in 1908 and she in 1916. They had three sons and two daughters.

1. Harry Lee Shaw, Sr., M.D. (born in 1865), married Jennie Wilson and they lived in Sumter, where he enjoyed a large medical practice for many years. They were the parents of three daughters and one son.

a. Lucile married (1) Marion Wilson, (2) Maxwell Jenkins, and (3) "Dick" Scott. By her first marriage there were two children – William Marion and Jean.

b. Harry Lee, Jr. (born 1905), married (1) Marie Louise Ragsdale in 1931. Their children are Harry Lee, III, Edward S. and Stephen Willard. His second wife is Joy Thomas and they live in Fairfield, Connecticut. Their children are Jay and Thomas.

c. Margaret Shaw married Bolling Gay, M.D.

d. Dorothy Shaw married Murdoch McLeod.

2. Lina Shaw, daughter of A. Leander Shaw, was born in 1879 and died in 1933. She married Fred Stuckey and there were two children in the family – Ashby Lee and Harriett.

3. Robert Lee Shaw (1870-1951). He lived in Lubbock, Texas.

4. James McKay Shaw (born 1874) married Mary Muldrow, daughter of Edward and Elizabeth Muldrow. They lived in Mayes-

ville, where he was a devoted member of the Mayesville Presbyterian Church and served as an Elder for many years.

They had three adopted children:

a. W.D. (Billy) was born in 1917 and lives in Sumter.

b. Mary Frances (born 1923) married Martin B. Tiller and they live in Summerville. They have two children, Kay and Martie.

c. Henry G. ("Sonny") was born in 1934. He lives in Columbia.

5. Jennie Flynn (born 1870) married J.M. Simpson and moved to Amarillo, Texas.

William A. Shaw's son, Theodore Munson, was thought to have been the twin brother of Augustus Leander. He married Margaret Saye in 1859 and received his degree in medicine the same year. Their children were Elizabeth R. (1864-1869) and Sue Montgomery (1866-1867).

William A. Shaw's son, Robert Dwight, was born in 1839 and died in 1864.

Edward Lawrence Shaw, another son of William A. Shaw, was born in 1841 and died in 1845.

Henry G. Shaw, son of William A. and Elizabeth Bradley Shaw, was born in 1847. He married Sarah ("Sallie") Saye in 1867 and they lived in Carter's Crossing Township. He died in 1908, and she in 1921. Both are buried in the Mt. Zion cemetery. They had three daughters and one son.

1. Lula Dwight Shaw (born 1868) married C. Benjamin Dusenberry.

2. Emma Rebecca (born 1872) married Thomas Chiles Perrin of Bishopville.

Their issue:

a. James Wardlaw Perrin

b. Lula Dwight Perrin married Harry Camnitz.

c. Mary Perrin married Bob Griffin of Florence.

d. Henry Shaw Perrin of Atlanta, Georgia, and Jacksonville, Florida

e. Sarah Perrin married W.H. Thrower, Cheraw.

f. Col. Thomas Cothran Perrin of Bishopville

g. Rebecca Perrin married Henry Giles of Forest City, North Carolina.

h. William Alford Perrin of Fort Lee, New Jersey

i. Jack L. Perrin of Augusta, Georgia, and Bishopville, died in 1976.

j. Rosa Margaret Perrin married Carey Rogers Kilgore, Jr., of Bishopville.

Third daughter of Henry G. Shaw was Rosa, who married G. Edward Grier. Their children were Moses Edward and Henry Shaw.

Jamie Shaw, only son of Henry G. Shaw, died young.

William A. Shaw's daughter, Lillis Elizabeth, was born in 1832. She married James Harvey DuBose and they lived in the Mt. Zion community. She died in 1909 and he in 1863. Their children:

1. Vara Jane DuBose married John J. Shaw.
2. Alice Cynthia DuBose (1853-1882)
3. William Shaw DuBose (1857-1927)
4. John Frank (1861-1927)

John Shaw, Sr., and Lillis Mitchell Shaw's daughter, Elizabeth, was born in 1797. She married William Wilson Bradley, Sr. (born 1783), son of James and Mary Wilson Bradley. He died in 1854 and she in 1865. Both are buried at Salem Church. They were the parents of 14 children and they also reared the four sons of her sister, Lillis Shaw Cousar, and Rev. John Cousar, who died when the boys were young.

1. John Shaw Bradley, oldest in this family, was born in 1813. He married Eugenia English in 1840. He died in 1884 and she two years later. Both are buried in Bishopville.

2. The next child died as an infant in 1816.

3. Samuel Bradley, M.D., was born in 1817 and died in 1843, soon after graduation from medical school in Charleston.

4. James Bradley was born and died in 1819.

5. William Wilson Bradley, Jr., was born in 1821. He married Martha Jane Wilson in 1843. She died in 1877 and he in 1878.

6. Elizabeth Bradley, born 1823, married Robert Carter McCutchen. They had one son, Robert Carter McCutchen, Jr., who married "Sallie" Shaw.

7. Mary Wilson Bradley died as an infant in 1825.

8. Lillis Jane Bradley was born in 1828 and married John Shaw Whitworth. She died in 1884 and is buried at Salem Church. He died in 1862.

9. James Bradley (1826-1878). Unmarried.

10. Robert Bradley was born in 1830 and was graduated from Columbia Seminary. He married Sarah Elizabeth Tyson Bradley, daughter of James Bradley, M.D. He died in 1906 and is buried at Midway Presbyterian Church and she is buried near Bethune.

11. Mary Stewart Bradley, born 1832, married Thomas James McFaddin (his first wife). They had one daughter, M.S.B. McFaddin.

12. Leighton Wilson Bradley (1834-1850)

13. Isaac Whitworth Bradley, born 1837, married Elizabeth Shaw Rhodes, daughter of Martin L. and Elizabeth Shaw Rhodes. They were the parents of a number of daughters and one son. One daughter, Louise Lillian, married Henry Hawkins Corbett

and their daughter, Mary Jeanette (Netta) Corbett, who married P.M. Tiller, has done much research and furnished considerable information on the Shaw family and connections.

14. Edwin Bradley (1838-1855)

Sarah Elvira, daughter of John Shaw, Sr., and Lillis Mitchell, was born in 1807. She was the first wife of Isaac DuBose Whitworth, descendant of Isaac DuBose and Suzanne Couillandeau, French Huguenots, who came to South Carolina in 1686.

There were five children in this family:

1. Sarah Elizabeth Caroline Bradley Whitworth, born 1827, was the second wife of Martin L. Rhodes.

2. John Shaw Whitworth (1829-1862) married Jane L. Bradley (1828-1884).

3. Mary Ann Magdeline DuBose Whitworth was born in 1831. She married ___ Goddard and their son was John Gee Goddard.

4. Lillis Hester Jane Whitworth, born 1835, married Ervin James Shaw. (This line has been given.) Thus the Sumter Shaws are descended from John Shaw, Sr., and his first wife, through David, and his second wife, Lillis Mitchell, through their daughter, Sarah Elvira, who married a Whitworth.

5. Elvira Theresa Whitworth, born 1836. Isaac DuBose Whitworth married (2) Amanda ___ ___ and there were two children from this marriage: Julia and Amanda.

Lillis Shaw, daughter of John Shaw, Sr., and Lillis Mitchell, was born in 1804. She married the Rev. John Cousar (born 1772).

She died in 1836 and he in 1837, leaving four young sons, who were reared by her sister, Elizabeth Shaw Bradley. They are both buried at Midway Presbyterian Church.

The eldest of the four sons was John Shaw Cousar (1825-1841). He was unmarried.

The second was Andrew Flynn Cousar, born in 1826. He married Theodosia Bradley English (born 1824), daughter of James Wilson and Mary Jane Bradley English. He died in 1896 and she in 1889. Both are buried at the Bishopville Presbyterian Church. There was no issue.

Rev. James Archibald Cousar (born in 1829) was the third son. He married first Martha Jane ("Patty") English, daughter of James Wilson and Mary Jane Bradley English. They had two sons.

John Richard Cousar (born 1861), older son, married Mattie Jane English, daughter of Robert Manton and M.B. Shaw English. Both died in 1909 and are buried at Mt. Zion Presbyterian Church. They had one son, Richard Flynn Cousar (1896-1916).

The second son of Rev. James A. Cousar was James English Cousar, born 1864. He married Leonora Muldrow, daughter of

William J. and Mary M. Muldrow. He died in 1929 and she in 1951. Both are buried in Bishopville. They were the parents of four: Rev. James English Cousar, Jr., a dedicated Presbyterian minister, is now retired, living at the Presbyterian Home in Summerville. He has done extensive research on his family connections and has written at least two books.

The second son of Rev. James A. Cousar was George Cousar, a missionary to Africa.

Rev. Wilbur Cousar was third in this family and John Cousar, M.D., was the fourth.

Rev. James Archibald Cousar's second wife was Mary Jane McLucas (1836-1912).

The fourth son of Rev. John Cousar and Lillis Shaw Cousar was Nelson Richard Cousar, born in 1834. He was only two years old when his mother died. He married Mary Jane Epps, born 1837. She died in 1880 and he in 1896. Both are buried at Midway Presbyterian Church.

Mrs. Anne McCutchen McDonald (wife of Olin McDonald), one of Sumter's outstanding teachers, is a descendant of John Calvin Shaw. (One of his daughters, Mary Susan, married Robert A. Carnes. Their daughter, Anna Estelle Carnes, who married Eugene Bradley McCutchen, was Anne McDonald's mother.

Lillis Mitchell Shaw, second wife of John Shaw, Sr., outlived her husband many years. She made an interesting will in 1839. First she stated that her estate was to be divided into six equal parts – one part to her stepson, David, and one each to her five children. If any of the children were deceased their shares would go to the grandchildren.

She also requested that her lands be appraised at $3 an acre. One stipulation was that $200 be given to Salem Church "to be added to the permanent fund of the church." In a codicil attached later, she said that nothing was to be given to the church since she had "paid her full portion in building the new church."

There were five codicils to the will, the last one being signed in 1853; each one making some change in the legacies that she had mentioned in the beginning.

Lillis Mitchell Shaw must have been a very remarkable woman. She was left a widow when her youngest child was only three years old. Therefore, she had the responsibility of rearing a family and of managing an estate. No doubt she had learned much from her husband, who must have been a very successful businessman, judging from the amount of property he accumulated.

The Shaw descendants have indeed a rich heritage. Not only were their ancestors successful in business, but more important, they were leaders in four of the old Presbyterian churches in the area.

PART III. PERSONS

Glimpses Into Lives Of Early Citizens

Coming to Sumter District from Darlington County where he was born in 1848, John Julius Dargan was active for many years in both educational and political fields.

After he was graduated from Furman University, he began teaching, and although he left this profession for a time to practice law, it is said that teaching was always his greatest interest.

Having been admitted to the bar in 1874, he went into politics two years later, running for solicitor from his circuit. He was defeated in this venture, but in 1878[19] he won the election for the House of Representatives from Sumter County where he was then living.

During Reconstruction he was a staunch follower of Wade Hampton and worked diligently for his election as governor. In return he was made a full colonel on Hampton's staff. Later he was elected solicitor.

Colonel Dargan is credited with the founding of the Pee Dee Historical Society, thus showing interest in the history of his state and the cultural development of its people. Returning to his first love, he became principal of the General Sumter Memorial Academy. Being a zealous worker for universal peace, he dedicated his school to this pursuit, and at his own expense attended a peace conference in Boston as the only delegate from the South.

Interested in writing, Colonel Dargan worked with the press for some time in Sumter. He published in **The State** of October 9, 1904, the life of a Presbyterian missionary who was respected and loved in this area, Dr. John Leighton Wilson. Another publication, prompted by the fact that he found errors and omissions in the history textbook being used in the schools, was his own School History of South Carolina. This book came off the press in 1906 and was adopted as the school text for some years.

He was an advocate of equal rights for men and women in the churches. It was always his desire to recognize the ability and worth of individuals, and it was he who was responsible for the erection of a monument to Gen. Thomas Sumter, serving as chairman of the commission appointed by the General Assembly for that purpose. In a tribute paid to John Julius Dargan at the celebration of the 200th anniversary of Sumter's birthday, it was said: "Colonel Dargan loved his state with a deep devotion and was ever anxious that her heroes should receive the honor due them."

HORATIO LINCOLN DARR

One of Sumter's colorful citizens of the long ago, Horatio Lincoln Darr, born in 1825 in Charleston, though not a native son of the young town of Sumterville, made a distinct contribution to the life of the town, especially in the growth of the Fourth Estate.

He received his training as a printer through an eight-year apprenticeship with his foster father, Isaac C. Morgan. As a result of this practice, he became recognized as one of the most skilled and "fastest" printers of his day. The story is that he exhibited in one of the first fairs sponsored by the old South Carolina Agricultural Association an issue of his paper printed on white satin. Though he was discouraged in this undertaking by his foster father, who was also entering the contest, the young man walked away with the medal and the admiration of all.

Before coming to Sumter in 1856 to begin his long and successful career in newspaper work, he had held responsible positions with papers in Charleston and Columbia.

According to Dr. Anne King Gregorie's book, **The History of Sumter County**, Darr was a "short, florid, very energetic and rather talkative man. . . . " He "had a fringe of red hair, restless blue eyes and a passion for keeping ahead of his work."

H.L. Darr was not only a printer of unusual ability, but he was also a man who stood high in the esteem of his fellowman. He was chosen to fill many offices of trust in his community, and he was never found wanting in the fulfillment of his obligations to these trusts. As an example of his integrity and loyalty to his convictions is an event that took place just after the War Between the States. He was asked by the clerk of the House of Representatives to print and publish the Acts of the General Assembly. His reply was that if this position in any way comprised his loyalty to his state and people, he could not accept. The request was not repeated. It wasn't easy for a man in moderate means to turn down an opportunity to make a sizable sum of money, but Darr placed a higher value on his integrity than upon any money that he might receive.

He died on June 20, 1888,[20] survived by three children – Mrs. L.W. Jenkins, Mrs. F.D. Knight, L.B.H. Darr. Many of Sumter's older citizens remember "Mr. Louis" Darr, who was evidently "a chip off the old block;" for he was a man of character, beloved by all who knew him.

REVEREND NICHOLAS WILLIAM EDMUNDS

A man who had a lasting influence on the religious life of Sumter in days gone by was Dr. Nicholas William Edmunds. He came to the town as a teacher in the Sumter Institute in 1875, having previously taught in the then famous Barhamville School near Columbia.

In 1880[21] he was called to the pastorate of the First Presbyterian Church (remaining as chaplain of the Institute), where he served until 1905. On account of failing health, he had to give up active duties, but he was pastor emeritus until his death in 1907.

At his funeral his friend, Dr. W.J. McKay, said he "walked our streets for thirty years, 'going about doing good.' "

His name was cherished by all who knew him, and there are still those living in Sumter who accord him a place among those who did much toward the building of a better world for their descendants.

Not only did Dr. N.W. Edmunds leave an imprint on Sumter in his own person, but he left a son, the beloved Dr. S.H. Edmunds, known to countless citizens of this area as the symbol of education in its true sense – an education for the physical, mental, and spiritual development of each boy and girl in the community.

Spotlight On Some Early Sumter Lawyers

The practice of law was indeed a popular profession with the young men of Sumter District. From the earlier records of settlers in the area there were many who chose this profession, some becoming prominent as lawyers and judges, not only in their own district but throughout the state.

The earliest of these lawyers was Thomas Waties of Marden Plantation, who came to Sumter District from Georgetown. He was admitted to the bar in 1785 and four years later was elected an Associate Judge. Thus at the age of 29 he "attained to the highest legal distinction." He resigned this position in 1811 to become a Judge of the Court of Equity, which office he held until 1824 when he was assigned to the Circuit as a Law Judge. The arduous duties of this office he performed faithfully until his death in 1828.

The book, **Bench and Bar**, by O'Neall, speaks of him as "one of those men, who, in a quiet and unobtrusive way, won upon the hearts of all men. He was a most distinguished judge; he loved the right and sought to do right . . . ."[22]

In the 1790's John Smyth Richardson of Bloom Hill Plantation was reading law in Charleston and began practice in Sumter in 1799. He, too, became a judge and won the reputation of being "honest and just." O'Neall said of Judge Richardson, with whom he was closely associated in the same court for 15 years, "He was firm and immutable in what he believed to be right."[23]

Though not a native of Sumter County, Joseph Haynsworth Earle enjoyed a successful practice of law in Sumter, having come from Greenville in 1872. When he was elected Judge of the Eighth Judicial Circuit from his native county, he returned there in 1891. In 1886,[24] while in Sumter, he was elected Attorney General of South Carolina and filled the office with "distinguished ability."

One of "the big four" of Sumter Democracy, James Douglas Blanding was one of those "largely influential in guiding the destinies of a down-trodden, discouraged and severely tried people." The time was between 1876 and 1884. James D. Blanding was at that time a veteran of the legal profession, having been practicing in Sumter for approximately 35 years.

Born in Columbia in 1821,[25] he studied at the Academy in that city and after graduation from South Carolina College in 1841 read law with his uncle, William F. DeSaussure. He was admitted to the bar in Sumter and became a member of the firm of Blanding and DeSaussure in 1843.

His law practice was interrupted by the Mexican War, during which he served first as adjutant and was mustered out in 1848 as a captain.

In 1852 he was elected to the Legislature, remaining in this office for six years. He was also intendant (mayor) of Sumter from 1852 to 1858; he served as chairman of the Committee on Education and was also on the Judiciary Committee while in the Legislature.

This dedicated patriot was colonel of the 22nd South Carolina Regiment of Militia in the 1840's, and even before the signing of the Ordinance of Secession raised the first company in Sumter District — Company D of the Second Regiment, later becoming lieutenant colonel in the Ninth Regiment.

After the War of Secession his efforts were untiring to place the government of his county once more on a firm foundation. From 1876 to 1890 he was a delegate to every state convention.

His law firm for many years had the largest practice in Sumter, it has been said.

Colonel Blanding was devoted to his church and the Calvinistic doctrines which had been ingrained in him from generations of loyal Presbyterians. "He was a Godly man, a wholesome, old-fashioned Christian . . ."[26] For 40 years he served First Presbyterian Church of Sumter as deacon and elder.

So strong was his belief in the importance of education that he provided for each of his 13 children who reached adulthood a college education. It was his conviction that he should leave his children, instead of money, "something infinitely more valuable which an enemy could not take away from them."

As to the character of this outstanding citizen of Sumter County, Bishop Ellison Capers said of him: "Col. Blanding and I were friends and I had a very high regard for his character, his spirit and his gallant life."

Thomas Boone Fraser, another of Sumter's native sons, who lived and served during that crucial period of history following the War Between the States, was noted for his "cool head" in helping to save his country from "Radical Rule."

He was born in Sumter District in 1825 and admitted to the bar in 1847, beginning practice at once in Sumter. Elected to the Legislature in 1858, he served four terms, and was a member of that body which called the Convention of Secession.

For ten years (1868-78) he was a member of the State Democratic Executive Committee. In 1878 he was elected as Judge of the Third Judicial Circuit,[27] retaining that office until 1894. Sumter County chose him as a delegate to the Constitutional Convention in Columbia in 1895.

He is said to have been a "power of strength and an inspiration of wisdom."

A brief sketch of one other of Sumter's well-known lawyers can best be given from a resolution passed by the Sumter Bar and read by W.F.B. Haynsworth. This highly respected member of the bar was James S.G. Richardson, who was born in April, 1815, and died in August of 1879.

Though in young manhood he spent weary months of agonizing pain, confined to his bed, he fought against becoming an invalid, keeping his mind "superior to suffering."

"They (members of Sumter Bar), unitedly and individually, bear testimony to the nobility of his character, the unsullied integrity of his life, the attractive refinement of his nature."

He was said to have been very thorough, his first aim being "to master the great principles of law" and then to follow them without deviation. He was known especially for his skill in handling real estate cases. "His memory was remarkably ready and accurate . . ."

Summarizing the life of this esteemed friend and respected legal associate, the tribute ended thus: "Resolved therefore, That we cherish the memory of our departed friend: that we hold up his life as an example of high aims and well-directed efforts, and present to ourselves and our successors, his industry, his patience, his gentleness, his firmness, his generosity, his high sense of honor, his integrity of life as a model for the foundation of character, both individual and professional."

Space forbids the recounting of services rendered to Sumter County by Stephen D. Miller, Samuel Mayrant, A.C. Spain, Charles Mayrant, E.W. Moise, John S. Richardson, F.I. and Montgomery Moses, John Thompson Green, Robert Obadiah Purdy and others of outstanding legal ability.

R.J. Aycock (Profile)

Robert James Aycock, a member of the South Carolina House of Representatives from Sumter County for almost 30 years, was born July 27, 1893, in Clarendon County, the son of the late Robert James and America Fair Jones Aycock.

From 1913 he lived in Pinewood, and for a number of years was employed in a bank. He also held partnership in a mercantile business and ran a farm.

In 1928 he became mayor of Pinewood. In 1934 he was elected to the state legislature but at that time served only one term, not offering for re-election. Then for 12 years he was postmaster of Pinewood and at the same time continued his farming and mercantile interests.

In 1948 he returned to politics, winning election to the House. He was soon named to the powerful Ways and Means Committee and became its chairman in 1960, holding that position 14 years.

His influence on the committee was instrumental, it has been said by many, in keeping the state "financially sound."

Through his legislative efforts "Mr. Jim" was able to bring about the formation of the South Carolina ETV Commission.

Many honors have been accorded Mr. Aycock, among which were the naming for him of the Aycock Building on Bull Street in Columbia, which houses the S.C. Department of Health and Environmental Control, and the Aycock Building at the Career Center located on McCray's Mill Road, associated with School

Districts 2 and 17.

"Jim Aycock Day" was celebrated in Pinewood on July 28, 1973, at which time he was presented a plaque by the Sumter County Delegation, giving him the official name of "Gentleman Jim."

Just one week before his death, in September, 1975,[28] Station WRJA-TV was dedicated in his honor.

Among the countless tributes paid R.J. Aycock was one voiced by Senator T.O. Bowen, which is here given in part: "A stalwart legislator, a gentleman of the first order and a statesman, he will go down in the history of South Carolina as one of her greatest men.

"His gentleness and many kindnesses, his honesty and integrity shall be remembered for years to come by all of us who have been closely associated with him."

J.O. Barwick (Profile)

A joyous occasion for the family of John Oliver Barwick was the celebration of his 90th birthday on November 16, 1974.

He was born in a country community near Paxville in Clarendon County in 1884,[29] the son of Lawrence Sinclair and Susan Gibson Barwick. The oldest of ten children, he learned early the meaning of shouldering responsibility, a characteristic that has proved a valuable asset through the years.

As a boy he helped his father on the farm and attended Home Branch and Paxville Schools. At the age of 19 he entered Osborne Business College in Augusta, Georgia. So outstanding was his record at Osborne that he was offered a position in the bookkeeping department of J.B. White Department Store, one of the large business concerns in Augusta. However, he felt that he should return home to help his father on the farm and in the general store known as Barwick and Mims. Later the name of the store became Barwick and Sons.

On December 26, 1905, he married Annie Lou Smith, daughter of William Franklin and Sallie Gregory Smith of Baton Rouge, S.C. She came to Paxville to teach and when young Barwick saw her get off the train, he decided then and there that she was the one for him.

He was associated with his father until 1909, when he took a position with the Sumter Railway Express. Having moved to Sumter, he began work on Thanksgiving Day of that year.

After three years, he began working for the late Neill O'Donnell. In addition to his bookkeeping duties in the office of his employer, which was located in O'Donnell's Dry Goods Company Store, he, upon the request of Mr. O'Donnell, took on the responsibility of collecting from renters and sharecroppers on the Bell Mill plantation.

His responsibilities continued to expand and soon he was accountant for three very large estates, Neill O'Donnell, Tuomey and Arthur O'Neill. His office, since the closing of the O'Donnell Dry Goods Company around 1938, was located at 21 Dugan Street.

In the business world he exhibited a stern and uncompromising attitude. There was no deviation from what he knew to be right. Through all the years an auditor never found a mistake in his accounts. His aptitude with figures was phenomenal. It is said that he could add three rows of figures at the time and never use an adding machine. Though he enjoyed many forms of recreation, he always kept work before pleasure.

Well past retirement age, J.O. Barwick still worked five days a week, spending about five hours at the office, carrying on the duties that he had enjoyed so many years.

In fact he worked on the day before his death, November 14, 1976, completing the balancing of all his books.

A dedicated Christian, he was ever loyal to his church. When he came to Sumter, he brought his letter from Paxville to the First Baptist Church and at the time of his birthday was the oldest member in the church. He was active in many phases of the church program. He long served as a deacon and shared responsibilities as teacher of the Baraca Class for many years. Lay evangelism also claimed his interest and dedication. A devout student of the Scriptures, he was said by those who knew him to be a true Bible scholar.

After the death of his beloved companion in 1964, he lived alone; but there was no time for loneliness. He was a man of many talents and with many hobbies. One gift that may be a chore for some was a fascinating pastime for him. He liked to cook! He had a pound cake recipe that was matchless. Two of his granddaughters called on him to make their wedding cakes. Included in his specialties were cookies, jams, jellies, and many other goodies.

He gardened, too, and was a flower enthusiast, as one visiting his yard could readily see.

In evidence throughout his home were books, magazines and newspapers through which he kept informed on a wide range of subjects. His chief interest, however, was in studying his Bible and reading Christian literature.

Versatility was the "name of the game" with this extraordinary nonagenarian. He greatly enjoyed outdoor sports such as hunting and fishing. A deer drive or bird hunt brought a special thrill. He was always a good shot, too!

He was a "born fisherman." One of his friends who fished with him often told of the great fun he got from this sport. Though adept in the use of modern fishing tackle, he enjoyed using an old-fashioned cane.

This friend told of how Mr. Barwick talked to the fish. That tactic must have worked, for he is said to have been the best fisherman in Sumter County. Nor was it necessary for him to tell the legendary tale that the "big one" got away. Once he entertained some of his family for supper and served a six-pound trout baked just right.

Mr. Barwick was a charter member of the Sumter-Columbia Fishing and Hunting Club, a private organization. He also belonged to the Sumter County Game and Fish Association.

Many honors came his way, two of which will be mentioned here. In 1970 he was honored by the Board of Trustees of Tuomey Hospital for 60 years of dedicated service to that institution. Among the gifts that he received in connection with this celebration was a beautiful silver tray appropriately inscribed.

Then in 1972 a dinner in his honor was given at Cain's Mill by members of the Sunday School class that he had served for many years. Appreciation was expressed in numerous ways, including the presentation of a silver tray with an inscription showing the gratitude of those whose lives he had touched.

Mr. Barwick was the father of three living sons and one daughter: Leon Sinclair, Charleston; Gregory Bernard, who lives in Petersburg, Virginia; Raymond Carlisle of Pensacola, Florida; Eleanor Michalowski Gibson, Sumter. (One daughter, Aurelia, died at 17 months and the oldest son, John Oliver, Jr., died in recent years.) He also claimed with much pride many grandchildren and great-grandchildren.

It can be said of John Oliver Barwick that in his youth he was a dutiful and faithful son; in manhood he was an indefatigable worker, a generous and loving husband and father, a kind and faithful friend, a dedicated Christian gentleman. His influence for good has been felt far and wide and he was ever an inspiration to those who knew and honored him.

Dr. C.W. Birnie, Prominent Sumter Citizen

Charles Wainwright Birnie, born in Charleston on May 15, 1874, was one of Sumter's well-known and respected physicians for 40 years.

He was the son of Richard and Anna Frost Birnie. His father was a cotton classer, who was known over the state and was highly successful in business. He was able to afford an adequate education for this large family.

Having received his earliest education in Charleston at Avery Institute, C.W. Birnie later was graduated from Wilbraham Academy, a preparatory school in Wilbraham, Massachusetts. He then attended Oberlin College in Ohio, and following his graduation there, he received his medical training at University of Pennsylvania School of Medicine.

Having received his degree in medicine, he came to Sumter in 1898 and began a very successful practice which continued until his death in 1938.

Around 1902 Dr. Birnie married Ruth Gardena Harrison, daughter of Moses and Gardena Harrison of Sumter. After teaching a short while at Lincoln High School in Sumter, she and her husband decided that it would be worthwhile for her to study pharmacy since there was no black-owned drug store in the Sumter area at that time.

First she attended Benedict College in Columbia. Then she went to Temple University in Philadelphia, where she received her pharmaceutical degree. She was one of the very few either female or black pharmacists in South Carolina.

Dr. Birnie, the first black physician in Sumter County, was a general practitioner and family doctor, who was known among his professional peers for his diagnostic skill. The basis of his philosophy of life was the Hippocratic Oath which contains the ideals to be followed by every good doctor. By day or night he never refused to minister to anyone in need of attention. Since much of his practice was in the country, he made his calls on a bicycle or in a buggy.

The health team, comprised of Dr. and Mrs. Birnie, brought medical aid and comfort to many in Sumter and adjoining counties. They operated a drug store, the People's Pharmacy, on West Liberty Street until his death. His office was located above the drug store. Mrs. Birnie often accompanied her husband on night calls in rural areas to assist in the delivery of a baby.[30]

So dedicated was this husband-wife team to the practice of medicine for all who needed treatment and so firm in their faith in human nature that bills for their services were never sent. They believed that those who would not pay could not pay.

Recognizing the need for post-medical school training, when internships were hard to get, Dr. Birnie took many black medical school graduates into his office for the supervision needed before they were ready to begin practice on their own.

Dr. Birnie researched black history before reconstruction as a hobby and had published some valuable articles on the subject.

Deeply interested in the education of black youth, he used his influence for the improvement of school facilities for the blacks; and he was constantly striving to encourage and motivate youth to continue their education, especially in science and mathematics. He and his wife sponsored frequent social events to help the young people to become well-rounded individuals. And he constructed a tennis court in his back yard that black youth might have access to a recreational facility. Croquet was also made available for older people. In consequence of his interest in the welfare of others, Birnie Community Center was later named in his memory.

To nurture a love for reading, he opened his extensive library to anyone wishing to use it. Readers found there not only worthwhile books, but more than 20 monthly magazines and such newspapers as **The New York Times, The Charlotte Observer, The Charleston News and Courier, The State** and others.

Another service rendered by this kindhearted man was the establishment of a day care center in the Savage-Glover community, supported partly by the city and partly financed by him.

Dr. Birnie was active in many medical, civic, and fraternal organizations, local and statewide. Taking a leading role in politics, he was elected more than once to the National Republican Convention.

He was a guiding spirit in the establishment of the Good Shepherd Episcopal Church in Sumter. He was Senior Warden for many years and a most active communicant in his church.

A devoted family man, he found time in his very busy schedule to give of himself to his wife, his daughter and other relatives.

His daughter, Annie Birnie McDonald, who lives in Sumter today, says of him in part: "He had a love for and an understanding of people that is rarely found, and people usually responded with respect and affection. 'A man's truest monument must be a man.' "

Hamilton Carr Bland

"O the green things, the green things growing,
The faint sweet smell of the green things growing!
I should like to live, whether I smile or grieve
Just to watch the happy life of my green things growing."

This bit of verse by Dinah M.M. Craik is descriptive of the love of natural beauty that filled the heart and life of that generous one who gave Swan Lake Gardens to the people of Sumter – Hamilton Carr Bland.

Life was not always easy for this unusual man, but in spite of hardships along the way, that spirit of determination and hope which he, no doubt, inherited from his father and mother, kept him going.

After the War Between the States, his father, Capt. James F. Bland, who gave of his best to the Confederate Army, came to his home in New Hanover County, North Carolina, to find his home pillaged and his horses gone. He was physically unable to cope with this situation.

When he was told by his physician to seek a dryer and more healthful climate, he took the train in Wilmington to come farther South, not knowing where he would land. In talking with the conductor, he learned that more fine horses and rigs driven by prosperous-looking people met the trains in Mayesville than at any other place on his Wilmington-Augusta run.

Forthwith, the traveler got off the train in Mayesville, though it was 4:30 in the morning; and the town was dark and cold. Looking around, he saw a light at some distance on the left of the depot, at which place he thought he could at least get warm and learn something of the town.

And a fortunate decision he made, for he went straight to the home of one of the leading citizens of Mayesville, Mr. Thomas Alexander Mayes, son of Squire Mayes, founder of the town. Mr. Mayes graciously invited him in to have breakfast with the family. Such treatment convinced this man without a home that Mayesville was the place for him.

Determined to make a living, he began cutting crossties for the railroad, no doubt finding this work because Mr. Mayes was the depot agent.

The fact that he had had to leave his sweetheart in North Carolina no doubt was a strong incentive for his zealous application to this strenuous work. After some years, feeling well enough established to support a family, he returned to North Carolina and married Miss Mary Johnson.

Since she was such a great help, his lumber business grew. Continuing his original work of cutting crossties, he added other interests, such as cutting heavy construction timbers. He was able gradually to buy large plantations to tap the pines for turpentine and to cut more lumber.

In the meantime, Mrs. Bland rented rooms to traveling men. Mr. and Mrs. Bland opened a stall where they could sell vegetables from the garden they tended. She eventually had to keep the store since his asthmatic attacks returned, and he was forced to spend time in bed. To add to her stock of goods, Mrs. Bland ordered material to make a few hats for sale. So proficient did she become in the millinery business, that people came from far and near to buy her hats.

With such a background, "Hallie" as he was called, born September 20, 1880, had all the "makings" of a successful businessman; however, at the age of seven he had a very serious illness that caused him to spend much of his time in a wheelchair until he was 17. Fortunately, he was finally able to receive therapy from a man from Atlanta, Georgia, and was improved enough to walk with a cane, which he used most of his life.[31]

Though handicapped physically, he kept up his school work and used his hands tinkering with clocks and watches. As a result he was able to do intricate repairs on all types of timepieces. His ambition was fired even more by a trip to Chicago for the World's Columbia Exposition, where his alert mind captured many worthwhile ideas. He continued his work with clocks and watches, in the meantime going to Philadelphia to study jewelry making and watch repairing. He attended Furman University for two years, but he left college to marry Miss Coralie Holly of Fairfield County. He opened a jewelry store in a corner of his father's store and later added to his other interests, the sale of Delco Lights.

Their home was burned, destroying all of their possessions. He then built a large attractive house, which P.M. Tiller later bought.

Another of his special "loves" was the automobile. In 1901, he bought the third car brought into South Carolina, a "locomobile Steamer." So fascinated was he with the mechanics of cars, that he built a car in his back yard, using old automobile parts that he gathered from various places. His car was known as the "Bland Horseless Carriage."

Mr. Bland moved to Sumter in 1917 to sell cars, first with a Hudson-Essex franchise, locating his business on the corner of Liberty and Sumter streets. In 1922, he took over the Ford Agency and his business covered almost a whole block.

Having reached a point where he had more leisure time, he purchased "The Pond" on the western part of the city, thinking to develop it as a fish pond and also as a garden and bird sanctuary. He worked tirelessly building little islands with old magazines, newspapers, weeds, brambles, even dirt from Hampton Avenue, where paving was being done, trash – in short anything available.

He brought in many fine birds, but the alligators destroyed many of these. He ordered black swans from Australia and white swans from the state of New York. Other types of birds were added from time to time – brown Chinese geese, wild egrets, and blue herons.

On Hampton Avenue, across from his home, he developed a beautiful flower garden where bloomed roses, lilies, daisies, camellias, azaleas, etc. Intrigued with their beauty, he attempted to grow the Japanese iris, but he was unable to succeed. He wrote the Horticultural Magazine in Boston to get some advice and was told to contact Mr. George M. Reed, curator of Plant Pathology of the Botanical Gardens of Brooklyn. Mr. Reed, he said, spent three months each year in Japan, studying the culture of this flower and was therefore the expert in this field. After a trip to the Botanical Gardens to see Mr. Reed, he decided that this lovely flower would not grow in Sumter.

He dug up the plants and along with trash and clippings took them out to the lake and threw them along the edge to build up the land, "The rabbit had been thrown into the briar patch." This was just the place for the iris. The following year he discovered thriving plants with blooms from six to ten inches across. What they needed was a damp acid soil and the problem was solved.

When Mr. Reed heard, he came to Sumter and found Japanese iris finer than his in the Botanical Gardens. The two flower lovers became fast friends and visited back and forth to watch the progress of the flowers in both places. The blooming season here is the last week in May and the first two weeks of June; in New York, these flowers are at their peak the last of June.

Mr. Bland ordered many more plants and set them in groups of fifty of a kind. At first, they were white or deep purple, but more and more he expanded his color range with more and more varieties such as Blue Giant, Margret, Moonlight Waves (pink and opal), Painted Lady and many others. He kept adding until he had about 250 varieties, many of Japan's best. Some of the islands were connected with arched bridges, and he began to achieve the appearance of a rainbow, of which Iris is the goddess in Greek Mythology.

When Swan Lake was first opened to the public, enthusiastic flower lovers came from five countries including Japan. These Japanese were amazed to find larger flowers than they were growing.

Each year the cultivated part of the lake was extended, with great care that the native trees and flowers be preserved. Oaks, pines and cypress furnish a natural background for the native woodbine, yellow jessamine, myrtle and willows. Other flowering plants were added – roses, azaleas, camellias, lilies, wisteria, to name a few.

Mr. Bland, ever a bird lover, planted shrubs bearing berries – pyracantha, nandina, and holly. The air is fragrant with sweet olive, oleander, mimosa, banana and strawberry shrubs. He also added varicolored water lilies.

Following another hobby, Mr. "Hallie" many afternoons

went out into his garden to photograph clouds that were in the shape of faces. Among other faces that he "captured" were those of Abraham Lincoln and Franklin D. Roosevelt.

In 1938, Mr. A.T. Heath bought 70 acres across the road from Swan Lake and deeded it to the city to be developed under the supervision of Mr. Bland. The city furnished help in laying out paths, developing tennis courts and a recreation area with picnic tables. Here there are swans, geese and ducks that enjoy food from the hands of children.

Hamilton Carr Bland died in 1967[32] at the age of 87, but his memory lives on in Sumter and beyond as year after year throngs of old and young come from Sumter, other parts of South Carolina and the United States and even from other countries to enjoy the beauty of nature which he loved and unselfishly provided for others.

Albertus Spain Brown

Better known as Bert Brown, Albertus Spain Brown was born in Sumter County May 2, 1852,[33] the son of Leonard and Marian Michau Brown. He was one of 15 children.

After finishing the free school in his home community, he attended the Military Academy in Mayesville.

He built up a good business in the county and then in 1875 moved to Sumter, where he prospered in several business interests. He owned a lot, which was later sold, on the Northeast corner of Main and Liberty Streets. Behind the Sumter Dry Goods Company, which was on the Southeast corner of Main and Liberty, he carried on a lien business for farmers. He was successful in other business ventures in the city, including a large warehouse for the storage of cotton, one of the first in Sumter. He also had an interest in the Sumter Telephone Company.

On October 26, 1887, Brown was married to Miss Lillie DuBose, daughter of T.D. DuBose of Sumter County. They were the parents of three children: Marie, Holly and Albertus Spain Brown, Jr., who died at the age of 13 months.

Highly respected, Brown played an active role in governmental and civic affairs of the city. He was elected alderman in 1890 and was chosen to represent Sumter as a delegate to the South Carolina State Convention in 1884 and again in 1886.

At his death in 1898 **The Southern Christian Advocate** paid tribute to him, saying that he was a man of purest morals. Integrity and uprightness were shown in his business operations, the tribute continued. He was said to be a "good man and people loved him."

The Sumter Daily Item spoke of him as "progressive, enterprising, public spirited and highly esteemed."

The Freeman, one of Sumter's newspapers at that time, spoke of his interest in the progress and improvement of the city.

Through the long months of his illness he was said to have been always cheerful, and he helped others with his bright outlook. He made a strong impact for good on all who knew him.

Dr. John Alexander Brunson (Profile)

John Alexander Brunson, "a prince among men, a great Bible scholar, a powerful preacher, a loving and loved pastor, a consecrated servant of God," was born in 1862 between Darlington and Florence. His father was killed in the War Between the States, leaving his wife, the former Hannah Maria Burch, and this tiny four-months-old baby son.[34]

As a boy "Jack." as he was called, studied under his aunt and worked on his uncle's farm, saving his money toward an education. He later attended a private school in Florence, going from there to Furman University.[35] There he was graduated with highest honors. It is said that one year his average was 99.

After graduation from Southern Baptist Theological Seminary in Louisville, Kentucky, he was sent to Japan by the Foreign Mission Board to begin a new work for Southern Baptists. When he had completed his assignment there, he returned to America to take up pastoral and evangelistic work.

He pastored churches in Cheraw, Asheville, North Carolina, Elloree, St. Matthews and did evangelistic work in Tennessee and several Northern states before becoming pastor of Grace Baptist Church in Sumter January 1, 1916.

He remained on this field until his death in 1943, preaching as long as he was able. When he became too weak to stand, he sat, using a lap board for his Bible and whatever notes he might have. Before his death, when he became unable to preach, he was made pastor emeritus.

Dr. Brunson was married to Sophia Boatwright from Ridge Springs, a well-known and respected physician in Sumter for many years; and he was the father of one lovely daughter, Sophia Boatwright Brunson, a beloved teacher in Sumter.

It is said that Dr. Brunson always received rapt attention from his congregation and one who listened to him Sunday by Sunday says that he always "taught us something." She says that after these many years things that he said still come to mind often. He loved to preach from the prophetic books of the Bible, she recalls, and his preaching is still bearing fruit in the lives of those who sat under his teachings.

Another says that he had the gift of seeing into the future. Many of his prophecies are being fulfilled in America today.

He wrote in 1938 a paper on Communism which was given first at Grace, then by the request for the Bible classes of the city meeting at Trinity United Methodist Church, and later still before the American Legion.

In this treatise he said that Communism went back to Adam Weishaup, "the profoundest conspirator that has ever lived." His aims, said Dr. Brunson, were to abolish – 1. all ordered government; 2. private property; 3. inheritance; 4. patriotism; 5. the family, marriage and morality; 6. religion.

At the time of his writing, Communism was active in the United States, trying to dominate the labor unions and in other ways seeking to overthrow America. These Communists, he said, are "keen, clever, intelligent educated men and women."

He went on to say that by conservative estimates at the time of his writing there were 3,000,000 revolutionary Communists in the United States.

He believed that, "If professing Christians throughout the world were thoroughly loyal to Christ, Communism would quickly die."

Dr. Brunson was a man beloved by all who knew him. He was a friend to all, kindhearted and ready to serve wherever there was need.

When the depression came, he announced from the pulpit, "I am cutting my salary to $100 a month."

Wilhelmena Murray, who worked for the family 47 years, keeping house, tending the lawn, helping Dr. Brunson with his patients and whatever else needed to be done, recalls that he was very quiet in the home, talked little, prayed and read the Bible much. He said to her before his death, "Willa, you don't get as much money as you deserve. The Father in heaven will repay you. I appreciate all you have done for me."

After his death, the church dedicated a bronze tablet as a memorial. On the occasion of the dedication, the bulletin carried a beautiful tribute to him. It read in part:

"Dr. Brunson gave himself unselfishly and untiringly to the ministry of the Word. He was a profound student of the Bible and was at his best as an expositor of the sacred Book. He proclaimed the Gospel fearlessly, effectively and lovingly. He loved the Word passionately and cherished the great truths and doctrines embodied in it. He demonstrated in his life and preaching the power of the Gospel of the Grace of God. In his ministry as pastor he had the passion to be like Christ – he went about doing good. He sought to lead the people into an intimate and vital relationship with God. He was indeed a wise counselor, a sincere and trusted friend, kind, true, sympathetic. He knew the Lord because he lived with Him. He talked much with the Lord. When he prayed, the gates of heaven seemed to open, and at the throne of grace he talked humbly and simply with the Father as in His very presence.

"In both private and public life, he was a man among men, wielding an influence for righteousness in the church and in the city. He lived his life on high levels, physically, mentally, spiritually – his life was a sermon in itself. While he was brilliant in mind and scholarly in attainments, no gentler spirit ever moved among us. He was held in the tenderest affection, not only by his own church but by the entire city."[36]

Miss Abbie Bryan – Great Educator

After lighting the road to learning for many people in Sumter as well as in more distant places, Miss Abbie Bryan, Sumter's respected, admired and much loved veteran teacher has passed on the torch of learning to others and gone to her reward.

"Miss Abbie," as she was affectionately known by old and young alike, was born in Dalzell in 1888,[37] and there she began her formal education in a little one-teacher school. When she was 10 years old, her family moved to Sumter, where she was graduated at the head of her class in 1905.

She went on to Winthrop College with the help of her "Aunt Abbie Dukes." Since her consuming desire was to be a teacher of little children, she specialized in kindergarten training and was graduated in 1909.

In the fall of that year her dream came true. She began teaching. For some years she taught kindergarten in Granby Cotton Mills in Columbia, Monaghan Mills in Greenville, Edgefield Cotton Mills and in public schools in Chester and Columbia.

For one year she left the classroom to serve as YWCA secretary in Monaghan Mills. She taught night school, coached basketball and played games with girls teams from another mill village, organized Mother's Clubs, coached debating teams and was involved in other worthwhile activities. Though she found this work rewarding, she loved little children and teaching too much to give it up permanently. Therefore, she returned to the classroom.

In 1927 she came home to Sumter where she taught first grade (with the exception of one year when she was a second-grade teacher) until her retirement from the public school system in 1954.

Many in Sumter and in other places as well look back with happy recollections of those days in "Miss Abbie's" room. There was always a long list of those desiring to be assigned to her room, but she could not take all, as much as she would have enjoyed having them. But those in other rooms were given a special treat occasionally when they were taken to "Miss Abbie's" room to hear her tell a story, a gift of hers that no one could surpass. Many older folk still recall the thrill these visits afforded them as children.

As she taught, this ambitious teacher continued her education, studying at Winthrop, Wofford, Coker, Columbia University (New York), Appalachian State for Teachers (Boone, N.C.), accumulating 21 hours of graduate credit in Child Psychology, Child Development and Bible.

But these studies would have been of little value without "Miss Abbie's" love of children. This was indeed the secret of her success as a teacher. Someone has said that if one would light a spark in another, he himself must glow, and she truly lighted the way of learning for her pupils.

She used every means possible to plant in the minds of the little ones seeds of desire for learning. Her room was filled with pictures and objects that served to encourage creativity.

Field trips were used to teach about trees, flowers and animals. She pointed out to them important buildings, teaching the reasons for their importance.

Patriotism was another theme stressed by "Miss Abbie." For George Washington's Birthday pupils learned poems, songs and stories that stressed not only love of country but also commendable qualities of citizens.

The climax of the celebration was the parade that no one living in Sumter in those days could ever forget whether he was a pupil or not. The picture of Miss Abbie marching down the street proudly waving her flag, followed by all the first grades of the city schools, wearing their little paper hats which they had made themselves and waving their little flags "just like Miss Abbie" was indelibly impressed upon the minds of all who were privileged to see the parade.[38]

For many years Miss Abbie shared her wonderful ideas with other teachers as she taught in summer schools at Winthrop, Wofford and Converse, thus extending her influence, inspiring others in their teaching experiences.

At Wofford she was editor of a newspaper that those attending the summer session produced. It contained editorials, news items and articles by guest contributors. One issue told of Miss Bryan's Demonstration Class, composed of pupils from the first three grades of one of the elementary schools in Spartanburg at that time. Some of the activities listed were excursions on the Wofford campus, studying trees, plants etc.; a radio program; a trip to a farm near the city. Thus this master teacher was sharing with others some of her ideas for kindling the desires for learning in their pupils.

During the summers at Wofford she also was responsible for a paper to which she encouraged the children to contribute. It was called "Just Children."

When the time came when Miss Abbie had reached retirement age (according to state law) she was not ready to retire. Therefore she established a kindergarten in her home. It was a kindergarten that only one with her love of children and her ingenuity and creativity could have conducted. Those children who were fortunate enough to be enrolled still talk of those days filled with joy and excitement, with something new and different for each season.

One project that they especially enjoyed was "Be Kind to Animals Week." At an improvised microphone each boy and girl was given an opportunity to sing, recite a poem or tell a story. This program they gave on radio station WFIG.

But with all her interest in teaching, Miss Abbie did not spend all her time in the classroom. She was instrumental in forming the Winthrop Alumnae Association and organized the Sumter Chapter. She served as director of the central district and was vice president of the Association.

So loyal was she to her Alma Mater and so diligently did she work in its interest that in 1969 she received the highest honor bestowed by that institution – the Mary Mildred Sullivan Medallion, given to those possessing "fine humanitarian qualities."

With deep Christian devotion "Miss Abbie" served her church, the First Presbyterian of Sumter, as well as churches in other places where she taught. In one community she taught Sunday school in a Baptist and a Methodist Church. And her Christian influence was always manifested in her classroom teaching as well as in all her contacts with others.

On Feb. 23, 1981 "Miss Abbie's" earthly life came to an end.[39]

At the age of 93 Miss Abbie Dukes Bryan completed a full, unselfish, dedicated life of service to others. Her memory will ever be kept alive by those whose lives she touched in any way.

The following poetic lines will tell something of her life:

"The life that counts must helpful be;
The cares and needs of others see;
Must seek the slaves of sin to free –
This is the life that counts.

"The life that counts is linked with God
And turns not from the cross – the rod,
But walks with Joy where Jesus trod
This is the life that counts."

L.C. Bryan Made His Life Count

"Listen, my friends, and you shall hear
Of the long useful life of one we revere."

Thus began a tribute to Louis Cain Bryan, given at a celebration in his honor at the Holy Cross Presbyterian Church in 1963.[40]

Since that time more years of usefulness have passed and more deeds of loving service have added honor to his name.

Another of Sumter's outstanding sons, Mr. Bryan has long since won the admiration, respect and love of his fellow citizens by his loyalty to his hometown, his active interest in its growth and development, his appealing personality and his consecration to his church in its Christian witness.

Son of William H. and Susan Carson Bryan, Louis Cain was born on old Homefield Plantation near Dalzell on September 16, 1885, one of eight children – three boys and five girls.[41]

Conveniences were few in the country in those early days and young Louis walked three miles with his brothers and sisters in order to attend school at Tirzah, but there is no record of any complaint on his part.

Evidently he was an ambitious scholar (as pupils were called in those days), for in addition to regular studies, he is said to have memorized a long, hard classical poem to recite at a "Friday Night Speaking." However, the learning proved to be the least difficult part of the experience. When the time came for him to "show off" his intellectual skill, his innate shyness tied his tongue completely and he was unable to say a word.

His educational pursuit became somewhat less arduous when his mother moved to Sumter with the children in order that they might attend the graded school there. His father remained in the country to run a store at St. Charles for Mr. Maxwell Jenkins, Louis' uncle, thus meeting the financial needs of the family.

While in high school this ambitious lad, seeking to add to his finances, became sexton at the First Presbyterian Church in Sumter. His duties included cleaning and filling with kerosene 52 lamps each week, ringing the church bell for all services, keeping the church building and grounds clean and pumping the church organ at each service.[42]

Alert to every opportunity to earn a little money, either by physical or mental effort, he took advantage of an offer made by his Sunday School teacher, Dr. George W. Dick, who promised $5.00 to each of his pupils who would learn the Shorter Catechism. Louis was one of the first to complete the assignment.

Apparently, however, nothing interfered with his regular school work. At his graduation from the tenth grade (the highest at that time), he was the recipient of two medals, but he was so exhausted he had to be awakened to receive both of them.

Through examinations the young Louis won two scholarships – one to the University of South Carolina and the other to the South Carolina Military Academy (The Citadel). He chose the latter and made an excellent record in his studies, in addition to outside activities. He took an active part in Y.M.C.A. work, serving at one time as vice president, and he was a member of the Calliopian Society. According to Louis himself, however, the "crowning event" of his cadetship was his appointment as sergeant.

His first work after finishing college was at Fort Motte High School, where he served as principal and teacher for two years. Since it was a requirement that one finishing The Citadel on a scholarship teach two years in South Carolina public schools, Mr. Bryan thus fulfilled his obligation; but those two years ended his teaching career. His evaluation of the experience was that he liked the pupils and the people in the community but he did not like teaching.

His next work was in journalism. Several very successful years he spent as a reporter for **The Sumter Daily Item**. Although he was very happy in newspaper work, when the United States entered World War I in 1917, he felt it his duty to volunteer his services. After spending some time at Fort Jackson and receiving a commission as 2nd lieutenant at Officers' Training School, Fort Sill, Oklahoma, he went to France as 1st lieutenant in the fall of 1918. He was never engaged in actual combat, however, since the Armistice was signed soon after his arrival in Europe.

Many boys coming home after the war found it somewhat difficult to get work. Those were the years that marked the beginning of the "Great Depression" in this country. And along with others, Louis Bryan was caught in the slump. For some years he was the Sumter representative of the **Charlotte Observer** and the **News and Courier**; riding his bicycle in rain or shine, heat or cold, he delivered the papers with his usual conscientious application to his work, whatever it might be.

In 1934 at the suggestion of his friend and fellow World War I Veteran, George Levy, he applied for the newly-created office as County Service Officer. His application being approved by the County Delegation, he became Sumter's first County Service Officer, holding the position in a most creditable manner for 30 years. At his retirement in 1964, he held the distinction of being not only the first in his own county but the oldest in terms of service in the state.

As Service Officer he was able to help many veterans – more than 3,000 of them – in many ways. Whether it was the service of a minister, a doctor, a lawyer, a social worker, or a friend in time of need that was required, he was always equal to the occasion.

When he retired, he was awarded a certificate of life membership in the local Post of the American Legion. He had the honor of being only the fifth to receive such an honor in the history of the organization.[43]

In 1925 Mr. Bryan was married to Miss Clara Hudson Jordan of Sumter, and they became the parents of two children – a son and a daughter.

From early childhood, Louis Cain Bryan was a faithful attendant at Sunday School and church services. In those early days in the country, his father, an elder in Tirzah Presbyterian Church, took his family to church services each Sunday in a wagon. Louis became a member of this church at an early age. When ten years old, he pleased his Grandmother Carson greatly by memorizing one of the longest Psalms.

In later years he was vitally interested in the work of the First Presbyterian Church of Sumter. He served as deacon and elder, and at the suggestion of his pastor, Rev. Lewis Lancaster, he began working as superintendent of Lemira Sunday School. After Lemira became a church, Mr. Bryan transferred his valuable services to Miller Outpost. As an indication of his devotion to Christian service, he could be seen on many a freezing morning riding his bicycle and carrying a large bucket of coal to Miller Sunday School so that the children (and grownups, too) might find a warm building when they arrived. Then in warm weather he was carrying flowers to make the Sunday School room more attractive. He was always going that "second mile" to bring comfort or pleasure to others.

Mr. Bryan was a faithful and dedicated worker at Holy Cross Presbyterian Church, which he helped to establish. He served as superintendent of the Sunday School, pastor's assistant, a tireless member of numerous committees, assistant janitor, always ready to fill in anywhere he was needed.[44]

One of the services from which he derived the greatest joy was his work with the children – planning and helping to carry out the Halloween party each year, the Easter egg hunt, the watermelon cutting in the summer. Another of his chief interests was the beautification of the grounds.

His Christian character shone forth in his attentiveness to the old, sick and lonely in the community, but everybody — old, young, middle-aged — looked forward to his visits and his cheery heartwarming smile.

In addition to his church centered interests, Mr. Bryan continued his activities in the American Legion Post No. 15, of which he was a charter member and in which he held various offices, including that of Post Commander. He also served as State Historian. A member of Veterans for Foreign Wars, he was chaplain and adjutant of Veterans of World War I.

In his younger days, Louis was an enthusiastic hunter, having perfected his marksmanship by shooting beans from a peashooter at his little sisters' bare legs. Later he killed partridges, rabbits and squirrels in the woods near his country home.

As a sportsman he excelled in tennis, basketball and swimming; and his favorite indoor pastime included chess and bridge.

Someone has said that it is not so much the years in your life but the life in your years that count. Though Louis Cain Bryan's life on earth came to an end November 5, 1971, his influence lives after him.

Dr. Warren Hamilton Burgess (Profile)

"Your heart's doing fine. It'll last you as long as you live."

"People are dying now that never died before."

"You ain't gonna die. Call me in the morning."

Who was the doctor who would give such answers to patients who would want to call him in the middle of the night or at some other inopportune time, when he knew they were not really sick?

Many of the oldtimers in Sumter would know immediately that he was one of the most successful, unselfish, beloved medical men that ever practiced in this county — Dr. Warren Hamilton Burgess.

This unique man was born in Stateburg on Enfield Plantation on July 7, 1888, the son of Warren Hamilton and Margaret Pinckney Burgess. He took great pride in his aristocratic ancestry. He had one brother, Sidney (deceased), who was a surgeon in Sumter, and two sisters. Daisy married Hal Harby, and lives in Sumter. Mary is the widow of Guy Warren. She was a beloved teacher in the Sumter Elementary Schools for many years and now lives in Columbia.

Doctor Warren Burgess, the subject of this sketch, was graduated from Charleston Medical School (now Medical University of South Carolina).

After graduation he served as a physician for a railroad company in Andrews. While there he married Miss Daisy Munnerlyn, a teacher from Chopee in Georgetown County. They were the parents of two daughters – Mary (Mrs. Murray G. Fant) and Margaret (Mrs. R. Kirk McLeod) and a son, Francis M., better known as "Sonny."

During World War I the young doctor served in the Medical Corps.

Returning to Sumter after the war, he became City Physician and began general practice as well. He became a vital part of his community. He was a loyal member of the Episcopal Church of the Holy Comforter and also made his contribution to the town through membership in the Elks, the Rotary Club and Woodmen of the World, by which organization he was honored in 1966 for the service he had rendered.

All of his contemporaries agreed that he was indeed the town "Character." He was welcomed into any group and was always the center of attention. His humorous stories could captivate any audience.

But he was equally well known as an excellent physician, especially skilled as a diagnostician. One example of his keen diagnostic perception was the case of Billy Gibson's little daughter, who became very ill with a disease that a local specialist was unable to diagnose. Doctor Burgess, upon seeing the child, immediately said that she was suffering from typhoid fever. The correct treatment was used and she was soon well.

Plagued, as many physicians are, by the complaints of hypochondriacs, Doctor Burgess, through his unusual concept of human nature and a keen sense of humor, usually saved himself from unnecessary responses to calls.

Once at an inconvenient time a lady, whose "ailments" he knew quite well, called to say that he must come at once. His answer was that it would be an hour before he could come. "I'll be dead by then," she said. "In that case," he said, "you'd better call Shelley-Brunson (Funeral Home)." That apparently was the right answer.

One of his "patients" would go to a specialist in Columbia for her "illness." The specialist, finding nothing wrong, would slip out and call Doctor Burgess to find what to tell her. She would come home satisfied that she had received expert advice.

However, when there was real need, he was on hand to give assistance. Kindhearted and unselfish, he spent much time with the poor of the city. He gave of himself unreservedly to the sick and indigent. Miss Antonia Gibson, city nurse, who worked very closely with him, told many stories of his kindness to those in need. One such story tells of the time he left his new overcoat to cover a poor sick woman who had no covering. And another time he ordered two new blankets for a family in need.

However, he was never wealthy, for his visits to the poor and sick were often never paid for with anything except genuine appreciation.

For his large private practice he never sent bills, especially during the depression years, and his charges were never exorbitant when people offered to pay.

Mortimer Weinberg met him on the street one day and reminded him that he had never sent a bill for the several times he had made doctor's calls to his home. He looked down at his light bill which he had just received and said, "You owe me $16.37." That was the amount of the bill. And many other charges were treated much the same way. He knew the patients would pay when and if they could. Such was his trust in people.

A story told by his daughter best illustrates his thoughtfulness and unselfishness.

"Every Sunday we had our big meal in the middle of the day – always rice and macaroni. Mother made the world's best macaroni! But we never had a macaroni pie on the table without a hole in the middle. Before we could sit down to Sunday dinner, Daddy fixed a tray (fork, knife, spoon, napkin and tea) and a plate of dinner – especially the plug from the middle of our macaroni. He would take the tray to Mrs. Jenkins, who lived in the house opposite the National Bank of South Carolina where Polly and Sally had their antique shop (later). Every Sunday, Daddy would wait in the car, and I would give her the tray and pick up the tray from last Sunday. Then we could go home and have dinner, until the phone called Daddy away."

He loved life and constantly found opportunities to play jokes on his friends. For example, he once invited several of his good friends for a fish supper. When they entered the dining room, they found – six cans of sardines! and nothing more.

He was a well-known lover of "chitlins." One night he received a call from the Rev. Knox Lambert, pastor of Grace Baptist Church, inviting him to eat this delicacy with him. Sure that the caller was none other than Julian Seale with whom he carried on a continuous "battle of wits," he used some strong language. But just in time he realized his mistake and stammered out an apology and an acceptance to the invitation. These "chitlin" lovers became great friends.

Many other stories could be told of his love of life, his skill as a physician, his never-ending kindness and generosity to those less fortunate, but the few incidents herein included will give a very slight idea of his impact on those who loved and respected him, and this number was great. As an indication of the high regard with which he was held, he received in 1945 Sumter's highest civic award, the A.T. Heath award, which was given for community service.

Before his death, May 18, 1968, Doctor Burgess lost his sight, but he kept his sense of humor.

A quotation from a paper written by Robert Moise for the Fortnightly Club from which most of the information for this sketch was obtained, says: "He was a man who loved his God, his family, his community and his fellowman. He was abundantly loved in return."

From an editorial in **The Sumter Daily Item** of May 26, 1968, is the following statement: "This community is a better place for having had Dr. Burgess as a resident. He will long be fondly remembered by an untold number of people with whom he came in contact during his long years of service in our city and county."

Fulton B. Creech (Profile)

A government, civic, business and church leader, Fulton B. Creech gave of himself unreservedly for Sumter and its citizens.

Born in Barnwell County, son of the late William S. and Carrie Kearse Creech, he came as a young man of 19 to Sumter after graduation from the public schools of Barnwell and Orangeburg Business College.

He began work with Trexler Lumber Co. and after four years went into partnership with C.D. Brunk to form the Imperial Lumber Company of Sumter. From that time his independent interests grew. In 1921 he organized the Creech Lumber Company and later he and his two sons, Fulton B. Creech, Jr., and John S. Creech, formed the Creech Holding Corporation.

In other business relationships in Sumter he served as vice president of First Federal Savings and Loan and was a director of Carolina Power and Light Company for almost thirty years.

During World War I he was an Army field clerk in this country and in Europe, receiving a Silver Star. As a veteran, he took a leading part in all the activities and services of the American Legion, serving as past commander of Sumter Post 15 and past district commander.

In his role as a leader in governmental circles, he served first as a member of City Council and became Mayor in 1932, which position he held until 1944.[45] It was during his years as mayor that he was instrumental in having Sumter selected as the site for Shaw Air Force Base.

He is remembered for his conservative stand as mayor, always endeavoring to keep a balanced budget. Though he favored holding taxes as low as possible, he didn't hesitate to make improvements when needed. It was he who was credited with having sewerage plants installed in the city.

His governmental influence extended beyond his home town. He was chairman of the State Forestry Commission from 1954 until 1975, and was named chairman emeritus in 1980. He served also as executive committeeman to the Democratic Party from Sumter County.

He was awarded the order of the Palmetto by Gov. "Dick" Riley in recognition of his service to the state.

As a civic leader, his activities were varied and influential. He was president of the Sumter Chamber of Commerce, director of the YMCA for 20 years, a charter member of the Kiwanis Club and was awarded the Kiwanis Plaque. He also received the Heath Award for "outstanding and unselfish service to the community."[46] He was a Mason and a Shriner. He was the first president of Sumter Executives Club.

Mr. Creech was a dedicated member of First Baptist Church of Sumter. There he was chairman of the board of deacons for more than 30 years. He taught the Men's Bible Class, and served his Lord and fellowman in many other ways.[47]

The contributions made to Sumter and South Carolina by Fulton Bethune Creech will bear fruit in years to come, and he will be remembered as one of the community's outstanding leaders in all aspects of life.

John K. Crosswell, Friend Of Children

Founder of the John K. Crosswell Home was a man of unusual interest and unique personality — a man who had exceptional business ability and at the same time one who had time to be concerned about the welfare of others, especially children.

He was a native of Lee County north of Bishopville near what is now Lee State Park. His family lived in a country community known as Cypress. He was the son of John R. Crosswell (1827-1889) and Susan Wright Crosswell (1831-1896), both of whom are buried in the Cypress Church Cemetery. As a token of his love for his parents he engaged someone to care for their graves as long as he lived and made provision in his will for their continued upkeep.

Little is known of his life prior to his coming to Sumter around 1900. He was approximately 30 years old at that time. A relative of Henry D., a brother of John K., thought that the brothers had worked in Georgia during a part of this time for which there is no record.

The firm of Crosswell and Company was begun in Sumter in 1901, the largest wholesale business in eastern South Carolina. For some years, it has been operating in a 50-mile radius of Sumter, with the use of a number of large trucks which deliver products to customers in a large number of towns, among which are Camden, Rembert, Bishopville, Mayesville, Manning, Summerton, as well as in Sumter.

Early salesmen for the company were B.R. Compton and W.O. Staley, who would go by train to other towns, hire a horse and buggy and make calls on customers during the day. At night they would take a train back to Sumter.

At first the business was located on the southwest corner of Main and Liberty Streets; howver, Crosswell later constructed on South Sumter Street three buildings; one has since that time, been used for the Warehouse of Crosswell and Company. One became the Seaboard Coastline freight depot and one, the old Southern Railroad station.

Mr. Crosswell made frequent trips to New York, sometimes spending several weeks. It was thought that these trips combined business and pleasure; however, his associates said that after each, several freight cars of merchandise would arrive in Sumter. He also made trips to Chicago and Atlanta.

When in Sumter he lived at 5 West Oakland Avenue in one of Sumter's finest homes, known as the Henry Ligon Home, built as many were at that time, near the railroad tracks. This lovely old home was recently condemned since it had fallen into a state of disrepair.

In addition to his business in Sumter, Mr. Crosswell, together with his brother, Henry, owned the Coca-Cola rights on syrup sold to bottlers in many cities. The firm, known as H.D. and J.K. Crosswell, Inc. of Columbia, bought the rights from a company in Greenville. From these rights H.D., president, received $11,500 a year and J.K., vice president, realized $9,000. At the death of his brother in 1911 John became president. He already owned the bottling rights for the cities of Sumter, Bishopville, Hartsville, Florence, Marion, Dillon, Lake City and Lanes.

In 1903 he began bottling Coca-Cola in Sumter in his own plant, the Crosswell Company. This business was later sold to a company in Cartersville, Ga., who later sold to Carolina Coca-Cola Bottling Company. The operation was then moved from the Sumter Street location.

In 1915 the stock in the Crosswell Company was divided into five equal shares. Crosswell was president and other stockholders were J.H. Strong, manager; C.B. Yeadon, office manager; B.R. Compton and W.O. Staley, salesmen.

In that same year Crosswell had a will drawn by Judge Robert O. Purdy, in which he remembered his living brother, T.M. Crosswell, and the immediate descendants of his deceased brothers and sisters.

He named as executors of his will C.B. Yeadon, J.H. Strong and the Sumter Trust Company. He later (1928) added a codicil naming R.R. Bruner, manager of the Coca-Cola plant in Columbia, instead of the Sumter Trust Company, which had ceased to operate.

After settling the estate, the executors, named as trustees, along with two others whom they would appoint, were instructed in the will to carry out the work of building and operating an orphanage for the white children of Sumter County, for which purpose the bulk of his estate was designated.

In 1929 John K. Crosswell died, a comparatively young man. Since his death, his assets have increased in value making his estate worth several million dollars.

Five years after his death the trustees who were at that time C.B. Yeadon, R.R. Bruner, J.H. Strong, John J. Riley and C.G. Rowland, purchased approximately 100 acres on North Main Street at a price less than 10,000 and let a contract for building the first unit of the orphanage that Crosswell, the great-hearted philanthropist that he was, had planned for the orphans of Sumter County.

At first the plans called for the building of two cottages, each to house 16 children and two house mothers.

In May 1935, 19 orphans or half orphans, were given a home. The first director was Dr. Theo Quattlebaum, who remained in charge until 1947.

Two more cottages were built in 1936, each to accommodate 14 children. The largest number of children that have lived at Crosswell Home at one time was 67 during World War II.

In 1952 the trustees appealed to the courts for the authority to accept children from broken homes.

The youngest child to enter the Home was 13 months of age and she remained until she graduated from high school.

The children in Crosswell Home attend the city schools and are regular attendants at churches in the community, each according to his or her choice.

House parents strive to make life for the children in each cottage as nearly like real home life as possible, giving them the best in love and good training.

W.C. James became director in 1947 and gave himself unselfishly to the management of the home and to the Christian leadership of the children even as a father for his own children until his retirement in 1972. His successor, James McGee, is now carrying on worthily the work begun more than forty years ago. He says, "Fruits of the Spirit may not be seen now, but I am trying to plant seed that will come to fruition in later years." [48]

Thus the work of making a worthwhile home for children envisioned and provided by John K. Crosswell goes on. Surely he was a great man. He is gratefully remembered by men in Sumter today who often played around his warehouse as children and were given fruit and candy from his generous hand. And that love of children was shown by his provision of a place for those deprived of a place; for those deprived of the joys of a home. His thoughtfulness and generosity have brought comfort and enrichment to more than 300 children.

Thomas M. Dabbs summarized the life of this unusual man in his paper given at a meeting of The Fortnightly Club (from which most of the information here given comes) in these words: " . . . the true measure of a man is the love that is within his heart. Here is a man who had a big heart – and he gave it to the children of Sumter."

William H. Cuttino

One of Sumter's early men of distinction was William H. Cuttino, a direct descendant of Jeremie Cothonneau who came to South Carolina in 1687. The name of this immigrant is inscribed on a marble tablet in the old Huguenot Church building in Charleston, S.C.

William Henry Cuttino, son of David William Cuttino, was born 18 Sept., 1841, in Richland County and was educated at the Indigo Society School in Georgetown.[49]

He married Eugenia Ann Connors from a prominent family of Clarendon County (born 9 Oct. 1843). They were the parents of four sons and seven daughters, three of whom – Anna Maxwell, Annie Hickman and Mable died young.

Others in the family were as follows: Henry Connors (m. Sallie Nettles McKellar), David William (m. Augusta Black Shingler), Elizabeth Thomas (m. LaMotte Lesesne), Margaret Graham (m. Samuel Sanders), Julia Agnes (m. Robert A. Church from England), Thomas Connors (m. Margaret Rose), William Henry (m. Rosa Lou Folsom). [50]

At the beginning of the War Between the States, William H. Cuttino joined the Hampton Legion and was wounded in the Second Battle of Manassas.

After the war he farmed for a while in Williamsburg County.

Then in 1870 he came to Sumter.

He was elected clerk of court of Sumter County in 1880, which position he held for some years.

When Mr. Cuttino came to Sumter he was received into the First Baptist Church at a special meeting on May 16, 1870. He came into the membership of this church on a certificate stating that he was in full fellowship with Georgetown Church when it disbanded. Mrs. Cuttino came from Taw Caw Church in Clarendon County.

He taught a class of young ladies, which was the banner class in 1882.

In 1875 he was elected clerk and served until his death June 5, 1886. In the church record it was stated that his death was "a severe blow to the church and community."

A page in the minutes was dedicated to his memory. It was a curtained scroll designed by the pastor, Dr. C.C. Brown, with the following inscription: "In Memoriam W.H. Cuttino. Born Sept. 18, 1841. Died June 5, 1886. Church clerk for ten years. Generous, Godly, Gracious and Good. Resting now in peace with Jesus. Loving hearts remember you."[51]

Dr. Thomas Jefferson DuBose

Unfortunately the present generation knows nothing of the virtues of the old country doctor – a person whose chief interest in life was that of being a friend to man. Night and day, early and late, he could be seen either in a buggy or on horseback hurrying over the sandy or muddy roads to answer a call of distress from some sick man, woman or child.

When not on the road, he could be found in his little frame office diagnosing and dosing those who were able to visit him.

Back in those early days, Walter B. Pitkin said, "A country doctor needs more brains to do his work passably than the fifty greatest industrialists in the world require."

Such a person was Dr. Thomas Jefferson DuBose, who practiced medicine for many years in Sumter County. It is said that he wore down six horses during his busy life.

Born in Darlington June 5, 1804, he was the son of Daniel and Jane Shakelford DuBose. His father was a highly respected citizen of Darlington County and one of the first elders of the Presbyterian church there.[52]

Thomas Jefferson DuBose received his diploma from the Medical College of South Carolina in Charleston in 1835. This diploma still hangs in the home of his granddaughters on the same plantation where he spent his adult life. He built a home in the "Pines" near a spot where cross the roads from Mayesville to Camden and from Sumter to Bishopville.

Though he loved his home and was a devoted husband and father, he felt so strongly the call of duty to bring healing and comfort to his patients, that sometimes he even remained overnight with a sufferer. The story is told that one rainy night he was called to the side of a very sick child. The crisis being expected that night, the distraught mother begged him not to leave since her husband was away. She showed him to a room where he could sleep when not needed at the bedside. During the night the father returned and was so grateful to the good doctor that he crawled into the bed with him, wet and cold as he was.

On October 4, 1838, he married Eliza Holly Kennedy, daughter of Francis L. and Holly Young Kennedy. His father-in-law was a very wealthy planter in the area. On his gravestone in the DuBose (or Young) cemetery, located in the Ashwood area, is the following epitaph:

"As a citizen he was beloved and influential, party only to the common worth. As a master, humane and cheerfully obeyed; as a husband and parent, loved, esteemed, honored."

Thomas Jefferson and Eliza Holly Kennedy DuBose were the parents of eight children, six of whom lived to adulthood and were highly esteemed in the neighborhood in which they were born and where they lived throughout their lives, having inherited lands from their father. Most of them added to their inheritance by buying additional tracts.

The children were as follows:

1. Francis Kennedy DuBose (1839-1840)
2. Thomas Daniel DuBose (1841-1929). He married Ida Freer of James Island.
3. Henry Young DuBose (1846-1917). He married Martha Anna DuBose of Darlington and followed the example of his father in becoming a doctor. He also farmed and taught school.
4. William Robert DuBose (1850-1924). He married Mary Atkinson Fraser, Sumter County.
5. Eliza Jane DuBose (1853-1892). She married Thomas Chalmers Law of Darlington.
6. Theodore Scott DuBose (1855-1933). He married Louisa Antoinette Chandler of Manning and Mayesville.
7. Julia Abigail DuBose (1857-1919). She married Ladson Lawrence Fraser, Jr., of Sumter County.
8. Francis Kennedy DuBose (1860-1860)

All the sons and one son-in-law were planters and one son-in-law was a lawyer. The two older living sons fought in the Confederate Army.

Dr. DuBose was blessed with 70 grandchildren.

While still a young girl, his wife had become subject to attacks of asthma "of the most formidable, malignant and stubborn type," and she suffered all the rest of her life from this malady. At times one would think she would be unable to get her breath. Nothing was known in those days of allergies, and thus she suffered with no real treatment at hand. Tea made from Jimson weed was her only remedy. In spite of this disabling disease, however, she made the good doctor a loving and faithful wife and reared her children as all good mothers should, "in the nurture and admonition of the Lord."

The will of Thomas J. DuBose gives evidence of the thrift with which he managed his affairs. He was able to leave each of his children several hundred acres of land as well as other valuable property. His entire estate included 2,481 acres.

To his son who became a doctor, he willed his medicine library, medical instruments, shop furniture and medicines, as well as some choice pieces of furniture, and some silver.

To another son "his mother's physic stand and physic," the parlor furniture, the "Brass Dog Irons in the dining room," the money trunk, other furniture and part of the family silver, "my gold spectacles," and his Resuscitator. To this son, Scott, who had stayed at home after the others were married and taken care of, his parents as long as they lived, he left also his home place of 684¾ acres.

To a daughter, Julia, he left the furniture in her room, as well as other valuable pieces of furniture and some choice pieces from her mother's room, including the "iron dog irons" with shovel, tongs and fender, some china, silver and her mother's gold spectacles.

As a final stipulation noted in his will, he forbade his land to be used for "turpentine or turpentine purposes."

Not only does the will demonstrate the thrift and business ability of Dr. DuBose, but it shows his understanding of his children in the discriminating choice he made in the selection of each article to go to each child.

Many of these cherished articles were burned when his second home was destroyed by fire, but some were saved and placed in the home built by his son, Scott, who inherited the home place, for his wife and children. Two of these children, who now live in the old home, cherish these old family heirlooms. Miss Sarah DuBose and Mrs. Lou Cain, widow of Lawton Cain, are the only two surviving children of Scott and Louisa DuBose. The other daughter, Julia, lived in the home until her death a few years ago. The only son, who married Vermelle Montgomery, daughter of Mr. and Mrs. Ladson Montgomery, is also deceased.

The children of Mr. and Mrs. Lawton Cain are Richard Lawton Cain, Jr., who married Edna Geddings; Louisa Antoinette, who married Donald Jackson Clark.

Mr. and Mrs. Thomas Alexander DuBose adopted two sons: Thomas Alexander DuBose, Jr., married Virginia Green and Laddie Montgomery DuBose married Virginia LeNoir.

The other children of Dr. Thomas J. DuBose reared a large number of sons and daughters who had large families, many of whom live in Sumter or Lee County. One of his descendants is Mrs. Holly Beck, well-known and highly respected citizen of Sumter. She was the granddaughter of Thomas Daniel DuBose, who married Ida Freer. Her mother was Eliza Holly DuBose and her father, Albertus Spain Brown. She married Frederick Baggs Beck. Her son, Frederick Baggs Beck, Jr., was born in Indianapolis, Ind. He married Mary Alice Siddall.

Mrs. Beck has one daughter, Holly DuBose Beck, born in Indianapolis. She married William E. Broadwell.

The obituary of this good man and beloved doctor gives a perfect picture of his life and the contributions he made to the lives that he touched in his 79 years.

"Departed this life on Sunday, the 13th of January, 1884, Dr. Thomas J. DuBose, a venerable and highly esteemed citizen of Mechanicsville in this county.

"Born at the opening of the century, had he survived until the 5th of June, next, he would by reason of strength, have attained to four-score years, the extreme measure of human life. He was a native of Darlington County, but soon after receiving his degree from the Medical College of South Carolina, at Charleston, he emigrated to Sumter and located at Mechanicsville, where he engaged in the practice of his profession, which he so adorned throughout a long and checkered life. Soon after establishing himself in that neighborhood, he married the third daughter of the late Captain Francis L. Kennedy, from which union he raised a large family of children, highly respected in the community where they reside. He was eminently successful as a physician and practiced medicine, **con amore**, until a few years ago, when he was stricken down by an attack of paralysis which incapacitated him for the active duties of his profession. Since then he was a confirmed invalid, and martyr to disease and suffering, which he bore with wonderful fortitude and patience. In the bloom of health and strength of manhood, he was a power in the land. Well and vividly, do his friends remember him, in his palmy days, in the full tide of an extensive practice, traveling day and night, through summer's heats and winter's snows, carrying everywhere with him the kindliest sympathy and most efficient aid to his suffering patients. They placed implicit confidence in his skill and his very name seemed to charm away disease, like some blessed talisman. He was a welcome guest, alike in the mansions of wealth and the humble abodes of poverty. His own house, too, was the home of hospitality where every visitor received a cordial greeting; and a genial welcome open-handed hospitality he deemed a cardinal virtue. And honesty of principle was his grand distinguishing and characteristic attribute. A profound thinker and writer says that 'an honest man is the noblest work of God,' and if this enunciation be true, the subject of this tribute, occupied a proud and exalted niche in the temple of Divine Creation, for he was scrupulously upright in all of his dealings with his fellowmen. His sterling uncompromising honesty was proverbial, among all of his acquaintances. We do not pretend to say that he was impeccable and that no shadow ever darkened the brightness of his fair fame, but we do assert that his faults were few, while his virtues were many, and that his genial disposition and habitual good humor and kindness of heart gained for him the affection of the entire community.

"In all of the relations of life, he was indeed a **preux Chevalier, sans peur et sans reproche**, and few men have gone down to the grave so universally beloved, respected, almost revered by their contemporaries. We trust that he has found mercy at the hands of the Eternal Judge of all, the living and the dead, and that his rest will be as peaceful as his life-labor was arduous."

Another tribute paid this beloved man said in part: "Dr. DuBose was a representative of a high type of manhood which I fear is getting painfully scarce in our day. His was an outspoken, generous, sympathetic nature and to know him well was to like him better."

In a letter to the family after his death, a doctor friend in the community said, "As long as life lasts, will I ever cherish with feelings of the liveliest emotions the many acts or professional kindness I and members of my family have received at his hands, as well as the wise counsel oft repeated, of which I have been the recipient . . ."

F.M. Dwight
Was Beloved Horse And Buggy Doctor

Born to the medical tradition, Francis Marion Dwight, a descendant of Gen. Francis Marion's brother, Isaac, grew up in the Sand Hill section of Sumter County.

His father, Samuel Jamison Dwight, was a graduate of Philadelphia College of Medicine, where his grandfather, Samuel Broughton Dwight, and his great-grandfather, Samuel Dwight, had completed their medical studies. It is easy to see that doctoring was in his blood and he could but follow the examples of his ancestors.[53]

Grandfather Dwight had such a large practice in Orangeburg County that in his later years he was forced to retire from practice and move to Georgia for the remainder of his life. His son, Samuel Jamison, Francis Marion Dwight's father, served as a surgeon in the Confederate Army until his death in 1862. He left his young wife, Sarah Ann Scott Dwight, and six small children, the youngest, Matilda, only six weeks old. The oldest was nine or ten and Francis Marion, only two.

The young widow sold the home in Georgia and moved to Sumter County, bringing her little family, her faithful old "Mammy" and the coachman. Because of unsound advice from her lawyer, she invested what cash she owned in Confederate bonds, which were soon entirely worthless. By taking in sewing and practicing great thrift, she was able to buy enough necessities for the family. As each son became old enough, he obtained some kind of work to supplement the meager income. Francis Marion worked in a neighborhood store at Eastover, three miles from his home. During the week he spent nights at the store, but walked home for Saturday night and Sunday. In addition to his clerking duties, he had charge of the cotton pickers, "weighing up" the bags and sheets of cotton that had been picked during each day.

When Mr. Oakman sold his store, the young man obtained work at Kaminer Brothers store in Gadsden, eating and sleeping with the Kaminer family.

His education thus far consisted only of some years at Palmetto Academy, a school near his home. Eager for further knowledge, he saved enough to attend Eastman Business College in Poughkeepsie, New York.

Still not satisfied, he borrowed money from Kaminer and entered medical school at the University of Maryland in Baltimore. Upon completing his course, he established his country practice in the Wedgefield area in 1889. After boarding for a year with Mrs. Harvin, he bought a two-story house where he set up housekeeping with his youngest sister, Matilda, doing the housekeeping until his marriage in 1892 to Miss Mary Carter Singleton, daughter of John Coles, Jr., and Harriett Brown Singleton and great-granddaughter of Col. Richard Singleton.

Dr. F.M. Dwight was truly one of the county's beloved "horse and buggy" doctors. In the first few years of practice, however, he used a little road cart in lieu of a buggy. It was during this time that on one of his trips, he attempted to cross Cow Branch which was greatly swollen because of recent rains. In the middle of the stream the water filled the floor of the sulky. The water was so deep that it was necessary for the horse to swim. The doctor's instrument case was washed out of the cart, but he managed to rescue this valuable part of his practice, though with considerable difficulty.

Later he was able to purchase a "top buggy" and was then able to ride in style. His horses were always "blooded and spirited animals." They were sleek and shiny, for he kept them in perfect condition. It is said that his practice was so widespread that he needed three horses to take care of his day and night visits.

Always impeccably dressed, the doctor made an impressive appearance as he drove through the country. As long as he practiced medicine, he was never seen in public without a coat — a Prince Albert in winter and a linen coat in summer. According to his wife, he was always orderly and systematic, even at home. Everything was in its proper place at all times. He did have a saving sense of humor, however; for once when he found a sachet in his shoe, he laughed heartily, knowing that one of the children was responsible.

A man of tireless energy, Dr. Dwight, for some years, ran two farms, a store and for part of the time a drug store — all in addition to his medical services. He provided all medicines for his patients for a time, making the pills himself.

Dr. Dwight purchased half interest in McRae's Mill, long abandoned, from Mrs. Dwight's mother in 1892 and immediately began renovating the millhouse and rebuilding the dam. Taking charge of the work while the doctor was attending to this large country practice was John Bradley. When the mill was ready to operate, Dr. Dwight obtained the services of a Mr. Windham, who was his miller for 20 years. This venture proved very profitable for the Dwight family, for they received all the meal, hominy, and graham flour they needed and were able to feed the horses, mules, hogs and chickens with cracked or whole corn.

In 1903 the Dwights left Wedgefield, moving into a spacious new home known as Sherwood, in Stateburg. Since collections were very poor at times, the construction of their lovely home was slow, taking several years, in fact. In those days the money crop — cotton — was bringing a very low price, and the patients really had little with which to pay. Be it said to his credit that the faithful doctor never failed to answer a call of distress, whether he was paid or not.

During the years when he was trying to construct his home, a small windfall came his way that provided some help. An aunt died in Hopedale, Georgia, leaving her possessions to her many nieces and nephews. Dr. Dwight's share was $60; but when he returned from the funeral, he brought enough soapstone brick, made in the aunt's talc mill, to put hearths in several chimneys.

The home in Wedgefield was sold to Dr. M.L. Parler, who had come as a young doctor to assist Dr. Dwight in the extensive country practice which was becoming too burdensome.

A tragic accident befell Dr. Dwight while he was still a young man. While opening a bottle of carbonated water, the cork popped out and flew into his right eye. This caused terrific pain at the time and sometime later resulted in a cataract. After surgery in Columbia, he returned home to recuperate. Before the eye had healed, a fire broke out on one of his farms. Though he had been cautioned against activity, he insisted on helping in the emergency. As a result, his eye became so irritated and inflamed with so much accompanying pain that its removal became necessary.

Soon after this tragedy, he walked one night into a nail that injured the other eye. A cataract formed and though it developed slowly, it became more and more of a handicap, finally forcing the dedicated doctor to give up his practice. In those last years one of his children or his wife would often drive him on visits to his "old" patients – those whom he had treated for many years. Often his very presence, along with generous doses of friendliness and optimism, would bring relief to the suffering.

Even after giving up for the most part his medical practice, he was still able to get around on his farms, driving Celeste, an intelligent horse that he had raised. She knew her way around and he could trust her to follow the familiar roads. Since his other horses were too highstrung for him to manage, he sold them to Dwight Cain.

Dr. Francis Marion Dwight was a devoted member of the Church of the Holy Cross at Stateburg, having served as vestryman, junior warden, senior warden, warden emeritus. For 20 years he was Sunday School superintendent and was always a delegate, and often the only delegate, to the Diocese Convention of his church. Even after his sight had failed, he was elected as delegate, his son or Mrs. Dwight going along to guide him. Bishop Capers made the Dwight home his headquarters when he came to visit the parish, for there he always felt a special welcome awaiting him.[54]

Dr. and Mrs. Dwight had large family connections, and the latch-string was always out for relatives, and most of the time there were several visitors at the dining table. They had a large immediate family and the friends of their many sons and daughters were made welcome at any time. Young people found the Dwight home especially attractive, for here they could enjoy innocent fun in which the grown-ups entered with enthusiasm.

In 1942 Dr. and Mrs. Dwight celebrated their 50th wedding

anniversary though at the time the doctor was a semi-invalid. The following year he passed away, after a long and useful life, having been a devoted husband, a loving father, a compassionate physician and a dedicated Christian.

The Influence Of Dr. S.H. Edmunds Lives On

Standing in front of the high school that was named in his honor is a monument erected to Dr. S.H. Edmunds. The name of the school has been changed, but the name of this eminent educator should be kept alive in the minds of each generation of the citizens of Sumter.

Samuel Henry Edmunds was born at Mill Grove in Richland County May 28, 1870, son of Rev. Nicholas William and Mary Claudia (Leland) Edmunds.[55] Reverend Edmunds taught for some years in the Sumter Institute, where his subjects were Latin, Greek, literary subjects and the Bible. He was a pastor of the First Presbyterian Church in Sumter for 25 years.

Young Samuel Henry spent his boyhood in the country or village and attended the early schools of Sumter. In 1890 he was graduated from Davidson College with an A.B. degree and later attended Columbia University in New York and the University of Chicago. In 1914 he received an honorary Litt.D. degree from Presbyterian College and was given the same recognition by Wofford College in 1916.

He began teaching in Sumter in 1890, but left in 1893 to have charge of a Presbyterian High School for Boys in Rock Hill. However, in 1895, he was called back to Sumter as superintendent of the Sumter City Schools, remaining in that position until his death in 1935.

In 1896 Samuel H. Edmunds married Miss Eliza Champion Davis and they were the parents of six children.

He was always alert to the needs of the pupils and it was through his efforts that many improvements were made from time to time, in the physical facilities, as well as in the curriculum.

One of the most popular innovations was the beginning of military training. He procured well-trained commandants and was instrumental in supplying military equipment needed for the program. Boys were well trained for military service in World War I. According to Snowden's sketch of the life of Dr. Edmunds only one failed to receive a commission in training camps.

The plan was copied by other schools and in 1912 Dr. P.P. Claxton, U.S. Commissioner of Education, issued a bulletin on the Sumter schools which was read and published throughout the country.

Dr. Edmunds became a member of the State Board of Education by appointment of the governor in 1916, and in 1918 he was chosen state director of the U.S. Boys' Working Reserve. He served as chairman of the Educational Research Commission of South Carolina.

Though the City Public Schools, of which he was superintendent for more than 40 years,[56] claimed most of his attention, he gave of himself to the people of Sumter and South Carolina in many other ways. As a member of the First Presbyterian Church of Sumter, he dedicated himself to its work, serving for many years as an elder and as teacher of the Men's Bible Class. He was a member of the Board of Directors of the Columbia Theological Seminary.[57]

Held in high esteem throughout South Carolina, he was chosen to serve as a member of the State Board of Education, a member of the Commission for the Revision of State School Laws and a member of the Illiteracy Commission for the State of South Carolina.

Other activities of this busy man included the presidency of the Y.M.C.A.; chairmanship of the Carnegie Library Committee; membership in the Rotary Club, the Masonic Order, the Knights of Pythias.

Dr. Edmunds died on September 14, 1935, and countless tributes of love and appreciation were voiced by young and old alike. Respect for his strong character and power of leadership felt by his fellow teachers may be summed up in these words from one of those who served under him: "Dr. Edmunds was a great leader because he was a great man. In trying to teach those more important lessons: kindness, courtesy, clean-mindedness, reverence, honesty and dependability, having held up the ideal before the child, how often we have said, 'You may forget my words, but watch Dr. Edmunds. Live as he lives.' . . ."

Someone expressed most aptly his relationship to small children in these words: "The treasures of his heart and mind he gave quietly, lovingly, wisely, fairly, and freely to every little child. Instinctively the children felt this bigness, this generosity which embraced them all in the great rich heart of him."

The older boys and girls, too, loved him devotedly. The following sentence summarizes the high regard they always had for him: "In the mornings, when he would read the Bible and lead in the Lord's Prayer, or when he would make a little talk on morals, what he was and what he stood for spoke a great deal louder than what he said."

A sonnet written by one of his teachers seems a fitting tribute for Dr. Samuel Henry Edmunds, that one who exemplified the true image of public school education. Some lines from this sonnet read:

"... How truly great, how truly great he was,
So wise, so gentle, so benevolent,
So fearlessly he fought for every cause
That lifted fellowman! He found content
In service. Following him was joy to me
For in his life I saw nobility."

What he accomplished for the education of Sumter's youth has lived and will continue to live after him. Many can say with Daniel Defoe, "We loved the doctrine for the teacher's sake."

The monument erected by appreciative citizens of Sumter County carries the following inscription:

"Faithful in the discharge of every duty; unselfish civic leader, distinguished and trusted teacher, his fellow citizens and his pupils call his life-work blessed and revere his memory. As a token of their affection and as a testimonial to future generations of the appreciation of the community, this memorial is dedicated by the Citizens of Sumter."

McDonald Furman – A Sketch Of His Life

On Cornhill Plantation, Nasty Branch, Privateer Township on March 1, 1863,[58] was born Charles James McDonald Furman, who, in the words of a friend "lacked only a little of being a genius." Coming from a century of leadership in education and religion, he was carefully trained and nurtured by parents possessed of pride of ancestry and devotion to high ideals.

McDonald's mother was Susan Miller, daughter of the eminent lawyer, John Blount Miller. His father's ancestry went back to Stokes County, Suffolk, England. From there John Furman came to America in 1631, settling in Massachusetts. His descendant, Wood Furman, came to South Carolina, where he received a royal land grant in Craven County in 1756.

Son of Wood Furman was Richard Furman, that eminent scholar and theologian of whom Sumter County and South Carolina are justly proud. His son, Samuel, educator in Sumter District, married Eliza Scrimzeour, from a royal family in Scotland; and their son, John Howard, father of McDonald, practiced medicine and ran his plantation for many years in the Privateer section of Sumter County.

Through McDonald's diary much is learned of the dreams and ambitions of this young lad. His formal education began at a small neighborhood school taught by J.T. Ramsey, through whose teaching he became especially interested in South Carolina history and literature.

At an early age he manifested an intelligent curiosity and thus learned much through observation.

McDonald was an avid reader, choosing for the most part historical writings and the best in literature. His parents gave him books as birthday and Christmas presents; he also borrowed from friends and bought some with his "cotton money." Judge Pressley took an interest in his education, encouraging him to read and lending him books from his extensive library.

After completing all available training from the country school, he entered Greenville Military Academy in 1880, where he excelled in composition work on subjects dealing with South Carolina history and genealogies. In Greenville he became a friend of Benjamin F. Perry and was allowed the use of his library.

In 1882 he returned home thinking that he would take over work on the plantation, but he was soon enrolled at South Carolina College in Columbia, where he studied for three years.

From letters[59] written to his parents at this time, one can see many facets of his character. Between the lines could be read his great love of home and devotion to his family. He was quite solicitous of his mother's health and showed great interest in the activities of his brothers and sisters. The letter that contained the report on the purchase of furniture for his room revealed his bent toward strict economy. He rendered a strict accounting for each article: bedstand and mattress $5.25; two chairs – $1.40; water stand, pitcher and basin – $2.50; oil can and lamp – $1.80; pail and dipper – $.75; looking glass and table – $2.30; washtub and broom – $.65. For school books he spent $6 and bought an umbrella for $.75. He said that he had paid the lowest price possible.

At first he and one other boy took meals at Mrs. McMahon's, but later he ate at "Steward's Hall" with other students. The eight at his table paid ten cents extra to have ice water.

Soon after entering the college, he wrote his mother that he had joined the Clariosophic Literary Society as she had directed. He was immediately nominated for several offices but declined the honor because he felt that he was "too new" to undertake such responsibilities. He later was chosen as orator for the Society.

In his early youth McDonald was quite shy, but he soon overcame his timidity. At the age of 15, he was taken by his father to an agricultural meeting where he met the "Bald Eagle of Edgefield," Martin W. Ary. Not agreeing with some of that gentleman's views, he courageously presented his own. His correspondence shows that he readily made friends with lawyers, statesmen, journalists, and others. He counted among his friends such men as B.J. Lossing (historian); Governors Bonham, Perry, Thompson, Hagood; Gen. Robert Toombs; poet Paul Hamilton Hayne.

During his third, and last, year at South Carolina College, he was editor of "The South Carolina Collegian," the college newspaper, writing many of the articles that appeared in the paper.

Having decided not to return to college in the fall of 1885, he took up the many duties and responsibilities of plantation life, and made plans to write. His first articles were not accepted, his first successes being two newsletters giving local items signed with pseudonyms. The first appeared in the "Spirit and Times" and he was so happy that he "had to go out in the yard and have a sort of dance." This was the beginning of his news column "Privateer Notes," which he continued as long as he lived.

His articles were later published in several Southern magazines. He also established a correspondence in the **Atlanta Constitution** as well as in leading newspapers in South Carolina. The young author received his first money from his writing when the **New York Herald** in 1889 paid him two dollars, which he gave to his parents, saying it was too "sacred" for him to keep. His two attempts at fiction were published in **The Watchman and Southron**.

An article telling of the Furman family, titled "A Family of Educators," he had published in the magazine, *Education,* Boston, Massachusetts. His articles often appeared in *Homestead Magazine* and in publications of the Southern and American Historical Associations.

Most of his writings centered around South Carolina's history and people. He wrote archeological and ethnological studies of the Catawba Indians and of the "Redskins," a mixed ethnic group found in Privateer Township.

He felt that he was not fitted to write a book, but said that the aim of his literary career was "every now and then to write short and pointed articles about some historical subjects."

In evaluating his writings, a fair critic would say that his was "a greatness of aim rather than one of accomplishment." And what was his aim? One opinion expressed was that his guiding motive was to inspire as many as possible to a greater love for and pride in South Carolina upon whose "glorious past" could be built a great future.

The general lack of interest in preserving and studying the historical records of the state was heartbreaking to Furman. He wrote to many influential friends throughout South Carolina, deploring the apathy of the times and appealing for help. He received many letters in reply, one of which stated in part: " . . . There must be some sentiment and some state pride . . . and I hope that the generations now coming on the stage of active life will furnish men who will have the good sense and the influence to accomplish more complete results."

Another letter voicing a similar view was received: "Aye! You are right! If Camden were in Massachusetts or Connecticut, its fame would be world wide! Why are our people so indifferent to our glorious past?"

In order to create interest in history, the enthusiastic Furman suggested a celebration of conspicuous anniversaries. In 1889 he mentioned to the editor of **The News and Courier** the idea of a centennial celebration of the first meeting of the General Assembly in Columbia. There was a favorable response and the "Furman Movement," as it was called, resulted in "the biggest celebration which has ever been in Columbia." Sumter's part was "second only to Columbia and in some things ahead of her." Sumter saw the commercial advantage in such an affair and went all out in advertising the town. Furman's aim, of course, was to revive an interest in "our State History."

Though McDonald Furman seemed more inclined toward history in his writings and activities, he had an abiding interest in good literature, an interest that must not be overlooked in giving a sketch of his life. In his correspondence with Paul Hamilton Hayne, he received a letter which read in part: "I have read, and read with pleasure your letter . . . with pleasure because it shows a literary taste, unfortunately quite rare among our people, especially the young generation to which you belong . . . "

Mrs. Hayne wrote him as follows: "My husband is always kind to the young, and when they take an interest in literary matters, he has never failed to foster such taste. It is rare indeed for Southern boys to manifest any pride in their great men, or any interest in cultivating a literary education. And no people are ever a great people who neglect aesthetics."

An outstanding facet of Furman's personality was his friendliness. In his first letter to his mother from South Carolina College he told of all those whom he met on the train going to Columbia and of one with whom he shared his lunch. His college friends were numerous. Some of those he spoke of were "Billie" Ball, Shirley Hughson, Eugene Dabbs, Don Blanding. There were many whose last names only he mentioned: Scarborough, Pringle, Edmunds, McBride, James, Spencer, Pinckney, and others.

A kind, warm heart moved McDonald to sympathize with those less fortunate than he and to take time for many thoughtful, unselfish deeds. One such kindness was shown when he sat up with Blanding one night when he was ill.

He not only wrote about the Catawba Indians, but he tried to help them. Through his articles he hoped to arouse interest of others in making an education possible for these people. He made an effort to get Governor Evans to visit these Indians, hoping to stir his sympathy for them. No doubt because of his writings, Bethel Presbytery established a school for them in 1897.

His research into the history of the "Redskins" was considered by many as useless, but it caught the attention of the Smithsonian Institute, the Bureau of Ethnology and several noted ethnologists. One wrote him: "We owe much to those isolated workers like yourself who gather up what is near them and save for the use of future students what would otherwise be lost . . . it is upon the good work of local specialists that the general history must largely stand."

This man of varied interests showed a desire to help the Negroes of his day. In fact, he had been reared to have a kindly feeling toward them, since his father had always treated those on his plantation with consideration. Each year they had a "Lay-by Dinner" at which white and black made speeches and useful gifts were distributed. McDonald often talked to Negro meetings and encouraged these people to try to improve themselves. Appreciation for his interest was spoken by Charleston pastor and poet George C. Rowe: "As a people we are grateful to you."

Any phase of education attracted his attention. In 1896 he visited the schools of Sumter County to discover ways by which he might improve the public school system. In a small book he kept notes on his observations. One visit may be mentioned to give an example of what he found and also to give an idea of the curriculum followed in that day: The school of Miss Manette McCutchen – 30 pupils enrolled, 13 present. Subjects taught – South Carolina history, United States history, algebra, music (taught from charts), physical geography, Spencerian writing, spelling, reading. At the one blackboard were George Nettles and Annie Whilden.

On the political stage Furman played his part. Through the newspaper he waged a "personal anti-Tillman campaign" and was elected as a delegate to the Conservative or Anti-Tillman Convention.

In 1895 he wrote about issues considered in the Constitutional Convention and agitated for a two-mill educational tax without which "the free school systems will be nearly wiped out."

He ran for the House of Representatives in the following year but was defeated. His platform advocated biennial legislative sessions, four-year terms for all state offices and equal pay for equal work regardless of sex. As early as 1888 he said that it was "only a question of time before we have a qualified suffrage of both sexes in this state."

Of an outgoing personality, McDonald enjoyed social events, concerts, and casual visits with friends. His letters home during his college days were filled with accounts of various social affairs.

But with all his socializing he did not neglect his religious life. He was faithful in his attendance at church and Sunday School while in Columbia. After coming home, he was a regular attendant at Bethel Baptist Church.

During his last years, this young man, who had led usch an active life, was confined to his home much of the time because of ill health. He spent many lonely hours after his sister, Sudie, left for Cuba as a missionary. His parents had died and his brother and sister had moved into other homes, leaving him in his bachelor quarters on Cornhill Plantation, where he died at the age of 40 on February 19, 1904.

In newspapers over the state appeared obituary notices paying tribute to a man who was known and loved by scores of acquaintances and friends.

From the **St. Matthews Recorder** came these words: " . . . Mr. Furman had his peculiarities, but was a gentleman of the old school, and was fearless and honorable in his dealings with mankind."

The State said of him: " . . . Upright and sincere, independent and original in his views, indefatigable and untiring in his researches into South Carolina history and genealogy . . . "

"There was but one McDonald Furman," said a friend, "and we cherish his memory with peculiar tenderness."

Memories Of Dr. R.B. Furman

All but hidden from view by trees and underbrush in the Privateer section of Sumter County stands a forlorn weatherbeaten little two-room cabin that was once the center of activity for the entire neighborhood.

In the late 1800's and well into the 1900's, this little building was a witness to many expressions of pain and signs of relief, for it was the office of the beloved Dr. Richard Baker Furman.

During the years of his practice, the small cabin was surrounded by a large yard dotted with trees of various sorts that served as convenient hitching posts for the horses (or mules) that had drawn the wagons or buggies of the patients. Of course, in the latter years there could be seen automobiles among the other vehicles.

The "waiting room" was a narrow porch on the front of the office where there were a few chairs. Most of those who came to see the doctor, however, remained in the vehicles in which they were riding until their turns came. In good weather the "men folk" – those who had brought wife or children and the less ill patients themselves – would collect in groups around the clearing and discuss crops, weather, politics, their assorted ailments, etc.

When one patient would come out, another would enter the little front room, each one knowing his time without benefit of nurse or appointment record. (There were no appointments. It was "first come, first served.") In the front room sat the doctor by his desk, which was cluttered with books, papers, letters, pipes and other objects that had been dropped there sometime in the past. When the patients had been seated, the "inquest" began. When questions had been asked concerning the affected parts of the anatomy, he was ready to prescribe. Though he had none of the modern scientific equipment, such as an apparatus for taking blood pressure or a cardiograph, he was usually able to detect hypertension, heart trouble, typhoid and all the other diseases that were common – and surprisingly those that were rare. Since he was familiar with the medical history of the people in the community, he knew what symptoms to look for. However, he had many patients from a distance who had somehow heard of his ability as a doctor.

The diagnosis having been completed, he went into the back office where his medicines were kept. To the unpracticed eye this department was in a state of complete confusion, but he knew exactly where to find the calomel, paregoric, or other drug that he needed at the time. He prepared the medication, bringing it out to the patient with verbal direction. One of his favorites was: "Put this powder in a pint of water and take a teaspoonful three times a day before meals."

When asked the price of office visit and medicine, his usual reply was, "That will be a dollar and a half." Sometimes he charged more if he gave more than one medicine. If a person was unable to go to the office, Dr. Furman would visit in the home, going from place to place around the countryside by horse and buggy. His home visits were not expensive usually.

In view of all the modern scientific knowledge of diseases and their treatment, one would think that Doctor Furman's methods were primitive, but anyone living today whom he treated will readily agree that he was among the best. According to a trite expression that can convey a truth, he was a "born doctor."[60]

Who was this man who for many years held the respect, admiration and love of countless people in his community and elsewhere?

His family can be traced back to Naylandhy, Stokes County, Suffolk, England, whence his ancestor, John Furman, came to Salem, Massachusetts, in 1631. From a line of distinguished forefathers, Wood Furman was the first of the name to settle in South Carolina. A grant of 250 acres to this newcomer from King George II is recorded in the office of the Secretary of State, dated August 13, 1756. This land is situated on both sides of Beech Creek at the foot of Borough Hill, Stateburg. In 1768 he received a second grant containing 300 acres in the same section.

Son of Wood Furman was the illustrious Biblical scholar and theological Richard Furman, who was twice married – first to Elizabeth Haynsworth and after her death to Dorothea Burn. The second son of the second marriage was Samuel, a teacher, writer, minister. He was at the head of Furman Institution, which was the first school to train ministers in the South, having been founded by his father, Richard Furman.

Samuel was married to Eliza Scrimzeour, a descendant of the earls of Scotland and heir to a large fortune. Samuel and Eliza were the parents of nine children, the seventh being John Howard, born in 1824 at Coosawhatchie (Beaufort County). He spent his early manhood in Scotland where his mother was trying to establish her title and receive her estate. For a while he lived in Milledgeville, Georgia, where he was married to Catherine Carter and had two sons. After her death he came to Sumter County and acquired Cornhill Plantation. He married Susan Miller, daughter of Col. John Blount Miller, one of Sumter County's leading citizens. It is not clear to the writer where he received his medical training, but he began the practice of medicine in Privateer Township, and he also became a successful planter there.

With a rich heritage on both sides, Richard Baker Furman was born in 1866,[61] the son of Dr. John Howard and Susan Miller Furman. After his graduation from The Citadel and the Medical College of South Carolina, he began to practice with his father on Cornhill Plantation in the Bethel Community. His father was then called "old Dr. Furman" and he was known as "Dr. Richard." By the turn of the century the son had taken over the practice of his father who was in failing health and whose death came in 1902.[62]

Richard was married in 1905 to Katherine Lide, daughter of Rev. Tom Lide, who at one time was pastor of Bethel Baptist Church. He built a home for his bride near his father's plantation home and named it "Australis." They had one daughter, Katherine, who died during her college days.

"Doctor Richard" kept up his office practice until a short time before his death in 1958 at the age of 91.[63] For some time, however, he had been unable to make house calls. His wife survived him by several years, but the three now lie buried in the Bethel Cemetery with identical flat stones over the graves of all. In the plot, surrounded by an iron fence, which shows the effects of time and weather, are stones marking the resting places of many of Dr. Furman's relatives.

During his years of practice, "Dr. Richard" won the esteem of medical men because of the accuracy of his diagnostic ability, his skillful use of medication, as well as his professional spirit. His wonderful "bedside" manner, which he displayed at all times, appealed to all.

In 1953 he was accorded the honor of being named "dean of practicing physicians" in the state. His neighbors paid tribute of their loyalty and love by naming the new consolidated school that was built some years ago the "Furman School."

For years to come the memory of this man will linger in the minds and hearts of those who from childhood were familiar with his tall aristocratic figure, his little goatee and his tender half-humorous smile. His gentle voice could calm distraught parents and soothe the ill child. His psychological approach was able to win part of the battle before a diagnosis was made.

The name of Dr. Richard Baker Furman will long be a tradition in the community where he spent his life and was spent for his friends.

Miss Antonia Gibson, Dedicated Nurse

"Where love and skill work together, expect a masterpiece."

No better example of this truism can be found than in Sumter's own Antonia Gibson, who was highly skilled as a nurse and whose every deed was actuated by love.

The story of Miss Antonia began September 22, 1875, in Charleston. She was the daughter of Bentley Gordon and Mary Tennent Gibson. The Gibson ancestry had its roots in Scotland, the great-grandfather of Antonia coming to Carolina at least a century before her birth.[64]

Her father was in the cotton business with Maybank and Co. in Charleston and was transferred to Sumter as an agent of the same company when Antonia, the second of nine children, was 12 years old.

She attended the Sumter Institute, a very reputable school of the time, and was graduated in the class of 1893. Her formal education was then interrupted for a while by the illness and death of her mother.

In 1897 she entered nurses' training at the Baker-Dick Infirmary and received her degree in the school's first graduating class in 1902. For four years she did private duty nursing. Though her first case, a patient with rabies, was a most difficult one for a young nurse, she proved equal to the task.

The Civic League, Sumter's first public welfare organization, employed Miss Gibson in 1906 as a visiting nurse – a position that kept her busy, working with the poor and needy wherever and whenever there was a call for help. She could be seen day and night on her bicycle, hurrying from one part of town to another, answering distress calls.

So widespread were her contacts that it became necessary to create the City Health Department to care for all the needs she found and served. Later the responsibility was extended to a City-County Health Department.

The city employed her as city nurse in 1917 and assumed responsibility for her salary. At that time, she laid aside her faithful bicycle and with determination learned to drive the "Model T" which the city gave for transportation. After she had put many miles on the Ford, she was given a new car, which she drove until she had to give up her work.[65]

Many families in Sumter looked to Miss Antonia for friendship and advice in all kinds of difficulties. She assisted at the birth of 1800 babies, nor did she merely help to bring these children into the world and then leave them on their own. She kept up with their every need. When they were old enough to go to school, she saw that they had the required physical examinations and insisted that they attend school regularly. In order for them to have enough food to keep up their strength, she worked with a committee to set up a lunch program. If clothes and shoes were lacking, she made arrangements for these, sometimes at her own expense.

It is said that one Easter morning a little girl called and said, "Miss Antonia, I can't go to church today because I don't have any shoes to wear."

What did this kindhearted friend do? She went to see one of the merchants (who was also kindhearted) and got him to go to his store and let her have a pair of shoes. She then took them to the child so that she would not have to miss church.

She sponsored a two-week camp for underprivileged children in the High Hills area. At this camp at least one summer there were 17 boys ranging in age from about six to 17. They were given plenty of wholesome food, rest, body-building exercises, mental and spiritual training.

Going into all kinds of situations in some of the most dangerous parts of the city, the fearless little nurse demonstrated matchless courage. Once she was called by a desperate mother to say that her baby had no milk and her drunken husband had gone out with the last of the money to buy more whiskey. As always, meeting the challenge head-on, Miss Antonia hurried to the home to lend whatever assistance she could. Soon after her arrival, the husband staggered in with a pistol in hand and so intoxicated he was likely to shoot at any moment. Miss Gibson demanded that he hand her the gun, and surprisingly he obeyed. She walked to the window and threw it as far as she could out into the weeds. Turning, she ordered him to go immediately and get milk for the baby. Meekly he left and soon returned with the milk. The crisis was past, the victory won and a tragedy averted, all because of the dauntless courage of Miss Antonia Gibson.

"Tony," as her family lovingly called her, lived for many years with her sisters – Mattie, Mae, Hattie – and her cousin, Daisy Yeadon, who was like a sister, in the old Haynsworth home on the corner of Salem and Haynsworth Streets (where Dr. R.B. Bultman later lived), which belonged at that time to Miss Yeadon. Later Miss Antonia bought a lot on Anne Park and built a home for her "family."

Selected by the Pilot, Lions, Kiwanis, and Rotary Clubs for the honor, she received, in 1944, the A.T. Heath Outstanding Citizens Award for Unselfish Service to the Community. A beautiful silver service was presented to her as the tangible token of the award, a gift that could not have been better chosen. It had been a special desire of hers to own a silver service from the time of her childhood when she had admired the one brought from Scotland by her ancestor. However, the heirloom had gone to another branch of the family. Therefore, this gift brought added delight.

Realizing that her strength was failing, she retired in 1949, after 42 years of tireless and unselfish service to those in need.

Miss Antonia Gibson was more than a nurse. She was quick to see opportunities for service and was ever ready to take advantage of each one. It could well be said of her that she went about doing good.

One of the many appreciative citizens said of her in 1939: "Miss Gibson speaks of her work as just a nursing job, but it is much more than that. Most of her families of meager means look up to her as they would to a kindly aunt who would take an interest in baby's first tooth, what Sonny made in arithmetic, and where Grandpa's sorely needed pair of shoes were coming from. Miss Gibson's interest is a real one, her sympathy broad and genuine, and years of experience have given her the wisdom to deal so wisely with people that the help which she renders builds self-respect rather than encouraging dependence and desire for coddling. Her keen discrimination, accurate diagnosis and wholesome sense of humor make her uniquely well fitted for the position of city nurse."

Miss Antonia died on October 12, 1949, and is buried in the Sumter Cemetery. The marker at her grave was given in her memory by the Pilot Club, of which she was an honorary member for many years.

There are many living in Sumter today who recall her bright smile, her energetic personality, her marked efficiency and her friendly attitude toward all, but especially toward those in distress. Brothers, sisters, nephews, nieces, cousins, friends — all loved her and those living today who knew her cherish her memory. It can truly be said that she used time "to weave tapestries of enrichment that last."

Gorgas Had Roots In Sumter

A brief sketch of the Haynsworths and something of the direct impact made on the history of Sumter County by this family were undertaken. But members of the family have indirectly reflected honor upon the area in that many of the Haynsworth line, who made their homes in other cities and states, had descendants of great renown in other parts of the world.

Richard Haynsworth, eldest son of Henry and Sarah Furman Haynsworth, was the great-grandfather of one of the world's great benefactors, the eminent Surgeon-General, William Crawford Gorgas.

Richard, as a young man, is described as a planter, owner of many tracts of land in Sumter District. At the age of 34, however, the early pioneering spirit possessed him, causing him to sell his holdings in 1808 and, with his wife, the former Sarah Ann Pringle James, and his young daughter, Sarah Ann, move to Alabama.

Among others who had previously "gone west," stopping in Alabama, was John Gayle, son of Matthew and Sarah Rees Gayle, also of Sumter District. Having graduated from South Carolina College in 1813, Gayle entered politics in his adopted state and was elected to many important offices. He served one term as governor and later became Judge of United States District Court.

He visited the Haynsworths soon after their arrival in St. Stephens (Alabama) and immediately fell in love with the lovely young daughter.[66] He wasted no time in wooing and winning her, for they were married in 1819 before she reached "sweet sixteen."

Six sons and daughters were born to this union before the young wife and mother died of lockjaw while her beloved husband was away on government business.

The second daughter, Amelia, while visiting at Mt. Vernon, an Army Camp near Mobile, and taking care of her sister's children, met Capt. Josiah Gorgas, a West Pointer, stationed at the arsenal. According to an account by Captain Gorgas, he heard her voice one day as she was reading to her little charges and thought it the most beautiful he had ever heard. When he met the young lady, he found her as charming as her voice. Though he was 35, he had never found a girl to his liking. Amelia Gayle, granddaughter of Richard Haynsworth, proved to be "the one."[67] She must have been equally impressed, though she too had been hard to please, for they were married in 1853 when she was 27. It is said that, although she was not beautiful, she "had a way with her." She is portrayed as having humor, tact, repartee, talent for telling anecdotes and sweetness of disposition.

October 3, 1854, was a momentous day for Josiah and Amelia Gorgas because it was on that day that their eldest son, William Crawford, was born, and a great day it was for people far and wide.

When the young lad was three, his father was transferred from Alabama to Maine. Josiah noted in his journal that the small boy was "very bright, quite grave, and tolerably mischievous and troublesome."

At the beginning of the Civil War, Captain Gorgas was stationed in Charleston, where he observed the beginning of hostilities. Though he was a member of the United States Army and as an officer had pledged his loyalty, he gave up his commission and joined the Confederacy. Jefferson Davis immediately made him brigadier general and put him in charge of ordnance. This position he filled so successfully that Gen. Joseph E. Johnston said, "He created the Ordnance Department out of nothing."

During the war years, son Willie became acquainted with such men as Robert E. Lee, Stonewall Jackson, Albert Sidney Johnson, all of whom he greatly admired. The respect he had for his father and his admiration of the Confederate leaders early instilled in him a desire to be a soldier.

The sensitive boy was deeply involved in the suffering of the Confederates. It is said that when he saw men walking on the streets of Richmond with worn shoes or barefooted, he refused to wear shoes for a whole winter.

When Richmond, where the family lived during the war, fell

to the enemy, he, at the age of 11, was responsible for the care of his mother, sisters and brother and the family cow, since his father was in the Army.

After the war, Josiah Gorgas, penniless and weary, returned to Alabama with his family. He tried to find a livelihood by working in a blast furnace, but this venture failed.

In 1870 the University of the South at Sewanee, Tenn., opened, under the auspices of the Episcopal Church, with a few students and limited facilities. The ex-Confederate officer was asked to become its president, which position he accepted and held for ten years.

On the college campus William, a slender youth, grew up. At first he was not interested in studying, but in his last year he became an avid student, a baseball star, and a class leader. His ambition to become a soldier was still with him, but every attempt he made to get an appointment to West Point failed. Finally he decided that if ever he was able to get a commission in the Army, it would be as a doctor.

Against his father's wishes, he enrolled at Bellevue Medical College in New York in 1876, where he labored for four years to complete the course. But sometime during those years he became vitally interested in what he was doing and his medical study was no longer only a means to become an Army officer.

Upon his graduation he served for a short time on the staff of Blackwells Island Insane Asylum and then for another short period as an intern at Bellevue.

In June of 1880 the young man's lifelong dream was realized. He joined the Medical Corps of the United States Army. His father, at this time president of the University of Alabama, was still against the idea of his son's being an Army doctor. However, this was what William wanted above all else.

He became a second lieutenant and his assignments during the first five years included three frontier forts in Texas and one in North Dakota, and one in Florida.

There was one disease running rampant over the country for which no cure had been found. Yellow fever was ever on the increase. In Brownsville, Texas, near the Mexican border, the dread disease came in epidemic form. When Gorgas reached Fort Brown, there were 2,300 cases in the area. Mosquitoes were swarming, but no one thought of a connection between these insects and yellowjack.

In this pestiferous place, the young doctor was busy day and night, applying all the medical aid he knew, digging graves for the victims (who were buried within a few hours after death), conducting funerals and doing whatever else came up to be done.[68]

His bachelor quarters, it so happened, were next to the colonel's home, where Marie Doughty, sister-in-law of the colonel, lived. When she became ill, he was called in and, though she was gravely ill, his medication evidently helped, for she recovered. In the meantime, however, he was stricken, though his case was mild. The two carried on a quiet courtship during their convalescence and were later married.

In 1883 William's beloved father died, without seeing all the accomplishments of his famous son and the honors heaped upon him. Amelia Gorgas lived on for many years working as librarian at the University of Alabama, and giving inspiration to her son.

When the Spanish-American War began and the United States Army entered "pest-ridden" Cuba, Gorgas was a "natural" for an assignment there, since he was immune to yellow fever. At that time, though, he had studied the disease and was given the name of "yellow fever doctor," he was not yet an advocate of the mosquito theory. Dr. Carlos Finlay, a Cuban doctor, was convinced that mosquitoes were carriers, but he could not prove his belief.

Many groups had attempted to solve the puzzle, but to no avail. Finally Dr. Walter Reed came to Havana and began experiments. Gorgas watched and waited until it was proved that the Aedes Aegypti mosquito was the culprit. Then the indomitable doctor went to work to rid Havana of mosquitoes. The task looked hopeless and indeed it was exceedingly difficult for the city was swarming with the insects. The opinion was that there had always been mosquitoes there and they would always be there.

Nevertheless, in the fact of great odds, Gorgas, as sanitation officer of Havana, was determined to clean up the city, one of the dirtiest in the world. His campaign went into streets, public buildings, private homes — everywhere. Some of the citizens at first rebelled, but as the young doctor "had a way with him," a trait inherited from his mother, he mollified the recalcitrants and proceeded with his task.

In the meantime he studied the habits of the yellow fever carriers, finding that they were very "intelligent," since they usually bit on the underside of the wrist where the flesh is tender, seldom on the face or body where they could be killed. These habits posed an additional problem in ridding the city of the carriers.

The struggle against yellow fever was long and discouraging, but finally in the last months of 1901 and for four years thereafter, no deaths from the fearful plague occurred. The battle was won!

In 1902 Gorga, then a colonel, was recalled to Washington

and sent to Egypt, Suez and Paris on an official journey. His next assignment was a preliminary trip to Panama.

Later, in 1905, he landed in Panama with seven helpers to undertake the gigantic task of cleaning up the dirty, disease-plagued country and make it safe for the building of the canal.

The fact is well known that the French had attempted to build this canal, using the same methods that had been successfully used in building the Suez Canal. But there was a difference. And what a difference! On the Suez project they faced no epidemic of yellow fever. The tiny Aedes Aegypti stood guard in Panama, and the French, after losing thousands of their men, abandoned the project, selling their equipment to the United States while Theodore Roosevelt was President. And when American engineers and workmen landed in the Canal Zone, the mosquitoes were still on guard, just waiting for fresh blood to begin multiplying again.

In spite of the Herculean effort put into the task by such eminent engineering experts as Gaillard and Goethals, the whole enterprise would have been a dismal failure had not Gorgas and his assistants supplied the sanitation measures and medical skill needed to save the lives of the workmen.

In the face of opposition that would have stopped a lesser man, Gorgas set to work with a will. Considering the mosquito theory all "poppycock," the Canal Commission and Congress delayed all supplies that he requested in an attempt to discourage his expensive requests. When he continued to persevere in his efforts to save the lives of the workmen, one member of the Commission insisted that Gorgas must go and a more "practical" doctor be engaged in the place of this "theorist."

Needless to say, Roosevelt was in a dilemma, wanting to agree with the wealthy men who were supplying funds, but knowing that Gorgas must be right, since the medical profession had finally agreed that the disease was definitely carried by mosquitoes. When the President asked one of his trusted advisers for his opinion, he was told, "Mr. President, you want your canal. Dismiss Gorgas and you won't get it." President Roosevelt made the right decision. The rest is history.

When yellowjack was conquered and the Canal Zone was made a healthful place (the annual death rate in Panama in 1914 was six per 1,000 inhabitants and the general death rate in the United States was 14.1 per 1,000) so that the canal could be completed, the world took notice and other countries sought the services of this great doctor.

He became Surgeon-General and by a special Act of Congress was made Major-General, a rank never given before in the medical department.

Invited by Great Britain to go to Africa to study the great incidence of death from pneumonia in the diamond mines of South Africa, he set sail for that continent. In three months he made a survey of much of the affected area and made recommendations to the Transvaal Chamber of Mines. Dr. Lewis Ornstein, an assistant of Gorgas in the Canal Zone, was made sanitation director of the Central Mining Company of the Transvaal.

In 1915, under the auspices of the International Health Board in New York, Gorgas, with two other doctors, toured several countries in South America to learn the exact locations where yellow fever was still a health problem. They were received with open arms and plans were made for a crusade against the disease in these countries.

However, in 1916, America became involved in World War I and he felt it his duty to serve in this crisis. His accomplishments were beyond belief. At the beginning of the war, the Army Medical Corps had only 435 medical officers and a medical reserve corps of 2,000 civilian doctors. When hostilities ceased, Gorgas was commander of 32,000 medical officers and a medical reserve corps of about 35,000 doctors and dentists and about 22,000 nurses. This was the largest command ever assigned to a Major-General.

Retired by the Army after the Armistice, Gorgas started on another mission to Africa where a new epidemic of yellow fever was reported. On his way, he, with his wife, stopped in London. Soon after his arrival there he was stricken with paralysis and was taken to a military hospital at Willbank.

One day King George V visited him in his hospital room. After talking with Gorgas for some time about the great services he had rendered in Cuba, Panama and Africa, the King presented to him the insignia of the Knight Commander of the Most Distinguished Order of St. Michael and St. George.[69]

William Crawford Gorgas died on July 3, 1920, facing the end "like the good Christian he was." A London newspaper, in reporting his death, noted that, "He was the best known and most uniformly successful medical administrator, not of his age alone but of any age, and his work is comparable only with that recorded of Moses."

After the great humanitarian service he had rendered in Panama, Gorgas was accorded many honors, beginning with his election as president of the American Medical Association. He received honorary degrees from Harvard, Brown, the University of Pennsylvania, the University of the South (his Alma Mater). He received from his former teacher at Bellevue, Dr. William H. Welch, "dean of American physicians," the Johns Hopkins degree of Doctor of Letters. Belgium awarded him the Harbin medal for "services to mankind." He passed away, however, before the International Hygiene Conference at Brussels, at which time he was to have received the medal from King Albert.

A state funeral in St. Paul's Cathedral was ordered for him. It was written of him, "It seemed good that death should find him here, for so there came our opportunity to do a great man honor . . .

"They will take him to his own land, but in truth he belongs to us all. He was one of life's great helpers, for he cleaned up foul places and made them sweet, and now as they said of Lincoln 'he belongs to the ages.' "

He was brought to America and buried in Arlington after memorial services which were attended by representatives of all American republics and many European countries. Panama proclaimed a three-day period of mourning with flags at half-mast. Both houses of Congress voted to establish in his memory the Gorgas Memorial Institute for the study of the prevention of tropical diseases.

Is it not fitting that Sumter pay tribute to the memory of one of the world's great? One whose lineage is traced to a distinguished and honorable family which the county is proud to call her own.[70]

Alfred Taylor Heath (Profile)

A man of many talents and achievements, Alfred Taylor Heath began his successful business career in Sumter, when in 1918 he bought from E.D. Cole the Sumter Coca-Cola Bottling Company, having been in Coca-Cola business for six years prior to coming to Sumter.

Born in Rosswell, Georgia, September 27, 1881,[71] he was the son of Alfred Taylor Heath and Katherine Quintard Pratt. He received his early education in the Rosswell and Atlanta Public Schools, later attending Georgia Tech in Atlanta.

In 1903 he was married to Ann D. Howell and they were the parents of four sons and three daughters; there are eight grandchildren.

He was a member of the Presbyterian Church.

In 1920 he organized the Carolina Coca-Cola Bottling Company and became its president, which position he held until his death, which came April 12, 1950.

His matchless success as a businessman was demonstrated in the growth of his company. The territory served under his leadership was expanded to include Lee, Kershaw, Lancaster, Chester, Clarendon and Williamsburg Counties, as well as sections of

Florence, Darlington, Fairfield, Newberry and Union Counties.

Not only did A.T. Heath add much to the economic growth of Sumter, but he served the community in many other ways. He believed that if a person lived in a community and enjoyed its privileges, he in turn owed the community every contribution he could make toward the improvement of life for all.

First of all, he felt it his duty to take care of his employees, believing that next to the product he sold they were the most valuable asset of the company. Each one was paid full salary when sick and, in addtion, his doctor's and hospital bills were paid. If a person was called into service while employed by his company, the difference between military pay and his salary with the company was paid while he was in the service.

With an especially warm love for young people, he helped many get an education who could not have afforded the cost without help.

As another indication of his interest in young people who needed a place for wholesome recreation, he provided the first "Teenage Canteen" in Sumter.

Seeing that the various clubs needed a meeting place, he provided for public use the "Coca-Cola Community Room" on Liberty Street.

Mr. Heath was a man of many interests, among which was baseball. He enjoyed giving members of athletic teams souvenirs. It was he who organized professional baseball in Sumter; his team was the "Sumter Chicks." It was through his connection with the New York Yankees that Bobby Richardson became a member of that team.

Through his strong influence, the Sumter Telephone Company was able to receive better service by being placed under the Public Service Commission.

The Community Chest, one of Sumter's most successful charity drives, owes its inception to this public spirited citizen.

Ready at all times to add a helping hand when financial aid was needed, he learned of the difficulties being faced by the Sunset Country Club. He promptly came to the rescue by buying the outstanding stock. Then when the membership had weathered the financial storm, he returned the stock to the original owners.

Believing that honor should be given to those who were serving others in a noteworthy manner, he began the "Heath Outstanding Citizen Award." Some of those receiving this honor were Mr. Hallie Bland, Congressman John J. Riley, Miss Antonia Gibson, Dr. Warren Burgess, Mr. Fulton Creech, Mr. W.E. Bynum and Mr. T. Doug Youngblood.

Perhaps the contribution that more people – young and old

alike – have enjoyed was the gift to the city of the Southside of Swan Lake Gardens, known as "Heath Side." With the help of H.C. Bland and at the expense of the city, he developed a lovely garden with a picnic area which the people of Sumter continue to enjoy.

One year Mr. Heath was the choice for the Kiwanis Outstanding Citizen Award. How fitting that one who always thought of serving others should thus be honored.

Another honor that spoke of the merits of this good man was his being named as an honorary member of Rotary.

Quiet, retiring in nature, A.T. Heath never sought the limelight. The service he rendered the people of Sumter, both as a businessman and a citizen, can never be estimated.

Fannie Spots Ivey, Beloved Teacher

Fannie Spotts Ivey, who served as a social studies teacher in Sumter School District 17 for 30 years died a few months ago (July, 1980) after a full life of service to her fellow man.

She was born in Georgetown, Ky. in 1918,[72] daughter of the late Henry S. and Margaret C. Generals Spotts. She was a graduate of Kentucky State University and received also a social studies certificate from Fisk University and a masters degree in library science from the University of Chicago. She took special courses at the University of Hawaii, Hampton Institute and the University of South Carolina.

She began work in Sumter in 1934 at Morris College where she was in charge of the first library there. During the summer sessions she taught classes at the college.

Dr. Luns C. Richardson speaks highly of her ability as an educator and one who was deeply interested in the education of young people.

As a great humanitarian she was interested in the development of the whole child her fellow workers say of her. Because of this love of young people she organized the first Girl Scout Troop in Sumter County. A year before her death she was given a citation for 30 years of leadership in Girl Scouts, and in recognition of her service the Sumter Scouting program was named the Fannie S. Ivey Girl Scout Neighborhood in her honor.

There seemed no limit to the extent of her interest in and service for others. She was founder and past president of the Mary McLeod Bethune Branch of the YWCA, former state president of the South Carolina Federation of Women and Girls Clubs, Southeastern vice president and board member of the National Association of Colored Women and Girls Clubs.

In professional organizations she served faithfully and well, having been a member of the South Carolina Education Association, the State Textbook Commission, the P.T.A. and the South Carolina Association of Human Relations. After retirement she became an active member of the State and National Retired Teachers Associations.

As a loyal member of the Study of Afro-American Life and History she was honored by being named secretary emeritus of the Sumter Chapter. She was also a member of the National Council of Negro Women. SCEA gave her the State Human Relations award in 1978 and the same year she was named "Woman of the Year" by the local YWCA. She was a member of Sigma Gamma Rho Sorority.

Her interest and influence extended also into civic and political activities. She encouraged voter registration. She served at one time on the Sumter City Council Advisory Board, as a commissioner of the Housing Authority and as co-director of the March of Dimes at one time.

In recognition of her dedication to these responsibilities, Mayor W.A. McElveen said of her: " . . . She had a special way of getting along with people and getting the job done . . ."[73]

That Mrs. Ivey went beyond the call of duty in every phase of her service to the youth of Sumter County is the feeling of Dr. Harold Patterson, superintendent of District 17 Schools.

Fannie S. Ivey's place is hard to fill and she will continue to be greatly missed by young people and adults because of her great love for others which she expressed in countless ways.

Wendell Mitchell Levi (Profile)

A noted son of Sumter, Wendell Levi was nationally known as lawyer, author and naturalist.

Born in Sumter September 28, 1891, the son of Mitchell and Estella D'Ancona Levi, he received his education at the College of Charleston and the University of Chicago Law School. Admitted to the bar in 1915, he practiced law in Sumter for 60 years, serving for a time as president of the Sumter County Bar Association.

He was engaged in active military duty during World War I, serving as an officer in charge of the Pigeon Section of the U.S. Army Signal Corps. He organized the 321st Labor Battalion and was captain and commanding officer of Company L of the 323rd Infantry, 81st Division, having a part in the Vosges and Meuse-

Argonne Campaign. In 1920 he was the recipient of the Cross of Military Service conferred by the United Daughters of the Confederacy.

Organizer of the Palmetto Pigeon Plant in Sumter, he served as president from 1923 to 1956 and after that was chairman of the board. It was essentially through his efforts that the plant became the largest Carneau squab market in the United States.

Because of his vast knowledge in this field, he held membership in a number of scientific organizations among which was the National Pigeon Association of which he served as president for a time. From this organization he received the Hall of Fame Award in 1958 and the Service Award in 1967. He was chosen as First Man of the Year of the International Federation of American Homing Pigeons.

He published many outstanding works on pigeons, among which was **The Pigeon and Encyclopedia of Pigeon Breeds**, a definitive authority on the subject.

In addition to all his other accomplishments, Mr. Levi was a noted naturalist, making a special study of camellias. He was at one time president of the South Carolina Camellia Society, contributing many authoritative articles on this plant to various journals.

He served as Commander of the Sumter County Post and South Carolina Department of Veterans of Foreign Wars and was chairman of the National Membership Committee of that organization.

Active in Boy Scout activities, he wrote the Merit Badge Pamphlet on Pigeon Raising.

He was an active member of the American Legion, was one of the founders of the Sumter Kiwanis Club, a life member of the Alumni Association of the College of Charleston, a Mason and a Shriner.

Dedicated to the work of Congregation Sinai, Mr. Levi was president of the congregation for many years and served a number of times on the Board of Trustees.

In 1968 his alma mater, the College of Charleston, conferred on this eminent alumnus a Doctor of Literature degree and in 1975 a wing of the library was named in his honor.

Levi was married in 1921 to Bertha London of Pittsburg, Pennsylvania, and they were the parents of two daughters and one son.

Wendell M. Levi died at the age of 84 after a long and useful life, leaving many reminders of the outstanding contributions made to countless persons and communities through his personal contacts as well as his valuable writings.

George D. Levy

George Davis Levy practiced law in Sumter for 65 years and from the beginning he stood at the top of the ladder in his chosen profession.

For many years he served as president of the County Bar Association as well as vice president of the South Carolina Bar Association. He was a member also of the American Bar Association and chairman of the State's Bar Committee on professional ethics in 1957.

Born in Petersburg, Virginia, July 16, 1883, Levy as a boy of nine came to Sumter with his parents, Julian H. and Corinne Davis Levy, and his two brothers, Julian Henry and Waverly Bertram.

He was graduated from Sumter High School in 1899, attended Clemson for three years, and in 1904 received his law degree from the University of South Carolina, where he was a member of ODK, leadership fraternity.

His law practice was interrupted by World War I. True patriot that he was, he left for military training at Fort Oglethorpe, Georgia, and was commissioned as a 2nd lieutenant. His assignment was in Company A. 323rd Infantry, 81st Division at what is now Fort Jackson. In 1918 he was made the 1st lieutenant and was shipped overseas. He served in France for more than a year.

After the war, he served as assistant trial judge advocate of Division General Court. He received a divisional citation for his services in that capacity.

In the early part of his military assignment at Camp Jackson, Mr. Levy married the former Pauline Greenwood Gardner of Savannah, Georgia; and when he finished his tour of military duty, he returned to Sumter and saw his seven-month-old daughter whom he had not seen before. This daughter, Polly Anne, is now deceased.

After four years another daughter, Corinne Alice, was born. She is now Mrs. John Jay Philips and with Mr. Philips lives on Swan Lake Drive. One of their sons, George Davis, is in the automobile business in Columbia. The other son, John Jay, Jr., is a partner in the law firm of Goldstein, Bowling, Douglas and Philips in North Charleston. Mr. Levy delighted in the accomplishments of his grandsons.

It was George D. Levy who organized American Legion Post No. 15 and it was through his efforts that this unit of the prestigious national organization has made an outstanding record of service to the country. His dedication to its activities (he was proud of the fact that he missed only six meetings as long as he was able to attend) are well known to people in Sumter. Through his service as the first commander, he set an example for others to follow. He later served for two other terms.

Nor were his services confined to the local organization. He was known, admired and loved throughout the state and nation. For a number of years he was a member of the Department Executive Committee, was judge advocate for six years. From 1934 until his death, June 13, 1972, he was National Executive Committeeman. He was so highly regarded as a man of wisdom and perspicacity that he was placed on a committee of five to rewrite the constitution and by-laws of the Legion. Recognized also as a gifted writer, he was placed on the National Publications Commission.[74]

In 1963 he received the Distinguished Service Award for the Department of South Carolina and in 1969 he was honored by being named the first emeritus member of the National Publications Commission.

He was a member of the Columbia Chapter of Military Order of World Wars.

This indefatigable worker also found time to serve on the County Draft Board for five years during World War II.

It was largely through his work as a member of a committee that Shaw AFB was brought to Sumter. He made many trips to Washington in the interest of this great boon for Sumter.

With all of his legal practice and his work for the American Legion, Mr. Levy still had time to serve his fellowman through many channels. He served as a member of the advisory boards of Boy Scouts of America and the Salvation Army. He was chairman of Red Cross and T.B. Drives, as well as the United Appeal (1959). He was one of the civilian appointees of Governor Byrnes for five years.

Work in various clubs also claimed the attention and service of this remarkable man. He was a life member of Sumter Elks Lodge No. 855, serving in all chairs besides being Exalted Ruler at one time; he was also appointed District Deputy to the Grand Exalted Ruler; was state president (1913-14); trustee for the local lodge and chairman of advisory board of governors of the Shriners' Hospital for Crippled Children in Greenville. He was past director of the Jesters, an organization within the Shrine.

He was first chef de gare of Voiture 1254, 40 & 8 and grand chef de gare passe of Palmetto Grand Voiture of the same organization.

Other organizations in which he held membership were Sumter Rotary Club, Sunset Country Club, the Assembly, Claremont Lodge No. 64.

As a devoted member of Temple Sinai, he was at one time president of the Congregation and of the Men's Club.

Mr. Levy, in addition to all his other accomplishments, was a gifted speaker and was in great demand by various groups over the state.

His sound advice as a legal counselor brought him many clients, who admired and honored him through all the years of his long practice. So highly regarded was he as a lawyer that at his death a sketch of his achievements was included in the memorial book, "Memory, Hold the Door," which is kept in the law library at the University of South Carolina.

The memory of this great man who made so many worthwhile contributions to life in Sumter, as well as in other parts of the state and nation, will live on not only in the book of remembrances but in the hearts of those he touched directly or indirectly.

John Alexander McKnight (Profile)

Living in Sumter during the first half of this century was a man who was highly respected and greatly admired by those who knew him — and he was known of many throughout Sumter County. This man was "Mr. Johnny" McKnight.

John Alexander McKnight was born in Clarendon County near the little town of Paxville on March 17, 1886.[75] His parents were Charles Peter and Sarah Lois ("Lula") Cuttino McKnight. Their home was on land that was part of a grant from the King of England to Joseph Pack. It came down through the Kellys to the Cuttinos.

His grandfather, James Harper McKnight, was at one time the owner of a large cotton and rice plantation near Summerton. After the War Between the States, however, he found himself in much the same condition as other Southerners of the time. In addition to his losses caused by the war, his plight was made worse because he signed a security paper for his neighbor, who failed to pay the note. Therefore McKnight was left with nothing except the home in Summerton. He, therefore, had no means with which to rear a large family.

His brother, John Alexander, who had extensive holdings, gave to him title to 1,000 acres of good farming land, the only condition being that his oldest grandson be named John Alexander.

Therefore when the oldest grandson, son of Charles Peter and "Lula" McKnight, was born, his name had already been chosen and he grew up to be Sumter's own "Mr. Johnny."

In this family of nine boys and girls, John learned early how to love and share. He unselfishly stood aside for the others in the family to continue their education. (Eight finished college and two received medical degrees.)

Because of the prevalence of malaria in the lower part of the state, Charles Peter with his large family moved to Ridgeway in 1904.

At the age of 19, in 1905, John came to Sumter and became a partner in the Cuttino-McKnight Grocery Store. After operating this business for six years, he became associated with Jefferson Standard Life Insurance Company.

So successful was he in the insurance business that in 1920 he founded the Central Insurance Agency with the late W.B. Upshur and Cecil Wilson as partners. (This company is now run by Thomas R. Parker.) He continued in this firm and as a special agent for Jefferson Standard until his death.

In 1910 "Mr. Johnny" was married to Miss Edna Hughson, daughter of Dr. John S. Hughson and Celeste E. Quattlebaum Hughson of Fairfield County. His sister, Lois McKnight Tolleson, who made her home with them for some years, says of her, "She was a wonderful companion and helpmate to him and they kept open house for friends and family."

In addition to his insurance business, he had extensive farming interests which he operated successfully.

He was elected to the County Board of Commissioners on June 15, 1928, and served on this Board for 27 years, filling the place of vice chairman from July 3, 1928, until Feb. 4, 1941, when he became chairman, holding that position until his death.

Always interested in the improvement of his city and county, he played a very active role in civic activities. He was a member and past president of the Kiwanis Club, a Mason and a member of the Executives Club.

He was a dedicated member of Grace Baptist Church. He was for many years a deacon, serving for a time as chairman of the board of deacons. When a building program was planned, he was chosen to serve on the committee to carry out the plans.

In 1948 Mr. McKnight was the recipient of the coveted Coca-Cola award, which was presented to "Man of the Year in Sumter."

He was lieutenant colonel on the staffs of several governors, and in 1945 Shaw Field presented him a certificate for service rendered during World War II.

The Shaw-Sumter Community Council, which came into being Nov. 24, 1953, established an award to be given to the citizen of the county making noteworthy contributions toward the promotion of good public relations between Shaw and Sumter

County and rendering exceptional service on the Council. The first recipient was Mr. McKnight and so outstanding was his service that the award was given the name the "John A. McKnight Award" in his honor, and a John A. McKnight plaque was put on display in the base commander's office, the name of each subsequent winner being placed on the plaque.

In the history of the Council the following tribute was paid to this outstanding leader: "The Council and the entire community have greatly benefited by contact with Mr. Johnnie."

Mr. McKnight died Aug. 28, 1955,[76] after a full and useful life.

Billy Gibson, well-known and respected citizen of Sumter, who at an early age began working with Mr. McKnight in the insurance business, recalls the great impact made by him in all circles of life in Sumter County. His business ability was viewed with respect by Jefferson Standard Life Insurance Company. He was often called to the main office in Greensboro, N.C., by Julian Price, president of the company, for consultation.

He was known, said Mr. Gibson, as "Mr. Sumter County," and was usually consulted by those running for office because all knew that Mr. Johnny's approval was a "big plus" in their favor.[77]

Many others who knew him have kept his memory alive by words of affection and respect.

Annie McLaughlin, Friend To The Needy

"You just can't get good medicine any more," complained Mrs. Annie McLaughlin, a beloved friend of all sick people in and around Dalzell. "Why I even have to mix my own ammoniated mercury," she continued.

In 1912 when she first came to Dalzell as the wife of Dr. Bush McLaughlin, this unusual person opened her arms and heart to the poor, the sick, the friendless, as well as to those of more fortunate circumstances.

Born April 4, 1887, in Kershaw County, daughter of Alexander C. and Tammie Gardner Watts, Annie received her early education in a log cabin. Having completed all the "learning" she could acquire in this little country school, she entered nurses' training at the State Hospital in Columbia in 1908. After a year in that institution, she transferred to Magdalene Hospital in Chester and finished the requirements for an R.N. degree while working with Dr. S.W. Pryor.

"In those days," she says, "there was no capping ceremony. I got off duty at 7 a.m. and was handed my diploma and an assignment for my first case, a doctor's widow in Whitmire."

Seeing her hesitancy about accepting the case because she had no uniforms, the doctor assured her that it was better to wear regular clothes since the patient was opposed to nurses. With this doubtful encouragement and the added assurance that the patient was going to die in a short time, she accepted the case and after a week left the patient much improved and on the road to recovery.

After this experience the brave young lady, the 118th registered nurse in South Carolina, settled in Bishopville in 1910, living with her pastor, the Rev. J.W. Davis, and his family, doing private duty nursing in the surrounding community. (There was no hospital in Bishopville at that time.)

During that year she met Dr. McLaughlin on a labor case and later was employed on one of his long-term cases. A romance blossomed, and giving up the dentist to whom she was engaged, she married the doctor instead in November, 1911.

Soon after coming to Dalzell, she was called on to nurse several typhoid fever cases attended by her husband. Having had experience in an epidemic of hemorrhagic typhoid in Wagner before her marriage, she had gained much valuable information, some of it contrary to the holdings of medical science at that time. Doctor's orders were that patients be given practically no food, but this nurse believed that if the patient did not have nourishment, he could not withstand the disease. In those cases she won the argument and saved the patients.

Not only did she practice nursing, but going with Dr. McLaughlin on his calls and assisting in his office, she learned the fundamentals of medical practice. Therefore, when his health failed in 1929, she was able to carry on the practice under his directions until his accidental death in 1941. He was hit by a car in the road near his home and lived only a short time.

Since that time "Miss Annie," as she is known throughout the community, has done much emergency treatment of patients in addition to her nursing and her obstetric work for which she holds a license. Her practice extends over Sumter, Lee and Kershaw Counties; and on occasion she has gone into Richland County.

Her experiences in midwifery have been varied and interesting as well as, in some instances, heartbreaking. Once when she was sick, a mother was brought to her office and she got out of bed to deliver her baby; however, most of her work is done in the homes — all kinds of homes. Of necessity she carried safety pins and other supplies when she went to a home, for in many cases no preparation whatever has been made for the arrival of the newcomer.

She recalls that her mother, as long as she was able, delighted in making baby clothes for "Annie" to take to the "little things" that came into homes that were too poor or too ignorant to make provision for them.

During her long career of dealing with physical needs, Mrs. McLaughlin says she has pulled out splinters, sewed up cuts, set broken bones, extracted teeth, or performed whatever task the occasion might demand. With a chuckle she says that she even lays claim to a little fame as a veterinarian since she has treated a hog, a cow, and a horse.

In addition to her nursing duties, her work as a midwife, and the constant calls for being a "friend in need," she ran her 140-acre farm until 1946 when her son returned from the duties of World War II and took over the responsibility.

The McLaughlins reared six children. Louise (Mrs. T.E. Beard), the oldest, and also an R.N., teaches in Duke Hospital. As manager of a grocery business, the oldest son, J.B., lives in Baltimore, Maryland. Managing her own grocery store at Hillcrest is Annie Lee (Mrs. Allen Harris). Three are in Sumter: Clarence, working in the General Telephone office; Fred, general manager of McLaughlin-Ford; Elizabeth (Mrs. W.L. Kennedy), working with Fred in his business.

Though past threescore years and ten, Mrs. McLaughlin is in good health and still works regularly, delivering an average of 100 babies each year, 1959 being the peak year with 129.

Living in a comfortable home in the heart of the little town of Dalzell, she enjoys the companionship of her niece, Mrs. Marie Felder, who lives with her. In her "spare" time she raises lovely flowers and prize tomatoes.

A loyal member of the Horeb Baptist Church, "Miss Annie" was president of the missionary society for 27 consecutive years. From comments of others, one can easily believe that she daily puts her Christian faith into practice. Someone said that she voluntarily returns to see her patients, taking appetizing dishes, especially to those in need.

A person of strong convictions, Mrs. McLaughlin is not afraid "to stand up and be counted," whether the issue be political, economic, social, or religious.

Her keen sense of humor has "saved the day" in many trying experiences. Her love of life is manifested in the zest and enthusiasm with which she enters into the program of the Golden Age Club. She recalls with pleasure the "fun" she had taking the part of the groom in a mock wedding staged by the club.

In the many facets of her long and exceedingly useful life can be seen what some philosopher calls, "The Triple Alliance of the three great powers: Love, Sympathy and Help."

(Note: This sketch was written in 1968. Mrs. McLaughlin continued her active life until approximately six months before her death in August of 1975 at the age of 85.)[78]

Miss Linnie McLaurin's Influence And Example Still Inspire Many

"Where there is hatred, let me sow love.
Where there is injury, pardon,
Where there is doubt, faith."

These words from St. Francis of Assisi have been very aptly used in describing Miss Leonora C. McLaurin, that great educator whose influence for good continues to live through the lives of countless ones whom she taught.

In 1896[79] Miss McLaurin, recommended by Dr. S.H. Edmunds, superintendent, was employed as a teacher by the Sumter City Schools. After one year, however, she left Sumter to teach in the science department at Winthrop College; but because of a health problem, she returned in 1902 to her home in Sumter to recuperate.

A group of neighborhood mothers, led by the mother of Miss Julia Reynolds, persuaded "Miss Linnie" to begin a private school in her home for their children. She consented and for four years she was a guiding star for these small boys and girls – first in the family living room and then in a small building in the back yard.

In 1906 she again accepted work in the city school system, where she and Dr. Edmunds, a master teacher and superintendent, built a name for the Sumter schools. They were a matchless team in the field of education.

Miss Linnie knew her pupils so well that she was able to detect the cause of their problems and to help in the solution of most of their difficulties. Somehow learning the background of each, she could identify with each one, though she had large classes; and even during her many years as principal of the Girls High School, she seemed to understand each pupil under her care and showed a special interest in the physical, mental, and spiritual welfare of all on a one-to-one basis.

Tall, with an imposing stature, she commanded the respect of all whom she met. But her sweetness of character and her keen sense of humor quickly dispelled any fears one might have in her presence.

Her keen mind made clear any mental problems faced by her pupils in their classwork.

In an article written by Miss Julia Reynolds for the **Sumter High News** after her death were these words which tell of her idea of discipline for young people: "She never condoned wrongdoing or minimized it; but also she never failed in kindness to the culprit, making him feel that there was still a chance for him, building up his faith in himself."

In 1935, upon the death of Dr. Edmunds, Miss Linnie was made acting superintendent, serving until Mr. Loggins came the following year.

She resigned from public school work in 1937, and with her sister, Miss Ruth McLaurin, conducted a private business school in the little building in her back yard which she had used years before.

In 1949 death came, ending a span of 53 years as teacher, principal and superintendent. But the influence exerted in those years will continue to live in Sumter and wherever those whose lives she touched may be. And as those who knew her tell their children of her influence, her great example will continue to inspire.

On the day following her death, a memorial service was held for her at the Junior High School where she had spent so many hours lovingly ministering to the youth of Sumter.

A beautiful tribute was paid her memory by Hugh T. Stoddard, who had worked with her for six years and knew her many fine qualities. He closed his remarks with these words:

"Born for service, she lived in service. Because of Miss Linnie C. McLaurin, Sumter is a better town in which to live."

A resolution of sympathy passed by the Sumter Class Room organization contained these words:

"In scholarship and ability to teach, in leadership and administration she was outstanding; in character, a rare combination of integrity, loyalty, devotion to duty and kindness . . . "

On April 16, 1950, a little more than a year after her death, a memorial service was held at the Junior High School, at which time a plaque was unveiled, naming the building the Linnie McLaurin School.

As a further indication of their respect, esteem and devotion, the many whose lives she had touched and inspired presented on October 28, 1951, a portrait of Miss Linnie to the school named in her honor.

Expressive of the character of Miss Linnie McLaurin is a poem written by a fellow teacher, L. Clifton Moise, one stanza of which reads:

"Housed in her body was a brilliant mind,
Obedient servant to her noble heart,
These taught her well to match the scales of justice,

To gauge the unfilled pail, to winnow chaff
From grain, to deal unyielding with deceit,
To trust in triumph fo good o'er ill, to keep
Unfaltering faith in God and love of man."

Dr. McLaurin Left Lasting Imprint

As a skilled physician and surgeon, a courageous soldier, a successful businessman, a devoted husband and father, a Christian gentleman, Henry James McLaurin made a lasting imprint on the history of Sumter County.

Son of Daniel Benjamin and Agnes Chandler McLaurin, he was born in Sumterville on January 16, 1838,[80] and spent his boyhood days in what was then a very small town. His early education was obtained in a private school on the corner of East Liberty and Reardon Streets. The school was run by a Mrs. Rice.

Somewhat later, when his father was employed as contractor for the Manchester-Augusta Railroad (the first railroad to reach Sumter), the family moved to Manchester and lived in the old Matthew Singleton home, "Melrose." In those days country schools were few indeed. In order for the McLaurin children to get an education, D.B. McLaurin and the Ramseys who lived nearby, employed a tutor for the two families. This "live-in" teacher was Miss Vermelle Arthur, sister of Chester Arthur, who later became President of the United States.

Her instruction must have been thorough, for Henry was able to enter Davidson College with her preparation. He later transferred to the University of Virginia for his pre-medical training. He then entered the Medical College of South Carolina in Charleston, where he received his degree in internal medicine and surgery in 1857.

His first practice was in Manning, where he remained until the outbreak of the War Between the States. One of the first to volunteer in the defense of his state, he joined Company C of the Manning Guards. Finding that the conflict was destined to last longer than he had at first thought, he stood an examination and was appointed Assistant Surgeon in the Hampton Legion. In October, 1863, he received an assignment with the 7th South Carolina Cavalry, Haskell's Regiment, Gary's Brigade, later becoming Surgeon in that command and remaining at this post of duty till the end of the war. He was present at the fall of Fort Sumter and in the Battle of Manassas, as well as in many other engagements.

While in service he showed compassionate concern for all – Southerners and Northerners. Some years after the conflict had ended, he had a letter from a former Northern soldier whose arm he had set after one of the battles, inviting him up for a visit. Of course, it was too soon after the war. All the atrocities that the Federal troops had inflicted on the South were still fresh in his mind. Nor had the South yet recovered from the indignities perpetrated during the Reconstruction (as it was called) era. Dr. McLaurin just couldn't picture himself making a social visit with a Northerner.

Many times he referred to the surrender of General Lee at Appomattox as one of the saddest experiences of his life. It was heartbreaking to see his beloved general humiliated. However, he also recalled with appreciation the generosity of General Grant in allowing the officers to keep their mounts. Thus he was able to ride home on a gray horse to be reunited with his young wife.

He had married on August 20, 1863, Elizabeth McFaddin, daughter of Hugh and Margaret Montgomery McFaddin. It was said that "Bessie" in her youthful days was much sought after by the young gentry, but eventually she made a wise choice by accepting Dr. H.J. McLaurin, by whom they have a large and interesting family, mostly daughters.

She had remained at her father's home, "Fullwood," near Midway Presbyterian Church in Clarendon County, until her young husband returned from the war. They continued to live in the same community until their fourth child was born.

Seeking better educational advantages for his children, he moved to the High Hills section of Sumter County, occupying for a while his father's plantation home "Argyle," near Wedgefield. He later built his own home, "Sterling," across the road from his father's home. Here he lived and practiced medicine from 1869 until December of 1886.

Those were difficult days, but dedicated to his profession and sympathetic with all who suffered, Dr. McLaurin spent himself in service for others. He traveled by buggy over unpaved roads, which in bad weather were rough indeed. Or he rode horseback with his instruments and medicines in saddlebags. He traveled from Manchester to Hagood, sometimes 15 or 20 miles on a single call.

He dispensed such medicines as quinine, calomel, castor oil, rhubarb, Dover's powder; and his best antiseptic was turpentine. Whenever necessary he performed operations or set broken bones, using often the kitchen table as an operating table. Since hospitals were few and far between, he often took very ill patients to his home to be nursed by his efficient wife. No situation was too difficult for him to handle and usually the result was successful.

It could well be said that he did not work for money. It was considered unethical for a doctor to send a bill to a patient, but he answered the calls of distress nonetheless. Many patients were unable to pay anything, and others paid with pork, beef, poultry or other farm produce.

This strenuous life broke the health of Dr. McLaurin, and upon the advice of Dr. John A. Bossard and Dr. Julius A. Mood, he gave up his practice and moved back to Sumter.

In order to support his family and educate his ten children, he established a lumber business with his son as a partner, the name of the firm being Henry J. McLaurin and Son. Since his mill was built in the pine woods of Sumter County, he named the little town that grew up Pinewood, the name being suggested by the location.

There was only one small school in that vicinity at that time and his mill supplied the lumber for the benches and desks. The teacher of this little school was Miss Lizzie Moore, a friend of the McLaurins.

Desirous that his children should have better educational advantages, he continued to live in Sumter, though his business was some distance away. The Sumter Institute, run by Mrs. Eliza Brown, offered splendid educational opportunities for the eight girls, and the two sons attended a good private school for boys which was under the direction of Mr. Len Dick and his brother, Dr. Aleck Dick.

In 1888, soon after returning to Sumter from Wedgefield, he bought the large home on "New" Street, which is now Salem Avenue, from Mrs. McConico Haynsworth.

Interested in the civic progress of his town, Dr. McLaurin served as an alderman for several years. He was a loyal and devoted member of the First Presbyterian Church of Sumter and took an active part in its work, serving as ruling elder until his death.

Highly respected and loved by those who knew him, he left many friends to mourn his passing on May 7, 1921.[81] The beloved wife and mother of this home died in 1918.

Dr. McLaurin and Mrs. McLaurin were buried in the cemetery near the quaint little Presbyterian Church in Wedgefield – a church that he had helped to build and which the family has loved through the years.

Surviving father and mother were the ten children: Henry J., Jr., Hugh, Mrs. J.D. Ryan, Mrs. W.J. Shaw, Misses Helen, Catherine, Leonora (Linnie), Isabel, Ruth and Cornelia. And through these sons and daughters the influence of Dr. Henry J. McLaurin and Mrs. McLaurin was passed on to the following generations. McLaurin Junior High School is a monument to the memory of "Miss Linnie," who stood for education at its best. Other members of the family, too, played their respective roles in making Sumter County a better place in which to live.

Richard Irvine Manning (Profile)

Richard Irvine Manning, born of an illustrious family in 1859 at Holmesley Plantation in Sumter County,[82] was said to have had within his person much of the aims, purposes and culture that made South Carolina distinctive at that time.

He was educated in local schools, Kenmore Preparatory School in Virginia and after completing a pre-law course at the University of Virginia, he returned home where he immediately became interested in public affairs, especially the farmers' concerns.

In 1892 he was elected to the State House of Representatives and to the Senate in 1898. In these offices he worked for improved public education, fiscal reform, better roads and county health service.

Coming from a long line of governors on both sides of his family, he naturally had ambitions for that office. Therefore, in 1906 he entered the race but was defeated.

Not discouraged, however, he ran again in 1914 and was elected. He served two two-year terms, 1915-1919, and his accomplishments were indeed noble.

Though interested in public affairs, Manning was not considered a politician. In his first inaugural address he said, "From my earliest youth the ambition to be governor of South Carolina has filled my breast. To serve my state is my ardent desire – to join all other patriotic citizens in the effort to do her service – and to help in the upbuilding of her resources and in the character of her citizenship."

He was able during his time in office to bring about many changes needed in the government of the state. He is credited with reform of the State Hospital, the improvement of law enforcement, the abolishment of race-track gambling, creation of a state board of arbitration and conciliation, reinstatement and reorganization of the National Guard, creation of a tax commission, establishment of a state board of charities and corrections, founding of an institution for the feeble minded (Whitten Village), opening of the State Tuberculosis Hospital. He promoted broadening of town and country educational opportunities. He led in securing the first appropriation for the "moonlight schools" initiated by Wil Lou Gray in Laurens County. This was the beginning of adult education. Today thousands of adults receive high school diplomas through this program.

While in office, Governor Manning worked for and obtained many other worthwhile changes for the citizens of the state. He was especially interested in the improvement of the needy.

During World War I he set an example of patriotism that all could have well emulated. Six of his sons volunteered for service and one gave his life. He himself served as aid and advisor to President Wilson.

He was dedicated to his church, holding a place of leadership in the Episcopal Church of South Carolina, and after the division of the church, he was an outstanding layman in the Diocese of Upper South Carolina. It was said by one who knew him, "His faith in God and devotion to the work of the church were apparent to all who knew him. In the best sense he was a religious man."

His son spoke of his faith as "the faith of a child in its simplicity; his absolute dependence on his Maker and his absolute belief in the efficacy of prayer."

Mr. Herbert A. Moses, one of Sumter's own, who served as Governor Manning's secretary, said of him: "He was liberal with his means. He was always a generous giver . . . particularly in matters that he thought were for the upbuilding of the community, city, state and nation."

Another spoke of his gentleness and thoughtfulness.

An alert businessman, Governor Manning managed successfully several plantations, was a successful bank president, a director in a number of business corporations, active in local and national church affairs, active in the state Democratic Party, and a trustee of Clemson College.

Richard Irvine Manning was Sumter's last governor and one of whom the county can well be proud.

John Blount Miller, A Founding Father

A simple epitaph on a simple monument in the cemetery of Bethel Church, Privateer, marks the resting place of one of the guiding spirits in the early development of the city of Sumter, then known as Sumterville.

This man was John Blount Miller, born in Charleston October 16, 1782,[83] of Scotch ancestry. His father, Andrew Miller, had come from Scotland to North Carolina in 1763.

Although little is known of his early life and educational advantages, it is certain that he received the best instruction available at the time. After a few years as a merchant in Augusta, Georgia, he began the study of law in 1801 with his brother-in-law, Samuel Mathis, Esq., in Camden. He later continued his study in Charleston.

Admitted to the Bar as an attorney-at-law in 1805, he came to Sumterville, which had been selected as the seat of justice for the Sumter District in 1800. At this time the town was very small. In fact, it is said that 12 years after the town was first settled, a lady passing through was "much surprised to learn that it was really Sumterville."

John Blount Miller was possibly the first resident lawyer in the town. He was the first Notary Public in the district, and in 1807 he began practice as Solicitor of Equity.

In July, 1808, John B. Miller was married to Mary Murrell, daughter of William Murrell, Esq., one of the last three judges of the county court before the consolidation of Claremont, Clarendon, and Salem Counties into the "new circuit court unit known as Sumter District." Mr. and Mrs. Miller were the parents of seven daughters and two sons.

Gaining in prestige as an able lawyer and gifted orator, he extended his legal practice year by year. In 1817 he was appointed by the governor as Commissioner and Registrar of the First Court of Equity in Sumter District, holding this position until his death.

Testifying to the meticulous care exercised by John B. Miller in keeping records was the method used while Commissioner in the Court of Equity. At his own expense he had bags of cloth in which he placed all papers pertaining to each case, labeling and filing each packet so that it could be found easily. A system growing out of the method was later adopted by law for all equity offices in the state.

A man of tireless energy, he took an active part in the political life of his district and state, serving as a member of the legislature at one time and also as a member of the Nullification Convention of South Carolina.

During the War of 1812 this loyal patriot was a captain of Light Infantry, later becoming a major, and finally lieutenant-colonel; thus the title of "Colonel" was his for the rest of his life.

Ever a great influence in the cultural development of the village, Colonel Miller was president of the first Library Society, known as the Sumterville Circulating Library Society. He and Mrs. Miller donated nine books as a supplement to the first purchase of books, which included only ten titles.

Public education in Sumterville received a very strong boost from Colonel Miller. When the General Assembly passed an Act in 1811 stating that "Free Schools were to be established in each election district," he was one of the first Board of seven Free School Commissioners for Claremont election district.

Later, recognizing the need for schools and desiring to promote this worthy cause, he signed a deed of conveyance to the Trustees of the Sumterville Academical Society for the "improvement of the children of said village and its vicinity," for the sum of one dollar, one acre of land on the corner of what is now Liberty and Washington Streets for the "purpose of erecting a suitable building for an Academy." This square was known for many years as Academy Square.[84]

The Academical Society held its first meeting in 1837 and elected John Blount Miller as president.

Judging from these examples, one can see that Sumter owes much to this public-spirited citizen for his worthwhile contributions to the early educational growth in this town.

In addition to all of his many civic responsibilities and interests, Colonel Miller found time to publish two books – **A Collection of the Militia Laws of the United States and South Carolina, That Are of Force** and **Instructions for Guardians and Trustees.**

Colonel Miller's religious life was of paramount importance to him and a strong influence in the life of the community. According to the records, he was the guiding spirit in the organization in Sumterville of a branch of High Hills Baptist Church. (This branch later became the First Baptist Church of Sumter.) John B. Miller became the first clerk of the church and he is said to have filled the office with "peculiar efficiency," keeping an exact record of every meeting, giving texts of sermons, and listing items that make the record of this church of great value today – more than 100 years later. He was known also for his liberality in all contributions made to and through the church.[85]

In 1837 Colonel Miller moved with his family to his plantation in the Privateer section of Sumter County. There he proved a devoted member and faithful deacon of Bethel Baptist Church, where his former evidence of generosity were no less pronounced.

Included in the records of the church are copies of deeds of conveyance for a plot of two acres adjoining the churchyard to be used for a cemetery and nearby a one-acre plot for the Negroes of the community.

The death of Colonel Miller on October 21, 1851,[86] brought to a close the earthly life of one who had lived in such a manner that his influence, demonstrated in many ways, is felt even today.

Tributes from far and near have been paid this great benefactor of mankind. "In order to perpetuate his memory," the Sumter Bar Association passed a resolution asking that William Harrison Scarborough, son-in-law of Colonel Miller, paint a portrait of him. This portrait when completed was hung in the office of the Commissioner in Equity in the old courthouse.

A tribute that might best summarize the life of this great man is found in the history of the First Baptist Church of Sumter: "After a long life of usefulness, the Colonel died in 1851. But he has left a worthy record, not only in words written with a pen, but in works which are imperishable. Life is a real privilege when spent in a noble calling, and it should be a source of great satisfaction to know that we can direct our efforts as to compel others who come after us to rise up and call us blessed."

Perry Moses, Sr. (Profile)

Perry Moses, Sr., was born in Sumter in 1843,[87] one of the 17 children of Andrew Jackson and Octavia Harby Moses.

He was a student at the Citadel when the War Between the States began, and though quite young, he joined the Confederates as a member of Palmetto Guards of Charleston. From there he went to Virginia in Kershaw's Second South Carolina Regimet.

He fought in the First Battle of Manassas, Manchester and Falls Church before being transferred to Culpepper's battery and was staioned at James Island for one year. He then joined McNair's Arkansas brigade, going into the campaign to relieve Vicksburg. Culpepper's battery was sent to Mobile for the defense of that city.

The great battle of Chickamauga was the next major engagement in which Moses took part. Again his unit was ordered to Mobile and divided into three parts to man the forts defending Mobile. Having been promoted to the rank of lieutenant, he was put in charge of one of the forts, Fort Powell. Admiral Farragut ran past the three forts, however, and captured Mobile. The Confederates were forced to evacuate the forts and swim back to the mainland.

Moses was wounded at Fort Blakely. His younger brother was wounded and his older brother killed. In a hospital in Mobile, where he was taken for treatment, he was married to Miss Rosalie Virginia Levy, daughter of Mr. Jack Levy of New Orleans. The family were refugees in Mobile.

Almost immediately he was forced to flee from the Federal troops who had entered the city. On this same day, Lee had surrendered in Virginia, but the news had not reached Alabama.

It was three months later that he returned to claim his bride, arriving in New Orleans by stage.

They settled in Sumter, but for some reason he was unhappy with conditions in his home town, and after some months they returned to Louisiana. There he became a planter, growing cotton and sugar cane for eighteen years. While there, Mr. and Mrs. Moses became the parents of four sons and three daughters.

Returning to Sumter he became engaged in the sawmill business and somewhat later in the oil mill business, accumulating from these endeavors considerable property. Some years before his death, in 1916, he retired, but he still kept an interest in business affairs, operating a small farm near town and holding the presidency of the Sumter Roller Mills Company.

Always interested in the meetings and activities of Confederate Veterans, Mr. Moses held the office of Commandant of Dick Anderson Camp, going as a delegate from the camp to most of the meetings.

An honor that came to him was the appointment on a commission sent to Chickamauga to help mark the lines of the South Carolina troops on this important battlefield.

Perry Moses, Sr., was said to have been "a man of strong views and plain words"; and he was always ready to state his views and defend the side of a question on which he stood, it is recalled by those who knew him. This trait was admirably shown in his loyalty to the Confederacy, serving honorably as he did throughout the War of Secession.

George Washington Murray

Congressman from the 7th District of South Carolina, 1893-1897, George Washington Murray was the last of eight black Congressmen from the state to serve in this capacity during the Reconstruction period.

Murray was born a slave in 1853 in the area of Rembert in Sumter County, but he became the largest landowner in the county. In a paper given in March 1980 by John S. Hoar at a meeting of The Fortnightly Club, the writer gave several sources of information. Among them was *History of Sumter County* by Anne King Gregorie, which gave H.G. Osteen, founder and editor of the **Sumter Daily Item**, as her authority.

Murray was described in this book as being "not an ordinary Negro in appearance, intellectual ability, education, or attainments and business . . . " in the era in which he lived. He became a leader in politics, having a voice in Republican conventions both local and state. In 1890 he was appointed Inspector of Customs at Charleston.

Having proved his ability among the Negroes of his community, he ran for Congress in 1892 against Gen. E.W. Moise, a lawyer of recognized ability in his community, and "was given the certificate of election by the Tillmanites" by a margin of 40 votes.

Hoar expressed surprise that a black Republican candidate "could have survived politically so many years after the overthrow of radical Republican rule by Wade Hampton."

In Washington, Murray fought for the common people, making some very strong speeches. He believed that the "financial system of the time was producing a 'small group of millioniares and an abundant harvest of paupers'." His speeches were strong and eloquent, hardly indicative of a man with little formal education.

Since he apparently had no white blood in his veins, he appealed to a large group of voters that put him into office.

During his years in Washington he made strong arguments against the "Silver Purchase Act of 1890." His appeal for the common man received prolonged applause, but it failed to win necessary votes for repeal of the measure.

Murray was reseated in 1896 for another term in Congress – his last.

No longer in politics he turned his attention to land development. Gregorie says he returned "to the Rafting Creek community with a good deal of money. He purchased tract after tract of land . . . " It seems that he divided his land into small tracts which he sold to Negroes. They were to pay for their tracts on the installment plan, forfeiting their ownership if they failed to keep the terms of the contract.

William Gaboury, a history professor at Southern Oregon State College, quoted by Hoar in his paper, said that "by 1902 he had placed up to two hundred families on nine thousand acres of land."

It was apparently one of his land deals that brought an end of Murray's career in South Carolina. In 1903 he brought a suit against a man and his son who had purchased 25 acres of land and had defaulted on the contract. In the suit, however, there was a discrepancy between the contract he held and the one in the possession of the other man. He was accused of forgery, though he denied any intention to defraud, and was prosecuted in 1904.

The case was tried by Judge Robert O. Purdy. Murray's lawyer, Marion Moise, son of General Moise, asked for a directed verdict in favor of the defendant on the grounds that "nothing but an innocent mistake had been shown." However, the case was sent to the jury who found him guilty. He was released on a bond of $2,000 and Mr. Moise made an appeal to the South

Carolina Supreme Court, which upheld the lower court verdict.

According to some sources, Mr. Hoar said, the bail was raised to $10,000. However, he forfeited the bail, whatever it was, and left for Chicago.

He later made a deed for a large acreage to his lawyer and gave him power of attorney to dispose of the remainder of his land.

Mr. Hoar, giving *History of Sumter County* by Gregorie as his source, said that this remarkable man in his earlier days went to the local public school for Negroes established soon after the Civil War, and from 1874 to 1876 he was a student at what is now the University of South Carolina. So far as is known this was the extent of his formal education, but he apparently made the best possible use of his opportunities, appropriating every opportunity for adding to his intellectual growth.

He later taught school and farmed for a period of 15 years. Dr. Gregorie says, "Out in his field at dawn, he followed his furrows until time to walk to school, several miles away. There he taught the swarming children the required number of hours, then hurried to his farm to work until dark, and on moonlight nights for many more hours."

Though Murray had little formal education, his breadth of knowledge and his ability to express his ideas in polished language would put to shame many today who have had the best in educational advantages.

Hoar in concluding his paper on Murray quotes Gahoury as saying: "Certainly George W. Murray played a more dynamic and constructive role in American history than published accounts have indicated thus far."

Shepard Kollock Nash (Profile)

Here was a man who stood high in the legal profession not only in Sumter but throughout South Carolina. He had, too, a special place in the affections of those who knew him.

Mr. Nash was born in Sumter December 13, 1893, the son of the late Shepard and Ann Nash. He was graduated from the local city schools and Davidson College.[88]

Unique in his manner of receiving a legal education, he read law and passed the South Carolina Bar without ever attending a law school. A fellow member of the legal profession said of him that he knew more law than the law schools taught. During his 60 years of legal practice, he was one of South Carolina's most highly esteemed in the profession. He was qualified to practice before all state and federal courts and was a special judge for common pleas and general sessions court on several occasions.

Interested also in politics, he was chairman of the Sumter Democratic Party for 18 years. He served in the South Carolina Senate for three terms and in the House of Representatives for one term.

In his busy legal and political life, he also found time to become involved in a number of businesses. He served on the board of directors of the National Bank of South Carolina for 22 years, and at the time of his death, he was chairman emeritus of that board. He was also on the board of directors of First Federal Savings and Loan.

Mr. Nash took great interest in civic affairs, giving of his time and effort to the growth and improvement of his city. He was instrumental, for instance, in raising funds for the YMCA and was on the board of directors of that institution for 14 years. He was always ready to lend his aid in the Community Chest and other fund-raising projects for the community. He was a Kiwanian, a Mason, a member of the Elks Club and a Shriner, taking an active part in the work of these organizations.

Willing to make a contribution toward the education of the youth of the city, he served on the board of trustees for some time.

He held leadership positions in his church, The First Presbyterian.

It was said of Mr. Nash that whenever anything needed to be done for the good of others, he was available to fill the need. What a tribute this is! It implies that whenever a service could be rendered, he was not only willing, but he had the wisdom and ability to meet the need.

Sumter will rightfully revere the memory of Shepard K. Nash.

Neill O'Donnell (Profile)

Neill O'Donnell, one of the acknowledged leaders in the early years of Sumter's history, lives on today in the educational, business and humanitarian life of the city and county.

He was born in Ardora Parrish in the County of Donnegal, Ireland, in the year 1859. Fifteen years later the family came to America, settling in Pennsylvania. Young Neill continued his education at Wyoming Seminary.[89]

Influenced by some relatives living in Anderson, South Carolina, he came to that town and began work in the textile industry. It is thought by some that he came to Sumter while traveling for George W. Wagner and Company of Charleston and called on William Bogin, a merchant operating on Main Street near

Dugan. The story continues that he began work as a clerk for Mr. Bogin; and when the owner died in 1887, O'Donnell became manager of this highly successful business.

It has been said that the stores on Main Street from Hampton to Liberty catered to the more urban citizens, while those below Liberty served agricultural interests. Many living today recall buying merchandise of practically every kind and of the finest quality from O'Donnell and Company, located on Main Street between Liberty and Dugan.

In 1887 the young merchant was married to Kate Bogin, second daughter of William and Johanna Dowling Bogin. The older daughter was married to Timothy J. Tuomey and the youngest Bogin sister was the wife of Arthur O'Neill. The Bogins had one son, William, who was married to Agnes Moise. Little is known of him.

The Bogin home was adjacent to the store but was later moved to East Liberty by Neill and Kate O'Donnell. Still later it was extensively renovated, becoming one of the finest homes in Sumter. It was furnished throughout with beautiful and expensive antiques.

According to Mrs. O'Donnell's will, the home was left to the Catholic church and became St. Catherine's Convent, but was later sold and became Shelley-Brunson Funeral Home.

While the O'Donnells were living there, other fine homes were built and the area was referred to as "Little Dublin." The social life of the O'Donnells was for the most part connected with St. Anne's Catholic Church.

O'Donnell and Company was incorporated and a charter was granted in 1906 and the business continued under the capable leadership of the president, who was always Neill O'Donnell. Vice president of the new corporation was S.R. Chandler; treasurer was David W. Cuttino. J.O. Barwick was bookeeper and later manager of the real estate properties. These officers remained in charge until Mr. O'Donnell's death in 1937. At that time, Messrs. John D. Lee, J.B. Britton, W.E. Bynum, F.B. Creech, T.H. Parker and Messrs. Chandler and Cuttino became the Board of O'Donnell and Company and this committee was instrumental in carrying out Mr. O'Donnell's will which called for the dissolving of the company within a three-year period after his death and stipulated that all assets of the corporation be turned over to Tuomey Hospital.

Before his death, Mr. O'Donnell had great influence and exerted strong leadership in the establishment of Tuomey Hospital. He worked conscientiously in carrying out Mr. and Mrs. Tuomey's wills in regard to the establishment of a hospital for the "benefit of the respectable sick and poor people of the city."

He spent time and money in improving the properties left by the Tuomeys for this purpose.

For eight years he was president of the Board of Trustees and in 1921 when Mr. I.C. Strauss was made president, he became treasurer, which position he held until his death.

In 1930 when there was need for expansion of the hospital and funds were being sought, he gave $10,000. The O'Donnell Wing was built in 1961 and the Nurses Home was named in his honor. The value of the O'Donnell estate now held by Tuomey Hospital is said to be approximately $1,300,000.

Not only was Mr. O'Donnell a successful businessman, but he was a proficient financier, being considered one of Sumter's leading banking figures. He became president of the First National Bank in 1910 and remained in this position until the bank became a part of South Carolina National in 1930. He remained on the Board of Directors until his death. He was always found to be fair and ethical in all his financial dealings.

In 1894 he became a member of the Sumter City School Board and remained in that position for 43 years, serving part of the time as vice chairman and part of the time as chairman. He was keenly aware of the educational needs of the community and intensely interested in making opportunities available for all the youth of Sumter.[90]

He exerted considerable influence on city government, serving one term on the city council. On countless occasions, elected officials conferred with him concerning the resolution of important problems facing them.

His guidance was sought by many businesses of the city. For instance, he was largely responsible for the organization of O.L. Williams Furniture Corporation. He served on the boards of the Sumter Casket Company and the Sumter Machinery Company. He was president of the Sumter Ice and Fuel Company, although the controlling interest was owned by the E.H. Moses family.

It was Mr. O'Donnell who assisted in the establishment of Gallagher and Foxworth, a very successful clothing store on Main Street in the past, and he was instrumental in the formation of Commins Grocery Store that had a thriving business at one time on Liberty Street.

Always kind and sympathetic, he tried whenever possible to avoid foreclosing mortgages while president of the bank. On one occasion he was known to have paid $10,000 from his own account to keep a man from losing his home.

His humanitarian and generous spirit was shown in the influence, interest and leadership he exerted in the establishment and supervision of the financial foundation of Tuomey Hospital.

He was always considerate and sensitive to the needs of others, often giving anonymously to meet an emergency. He arranged a $3,000 trust fund for the income to go to needy families at Christmas, a gift which is usually used by the Salvation Army.

Though somewhat retiring, he had a warm and friendly nature. He was highly respected and those who knew him counted themselves privileged.

It can truly be said that the good that Neill O'Donnell did lives after him.

Noah Graham Osteen (Profile)

One of the pioneers in the history of Sumter's Press was Gen. Noah Graham Osteen born January 25, 1843, son of Charles LeRoy and Elizabeth Weston Osteen. His maternal grandfather was Jonathan Weston, at whose home in the Concord section of Sumter County he was born. His maternal grandmother was Mary Pringle, daughter of William Pringle, from the same section of the county.

His paternal great-grandfather came from North Carolina and settled in the Privateer section of the county near Bethel Church, but later he moved to Mississippi.

Jacob Osteen, the paternal grandfather of Noah, remained in Sumter County and his wife was Elizabeth Hilton.

As a young lad, Noah lived on his father's farm and took advantage of whatever educational opportunities were available at that time.

Somehow he was greatly interested in printing, and whenever he was able to get to Sumter, he would visit the printing office. It was then that he decided definitely that he wanted to be a printer.

And so it was that in 1855, when he was only 12 years of age, he learned that the **Sumter Watchman** wanted two boys, preferably from the country, to learn the printing business.

Accompanied by his father, young Noah Osteen went to see Mr. A.A. Gilbert of the firm of Gilbert and Richardson. Although there was some objection to his small size, he was taken on trial. Later he became an apprentice with a five-year contract with Gilbert and Darr, Richardson having sold his share of the paper to H.L. Darr. The first year he received board, clothes and 25 cents a week. After that his monetary remuneration increased somewhat, but it was never over 50 cents a week. The last year he received $50 to buy his own clothes.

When he had completed his apprenticeship, he was sent to Conway to publish a paper which the company owned there. In 1862, however, the publication there ended, and he joined Col.

J.P. Thomas' Battalion of Reserves and was sent to a printing office to print Confederate money. After that he worked on a paper edited by Henry Timrod.

At Sherman's approach to Columbia, he went into active service. Printing presses and other equipment were hidden in Chester and Charlotte during the raid.

The paper began publication again in Charleston in 1865 where General Osteen worked as foreman of the press. (After the paper ceased publication in Charleston, he returned to his home in Sumter.)

While in Charleston he married, Mar. 6, 1866, Mrs. Esther Anne Doar Anderson, daughter of Thomas and Louise Ann Doar of Christ Church Parish, Charleston County. Into this family were born three sons and one daughter; namely N.G. Osteen, Jr., Charles P. Osteen, both of whom became doctors; Hubert G. Osteen, who followed his father in the newspaper business; and Mrs. E.H. Schirmer of Columbia.

Upon coming back to Sumter, he bought half interest in **The Sumter News** (1866), being published by H.L. Darr. Later the name of the paper was changed to **The True Southron** and it fought vigorously against the "carpetbag" and "scalawag" rule that was taking over in the South at that time, and the ownership worked tirelessly for the election of Wade Hampton as governor of the state.

In 1881 General Osteen purchased from Mr. Darr his interest in the **True Southron** and purchased at the same time **The Sumter Watchman**, later consolidating the two papers into **The Watchman and Southron.**

In 1894 he began the publication of a daily paper, **The Sumter Item**, and **The Watchman and Southron** was subsequently changed to a semi-weekly and continued until 1933.

From this brief look at the life of Noah Graham Osteen, one can see that his deep and dedicated interest in newspaper publication grew steadily from his early youth. Until his accidental death, which came Sunday, November 8, 1936, he worked continuously on his paper, even to the last. In fact, on the day when he suffered his fatal accident (November 5), he had worked all morning at his office reading proof for the paper. He seldom took a holiday and missed very few days from his work.

During the War Between the States, he served as Brigadier General of the Second Brigade, C.S.A., and as Major General was commander of the South Carolina Division, U.C.V. After the war he was a member of Camp Dick Anderson United Confederate Veterans of Sumter, and he attended most Confederate reunions, where he enjoyed seeing many of his close friends from all parts of South Carolina.

General Osteen had a long, busy and useful life, serving unselfishly his community to which he was deeply devoted. He was the epitome of good journalism, and Sumter can always be grateful to him for his years of devotion to his calling and the important contributions he made to life in this area.

Theodosia Dargan Plowden

Born in Darlington March 9, 1884,[91] Theodosia Dargan Plowden, daughter of Col. John J. Dargan and Theodosia Green Williamson, came to Stateburg with her family while she was still young.

She studied music in Columbia and taught in her father's school, the General Thomas Sumter Academy.

After her marriage to S. Oliver Plowden, a successful planter in Sumter and Clarendon Counties, she lived in the country for some years. It was during this time that she became interested in the life of farm women and began pioneering in the advancement of club work among rural families. She was one of the organizers of the Farm Women's Council of South Carolina in 1921. Through her influence, interest was growing rapidly in the Home Demonstration Club movement. In fact, she was so dedicated to the cause of improving rural family life that she went into full-time work as a demonstration agent under the Clemson College Extension Service.

She advanced from a local to a district agent and in this capacity she supervised the Home Demonstration Club work in 15 counties in the Pee Dee area of the state. She gave herself untiringly to this worthy cause and her efforts meant much to farm homemakers in the important task of food preservation and nutrition.

In the meantime, she and Mr. Plowden moved to the Dargan home in Stateburg, "Marston." From there she carried on her work and he commuted to his other farms.

But Mrs. Plowden was a woman of many interests and talents and was engaged in numerous activities. A gifted musician, she led the choir in the Episcopal Church of the Holy Cross in Stateburg for many years.

She was an active member of the Sumter County Historical Society and served as president at one time. She was also a member of the Sumter County Historical Commission, a charter member of the Stateburg Literary and Musical Society, serving as president. She also had the honor of being chosen as president of the State Federation of Women's Clubs.

Mrs. Plowden died February 21, 1975,[92] leaving a legacy of much good accomplished in her long and useful life.

Poinsett, Man Of Varied Interests

In the graveyard of the Church of the Holy Cross in Stateburg stands a simple tomb marking the resting place of one of South Carolina's greatest patriots.

Though Sumter County cannot claim Joel Roberts Poinsett as her very own, she proudly hails him as one who represented the state worthily in many ways.

This versatile Carolinian was born in Charleston on March 2, 1779,[93] amid the noise of guns and shouts of confusion caused by the war of revolt against Great Britain.

Seeking religious freedom after the revocation of the Edict of Nantes in 1685, French Huguenots came to America, many finding homes in South Carolina.

One of these refugees was Pierre Poinsett. Among his children was a son, also named Pierre, who was the progenitor of the Poinsett family in this state. It is said that the first Pierre was very poor, coming over probably as an indentured servant. Like all Huguenots, he taught his children thrift and industry; and they soon made a place for themselves in the colony.

In the mid-eighteenth century, Elisha Poinsett, descendant of Pierre (Peter), sent his two sons, Joel and Elisha, to England to study medicine. After spending several years there, they returned to Charleston, each bringing an English wife. Elisha, according to plan, began the practice of medicine; but Joel ran a tavern that was well known throughout the state as a center of political controversy. The latter died without leaving any children.

Doctor Elisha and his wife (who was a Roberts) had four children, three of whom died young. Joel Roberts, the only survivor of this family (the subject of this sketch), had a goodly heritage, for his father was highly respected and loved by his contemporaries. A tribute paid him in **The Charleston City Gazette** at the time of his death in 1803 stated: "Thus determined the life of one of the most valuable members of the community . . . "

Not only a good name did the young Joel inherit from his father, but a small fortune as well. From his ancestry he was heir to an industrious, generous, religious nature and a keen mind with an ambition to reach his highest potential in learning and culture.

While living in England with his parents between 1782 and 1788, he no doubt began his formal education. Returning to Charleston, he was tutored for a few years before being sent to

Connecticut to study under the famous Dr. Timothy Dwight. Since he had always had a frail body, the climate of New England was much too rigorous; therefore, he returned to his home in Charleston for a short time. To complete his education, he was sent to a private school in England, where his mother's relative was headmaster. Though a good scholar in all subjects, he was especially proficient in languages, learning in addition to the classics, French, Spanish, Italian and a knowledge of the Russian tongue.

Following the desires of his father, he enrolled at Edinburgh in courses leading to a medical degree. Again, however, he was forced to seek a milder climate because of his delicate health. A period of travel improved his physical condition remarkably. During this period he became interested in pursuing a military career, finding the combination of study and exercise a great delight.

In 1800 he returned to Charleston and revealed his new-found ambition to his father, who "objected sternly." Consequently, he was persuaded to take up the study of law, which proved extremely distasteful. He never advanced far enough to be admitted to the bar and was no doubt a great disappointment to his father.

He is described at this time as a "handsome young gentleman of 22, with lively dark eyes, wavy black hair, and personal charm far above the average . . . "

Though equipped to enter no profession, he had attained a wide range of learning: proficiency in languages, scientific skills, knowledge of military affairs, diplomatic finesse. In fact, he was perfectly equipped for the career he was destined to follow.

Instead of settling down in some profession such as medicine or law, young Joel, with the consent of his father, set out to "see the world." And for a decade he saw and learned many things that would be of use to him later; but his travels were far more important than the pleasure and educational value they afforded him. He was America's representative, "selling" his country to the political leaders of Europe and gaining their respect for the culture and political institutions of the republic, a form of government looked upon with disfavor by the European countries.

On a trip to Sicily, Poinsett absorbed the beauty of the mountains, sea and other gorgeous exhibits of nature. In contrast to the beauty, there was much ugliness of human suffering that stirred the sympathy of this humanitarian. His great heart was deeply touched as he viewed "hundreds of starved, half-naked figures scarcely human," fighting for the crumbs dropped by the rich.

On this extended tour the young Poinsett visited many countries, in each of which he beheld some wonderful sights, and learned many worthwhile lessons, but his journey came to a sudden end when he was called home by the death of his father. His sister, who was then ill with tuberculosis, soon followed her father, though her devoted brother took her to a different climate with hopes of restoring her health. Her death left him the only surviving Poinsett in America.

After her death he sought to relieve his loneliness by touring the northern part of the United States, learning much of his own country. He was impressed by the beauty everywhere he traveled, but the most awesome view was that of Niagara Falls. Of this he said in his notes, "I find language so feeble, so very inadequate to convey the impression made upon a mind alive to the beauties of nature by the grandeur, the sublimity of this scene, that I shall confine my description to simple facts." Among these "simple facts" were these words: "I gazed with silent rapture, the tears started in my eyes . . . "

This experience and others that he recorded reveal the deep feelings stirred in his mind and heart by scenes of natural beauty.

In 1804 Poinsett returned to his home in Charleston, where he lived a quiet life for two years. Not yet ready to settle down, he began another journey – this time to Russia.

This was a time of war in Europe. Napolean was on the march; and though Russia was in great danger of invasion, the people kept up their spirits by indulging in their habitual festivities. Poinsett was treated royally and entertained lavishly by Emperor Alexander or someone else almost daily. But in this country his sympathy was again aroused by the poverty of the masses, and he was repelled, too, by the abject obeisance of the people whenever and wherever the emperor appeared in public.

He observed the life of the Calmuch Tartars, Buddhists, who gladly explained their religious beliefs. In one part of the country he found Tartars, Russians, Georgians, Armenians – all living "without amalgamation," carrying on their separate customs. For a part of his journeys it was necessary for him to be accompanied by a strong guard because of the extreme danger of travel.

When he reached Kuban and approached the Khan, he found that he had never heard of the United States. When Poinsett finally made somewhat clear to "His Majesty" the geographical location of America and the military skill of her soldiers, he was duly impressed and entertained the stranger "in barbarous magnificence." The feast with its accompanying entertainment of music and dance began at five o'clock and lasted till long after midnight.

Before leaving Russia, he received an interesting request from Alexander, "Upon your return to Washington I beg you will expose to the President the esteem I have for his person, and the interest I feel for the United States. I hope the good understanding which exists between us at present will continue; our commercial interests are the same." That was in 1807. The Carolinian had represented his country well, but what changes have been wrought since that time!

His education, his knowledge of peoples and customs, his popularity with European monarchs – all fitted him admirably for a diplomatic post in one of the countries of Europe, but for some reason he was never given such an opportunity. Instead after a year at home he was appointed as "agent for seamen and commerce" to southern South America. He accepted this post with reluctance, since he still had hopes of a military career in his own country.

Upon arriving in Brazil, Poinsett made an acquaintance of Col. Thomas Sumter, spending some time with this South Carolinian, who held a diplomatic post in that country. (It was no doubt through this acquaintance that he later formed friendships in Sumter County.) He finally reached Chile, his destination, and was there received cordially.

In 1816 Poinsett was elected to the South Carolina legislature as a representative from Charleston. In the following year he was offered a position as a special commissioner of President Monroe to South America.

This offer he declined either through interest in his new political office or in the hope of receiving a more permanent diplomatic or military appointment. Because of his broad knowledge of Spanish-American affairs, he was convinced that his government would turn to him again.

When he entered politics, his friends suggested that he should not align himself with any party, but his reply was quick and definite: "It is not my character to hesitate on so important a question, and I would avoid the appearance of hanging on the favor of both parties. Through the whole course of my life I have been the advocate of Liberty, and I should blush to have my principles suspected in my own country." Though a member of Charleston's aristocracy, he had cast his lot with people, giving his allegiance to the party founded by Thomas Jefferson.

The South Carolina legislature created in 1819 a board of public works with Poinsett and Abram Blanding as the leading members, the former being elected president. The commission carried out a plan for linking the interior of the state with the seaboard, a plan which attracted nationwide attention. In addition to the opening of waterways for transportation, a road was built from Charleston through Columbia to the northwestern part of North Carolina for the purpose of bringing products of Tennessee and North Carolina to Charleston. When this road was completed, it was recognized as one of the best mountain roads in the country. At one site along the way, Poinsett built at his own expense a fountain known as "Poinsett's Spring."

Having an increased interest in politics, the public-spirited South Carolinian decided to run for Congress from the Charleston District to fill the seat left vacant by the death of Charles Pinckney. After a bitterly contested campaign, Poinsett won over his opponent, though by a small margin.

He made a definite contribution in this national body during his term of office; however, he is credited with few speeches. His work was done quietly, but efficiently.

Though elected to a second term, in 1825 he became minister to Mexico, after first refusing to accept the post. He was constrained to accept the assignment later, however, because of his sense of duty, knowing that he was better trained for the work than anyone else. He was given the difficult task of representing the democratic form of government, of supporting the Monroe Doctrine of America, of vindicating the "prestige of the United States," of presenting complaints regarding commercial regulations, of opposing Mexico's designs against Cuba.

When he returned from his assignment in Mexico, in 1830, hoping to devote time to his personal fortunes and to some well-deserved leisure, he found his state and country in a period of decline. Many of the citizens had moved westward and the economy was in a state of deterioration. He found that the great American institutions that he had represented so enthusiastically to the Mexicans were not working smoothly. One of the main causes of the downward trend was the threat of a prohibitive tariff to which he was unalterably opposed, but he disagreed with those who considered Nullification, which he thought would threaten the stability of the Union, the answer to the problem.

Faction fought against faction on the question, Poinsett throwing his every effort into his fight to hold the state to his line of thought. It was all in vain, however. The Nullifiers won out in the 1832 election and another step was taken, in the belief of Poinsett, toward final dissolution of the Union and imminent tragedy for all.

With a view to "prevent the impending evils of civil war," Poinsett and his Central Commission sent James Petigru and Abram Blanding to Columbia to seek to bring about a compromise, which, having been effected, restored a semblance of harmony. George McDuffie, a Nullifier, was elected unanimously as governor, but this move seemed to please the Unionists. However, it took time for the wounds inflicted on both sides to heal.

Poinsett's nationalism and administrative ability secured for him a lasting place of leadership in the Union Party of South Carolina and brought praise from many beyond his own state. But the cause for which he labored so faithfully was lost, and before his death he found himself almost alone in his convictions.

After serving one year of a four-year term in the State Senate, this dedicated patriot finally received an appointment in keeping with his training and ability. Under President Van Buren, he became Secretary of War. He came to this position at a critical period. There was threat of war with Mexico; England and France were showing an unfriendly attitude; hostile Indians were a threat to the security; the removal of more than 60,000 Red Men to lands beyond the Mississippi River was being undertaken.

In spite of the arduous duties of his position, he found time to make valuable intellectual and scientific contacts in Washington. In fact, it was chiefly through his efforts that The National Institute for the Promotion of Science was founded and he was the first president.

One of Poinsett's chief contributions during his years as Secretary of War was the adoption of European methods in all branches of the military. Especially noteworthy was his reform in the Artillery, though because of lack of funds, he was unable to carry out all of his wise planning.

In 1838 Poinsett recommended to the government that education for the Indians should be in the form of manual labor schools where the youth could receive, along with the rudiments of education and teachings of the Christian faith, knowledge of farming and useful arts, so that when he returned to his home in the "western wilds" he would be able to build a life for himself and family. His contention was that money expended by the government for the benefits of the Indian had hitherto been wasted to a great extent. He further recommended that "small schools with farms attached be placed in the more compact Indian settlements," that Christian mission schools be helped and that Indian girls be given training.

The years of his Cabinet position mark a dark chapter in American history, for in spite of Poinsett's compassionate attempts to help the Indians, little was done by the government to eliminate the tragic conditions under which these first Americans were forced to leave their homes and move, with untold suffering on a long journey to a bleak wilderness in the West.

As Secretary of War, Poinsett won the respect and admiration of all with whom he worked because of his "tact, wisdom, foresight and administrative skill." It has been said that of all antebellum war secretaries – though the list included such men as John C. Calhoun and Jefferson Davis – none showed more industry and originality.

The interests of Joel Roberts Poinsett were legion. His devotion to the pursuit of fine arts encouraged architects, and others, to come to him for advice and help. Though he wrote little for publication, he proved a benefactor to many writers and publishers. His interest in scientific farming was shown in his advocating "rotation and diversification for restoring the fertility of the soil."

Some of the new crops he suggested for cultivation in the South were grapes, cork, camphor and flax. He made a great contribution to botanical interests by the idea of exchanging plants with other countries. Everywhere in the country his name is known for his gift of the lovely Christmas flower, Poinsettia pulcherrima, which he brought from Mexico.

As an avowed advocate of better education for all, he said: "So important, so absolutely necessary do I deem education to be to the prosperity of the state that I could never find it in my heart to disapprove the decree of the Prussian Government which compels every parent to send his children to school . . . "

An address made in 1841 concerning the National Institution for the Promotion of Science (name changed to Institute the following year) was so well received, that for a short time Poinsett reigned as the intellectual leader of the nation. And when, in 1846, the Smithsonian Institution was formed, its scope, organization, and functions were determined by the versatile man from South Carolina. At his suggestion, too, another South Carolinian, Robert Mills, made drawings to be used in the building of the institution that is still a scientific center in America.

In his early fifties (on October 24, 1833), Joel Poinsett was married to Mary Pringle, beautiful widow of John Julius Pringle. She came from a distinguished family and was a woman of culture and refinement, a lover of the arts. Soon after their wedding, they settled on her plantation, the White House, on the Pee Dee near Georgetown.

In the early 30's Poinsett purchased a small farm near Greenville, "The Homestead," as a retreat for them from the unhealthy summer months in the low country. It was here in his last years that he spent many pleasant hours with friends who had stuck by him through some of his most trying experiences. Conversation naturally turned to conditions existing in the state and nation, and this great American spoke sadly of possible disaster that he felt would come unless the course of affairs should change. He often spoke in a reminiscent mood of his extensive travels and his contacts with important figures in other lands. Letters came, too, from old friends to brighten the dark days that came often as he felt forebodings of the tragedy that threatened his beloved land. In spite of the fact that he often disagreed with the views of many concerning secession and other crucial matters, most of them never lost their love and respect for him, though they would not be convinced by his logical reasoning. Former President Van Buren kept in touch, even coming to the White House on the Pee Dee to pay him a visit.

Miss Frederika Bremer, Swedish author and traveler, who visited the Poinsetts in 1850, later described their life at the White House, picturing this Southern plantation as one of great beauty and quietness. The home, furnished with exquisite antiques, was recessed in a park filled with trees, shrubs, and flowers, silent testimony to Poinsett's love of nature and interest in botanical research.

In characterizing this gentleman of the South, she said, "Mr. Poinsett is a French **gentilhomme** in his whole exterior and demeanor . . . and unites the refinement and natural courtesy of the Frenchman with the truthful simplicity and straightforwardness which I so much like in the true American, the man of the New World."

After Miss Bremer left the home of the Poinsetts, she remarked, "He seems weary of statesmanship and the life of a statesman. They are both aged and infirm and have arrived at that period . . . when the rest and life of a child are their highest happiness."

In the late fall of that same year (1851), Joel Roberts Poinsett became ill on a trip to the western part of the county. He was taken to the home of his dear friend, Dr. W.W. Anderson, in Stateburg, where he died on December 12.

On his marker in the cemetery of The Church of the Holy Cross in Stateburg is the simple inscription – "a pure patriot, an honest man, and a good Christian" – a beautiful tribute which, when considered thoughtfully, sums up the great life that he lived, the contributions he so unselfishly made to his beloved country and his devotion to the only one he claimed as Master and Lord.

Six years later, Mrs. Poinsett was laid beside her illustrious and beloved husband and together they rest in peace.

A few memorials here and there in South Carolina stand as witnesses of his greatness – an apartment house in Charleston, a hotel and cotton mill in Greenville, a State Park in Sumter County, a street in Sumter, and perhaps a few others – but he has not yet been given his rightful place among the great ones of this state and the nation – "perhaps at the head of them all in vision and versatility."

Attorney Mark Reynolds, Jr. (Profile)

Aptly called a "Gentleman of the Old School," Mark Reynolds, Jr., was a practicing attorney for almost 70 years, most of that time in Sumter.

Son of Dr. Mark Reynolds, an eminent and beloved physician in the Stateburg area, who came to this country from Ireland as a young man, Mark, Jr., was born December 3, 1860. His mother was Julia V. Rees Reynolds, who was also a Stateburg resident.[94]

He attended Mr. Neel's School, Kirkwood, Georgia, and the Bingham Military School in Mebaneville, North Carolina. Because of economic conditions after the Civil War, he was unable to enter college. Instead he began "reading" law in the offices of Lord and Hyde in Charleston and later in the offices of Pope and Haskell in Columbia. He described his legal training by saying that he "dug it out" for himself.

While in Columbia he resided in the home of USC professor, Dr. Alexander Nicholas Talley, and Mrs. Talley. Thus he gained entrance into the educational and social circles in the city.

Young Reynolds was admitted to the Richland Bar ca. 1883 and practiced in association with Col. John C. Haskell approximately six years.

In 1887 he married Elizabeth Waties Anderson, to whom he had been engaged for seven years. He said that when he began receiving for his work $50 a month he felt that he could afford marriage.

In 1889 he went to Florence, Alabama, advertised as a "boom town," but failing to find his fortune there, he returned to South Carolina after about a year and began the practice of law in Sumter. He was also editor of the **Watchman and Southron**, a weekly paper, for about a year.

His legal practice in Sumter proved very successful and he held the position of president of the Sumter Bar Association for many years. He was also a director of the National Bank of South Carolina. For some time he was legal counsel for the Southern Railroad Company and for the Southern Express Company.

Mark Reynolds, dean of the Sumter Bar, received the diamond-studded emblem of the Atlantic Coast Line Railroad in 1953 in recognition of his 60 years of service as local counsel for the railroad.

As a dedicated member of the Church of the Holy Comforter, Episcopal, he gave invaluable service as vestryman and warden continuously from 1890 to 1945. His dedicated Christian life was an inspiration to all who knew him.

Upon his death, February 7, 1955, at the age of 94, an editorial appearing in **The Columbia State** paid tribute to this sage of the legal profession along with his law partner in Columbia, Col. Haskell, in these words among other appropriate expressions of admiration:

"It was impossible to know such men without a feeling of honor and respect and veneration . . . Overtures to make tremendous profits in any manner not obviously and unmistakably above reproach were beneath their consideration . . .

"In the category of character, 'There were giants in the land in those days' . . . "

Probate Judge – Eleanora Richardson

Among the many distinguished citizens and colorful personalities that Sumter can claim is the former Judge of Probate, Miss Eleanora Richardson.

Born in the Sand Hills of Clarendon County, as she says "almost under the eaves of Saint Mark's Episcopal Church," she was one of the children of John Richard Charles Richardson and Elizabeth Sinkler Manning Richardson. The family lived with her grandmother in a beautiful old plantation home built in the late 1700's or early 1800's as a summer home by Gov. James Burchell Richardson. It was a three-story house originally known as Chateau de la Fontaine because of a nearby spring that resembled a fountain.[95]

In 1842 the home was somewhat remodeled; however, it was not changed significantly. Having been constructed of the best timber, it withstood the 1886 earthquake and a very destructive cyclone which uprooted 36 trees in the yard, but it was finally burned in 1906.

When their beloved home was no more, the family, including Mr. Richardson's mother, left the Sand Hills and their many relatives who lived in the same community in which they had made their home for many years, and moved to Sumter.

Since she came from a long line of outstanding political figures, there is little wonder that Miss Eleanora was inclined toward the profession which she chose. In her family were six governors of South Carolina; namely, James Burchell Richardson (1802-1804), Richard Irving Manning (1824-1826), John Peter Richardson (1840-1842), John Laurence Manning (1852-1854), John Peter Richardson, Jr. (1886-1890), Richard Irving Manning, Jr. (1915-1919). Though not in politics, Gen. Richard Richardson served his state well during the Revolutionary War.

With such a background "Miss Minna," as she was called by friends and family, had natural ability and personality for a successful life as a public official. She began her career in 1917 as a stenographer (at the "fabulous" salary of $25 a month) for the Hon. Thomas Eveleigh Richardson, Judge of Probate for Sumter County. As she looked back to those early days in the office of this distant cousin, she believed that she was indeed fortunate to start out in the business world under such a man. She paid tribute to him by saying that he was "a most wonderful, intelligent gentleman of the old school."

So valuable were her services that Judge Richardson appointed her deputy clerk, in which capacity she relieved him of many of his strenuous duties in his last years. At his death in 1933, she was named through the recommendation of the Hon. Shepard Nash to fill the unexpired term.

When election time came, she ran on her own record and was elected for four consecutive terms thereafter. After 46 years of public service, she retired in 1963.

Judge Richardson gave to her work a full measure of devotion and received much joy and satisfaction in return. In recalling the types of duties involved in the position, she remembered that she was called on to solve many problems for many people. She says, "The duties of the office were quite heavy, dealing with such things as wills and their administration, questions of guardianship, the task of admitting veterans to veterans' hospitals to be treated for alcohol addiction, and of committing patients (after examination by two physicians) to the South Carolina State Hospital." She even had the responsibility at times of sending delinquent children to correctional institutions. However, the Court of Domestic Relations took over that work toward the last of her tenure of office.

All of these tasks were physically and emotionally tiring, but Judge Richardson was always equal to the routine duties as well as any emergency.

One of the most rewarding phases of her work, she often said, was her contact with people; and the consciousness that she might be able to help those in need of friends also gave her satisfaction in her day by day effort to solve problems.

Numbers of people have always been ready to verify the fact that she was truly a friend in need. Her kind, honest and wise advice helped many a one over some difficult spot, nor was she ever too busy to talk over the troubles of her "clients."

But the position was not "all work and no play," for there were many happy occasions to relieve the tensions that can so easily build up under a heavy load of work and responsibility. "Miss Minna" chuckled over the tricks the lawyers were frequently playing on her. No doubt they would agree, however, that her sense of humor would always "save the day" for her, and their jokes were fully appreciated and enjoyed by the victim herself.

To show the high esteem in which these fellow workers held Judge Richardson, upon her retirement they presented her an engraved plaque which reads in part: "Commending her for her many years of assiduous devotion to duty as Probate Judge, which were ever performed with humane kindness, patience, wisdom, impartial justice and rare efficiency."

When she was planning to retire, she was asked what she was planning for her retirement years. Surely a person with the varied interests that Miss Richardson had would have little "spare time" to worry about.

She loved her home and got much pleasure from "puttering around" doing the countless chores connected with housekeeping. Too, she was involved in many outside organizations and activities, and she had more time to enjoy visiting the members of her family and chatting with friends. Her flowers, which she loved and to which she gave great care, claimed much of her time.

There is one thing that "grieved" her. She no longer had the quaint little Model A Ford car to which she was very deeply attached. After serving her faithfully for more than 30 years, the 1929 Ford coupe finally "chugged" out its last breath and could go no farther without being "hospitalized." Reluctantly she sold it and often she sadly sighed, "I wish I hadn't."

In a setting of beautiful old furniture, portraits and photographs of many ancestors, lovely paintings done by friends or relatives, Miss Richardson was representative of Southern aristocracy at its best. A visit with her was refreshing and enlightening for one who likes to catch glimpses of life in this area in bygone days. By recalling stories told by her illustrious ancestors, she was able in her charming and delightful manner to paint a picture for this generation of the priceless heritage coming from the pioneer settlers of South Carolina.

After several years of retirement, Miss Eleanora died at her beloved little home, but the memory of this fascinating, efficient and kindly person will continue to live in Sumter.

Gen. Richard Richardson

Among the outstanding families who settled in the Sumter District in the 1700's is that of Richardson.[96] Two of this name who were renowned during those critical years were Gen. Richard Richardson and his eldest son, Col. Richard Richardson.

General Richardson's role in the Revolutionary War was given briefly in a previous sketch, but other details of his life and his many contributions to his community and state may be of interest to some readers.

He came from an eminent family in Virginia. He received the best education "which the times and circumstances afforded," and became a land surveyor, a vocation pursued by many distinguished men of that time, including George Washington.

The rigors of outdoor life necessitated by his work helped to prepare him for his service as a soldier in the Revolutionary War; and the strict mental discipline required in mathematics, "mensuration, calculations and exact science," which gave him self-confidence, fitted him as a military leader.

After settling in South Carolina, he was able, through his knowledge of lands, to acquire for himself several valuable tracts of land, thus becoming one of the wealthiest men in the area. Richard Richardson has been described as prudent, firm, benevolent, frank. These traits "united with a courteous, friendly, engaging deportment, and a fine commanding person, soon won for him the confidence of the interior, particularly of Craven County, in which he resided."

When there was a feud or other type of dissension to be settled, it was Richardson who was called on to settle the differences. He "possessed an equity jurisdiction from the Santee to the North Carolina boundary of the state." It is recorded that his home often resembled the assizes, and of the countless litigations on which he passed judgment, few of those involved ever felt an inclination to disagree with his decisions or "appeal to the law."

He was actively involved as a soldier even before the Revolution. In fact, his ability as a leader of military tactics was shown in several conflicts with the Indians.

He was commissioned a Colonel in the Cherokee wars of 1760 and 1761. According to **The South Carolina Gazette** of September 25, 1762, "a very handsome service of plate was lately presented by the inhabitants of St. Mark's Parish to Col. Richard Richardson, as a mark of their gratitude and esteem; and to show their sense of the many services he rendered this province during the late unhappy Cherokee war, and to that parish, in particular, on every occasion."

In civil and governmental affairs also, Richard Richardson made many contributions. He was a delegate to the Provincial Congress;[97] he also helped frame the first constitution. He was a member of the legislative council, a body similar to the state senate.

With his assistance the new administration was formed March

26, 1776, with the appointment of civil and military officers, this being the first constitutional government established in the Revolution. It was revised in 1778 and continued as the basis for South Carolina Government until 1789.

When Charleston fell, General Richardson was taken prisoner with the privilege of remaining at his home in Sumter District until prisoners were exchanged. However, the British, upon taking command, ordered that men throughout the state take up arms in support of Great Britain. General Richardson was very indignant over this injustice and immediately expressed his views. Cornwallis, fearing the influence of this prominent leader, gave him an ultimatum in the presence of his family. Either he was to unite himself with the cause of the royalists or he would be put into "close confinement."

The great old general, true to his character, answered, "with great decision, in such dignified terms as to elicit an involuntary expression of respect and admiration from his lordship." His reply has been recorded as follows: "I have from the best convictions of my mind, embarked in a cause, which I think righteous and just; I have knowingly and willingly, staked my life, family and property, all upon the issue; I am well prepared to suffer or triumph with it, and would rather die a thousand deaths than betray my country or deceive my friends."

The remainder of the story is well known. He was thrown into a loathsome prison where his state of health rapidly deteriorated. So frail did the gallant soldier become that at the age of 76 he was sent home, where he soon died.

It is a familiar story of how Tarleton, six weeks after his burial, forced Mrs. Richardson to have her husband's body disinterred with the flimsy excuse that he wanted to look upon the face of a man "of his decided character." It was believed that the real reason was Tarleton's suspicion that the family silver might be concealed in the grave.

After much pleading the distraught widow was allowed to have her husband reburied. In the meantime the merciless soldiers burned all the buildings on the premises, including the home itself. Only a few pieces of furniture and a little clothing were left with Mrs. Richardson and her three small children. Spying his father's military saddle, seven-year-old James Burchell (later governor of South Carolina) jumped upon it and said that it was not to be taken. Somewhat amused by the impudence of "the little rebel," the soldiers gave up the saddle.

As long as the Green Dragoon and his men remained in the neighborhood, the Richardson family were kept alive by small bits of food brought by faithful slaves, who slipped away from their hiding places under cover of darkness to bring what they could to their beloved mistress and her family.

Col. Richard Richardson

Col. Richard Richardson, eldest son of Gen. Richard Richardson, was like his father, a gallant soldier and a loyal patriot during the struggle involved in forming a united and independent nation.

At the beginning of the Revolution, he was captain in the militia under his father. As such, in 1775 he was engaged in the fight against the Tories, led by Cunningham, Fletchall and Robinson in the famous Snow Campaign.

In 1776 he was made a captain in the second regiment under Thomas Sumter, and later, when Charleston fell, he was taken prisoner. Though under the agreement he was to remain with his family until the exchange of prisoners, this right was removed, as it was in the case of his father, and he was confined on John's Island. There he became ill with smallpox and was for a while near death.

Convinced that he was no longer bound by the original agreement, young Richard, as soon as he was able, planned to make his escape. The opportunity came through the help of a lady who had received permission to take the corpse of her father from the island.

It was rather easy for Richard to effect a disguise because his face was so scarred from smallpox that he was scarcely recognizable. Wrapping his head and shoulders in a blanket, he traveled on foot till he reached a hiding place in Santee Swamp near his home.

On the way he had one tense moment when he came upon a party of British soldiers. He knew that if he stopped or changed his direction he would arouse suspicion. Therefore, he continued on his way with a slow, tottering step as if he were very sick and weak. He approached some of the enemy, asking for help and saying that he was sick with smallpox. They gave him some trifle, and, expressing thanks, he went on his way.

His retreat in the swamp was called John's Island. In the same swamp was another retreat known as Beech Island because of the thick growth of beech trees. Here many found concealment and after many years initials could still be seen carved on the trees.

Somehow he was able to let his wife know of his safety and he received clothing and a little food from his home through the help of a faithful servant. Sometimes he was able to see his family, though this feat involved great risk. Tarleton and his men, about 800 of them, were occupying his premises, finding it an excellent station with plenty of food for men and horses.

Major Richard, as he was at that time, was ever occupied even while in hiding. In various ways he was able to get messages to his former fellow soldiers whom he could trust. These he collected and drilled as mounted militia on Beech Island. He had plans for using these men in the fight against the British and the Tories.

In the meantime Mrs. Richardson was treated with utmost contempt and cruelty by the Red Coats, who had taken complete possession of her home and plantation. The family was permitted the use of only one room in the spacious home.

Major Richardson, hearing of Marion's plan to encounter Tarleton, decided to join him. One of Marion's best guides deserted him to join the enemy. The Swamp Fox, having received the wrong estimate of the size of the enemy's forces, was forced to withdraw, pursued by Tarleton, who was guided by the deserter.

(This patriot-turned-Tory continued with the British throughout the war and then, under the legislative act which granted amnesty, he returned home and lived in peace.)

It is said that when Tarleton learned that Richardson was with Marion, he was very polite to Mrs. Richardson, offering to reward her if she would persuade her husband to come home and live with his family under the protection of the British, who offered him equal rank in their army or, if he preferred, retirement.

Mrs. Richardson tried to evade answering these requests, but Tarleton finally proposed that Edward Richardson, who was a prisoner on parole, be sent to take the proposals to his brother. Edward, however, reported directly to Marion, broke his parole and joined with the Swamp Fox.

Once when Major Richardson secretly visited his home, the same deserter led a posse of men behind him and shut off the avenue. Richardson spurred his horse and boldly dashed through the men to safety. None but the Tory fired, for the British wished to take Richardson alive to collect the reward offered for his capture.

Richardson once, with a group of his men, caught the Tory at his home. His men surrounded the house and began shooting. However, the deserter's wife came out and "on her knees implored" Richardson to save her husband. Because of his regard for the woman, whom all knew and respected, he called off his men.

On another occasion when Richardson, who had now been

made a Colonel, asked for a leave of absence to visit his home, General Marion reminded him of his narrow escape on a previous visit and sent with him an escort.

He and his escort had barely reached his home when a large party of Red Coats arrived. The men remounted their tired horses and raced for the swamp behind the house. One young patriot by the name of Roberts was caught and hanged near the door of the home. When Mrs. Richardson begged for his life, the soldiers told her that "she should soon see her husband kick like that fellow."

The only animal left from Colonel Richardson's "well-stocked plantation" was the horse he rode named Corn Crib for the fact that he was once hidden in a log house in the swamp that had been used for storing corn. The beautiful horse was killed under his master in the Battle of Eutaw when Colonel Richardson was holding a dangerous position on the right of General Greene.

In this, one of the most decisive battles fought in the South, Colonel Richardson "was seen encouraging and leading his troops, with cool and distinguished valor."

These few episodes are only examples of the many services rendered by Colonel Richardson to his state and nation and are indications of the sacrifices he was willing to make for the cause of freedom.

M. Priscilla Shaw

"She was a very able mayor who related to the total community. Her leadership set an outstanding example for all, especially women, in elective office." This tribute was paid by Sumter City Councilwoman, Coleen Yates, upon the death of Martha Priscilla Shaw, former mayor of Sumter, on Feb. 9, 1981.

Miss Shaw was born in Alcolu, a small country town in Clarendon County, August 29, 1904, daughter of the late David Charles and Lula Alderman Shaw and the granddaughter of the late D.W. Alderman, who built the town around his lumber business.

She had five brothers and one sister. The oldest brother, Ervin David, was shot down over France during World War I and Shaw Air Force Base was named in his memory.

The family moved to Sumter when Priscilla was five years old. She attended the city schools and upon graduation entered Agnes Scott College in Decatur, Ga., later receiving a degree in physical education at Sargent College, Cambridge, Mass. While pursuing her studies there she did social welfare work. Her graduate work was done at Boston University in 1937.

Returning to Sumter, she became the first physical educatio teacher in the city schools, serving in this capacity for 15 years. For one year she was acting principal of Girls High School.

During the summer for 25 years she owned and operated Silver Pines, a summer camp for girls at Roaring Gap, N.C.

Her great interest in sports continued through the years.

While on the faculty of the city schools, she had charge of the safety patrol, sponsored the junior-senior festivities, had charge of class day, promoted the lunch program, assisted the attendance teacher in keeping the daily attendance record.

Miss Shaw became more and more concerned about the manner in which the city government was being run. She expressed great disappointment that municipal affairs were not being conducted for the good of all.

She said, "I just wanted to see what was going on in our city government." She felt that there were too many incidences of "inefficiency and unnecessary secrecy on the part of the city government." Therefore in 1950 she decided to seek a seat on the Council.

There were five men in the race and she came out as one of the top two. In a runoff election she was victorious.

While on the Council she was often sought as a speaker for organizations. In an appearance before the Optimist Club, she spoke on the heritage of young men of America. During the talk she told of the desirability of a Citizens Planning Committee in order that more people might have a part in the government of the city.

In a talk before the PTA she emphasized the importance of giving children emotional stability, a responsibility that belongs to both parents and teachers, she said.

After two years on the Council Miss Shaw found that she knew no more about what was going on than she did before becoming a member. She said, "Important matters were being decided without any careful study. Sessions were called without my being notified. I decided to resign as a member of the Council and run for mayor." [98]

"There hadn't been any opposition for mayor for 30 years," she said, "A man just decided he wanted to be Mayor and that was it . . . " [99]

The slogan for her campaign was "Shaw for Mayor – Shaw for All Citizens." Some of the planks in her platform were the establishment of a Domestic Court and of a Citizens Committee. She wanted free enterprise, a better relationship between employer and employee. She wanted all Council meetings to be held in Recorder's Court and all minutes of regular and special Council meetings to be published. And she emphasized that all should get back to the foundation upon which the country was built – God, home and government.

When the votes were counted, it was found that Candidate Shaw had received an overwhelming majority – 2,189 against her opponent's 1,069. Thus Priscilla Shaw became the first woman mayor of Sumter, the first in the state and one of the few in the nation.

A business woman, Miss Shaw was bookkeeper for Alderman-Shaw, Inc., farm and timber lands, until her death.

She was a dedicated member of First Presbyterian Church of Sumter.

In addition she found time for many Civic and social activities. Among these were the presidency of the South Carolina Health, Physical Education, Camping and Recreation Association; work with the Red Cross, Community Chest, Salvation Army, T.B. Association. She also served as president of the YWCA and Pilot Club. She worked with the Memorial Homes and was a charter member of the Junior Welfare League, through which she performed countless services for the needy in Sumter County. She was also a member of the Tuomey Hospital Board.

During World War II she was chairman of Civilian Defense Services. She was a member of the Crippled Children's Association and the Girl Scouts Board of Directors.

Honors received by this outstanding Sumter citizen include: "First Lady of the Year – 1974," given by Beta Sigma Phi of which she was an honorary member. She was also honorary member of the Sumter Art Association. She received on Nov. 10, 1955 from United Church Women a Citation "For your Christian Citizenship Reflected in Your Active Participation in Making and Maintaining Good Government." She received National attention through ABC Television's "Woman's World" and Mary Margaret McBride.

From the President's Committee for Traffic Safety she was awarded a Certificate of Service. She was selected for Who's Who of American Women by **Woman's Home Companion.**

After her death members of the South Carolina General Assembly passed a Concurrent Resolution of sympathy for her family. One paragraph reads: " . . . the members of this body recognize the wonderful traits and characteristics of Miss Shaw and were influenced by her willingness to serve whenever her services were needed."

A final tribute summarizes the wonderful traits of character shown by Martha Priscilla Shaw and the faith by which she lived and served. It was written by Michael Karvelas for "Palmetto Profile" in the June 1953 issue of **South Carolina Magazine.** "Practical, quick-witted, dependable and gracious –

that's Sumter's lady mayor, to all who know her. She unassumingly shrugs off all credit for the success she has enjoyed in her various fields of endeavor and points to her life-long motto as her steadying influence — 'Our Guide - In God We Trust.' "

Though written many years ago, these words were also descriptive of Priscilla Shaw through the remaining years of her fruitful life.

George Decatur Shore, Sr. (Profile)

One of Sumter's most successful businessmen and community leaders of the past was George Decatur Shore. The son of Henry Washington Shore and Lavinia Elizabeth Boyer, he was born in Salem, a small Moravian town in North Carolina, on January 14, 1862, one of ten children.[100]

As a young man he kept books for Mr. Abe Ryttenberg, a native of Sumter, who had opened a store in the section known as Winston, where there was growing prosperity created by the Reynolds Tobacco Company's business there. It was then that the town became known as Winston-Salem.

When Ryttenberg decided to close out his business there and return to Sumter, he offered Shore a position as bookkeeper in the Ryttenberg Family Store located on the northwest corner of the intersection of Main and Liberty Streets in Sumter. Considering this a worthwhile opportunity for advancement since the Ryttenberg general store was about the largest of its kind in this section of South Carolina, George Shore came to Sumter by horse and buggy during a cold spell in the spring of 1887.

He worked for the Ryttenbergs for several years, but since he was possessed of an enterprising spirit, he decided to go into business for himself as a wholesale broker. Soon his brother, Bernard P. Shore, came to Sumter and the business continued under the name, George D. Shore and Brother.

Around 1900 Bernard P. Shore died and near the same time Theodore Roosevelt, who had become President when President McKinley was assassinated, appointed George Shore as Sumter Postmaster. He then sold his business to Graham Moses, who continued it for a while under its original name, but later changed the name to Moses and Company.

Mr. Shore was married on October 23, 1888, to Miss Charlotte Cordes Doar of McClellanville and they soon built a home on the southeast corner of the intersection of West Calhoun and what was then known as New Street. Later while A.B. Stuckey was mayor, the town wished to widen the streets. When Mayor Stuckey asked Mr. Shore about moving his fence to make room for the widening of the street, he agreed but suggested to the mayor that New Street become Salem Avenue, for his native home.

Civic-minded as he was, Mr. Shore was ever finding opportunities to serve his community. In 1905 he was one of the organizers of the Farmers Bank and Trust Company, now known as the National Bank of South Carolina, and remained a director until his death. For many years he was also on the board of directors of the First National Bank, now the local branch of the South Carolina National Bank. He helped organize the Sumter Machinery Company and remained a director for many years.

Always taking a keen interest in the concerns of farmers in the county, he and some others organized the Planters Mule Company. After he left the post office, he managed this company for a number of years.

Indicating again his desire to see Sumter grow and develop, he and R.I. Manning, C.G. Rowland and Thomas Wilson purchased property on the east side of South Main Street, which property they developed. The building on Law Range where his son, George D. Shore, Jr., has his office, was once located on Main Street. It is said to be the oldest building in use in Sumter today.

A lover of horses, Mr. Shore always kept some fine breeds on hand for riding and driving. His saddle horses won many ribbons in horse shows in and around Sumter. Automobiles were not for him. He never learned to drive, nor did he care to, though he kept several for Mrs. Shore to drive and enjoy. On seeing him pass one day during the Great Depression in his buggy, his friend, Mark Reynolds, heard someone say, "There goes George Shore out of date and out of debt." Both Mr. Reynolds and Mr. Shore were considered conservative in business.

Having grown up in Salem, Mr. Shore was reared as a Moravian and naturally was one of that faith; but after he married, he became an Episcopalian and was a loyal member of that church, serving on the Vestry as long as he lived.

In politics he was a Republican; but he was elected at one time to the City Council in a town that was at that time predominantly Democratic.

Mr. Shore had many friends in Sumter, and he enjoyed contacts with them through the activities of the Rotary and Fortnightly Clubs.

George Decatur Shore, Sr., died in 1935 after a long and useful life. His many worthwhile contributions to the business, civic, cultural and religious life of his adopted home have lived after him and will continue to be remembered by appreciative citizens of the area where he gave of himself for the good of others.

T.M. Stubbs, Man Of Many Interests

A man more loyal to Sumter County than Thomas M. Stubbs can scarcely be found, and though he lived out of the state for many years, no one was more dedicated to the preservation of historic lore of the area than he.

Born in Sumter on July 21, 1898, "Mac," as he was called by many of his relatives and friends, could lay claim to a most interesting and outstanding ancestry. He was the son of Campbell Laurence and Lillian Hoyt Stubbs. Campbell E. Stubbs, the only grandfather he ever knew, his father's brother and his mother's stepfather, came from Marlboro County in 1866, "fresh out of the Confederate Army," as the first cotton buyer in Sumter. At their home on the corner of Main and Caldwell Streets, Thomas' father and mother were married in 1895, with the bride's grandfather, the Rev. Henry M. Mood, performing the ceremony.[101]

On his mother's side his great-grandfather, Freeman Hoyt, was a merchant in Sumter as early as 1831, having come from New Hampshire on horseback. Another great-grandfather was the Rev. Henry M. Mood (mentioned above), a minister in the South Carolina Methodist Conference. While serving a church in Manning, he organized and directed the Manning Academy in which two of his sons and one daughter taught.

His paternal grandfather, Thomas Adams Stubbs, and his grandmother were both active in the Baptist and Methodist Churches in Marlboro County, rearing their children in those two churches, but Thomas became an Episcopalian.

After finishing high school in Sumter, he entered Washington and Lee University in Lexington, Virginia, where he received his A.B. degree in 1920, being graduated as life president of his class.

His college course was interrupted for a year of military duty in World War I.

Upon completion of his work at Washington and Lee, he enrolled in the Harvard Law School and received an L.L.B. degree.

Admitted to the Georgia Bar in 1923, he practiced in that state with the firm McDaniel and Neely (later Neely, Marshall and Greene). While in Atlanta, Mr. Stubbs was active in several organizations, including the Georgia and Atlanta Bar Associations; Atlanta Lawyers' Club, of which he was president from 1934 to 1935, Palestine Lodge No. 486 F. and A.M.

After practicing law for some years, Mr. Stubbs accepted a

position as professor of law at the University of South Carolina, which position he held until the mid-fifties.

Not only was he a successful lawyer and teacher, but he received recognition for his writings as well. Many of his legal compositions were published in "The Encyclopedia of Georgia Law." His history of the Supreme Court of South Carolina and Appellate Courts and of the federal courts, written by request in 1951 while teaching at the University of South Carolina, was published in **The South Carolina and Southeastern Digest**, a set of books in common use among lawyers.

In addition to his legal writings, books and articles on various other subjects were credited to this talented author. As a genealogist, he published one book, **Family Album: The Moods of Charleston and Related Families**, and contributed to **The Silversmiths of South Carolina** by Burton. He also wrote papers tracing family lines.

Other publications from the pen of Mr. Stubbs include: "Early History of Sumter Churches," "A History of Claremont Lodge No. 64, A.F.M. and Affiliated Lodges," "The Fourth Estate of Sumter, S.C." in the *South Carolina Historical Magazine* (October 1953). Since its beginning in 1954, he was a regular contributor to **Names in South Carolina**, said to be the first place-name journal in America.

On of his greatest interests was history. Endowed with a remarkable memory, he had "at his fingertips" facts, anecdotes, legends concerning persons, places and events in the Sumter area.

Sumter County will ever be indebted to Thomas M. Stubbs for his assistance in keeping alive an interest in the early life of the community. Instrumental in organizing the Sumter County Historical Society, he took a leading part in the work accomplished by the organization. He served for seven years as chairman of a committee to research and organize data for historical markers throughout the county, writing the first 12 himself.

He was a recognized authority on families, homes, organizations, businesses, churches, etc., in this area, and he gave gladly and generously of his time to anyone seeking information.[102]

Mr. Stubbs married the former Beatrice Whitney Jefferson of Oldham County, Kentucky. Mrs. Stubbs is a graduate of Wellesley and a talented writer. There are three sons – Thomas M., Jr., William Jefferson and Campbell Laurence – in this family.

In 1955 Mrs. Stubbs suffered an illness that necessitated a move to a cooler climate. Impressed by the beauty of the North Georgia Mountains, they decided to settle in Dillard, Georgia.

Loving the mountains and mountain people as he did, Mr. Stubbs took great delight in writing his regular column, "Mountain Wise."

Numerous honors came to Thomas M. Stubbs and verily each was merited reward for his many worthwhile contributions to society.

In 1969 he was awarded the Doctor of Jurisprudence degree from Harvard Law School. He served as National Historian for his fraternity Sigma Phi Epsilon. Who's Who in South Carolina included him among the outstanding people listed there. *Georgia Magazine* featured a profile of him in its November, 1971, issue.

These are only a few of the tributes of recognition accorded this man of many interests in South Carolina, Georgia and elsewhere.

Touchberrys Held In High Esteem

Having lived in the same community for more than 40 years, Mr. and Mrs. S.L. Touchberry have won the esteem and affection of all those who have had the privilege of knowing them or of being their neighbors.

A little more than 80 years ago these two were born in the same community in Clarendon County. This section was known as the Big Branch Community. "Mr. Sam," as he was often called, lived on the old Touchberry place. He was the oldest son in a family of seven boys and three girls. His parents were William Thomas and Henrietta Rich Touchberry.

When in a reminiscent mood, he liked to live again those days of the long ago. As he looked into the past, he recalled the good times he had with his six brothers. Though they lacked the wealth that would have afforded them more leisure time and perhaps more educational advantages, they did not mind the work, and at night they enjoyed their simple fun in their "castle" in the back yard, which was a "hulled-in" building with plenty of cold air, admitted through cracks in walls and ceiling and windows without panes of glass. A clay chimney provided the warmth for the room. With a bit of ingenuity, they always found a way to "make-do" with whatever they had instead of pining for what was not. For instance, one of them conceived a plan for providing hot water in their open-air retreat. Into a tub of water, they plunged a seven-pound axe that had been heated in the fireplace; and instantly they had hot water for bathing.

Their fun was kept within bounds at all times, for the father in the main dwelling could detect any disorder; and the culprit was forthwith called "on the carpet," the chief punishment being banishment to the barn to shuck a barrel of corn.

One of the chores on the farm each week was the shucking

and shelling of two bushels of corn – one for grits and one for meal – which they took to Tindal's Mill for grinding. The food that was prepared for the table made up in quantity what it lacked in variety. There was always plenty of hominy and cornbread.

Schooling in those days was not so important for the boys. Young Sam went to a one-teacher school when he was not needed on the farm. When he reached 17 years of age and was quite grown in size, he decided that it would be to his advantage to get more education; therefore, he went to school in Summerton and was placed in the seventh grade. With a twinkle in his eye, he said, "The other pupils brushed around my knees." But the fact that he was larger than his classmates bothered him not at all.

At the end of that nine-months' term, his formal education abruptly came to an end. His father became ill; and since he was the oldest boy, the responsibility of running the farm fell on him.

In his very first year of farming he met disaster. Before he had ginned any of his cotton, the barn caught on fire and destroyed almost his entire crop. In the face of this great loss, the young man demonstrated those qualities of "a faith to live by and a purpose to live for." With a loan from his father, he was ready to make a new start.

Of course, by this time he was becoming seriously interested in girls, especially that young lady whom he had known all his life – Miss Linwood Gibson. And oh, how he wanted a buggy in which to take this girl to ride!

Bradham and Son in Manning was displaying the prettiest ones ever. He would often stand on the street, looking in at the different styles and wishing. One day Mr. Bradham came out and said, "Sam, I want to sell you a buggy." And surely Sam wanted a buggy; but the idea was beyond his fondest dream, for he had no money. Being a good salesman, as well as an understanding man, he offered young Sam the buggy of his choice on his own terms. The glow of pride and happiness he felt that day still showed on his face as he told of the experience.

"That was really a good community we lived in as young people," remembered this happy-hearted octogenarian. "We had at least two frolics a week – peanut boilings, box suppers, candy pullings, square dances." The older people in the home where a party was held would watch the young people until they were tired. They would then leave the boys and girls, telling them to play or dance as long as they wanted to and then before leaving see that the lights were out. The youth in this community had the perfect confidence of the elders and never did they betray this confidence. It was indeed a good community. As well as he remembered, there was a family altar in every home.

The new buggy evidently hurried along the course of events. On July 17, 1910, Sam and Linwood were married at her home. The wedding was on his 21st birthday and she was 20. As he expressed it, "We've been striving together ever since."

Life for the young couple was not easy. Mrs. Touchberry summed up the situation by saying: "We lived close to the earth and worked hard, but we were happy." They continued living in the same community for a while. They later moved to the farm owned by LeGrande Geddings near Calvary Church.

In early 1929 they moved into the home a few miles below Pinewood. Set back from the highway at the end of a long tree-lined avenue is this interesting old home that had been built many years before the Touchberrys purchased the place. Made of handhewn timbers fastened with pegs, the front part consists of four large rooms – two downstairs and two on the second floor reached by an odd-shaped stair. At the back of this another house, that at one time was separate, had been joined with a narrow filled-in space between. The Touchberrys some years ago built another section between this part and the old kitchen which they pushed up for a laundry room.

The farm has 200 acres with only a part tillable. Woods cover part and there are three lakes or ponds surrounded by sandy soil. In addition to this land, Mr. Touchberry rents two farms on the Belser property in Clarendon County. He also has charge of one of the George Rowland farms. Cotton, corn and soybeans were his chief crops.

This remarkable couple reared eight fine children – three sons and five daughters. The oldest son, Roger, has a grocery store in Sumter and is now managing his father's farming interests.

The next son, Miles, also lives in Sumter and at present is working with his brother in the grocery business.

Bob, the youngest son, has had a different life. After completing his junior year at Clemson, he entered the service during World War II. During a period of very rough training in Kentucky the young lieutenant was seriously injured by an explosion. After many heartbreaking months of recuperation and rehabilitation, he returned to Clemson. When he had finished his senior year there, he went on to Iowa State where he earned his Master's degree and his doctorate. He is now at the head of Animal Genetics in all the colleges connected with the University of Minnesota.

One daughter, Corinne, is married to J.M. Scott and lives in Madison, West Virginia. Esther became a nurse and worked at the hospital in Lancaster, later becoming superintendent of the hospital. She married Tom Myers and now lives on the Isle of Palms.

Living at home is Ruth, postmaster at Rimini. She is very active in the Pinewood Baptist Church, serving as clerk and treasurer.

Another daughter, Harriett, is now Mrs. Walter Mason, Jr., and lives in Silver Spring, Maryland. The fifth daughter, Linwood Myrtle, lives in Columbia. Her husband, Carl Cleveland, is Chief South Carolina Bank Examiner.

There are 16 living grandchildren and two great-grandchildren. One grandson, Miles Touchberry, Jr., was killed in Vietnam.

The Triple Ponds are well stocked with fish and permits are sold to those desiring to enjoy the sport of fishing; however, these waters are not to be used for any other purpose. The permits specify no fishing on Sunday.

A successful farmer through the years, in 1964 Mr. Touchberry was named Master Farmer. The plaque that was presented to him bears the following inscription:

Master Farmer Award of Merit
to
Mr. and Mrs. Touchberry and Family
Outstanding Accomplishment in Farm
and Home Development, 1964
The Clemson College Extension Service
The Sumter County Agricultural Commission

"Mr. Sam" began teaching Bible classes in 1918. In Calvary Baptist Church and Manning Baptist he taught, and in 1927 accepted the Men's Bible Class in Pinewood Baptist with a wonderful record of faithful attendance. In 1952, on his 25th anniversary, the class presented him a silver bowl, and in 1970 he received a gold bowl, both suitably engraved.

Countless friends from many places and many walks of life sing praises of this couple and the outstanding children whom they have reared and sent out into the world to make worthwhile contributions to society. One of his former devoted friends, the late Mendel Rivers, highly respected Sam Touchberry for his Christian witness wherever he went. The Touchberrys cherished a handsome silver vegetable dish presented to them on their 60th wedding anniversary. On the cover the following words are inscribed:

Mr. and Mrs. Samuel Lee Touchberry
July 17, 1910 - 1970
Congressman L. Mendel Rivers

Now deceased, Mr. and Mrs. Touchberry have left to posterity an example worthy of emulation.

Rev. James Bentham Walker (Profile)

A dedicated, saintly servant of God walked the streets of Sumter for almost 47 years, bringing comfort, cheer and spiritual strength to all who needed his help.

This great-hearted, self-forgetful, princely gentleman was the Rev. James Bentham Walker, who came to Sumter as rector of the Church of the Holy Comforter in 1916.

Born in Charleston Dec. 11, 1869, he grew up during an interesting period. He remembered the first electric lights in Charleston. He remembered the cleanliness of the water in Charleston Harbor when as a boy he dived from a boat and swam to Fort Sumter, and before his death he regretted to see the contamination of these waters by atomic submarines. He remembered, too, the Charleston earthquake of 1886.

After completing school, it is thought at Porter Military Academy, he entered The Citadel to study engineering. He then transferred to St. Stephens (later Bard College) in New York State. While there he felt the call to the ministry.

He was graduated from Virginia Theological Seminary and was ordained to the priesthood in Trinity Church, Columbia, by Bishop Ellison Capers in March, 1901.

Before coming to Sumter, he served a number of South Carolina churches, including: Holy Communion, Allendale; The Cross, Bluffton; Holy Trinity, Grahamville; St. Edmund's, Hardeeville.

After these pastorates he was called to Philadelphia, Pa., where he served as first assistant priest at Holy Trinity and later as priest in charge of Zion Church.

While at Holy Trinity, he was married to Anna Gertrude Wilson in 1902. Still surviving from this marriage are five daughters and one son, 22 grandchildren and 30 great-grandchildren. The fiftieth wedding anniversary of the beloved couple was celebrated at the parish house of the Church of the Holy Comforter.

During Mr. Walker's rectorship, the church made many physical improvements. The debt against the building was liquidated and the church was consecrated; the old church building which was used as a parish house and for Sunday School rooms was enlarged, making room for an assembly hall, a kitchen and a few additional rooms.

Four young men entered the priesthood during his ministry.

He supplied at various times in area churches. These included the Church of the Good Shepherd in Sumter, All Saints Church in Manning, Church of the Holy Cross in Stateburg; and he held monthly services at St. Augustine's in Wedgefield, St. Philip's and Bradford Springs.

Mr. Walker was a proficient student and expounder of the Bible. His word pictures of Old Testament stories were said to have been "clear and colorful."

But above all, he was known in the family, among his flock and throughout the community as a consecrated man of prayer. One of his daughters said that growing up in his family was a great privilege. Each day there were family devotions and she remembers that he spent much of his time on his knees.

Whenever he was presented with a problem by a member of his church or anyone else (for he was a beloved counselor for all in the community), his first step was to bring the matter before the Heavenly Father in prayer.

Much of his parish work was done on foot and he was daily visiting the hospital and homes, bringing comfort and cheer to the sick, discouraged, sad and lonely. It was said that he was a "true shepherd" taking care of the sheep in his own fold and throughout the town.

Even in his youthful years, he was by nature courteous and kindly to all he met. The story is told that when he was a student at St. Stephens, he was walking down a lonely road on his way to church one day when he met a large bear. Politely tipping his hat, he went on his way – and so did the bear. This little incident showed not only his natural sense of civility, but his complete trust in God's care of him.

Growing older, he had difficulty remembering names, but still possessed with a gracious friendly manner, he called younger ladies "daughter" and older ladies "sister."

As the years passed, his work increased, and members of his parish, to whom he had grown more and more precious, persuaded him to retire in 1947 from active responsibilities and become rector emeritus. He remained in this position until his death on Oct. 6, 1963. But in his retirement years he continued to visit the sick, the old and those throughout the city who looked to him for spiritual guidance and strength.

The sketch of Mr. Walker in the bicentennial history of the Church of the Holy Comforter ends with these words: "Necessarily inadequate is this account of Mr. Walker's ministry, for it leaves out ' . . . that best portion of a good man's life, his little, nameless unremembered acts of kindness and of love.' (From **Tintern Abbey** by Wordsworth. 'They are **written not with ink . . . but in the fleshly tables of the heart.**' "

Harry E. Wilkinson, Jr. (Profile)

Harry E. Wilkinson, Jr., president of the National Bank of South Carolina in Sumter for 18 years, was born in Atlanta, Georgia, in 1918 and was reared in Charlotte, North Carolina.[103]

A graduate of the School of Banking of Rutgers University, Wilkinson received his prior education at Central High School, Charlotte, the University of Georgia and the University of North Carolina, where he majored in accounting.

For 16 years he was with the Wachovia Bank and Trust Company in North Carolina before coming to Sumter in 1955.

During World War II he served in the Navy, beginning as an apprentice seaman and advancing to the rank of Lt. Commander. For his bravery during the Normandy Invasion he received the Bronze Star and the Navy Commendation Ribbon for rescuing a sailor during the 1943 Cape Hatteras storm.

Prominent in the business world, Wilkinson maintained membership in the South Carolina Bankers Association and was elected in 1970 to the Executive Committee of the American Bankers Association's Marketing-Savings Division. He served also as president of the Charlotte Chapter of the American Institute of Banking. For 1968-69 he was chairman of the Federal Legislative Committee of the South Carolina Bankers Association.

Mr. Wilkinson served as vice president and director of the South Carolina State Chamber of Commerce, as vice president and director of the Investors National Life Insurance Company, director of the South Carolina State Chamber of Commerce, director of the South Carolina Association of School Boards, and a member of the State Committee for Technical Education. He was also a member of the Board of Business Development Corporation of South Carolina.

With all of these state obligations, he was never too busy to serve his community. Interested in the development of Sumter's boys, he served on the Board of Directors of the Y.M.C.A. and was chairman of the Mac Boykin Trust Fund, returns from which helped support Camp Mac Boykin for underprivileged boys. He was a trustee of School District 17 at one time and chairman of the Sumter Area Technical Education Commission and helped develop TEC plans in the Sumter area. In 1964 he was named chairman of the Advance Gifts division of the Sumter County United Appeal.

This energetic and public spirited man was involved in community improvement through his services to the Sumter County

Development Board and the Downtown Sumter Improvement Association.

Wilkinson was a member of First Presbyterian Church and the Rotary Club (past president).

For recreation he belonged to the Sunset Country Club, Sigma Alpha Epsilon social fraternity and the Palmetto Club.

In November of 1973, Mr. Wilkinson joined the Dutch Boling Company, an investment, commercial-industrial real estate firm based in Columbia, holding this position only a short while before his death, February 2, 1974.[104]

Mr. Wilkinson was married to the former Katherine DuBose of Athens, Georgia, and was the father of three daughters.

He will be remembered in Sumter for his outstanding services to town and community. The National Bank of South Carolina, which he served for 18 years, enjoyed great growth under his leadership, which was marked by foresight and good judgment.

Participation in civic campaigns was always gladly given and his response to requests for services was enthusiastic. His loyal friends in Sumter will ever have a warm feeling of devotion to his memory.

J. Frank Williams, Sumter's First County Agent

Just two weeks and one day after celebrating his 99th birthday, J. Frank Williams, who was an outstanding citizen of Sumter County for many years, died at Medic Home Health Center in Melbourne, Fla., where he had been residing since his health was impaired by an automobile accident.

Born in Pickens County, son of the late Barnett Holloway and Melissa Robinson Williams, he received his education in the Easley Schools and at Clemson, where he was graduated in 1904.

He was married to the former Florence Hendricks, who preceded him in death. They were the parents of eight daughters and one son.

Mr. Williams came to Sumter County as teacher of agriculture and mathematics at the Gen. Thomas Sumter Academy located at the historic Acton Plantation.[105] His students did their practice work in agriculture on the farm near the school and thus began the pioneer demonstration farm in the country.

In 1908 he became the first farm agent in Sumter County, which position he held until 1924. He then began his own farming operations on the Needwood plantation in the Stateburg area; and he and Mrs. Williams became Sumter's first Master Farm Family.

Contributions made by Mr. Williams in Sumter were limitless.

He was one of the organizers of the Sumter County Fair Association, serving as its president for several years. He was also instrumental in forming the County Farmers' Union and served as president. His influence reached beyond this county, shown by the fact that he was elected vice president of the State Farmers' Union.

He is credited with the organization of Union Brokerage Company and was president of that corporation, and he also helped in the establishment of Sumter Dairies and served for a time as its president.

John Frank Williams was a dedicated member of Wedgefield Baptist Church and was a senior deacon. Interested in the welfare of others, he was a charter member of the Kiwanis Club of Sumter, a trustee of Tuomey Hospital, and chairman of the board of trustees of the Stateburg School District for many years.

O.L. Williams (Profile)

Sumter owes much to the late Oliver Lafayette Williams, who came to this city in 1919 and founded the O.L. Williams Veneer Company.

Mr. Williams was born in the Fork community of Davie, N.C., November 16, 1865, the son of D.L. and Emma Rice Williams. He attended the University of North Carolina; and after completing his studies there, he began a business for the manufacture of plug tobacco in Mocksville, N.C. After a few years he sold his company to James Duke and started the Mocksville Furniture Company. Soon he sold this business also and built his veneer plant, also in Mocksville.

Sometime during these years he was married to Mattie Bahnson of Farmington, N.C., and there were three children from this marriage: Louise Bahnson, Charles Frank and Martha.

Hoping to find a greater supply of poplar timber for the making of veneer and plywood, he came to South Carolina, settling in Sumter. Here he established the O.L. Williams Veneer Company. In time he expanded his operations by acquiring the Sumter Veneer Company, the Veneer Manufacturing Company in Conway and the O.L. Williams Veneer Company in Montgomery, Alabama.

After taking over an unsuccessful local woodworking business, he organized the O.L. Williams Top and Panel Company for which he received a charter on August 8, 1925. The purpose of this plant was the manufacturing of lumber tops and panels for furniture makers. He was made president of the company. Other officers were Dr. E.S. Booth, vice president; Neill O'Donnell, secretary-treasurer; D.D. Moise, E.H. Moses, C.P. Gable, directors.

This company was reorganized in 1929 as the Williams Furniture Corporation and it began the manufacture of furniture. The plant was at first located on East Calhoun Street, but this building was completely destroyed by fire in 1936. A new site was purchased on Fulton Street (its present location) and a new and larger plant was built.

The company enjoyed rapid growth and expansion, becoming one of the largest manufacturers of bedroom and dining room furniture in the country. An outgrowth of this company was the Southern Coatings and Chemical Company, organized in 1938. This company was the largest manufacturer of lacquers, varnishes and paints in the state and one of the largest in the South.

Another expansion, coming in 1941, was a program of land and timber acquisition and lumber manufacturing which became the largest local South Carolina lumber company. It owned 186 tracts of land containing approximately 172,000 acres. Large sawmill complexes were operated in Russelville and Alcolu. There were also retail building supply outlets, manufacturing operations for flush doors, pre-finished plywood and a large business for lumber sales.

The O.L. Williams operations were merged into and became a part of Georgia-Pacific Corporation in 1967. At this time Williams was employing approximately 1,500 people in its Sumter operations, about 200 in Alcolu and more than 2,000 in South Carolina.

The Williams operations for more than 50 years had a tremendous economic impact on life in Sumter, especially during the depression of the 1930's and in the years before Shaw Air Force Base was built and before other important industries established plants in the city and county.

To the dedication, industry, sound business acumen and high moral integrity of its founder and the industry of its many zealous employees the Williams Furniture Corporation owes its phenomenal success. Other officers of the complex were Julian T. Buxton, general manager and later president; W.E. Covington, sales manager and executive vice president.

Mr. Williams was a member of the Board of Stewards in Trinity Methodist Church and a member of the Sumter Rotary Club. A loyal Mason, he received a 50-year membership pin from his lodge in Mocksville, North Carolina, in 1945.

O.L. Williams died November 20, 1952,[106] at the age of 87, having lived a long and useful life. Through his outstanding business efficiency, he brought better economic conditions for many families in Sumter and elsewhere and helped make Sumter known throughout the country.

Thumbnail Sketches Of Leading Citizens

"The roads you travel so briskly lead out of dim antiquity and you study the past chiefly because of its bearing on the living present and its promise for the future."

– Lt. Gen. James G. Harboard.

Many of those who lived and served in Sumter District and the city of Sumterville have been sketched in family and other settings; however, there are countless others about whom not a great amount has been written but to whom much is owed for the part they played in the development of life as it is enjoyed today. In this article a few of these will be spotlighted for the generosity with which they gave of themselves for the good of others.

JOHN LAURENCE MANNING

One to be cited especially for his political power in the mid-1800's was John Laurence Manning. A man of strong convictions, he had the courage to stand against opposing forces when he believed that he was right.

When the South was faced with a momentous decision in 1850 and it was the opinion of Calhoun and others, who were deeply concerned over the situation, that it was expedient for South Carolina to secede from the Union, John Laurence Manning was made head of a Committee of Safety.[107] Though feeling at that time that the secession of South Carolina would possibly be the outcome of the issue, he was able to bring about a period of peace among the state factions when he was elected governor in 1852. (He was the fourth man from Sumter District to be elected to his high office.)

Prior to this time (in 1847) when a decision was reached to build a railroad connecting Manchester with Wilmington, Manning was one of the ten astute businessmen in charge of getting subscriptions for the projected plan.

When it was decided in 1855 that the time had come for Clarendon, which at one time had been a separate county, to be separated from Sumter District, the new courthouse town was named Manning in honor of John Laurence Manning, former governor of South Carolina.

In 1866 Manning became United States Senator;[108] thus, he had continuing opportunities to use his political power.

Another facet of this Southern gentleman's influence was in his example of gracious living. His beautiful home, "Milford," built about 1840, though sometimes called "Manning's Folly," was symbolic of Southern life at its best.

However, the warm heart of John Laurence Manning went out to those less fortunate than he. His generosity was shown during Potter's raid when he brought unprotected families of the neighborhood into his lovely home and stood between them and the unruly mob that entered the mansion to plunder, steal, outrage and kill.

THE REV. JOHN SMYTHE RICHARDSON

Active in other developmental phases of life in Sumter District was the Rev. John Smythe Richardson, son of John Smythe Richardson of Bloom Hill. who studied law as early as 1790 and later became a judge in the district. The second John Smythe, though following his father in the study of law, became a minister, while showing a marked interest in other phases of life at the same time.

Throwing strong support to the cause of education, he was one of the first trustees in the Sumterville Academical Society[109] organized for the purpose of extending educational opportunities to the children of the area.

As an advocate of prohibition, Richardson was active in the Sons of Temperance, a national secret fraternity. The Grand Division of South Carolina met in Sumter in 1850, holding their sessions in the Methodist Church. A year later, the Temperance Hall was completed and at the dedication ceremonies, the Rev. John Smythe Richardson gave a "beautiful address on very short notice."

It seems that his love of public speaking was shown in many ways. He took an active part in the Sumterville Debating Society.[110]

Agriculture was another of his interests. At the last Sumter Fair before the War Between the States, he was "the orator." His articles appearing in **The Watchman** – "Use of Lime and Ashes as Fertilizers" and "Conversations on Agricultural Chemistry," gave evidence of his knowledgeable interest in the means of livelihood followed by most of the citizens of the area.

THOMAS JEFFERSON COGHLAN

A popular citizen of Sumter District, who saw the beginnings of the town of Sumterville, serving many years as intendant (mayor) was Thomas Jefferson Coghlan, born at sea on the way to South Carolina from Ireland in 1803.

After his parents died, while he was only a boy, he served for seven years as an apprentice to John Frierson of Cherry Vale. After marrying a young girl of that community, he came to Sumter and set up a shop "to do both blacksmith and whitesmith work." His shop at first was on Republican Street, which is now known as Hampton. He soon added a gun shop and a locksmith shop.

After some time, he established a lumber business for which he built a steam sawmill a mile from town and used the same power to run a mill for grinding corn.

He later (in 1858) added a foundry to his blacksmith shop.

Coghlan was ever an enterprising citizen, trying not only to better himself, but to bring recognition to his town as well. At a time when many were heeding the call to "Go West, young man," Coghlan, with his partner, G.C. Jones, was building new houses in Sumterville, featuring in their unique advertisements their desire "to wipe off the reproach attached to the noble old South Carolina and arouse her from her Rip Van Winkle slumbers and leave California to take care of herself." Another advertisement showing the keen wit of this Irishman was used when the railroad was being built. He advertised "a few dozen railroad carts with three-inch tires," at $300 a dozen and stressed that "the carts will not be built of green pine, but of the best River-swamp oak, ash and hickory, and will be suitable for plantation purposes when the road is completed."

Keenly interested in every phase of community life, Thomas Jefferson Coghlan took an active part in politics. In 1868 he was sent as a delegate to the Constitutional Convention meeting in Charleston.[111] In fact, he was so engrossed in politics after the war that he held at one time three offices – county treasurer, sheriff and United States deputy marshal, though he resigned his seat in the Senate.

At this time his popularity waned somewhat. **The Sumter News** referred to him as the "Ku Klux Exterminator." In the next election for sheriff, he was defeated, and Governor Scott removed him from the office of county treasurer. These moves caused "a howl," for as the Charleston **News and Courier** Sumter correspondent wrote, Coghlan was "an old, well-known and highly respected citizen . . . "

After losing his political positions, the indomitable Coghlan went back into the lumber business – five miles from town. By 1873 he had completed a wooden tramway to the Sumter depot on which to transport his lumber to market. At first cars were drawn by two oxen, believed to be able to do the work of 12 or 14 on an ordinary dirt road. He later used mules to replace the oxen. At the last, he returned to his first occupation – the blacksmith shop.

During his life in Sumter, Coghlan made many worthwhile contributions to the various civic organizations. In 1849 he was elected president of the Sumterville Mechanical Association.

When the State Division of the National Sons of Temperance held a colorful parade in Sumterville, as the Worthy Patriarch he made an "appropriate, humorous, and effective speech."[112] Those present were said to have "strongly manifested their approval of the speaker's sentiment." He also wrote many editorials for **The Sumter Watchman**, supporting the cause of temperance.

Though he may have made mistakes in the eyes of some, Thomas Jefferson Coghlan was a great asset to the growth of Sumter in the mid-1800's.

Ancestral home of Florence Pringle Shaw Shuler, who lived in the home until her death. It is located near the intersection of the old Brewington Road and Hwy. 76. Part of this home was built more than a century ago. (Photo: Courtesy of William S. Shuler).

Samuel Touchberry Home. Near Pinewood. Built of handhewn timbers, fastened with pegs, it is quaint and holds many memories of a devoted family. (Photo: Mike Lee).

Built in 1881: In 1979 placed on National Register of Historic Places. (Photo: South Carolina Department of Archives and History).

Small Office: Dr. Richard B. Furman practiced here for many years, treating patients in the Privateer area and beyond. (Photo: Mike Lee).

Monument at Intersection of Main and Warren Streets. In memory of Capt. Willie Graham who lost his life while fighting a fire in the early days of Sumter. Built by public subscription.

Dixie Hall, originally known as "Oakland Plantation." It was built around 1735 by William Sanders in western section of Sumter County. (Photo: Mike Lee).

William Dinkins Home, off Wise Drive in Sumter. This home dates back to around 1810 and was built on what was probably a grant to John Barden. (Photo: Mike Lee).

The Rev. James Bentham Walker: Former rector of the Episcopal Church of the Holy Comforter – saintly, beloved, a "true shepherd." (Photograph of portrait in Church of the Holy Comforter, Episcopal, made by Mike Lee).

B.J. Barnett, Inc. – (Inside View). This "general store" was begun in 1881 on Main Street, and still has thriving business at its location at 9 E. Liberty. (Photo: Mike Lee).

Mt. Pisgah Methodist Church. Organized in 1866. Present building completed in October 1971. Situated on northeast corner of Bartlette and Council Streets. (Photo: Mike Lee).

Original YMCA: Built around 1910 on the northwest corner of W. Liberty and N. Washington Streets.

Dr. C.W. Birnie: Physician, educator, humanitarian of Sumter. (Photo: Courtesy of Mrs. Anna Birnie McDonald).

Sumter County Historical Society Museum-Archives. Williams-Brice House. North Washington Street.

Research Center in Sumter County Museum-Archives. At right Mrs. Helen Malone, secretary.

Dr. S.H. Edmunds, 1870-1935. "Great educator, great leader, great man." (Photographed from portrait in Sumter County Library by Mike Lee).

Richard Irvin Manning, last governor from Sumter County (1915-1919). He has been credited with reforms in county and state brought about during his years as governor. (Photo: Courtesy John Adger Manning, Lexington, S.C.).

National Bank of Sumter, later Peoples State Bank of South Carolina. Now owned and being restored by Sumter County Historical Foundation. On. N.W. corner of Main and Liberty Streets.

Ellerbe's Mill. Since 1830, it has ground corn for citizens in the Rembert-Rafting Creek area. (Photo: Courtesy of James L. Haynsworth).

Wedgefield Presbyterian Church observed Centennial Anniversary April 6, 1981. (Photo: Courtesy Mrs. Hugh M. McLaurin, Jr.).

J.O. Barwick: One of Sumter County's outstanding business men, and a dedicated church leader. (Photo: Courtesy of Mrs. Billy Gibson, daughter).

Hebron Presbyterian Church: DuBose Crossroads, Highway 15. (Photo: Mike Lee).

Millford, built by former Governor Laurence I. Manning, now owned by William R. Clark. Of great historic interest. Saved by General Edward E. Potter from destruction by his followers in 1865. (Photo: Courtesy Mrs. Hugh M. McLaurin of Wedgefield).

Sumter Art Gallery — Home formerly owned and occupied by Miss Elizabeth White, world famous artist. (Photo: Mike Lee).

First in the World. (Photo: Mike Lee).

PLAT OF CITY OF SUMTER IN 1817

From Report Book "A" - page 138

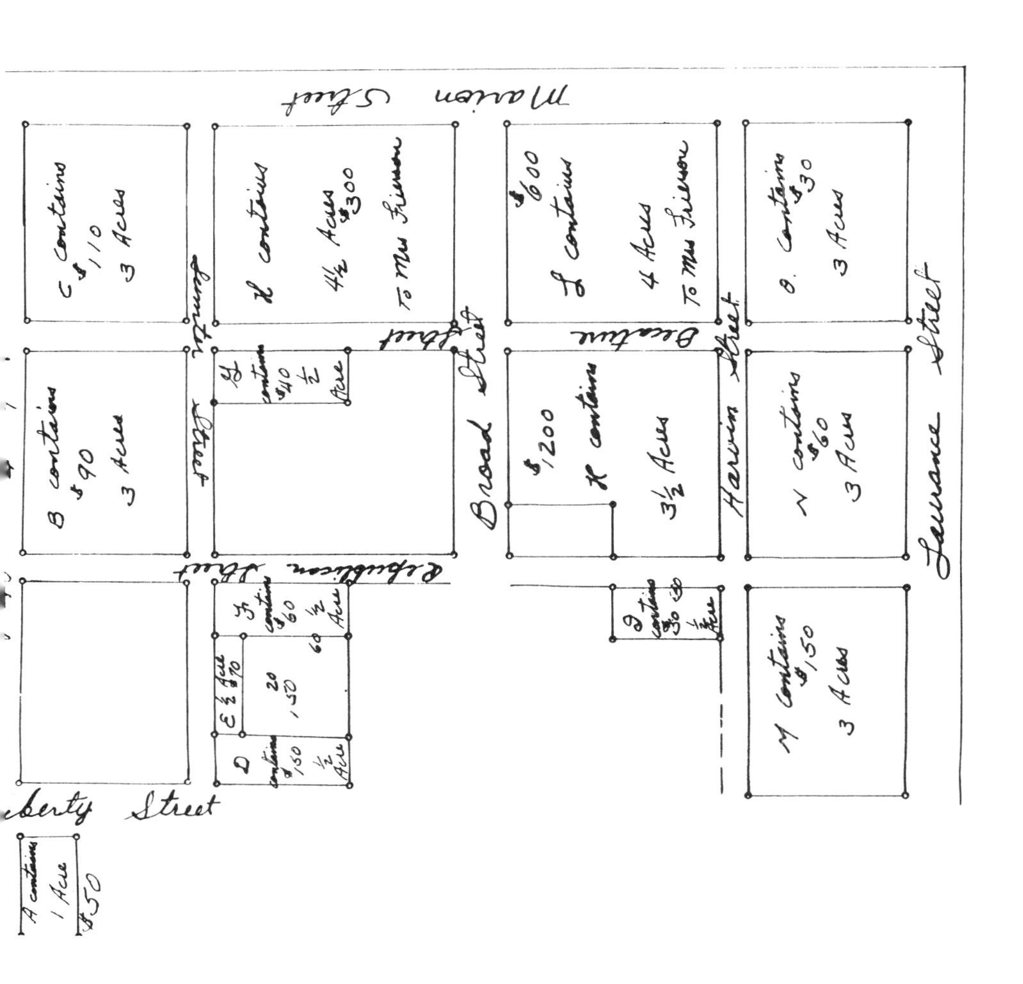

Pursuant to directions I have admeasured and laid out the Lots of land around the village of Sumterville represented in the above plan – containing in the whole Thirty Acres ——

Surveyed the 9 October 1817

W. L. Brunson D. Surveyor

1200	110
600	50
300	60
150	20
50	40
90	50
	150
2390	90
570	570
2960	

Recorded Sept 30th 1916
H. L. Scarborough
C.C.C.P.

Note: this is a true copy of a plat recorded in Plat Book 0-4 pg. 1 in the office of the Register of Mesne Conveyances in the Sumter County C.H.

H.S. Wilson R.L.S.
March 4, 1981

FILE No. 81-18

Home of Miss Maggie Pierce, near Concord Presbyterian Church. It was built in the early 1800's by Mr. and Mrs. Robert McFaddin ("Aunt Leah" as she generally known). (Photo: by Mike Lee).

Built in 1959 on Alice Drive. (Photo: Mike Lee).

Dedication of Park at Dingle's Mill, site of battle in 1865. Shown in foreground Mrs. Marilyn Ayers, president of Dick Anderson Chapter, UDC, sponsor of project; Mrs. Myrtis Ginn Osteen, co-chairman of crermonies; W.E. Brunson III, chairman; David M., Osteen Ch. of Honor Guard. (Photo: by Heyward Crowson).

Sumter Council of Garden Club Center: Built in 1964 near Swan Lake. (Photo: Mike Lee).

Historic home of Mr. and Mrs. Ansley L. Yates, on W. Hampton Avenue, moved from what became in 1920 Memorial Park and restored by the present owners. (Photo: Courtesy of Mrs. Yates).

Tirzah Presbyterian Church in Dalzell. Centennial Celebration observed March 21, 1976. (Photo: Mike Lee).

Unique home built by Mr. and Mrs. W.L. Miller from materials obtained from old freight depot and other old buildings. Near Dalzell. (Photo: Mike Lee).

Located in High Hills of Santee area. (Photo: Mike Lee).

Mrs. Daisy Wilson Cave, South Carolina's oldest Confederate widow. She lives in Sumter. (Photo: Mike Lee).

Original building, located on Liberty Street. (Photo: Sumter Chamber of Commerce).

Scene from Sumter Cemetery. Located W. Oakland Ave. (Photo: Mr. and Mrs. W.E. Covington).

This little club house near Cain's Mill is the place where many local men have enjoyed constructive programs and relaxation for a number of years. (Photo: Mike Lee).

Dignity Village: Apartment Complex, YWCA-HUD project on N. Blanding Street. In the foreground Mrs. Theo Palmer, director of YWCA and Mrs. Casey Reiling, president. (Photo: Mike Lee).

Sumter Towne Mall – Looking north. (Photo: *The Sumter Daily Item*).

Sponsored by Sumter County Commission; Sumter Area Technical College; Clemson University Ext. Service. Director of project is Agronomist Harvey W. Tiller, Jr. (Photo: Mike Lee).

This beautiful home on the northwest corner of Broad and Church Streets was built first as an office building for former Governor Franklin I. Moses around 1840. It later changed hands and was made into a home. Since 1921 it has had numerous owners and been used for various purposes. It is now owned by the Billy M. Harris family.

Swan Lake Iris Gardens, showing beautiful gate on left.

Winners in Trolley Parade, 1954.

Myrtle Moor, in Salem section of Sumter County. It was built more than 100 years ago. (Photo: Courtesy C. Rembert Skinner).

Oldest School Building, in what is now School Dist. No. 2. Located in Stateburg area. (Photo: Mike Lee).

L.C. Richardson-W.A. Johnson Learning Resources Center – W.H. Neal-Iola Jones Fine Arts Center – Morris College. (Photo: Courtesy of the College).

Built in 1892. On North Washington Street.

PART IV. OLD CHURCHES

Providence Baptist Church

Providence Baptist Church, begun as a mission of Bethel Baptist Church, was organized as a church on January 7, 1842, with 26 members.

Apparently there was no regular pastor until 1879, as the first pastor listed was B.C. Lampley, 1879-1882. However, a meeting house (as it was called in the records) was completed in March of 1842.[113]

In 1887 another sanctuary was built, but for that year there was no pastor listed. However, H.F. Oliver came in 1888, serving only a year. This old building was reroofed in 1929 or 1930 while Rev. P.O. Batson was pastor.

Around 1937 four Sunday School rooms were built while Rev. V.V. Raines was pastor.

Three more rooms were added in 1942. Apparently the Sunday School was growing.

In 1948, while G.T. Wilson was pastor, a pastorium was built and replaced in 1970 with a new pastor's home. Jack Hunter was pastor at that time.

The building program continued from year to year with new educational facilities added from time to time. A new sanctuary was dedicated in 1972.

Many other pastors have served this old church, but there were times when the church was without a pastor. Present pastor is Jimmy Atkerson, who has been with the church since 1976.

An excerpt from the report of the church in 1977 reads:

"The history of Providence Baptist Church goes on. We desire to honor those who worked with courage, faith and vision in the face of hardships and discouragements. We are grateful to God for his leadership. For 134 years this church has stood like a lighthouse for Christ in the community. The song rings out in our hearts, 'O Lord, our help in ages past . . . Our hope for years to come.' "

Mt. Pisgah A.M.E. Church

One of Sumter's old churches stands today on the original site, the northeast corner of Bartlette and Council Streets, though many changes have been made since that day just after the War Between the States when the desire was kindled in the hearts of a few ex-slaves to have their own church. They consulted the pastor of the church to which they belonged and received encouragement for such a move.

Therefore with his encouragement and under the leadership of Rev. Richard Cain of Charleston, the little group of 11 charter members began their own A.M.E. church on August 15, 1866.[114]

In this group were James White, Sam Burroughs, Elizabeth White, Mary A. Singleton, Molly Stewart, Eliza Brooks, Sallie Johnson, Ellen Levan, Abbie Spears, Charlotte and Abram Ruffin.

First pastor was Rev. W.A. Johnson and services were held in the Sumter Courthouse at first. They were soon able to raise $300 to purchase the property upon which the first church house was built in 1868 while Abram Powell was pastor.

The first Sunday School superintendent was Sam Lee (who became a member of the State Constitutional Convention). He was followed by W.J. Andrews who led the church school for 54 years.

In 1879 the second sanctuary was built while Rev. E.D. Spearman was pastor.

While Rev. J.C. Williams was pastor, in 1900, the third sanctuary was built and it was brick veneered in 1941, during the pastorate of Rev. R.L. Pope.

Fourteen years later, in 1955, an educational building was completed and in 1963 the mortgage on this building was burned. During the time of these improvements Rev. R.C. James was pastor. About this time the remainder of the lot adjoining the church property was bought.

In 1968, under the leadership of Pastor James, the church sponsored a low-rent housing project, the first in the state, on College Street for the accommodation of those living in the northern part of the city. Known as Mt. Pisgah Apartments, the project cost between six and seven hundred thousand dollars, but received aid for the construction through the Federal Housing Administration. It contained 60 units, with two or three bedrooms.

Rev. James began plans for a project in conjunction with Mt. Pisgah Apartments. Cooperating in this project were the Vocational Home Economics Department of South Carolina, the State Department of Education, Mrs. S.D. Ramsey and Mrs. H.W. Nelson from the Home Economics Department of Lincoln High School. He called for volunteers for the project, the first of its kind in the state.

Teen groups were organized as well as Boy Scout Troops, in addition to weekly classes which gave training in the use of modern facilities. Classes were held in office conference room – all-purpose building on College Street. Attendance, mostly female and adults, varied. Some classes were held at night. There were also courses on housing and home improvement, child care and guidance, family relations, management of time and energy, family financing, consumer buying, family health, foods and nutrition.

Though there was much sentiment involved, in 1971 members of Mt. Pisgah decided to demolish the sanctuary built in 1900 and loved for 71 years. When renovation was undertaken, it was found that the timbers had deteriorated to the extent that renovation was not feasible.

The new sanctuary begun in April was completed in October. A special service was held in which W.B. Boyle, president of Boyle Construction Company, was a special guest since it was his company that did the building. He praised the work and cooperation of the church membership, saying, "I personally feel that God ordained this building to be done."

The sanctuary is beautiful indeed, topped by a "perfect dome" with the huge stained glass windows from the old church and a cross on each side of the front entrance. Above the pulpit is the following inscription in large gold letters: "God Our Father, Christ Our Redeemer, Man Our Brother."

Soon after the completion of the new sanctuary at the 39th quadrennial session of the African Methodist Episcopal Church in 1972, Rev. James was chosen as one of the 18 bishops of that body. He was assigned to Southern Africa for a term of four years.

In the same year, Rev. J.L. Gillison became pastor of Mt. Pisgah and has been the dedicated leader of the church since that time. In the eight years of his pastorate much has been accomplished in Christian activity and growth.

In the spring of 1975, one-fourth acre of land adjacent to the church on Council Street was purchased with a view to future growth, and in December of 1978 the indebtedness of $20,500 on the lot was liquidated.

Always noted for its interest in young people, the church, led by Pastor Gillison, has launched projects in developing scholarship and talents of the youth.

There have been special efforts made to revitalize Men's Day and Women's Day programs, and counseling services provided by the pastor are being stressed.

An evangelistic thrust is being made by the Steward Board for the winning of the lost. More emphasis is being placed on the necessity for prayer in the work of God's kingdom by a special emphasis on the mid-week prayer service.

Pastor Gillison is exerting strong leadership not only in his own church, but in wider circles as well. In December of 1978, he was elected to the South Carolina Christian Action Council, the first black to hold this position.

Mt. Pisgah A.M.E. Church, having begun in the hearts of 11 dedicated men and women in 1866, has now 500[115] members. In these 14 years it has meant much to those who have been a part of its history, to the community in which it stands and to the city of Sumter. It has been led by many able and consecrated pastors and it stands today as a lighthouse for all who may be guided by its strong Christian influence.

Congregation Sinai

Observance of the Centennial of Congregation Sinai was held on April 4, 1976, which date was really two years after the 100th anniversary of the first Jewish organization in Sumter.

No doubt Jewish settlers came to Sumter from Charleston in the first days of the village of Sumterville, around 1801. According to the late Herbert A. Moses, one of Sumter's outstanding historians, the first permanent settler was Mr. Mark Solomons, who came from Charleston between 1815 and 1820.

The booklet, "The Early Minutes of the Sumter Society of Israelites," published by Mr. Moses in 1936, gives something of the activities of the first Jewish organizations in Sumter, organizations which were the real beginning of Congregation Sinai.

The first minutes recorded were of "an adjourned meeting" of the Sumter Hebrew Benevolent Society held on April 17, 1881,[116] at the office of C.H. Moise, Esq.

Prior to this there had been another group that purchased in 1874 two acres of land from John H. Furman, trustee, for a Jewish cemetery by a representative of a group known as the Hebrew Cemetery Society (or Burial Society). This took place seven years before the Hebrew Benevolent Society was formed.

According to the minutes as found in Mr. Moses' booklet, those present for the meeting of the Hebrew Benevolent Society on April 17, 1881, in addition to C.H. Moise, were: D. Rosendorf, G. Morris, Abe Morris, Altamont Moses, M.G. Ryttenberg,

B.J. Barnett, E.W. Moise, A.D. Moses, H. Goldstrom, Abe Ryttenberg, A.C. Phelps, E.W. Moise, Jr., H.D. Moise, C.H. Moise, Jr., J.E. Suares, Harry Ryttenberg, Perry Moses, M. Furstenberg, Herman Schwerin, Dr. Ed Solomons, Horace Harby, Marion Moise, and Isaac Sulzbacher.

On April 27, 1881, a committee from the two societies met to consider a merger. Representing the Burial Society were M.E. Cohen, A.A. Solomons and C.H. Moise and representatives for the Benevolent Society were E.W. Moise, Horace Harby and Altamont Moses. It was agreed that the two should merge under the name of the Hebrew Benevolent Society, and on May 2, less than a week later, the cemetery property was transferred to the Benevolent Society.

On May 1, 1881, the first officers were elected: C.H. Moise, president; Altamont Moses, vice president; J.E. Ryttenberg, secretary; B.J. Barnett, treasurer.

Soon a committee reported that the Masonic Hall had been rented for use of the Society for its meetings. This meeting place was used for many years by the Society.

The work of the Society covered a wide range of activities. There were committees appointed on Moral Improvement, Finance, Charity, Visiting the Sick, Burial and Cemetery, and Intellectual Improvement.

Though there was no resident leader at first, Rabbi David Levy of Charleston visited the Society, helping to train the young people. One class trained in Sumter was confirmed with a Charleston class in 1891. Rabbi Levy came to Sumter for perhaps a year or two, leading services and assisting with a Sunday School. Thus began the formation of a regular congregation which later called a resident leader and built a place of worship.

It was in the year 1885 that the name Sumter Society of Israelites was assumed by the Jewish residents of Sumter, and on December 7, 1891, this society received a charter from the clerk of court. The following are recorded as members: Altamont Moses, Marion Moses, M.G. Ryttenberg, Horace Harby, E.W. Moise, Abe Ryttenberg, V.H. Phelps, A.C. Phelps, Irving A. Ryttenberg, Louis Morris, Harry Morris, Henry Weinberg, H. Schwerin, I. Strauss, R.H. Moise, A.L. Moise, I.H. Moses, Jr., H. Ryttenberg, Louis Lyon, Moses Green, Joe Strauss, Gabriel Levy, H.J. Harby, C.D. Schwartz, Isaac Schwartz, D. Rosendorf, B.J. Barnett, H.D. Barnett, H. Karesh, H. Manheim, F.M. and M. Levi.

The first synagogue, a wooden structure, was built on the corner of Hampton Avenue (then Republican Street) and Church Street. The lot was purchased from Anna J. McCall in December of 1891.

Desirous of a more spiritual life for their congregation, the members in 1904 called Rabbi Jacob Klein to be their regular rabbi and live in the community. After serving four years, he was followed by Rabbi David Sessler, who remained for two years and was followed by Rabbi David Klein. Having served seven years, he was succeeded by Rabbi R.F.K. Hirsch. Rabbi Hirsch served the congregation for ten years and was then followed by Rabbi H.L. Freund who remained only two years and was succeeded by one who served the Congregation with devotion for many years – Rabbi Samuel R. Shillman.

In 1949 Rabbi J. Aaron Levy came and served until his retirement. Rabbi Edward Miskin then served for a short time.

On Sunday afternoon, December 10, 1972, Rabbi Avshalom Magidovitch was installed in an impressive service and he continued to lead the congregation until his death in 1979.

As the congregation grew, the wooden structure was replaced by a brick building which was dedicated in 1913. In 1907 two and a half acres were added to the cemetery property and in 1942 other property was acquired.

In 1960 property at the south of the synagogue, a lot 70 by 160 feet, was added to the holdings of the congregation and in 1971 another lot, 84 by 165 feet, was added at the east.

An addition to the synagogue was the Barnett Memorial Building, given as a legacy from Mrs. J.E. Barnett of Manning in 1932. This contains an assembly room and a stage. At the back is a kitchen built in 1956.

On November 22, 1956, the Hyman Brody Educational Building was dedicated. A. Brody presented the keys, during the service, to Jack Addlestone, who in turn gave them to Miss Ruth Lyon, superintendent of the Sunday School at that time.

A renovation and redecorating program was begun in recent years. A committee consisting of Harold Moise, Harry Berger, Abe Stern, Morris Mazursky, Herbert Moses, and Dr. Herman Rubin (chairman) was appointed to raise money for the building fund.

A committee for redecoration consisted of Robert Moses, Harold Moise, Mrs. Herbert Rosefield, Mrs. Jack Addlestone and Mrs. Reuben Brody.

The walls were repainted, a beautiful new chandelier replaced the old one, new carpet and new pews were added, a new ark was built (memorial gift of the family of Reuben Brody), and other improvements were made.

On February 7, 1969, a most impressive rededication service was held.

Officers of the congregation that year were: Robert Moses, president; Morris Mazursky, vice president; Ruth Lyon, secretary; David D. Kramer, treasurer; Herbert Moses, warden; and W.L. Hirshberg, trust officer.

Sisterhood officers were: Mrs. A. Brody, president; Mrs. Jack Addlestone, first vice president; Mrs. Abe Stern, second vice president; Mrs. John Philips, secretary; Mrs. Irving Yokel, treasure.

Men's Club officers were: Bennett Denemark, president; Max Edelsberg, vice president; Bernard Warshaur , secretary; and Myer Horovin, treasurer.

All of these worked with the committees to make the work on the Temple successful, and no doubt, the officers of the Temple Youth also had a part. These were: Anthony Kramer, Neil Dubin, Sheila Brody, John Philips, and Susan Freed.

Very active in community affairs is the Sisterhood, which was at first known as the Ladies Aid Society and was busy beautifying the Temple and grounds, as well as the cemetery. In later years, the organization's scope of community service has broadened. Members have made a wonderful contribution to the blind in the area by translating books into Braille to be used in schools and by reading books to be transferred to tapes for the use of students.

This group is affiliated with the National Federation of Temple Sisterhoods, and at one time Mrs. Herbert Rosefield served on the National Board. This Sisterhood is also a member of the Southeast Federation of Temple Sisterhoods and Mrs. Joseph Gilbert was formerly vice president of that organization. Through these affiliations they have contributed to worldwide Jewish causes.

The Men's Club is also very active in service in the community, as well as in other states and nations.

On January 12, 1972, a beautiful new Torah was dedicated by the congregation in memory of Rabbi J. Aaron Levy, the beloved Rabbi who served the congregation faithfully and well for 21 years. He lived only a short time after his retirement in 1970.

In the Brody Educational Building are classrooms, a library, office space – most furnished as memorials. One room has been devoted to an archives where many priceless books, papers, pictures and other mementoes of the early Jewish history are kept on display. Time can be well spent in going through these relics, many of which date back beyond the American Revolution, having been brought from Charleston by the descendants of those first Israelites who came to the New World. The first archivist was Mrs. Joseph Gilbert.

The interior of the Sanctuary has many outstandingly beautiful features. Among these are the magnificent stained glass windows portraying Biblical characters. To describe the tall colorful windows of matchless beauty would be impossible, but it is of interest to note something of their history.

One is in memory of Abraham and Fanny D'Ancona, the grandparents of Wendell M. Levi. Mrs. D'Ancona is buried in the Jewish cemetery in Sumter.

Another is dedicated to the memory of Andrew Jackson and Octavia Harby Moses, the parents of Perry Moses, Sr., Horace Harby and J.J. Harby. (Some in this family changed the name from Moses to Harby.)

Dedicated to Harry and Rose Ryttenberg is a third window. They were the parents of Irving A. Ryttenberg and the grandparents of Lydia Hirshberg and Harry Ryttenberg.

The parents of Isaac Strauss, Seligman and Yetta Strauss, are memorialized in the next window. They were the grandparents of Mrs. Eileen Rubin, a member of the congregation.

Next is a window dedicated to Moses and Hannah Levi, paternal grandparents of Wendell M. Levi.

The third window on the north was dedicated to Marion Moise, brother of Nina M. Phelps and Jessica M. Merrimon, father of Harold Moise and grandfather of Virginia Rosefield, Davis D. Moise and Marion Moise.

Next is a window dedicated to General E.W. Moise, one of the founders of the Hebrew Benevolent Society which later became Congregation Sinai.

In memory of Jacob Theodore and Julia Solomons, parents of Mrs. Isaac Schwartz, is the next window.

For more than 100 years Jewish settlers of Sumter have been organized, first as the Hebrew Benevolent Society, then as the Sumter Society of Israelites and now as Congregation Sinai; and under all names they have made their influence felt, contributing to the business, educational, cultural and moral improvement of community life in the Sumter area and beyond.

Tirzah Presbyterian

Beautiful old Tirzah Presbyterian Church has stood for a century in the little town of Dalzell as a witness for Christ and His kingdom.

A service of worship commemorating the 100th anniversary of its founding was held on Sunday, March 21, 1976,[117] with many former members, descendants of former members and friends attending.

A spirit of reverence was felt throughout the service and those present were made aware of the influence for good Tirzah has had through the years as the minister, Rev. T.L. Johnson, told something of its history.

Though no one really knows, said the speaker, who or why the church was given the name that it has had from the beginning, he told of the meanings of the word from Old Testament Scriptures.

From Numbers 27:1-11 he revealed that Tirzah was a woman, daughter of Zelophehad. He reminded his hearers that in those days the sons were the heirs of the father both in the matter of property and community standing and the rights of the daughters were not considered. But when Zelophehad of the tribe of Joseph died, leaving no sons, his daughters including Tirzah asked of Moses that they have the rights of heirs. Moses brought the matter before God and He commanded that henceforth the daughters of a man with no sons at his death were to receive the inheritance. Thus Tirzah is pictured as a woman of strength, with a sense of justice and not afraid to speak out.

Using 1 Kings 16:23, he pointed out that Tirzah was a city — not just a city, but a royal city, for there the king of Israel ruled.

Then in the Song of Solomon 6:4 it is implied that Tirzah was beautiful.

The pastor thus brought out some of the qualities demonstrated by Tirzah Presbyterian Church through its 100 years.

From the minutes of the church, which have been kept from the beginning and are now being preserved in the South Caroliniana Library in Columbia, he gave the names of the charter members who came from the Sumter church. These were Mrs. T.M. Jennings, Miss Mary Pelham, L.R. Jennings, Jr., Dr. L.W. Dick, Mrs. Ida Dick, J.J. Knox, Miss Minnesota Bryan, Mrs. Rebecca Ann Raffield, and Mrs. S.C. Bryan.

On the same day five were admitted on examination — Miss E.R. Jennings, H.A. Raffield, Mrs. S.C. Raffield, Miss R.E. Raffield and J.B. Raffield.

H.A. Raffield and J.J. Knox were elected, ordained and installed as ruling elders and L.R. Jennings became a deacon.

The first minister was William Boyd of Brazos, Texas. He was a student at Columbia Theological Seminary, located at that time in Columbia and preached at Tirzah for the three months of his vacation.

During the early part of the service the pastor recognized Miss Abbie Bryan who was baptized in Tirzah in 1887 and attended Sunday School and church services there during her early life. He also recognized Mrs. W.H. Stevenson, whose husband was beloved pastor of Tirzah for many years. Other guests were warmly welcomed.

Special music, including "How Great Thou Art" and "Sweet Hour of Prayer," was furnished by Mrs. Willie Dinkins, Mrs. Frances Dinkins Strong and Mr. Langdon Dinkins.

Wedgefield Methodist Church

In an overgrown spot in the little town of Wedgefield, once stood a church that was dear to the hearts of the few faithful Methodists living there. A history of this church from its very beginning was written by Mrs. Lizzie Moore Griffin and published in the **Southern Christian Advocate** on July 18, 1935. In this history, Mrs. Griffin states that even before 1876 Methodist ministers preached in homes of the area, in vacant houses, on the railroad depot platform or anywhere a group could congregate. Sometimes "a few ladies, some boys, and perhaps a man or two" would walk down to Camden Junction near Wedgefield to hear a sermon as a minister was passing through.

Only a dozen or so white families lived in Wedgefield at that time and only a sprinkling of these were Methodists. In 1877, a new school house was built in the town and a platform was placed at one end in order that the building might be used also as a community church. Several ministers preached for the faithful few gathered here. These were, according to Mrs. Griffin, Rev. D.D. Dantzler, Rev. Mr. Horton, Rev. J.C. Stoll, Rev. A.C. Legette and Rev. A.A. Gilbert. Some of these may have been of different denominations, since the building was used by the community.

Then in 1878 or early 1879[118] the Wedgefield Methodist Church was organized by Rev. A.C. Legette, with fewer than a dozen members, but these made up in interest and dedication what the church lacked in numbers. In 1881, a church building was begun. William W. Moore, William J. Graham and Isaac J. Wilson were the stewards and leading spirits in the building program which was a tremendous undertaking for so small a group.

A Sunday School was organized and literature, consisting of "Happy Voice" song books, catechisms for the younger children, "Union Question Book Two" for the youth and adults, and New Testaments, were brought and distributed by William W. Moore. So hungry were the people for worship services and so happy to have a place of worship that they would spend whole Sunday afternoons singing from their new song books.

After some years and many sacrifices, the church building was completed and dedicated by Rev. W.D. Kirkland.

For a while, the church "flourished." The reports given in the records of Sumter District of the Methodist Church show that the Wedgefield Church had 50 members in 1880, 60 in 1881; but in 1882 the membership dropped to 46, going up to 51 in 1884. In 1885 and 1886, there were 60 on roll again and in 1891 the membership was 63. When Mrs. Griffin's sketch was written, however, in 1935 there were only 32 members. Apparently, the population of Wedgefield must not have been very stable.

In fact, Mrs. Griffin bemoaned the changes in population. At the time when she was writing, she said that some had moved away and some had died. She said, "We are thankful that a faithful few are still holding up the total of Methodism in Wedgefield."

Some time along the way, a parsonage was built and furnished. An organ was bought for the church in 1886 and Mrs. W.D. Graham became the first organist.

Members took much interest in the church work. There was a wide-awake Sunday School with classes meeting in different parts of the auditorium or wherever they could find a place. Mrs. Griffin recalled that Children's Day was observed every May with an all-day picnic in a nearby woods. Those present would sing, recite and make talks. The pastor was always present for his part on the program. One feature of the day was the placing of a collection basket in a convenient place where money could be placed for the missionary work in Brazil. "Those were happy days for Wedgefield Methodist folks," remembered Mrs. Griffin.

In 1904, John C. Chandler came to Wedgefield and became moving force in the little church. He served for many years as steward, part of the time as chairman of the Board of Stewards. He was also the keeper of the records. In 1921, he became Sunday School superintendent and held this position along with that of steward and recorder until the church was closed, and he kept records beyond that time, showing churches to which various members took their membership after the disbanding of the congregation.

In the beginning, this church was in the Wedgefield or Spring Hill Circuit with three other churches – McLeod's Chapel, Providence and Bethesda. Preaching services were held twice a month in the afternoon; however, members held Sunday School every Sunday.

In 1894, Wedgefield Methodist was transferred to the Pinewood Circuit, according to records in the Historical Society of the South Carolina Conference of the Methodist Church.

In 1908 and 1909, it was recorded as "apparently" in the Providence Circuit. Then from 1910 to 1913, it was listed in that circuit; but in 1914 it was in the "apparently" status again. In 1922, the Providence Circuit was discontinued and Wedgefield was assigned to Broad Street Methodist (now St. Mark's) in Sumter; however, it remained there only six years. In 1928, it was assigned again to Pinewood Circuit, where it remained until 1941. A statement signed by John C. Chandler found in the Wedgefield Church Register reads: "Doors of the church closed in July 1941 on account of depleted membership."[119]

Many regular pastors, as well as supplies, served this old church in Wedgefield. Some of the earlier ones in addition to those named were Rev. Emory Olin Watson; Rev. J.H. Chandler, uncle of lay member John C. Chandler, who served from 1881 to 1884 and again from 1891 to 1894; Rev. James Whitefield Kilgo; Rev. H.C. Bethea; Rev. John Manning; Rev. W.B. Duncan; Rev. J.W. Dowell; Rev. Thomas White; Rev. Foster Speer; Rev. James R. Copeland. These were the pastors from the beginning till the end of the 19th century. At the time when the church was closed, there was no pastor listed.

When the church was organized, Rev. Thomas G. Herbert was the Presiding Elder; and when it was disbanded, the Presiding Elder was Rev. J. Ross Johnson.

At some time the organ was replaced by a piano and for a long time, Miss Mary Alice Chandler was the pianist. The church was lighted by hanging kerosene lamps and two beautiful lamps on the piano. Collection was taken in velvet pouches attached to long sticks, the type of collection "plates" often used in churches of the long ago. Another handsome piece of furniture used in the church was a lovely bookcase, which along with the lamps from the piano are in the home of Mrs. F.H. Suber, daughter of Mr. Chandler. There were also two marble-top tables, but it is not known where they are.

When the church was demolished, upon the decision of the presiding elder, in 1952, the pews and piano, as well as other furnishings were given, it is thought, to other churches in the community.

The old parsonage was no longer needed when the Church was transferred to the Pinewood Circuit since the minister lived in Pinewood. It was eventually sold and is now occupied by the George Hair family. It is still in good condition, though it is more than 75 years old.

To those living today who attended Wedgefield Methodist Church, the old parsonage and the overgrown site where stood the little church bring back poignant memories of those days and hours spent there and of the many joyous experiences that came to them through their Christian service fostered by pastors, Sunday School teachers and other leaders.

Mayesville Baptist Church

Though small in number from the very beginning, Mayesville Baptist Church has weathered the storms of more than 100 years.

Its origin dates back to the 1870's when under the leadership of Missionary M.L. Ball, whose salary was paid by the State Mission Board and Santee Association, those in the community who were Baptists met in the "Hall," a building used for various meetings in the little town, once a month. After two years these faithful few were led to organize a New Testament church. A covenant of the church, presented by the Reverend Ball, was endorsed by the members and the body was declared a "regular constituted" Baptist church. According to the record of a business meeting of the church held on October 1, 1883, the date of the organization was June 23, 1879, although associational minutes put the organization date in 1878.

In the fall of 1879 the church, having made application for membership, was received into the Santee Association.

For many years the State Baptist Board and the association assisted with the finances of the church by providing at least $100 each year for the pastor's salary.

On the first Sunday in June of 1881,[120] the new church building, with a capacity of 250, was dedicated by Dr. C.C. Brown, for many years pastor of First Baptist Church of Sumter, preaching the dedicatory sermon. The building was erected on land donated by C.O. Wheler; however, the title to the lot was not given to the congregation until May 9, 1916, when a deed to the property was presented to the trustees, W.S. Wheler, T.B. Fort and F.J. Bass.

Services were only twice a month most of the time until 1951. During the pastorate of Rev. S.S. Averitt, the congregation resolved to have worship services each Sunday and this schedule has continued. At times the church has maintained a well-attended Sunday School, but at other times interest in this part of the work has been lacking. The same situation has been true of the women's work. In 1890 there was a note in the minutes of one church conference stating that since the missionary society was giving all of its money to foreign missions, the church would give its contributions to state and home missions. Apparently there was an active society at that time.

Always a part of a field of two or three other churches, Mayesville has shared a pastor with the following churches at different times: Lynchburg, Salem Avenue, Bethany, Southside, Wedgefield, Providence and Mizpah.

In 1912 the church was disbanded and there is no record as to when it was revived; however, indications are that it must have been reorganized in 1916. During that year the building was repaired at a cost of $773.50.

Many ministers have served this old church since its beginning, some as supplies and some as regular pastors. Most of these, however, were connected with the church for comparatively short periods of time, but each doubtless made a worthwhile contribution to the life of the church.

The longest pastorate was that of the Rev. E.W. Reynolds, who served the church with great devotion for 19 years, preaching twice a month on Sunday afternoon. He was pastor of Salem Avenue Baptist Church in Sumter for many years and was greatly loved by his members in both Sumter and Mayesville.

Other pastors and supplies include the following: Rev. F.O. Curtis, Rev. J. Howard Carpenter, Rev. N.B. Williams, Rev. H.F. Oliver, Rev. Thomas H. Edwards, Rev. R.P. Galphin, Rev. William Haynsworth, Rev. J.H. Mitchell, Rev. J.W. Guy, Rev. George Hopkins, Rev. J.B. Caston, Rev. B.M. Davidson, Rev. Paul Bullington, Rev. S.S. Averitt, Rev. M.A. Hutto and Rev. J.O. Summerlin.

The second longest pastorate began in 1957 when Rev. Paul Kok came to the church. This minister had a unique background, having been born in Holland, reared in China, and educated in America. His father was in the diplomatic service of Holland in China for 27 years.

After completing elementary school in China, Mr. Kok entered Wheaton Academy in Wheaton, Illinois, and later studied at Chicago Art School. He then returned to the hill country of China as a missionary. The region lay beyond a wild mountain section of North China. There he preached the gospel and served a people where only two white men had ventured before him.

When the Communists took over China, he was forced to leave and was not allowed to return. Coming back to America, he studied at the University of South Carolina and Southern Baptist Theological Seminary in Louisville, Kentucky, before going into pastoral work. His last church was Mayesville from which he retired in 1975.

The church building has had many improvements through the years, some through the generosity of Mr. Warren Smith, who lived in Mayesville as a boy. After growing up, he went into the oil business in Venezuela. Since his mother was a member of Mayesville Baptist Church in his early life, he wanted to make improvements in her memory.

Rev. Leon Lowder became pastor in 1975 and served until June of 1980 when he resigned because of failing health. His spiritual leadership meant much to the little church. Rev. H.W. Granger is now serving the church as pastor.

The present board of deacons consists of Messrs. H.C. Partin, W.A. Riley, W.M. Riley, and D.C. Webster. Serving as clerk is Mrs. H.C. Partin. Mr. Partin is treasurer and Mr. Webster is superintendent of the Sunday School.

In 1979[121] the church was listed in the National Register of Historic Places.

New Hope Baptist Church

New Hope Baptist Church was organized in the year 1880. Land for the church building and cemetery was given to the community, it is said, by Mrs. Mattie Morris Cato.

Services were held in the home of Mrs. Betsy Morris until the men of the community were able to complete the building of the church.

Timbers for the framing were hand hewn and boards were sawed at the mill of Mr. Isaac Cato, Sr., son of Mr. Burrell Cato. It is believed that the pulpit table and pews were made by Mr. Haston Cato and Mr. John J. Cato, grandsons of Burrell Cato, Mr. Thomas Morris (also a grandson) and Mr. William J. Hatfield, with possible help from others.

The Rev. W.J. Hatfield is thought to have been the first pastor. There is little known about the first few years of the church.

Information from the curator of the Southern Baptist Historical Society at Furman University says the church applied for admission into the Santee Baptist Association October 26, 1888,[122] at Antioch Baptist Church, Kershaw County, where the Santee Association was meeting that year, and was admitted. First delegates were Mr. John J. Cato and Mr. J.A. Dawkins.

In 1934 or 1935, the original building was so in need of repairs (there were so few members and so little money available) the building was torn down and a 20- by 30-foot building was put up with the usable material. The work was done by W.P.A. workers, headed by Mr. James Reames. In 1935 the Rev. P.E. Blackmon became pastor.

Membership increased and other pastors followed. In 1953, a drive was held to raise money to build a new auditorium. In 1955 dedication services were held in the present building. Rev. Jim Birkitt was pastor at the time. The present Sunday School building was added later, while Rev. Earl Lamm was pastor.

Present pastor is Rev. Henry C. Bonner and the church seems to be wide awake and filling a real need in the community.

Mayesville Presbyterian Church

For many years Mayesville Presbyterian Church has stood as the center of life for many of the town's citizens.

Most of the first communicants were members of Salem Black River (Brick Church) or Mt. Zion, the first two churches of the Presbyterian faith in this area. A number of those living in the town, deciding that they needed a place of worship nearer to their homes, sent a petition to Harmony Presbytery, requesting permission for the organization of a church. Presbytery favored the request and sent a commission to activate the organizational procedure.

Mayesville Presbyterian was begun January 8, 1881,[123] with 34 charter members. The first elders were S.D. Pierson and Hugh H. Wilson; first deacons were S.W. Wilson and R.A. Chandler.

For a time the church had the service of a supply pastor, the Rev. J.L. Bartlette. In April, 1881, the Rev. James Cousar was installed as the regular pastor. However, his connection with the church was ended in less than a year by his untimely death. Stunned by the loss of their beloved minister, the church did not call another pastor until 1887. During the intervening years, the Rev. J.S. Cosby, pastor of Mt. Zion, supplied.

At first, services were held in the Masonic Hall, but the congregation grew rapidly and soon a building fund was begun. A spacious lot in a desirable part of town was donated by Matthew P. Mayes; lumber was provided by members who had timber land, and work was begun.

Interested friends made generous contributions toward furnishing the sanctuary. A.A. Strauss, a merchant in town, donated lights – large lamps (with glass prisms) suspended on long brass chains and small lamps on each side of the pulpit. These were made of frosted glass and were screwed to little tables. All, of course, burned kerosene.

A merchant in Charleston, with whom planters, including I.W. Bradley, Witherspoon Cooper, James Edgar Mayes and others of the area had traded for many years, gave the original communion set.

It was during the ministry of the Rev. W.C. Smith (1887-1894) that the sanctuary was completed.

A clipping from a newspaper (name not available) gives a graphic account of the dedication of the church in April of 1892.

"This Easter Sabbath morning will long be remembered by the good people of Mayesville, especially will it be looked back to by the Presbyterians as a day of joy and gladness. After more than 10 years of patient waiting and struggling have they been able to accomplish their hearts' desire and today to set apart for the worship of Almighty God this beautiful church.

"The house is built in Roman Gothic style, beautifully finished inside with our native pine and varnished. The pews are made of pine and varnished. The pulpit is finished with black walnut, furniture upholstered in crimson plush. The choir, placed back of the pulpit, is cut off by a balustrade; vestry rooms are on either side, with doors opening into the pulpit and choir."

The article continues with an account of the program, which was in charge of Rev. W.J. McKay, assisted by the pastor and by Reverends Bean and Galphin (from Mt. Zion Presbyterian and Mayesville Baptist). The church, with a capacity of 400, was filled.

"The services were opened by the choir under the leadership of Capt. (Henry) Corbett (organist). The 'Te Deum' was beautifully rendered as the opening voluntary."

The history of the church was read and the pastor made the announcement that although collections were unusual in such a service, it had been decided to take an offering for "Starving Russians." (The collection amounted to $40.)

Several times through the years the church was renovated and refurnished. Walls were redecorated, floors were recarpeted, new pews were added. Enhancing the beauty of the sanctuary were lovely stained glass windows given by members in memory of loved ones who were once faithful members of the church.

In 1894 Rev. J.E. Stevenson became pastor, serving the church for nine years. He was followed by Rev. H.A. Knox (1905-1912) during whose pastorate the manse was built next to the church. This, too, has been renovated and modernized during the years.

In 1913 the Rev. R.L. Grier became pastor and remained until his death in 1939. In the years he spent in Mayesville, he endeared himself not only to members of his own flock but to everyone in the community. To show their deep affection for this man of God, the church placed on the front wall of the sanctuary a plaque in his memory.

For more than a year after his death, the pulpit was supplied by the Rev. Charlie Evans and the Rev. L.B. McCord on alternate Sundays. But in 1940 the church called the Rev. John W. Groves, who proved to be the man for the hour. He served the church faithfully and well for eight years.

In 1948 the Rev. D.M. Morrison became the pastor. During his pastorate a Sunday School building was constructed. It contained a small auditorium (used for small gatherings and as a dining area for church suppers and other social events), classrooms and a fully equipped kitchen.

The Reverend Morrison left the pastorate in 1953 to enter the teaching field and was followed in 1954 by the Rev. Denny M. Hill, whose seven-year pastorate was one of definite growth and improvement for the church and Sunday School through his inspirational sermons, his interest in music and his special appeal to children.

In 1962 the Rev. J. Floyd Akin was called and remained with the church until his death. It was during his pastorate that the church took special interest in improving the cemetery.

Dr. D. McNab Morrison returned as pastor of the church in 1972 and is still leading in all phases of the work.

On May 23, 1975, the church was struck by lightning and the building was burned.

Services were held in the Educational Building during the ensuing months.

The women of the church, from the beginning, have had a very active part in the work of the church. The women have also propagated an interest in missions at home and in other countries. The W.O.C. works through three circles and as a unit.

Men of the church also work faithfully through their organization.

There is a senior Youth Fellowship which is very active, not only in local work but in affairs of Harmony Presbytery as well.

During the two years following the burning of the sanctuary, all of these organizations worked tirelessly in raising funds for the new church and a new pipe organ. Members and friends of the church made generous contributions toward the building of the new sanctuary and many of the furnishings were given as memorials.

The new church of modified Gothic architecture is of brick with an 85-foot steeple. The divided chancel has a white marble floor and the chancel window pictures the life and work of Christ. Other windows also depict biblical scenes.

First service in the new sanctuary was on April 17, 1977, and the service of dedication was held on December 4 of that year.

The church observed its centennial celebration January 10 and 11, 1981.

Wedgefield Presbyterian Church

Members of the Wedgefield Presbyterian Church for almost a century have sung in their hearts the great old hymn, "I Love Thy Kingdom, Lord, the House of Thine Abode . . . " For it was out of a great heart of love that the quaint little church was built.

Mr. James H. Aycock, an outstanding citizen of the community, gave three acres of land for the sanctuary and a cemetery. He was the first person buried there.[124] He died in 1895.

Miss Catherine Elizabeth McLaurin, one of the charter members, said before her death, "When the church became a reality, our delight knew no bounds."

It was on July 2, 1881, that 12 dedicated Christians met with a commission from Harmony Presbytery to organize this church.

Charter members in addition to "Miss Catherine" were Miss Mary McLaurin, Henry James McLaurin, M.D. Cornelius McLaurin, Mrs. Elizabeth McFaddin McLaurin, James Caldwell, Mrs. Sarah Caldwell, Mrs. J.H. Aycock, Miss Nora Aycock, Edward H. McCutchen, Mrs. E.T. McCutchen, Mrs. Olivia Kelley.

Elected and ordained as ruling elders were Cornelius McLaurin and James Caldwell. Deacons ordained were Henry James McLaurin, M.D. and Edward H. McCutchen.

The first service of the church was held the following day with the saintly Rev. James McDowell, the officiating minister. The celebration of the Lord's Supper was observed at the end of the service. For this occasion the First Presbyterian Church of Sumter graciously lent its communion service which was brought by Col. James Blanding, a ruling elder of that congregation.

A Sunday school was organized with Mr. Cornelius McLaurin as superintendent. It met in the nearby school house until the completion of the "Church in the Pines" in 1882.

The women of the church formed a Ladies Aid Society, and a great aid they were in helping to furnish the sanctuary. With their assistance pews were obtained from an old church; kerosene oil lamps on brackets, a reed organ and a communion service were purchased.

Rev. H.B. Garris, first pastor, was installed by a commission from Harmony Presbytery on May 24, 1885; and he served for a little more than a year, resigning in October, 1886.

From that time until the Rev. Joseph Crockard was called in 1895, the church was served by pastors Rev. James McDowell, Rev. J.L. Giradeau, Rev. J.S. Cosby, Rev. N.W. Edmunds, and others.

Stated supplies through the early years were Dr. C.B. Chapin, Rev. S.P. Bowles, Rev. Harold L. Bridgeman, missionary from China.

Coming as pastor in 1896 and serving till 1906 was the Rev.

John C. Bailey, Jr. who rode horseback from Summerton to preach.

From March 1, 1907 till December 31,1911, Rev. S.H. Hay was pastor. From that time the church was without a pastor until 1914 when Rev. J.R. Hay was called, serving the congregation for two years.

Rev. R.C. Reed, stated supply, filled the pulpit from 1916 to 1920 and he was succeeded by Rev. L.K. Martin who remained until August 1, 1924.

In January of 1928 Wedgefield, Hebron, Hephzibah and Tirzah joined to form a field and call a pastor to serve the four churches. It was then that Rev. W.H. Stevenson came, proving a great blessing to Wedgefield and the other churches and giving loving and dedicated service until 1944.

It was during his pastorate that the church entertained Presbytery (1935). The church was also blessed by protracted meetings held practically every year. These were always held during full moon so that those attending would have less difficulty walking or driving to the service. Some very inspiring speakers visited the church during these meetings. One of these was C. Richards of Davidson College.

According to church records preparatory meetings were held on the Saturday preceding each Sunday on which the communion service would be observed. Among these visiting ministers were the Rev. R.L. Grier of the Mayesville Presbyterian Church and Dr. J.C. Bailey, former pastor.

On March 30, 1947 Rev. P.H. Biddle was called as pastor of the four churches. He served most faithfully and acceptably, completing a long pastorate of 21 years, retiring in 1968.

From 1969 till 1972 Rev. Jack Spears was guest minister and was supply pastor until 1977.

Now serving as stated supply is Rev. Ashby J. Dick, a retired Army chaplain, who came to the church on Dec. 25, 1977. He is leading the church faithfully and well.

Others who served the church through the years as stated supplies were Dr. C.P. Chapin, Rev. S.P. Bowles, Rev. Harold Bridgeman, a returned missionary, and Rev. Ralph McCaskill.

Mr. Cornelius McLaurin served as superintendent of the Sunday school until his death in 1912. Elected at that time was Mr. Eugene Aycock, who faithfully guided this phase of the church work until his death in 1953. He was succeeded by Hugh M. McLaurin, Jr. who served faithfully for 25 years. He recently retired to be succeeded by Michael Anderson. (More recently Mr. Anderson moved away and Mr. McLaurin again took up the work).

First organist of the church was Miss Nora Aycock. She was

followed by Miss Betty Aycock, who played the reed organ for 50 years. Her brother, Eugene Aycock, led the choir and sang bass for the same number of years.

Others who have served as organists are Mrs. Hugh Pritchett, Miss Janette Aycock, Mrs. Walter Bailes, Mrs. Mac Johnson, Mrs. Greg Kemberlein, Mrs. E. Whilden Nettles, Sr., Mrs. Julia S. Talbert, Mrs. Michael Anderson (present organist).

The church had from the beginning a well stocked library in the session room. There have been excellent books for children and adults in this library. First librarian was Miss Catherine McLaurin and for many years Miss Denie Cooper also made a great contribution in service to this phase of the church program.

It was not until 1976 that the church installed a gas furnace. Up to that time the building was heated by an old fashion "pot belly" stove.

The original brass kerosene lamps on brackets around the walls are still used; however, they have been converted to electricity. Hanging on brackets on the walls of the sanctuary are the original velvet bags on poles used for collecting the offering. The first covered bread basket used for communion services is still in use. Recently Dr. Eddie C. DuRant, Sr. made from beautiful mahogany an additional tray for the communion set.

In 1950 the reed organ was replaced by a Hammond organ. However, it still stands on the right in the sanctuary with the Hammond on the left.

For the first time since its beginning the Wedgefield Presbyterian Church had a building program in 1980. The 99-year-old church was inspired to raise funds for the addition of an educational building. Under the able leadership of Dr. DuRant as chairman of the building committee the work was begun. He said, "We'll be following the same external scheme and design with a few modifications." And that is what they did, wisely preserving the historic plan of the quaint old church.

The addition has room for a nursery, rest rooms, a kitchen, a 24 x 30 foot assembly room and three classrooms.

In the removal of windows at the back of the church in preparation for adding the new rooms some wide boards of beautiful heart pine were found. Dr. DuRant with his great woodworking talent used these boards to make a lovely lectern for the assembly room.

Others on the building committee were Mrs. Hugh McLaurin III, Miss Dolly McLaurin and Gary Welchel.

The membership of the church has varied from time to time. Now in the 100th year of its history there are 53 active members with 37 enrolled in Sunday School. Over its century of life there have been a total of 285 who have been or are members; twenty-one men have served as deacons and eleven as elders.

Going out from the church for Christian service were Gertrude McLaurin Shaw (Mrs. R.J.), who was a missionary in the Philippines, and Rev. Russell Strange, who served as pastor of Presbyterian churches and is now working with alcoholics in Danville, Va.

Hugh M. McLaurin, Sr. was on the Board of Trustees of Presbyterian College and Thornwell Children's Home and Hugh M. McLaurin, Jr. has served in the latter capacity for many years.

Ruling elders at present are Hugh M. McLaurin, Jr. (clerk of the session), Hugh M. McLaurin III and Michael Anderson.

The board of deacons consists of R. Larry Dew, Reginald D. Goodman, Russell F. Jones, Richard Edmunds.

Organist is Mrs. Michael Anderson and choir director, Mrs. Richard Edmunds.

Grover Cranford is secretary-treasurer of the Sunday school. Teachers are Miss Dolly McLaurin, Mrs. Hugh M. McLaurin III, Mrs. Hugh M. McLaurin, Jr. and Grover Cranford.

President of W.O.C. and historian is Mrs. Gary Welchel, Mrs. Eulons E. Mosteller is vice president and Mrs. Hugh M. McLaurin III is secretary-treasurer.

Dedication of the new addition to the church was held on April 27, 1980.

Visiting ministers and other dignitaries present included: John M. Graves, moderator of Harmony Presbytery; the Rev. Cliff H. McLeod, D.D., pastor emeritus of First Presbyterian Church of Sumter; the Rev. Charles Robert Tapp, D.D., president of the Presbyterian Home of South Carolina; the Rev. Russell W. Park, D.D., stated clerk of Harmony Presbytery.

The hymn of consecration, "Lead on Oh King Eternal" has been and will continue to be expressive of the dedication and devotion shown by members of this little church, which has shed its light of Christian love through a century of dedicated service.

The Centennial Celebration will be held April 5, 1981. Speaker for the occasion will be Dr. McLeod Frampton, treasurer of the board of trustees of the Presbyterian Home of South Carolina. He was a recent interim pastor of First Presbyterian Church of Sumter.

Church Of The Good Shepherd

Standing as a witness to Christian concern is a small Episcopal church on the northwest corner of Wright and Dingle Streets, known as the Church of the Good Shepherd.

Though the organization of the church body took place in the early 20th century, the building has ties with an earlier era.

On the old Frierson plantation in Stateburg was an historic building known as St. John's Chapel, where the ladies of the Frierson family gave religious teaching to the slaves on the plantation.[125]

In 1886 the owner, John N. Frierson, transferred the property to a man by the name of Bowen, who moved the building to the neck of land where Highway 261 crosses Highway 76 to serve as a church for ex-slaves and their families. It was known as "Bowen Church." When the building had been abandoned as a church, it was used as a school until 1911.

It was then that the Episcopalians in Sumter, with Dr. C.W. Birnie as their leader, bought the building and moved the timbers, still in excellent condition, to Sumter to be used for a sanctuary for the Church of the Good Shepherd.

The story of this church, written by one of the faithful members, Mr. W.F. Bultman, is here given:

"If the Church of the Good Shepherd would set forth in her history its beginning as an organized mission of the Protestant Episcopal Church, it would take us back only about fifty years. But the nucleus of the present organization, or congregation, had its inception about 60 years ago, under the guidance and with the encouragement of the Rev. H.H. Covington, D.D., then rector of the Church of the Holy Comforter, this city.

"When we think of the beauty of our little church, our hearts swell with gratitude to our Heavenly Father and our thoughts go back to the little group which first assembled at the residence of Dr. C.W. Birnie, where for several months services were held.

"The few persons who gathered at Dr. Birnie's residence were all communicants of the Episcopal church before coming to Sumter, and like the exiles of Babylon who could not sing the songs of Zion in a strange land, remembered the beauty and order of the Prayer Book services and longed for the opportunity to enter in such a worship again. These few faithful souls were determined that a sanctuary would be erected in Sumter. They were ably led by Dr. Birnie, for whom, to those who were fortunate enough to know him, no words of praise can be added.

"Those who did not know him can be assured that he occupied a niche in the esteem of his fellowmen that few can equal.

"After having met Dr. Birnie's residence for several months, an abandoned laundry next to the Birnie residence was used for a meeting place. The two or three who had been meeting together in His name set about to make their place of worship churchlike and comfortable. Services were conducted at frequent intervals by the rector of Holy Comforter, the Rev. Mr. Covington.

"For about four years the little group passed through a period of corporate maturity. That, after all, marked the hours preceding the dawn of 1913, when the church went into quarters in the Lincoln Graded School. The first service there was held on December 14, 1913, the Rev. Robert T. Phillips officiating. According to the records, 'seven persons were present, and it was decided to have a service every second and fourth Sunday afternoon.' The first offering was taken up at the fourth service, January 11, 1914.

"But the little group was looking forward to more permanent organization and the erection of a place of worship. A church building fund was started in June 1914, with contributions amounting to $17.75. The organization of the mission took shape when on June 29 of the same year, Archdeacon Baskerville held a conference at Dr. Birnie's home. At this conference, it was decided to have 500 envelopes printed and distributed among members and friends for the purchase of a lot and for the erection of a church building to be known as the Church of the Good Shepherd. On September 13, 1914, the first service as an organized mission was held at Lincoln School.

"During the next three years, the coming of the Rev. J.B. Walker to the Church of the Holy Comforter and the Rev. J.C. Perry to the Church of the Good Shepherd marked the beginning of decisive things for the struggling mission. Under the leadership of the Rev. Mr. Perry, and with the cooperation of Holy Comforter, through its rector, serious efforts were directed toward the erection of a church building.

"It would take more than a brief history to set forth the indefatigable labors of the little group of members who have given of themselves throughout the years to the work; neither could we justly record how much we are indebted to our friends who have made sacrifices in our behalf. The decision was made to build in 1919 and the building was occupied in 1920.

"The Rev. Mr. Perry was the first resident priest assigned to Good Shepherd. It was under him that the church building became a reality. It is because of his efforts and his determination to fulfill a dream that recognition is due him in no uncertain terms. Rev. Perry left to accept a call to a church in Brunswick, Georgia.

"It had been learned that there was an old church building in the Stateburg section, that having served its usefulness, was now abandoned and no doubt could be purchased for a modest sum, torn down, and brought to Sumter to help in the erection of the new church. Quite a bit of the framing from the old Bowen

Church, as it was known, was used in the foundation and frame of Good Shepherd.

"Rev. Perry was succeeded by the Rev. W.H. Brown, followed by the Rev. William D. Turner, the Rev. R.B. Martin, the Rev. Quentin E. Primo, the Rev. W.C. Weaver, the Rev. Scott Peddie, and the Rev. George M. Foxworth. [126]

"Throughout the church's history there have been periods when there was no resident priest assigned to the church. Good Shepherd is grateful to Holy Comforter for allowing her rectors to serve at Good Shepherd during these interim periods. The Rev. Messrs. Frank V.D. Fortune, William Seddon Lee, Reid, and Philip Porcher are all remembered for their assistance to us. Major Kennickell, chaplain at Shaw Air Force Base, is also kindly remembered.

"But while the others faithfully ministered to our needs in spiritual ways, the memory of the Rev. J.B. Walker can never be erased from our minds. He served Good Shepherd from its earliest trying days through every period when we were without the services of a priest until the time he passed. With us, who had the privilege of listening to his wise and sage advice, unmatchable sermons interspersed with word pictures and illustrations that only a person with saintly qualities could give, the memory of him shall live forever. It was a great privilege to have him visit the home, to share the sunshine and radiance of his smile, and above all to have him kneel in prayer and intercede in our behalf to the Most High. His prayers were matchless gems of intercession and sources of much comfort to his listeners.

"Bishop Richard B. Martin was sent to St. Augustine's, Sumter County, and Good Shepherd from divinity school. He served these two charges well. He has now advanced to the Executive Council of the Episcopal Church and is Executive for Ministries. The memory of Bishop Martin serving his first churches can never be forgotten. It was evident by the manner in which he discharged his duties that he realized that he was about his Father's business. We are extremely pleased that he has made such a notable advancement in the ministry.

"In recounting the efforts of the many persons mentioned herein who labored and struggled to make the Church of the Good Shepherd truly the house of God, it can be seen that the blessing of the Almighty has been with them. Let us upon whose shoulders the work now rests realize that a kind providence still blesses His servants and assists them with their efforts."

Graham Baptist Church

In the lower part of old Sumter District is a church that has stood as a lighthouse of Christian witness for approximately 90 years. Graham Baptist Church was constituted in 1886[127] and a building was begun the day after the earthquake in the same year. Dr. C.C. Brown, long-time pastor of First Baptist Church of Sumter, was the temporary moderator and W.F. Cook was clerk for the organizational meeting.

Graham is a union of two very old churches in the area – Moriah, near Plowden's Mill Pond, and old Zoar, which stood near the spot where the Zoar Methodist Church stands. Charter members came from these two churches and eleven members of Providence Baptist on the old Georgetown Road between Sumter and Manning.[128]

First deacons of Graham were S.W. Davis, J.M.N. Wilder and Elias Hodge. W.G.S. Seymour was the first elected clerk.

Pastors who have served the church through the years include: Rev. B.C. Lampley, Rev. E.D. Wells, Rev. J.J. Myers, Rev. C.M. Billinger, Rev. D.W. Hiott, Rev. J.D. Huggins, Rev. W.D. Spinx, Rev. J.N. Booth, Rev. O.W. Triplett, Rev. J.S. Cobb, Rev. T.L. Willingham, Dr. P.O. Batson (35 years), Rev. C. Reid Williams, Rev. Hal Salisbury (interim pastor), Rev. W. Eugene Franklin and Rev. C.B. Smith.

Joe Wilder was the first Sunday School superintendent and Mrs. John I. Brogdon was president of the first W.M.U.

The first building, which was erected on land donated by Mr. Spencer Davis, soon proved too small for the growing membership, but a remodeling program was not undertaken for several years. The "L" was added and in 1941 a building program was begun. The old building was pushed back and was contained in the present handsome brick structure.

In 1960 the porch and the steeple were added, the steeple being given by Mrs. Essie K. Jones in memory of her husband, Robert M. Jones.

The education building, providing eight classrooms, a kitchen and assembly room, was begun in 1961 with dedication services in 1962. Later one room was equipped for a pastor's study.

A parsonage had been built in 1906 and the church began having services every Sunday.

Several have gone out from Graham as ministers, including W.J. Wilder, Lloyd E., Francis, Paul and Joel Chandler Batson. F.E. Seymour was ordained and planned to go out as a missionary to Siberia, but poor health and other troubles hindered his going. Miss Hannah Plowden served many years as a missionary in China and in Hawaii.

Hebron Presbyterian Church

According to tradition, Hebron Presbyterian Church came into being as the result of a heartfelt desire expressed in an exchange of notes between Mrs. W.W. Fraser and Mrs. Henry DuBose.

Mrs. Fraser came to the community from Williamsburg County, and Mrs. DuBose was a native of Darlington County; and these two, dreaming of a church in their community, spoke of their desire to their husbands, who were entirely sympathetic with the idea.

Only a short time later, the Rev. J.G. Richards, evangelist of Harmony Presbytery, while spending a night with the Frasers, was urged to hold one service in the school house at DuBose Crossroads. Doctor Fraser was said to have gone from house to house in his buggy, telling the people of the plan for a service.

And so, in December 1888,[129] Doctor Richards preached in the school house, and the following year came back, preaching each night for a week to ever-increasing congregations.

In March of 1889, the Rev. A.M. Sale, pastor of the Presbyterian Church of Camden, who was supply pastor for Hepzibah, agreed to hold services on the same Sundays that he preached at Hepzibah.

Encouraged by the interest shown, Harmony Presbytery in November, 1889, appointed a commission which organized a church, drawing members from Hepzibah. It has been recalled that Doctor Richards in his prayer asked that Hebron, the first-born of Hepzibah, would receive a double portion of blessings as did the eldest sons of the patriarchs in the long ago.

In addition to the Reverend Richards, the commission included the Reverend Sale, Rev. N.W. Edmunds and Ruling Elder Anthony White.

The newly organized church had as its first elders Dr. W.W. Fraser, Oliver McLeod and A.C. McKinnon; E.F. Burrows, L. Lawrence Fraser and James W. Dick were deacons.

Although the church grew in numbers and interest, it was not until 1893 that a sanctuary was built. At that time the present building was erected on land given by Dr. Henry Young DuBose.

In 1955 plans were begun for the building of Sunday School rooms on land donated by David M. Winkles; and on November 27, 1956, the new addition was dedicated. At the same time, repair work was done on the sanctuary and it was moved back and joined to the Sunday School building.

In addition to the necessary repairs, the church was painted inside and out. The floors and pews were sanded and finished in natural color, and a new carpet added to the beauty of the interior.

The first manse was built in 1897 on land given by Hon. R.I. Manning and Mrs. Adelaide Kennedy. This manse, owned jointly by Hebron and Hepzibah, was later sold, and a new manse, built on a two-acre lot given by Miss Sarah C. DuBose, was dedicated in September of 1948 and is still being used.

Hebron has had many pastors and supplies through the years, most of them serving only a short time. One of the best beloved was the Rev. A.M. Sale, who was instrumental in organizing the church. He served as supply until 1891 when he was called as regular pastor; however, death came before he was installed. To demonstrate their appreciation of this good man for helping lay the foundation for the work at Hebron and their deep love for him, the church placed on the wall an appropriately inscribed marble slab.

The first duly installed pastor of the church was the son of Dr. J.G. Richards, the Rev. Charles Malone Richards, who served from 1893 to 1900, when he accepted a call to Statesville, North Carolina.

The second longest pastorate was that of the Rev. William H. Stevenson, who served the church for 16 years — from 1928 until his sudden death September 21, 1944.

According to the church record, "This deep and profound scholar, close student of the Word, able preacher, humble servant of the Lord," was much loved and held in highest esteem by the members of his congregation.

Women's work, dating back to the beginning of the church, took the form first of a sewing circle to help raise funds for the construction of a sanctuary. After completion of the building, the ladies formed a Pastor's Aid and Missionary Society, promoting Foreign Missions especially.

In 1920 the women were organized according to the plan approved by the General Assembly, with Miss Julia DuBose as the first president. They have continued to be an active part of the work of the church.

On Thanksgiving Day in 1959, Hebron celebrated its 70th anniversary, with a threefold purpose: (1) to worship the Lord, (2) to honor those whom He had used in His service, and (3) to enjoy Christian fellowship. Many former members, including several former pastors, attended.

Dr. John C. Baily preached the anniversary sermon, ending with the challenge, "What can I render unto the Lord for all His benefits toward me?" And he answered in the words of the Psalmist, "I will take the cup of salvation and call upon the name of the Lord." (Psalm 116:12-13)

Hebron has made a great contribution to the Christian witness, not only in the little community where it stands, but in countless ways in many places.

Two ministers of the Gospel have gone out from its membership to extend its influence. One of these was Anthony W. Dick, who served as pastor in West Point and Moultrie, Georgia, Fayetteville, North Carolina, Spartanburg, South Carolina, and Memphis, Tennessee. He departed this life March 4, 1958, but his influence lives on through the service of others, including his daughter, a missionary to Japan, and his son, a Presbyterian minister.

Another son of the church who has gone out to serve in the Gospel ministry is Perry H. Biddle, son of the beloved pastor of the church.

In 1951 Hebron sponsored a Sunday School for Negro children, Hope Center. A one-room building was donated by Miss Julia DuBose, and various other church members gave pews, a piano and other necessary furniture. Each Sunday, volunteers taught the classes, and in the summer, a Daily Vacation Bible School was held. This school was discontinued in 1975 because of illness in the family of the director.

The church sponsored, under the leadership of D.T. DuBose, Jr., a Scout Troop for a number of years.

The church was without a pastor until the close of 1946 when the Rev. P.H. Biddle was called. He served the church faithfully and well until 1968.

After his retirement the church had as regular supplies Rev. Thomas L. Johnson and Rev. J. Ashby Dick until 1979. In June of that year, Rev. George G. Wilkes, III, was installed as pastor and is still serving.

The session is composed of J.W. Boykin; Sarah DuBose, clerk; Jerry Page, and J.T. Rivers, Jr.

Though Hebron is small, with only 50 members, it has a great influence on life in the little community where it stands as a beacon of light.

Goodwill Presbyterian Church

More than a hundred years ago, 100 Negro members of Salem-Black River (Brick) Presbyterian Church requested the Session of the mother church to grant them letters of dismissal in order that they might organize their own church.

Thus began historic Goodwill United Presbyterian, the first Negro Presbyterian church in the Sumter area. It was begun as part of the Northern Presbyterian Church now known as the United Presbyterian Church in the United States of America.

For a little over a year this congregation worshipped in the Old Goodwill Day School building. In 1868 the congregation received a two-acre tract of land from Hamilton Gaillard Witherspoon near what is now Dabbs' Crossroads upon which to build a sanctuary.

The church received an additional grant of 3.74 acres of land in 1890 from G.W. and A.M. McBride. The McBrides have been through the years one of the influential families in the area, and their interest in the growth of this church has been carried on by the Dabbs family, descendants of the McBrides. They have exerted a strong and supportive influence on church and school.

Upon this second tract the church soon was able to construct a manse and educational building.

There had come to the community from the state of New York a group of missionaries to organize and run a school for Negro youth. School and church were very closely connected. In fact the first minister of the church was also principal of the school. This was the Rev. Dr. West. The school was under the auspices of the church until it was consolidated with Eastern in Sumter School District 2 in 1960.

Countless boys and girls of the community received a good education from these Northern missionaries and as time passed, other teachers joined the faculty to help improve the educational status of the community. Teachers, doctors, ministers and farmers have gone out from Goodwill Day School from its earliest days to the time it was moved.

Second pastor of Goodwill United Presbyterian Church was the late Dr. Irby D. Davis, who was a graduate of Biddle University (now Johnson C. Smith University). He served the church faithfully and well for about 30 years.

A son and a daughter of Dr. Davis, following the example of their dedicated father, held responsible positions in the church. One of these, Dr. T.B. Davis, returned after retiring as a dentist. The daughter, Miss Nan Davis, served some time as a supervisor in Sumter School District 2.

Called to Goodwill as the third pastor was Dr. Warren J. Nelson, Sr. He served the church as minister and the school as principal for 36 years, retiring in 1960. Four sons of Dr. and Mrs. Nelson went into the ministry and on into education.

In 1961 the church extended a call to Rev. E. McKay Miller. In 1965 the church, under the leadership of Rev. Miller, renovated the sanctuary and completed an 11-room educational building, which was dedicated on November 7 of that year as the Davis-Nelson Educational Building. A new manse had been built in 1962.

The year 1967 marked the 100th anniversary of Goodwill Presbyterian Church and the occasion was observed with a three-day celebration. Descendants of former pastors appeared on the various programs.

The Rev. Franklin Delano Colclough is the present pastor, having been installed on Sunday, February 6, 1972; and he is leading the church in many worthwhile activities. An efficient secretary assits with office work.

Goodwill now has a membership of 361, with 140 pupils and teachers in church school. At present the pastor is leading the church in a land-development program in preparation for additional facilities for training as well as for recreation for the youth of the community. The church is also sponsoring a basketball team which will be following by a baseball team for spring and summer. An active Boy Scout Troop is another part of the church program.[130]

Goodwill provides a building for the Sumter County Child Care Uplift Program under the auspices of the Wateree Community Action program. Thirty children attend the Center daily.

Plans are in the making for an addition to the education building of the church.

Reverend Colclough, the fifth pastor that Goodwill has had in its 112-year history, is carrying on the traditional leadership of former pastors. He is a native of South Carolina, a graduate of Manning Training School. He has a B.A. degree from Johnson C. Smith University, with a major in French, the B.D. degree from Johnson C. Smith Seminary, and is a graduate of the United States Chaplain School, Ft. Hamilton, New York.

Goodwill United Presbyterian Church, established for the purpose of bringing spiritual help to man, continues as a strong influence on the Christian life in the community in which it stands.

St. James Lutheran Church

St. James Lutheran Church, one of Sumter's older churches, the history of which reaches back into the 19th Century, was organized under the leadership of the Rev. F.W.E. Peschau, D.D., pastor of St. Paul's Lutheran Church in Wilmington, North Carolina.

On March 11, 1890,[131] six dedicated Lutherans met at the home of Mr. J.F. Laughery and formed the first congregation.

Though a constitution and bylaws were adopted and on the following day officers were elected, the charter membership was left open until June of 1892 when the number had grown to 34. For the first public communion service, which was held in the Episcopal church on February 5, 1891, 13 communicants were present.

Small as it was, the membership purchased a lot on Washington Street in June, 1893, and began making plans for building a chapel, ground for which was broken on Monday, July 9, 1894.

Prior to this, on Sunday, May 13, 1894, a beautiful Communion set and Baptism Bowl, which were presented by the Ladies Aid Society, were dedicated.

It was in the early part of 1896 that Pastor Peschau resigned and the church was supplied for a time by seminary students and visiting ministers until the Rev. J.C. Trauger accepted a call to the church in the same year. During his service, which ended in August 1897, the church building was completed and St. James joined with St. Luke's of Florence to form a pastorate.

After the resignation of Reverend Trauger, Y. von A. Riser and Wilbur Riser, who were at that time seminary students, supplied the pulpit until February 1898, when the former, after completing his seminary studies, became the regular pastor.

In 1900 the pastorate with St. Luke's was dissolved and the church became associated with Orangeburg Lutheran Church. After a short time of service, Mr. Riser resigned and in 1902 the Rev. H.C. Grossman became the pastor. About the same time the Synod again joined St. James with the Florence church, which was soon dissolved. It was then that St. James became an individual pastorate, with the Reverend Grossman as minister. Soon he resigned to do a special mission assignment for Synod, and the church was again without a regular pastor.

Rev. Thaddeus B. Epting was called in May of 1904. During his ministry of approximately five years, many improvements were made in the church plant, including a recess room, a vestry room, and a robing room. The church was carpeted and a Mason and Hamlin organ was installed. Through a gift from Mrs. Maggie Laughery, the church indebtedness was paid.

On June 1, 1909, the Rev. E.H. Kohn of Cherryvale, North Carolina, became pastor, remaining until May 21, 1911.

The next pastor was the Rev. J.H. Wilson, who after serving five years, died on July 11, 1919, while still with this church.

St. James was without a pastor for almost a year before Rev. J.P. Derrick was called. It was under his leadership that the church became self-sustaining, no longer receiving aid from the Mission Board.

After the Rev. Mr. Derrick's resignation in 1924, Rev. Karl W. Kinard came as pastor, serving the congregation for eight years.

During his pastorate the church building was renovated and a parsonage was built on Haynsworth Street.

Following Reverend Kinard was Rev. William H. Stender of Charleston, who began work at St. James on October 1, 1933. Under his guidance the church was able to pay the mortgage on the parsonage; the church building and parsonage were renovated; an assembly room, four classrooms, a kitchen, and a pastor's study were added to the main building.

Following Reverend Stender was Pastor F. Frazier, who remained for about two years, and on August 15, 1947, Rev. J.E. Roof became the minister, serving the church for 17 years. This was the longest pastorate the church has enjoyed.

St. James grew in many ways under the dedicated service of Pastor Roof. Membership increased from 139 to 329. In January of 1950 six Sunday School classrooms were added to the main building. In 1954 a lot was purchased at the rear of the church at a cost of $8,500 on which was erected the Sterling F. Stoudenmire Educational Building at a cost of $47,500.

After Reverend Roof's resignation, Rev. Robert M. Weeks served for two years and under his ministry a new parsonage was built at 115 Benton Drive.

On May 1, 1967, Rev. D. Murray Shull became pastor of the church. The membership increased to 410 during his ministry, which ended in June 1971.

Dr. Carl A. Hunnicut, vice president of the congregation, supplied until December, 1972, when the present pastor, Rev. Alvin Haigler, was called.

In March, 1972, the Church purchased five acres on Alice Drive. A thorough study was made of the needs of the congregation and ground was broken for the new sanctuary August 29, 1976. The cornerstone was laid March 27, 1977.

Though the building was not complete, the first service was held November 20, 1977. Dedication services were held January 22, 1978. Present for this occasion were the Rev. Herman W. Caudel, D.D., president of the South Carolina Synod, LCA; the Rev. Karl Kinard, D.D., president emeritus of the Synod, and Dr. Carl Hunnicut.

Four of the beautiful leaded glass windows from the original church, after being worked over, were moved to the new sanctuary and placed in the Northex. There are three of the same type over the choir, which is in the back of the church.

As one enters the sanctuary, he sees the beautiful hand-carved wooden cross designed by artist Ray Davenport.

With Reverend Haigler as minister, the members of St. James carry on a very active church program. In the church school there are classes for all ages; there is also a men's club and the women carry on their work through four circles. As additional services the church sponsors an active Brownie Troop and a basketball team. In truth, the church is living up to its theme "Growing Together to Serve."

Wedgefield Baptist Church

At the 50th Anniversary Homecoming of the Wedgefield Baptist Church in 1935, Mrs. Peter Mellette told of the beginning of the church. The first gatherings of the Baptists in the community, she said, were held on the railroad depot platform where Rev. Noah Graham conducted services for the group as early as 1881.

Then the church was formally organized in the Methodist Church sanctuary, and it was given the use of this church as a temporary meeting place for the 14 charter members.

James H. Aycock, a large landowner, asked that the church be placed on his property. Many contributions were made by friends, one of which was a railroad car of lumber sent from Alcolu by the Alderman Lumber Company.

After much sacrifice and labor on the part of the faithful few, the church building was completed in 1885.

The following ministers have served the church as pastors: Rev. Noah Graham, Rev. W.L. Ball, Rev. M. Bishop and Rev. F.C. Hickson (all working under the State Board prior to the formal organization), Rev. B.C. Lampley, Rev. E.E. Ayers, Rev. R.P. Galphin, Rev. D.W. Hiott, Rev. Jesse Ayers, Rev. Thomas H. Edwards, Rev. Louis J. Bristow, Rev. Thomas P. Lide, Rev. William Haynsworth, Rev. J.H. Darr, Rev. Miller Jackson, Rev. Maynard Allen and Rev. Paul Kok.

The first deacons of the church were W.B. James and J.A. Harvin. L.D. Johnson was first clerk; Peter Mellette was first Sunday School superintendent.

The church is now in the field with Pinewood, and with Mr. Sim Smith as its pastor, the good work of this great old church moves on.

St. Mark's Methodist Church

Standing on the northeast corner of Broad and Church Streets is beautiful St. Mark's United Methodist Church, an edifice attesting to the fortitude, self-sacrifice, dedication of many devoted Christians, who lived and worked over a span of many years to establish a place of worship that would give glory to God and serve spiritual needs.

Though the present church plant with a lovely sanctuary, a well-equipped educational building and a modern parsonage is a powerful Christian witness in the section of Sumter where it stands, it came from a humble beginning in another part of the city.

As early as 1891 a group of dedicated laymen, including W.P. Smith, C.G. Rowland, C.E. Stubbs, held services in the old Curtis house on South Main Street. From this group came the idea of forming a mission.[132]

In December of 1893 Bishop Hargrove, at the meeting of the South Carolina Methodist Conference, organized the Sumter City Mission. Among the charter members were Mrs. Martha Booth Brinkley, Mrs. Bell Brinkley Grant, Mrs. Mamie Brinkley Lynam, T.B. Kennedy, Mrs. Janie M. Kennedy, R.J. Kennedy, Mrs. Eva Kennedy, Ed Strother, Mrs. Mary W. Strother, and Mrs. Lucy Brinkley Tucker. Rev. J. Grigsby Herbert was put in charge of the mission.

Early the following year the little group, under the leadership of Rev. Mr. Herbert, was able to build a little chapel.

The next pastor was Rev. William Aiken Kelly, during whose term of service an attractive frame church was built on the corner of Magnolia and Kendrick Streets in the year 1900 and the church became known as Magnolia Methodist Church.

During the next few years the struggling little church had five pastors: Rev. W.A. Fairey, Rev. J.H. Thacker, Rev. S.O. Cantey, Rev. J.P. Inabinet and Rev. S.D. Bailey. At this time population began shifting and because of that fact, and perhaps for other reasons, the membership fell from 166 to 84.

At the 1907 conference, Rev. J.B. Wilson was sent to pastor the little church. Because of the indebtedness of the church, its disorganized condition and the change of conditions in that part of town, it was decided at the Quarterly Conference on February 5, 1908, to change the location of the church.

A committee worked out a plan to move the church to the northern part of town. Soon members were able to secure a suitable lot on the southeast corner of Broad and Church Streets. They sold the old building, paid the debt and applied the remainder on the new lot.

However, there was no place in which to hold services. The small congregation, made up of moderate- or low-income members, had little money for building. But the Lord's work, in the hands of these faithful Christians, was to go on. The committee decided to build a small chapel for immediate use. Members began haulding lumber and with the willing help of the pastor, they all set to work with determination and faith. On March 12, 1908, prayer meeting was held in the completed chapel. There were now only 72 members, 12 having been lost in the move.

Approximately a year later (April 1909) work was begun on a church building. After much hard work and countless sacrifices the first services were held on June 26, 1910, in the nice brick sanctuary, valued at $10,000, with an indebtedness of $1,500. The name became Broad Street Methodist Church.

The membership increased from 72 in 1908 to 154 in 1913 when Rev. J.M. Rogers became pastor. During his ministry he published a church directory, giving names of officers and members.

In his message to the church recorded in the Directory, he said in part: "I am gratified to state that the work of the church is progressing hopefully. In all departments there is very good organization and along all lines there is promise of steady and healthy growth. Forty-four members have been added this year already (June 15). The Sunday School, the Missionary Society, the Ladies Aid Society and the Children's Society are all alive and at work. Current finances are in a better condition than has generally been the case heretofore at this time of year. The stewards have made an apportionment to each member of the amount expected on the salaries of the pastor and the presiding elder. The missionary and other benevolent claims, too, are being cared for. A plan is being put into operation for paying the debt on the church by small monthly contributions. In both financial and moral support of the church, I earnestly call upon every member to do something."

During the ministry of Pastor Rogers, Miss Attaway was sent from the church as a missionary to China; under the leadership of D.W. Brown and W.J. Rivers a Sunday School was organized at Winn School; a Juvenile Missionary Society was formed and conducted by Misses Anna Sanders and Ellen Beach; a Men's Wesley Adult Bible Class was begun; a Sunday School was organized at the County Home by J.D. Barnes, who was licensed to preach in 1914.

After these blessed years of growth in the church there came a period of regression. However, the words of Jesus concerning His Church, "The gates of hell shall not prevail against it," are wonderfully true. Rev. J.S. Rice was pastor in 1917 and Rev. S.W. Danner in 1918.

Then came Rev. J.G. Ferguson in 1919. He was a young minister, full of enthusiasm and dedication. With his coming the work began to revive.

This part of town was growing rapidly and the congregation was growing so fast that soon the building could not accommodate this membership. Since the lot was too small for the expansion of facilities, the property was sold in 1926 and the

Shaw home across Broad Street was purchased. This building was used at first for a sanctuary, Sunday School facilities and a parsonage. During this transitional period (1923-1926), Rev. S.D. Colyer, a progressive and dedicated pastor, a wonderful preacher and teacher, proved a great leader for the church.

The first service in the new church was held in 1927 by the new pastor, Rev. R.R. Tucker, who served the church until 1930. During his pastorate the membership of the church doubled and a large frame tabernacle was built to accommodate the large crowds.

From 1931 to 1932, during the depression, the Rev. Albert D. Betts was pastor. With a devout, unselfish spirit he insisted that his salary be reduced in order to cut expenses. His great desire was to build a new church, but his plans could not materialize because of economic conditions.

During the next pastorate, that of Rev. Robert P. Turner, the present parsonage was built and the minister and family moved in during the month of February 1935.

Rev. Paul Whitaker, remembered as a consecrated man of God, led his congregation in the steady purpose of magnifying the Kingdom of God through the church. During his ministry (1937-1939) a Young Adult Class was organized in the Sunday School and a Wesley Fellowship was formed. The financial standing of the church was good. Current expenses were met and payments were made on the indebtedness.

A man of mighty faith, Rev. Gobe Smith served from 1940 till 1942. He led his congregation into the belief that nothing is impossible with God. His first goal was to pay off the indebtedness. Then he asked for the gift of materials to be used in the new sanctuary. His enthusiasm led members to furnish whatever was needed. Mrs. H.M. Strange asked that she be allowed to buy the first thousand bricks, and others quickly followed suit in pledging needed materials. Thus the "Miracle Church" was completed and a communion service was held in October of 1942. The executive committee responsible for planning and construction consisted of T.B. Kennedy, H.L. McCoy, R.E. Weathersbee, J.I. Link and Roland Chewning.

These with many others did much of the actual work on the building. The Kennedy brothers made the pews for the sanctuary as well as other furnishings. They also furnished the sashes for the windows.

At the first Quarterly Conference after the completion of the church building, Harold L. McCoy made a motion that the name be changed to St. Mark's Methodist Church.

July 25, 1943, was designated as Homecoming. The church was then a little more than 50 years old. What great things had been accomplished during these years! Rev. Welborne Summers, a great spiritual leader, was then pastor.

There was a spiritual revival in 1945 with Rev. W.B. Garrett as visiting evangelist, and new members were added during Reverend Summers' pastorate.

On September 1, 1946, the new church was dedicated by Bishop Claire Purcell.

In 1946 Rev. Thomas Kemmerlin was appointed to pastor St. Mark's, and his four years of service were marked by much growth. Three hundred and fifty were added to the church during these years.

The next pastor was Rev. Pinckney Bauknight, who, because of poor health, served for only two years. He was a deeply consecrated man and was loved by all, especially the children. During his pastorate the church had a youth caravan and 125 were added to the church. A Fisherman's Club was organized for visitation and witnessing.

Rev. Bauknight was dedicated to the task of leading the membership to live consistently with the teachings of Jesus. The Woman's Society under his inspiration was very active with its six circles and a Guild.

During the next two years the basement of the church was improved to serve as a social hall. The system of rotating stewards was adopted at this time and a special pledge service was held at Easter. Leading the church during this period was Rev. J.E. Merchant.

In 1954 the church lost a devoted member and a former pastor, Rev. J. Marion Rogers, who had been living in Sumter since his retirement. At this time, Rev. S.D. Newell was serving as pastor of St. Mark's. A practical businessman, he led the church in achieving many material benefits. It was this good man who encouraged and urged the members to tithe their income.

Rev. J.O. Gilliam was pastor from 1958 till 1962. He encouraged the church to develop an outreach program to meet the needs of Shaw Air Force Base, and he was dedicated to winning the lost.

The years 1962-66 brought many improvements. The sanctuary was renovated with the installation of art leaded glass windows, the addition of new pews, pulpit chairs and communion table. The stained glass window in the front was given by Miss Rose Workman. Much of the work was done by J.C. Farmer as a contribution. Leading the church during these years was Rev. Clyde W. Allen.

The beautiful window was given by Miss Workman in memory of her father, Dr. J.F. Workman, and in honor of her mother, who "had probably the greatest all-time record of continuous, talented service and leadership."

Rev. Joe H. Sowell "rendered an ardent untiring ministry at St. Mark's for five years" (1966-1971). His Sunday morning services were marked by worshipful dignity and his sermons were inspiring.

It was during the pastorate of Rev. Barney F. Fowler, Jr. (1971-1975), that a bus was bought for church use. Another highlight of that year was the payment of all debts.

There was one sad occurrence for the church at this time. Mrs. Virginia Martin, who served the church as organist for 17 years, found it necessary to resign.

In August of 1973, Mrs. Carl Croft (Patti Hodge) accepted the position as organist.

The next pastor, Rev. S.O. Foxworth, began his ministry in 1975. Some of the activities of the church since his coming include the beginning of the observance of Harvest Sunday on the Sunday before Thanksgiving.

A highlight of 1977 that has meant much to the church has been work done by a summer assistant, Mike Henderson. During the 11 weeks of his stay he worked with all age groups. Several trips planned for Junior and Senior M.Y.F.'s have proved a great inspiration.

In 1978 Rev. Joe Pridgen became the pastor and the church is continuing its great work. Since its small beginning more than three-quarters of a century ago, St. Mark's has had a rich history. The dedication of many ministers, ministers' wives and lay members of the church has left an enduring influence on the life of Sumter.

Church Of The Ascension

A quaint little church in the Hagood section of Sumter County tells a story of sacrifice, courage and devotion on the part of a few who were dedicated to the task of building an Episcopal witness in their community.

The desire was born in the heart of William Crawford Sanders Ellerbe, a dedicated Christian and loyal Episcopalian as were his Ellerbe ancestors; while his maternal ancestors were equally devout Baptists.

After the War Between the States he lived in Camden until his children were grown. Then he decided to move to the country where he owned a mill, a store and a large tract of land on Rafting Creek.

He enjoyed life in the country on his plantation, but he missed his church. The nearest church to him was a little Baptist church between Hagood and Horatio, and he walked each Sunday to attend services there. He walked because he believed that animals should have a day of rest.

Somehow the idea of building an Episcopal church was born; and, though the Ellerbe family were the only Episcopalians in this vicinity, the idea grew. It was eventually decided that a fund should be started for this purpose. The story has come down that William's little daughter, Ellen, found a dime on the street in Camden and she promptly dedicated that coin to the building of a church. The idea caught on and soon enthusiasm began to mount among neighbors and friends who joined the Ellerbes in the raising of funds for the church.

Entertainments such as ice cream festivals, a strawberry festival and other similar events were organized. One lady made needlework which was sold in the North; one sent flowers to New York City for sale. The ladies bought no new clothes for themselves, giving the money instead to the fund. As the news of the heroic effort spread, gifts came from far and near.

Grace Church in Charleston sent the altar rail and an old pulpit which was made into the Bishop's chair. Another chair was brought from an old mill house in Waynesville, North Carolina. On and on stories could be told of gifts that came for the church.

Finally in 1895 the necessary amount was on hand and the church could be completed; but neither William Ellerbe nor his wife lived to see his dream come true, but the church was remained a monument to his name.

On June 30, 1895, the first service was held in this historic sanctuary with the Rev. James Stoney coming from Camden to conduct the service. However, the building was not completely finished until later. It is said that boards were laid down what would be the center aisle and Holy Communion service was observed without the altar rail, but with a beautiful silver communion set which had been given by St. Paul's Church in Boston.

The church was built under many handicaps with a number of disasters. The silver communion set mentioned above was stolen on the night following the first service. The building was struck by lightning while under construction. Later the roof caught fire and the building was saved only by the quick bold action of Marius Sanders who dared to climb quickly to the roof and tear off the burning shingles.

The first regular minister of the church was the Rev. William H. Barnwell. He was followed by Rev. C.W. Boyd and the Rev. William Stoney, son of the minister who preached the first sermon at the Church of the Ascension.

Then came Rev. Moultrie Guerry, followed by Rev. George Harris, who worked well with the young people of the community for 10 years. Others who have served through the years include: Rev. Eugene West, Rev. Claude Hobart, Rev. William Stoney (for a second term of service), Rev. Richard Sturgis and Rev. William Potts.

The church has indeed been a monument to William Ellerbe, but there are others, many of them, who in devotion to God and their fellowman have given of themselves through the Church of the Ascension. It is not possible to list all; however, a few must be mentioned: Theresa James Scarborough served for many years as organist and helped in many other ways; Samuel Gaillard was the first lay reader; Walter M. LeNoir was confirmed on March 8, 1896, the day the church was dedicated, the first to be confirmed in this church; Mr. Arthur Gaillard was one of the early lay readers. And many others made unselfish contributions that can never be forgotten.

The church stands on ground that was dedicated in 1807 as a burying place for the early families of the area, many of whose descendants now worship in the beloved sanctuary.

The desire to build the Church of the Ascension was conceived in one family, bound, not by blood, but by ties of love for and devotion to fellow Christians and by a common desire to serve God by serving others.[133]

PART V. CEMETERIES

The Bloom Hill Cemetery

This cemetery is situated on Milford Plantation in the Poinsett Park area. The plantation is now owned by Mr. William R. Clark.

The epitaphs show the burial places of members of the William Richardson Family, former owners of Bloom Hill Plantation.

The survey was made by Mildred S. Ducom and Jennie Smith Merritt, members of the Sumter Chapter of the South Carolina Genealogical Society, in February, 1978.

1. Anna Elizabeth, Dau. of John S. and Sophia Richardson, died: 25 April 1838, aged 7 years, 13 days.
2. Dr. Wm. J. Buford,
   died: 8th November 1845, in the 60th year of his age.
   Erected by his "Bereaved Widow."
3. Alester Garden,
   departed this life in the 30th year of his age,
   Sept. 4th. 1848

   "His widow erects this monument"
4. Judge John Smythe Richardson, son of
   William and Anna Richardson
   departed this life 8th May 1850 in the 74th year of his age.
5. Charles Rich, second son of WILLIAM AND ANNE M. Richardson
   b: 8th January 1776
   d: 15th January 1828
6. Luke Blumer Owen[134]
   b: 27th June 1849 at Dorking Surrey England,
   d: 17th December 1896 at Columbia, S.C., aged 47 years
7. John Smyth, a Native of Trowbridge Great Britain,
   d: in Charleston, S.C. on 14th day of May 1833,
   aged about Eighty five years (85 years)

8. Susannah, the wife of John Smyth, Esq. and sister of William Richardson the elder whose remains rest beside her,
d: Obil. 14th July 1815, aged 72 years

9. William Richardson
d: 17th of February 1786
Note: (No age or birth date mentioned – JSM)

10. Ann Magdalen Richardson, widow of William Richardson, departed this life 26th May 1810, 61 years, 6 months, and 15 days.

11. Harriet Richardson, wife of
William G. Richardson,
d: 25th of February 1804, in the twenty-sixth year of her age.

12. "By own Grave Stone . . . " (part is broken or worn off – not legible)
January 1849

Beneath this stone and between his two wives are the remains of William Guignard Richardson, d: 8th Sept. 1849 in his 77th year of his age.

13. Mrs. Emma Corbet Richardson,
d: 25th day of 1843
in her forty-fourth (44th) of her age. She was the daughter of Wm. and Frances Buford, and wife of William G. Richardson.

14. Thomas Couturier, 1st. child of John S. and Elizabeth Lucretia Richardson, b: 23rd. May 1804, d.: 28th October 1808

15. Elizabeth Frances, 1st. dau. of John S. and Elizabeth Lucretia Richardson,
b: 5th August 1807
d: 23rd August 1809

16. David Evans, fifth son of John S. & Elizabeth Lucretia Richardson,
b: 22nd. May and died 3rd. July 1813

17. Eleanor Lucretia, 3rd. dau. of John S. & Elizabeth Lucretia Richardson,
b: 18th May – died 17th December 1814.

18. Langdon Cheves, third son of John S. & Elizabeth Lucretia Richardson,
b: 24th Sept., d: October 1817

19. William Buford, 6th son of John S. & Elizabeth Lucretia Richardson,
b: 24th April 1813 d: October 1816

20. Maynard Davis Richardson,
b: 1st January 1812 d: 12th October 1832

21. Peter W. Fraser Richardson
son of
F.D. & Agnes Fraser Richardson
Born: April 2nd 1848
Died: May 5th 1849

22. Maynard Davis Richardson
son of
F.D. & Agnes Fraser Richardson
Born: Aug. 19, 1842
Died: May 5th, 1844

23. Agnes Fraser Richardson
wife of
F.D. Richardson
Born: March 23, 1822
Died: Feb. 15, 1849

24. Small stone (apparently broken off with W.T. White on it) W.T. White was the maker of the stone.

25. Built up grave with sandstone slab. Writing on the slab has faded. Writing not legible.

26. Belser
Hellen, J.V. – Daughter of Wm. S. &
Mary Jane Belser
Died: Sept. 27, 1832
Aged: 3 years, 4 mo. and 11 days.

27. Emma Louisa Belser
Died: 22nd Oct., 1831
Aged: 10 years, 8 mo. and 22 days

28. John Christain Belser
Died: 9th Sept., 1822
Aged: 10 years, 7 mo. and 3 days

29. (INFANT) Harriet Belser
Died: 8 Sept., 1819
Aged: 7 mo. and 13 days

30. (INFANT) Henry Belser
Died: 21 Sept., 1814
Aged: 6 mo. and 4 days

31. Jacob Belser
by his affectionate wife
Martha Belser
Died: 26th March, 1833
Aged: 51 years, 4 mo. and 3 days

32. Tarlton
Mary Martin – The child of
John & Caroline M. Tarlton
Who departed this life
Oct. 15, 1834
Aged: 5 years & 6 weeks

33. Tarlton
Alfred J.M. – The child of
John and Caroline M. Tarlton
Who departed this life
Oct. 15, 1834
Aged: 6 years and 10 months

34. **OUTSIDE THE FIRST MOAT, WITHIN THE SECOND**

DAVID, who was born 8th of February, 1747, O.S.

He served his Master
Wm. Richardson
Faithfully through the Revolutionary
War and up to 1786, and after
that his Master's widow &
eight children with the same
fidelity to January 1835 –
When faithful David died in peace.
Near him lies Binah his aged wife
who also served the same family well,
for nearly the same time.
Their example has been good & profitable
on the Plantation & we pray them Heaven –

W.T. White, Stone Maker.

35. **OUTSIDE THE FIRST MOAT, WITHIN THE SECOND**

HONEST JACK
Died: 15 May A.D. 1848, aged 77 years.
This trustworthy servant was the friend of his
owner, & watched his interest as if his own.
Ever thrifty yet sparing to himself. He left
86 dollars laid up from time to time for his
widow – Sally – & their children.
Condemn not his example in a lowly agent, High
& low in this world are terms of human note:

But, not to him with whom nothing is great, the nothing insignificant. To all men then must not this be the important question. Have the duties of life as assigned to each station by Providence, been conscientiously discharged.

36. Maynard Davis Richardson
son of
John S. & Sophia Richardson
Born: 10th April, 1833
Died: 5th August, 1834
Aged: 15 mo. & 25 days

37. Mary Sophia Richardson
Daughter of
John S. & Sophia Richardson
Born: 10th July, 1834
Died: 10th August, 1835
Aged: 13 months
"J. White" Tombstone maker.

Many sunken places like other unmarked graves are found here. This cemetery is very unusual in that it has a first moat around it and also a second moat. Reason for this is unknown.

Graveyard Survives Time's Ravages

In a wooded and weed-covered area in the southern part of Sumter is a small graveyard which was once lovingly tended. Here loved ones were tenderly laid to rest by devoted family and friends, and their graves were well marked and oft visited.

But as the years passed, the property fell into the hands of new generations who knew these ancestors only through family tradition, and the little country graveyard gradually lost its sacred significance. The town began to spread, enveloping the place where sleep the forefathers who had been, in great measure, responsible for the progress that marked the life of the community. The site became overgrown with weeds, brambles and bushes; and people who had no regard for the sanctity of the burying ground wantonly destroyed or removed most of the markers from the graves, leaving a forlorn scene of broken stones and desecrated graves.

But something happened recently that revived an interest in this historic spot. Engaged in "Operation Clean Sweep," a group of young people "discovered" the old buried site, where the few stones left indicate that these graves were made more than 100 years ago. The cemetery was once on Bradford property known as the Green Swamp Plantation and it was originally known as the Bradford-Brunson-Loring Cemetery since members of these families were buried here. In the beginning it is said to have contained 10 acres, but now it is the approximate size of a city lot and is on what is now Georgiana Drive.

Some of the few stones that are still left are toppled from their bases and broken. The only one bearing the Bradford name is that of Robert Dingle Bradford, "who was born the 2nd of June 1820.

And departed this life,
The 27th August 1853,
Aged 33 years, 2 months
And 25 Days"

Beneath this information is the following tribute:

"I loved thee fond Husband and love was thy due.
I loved thee fond Partner and tenderly too."

Robert was the son of Matthew and Harriet Dingle Bradford and grandson of Richard and Elizabeth Singleton Bradford, who came to South Carolina from Virginia and purchased land on Green Swamp around 1786. On his plantation Richard built a grist mill. This was located on the stream now known as Second Mill, and on the spot now known as Swan Lake Gardens he placed a saw mill. A canal connected the two streams. This wealthy planter also inherited lands from his father, Nathaniel Bradford, in the High Hills section of Sumter District and, it is thought, lived there for a time; but at the time of his death in 1825 he was living on the Green Swamp Plantation in the home that is still standing and some years ago became the possession of Mrs. John Snowden Wilson.

He donated the site for a chapel and according to his will this land was to "remain free to the use of the Methodist churches so long as they may continue the same as a place of religious worship."

Even though the stone marking Robert's grave is the only one now found bearing the name of Bradford, it is believed that others, including his wife, Mary McKnight Bradford, were buried here. All other markers are for those connected in some way with the Bradford family. One, for instance, bears the name of Richard B. Brown, the son of Adam Ervin and Sarah Bradford Brown, and likewise a grandson of Richard Bradford, Sr. His will recorded in 1864 designated that his estate, valued at $16,487.93, was to be left to Gabriel Wesley Bradford "in trust for the sole and separate use of my beloved wife, Caroline M. Brown."

On the stone was his name followed by these words:

"My loved Husband
May we meet in Heaven."

And above this tribute were carved two wedding rings intertwined.

Richard B. Brown (it is thought possibly the initial B was for Bradford) was born in 1820 and the time of his death is given as 1853. His family, according to records, were faithful members of the Green Swamp Methodist Church. His great nieces, Misses Anna and Rosalie Brown, are members of Trinity Methodist Church, which grew out of that first chapel on the Green Swamp Plantation.

Having withstood the forces of nature, two iron fences, sturdy and strong, stand today in the little graveyard. In one of these there are three stones that have remained almost intact, though darkened by age. One of these carries the following inscription engraved beneath a laurel wreath (the symbol of victory):

"To the memory of
Our beloved father
W.L. Brunson
Was born Oct. 6th 1789 and died Oct. 29, 1868."

William Leonard Brunson was one of Sumterville's leading citizens in those early days. He played a vital role in religious, educational and civic affairs and faithfully promoted the growth of his town and community.

He was a noted surveyor of his time and in 1817 laid out the town of Sumterville, making a map on which are given the original names of the streets. A copy of this map appeared in "Names in South Carolina, Winter, 1970."

In a sketch of "Some Early Methodists" the author, Rev. W.W. Mood, pictures him as a man of wealth who, with his wife, was constantly concerned with the welfare of others. Their doors were always open to traveling ministers of the day. He was a devoted member of Green Swamp Church, serving as steward, trustee and "class leader." His influence among his fellow Christians and church members was said to be very strong. He was instrumental in having the church site changed from Green Swamp in 1827 to a location nearer the outskirts of Sumterville. (It was moved at that time to the place on West Liberty where the Catholic church was later built.)

Interested in promoting education in his community, he was one of the 35 men and women who organized The Sumterville Circulating Library, serving as its first secretary. He was also treasurer of the Board of Trustees for the Sumterville Female Academy, which opened in 1832.

W.L. Brunson's home was located where Crosswell Home now stands, and the street which is now called "Crosswell" was then known as "Brunson." He owned land from the First Presbyterian Church to White's Mill. In an attempt to increase his wealth and probably open up new channels for the economic growth of his town, he sent slaves down to the Mississippi Delta in 1840, hoping to grow cotton on the rich lands there. However, when the location proved to be unhealthful, he brought his slaves home and gave up the venture.

For a wedding gift he built a home for his daughter, Charlotte, who married Joseph B. Roach, and the street on which she lived was named Charlotte.

As was the case with most people, W.L. Brunson lost everything except his land during the Civil War. It is said that Potter visited his premises during his ignoble raid and destroyed possessions as he did throughout the area.

Buried beside William Leonard is his wife, on whose gravestone the epitaph reads:

"Sacred to the memory of
Mrs. E.A. Brunson
Who died 13th May 1864 aged about 64 years.
She died in the triumph of the Christian faith."

She was a granddaughter of Richard Bradford, Sr.

A third grave in this inclosure is that of Manley A. Brunson, son of W.L. and E.A. Brunson. The inscription is as follows:

"To Cherish
In affection the memory of
One very dear
This table is erected over
The ashes of
M.A. Brunson
He left us in his 22nd year
8th January 1858."

Though there are no stones within the second iron fence, information found states that here were interred in the early part of the 20th century the remains of another son of W.L. and E.A. Brunson – Francis Lawson Brunson and his wife, Molly Alston Brunson. He died in 1900 at the age of 71. She, however, survived her husband by many years. Having been born in 1832, she lived until 1927- 95 full active years, those who remember her say. She was very fond of dancing and it is said that at the age of 95 she was chaperone for a square dance that lasted till midnight. This was only a very short while before her death.

Another grave in the old graveyard is marked by a stone bearing the inscription:

"In memory of
My Beloved Husband
Lucius P. Loring
God in His wisdom called him to His Heavenly Home
Oct. 10, 1886
In his 67th year
Oh, Father
Thy Will Be Done
Oh Blessed Truth, Tho we must weep
He Giveth His Beloved Sleep."

The wife of Lucius Pitts Loring was Mary Marsena Brunson, daughter of William Leonard and Elizabeth A. Brunson. She was born August 18, 1820, and died on April 9, 1898, and is no doubt buried beside her husband.

Lucius P. Loring was born in Alabama but was left in Sumter District with his grandparents — Jeremiah and Valentine Pitts — until his parents could become established in Alabama. According to Dr. Anne King Gregorie in "History of Sumter County," he remained in Sumter District, becoming a well-known planter and political figure.

In his public service, he was appointed jury commissioner by the governor in 1884 and at one time he was Clerk of Court of Common Pleas — General Sessions. He also served as registrar of conveyance and commissioner of locations, as acting ordinary in certain estates and magistrate ex officio in Sumter District.

During the Civil War he served as captain in Company K 23 South Carolina Volunteers.

He was a faithful member of the Presbyterian Church, serving as deacon and elder.

Near the grave of Captain Loring is a small stone bearing the names — Lucius, Mary, Fannie and Emma — children of Lucius Pitts and Marsena Brunson Loring — children who died very young. This little stone was removed once from the graveyard but was later returned.

Through the years many of Sumter's outstanding citizens have descended from William Leonard and Elizabeth A. Brunson, who set worthy examples for posterity to follow.

Two other markers in the cemetery have survived the destructive forces. One is inscribed:

"Sacred to the memory of
William Eldridge Mellett,
who died on Jan. 4, 1858
aged 39 years, 10 months and five days."

Though there is no marker for his wife, who was Mary Louise Bradford before marriage (thought to be the daughter of Matthew and Elizabeth Singleton Bradford), she was no doubt buried here also.

William Eldridge Mellett, the oldest son of the Peter Mellett who died in 1841, was an extensive planter, owning 6,000 acres of land in the Sumter area. One of his brothers, Francis Marion Mellett, was a colonel in the Confederate War. There are many descendants of this family living in Sumter County today. For generations Melletts have owned property in Wedgefield, Cane Savannah, Privateer and other sections.

The grave bearing the oldest marker is that of Harriet Angelina Mellett, who died on December 27, 1849, at the age of four years, one month and ten days. She is said to have been the baby daughter of William Eldridge and Mary Louise Bradford Mellett.

It is sad to think that there are those who would be so thoughtless of the feelings of others as to deliberately desecrate a cemetery, especially since the laying to rest of someone is an experience that is common to all.

Those whose ancestors are buried in this old graveyard began some years ago a movement to replace broken stones and restore the small part that still remains of the Bradford-Brunson-Loring Cemetery to something of its former appearance of quiet peacefulness and beauty.

Singleton Graveyard

In the long ago during the time when families amassed fortunes in lands and built large neighboring plantation homes, there were very close ties binding sons and fathers and brothers and sisters to one another. Then when the family circle was broken by death, the desire to keep the same nearness prompted the tradition of the family graveyard, which was kept with loving care by the survivors.

So it was with the Singleton family in the Stateburg-Manchester area. The plantation of Matthew Singleton, the sire of this branch of the family, was the logical place for the burial ground that received the earthly remains of many bearing the Singleton name, as well as those of other names who were of the same lineage.

However, Matthew's grave is not found in this historic spot. He lived his last years on a plantation at Cane Savannah which was given him by the state of South Carolina after the Revolutionary War. There he died in 1787, evidently before the graveyard at Melrose was begun.

When the Sumter County Historical Commission, present owners, and a committee from the Sons of the American Revolution were making a survey of the graveyard on August 2, 1980, with a view to restoring it, the name of Col. Matthew Singleton was found on a monument. It was apparently placed there in more recent years. The stone was old but the engraving was different from the type used on the other stones.

It is not clear when or why the name was placed there. However, his name is not included on the list given to the Historical Society when the graveyard was deeded to that organization.)

The graveyard is in Manchester Township and is shown on "that certain plot entitled Tiverton Farms, which was drawn by the United States Department of Agriculture District Engineer's office and dated April 7, 1941, said plot being recorded in Plat Book Z-7 at page 44, said tract containing 2.18 acres in Lot 7 Woodlot and measuring 208.56 feet on the North and South and measuring 418.44 feet on the East and West, said lot is given access to the Brohun Camp Road by a 15-foot-wide road which joins said tract on its Northern boundary at a point 75 feet from the Northeast corner of said tract and 118.12 feet from the Northwest corner of said tract and runs from said tract to the Brohun Camp Road for a distance of 513.41 feet more or less."

The foregoing is a quotation from the deed conveying this tract to the Sumter County Historical Society, Inc.

The oldest stone in the cemetery, that of Miss Martha A. Moore, is dated September 26, 1796. This young lady, age 19 years, 7 months and 2 days according to the inscription, was a granddaughter of Matthew Singleton, whose daughter, Ann (or Nancy), married Isham Moore, a very wealthy and influential citizen of the section East of the Wateree.

Mrs. Ann Singleton Moore was the next member of the family to be buried in this graveyard. Her stone bears the date July 1, 1798, and states her age as 48. The stone marking the grave of her husband, Isham Moore, is dated April 21, 1803.

Other members of the Moore family interred at this historic site include: Capt. M.S. Moore, Sr., whose epitaph, dated July 2, 1827, reads: "Beloved and respected for his many virtues, and the numerous acts of benevolence which characterized his life"; his son, Matthew I.S. Moore, who died at the age of 33 in 1829; the wife of Matthew I.S. Moore, who was Sarah Jane Cidelia Richardson, born March 27, 1798, and deceased March 19, 1869; Sarah J.C. Moore's second husband, Rev. Charles P. Elliott, who died on August 24, 1851, and whose epitaph reads: "Heaven, the element of love, was prepared for such as you"; Tabitha Polk, daughter of Isham and Ann Moore, who died in 1822.

John Singleton, Esq., son of Matthew and Mary James Singleton, who was born September 1, 1754, and died December 5, 1820, is buried in this graveyard. The tomb was erected, according to the engraving by "his affectionate consort."

His widow, Rebecca Richardson Cooper Singleton, died in Philadelphia on March 11, 1831. Her remains were later brought to this graveyard to rest beside the grave of her husband.

Perhaps the most illustrious person buried in the Singleton graveyard was George McDuffie, one-time governor of South Carolina. His monument just inside the gate was designed by O. Gorie of New York. On one side are given the date of his birth, August 12, 1790, and the date of his death, March 11, 1851. On another side is the well-known line, "The history of his country is the monument of his fame." His profile in bas-relief appears at the top and the torch of fame, at the foot.

Nearby is the grave of his young wife, Mary Rebecca, granddaughter of Capt. John Singleton and daughter of Richard Singleton and Charlotte Videau Ashley Singleton. She died on September 14, 1830, just a little more than a year after her marriage to McDuffie.

This first wife of Richard Singleton died in 1804, two years after their marriage and is buried in the family plot.

Col. Richard Singleton and his grandson, Robert Marion DeVeaux, who were killed on November 26, 1852, in an accident on the South Carolina Railroad, are buried in the same grave.

One of the twin sons of Col. Richard and his second wife, Rebecca Travis Coles of Virginia, Richard Richardson has a memorial stone dated 1833. He was only 16 at the time of his death.

An unmarked grave near the gate is said to be that of Videau Marion Singleton, daughter of Col. Richard Singleton and wife of Robert Marion DeVeaux and later of the Rev. Mr. Converse.

There are a number of stones marking the last resting places of Broüns, direct descendants of Capt. John Singleton, Esq. The oldest one of the name is that of Robert Broün, Esq., who died on September 19, 1809. The tomb was erected according to the inscription, by his mother-in-law, Mrs. Rebecca Singleton, "consort of John Singleton."

The body of Robert Henry Broün, who died in New Orleans on December 16, 1835, of yellow fever, was brought to Singleton's Graveyard for burial.

Caroline Belser Broün, mother of Thomas Day Broün and Matthew Singleton Broün, through whom the Historical Society has come into possession of the graveyard and the valuable land grant papers, was the last person to be buried in the old family plot; her stone bears the date of her death as May 27, 1944.

Erected by Mary Singleton Livingston and Julia M. Magel is a memorial stone for their father, Powell McRae, who died in 1844; another is to their grandmother, Mrs. Martha McRae, whose death is given as December 16, 1863; and a third to their aunt, Arabella McRae, who died at the age of seven in 1822.

Martha McRae, daughter of Capt. John Singleton, received some property through her father's will for her lifetime, but it was not to be "subject in any manner to the interference or control of her husband, Powell McRae." Her son, Powell, was to keep the property after her death during his lifetime, and his oldest male issue and his heirs were to "possess and occupy forever." However, Powell died before his mother and apparently left no male heir.

According to some old legal papers found in the Sumter Historical Society Museum, Col. Richard Singleton had his sister committed to an insane asylum. In spite of unfortunate circumstances, however, family ties were still strong and these three McRaes repose in the old graveyard along with other members of the Singleton and related families.

There are other graves, of course – 41 in all – found in the old graveyard, which was sacred to all who had loved ones buried there. It has come to this Society under certain well-defined conditions which follow:

1. Clearing the area enclosed by the walls surrounding the graveyard and the area immediately outside of the wall enclosure. Any trees or saplings or any other stumps or foreign growths to be cut off at ground level and treated with herbicides, and be it further specified that great care shall be used and every effort made not to disturb the stone wall or grave markers while this clearing is being performed.
2. Not cutting or removing any of the following trees, Dogwood, large Oaks, Crepe Myrtle, or Cedar.
3. Removing all rose bushes or bridal wreath plants in such a manner so that they may be replaced in the original places when all clearing has been completed.
4. Replacing all such plants removed by paragraph 3 above in their original locations.
5. While the clearing mentioned in paragraph 1 above is taking place, all gravestones and wall stones are to remain where they lay before the clearing began. After the clearing is complete, all gravestones and wall stones are to be returned to their original places.
6. All field stones and sandstones are to be replaced on the wall surrounding the graveyard.

7. The entire graveyard is to be returned, as nearly as is possible, to its original conditions.
8. No further burials are to be made in the graveyard.
9. The entire site shall be maintained in a manner that befits the reverence and dignity of a graveyard.
10. In the event the Sumter County Historical Society, Inc., ceased to function as an active society, the property herein devised is to be released unto the appropriate State Historical Society, the same covenants to remain in effect.
11. In the event that any of the above conditions are not fulfilled the property shall revert to the grantor, his heirs or assigns.

Now whether or not the shrubs and flowers listed are still in the cemetery or have long since been choked out by the weeds which infest the site will have to be determined. However, the Society is obligated to restore the plot as nearly as possible to its former beauty, and beautiful it must have been!

Sumter Cemetery Now Covers 40 Acres

Presenting an atmosphere of serenity and beauty is the well-kept Sumter Cemetery located on West Oakland Avenue, where the busy city street meets a wooded area of the countryside. Shaded by pines, planted some 20 years ago, native dogwoods, and other lovely trees, the 40-acre expanse gives a feeling of restful calm.

Plots and other spaces are covered with grass which is kept in excellent condition, and a pattern of paved roads provides easy access to all grave sites. Spots of color in the numerous "mini-parks" add to the overall beauty of the grounds. Mrs. I.D. Elmore, Jr., of the Garden Club Council, with the help of the custodian and other employees, is constantly working in these tiny flower gardens – planting, cultivating, watering, fertilizing – to insure the best results. There are multi-colored pansies, graceful shafts of princess feather, many varieties of coleus, and other low-growing blossoming plants. In one of these miniature "parks" is a statue of "Rebecca at the Well," which forms a fountain.

Here and there are camellias and other flowering shrubs. Small and large cedars give the desirable touch for a burial ground.

The beautification program began several years ago when Mrs. Martha Graham was chairman of the Grounds Committee. She worked tirelessly in landscaping and in planting many of the trees, shrubs and flowers that are in evidence today.

This burial place was begun many years ago when, according

to tradition, a public spirited citizen, Thomas Flowers, gave five acres of land for this purpose.

There were no records kept in those days; therefore, little is known of the early history of the cemetery. As time passed, some of those having a special interest in the cemetery conceived the idea of forming an association to carry out the affairs of the cemetery in a more business-like and efficient manner. A charter was granted in 1857 and the Sumter County Cemetery Association became a reality, the first president being Sheriff Hurst.

Other presidents who filled the office through the years included Arthur Hatfield, John D. Lee, Sr., C.G. Rowland, Jr., John D. Lee, Jr., who is in the office now (1971). The current vice president is J.W. Scarborough, who was preceded by J.L. Mooneyhan.

Executive Secretary-Treasurer is William M. Crawford, who has served the association faithfully and well for 30 years, having succeeded W.H. Seale in this office. Services of all officers, except secretary-treasurer who works in his office at the cemetery on a regular schedule five days a week, are rendered on a voluntary basis.

At first each family was responsible for the upkeep of the space where loved ones were buried. It is said that in 1880 a German came (no one seems to know whence or why) and asked to become a caretaker for the graveyard, to be paid by the individuals who were responsible for graves in their area. He had no family and lived alone in a nearby cottage.

In the 1920's the association decided to adopt the perpetual care plan for the Sumter Cemetery. In order to follow this plan, the association was required to build up a $5,000 Perpetual Care Trust Fund from fees paid for grave sites, each costing $100.[135] The cemetery was laid off in 16-grave plots, but one can buy the number of grave spaces desired. Of the amount paid for each space, $25 is placed in the trust fund, ten percent of the remainder is placed in a real estate fund, and the rest is used for general upkeep of the grounds. No grave sites have been sold since 1950 except on the perpetual care basis. Families who buried in the cemetery before 1950 are charged $1.25 a year for upkeep. Old graves without markers are kept clean at the expense of the association.

The association has built up a trust fund of $115,000, only the interest on which may be used for upkeep. The executive secretary-treasurer keeps a strict record of monies received and disbursed by the association and his books are audited annually.

Directing the affairs of the association is a board of eight trustees, with two retiring and two elected each January. Those retiring are not eligible for reelection until after the lapse of a year.

The present board consists of the following members: B.L. Williams, Roy H. Tucker, Irvin B. Shaw, Charles L. Shaw, W. Burke Watson, Mrs. R.A. Geddings, Mrs. I.D. Elmore, Jr., and Mrs. Myrtis Osteen. Officers and trustees are elected by lot owners.

After the death of the German caretaker (whether it was immediately afterward is not known), John S. Kennedy was in charge of cemetery work for a number of years. He was followed by A.L. Gibson, who died in 1948. G.R. Leatherwood became custodian in November of that year and served till July of 1967, when Freddy C. Burke, the present caretaker, was employed. He has under him from four to six workers to mow the grass, trim shrubbery and do whatever else is necessary to keep the grounds in good condition. The maintenance crew will also open and close graves for a fee to be paid to the association. The cost of this work on Sundays or holidays is $60 and at other times it is $50.

There are two general sections[136] in the cemetery – the Bronze and Monumental – so named from the type of markers used. The flat bronze markers have been in use in this burying ground only about 20 years. These lawn-type markers are ordered by the association and sold to the families desiring them.

In the monumental section there are granite and marble markers of various shapes and sizes. Some are so blackened by weather and age that the inscriptions can no longer be read. There are slabs covering graves, and there are upright stones of varying styles – some large and some small and modest. Some of Sumter's prominent citizens have provided impressive mausoleums of brick, granite or marble for members of their families.

The oldest marker found by this writer in the cemetery bears three names: John Haynsworth, Born February 19, 1782; Died January 27, 1831; M.M.H. Haynsworth, Born December 27, 1789, Died October 15, 1858; William Haysworth, Born in 1815, Died September 1831. The names are followed by the Scripture text: "Blessed are the pure in heart for they shall see God." It is likely that the remains of these may have been brought from elsewhere and placed in this one grave, and the marker was placed after the early dates indicated on the stone, though the slab shows that it is very old.

Another very old stone found nearby is inscribed with the name Mary H. Vaughn and the date of death is given as 1852.

Two other stones were apparently erected in the 1850's. One of these is of S.E.W. Clarkson, who died in 1855. He was born on Wadmalaw Island in 1828 and must have made Sumter his home at some time since he was a member of Claremont Lodge No. 64, as recorded in the book by Thomas M. Stubbs.

The other marks the resting place of one of Sumter's celebrities, Mrs. Elizabeth Ann Spain Chambers. She was a prolific writer under the pen name of "Lizzie Clarendon," contributing stories, articles and poetry to **The Southern Christian Advocate, The Home Circle, The Columbia Times, The American Courier** in Philadelphia, **The South Carolinian** and other periodicals both in Sumter and elsewhere. When she died in 1857, while on a visit at the home of her father in Sumter (she was living in Florida at the time), she was buried in the Sumter Cemetery.

There are some interesting multiple-grave lots in the cemetery, dedicated to different purposes. The American Legion, for instance, purchased a 16-grave lot for veterans of foreign wars who had no family plot in which to be buried. Most of these were from other states; they died, no doubt, while in training in this area. Likewise the Dick Anderson Chapter of the U.D.C. bought a lot where 25 Civil War veterans have markers. In the center of the lot is a large granite monument erected in 1951 with the inscription, "In memory of Our Confederate Dead."

The South Carolina Methodist Conference owns a lot on which are buried several old preachers. Among these is Rev. Bond English, who died in 1868, having served as a minister of the Gospel for 48 years. Another grave on the lot is that of Rev. Lewis M. Little, who was buried in 1888.

On the right side of the cemetery is a section where slaves were buried before the Confederate War, and some ex-slaves were laid to rest there after the war by former masters. Now the Negroes have a well-kept beautiful burial place, known as Walker Cemetery, east of the Sumter Cemetery on Oakland Avenue. Through the efforts of a retired mail clerk, W.F. Bultman, father of Dr. W.F. Bultman, Jr., the cemetery is now under the perpetual care plan. The remains of some of the former slaves have been removed to Walker, but some are still resting under the pines where they were laid more than a century ago.

Another special little section is known as "Babyland." For the most part infants of families that plan to remain in Sumter for only a short time are buried here, most of them being moved later. The price for these tiny grave spaces is $15.00, which includes perpetual care.

Some of Sumter's first ministers were buried in this cemetery. One of the earliest of these, if not the earliest, is Dr. Donald McQueen, whose monument, giving the date of his death as 1880, was erected by the congregation of the First Presbyterian Church, which he served as the beloved pastor for 43 years.

Other graves of interest include that of George Edward ("Tuck") Haynsworth, who was said to have fired the first shot of the Civil War, buried here in 1887. Also there may be seen the grave of Lt. William Alexander McQueen, who was killed in the Battle of Dingle's Mill, when a few brave men tried to defend Sumter from Potter and his army. He was buried in 1865 on the square where his venerable father was later placed.

Two graves that memorialize pathetic circumstances are found in the Sumter Cemetery. One is the grave of the outlaw who was killed on Main Street. Some will recall that Officer Kirven, in attempting to arrest this criminal, found it necessary to shoot. The man's brother, a well-dressed, seemingly prosperous businessman, came down from Chicago to bury this recreant member of his family. He said that the dead man's daughter was looking forward to graduation in a short while and rather than hurt by her by taking the body home, he arranged for the burial in Sumter.

Another lone grave in the midst of family plots where loved ones lie side by side is that of a man who was traveling on foot from somewhere to an unknown destination when he was taken ill with smallpox just as he reached Sumter. Across the road from the cemetery was an old house used by the county as a pest house where victims of smallpox were placed and nursed by an old Negro who had survived an attack of this dread disease. The traveler was taken to the pest house where he soon died. The authorities, it is presumed, buried him in this community burying ground and placed a marker at his grave, bearing the word "Stranger."

So here rest high and low, rich and poor, renowned and humble, beloved and friendless, good and bad – all lying together in the "silent halls of death" – a place described by Longfellow in the following lines:

> "I like that ancient Saxon phrase which calls
> The burial-ground God's Acre! It is just;
> It consecrates each grave within its walls,
> And breathes a benison o'er the sleeping dust."

Jewish Cemetery

In 1874 the Hebrew Cemetery Society, or Burial Society, in Sumter purchased two acres of land for a Jewish Cemetery. Later this Society merged with the Benevolent Society and the cemetery property was transferred.[137]

This cemetery, located on the northeast side of West Oakland Avenue and Artillery Drive, has a grave with an epitaph dating back to 1858. This stone marks the resting place of Aurelius Aaron Solomons, son of A.A. and Kate Solomons. There is a stone bearing the date 1862. This marks the grave of Rosalie Eliza, daughter of A.A. and Kate C. Solomons. The marker at the grave of Caroline Solomons gives the date of death as 1874.

There is a stone with the simple identification "Our Father," June 21, 1830-June 28, 1886. And beside it is one marked "Mother," August 25, 1831-1889.

One dated 1875 carries the name Julius Schwerin, born in Kurnich, Prussia.

There are a number of other graves with dates before 1900.

A U.D.C. marker is of interest in this cemetery. It bears the following inscription: "Ancestor Capt. Edwin W. Moise, soldier 1861-1865, Real Daughter, Nina Moise S. Phelps."

Another old stone is inscribed as follows: Marx E. Cohen, B. Charleston, S.C. July 25, 1810-D. Sumter, S.C. February 24, 1848.

The grave of Rebecca Phillippa Moses, daughter of Montgomery Moses, is dated 1882 and Catherine Moses bears the dates 1843-1848.

A marker shows the grave of Kate, wife of A.A. Solomons, nee Cohen, with the date 1876.

Two died in New York City, one on July 7 and one July 14, both dated 1881. They were Anita Moses, age 16 years 6 months and the other Albert Luria Moses, age 18 years 9 months.

These gravestones bear the oldest dates. There are many other graves in the cemetery – some old and some of more recent dates. One can readily see the loving care given to the upkeep of this sacred spot where loved ones and ancestors of many generations are buried.

In 1977 the cemetery purchased the adjacent corner lot, enlarging area of original grounds to insure land protection and meet future needs.

St. Lawrence Cemetery

Catholics in Sumter purchased in 1848 from the Methodists their small church on West Liberty Street. Along with the church building came an entire block bounded on the east by Church Street, on the west by Salem Avenue and on the north by Hampton Avenue (then Republican Street).

They added to the small church building and enclosed the block by an attractive fence, using part of the property as a cemetery.

In 1849 the church was dedicated to St. Lawrence and the cemetery was given the same name.

Sometime after 1875, when a new church was built on East Liberty Street, the property on West Liberty was sold to the city. However, the Catholics moved at that time the St. Lawrence Cemetery to West Oakland Avenue adjacent to the Sumter Cemetery.

Many who were early settlers of Sumter are buried in this old cemetery. The oldest grave, according to a survey made by a committee from the Sumter Chapter of the South Carolina Genealogical Society, is dated 1834. It marks the grave of John Carr (erected by his comrades) of Croughbed, Kilgar Parish, County Donegal, Ireland.

Dated in the 1850's were two stones: Mary Ellen O'Conner (1856), Mary Bryan (1859).

There are several in the 1860's, the oldest being that of Ellen O'Conner (1861). Others are Mary Frances Moran (1864); Catherine O'Brine (1864), consort of George W. Reardon; William B. Kavanagh (1865); Timotheus B. Sullivan (1865); Mary B. O'Brine (1865); Henry Hurst (1867); Joseph Edward O'Brine (1868); Mary E. O'Conner (1868); Joseph Edward O'Brine (1868); and John O'Conner (1868).

The oldest stones in the 1870's are those of John Brennan (1870) and Thomas Monaghan (1870). Others interred in that decade were John E. Dowling (1871), 22nd birthday; Henrietta E. Morrissey (1873, age 16 years); Eliza H.J. Kennedy (1872); Agnes Johanna O'Brine (1877); Margaret Hennagan (1871); George W. Reardon, husband (1877); Margaret Monaghan (1879); John Monaghan (1872); Patrick Egan (1872); Margaret Hennagan (1871); William Patrick Hennagan (1872); Franklin Joseph Moran (1875); Agnes Johanna O'Brine (1877); John Tuomey (1871); John Holt Feriter's stone was marked 1886 and Julia Kavanagh was buried in 1881.

There are a few graves dated in the 1890's: Sallie A. Poole (1892), Annette J. Hurlburt (1896), John Herbert Madden (1897), and Sallie Cobb (1893).

There are some stones without dates. And many were placed in the burying ground since 1900.

Some stones are very simple, while many are large and imposing. Shrubbery, trees and flowers planted and tended by loved ones make this cemetery an attractive and peaceful resting place for those who have made their contribution to the world and have passed on to another life.

Walker Cemetery

Located on the south side of West Oakland Avenue, neighbor to St. Lawrence and Sumter Cemetery, is historic Walker Cemetery. It is under the devoted care of the Walker Cemetery Association, which was organized on January 24, 1895. Responsible for the forming of this organization was Mr. Z.E. Walker.[138]

The first person buried in this cemetery was Cassandra Maxwell, who died on December 27, 1893. Either she was buried elsewhere and her remains moved after this cemetery was begun, or the cemetery location was chosen because of the place of her grave.

Others who were buried here before 1900 were Malvena Walker, December 18, 1895; Samuel Z. Walker, October 2, 1896; Laura Wesley, October 15, 1896 (90 years of age); Mary Virginia Lee, May 18, 1898; Sarah A. Davis, October 16, 1899; Walter Peters, October 21, 1895; and Hattie P. Commander, November 25, 1897.

Many have been laid to rest in this lovely old cemetery in the 1900's. Mary Dyson's stone bears the date of death, February 22, 1900. Z.E. Walker, the one who organized the cemetery association, died in 1916.

This cemetery shows great care from those who have loved ones buried here.

PART VI. HISTORIC BUILDINGS

Aycock's Store

The doors have long been closed to a quaint old store on a prominent corner in Wedgefield.

Although the marks of time are indelibly impressed upon the building, it still stands as a relic of bygone days in this little town. Members of the older generation recall often, no doubt with a feeling of nostalgia, the good times centered around this popular gathering place, which had the official name of J.H. Aycock and Sons, but was known locally as "Aycock's Store."

This building was erected around 1879 by the late J.H. Aycock, who came to Wedgefield from Rockingham, North Carolina. He was twice married: first to Miss Elizabeth Fullwood from the Brogdon section of Sumter County and after her death to Miss Henrietta Brogdon from the same community.

By the first marriage there were three children: James H., Jr., Albert and Leonora. There were also three from the second union: William Thomas, Eugene E. and Elizabeth (affectionately called by her friends and acquaintances "Miss Betty").

Mr. Aycock bought property in Wedgefield and built a saw-mill. He prepared the lumber there for his store. (The mill later was replaced by a gin.)

Around 1889 he built a beautiful two-story house where the family lived until all had died or moved away except Eugene and "Miss Betty." They later moved into a small house across from the Presbyterian Church. They, too, now have passed away.

After the death of their father, sons Eugene and Albert continued to run the store for several years.

Miss Betty, for a number of years, was a correspondent for **The Columbia Record** and **The Sumter Daily Item**.

A poem in blank verse written by Mary Celestia Parler and published some years ago gives a peek into the magic that this store created for the children of the community:

Christmas in Aycock's Store

Inside the big and barnlike village store
Heated by a huge pot-bellied stove
And the sweat of many bodies, brown and white,
Swinging tin kerosene lamps lighted up a glorious place,
My idea of Paradise when I was young.

Toys strung on cords above the busy counters,
Rubber dolls, tin whistles in their backs,
Tin horns striped red and white and blue,
And Jacks-in-boxes, monkeys-on-a-string
Drums and drum-sticks, toy soldiers,
Butterflies that flap their metal wings,
Watches always twenty after eight.

And Fireworks!
Red packages of tiny crackers with mysterious Chinese characters,
One-inch crackers, two-inch crackers, six-inch giant crackers,
Sparklers, son-o'-guns, torpedoes, sky-rockets,
Beautiful long Roman candles, pink, and green and yellow,
All strung on cords among the hanging toys.

The candy counter! Oh, the candy counter!
Brazil nuts, pin wheels, Tootsie Rolls,
Sticks of candy wearing finger rings,
Gumdrops and sugar plums in sturdy wooden pails,
Strips of chewey coconut, pink and white,
Pound boxes (for a quarter) of chocolate covered cherries.
Fat bunches of bananas swinging high
Looked down on apples, oranges, tangerines,
Boxes of raisins, and mixed nuts — almonds, walnuts, pecans, Brazil nuts.

Behind an iron grill great tables spread
With china dolls, with curls and sleepy eyes,
Tea sets, and sewing machines that really sew,
Rocking horses, pop guns, Indian suits,
Automobiles, and trucks, and trains,
All sorts of things that run alone when wound.

No hired Santa Claus in soiled red suit
Dispelled the spirit of Christmas in this enchanted place.

If heaven is as joyful as I think,
Some day I'll find again the magic glory,
The Paradise of Aycock's store at Christmas time
When I was very young.

Mortuary Housed In Historic Home

Sumter's lovers of historic lore and landmarks rejoice as they ride or walk up Church Street or out Broad to see the restoration of an edifice, part of which was built more than a century ago. All the charm and beauty of the original home has been kept in the renovation of the structure which now houses the Harris & Sons Funeral Home.

Not only the building itself, but its setting holds historic significance. Set back in a lot that extended from Broad Street to Haynsworth was a large, two-story frame home that was built for Franklin Israel Moses, Jr., by his father around 1840,[140] it is thought. The spacious grounds were landscaped and tended by an "imported" gardener who lived in a cottage at the back. The grounds were enclosed by a "handsome" iron fence.

In this home Franklin Moses, while governor of South Carolina, entertained political friends in a series of sumptuous receptions. In fact, he considered this home in Sumter as his headquarters for official society. The mansion was said to have had a beautifully furnished drawing room, library, dining room, the "Crimson Room," "The Family Room," "The Blue Room" and "The Oak Room."

A two-story office building for young Moses was erected, complete with a bar, a billiard table, and bedrooms. On the west side of the grounds were large stables for the dashing horses and handsome carriages used by the governor. Above these were living quarters for the coachman.

In 1880 Joseph Haynsworth Earle, who became state senator in 1882 and state attorney general in 1886, bought this magnificent residence. After the home was burned in 1889,[141] Earle moved to Greenville.

The office building, which had been used by both Moses and Earle, was saved when the home burned and was sold apparently to Dr. James L. Haynsworth, whose widow, Mrs. McConico Spann Haynsworth, sold it in 1901[142] to H.M. McLaurin, who built a beautiful home around the old office. After the death of Mrs. McLaurin the home was sold in 1921. Since then it changed hands, it seems, several times until it was bought by the Ben H. Rutledges in 1942.

Tied in with the history of the house and location is an added interest in that the company which has renovated the building and made it into a beautiful modern mortuary, retaining its original charm and beauty, is a continuation of Sumter's oldest funeral home and undertaking establishment. The family ties reach back from the Hurst who recently sold the business to the present owners and whose name remains with the company to the business that was begun in 1859 by J.D. Craig on the northwest corner of Main and Canal Streets.

Mr. Craig was first a finished cabinet maker and later went into the furniture and undertaking business. He advertised in 1889 caskets that he had made at a price of $3 and up for children and $5 up for adults. At some time he had taken the agency for famous makes of furniture and had a cabinet repair shop on the side.

When George H. Hurst married Mr. Craig's niece, the business became known as J.D. Craig Furniture Company and Undertakers. And in 1919, Hurst Funeral Home was established in a wooden building behind the furniture store on Main and Canal, with George H. Hurst as owner and manager.

At first horse-drawn vehicles were used for funerals. In addition to the hearses, surreys provided transportation to the funeral for the family. Serving Sumter, Lee and Clarendon counties, when notified by the family of a deceased one, they would take the casket (coffin in those days) requested, go to the home of the person who had died and stay with the family until after the funeral. Instruments and other materials needed for embalming the body were carried in a small case or kit. Sometimes in case of storms or high water they were stranded for several days. Always abreast of the times, however, Hurst was the first in Sumter to use motor vehicles in his business.

As time passed, Mr. Hurst took his sons into the furniture and undertaking business and the firm became known as George H. Hurst and Sons. In 1946 George H. Hurst, Jr., became manager of the business with the retirement of his father; however, the name remained the same.

In 1958 the Hurst Funeral Home was moved to 25 East Calhoun Street, where it remained until it was removed to the present location. The furniture business remained in the same name and location till 1962. After it was closed, Craig Hurst inherited the Hurst Funeral Home, running it until it was bought by Parnell and Rutledge, licensed morticians, and moved in December 1969, to the present location.

In the renovation of the home, the original rooms used for Governor Moses' office have been identified. The opening which led into the wine cellar has been closed and the cellar itself filled in. Timbers used in the building are of solid pine, handhewn, and the original part was put together with pegs. The mantle in the front is beautifully hand carved, and other mantles added by Mr. McLaurin are unusual and attractive.

Apparently at sometime the kitchen was separated from the house, since there are indications that it had been rolled up and attached to the main house at a lower level than the main part of the structure. In the front are large bay windows that no doubt were added by Mr. McLaurin.

The iron fence that surrounded the original Moses gardens is still on the south side. The present owners have removed the front section to afford a more spacious front entrance to the funeral home, but it will be placed on the north side of the grounds.

Howard Parnell and Ned Rutledge, with a fine sense of the loveliness of historic homes, have gone to infinite pains to restore the original beauty of the old home. Flowers and shrubbery will add greatly to the overall effect. Unfortunately a beautiful camellia, the seed for which was brought from Brazil many years ago, was accidentally destroyed by the tractor in the preparation of the soil for further planting.

The owners, too, are striving to carry on the tradition begun by J.D. Craig more than 100 years ago and improved from time to time by the Hurst family. The inside of the building is conveniently and appropriately arranged and decorated to give the best service to sorrowing loved ones. The directors have planned the funeral parlors to the best advantage and the decor is subdued and lovely.

Eli Kennedy, funeral director for the firm, was the earliest to qualify as a licensed director in Sumter and one of the earliest in the nation, his license number being 89.

The business has again changed hands. Billy Harris, with his sons, now operates an up-to-date mortuary in this beautiful old home.

Many in this area will agree with the sentiments of one who said: "Let us hope that owners of other old homes will see the possibilities of remodeling the old houses of such good construction into comfortable, modern homes or business houses, thus adding to the beauty and individual charm of Sumter."

New Life Comes To Old Plantation

As one travels along Highway 15, south of Sumter, he would likely not guess that behind a high hurricane fence, backed by trees and undergrowth, stretches a 600-acre plantation of unusual interest and great beauty, a recent owner of which was a most remarkable person – James Wilcox DesChamps.

This plantation, though now pervaded by an atmosphere of modern living, is still reminiscent of pre-Revolutionary days when the land was granted to early colonists by the King of England for the payment of a small sum.

The first recorded owner of a part of it at least was a Mr. Dugan, who built a home on his holdings. According to tradition he had a well in his back yard in which he buried his treasures and for some reason never recovered them. There can still be seen evidences of the home site, and a small depression nearby marks the spot where the well was thought to be.

As time went on, Dugan sold his land to a Mr. Maverick and moved to Sumterville to enter the merchandising business. It is thought that Dugan Street was named for him.

Then in 1837 the land was bought by Henry Haynsworth Wells, who built a four-story home in the prevailing architectural style of that day. At some time the place was given the name Mt. Hope Plantation.[143]

In due time the estate passed to the Wells heirs, the land being divided except for the house and some farm land. This was to continue as the home of three unmarried daughters during their lifetime. One of the daughters, Martha, known as "Aunt Matt," being in poor health, lived with her nephew and his family; another sister, Lydia, died; and that left one, Caroline, to occupy the large house alone. She was well known in the Privateer community as "Miss Callie," and the family called her "Aunt Cal." She was truly an individual, lending to the old home and its surroundings her unique personality. After her death (around 1919 or 1920), the homestead reverted to the estate to be settled by the heirs. Some years later the house burned, leaving an old barn, vestiges of which still remain.

When the estate was finally sold for settlement in 1937, Mr. DesChamps purchased the land.

He did much work on the old plantation, making lakes, planting flowers and shrubbery and building an attractive and convenient home.

At the death of Mr. DesChamps the place was sold to a group of Sumter businessmen who have formed the Lakewood Partnership. They are now converting the 600 acres into a residential development.

Thus the pre-Revolutionary plantation continues to bring pleasure to its owners though living conditions follow the customs of another era.

PART VII. INTERESTING HOMES

Chandler-DuRant Plantation Home

Almost completely hidden from the eye of one traveling on the old Brewington Road is the historic James Rembert Chandler home, where two of his great-granddaughters, Misses Marie and Hattie DuRant, now live.

This old home, built, it is thought, in the 1820's, gives a perfect picture of the antebellum plantation life in the South. Though having long since passed the century mark and having lost much of its youthful beauty, it stands proud with the dignity and charm which come from years of usefulness.

It is some distance from the road, which has for a long time been the main thoroughfare for those living in this part of old Sumter District. Ancient trees spread their branches to furnish shade; while tall and low-growing shrubbery add to the restful scene, welcoming the visitor to the Chandler-DuRant home.

Mounting the original steps that lead to the main story of the old home, the guest, upon the hospitable invitation of the hostesses, enters a spacious living room with high ceilings, typical of the old plantation homes, giving a feeling of a roominess that seems to hold out open arms of hospitality.

Opening into this room on the left is another large room which was no doubt used when crowds gathered for an evening of "fun and frolic." Behind these rooms were three others in the original structure. On each end was a tall chimney. These chimneys were cracked by the 1886 earthquake. One has been replaced, but the other repaired and the long crack can still be seen.

Through the years as the house passed on to larger families, more rooms were added at the back.

Originally, as was always the case, the kitchen was on the outside, where food was prepared and brought into "the big house" by slaves. Later the basement was used as the kitchen.

This house, characteristic of the times, was built high off the ground. Therefore there was plenty of room for cooking. Later still a kitchen was added to the back of the home.

Some of the furniture now being used came down from the original owners, and some was added through the years by other ancestors of the present owners.

There is a most interesting sideboard that must have been among the first furnishings of the house. Other pieces of unique interest are a hall rack; several chests; a bed, the parts of which are held together by rope; an old Gilbert clock; a Sleepy Hollow Rocker; a set of six small straight chairs with very graceful backs. There are dressers and washstands to match and old tables. Among smaller pieces is an interesting old pepper mill. All these tell a silent story of the charm of this home through the years.

In the back premises can still be seen the old kitchen (later used for a barn), the carriage house, the smoke house, part of an old gin. These ancient structures have fallen into decay, but they are vivid reminders of the past.

Beyond the yard was the lane on each side of which were the slave quarters. Some of their homes have been removed and some used for tenants on the farm after the Civil War.

James Rembert Chandler's gravestone bears the following inscription:

"He had the meekness of the Christian,
the energy of the man of business.
The independence of the good citizen.
His children rise up and call him blessed.
He died as none but Christians die.
With hope fixed firm on Canaan's shore.
His ashes here in silence lie,
To rise ere long to die no more."

James Rembert Chandler was the father of three daughters and one son. The son, Samuel Edward, was a doctor. He is buried at Concord Presbyterian Church. Mary (Pattie) Chandler married Thomas Alexander Mayes, son of Matthew Peterson ("Squire") Mayes, and lived in Mayesville in the old home now owned by Mrs. Glenn Kiser.

Maria Chandler became the wife of Lemuel Ira Reames, for whom Lemira School was named. The school was originally built on the Brewington Road on land belonging to Lemuel Ira Reames. It was later moved to Charles Chandler's place. This school is now located on Boulevard Road and is in Sumter School District 17.

Sally Jessie Reames, daughter of Lemuel and Maria Chandler Reames, married Joseph Henry DuRant. They were parents of several children, including Marie and Hattie.

Sarah Chandler, another daughter, also married a Reames and lived in the same community.

Signing his will in 1860, James Rembert Chandler mentioned special legacies to his children. To each he left a number of slaves. He requested that his land, crops, mules, plantation tools be sold. From the proceeds his debts were to be paid, $1000 given to Samuel Edward, and the remainder divided equally among others of the family.

To Sarah he left his carriage and horses and to Maria, the piano.

The land was apparently bought by Lemuel Ira Reames, and the home place passed down to Sally Jessie Reames, who married Joseph Henry DuRant. Their heirs now occupy the historic site, which they have loved from their earliest recollection and which still holds for them many cherished memories.

Dixie Hall

Home is a word fraught with meaning. It inspires thoughts of happiness or sorrow, companionship or loneliness, activity or relaxation or other sentiments. But when the walls of a home have heard the cries and laughter of babies, seen the disappointments and happiness of young people, the sorrows and joys of older folk for six generations of the same family, it really has a story to tell.

Such a home is "Dixie Hall," originally known as "Oakland Plantation," which stands proud and magnificent in the Hagood section of Sumter County, on Highway 261. It was built around 1735 by William Sanders I on a grant of land from the King of England.

In **Red Carolinians** Dr. Milling says that excellent farm lands along the Indian Trails near Wateree River had already been cleared, but were not planted. However, William Sanders I built his home and began making friends with the Indians by trading with them.

The home today has essentially the same form in which it was originally built, though some remodeling was done by William Sanders IV just before the War Between the States. He replaced the spiral staircase used by his ancestors with the handsome sweeping staircase now in use. The chimneys, which were originally on the north and south ends of the structure, he moved to furnish fireplaces in four rooms. He also remodeled the front porch.

Large timbers, adz-tooled, 21 inches thick, are still visible in the basement, which has two large storage rooms. There are also two rooms with brick walls and iron bars at the windows where unruly slaves were confined.

In 1807 the owner deeded two and a half acres near the home for a community burial plot. For a century it was known as "Shiloh." It is now the cemetery for the Church of the Ascension. For so many years bodies were buried with no markers that those digging graves today often dig into other graves. In the past buggies were known to sink into the graves.

Near the burial plot were built many years ago a meeting house and blacksmith shop.

On February 20, 1826, Sarah Sanders' will was recorded. She enumerated slaves and other possessions of "Oakland Plantation," as it was still called at that time. She was the widow of the eldest William Sanders.

William IV and William V both died at Dixie Hall. It is not known about William II and William III, but both lived there as the property was willed to each in turn. During Potter's Raid through central South Carolina, he dispatched soldiers to destroy homes and possessions in Stateburg, Bradford Springs, Spring Hill by Boykin's Mill and Camden. When they came to this area and to "Dixie Hall," however, Georgiana, the lovely young daughter of William V, met the officer in charge as he advanced toward the house and begged him to spare her home. He was so charmed by her beauty and gracious manner that he gave commands for the place to be spared. After the war he came back to woo the lovely young lady, but she had other plans. Her hand and heart had been won by a Southerner, DuPree Graham of Sumter.

Though the home had been spared, one cannon ball made a hole in the upstairs piazza. The ball was kept by the family as a relic.

William IV was so angry because one of his lovely daughters married against his will that he is said to have cut his throat. He immediately regretted his hasty action and called for help, but it was too late. His ghost has been known to wander around the home.

Emma R. Sanders, daughter of William V, inherited the home after his death. She married Dr. John Ashe Alston, who began practicing in the area. He built his office at the back of the house.

Their daughter-in-law, Mrs. Frances Poole Alston, was the next owner. She, too, did some remodeling. Since the kitchen was in the yard, as were most kitchens in the early days, she added a lovely pine-paneled kitchen, breakfast room and enclosed porch on the second floor (if basement is considered the first floor).

Since the old portraits and handsome pieces of furniture have been divided among other descendants, Mrs. Alston has collected many old pieces that fit into the decor of her rooms and most have interesting historic backgrounds.

(Mrs. Alston died October 12, 1979, and the place is now owned by her son, William P. Alston.) [144]

"Shalom," House Of Peace

Greeted at the top of the high front steps of "Shalom" by the charming owner, Mrs. F.M. Cain, Sr., a visitor is indeed enchanted with the peaceful atmosphere pervading the beautiful old home.

Upon entering the living room, one may exclaim, "How restful are the soft colors of the walls." And Mrs. Cain's answer would be that when she came to the home, the walls were all calcimined yellow with two shades of blue above the picture molding; and the mantels, doors, wainscoting and other woodwork in the entire house was varnished a dark brown. Floors were painted red.

The guest is amazed when told of the tremendous, backbreaking effort that went into the transformation of this old home, which had been "modernized" through the years until it had all but lost its original beauty.

Mrs. Bertha Sweet Cain grew up in the country, and she always wanted an historic plantation home of her own. Therefore, when she and Mr. Cain saw this place advertised for sale, they bought it and moved in on December 26, 1934. He was told after he bought it that the plantation was nothing more than "doodle bugs and frogponds" and that the house was falling down.

Though no doubt discouraged at the appearance of their purchase but not in despair, the couple set to work to make over the house and improve the surroundings. Yes, Mrs. Cain had always wanted an old house to restore and this she had indeed!

The house was started in 1837[145] by James Burrell Fort, who was married to Cecilia McCoy, for their daughter, Sarah Pyrene, who married Moses Brogdon in 1838. The long leaf pine timbers were hand-hewn and put together with pegs. It was a large house and the work was done with painstaking care; therefore, it required much time to complete the two-story house. In fact, two of the Brogdon children were born before the young couple was able to move into their home.

But what changes almost 100 years had wrought! The home passed into other hands as time went on. Some of the occupants tried to make the home conform to more modern ideas, and others didn't really seem to care how the house and its surrounding appeared.

The original blinds had been removed from most of the windows; the original handmade front door had been replaced by a half-glass door; the plastering overhead had been replaced with narrow ceiling; there were ugly, gaping holes in the plastered walls; panes of glass were out of the windows and cardboard had been tacked over the holes; rain poured through the roof.

The house was in bad enough repair, but the outhouses were impossible. In front of the house was an old barn on the verge of collapsing. The woodpile, wash pot and tubs and a scaffold on which hogs were butchered were all in the front side yard.

The first order of business was to build a walled-in shed for the mules; the cows were put into two old chicken houses. Ditches had to be cleaned out and weeds and small trees to be cut to prepare the land for the spring planting. Tenant houses had to be repaired.

Finally, however, they were able to begin work on the house. Since Mr. Cain was busy on the farm, the greater burden of restoring the home fell to Mrs. Cain.

To make the prospect more dismal, their furniture which had been sufficient for the small cottage-type home they had lived in previously was lost in the big rooms; and the curtains and shades were far too small for the large, old-timey windows.

With some extra money that she made by nursing and working for a few months as assistant supervisor of a consumer purchase survey, Mrs. Cain went to work with a will. With ingenuity and good taste, strengthened by a firm determination to have what she wanted, she began to get results.

The house having been wired by previous occupants with a drop cord in each room, the Cains installed a Delco plant and put in some wall outlets. A roof also had to be provided to keep out the rain.

Before spending too much time on the house, they decided that it was necessary to move the old barn from in front of the house to the back and rebuild it for use. Finally, she was ready to begin work on the house to restore it to its original historic look.

Using some old molding that came from her grandfather's house in Williamsburg County, with the help of a man from the place, she built a mantel for the living room to harmonize with the age and style of the home and the fireplace was opened for use.

The next task was removing the ugly brown paint from the woodwork. Mrs. Cain said, "I scrubbed and scraped until I ached when I got up in the morning!" Then the dirty, yellow calcimine had to be washed from the 13-foot walls. Since Mr. Cain had given her a 10-foot stepladder for her birthday, she was fully equipped for the task. She had a man to wash the ceilings in the four front rooms, but she was able to reach the overhead of the shed rooms.

Looking at the walls today one could never visualize what they were like when the Cains bought the place. The living room walls have been finished with paper in light taupe and the woodwork is ivory. The half-glass door has gone to the back and the old handmade wooden door has come to the front. Harmonizing with the walls are rugs, as well as draperies, hung from poles with rings.

The furniture consists of a couch (bought from a second-hand store and redone with new cushions and covers); an old overseer's desk that belonged to Mrs. Cain's father; bookcases and tables in keeping with the room; three large chairs, a deck chair and a child's rocker.

Amazingly it cost only $46.49 to furnish this room because much of the furniture came from their parents and grandparents.

The dining room is 13½ by 17½ feet. It, too, has an open fireplace with a pretty mantel that came from an old home that had been torn down. This mantel she bought for $3.00. She papered this room with a light scenic paper. In winter, straight curtains hang from under old golf leaf cornices, and in summer, ruffled marquisette curtains, hanging to the sill, are held back by brass arms.

The dining table is a family heirloom and the chairs are of the plain Windsor type. There is also an old hand-made high chair that came down through Mr. Cain's family. An old mahogany sideboard and an Empire couch completed the furnishings in this room, and a soft green rug was chosen to complement the decor. The chandelier, which is just right for this room, was found by the alert Mrs. Cain for a small amount.

The 17½ by 17½ foot front bedroom with ivory walls and woodwork presents a most inviting appearance. It has four large windows and three doors, allowing plenty of light to add to the cheery atmosphere. To enhance the antique look, Mrs. Cain chose rag rugs.

In keeping with the period of the house is a beautiful French bed of early 1800 vintage. To take the place of a closet which the room does not have, Mrs. Cain brought from her grandfather's an old wardrobe built by her great-grandfather's plantation carpenter. In the corner is a quaint round table that was brought in 1873 by her grandfather for the children to sit around for study.

A lovely chest of drawers adds to the antique atmosphere of the room. Other old pieces, together with lamps, vases and pictures, complete the attractiveness and comfort of the room.

The middle bedroom is also large and airy and is furnished with family heirlooms. Adjoining is a small bath built under the staircase. The bedroom has lovely curtains and is attractively decorated with pictures, lamps, etc., in keeping with an appropriate color scheme.

At the back of the house is a small 10 by 10 foot bedroom. Though smaller than the rooms in the main part of the house, it is furnished most attractively with old furniture and colorful accessories. Next to this room is a bath.

Across the small hall is the kitchen, which, though having very modern furnishings, has other accessories that tie in with the decor of the rest of the home. The back wall in the kitchen was cut down to counter height that a small breakfast nook might be added. To give an idea of the strength of the house, the studs to be cut were five inches thick.

The Cains also built a back porch, which, furnished with comfortable rockers, offers a place for relaxation on a hot summer day. There is a pump to furnish fresh drinking water.

The narrow hall, once dark and gloomy, is now painted ivory and has two half-glass doors to give plenty of light. There are attractive pictures on the walls to add color.

The upstairs rooms have been repainted, but they are used for the most part for storage now.

There was no running water in the house when the Cains first moved there. They used the old well that was dug in 1837 until they brought their windmill from their former home. This furnished water for the kitchen until they were able to install more modern equipment.

Materials for improving the house came from many sources. Mrs. Cain was ever looking for opportunities to obtain anything that would be suitable for the home and she always knew exactly what was suitable.

The banisters, for instance, on the front of the porch and down the steps came from her grandfather Holleman's house. Those on the sides came from an old Brogdon home and she changed them to match the others.

The wide boards in the shed room came from Carew Rice's great-grandmother's old school house on East Liberty Street. On the back porch is an old roller towel rack from her grandfather's home. She found a Victorian door stop that had been plowed up in the field. The pretty cornices came from Charleston. A lovely old wall chest is a family piece.

On and on the list could go of places and persons whence

came materials and furnishings for "Shalom." The renovation of the home and the collection of furnishings and decorations show something of the skill, taste and perseverance of Mrs. Bertha Cain — a most remarkable person.

She served several years as president of the National Master Farm Homemakers Guild and for some years as chairman of Exterior Beautification for Sumter County Council of Farm Women. As such, she was well qualified to improve the grounds around their plantation home. The drab picture that faced the Cains when they moved in is no more. Trees, shrubs, flowers — everything to make the place a beauty spot — have been planted and tended with care. On the sides and back of the spacious grounds were placed grape arbors, pecans, walnuts, fruit trees. The front, shaded by oaks and other trees, has crepe myrtles, flowering almonds, large camellias, azaleas, fragrant roses, hydrangeas, gardenias and other flowering plants. Bulbs of many varieties were used as borders for the beds. The dream of a beautiful historic home on a plantation truly became a reality. The past 40 years have brought some changes in the inside and outside, each adding to the charm of the home and surroundings.

In 1952, Mr. Cain passed away and Francis, their son, while in service met and married a lovely girl, Peggy Wright of California. The young couple built a home across the road and Mrs. Cain was left alone in the beautiful home in which she had expended so much of herself through the years.

Then in 1954, a happy solution was found. Mrs. Amy Wright, mother of Peggy, upon Mrs. Cain's urgent invitation, came from California to live with Mrs. Cain and be near her daughter. Since that time the two mothers-in-law have enjoyed the beauty and comfort of "Shalom," a name denoting peace. The place was so named many years ago by Dr. John A. Brunson, former beloved pastor of Grace Baptist Church.

As Bertha Sweet Cain looks at her surroundings today, she knows that the following lines are really true:

"Houses are made of brick and stone,
Homes are made of love alone."

Home Occupied By Sixth Generation

Picturesque in its setting on the corner of Magnolia and Kendrick Streets is a home of great historic interest. The captivating story of this old home goes back to the very earliest days of the little town of Sumterville. The story begins when in 1811 Daniel Rose bought 219 acres of land from Spencer Wilder and John Blount Miller, executors of the estate of John Mullin, on what was then known as Laurence Street in the southeastern part of the village. The street later became known as Magnolia because of the large magnolia trees growing on the property, a part of which is now owned by St. Anne's Catholic Church.

On his land, Mr. Rose built a home of pegged timbers. This house was later sold to Daniel Norton, who is said to have been a wheelwright in Sumterville at this time. It later became the property of Jabez Norton of Charleston, son of Daniel. Later still, Judge William Lewis became the owner. He was the ordinary or judge of probate.

It was in 1854[146] that James Richard Kendrick (1824-1875), a native of Mecklenburg, North Carolina, bought 12½ acres along Mill Street, which later became Kendrick Street. He became commissioner in equity for Sumter County and during this time he lived on the property and had a school there.

During the Civil War the house was used as a relief hospital for Southern soldiers being brought through Sumter on the Wilmington-Manchester Railroad which touched on the edge of the Kendrick property. The story is that some of those wounded by the guns of Potter's raiders were also cared for there. Makeshift beds were hurriedly made from boards laid across sawhorses with mattresses of pinestraw and cotton.

During the harrowing aftermath of the war when everyone had lost practically everything, many homes were lost. James Richard Kendrick, however, was able to keep his home, which he deeded in 1872, only three years before his death, to James Diggs Wilder (1840-1910), who had married Kendrick's niece, Sarah Moore Roach (1840-1922), in this home in 1869. Rev. Samuel Furman performed the ceremony. She was the daughter of Stark Hunter Roach (1813-1872) and Martha Moore Kendrick (1816-1841).

The first of the Wilder family to come to South Carolina from Virginia was Spencer Wilder, who was listed in the census of 1790 as living in Clarendon County. He, with his wife, Sarah Yopp Wilder, left Virginia soon after the Revolutionary War. She, as a girl of 12, had witnessed the surrender of Cornwallis at Yorktown.

Son of Spencer and Sarah Yopp Wilder, James Thomas Wilder (1794-1850) lived to the south of the Kendricks. His land holdings extended nearly to Dingle's Mill. The school that still bears the name of Wilder was built on his land. His wife was Amanda Diggs, who traced her ancestry to King Edward III of England.

He was an important figure in Sumter County, during his life, holding the office of clerk of court from 1831 to 1835. He was elected to the state legislature several times and served as sheriff of Sumter County.

Son of James Thomas Wilder was James Diggs Wilder, who saw service throughout the War Between the States. He was in the Battle of Fort Sumter, first in the war, and in the Battle of Cold Harbor, the last of the war. After the conflict ended, he lost his farm near Hagood to a Mr. DeSaussure because he couldn't pay taxes.

He then studied photography and opened a studio in Sumter. Active in the field of education, he served two terms as school commissioner, beginning in 1869 and up to 1888, he was principal of a five-room school on East Hampton Avenue. Entering politics, he served as Sumter County auditor from 1896 to 1910.

The house, which was deeded to James Diggs Wilder in 1872, was remodeled several times. The first renovation was done by the owner about 1890. Then in 1926 Arthur Hunter Wilder (1877-1931), son of James Diggs and Sarah Moore Roach Wilder, remodeled again. The house had been conveyed to him, the middle of five sons, in 1922. Their other sons were Richard Kendrick Wilder, James Guignard Richardson Wilder, Robert Eugene Wilder, and Julian Diggs Wilder.

This Wilder spent many years in the men's clothing business, first as a member of the Sumter Clothing Company with Alston Stubbs and Claude Hurst. After 1913 he joined the business known as Stubbs Brothers. He also worked at the Sumter Casket Factory and the Sumter Insurance Company.

It was Arthur Hunter Wilder, who removed the back portion of the home and used it in building a duplex next door on Kendrick Street. In 1932 Mrs. Arthur Hunter Wilder changed the front and extensively renovated the home. She added four columns at the front and installed four bathrooms.

This Mrs. Wilder was the former James Athalia Robbins, daughter of James Washington Robbins (1841-1909) of Orton Plantation, Southport, North Carolina, and Caroline McDaniel Robbins (1847-1892) also of Southport.

After the death of Arthur Hunter Wilder, the place belonged to his estate, consisting of Mrs. Wilder and their two children, Mrs. N. Roland Goodale of Camden, the former Sarah Kendrick Wilder known as "Happy," who was born in 1909, and Arthur Harrison Wilder (1921-1970), attorney at law and master of equity in Sumter County. He was appointed to this position by Gov. Robert McNair April 1, 1968, to succeed William Reynolds, who was retiring.

The house now (in 1979) is owned by Mrs. Arthur Harrison Wilder, the former Josephine Williams, daughter of J. Frank Williams, Sumter's first County Farm Agent, and Florence Hendricks Williams, of "Needwood Farms," Stateburg, and her three children — Arthur Harrison Wilder, Jr. (1952), and twins, James

Robbins Wilder and Martha Josephine Wilder, born in 1956.

Josephine Wilder taught foreign languages at Sumter High School for 23 years; she is now an assistant professor of French and Spanish at the University of South Carolina at Sumter.

Occupying the home are Arthur Wilder, Jr., and Mrs. Wilder, the former Linda Leonard. He is municipal judge and practicing attorney; she is a teacher at Willow Drive Elementary School in District 17. They have a daughter, Ashley Hope, born September 25, 1978. She is of the sixth generation to live in the ancestral home.

The architectural style of this historic home, dating from the early Republican Period is a combination of the American Federal Classical revival and the middle Georgian Period.

The entrance features double doors over which is an Adam style fanlight. Supporting the roof over the two-story front piazza are four Roman Doric columns of plaster covering brick. The central hall once extended from front to back with a stair and landing in the middle, but in the latest renovation the stair hall was divided into a front and back area.

The upper walls of the hall are plain plaster with wooden wainscoting from the chair rail to the baseboard. The plastered walls in the rooms are painted. Placed diagonally in the center corners of the front rooms are chimneys. The mantels are of wood in a "plain but genteel style." Crossing in the center of the ceiling is a design of single beaded boards with wider diagonal strips coming from the four corners. Most of the ceilings are high as were all ceilings at the time this home was built; however, some have been lowered to 10 feet. The front rooms have the original 14-foot ceilings.

The house rests on a solid foundation of timbers, that were hand-hewn and measure 10" by 12" and 4" x 12" and 2" x 10" beams, also hand-hewn.

The original house was one story high in an L shape with two main chimneys. It is thought that it faced Kendrick Street, then known as Mills Street.

The most enjoyable room in the house is what is called a living room-solarium which Mrs. Arthur Hunter Wilder planned to replace the back piazza. It has five double windows and two double French doors. A mirror in a gold leaf frame extends from floor to ceiling. It reflects more light into the room. The molding at the top was cut with a hand saw by Lucius Hammond, a skillful carpenter, under the supervision of Mrs. Wilder.

Not only is the Wilder home a most interesting and historic house, having been beloved for six generations, but it still has some very unusual pieces of furniture that have been in the family for many years. For instance the grandfather clock in the front hall. It was built by the Seth Thomas Clock Company and has wooden works. It was still in running order until a child pushed it off the stair landing some years ago. In 1978 it was repaired by Ray Wilcox, who hand carved some of the parts that had been damaged by the fall. A clock like this one gave prestige to a home in those early days since it was made by a clockmaker who made the parts by hand and it took months to complete the intricate work involved (page 2, **Palmers Book of American Clocks**).

In one room is an original Hepplewhite end table over which is an old mirror and two ladderback chairs. In this room also hang old photographs, among which is one of Hon. Greene Kendrick (1798-1877), governor of Connecticut, uncle of James Richard Kendrick. It was he who helped save the home when after the war he sent $1000 to Sallie Wilder, wife of James Diggs Wilder.

Unique in style is a nest of four mahogany tables with inlay of holly. These are in the front parlor along with a Duncan Phyfe mahogany couch which is said to be "graceful in line, robust in carving and very uncomfortable." It has carvings of acanthus leaves, sunflower blooms, melon and cornucopias and the clawed feet are lion's paws.

A Hepplewhite mahogany fall-front bureau serves as a desk.

For more than 100 years two oil portraits hung on the wall in this room. They were of the parents of the first Kendricks to live in the home – James Kendrick and his wife, Sarah Ann Moore. The portraits are now owned by Sarah Wilder Goodale, the first girl born into the Wilder family for over 75 years.

In the dining room is a genuine Hepplewhite dropleaf table with two matching rounded ends to complete a handsome banquet table, and the sideboard is of crotch mahogany veneer with four front cabriole legs with claw and ball feet.

Still used in the master bedroom is a mahogany four poster handcarved in a pattern of acanthus leaves. The marble-top bureau has come down in the family from the grandmother of Mrs. Arthur Hunter Wilder. In this room also is a cheval full-length mirror mounted on a wooden support carved in a pineapple design.

There are other pieces of antique furniture that came from past generations of those who owned and loved this old home through the years.

Not only is the house with its well-preserved pieces of antique furniture of great interest today, but the two-acre yard draws the attention of flower lovers. Unusual and lovely plants include a true laurel, a bay-blossom tree, a popcorn tree, a banana shrub tree and a huge holly under which children of another generation had a playhouse. Here, too, may be seen a gardenia bush that was rooted from the original species that the Scot botanist, Dr. Alexander Garden, propagated in this country. His nephews formerly lived on Magnolia Street near the Wilder home.

Some of the other rare plants found in this expensive garden are the blue scilla brought from England by Kendrick. In the spring the air is fragrant with the perfume of the Carolina yellow jessamine blossoms that have an unusual double trumpet-shaped corolla.

There are many species of camellias that have grown into trees and a variety of azaleas and bulbs that were added by the different families that have enjoyed this garden.

Mrs. Arthur Hunter Wilder and her son began specializing in bearded irises in 1930 and added from time to time till in 1970 they had acquired over 200 name brand varieties of rhizomes. Mrs. Arthur Harrison Wilder, who lived in the home a short while after marriage, has been equally interested in this project.

During the South Carolina Tricentennial celebration, the Sumter County Historical Commission placed a plaque on the front of the home telling something of its history.

A Lovely Antebellum Home

"But what on earth is half so dear – So longed for as the hearth of a home?" – Emily Bronte

And what can stir the imagination of one as can an old, old home that has seen the joys and sorrows of those who have lived out their lives within its walls.

Sumter still has a few of these landmarks among which is one now standing on Hampton Avenue and for the past 20 odd years has been the home of the Ansley L. Yates family.

The history of this house dates back to antebellum days, but it is not certain who really built this lovely and unusual old home. It originally stood on the spacious grounds where Memorial Park is now located. The earliest transfer of the property that has thus far been found was from Leonard W. and Lenora Ida Colclough Dick to W.E. Dick in 1860, but Mrs. Dora DuBose, granddaughter of W.E. Dick, said that he did not build the house. He lived there a comparatively short time for in 1864 he died at Green Pond of a fever contracted in the Confederate War.

Mrs. Edward Dick was Posthuma Evelyn Colclough, who died when her daughter, Gertrude, was eight months old. Gertrude, Mrs. DuBose's mother, married Guignard Richardson while her father was still living on Dugan Street, but she visited him after he moved to Hampton Avenue.

After the death of W.E. Dick, the place was sold to James D. McFaddin in trust for his daughter, Leonora, wife of James Douglas Blanding, in 1866, the selling price being $3,500. The Blandings had been left homeless when their plantation home, Millgrove, three miles from Sumter on the Wedgefield Road in the Jordan community, was destroyed by fire.

In the **Biography of the Blanding-McFaddin Families**, written by A.L. Blanding, one of the sons of the family describes the home and surroundings. While sitting in Memorial Park, he reminisced on his young manhood memories of the old home and its surroundings: "On this spot in days gone by there stood a home, a monument to a devoted life, and a happy family. . . . Here in this beautiful municipal park once stood a spacious Southern home, and while sufficiently expansive to shelter a large family — and all friends who came that way — its spaciousness was more fittingly reflected in the hearts of its host and hostesses, than in the physical dimensions of the house itself. Here on this spot stood the homestead of the Blandings. Their children happily played among these very trees, children who in future generations should play their part in molding the destinies of the nation; children whose progeny were destined to inhabit the nation; children whose children were to walk the earth permeated with the sound Christian principles, illuminated by those glorious old family traditions, and strengthened by the memory of that remarkable old family home life that emanated from this very spot."

These memories give not so much a description of the house itself, but a picture of the devotion of the family to the home and to one another.

Many of the beautiful trees that still stand, furnishing comfort and enjoyment to those who visit the park, were planted by James Douglas Blanding for the pleasure of his family.

A large house and grounds were needed for this unusual family, for there were 15 children born to James Douglas and Leonora McFaddin Blanding, thirteen of whom grew to adulthood.

"Born in 1865 my early outstanding recollections are of the nervous tension all of us lived under during the Ku Klux Klan regime. Those were the times that tried mens (sic) souls and brought out what was noblest and bravest in womens' (sic). . . . I went out in the grove one morning where Father had made us a lovely playground, equipped with swing, "Flying Jinnie," Jinnie board, "Fly around pole," and different height gymnastic poles and a croquet ground. Rob or perhaps Louis and I stood in the swing and "pumped" until we would go high among the treetops. We sang vigorously and loudly as we pumped, "the Ku Klux will catch you if you don't be good" until Mother called from the dining room window, 'Children, stop singing that, the Ku Klux might hear you.' "[147]

The mother of the family, Leonora McFaddin Blanding, died in 1886. She lived in this beloved home until her 15th child was 15.

The father of the family lived on there until 1892 when the place was sold to A.C. DuRant for $1450. (In 1890 the Blandings had sold an acre of land to Mark Reynolds.)

Thus the Blandings had occupied this home for 26 years and for a number of years it was still called the Blanding house.

Mrs. Annie Randle bought the house and land from A.C. DuRant in 1899 for $3,750. This family occupied the home for only two years. It was sold to William A. Bowman on August 16, 1901, for $5,500.[148]

Mr. William Bowman was married to Mary Ellen Dick; thus the home once again welcomed a member of the Dick family.

There were six children in the Bowman family. The late Paul Bowman recalled with delight the happy times they had playing under the house and over the expansive grounds. He remembered especially the large grape arbor in the rear of the home.

The home was built of hand-hewn heart timbers as most homes were in those early days. The sills were 14' x 14' and the joists 4 x 12. Whether changes were made by Blandings is not known, but in the time of the Bowmans there was a hall down the middle with rooms on each side. Later the partition was removed on the right. Thus one large room was at the front. The porches were said to have been 12 feet wide. There were two wings on the original building and the Randles added a bathroom on the back. There were three rooms upstairs and at one time they were occupied by two Scotch servants.

Not only the home itself is a landmark in Sumter, but the six and a half acres of land, a part of the beautiful homesite were enjoyed by the Blandings for 26 years and the Bowmans for 19, as well as by others for shorter periods of time between these two families.

Of such esthetic appeal was this beauty spot on Hampton Avenue that it was bought in 1920 by interested citizens and presented to the City of Sumter to be made into a park in memory of those brave young white men who gave their lives for the fight for freedom in World War I.

One paragraph from an article written by Mrs. Julia Dillon, that one who contributed much toward the beautification of Sumter, gives a glimpse of the beauty found in Memorial Park.

"It is a sanctuary for the birds, as well as for the children.

Each season brings its own panorama of unfolding blossoms and foliage and fruit. There are rich backgrounds of evergreens that frame as well as screen. Magnolias, Hollies, Photinias, Ligustrum, Japonicums, Carolina cherries, and Japanese oaks are planted on the boundary lines. For accents there are tall and stately Himalayan cedars and Italian Cypresses, with junipers, retinesporas, thuyas, biotas and spruce."

It was in 1920 that the beloved old home and the equally loved grounds parted company. The city sold the house to the George C. Warrens (for $800 it is said) by whom it was then moved farther down Hampton next to the home of the L.I. Parrotts. Mr. Parrott (Mrs. Warren's father) gave his daughter and her family the lot on which to place the historic home. Before the moving began, one wing and the back porch were removed from the house. The building was moved by a team of mules and quite an undertaking it proved to be. Mrs. Warren recalls that it took the better part of a day to saw one of those solid pine sills in two.

The Warrens effected a number of changes in the home, making it more convenient for their particular needs. One of the most significant changes that added convenience and comfort was the digging of a cellar, which was entered by a stair in the back hall, near the steps leading to the second floor. Another improvement was the addition of a bathroom in the back hall, completing a small apartment.

Dormer windows were made across the front and back, giving added light and sunshine to the upstairs area.

When asked about the presence of ghosts, Mrs. Warren said that there were lots of strange noises but no ghost had actually been seen. She pointed out, however, that there is a dark stain on the floor near the left front window. The story has been handed down that someone was murdered in the room and this stain was left by a spot of blood. But no one has ever solved the mystery.

The Warrens moved in 1933 and during the next 22 years several families occupied the house at intervals for comparatively short periods of time — the Francis K. Holmans, the Ervin Shaws and perhaps others. Then Miss Mamie Gunter converted the house into apartments, replacing the partition at the front, thus restoring the original arrangement of an entrance hall with a room on each side.

The Ansley Yates family bought the house in 1955 from Miss Gunter. They have also made changes in the 20 years since they moved into the home, but in no way have these changes detracted from the historic interest of the home. They designed the attractive front entrance, mentioned earlier. The beautiful door was brought from the old Yates home, which once stood on Calhoun Street. Thus a bit of family history is added, making this home mean even more.

From the large entrance hall, one enters on the right the formal living room (parlor). At the tall windows reaching almost to the 12-foot paneled ceiling, are lovely draperies chosen with care to give just the right touch to enhance the historic charm so evident in every part of the room.

This room opens into a similar one which the Yates family use as a formal dining room, and the same meticulous care in decorating and furnishing is apparent here.

Though the present owners have installed central heating to make the home more comfortable, the old fireplaces in these rooms are kept with their lovely old mantels, reminding one of those days long ago when members of a family gathered around the open fire to discuss the happenings of the day – a custom which brought the family closer together.

The room beyond the dining room has recently been extended, but this addition has the same high ceilings, the same windows with small panes, floors made of old-fashioned wide pine boards, high wainscoting – all typical of the original home. These materials were found in an old house of the same period in Clarendon County.

The kitchen, though modern and convenient, has a counter of wood such as was used for the chopping boards of long ago, and the cabinets are boarded to match. A replica of an old kerosene lamp furnishes light, and the windows have homespun curtains. Completing the antique decor is a stencil pattern of wallpaper.

In this new extension also are the breakfast room and a large family room, light and airy. Giving the atmosphere of home is another fireplace, made of old city brick, bought for the purpose when they were unearthed on Main Street.

Furnishings in this recent addition are in keeping with the historic tone. Holding a prominent place is an old buffet (sideboard) with which Mr. Yates' grandmother began housekeeping. In a nook between the kitchen and the bedroom there stands a quaint old bookcase.

The house has five bedrooms, three and a half baths, a den upstairs, a study, a living room, in addition to the rooms already mentioned – all giving a feeling of "hominess" and old-time hospitality.

Mr. and Mrs. Yates have four children – two boys and two girls. All are keenly interested in the restoration of the old home and take an active part in all the plans for its beautification.

This historic home has made its contribution to the happiness of many lives; and though it is in its second century, it's still fulfilling its mission as a beloved home. The Yates family feel that there is a joy and satisfaction in the owning and restoring of an old home that can never be found in buying a new house in which there is no feeling of warmth that comes from having been lived in and loved. As William Camden once said,

> "He that buys a house ready wrought
> Hath many a pin and nail for naught."

Modern Home Built From Old Materials

Standing on a wooded knoll in a picturesque setting off Highway 441 in Sumter County is the unique home of Mr. and Mrs. W.L. Miller. As they say, it is a house that "just happened." The materials, salvaged from an old building, lent themselves to a construction that is "different" indeed, but one that is comfortable and charming on the inside and "eye-catching" and attractive on the outside.

But the story of this house goes back to the turn of the century, even before the time of the present owners, who drew the plans and constructed the house as it is today with practically no outside help.

The solid pine timbers of which the home is built were once upon a time used in an old railroad station of some kind on the Atlantic Coastline Railroad between Wilmington and Augusta, near where Guignard Drive now runs, according to information given to the Millers. No one has been found who knows the name of the station; however, old shipping tags and bills of lading found in the walls bear the name of this railroad and give the date as "19–," showing that the building was used by the railroad before 1910. There was also found a heart-shaped lock on a chain. On the lock were the words, "Property of the Atlantic Coast Line Railroad."

Sometime in the early 1950's the Southern Methodists bought the old T-shaped station, moved it to 113 Highland, added some rooms and used it for their church till they constructed their new sanctuary on Miller Road. Later they sold it to the Assembly of God Church, which soon moved.

Then it apparently stood for sometime without being used, since it was said to have been inhabited by squirrels, opossums, cats and perhaps other animals.

It was bought by the Millers, who were at that time living next door. They paid $700 for the building with the understanding that they would tear it down and remove the materials. This the two of them did, and it was a monumental task. It took six months to complete the work.

The timbers in the 32 feet by 50 feet building were solid heart pine that had been creosoted and there were several thicknesses of the walls. The outside was asbestos siding beneath which was siding and on the inside were ceiling boards, sheet rock (10 loads of it) and paneling.

The sills were 20 by 12 feet and three inches thick. The Millers burnt out two chain saws and one circular saw, cutting the solid timbers. From the top they secured a piece large enough and long enough to make two columns for the front of the house.

"Generations" of soot had accumulated inside these old walls, and Mrs. Miller said that at the end of each day they were a sight to behold. The smell of smoke was everywhere, too.

As the task of wrecking the building was being completed, materials were taken to the spot which they had chosen and bought for their "new" home. That step in the project presented another problem. The hill was covered with trees. Three trailer-loads of trees had to be cut down and moved out before any of the lumber from the church could be moved.

Surprisingly, the plans which they had drawn could be followed fairly closely, but some phases had to be changed to fit the size and shape of the timbers. Genius will always find a way, however, and these two builders showed unbelievable skill, ingenuity and genius in adapting the materials to the plans or vice versa.

At last they were ready to welcome visitors to their home. As the front door is opened in welcome, one enters a roomy vestibule which has an inviting decor.

On the right is a long room which serves as a living room and dining room with a piano as the divider. In the living room is a large open fireplace, having an artistic mantel skillfully designed from two old church pews. (What was left of the pews was made into an umbrella rack on the wall of the vestibule.) The bricks of the fireplace came from the pillars of the old station. They have been cleaned and polished in keeping with the room. (The brass fender and andirons Mr. Miller had made for a former home.)

At the entrance to the living room are two white pillars from the floor of the vestibule to the high ceiling. These with the white railings on each side came from the old parsonage of the Dalzell Baptist Church and they form a unique division between the entrance hall and the living room-dining room area.

Two wrought-iron "Columns" mark the entrance from the dining room into a very modern and convenient kitchen.

At the back of the kitchen is a door leading to a large bathroom, which has plenty of light. It opens into a spacious master bedroom, which is beautifully and comfortably furnished. The bedroom is next to the vestibule and is used often as a sitting or family room.

Another door in the vestibule opens to reveal a staircase, leading to the second floor. There is a sewing or workroom at the head of the stairs and beyond is another bedroom tastefully decorated and furnished. Also on the second floor is the furnace.

On both floors there is ample closet space. The floors throughout are from the old tongue and grooved boards from the original building.

There is still some work to be done before the home is entirely complete. The back porch is in the process of being added. When it is finished, it will bear at the top of the steps an inscription in Greek that was on the stoop of an old parsonage. Translated it reads: "The house of the servant of the Lord."

The Millers are both from Georgetown but have been living in Sumter for a number of years. She is the former Elphena Carraway and is accomplished in many areas. Mr. Miller is professor of automotive technology and related subjects at Sumter TEC. They are members of Dalzell Baptist Church and are very active in the various phases of the work there.

They have two children – Mrs. Kay Vinson, Camden, and W.L. Miller, Jr., who is minister of music in a Columbia church and also teaches organ and piano.

The Millers can surely look on their accomplishment with just pride and say with Cicero, "No place is more delightful than one's own fireside." And this home is doubly delightful because it represents part of themselves.

(Written in 1977)

PART VIII. MUSEUMS

Sumter County Historical Society Museum-Archives

"It is delightful to transport one's self into the spirit of the past, to see how a wise man has thought before us and to what glorious height we have at last reached." — Johan Wolfgang von Goethe.

With a great desire to make the past of Sumter County come alive for future generations, a group of history-minded citizens met on March 4, 1950, at the home of and upon the invitation of Mr. and Mrs. V.C. Barringer for the purpose of organizing the Sumter County Historical Society.[149]

Those attending that meeting were, in addition to the Barringers, C.D. Cooper, Jr., Mrs. Harry E. Drevenstedt, John D. Lee, Maj. W. Loring Lee, Sr., Herbert A. Moses, Miss Julia Reynolds, T.M. Stubbs, and Mrs. S. Itly Wilson.

Others who were invited but could not attend were R.D. Blanding, Paul K. Bowman, S.K. Nash and Earl Rowland.

They agreed that each would invite five others for the next meeting which was held on April 22 of the same year and the Sumter County Historical Society came into being.

At that meeting a constitution was adopted and officers were elected. It was the purpose of the society "To discover, preserve and study all books, pamphlets, papers and traditions touching on, or pertaining to the history of Sumter County and to aid and encourage individuals and associations in the compiling and publishing of historical data covering Sumter County."[150]

Therefore the dream of some day having a museum in Sumter was in the minds of these founders, even from the beginning of the Society.

It was 12 years later, however, before the first public step was taken toward accomplishing this long nurtured purpose.

A request presented to the Sumter County Board of Commissioners in 1962 at the time of the remodeling of the courthouse was favorably received. Room 103 was furnished by the Society with custom-made cabinets, office-type tables, chairs, a storage cabinet, a secretary's desk and other equipment suitable for a small museum. Materials collected through the years and carefully filed by Mrs. Myrtis Ginn Osteen at her home were transferred to this room. Mrs. Osteen served as secretary-treasurer-custodian-archivist from 1951 to 1975.[151]

The room was opened July 7, 1965, while Dr. Edward C. Gilmore was president of the society. Hours for use were on Wednesdays from 3:30 to 5 p.m., with Mrs. Osteen in charge.

August 31, 1967, the executive committee of the Society authorized "Archives" to be added and the official name to be Museum-Archives.

For a number of years this little room was used by many interested people. Though small, it served a useful purpose.

At last the dream of so many for so long came true, even beyond expectations.

In 1971 an historic home, 122 North Washington Street, was presented to the Society to be used as a Museum-Archives. The donors were Messrs. Philip L. and Thomas W. Edwards and their families. The Edwards brothers had inherited the property from their aunt, Martha Williams Brice, daughter of O.L. Williams, founder of Williams Furniture Division of Georgia Pacific. He had purchased the home in 1922.

The first owner of the property as far as records have been established was C.W. Miller. It was bought ca. 1845 by Andrew Jackson Moses, who either built or reconstructed the home in the basic form it has now.

In 1889 it was rented or leased to the Sumter City Schools.

Perry Moses, son of A.J. Moses, bought the home in 1892, deeding it in 1915 to his daughter, Virginia, and her husband, Aaron Cohen Phelps. They did extensive work on the home. It has been said that it was torn down to the foundation. At any rate it has the same style as it had before.

It was brick veneered, however, and the "welcoming arms" curved steps were added at the front and some other changes were made.

When the Messrs. Edwards offered the property to the Sumter County Historical Society in 1971, plans were begun for raising funds for the administration and upkeep of the property. The deed was signed August 31, 1972.[152]

In April of 1973 the materials that had been in use in Room 103 at the courthouse were moved to the ground floor of the spacious Williams-Brice home with Myrtis Ginn Osteen assisted by Margaret R. McElveen empowered to arrange the archives section of the complex. The facility was opened to the public on

Wednesday from 3:30 to 5 p.m., and in August of that year the Board of Governors authorized a Saturday opening from 10 a.m. to 12 noon. Members of the Sumter Chapter of the Genealogical Society of South Carolina kept the archives during these hours. Prior to this, the SCHS had sponsored the organization of this chapter; and until the group grew too large, it held regular meetings in the museum.

On April 11, 1973, the Museum-Archives held a very successful "Open House."

The dedication of the facility took place in a very impressive meeting in 1976. Harold Moise, who from the beginning of the Historical Society had worked toward this end, said it was "a day long to be remembered," and Sherman Smith, director, declared the occasion "one of Sumter County's finest hours."

The climax of the dedication ceremonies was the unveiling of a wall plaque by Myrtis Ginn Osteen, who had served the society as a dedicated volunteer since its beginning in 1950.

In the Archives is a wealth of helpful materials, such as census records back to 1890 on microfilm. The Janie Revill Files, kept by Miss Revill over a period of 40 years, were purchased in 1969. These have proved a definite asset, for visitors from far and near have found them helpful. The Lecoq photography files are also a valuable part of the treasures owned by the Society. There are countless files of newspapers, letters and manuscripts of historical interest and value. There are also numbers of valuable books for research and reading enjoyment.

The Archives section of the Williams-Brice complex is now in charge of W. Esmonde Howell. It is equipped with a fireproof safe where land grants and other valuable papers are kept, a microfilm reader, fluorescent lighting, comfortable chairs and tables.

On the ground floor also is a large display of antique irons on loan by Mr. and Mrs. Warren Carraway.

At the front entrance to the Archives on the ground floor is the last one of the section boats used by fishermen, plying the waters of the Wateree River back in the first of the century. These unusual boats were long enough to accommodate several men, but for the convenience of transportation from one location to another by wagon or train, they could be separated into three parts and stacked, each piece fitting perfectly into another.

The designer for this unique boat was Edward Richardson Sanders, better known as "Toot" Sanders, who was a master carpenter born in Sumter County in 1845.

The one on display, believed to be the last one in existence, was placed in the Museum-Archives by the family of Julian M. Sanders, Jr. Mr. R.N. Moore is due thanks for transporting it to its present resting place. The seats are missing, but one can readily see how it came to be known as a "Section Boat."

Upon entering the front door of the first or main floor of the Museum, one is charmed with the furnishings of the drawing room. There are a number of chairs, anyone of which is of great beauty and value. Attracting immediate admiration are several portraits done by masters. One of these is the Thomas Sumter portrait done by Rembrandt Peale which the Society was fortunate in being able to purchase a number of years ago. By the door is an old school master's desk. Near the door is an antique whatnot with many interesting pieces of china. Several fine rugs enhance the beauty of the room. These are only a few of the attractions for the interested visitor.

The original dining room on the right of the hall is used for social meetings. However, there are a number of eye-catching displays. Near one wall is an interesting collection of old dispensary bottles. In several wall cabinets are lovely sets of fine old china and glassware, and on the walls are portraits of Sumter's great educators of the past.

On the left of the hall is the War Memorial Room where may be seen 18 firearms, including pieces ranging from the American Revolution through World War II. These were collected and arranged by William E. Brunson, III, and Lewis E. Leavell. In this room are also 250 antique miniature soldiers, a portrait of Gen. Robert E. Lee, by South Carolina Artist Albert Capers Guerry, and many other priceless mementoes of early Sumter's military history.

On the second floor one enters, first, Gallery No. 5 where there is a lovely four-poster bed and other complementing furniture of days gone by. Displayed here, too, is a beautiful wedding gown of the past.

In the next room are maps, land grants, and other valuable historic treasures.

On the third floor is a room that is of special interest to doll collectors. The museum proudly owns 100 antique dolls arranged by Mrs. Harrison Harp, Miss Margaret McElveen, Mrs. Frank McMillan and Miss Sallie Rembert in "a trip around the world."

Attracting special attention is an arrangement of fossils, collected and donated by Kinson Cook of Florida.

Then for the children's enjoyment is a toy room containing a toy steam engine, a sewing machine, playhouse furniture and many other toys that delighted the hearts of children of long ago. Enhancing the attractiveness of the room are a number of portraits of children painted by Miss Elizabeth White, Sumter's own gifted artist.

Next to this room is Gallery No. 1, dedicated to the works of

Miss White. At her death she left to the museum a number of her etchings which are known in many parts of the world. Other art lovers have donated additional paintings done by Miss White.

Near the main part of the Museum is the Country Life Collection. Here may be seen the James E. Morgan collection of farm machinery used by the early settlers. There are tools for cutting logs or splitting shingles, as well as harvesting tools. The old yokes, collars and other pieces worn by the farm animals are on display.

In the collection are implements for cutting grain, kitchen utensils, a scrubbing board and clothes wringer and many other things to remind one of the hard life of the original citizens of the area.

The Museum is surrounded by a beautiful garden of an acre and a half. It was planned by Mr. Robert Marvin, a nationally known landscape architect, who was engaged by Mrs. T.H. Brice during the Brices' ownership of the home.

The Museum owns the carriage that belonged to former Gov. John Laurence Manning. It has been restored to its original grace and beauty and can be seen on the premises of the Museum-Archives.

The latest addition to the Museum is the historic James Cabin built near Rembert between 1740 and 1760. According to Director Sherman Smith "... It is a piece of our early culture and a reminder of an effort to settle and be successful in this area."

For the acquisition of this cabin, credit is given to the James family, and for the difficult task of moving it to the Museum grounds, special recognition goes to Mr. Willie Dinkins and Mr. Arthur James. They personally labored tirelessly in preparing it for the move, and they continue the work necessary for its restoration.

The skill with which Mr. Dinkins has worked to restore the various parts of the cabin in authentic 18th century form is of special note.

Those who help also deserve appreciation.

Mr. Sherman Smith, who was appointed acting director by the Board of Governors in 1975 and director in 1976, merits the thanks and praise of Sumter citizens for the efficient manner in which he has directed the work that has been done to make Sumter's Museum-Archives what it is today and the enthusiasm with which he continues to look to the interests of the institution.

Something must be said, too, for those who in the early days kept the "dream" of a museum alive. In addition to Myrtis Ginn Osteen, Honorary Life Member, who has already been mentioned for her tireless efforts for the Society, there are two others who especially deserve the gratitude of Sumter for their untiring efforts in making the museum a reality.

The late Herbert Moses, one of the organizers of SCHS and first president, was "most dedicated and active, with his contributions, experience, guidance and firsthand knowledge of history and its potential."

The other is Harold Moise, a charter member of the Society and long-time chairman of museum-archives affairs. He has through the years ably guided the ongoing plans for a museum and is still giving of his time and effort toward its continued success. He was recently honored by being named Life Time Member of the Museum-Archives Board of Governors.

Sumter County has reason to be proud of its Museum-Archives, and public-spirited citizens will doubtless continue to contribute toward its maintenance and growth.

Museum hours are from 2 to 5 p.m. Wednesday through Sunday. Archive hours are the same on Wednesday through Saturday.

Arrangements may be made by schools or organizations for group visits.

Museum Shows Highlights Of Trinity Church

There is no greater incentive for building a worthwhile future than to look at the past, profiting by the wisdom of those who have gone before and gaining inspiration from their courage and faith.

And that is what Trinity United Methodist Church is doing through the establishing of an Archives Room. Here they have collected pictures, documents, church furniture and other mementoes that throw light on the years that have passed since the roots of this great church were planted in this community almost 200 years ago.

Responsible for the collection and preservation of these valuables are Mrs. Lena Hill, chairman of Records and History, and Mrs. Katie Allen. After the revision of the church roll in 1972 by Mrs. Allen, Mrs. Hill began the research necessary for writing the history of the church; and since that time they have collected from willing donors many relics of historic value for the Archives.

The first exhibit pointed out by Mrs. Allen is a copy of the petition from male members written in 1851 asking that this church be taken from the Santee Circuit and made a station church. Santee was a very large circuit extending from Charleston to Charlotte, North Carolina, including Sumter District, which alone contained 1,070,080 square acres. Some of the ministers serving this large area were Reverend Swift, Bishops Asbury and

Thomas Coke, and Rev. James Jenkins. One can imagine how difficult it must have been for the ministers to visit all parts of the Circuit with any degree of regularity. First services in the vicinity of what later became Sumterville were thought to have been held at the home of a Mr. Maple before 1786. The first meeting house was Green Swamp, built on land belonging to Richard Bradford through the efforts of Mr. Bradford and Robert Singleton. (The location of this meeting house is indicated by a historical marker west of Sumter beyond Swan Lake.)

Then in 1823 a small church house was erected in the village and the Green Swamp Church was apparently discontinued.

The membership of the little village church steadily increased, outgrowing its house of worship. Around 1844 the property was sold to the Catholics and the Methodists bought two acres of land across Liberty Street on the spot where the present church stands.

But the church was still served by ministers of the Circuit, hence the petition of 1851 to the South Carolina Conference. The petition stated that since Sumterville was becoming a place "of great resort," and since other denominations had resident pastors and "that the voice of Methodism be often heard, its faith defended and its true character appreciated," they were making the request. The petition (the original of which is in the Methodist Archives at Wofford College) was signed by Messrs. W.L. Brunson, J. Harvey Dingle and W. Lewis. Hanging on the wall along with the petition is a photograph of the original portrait of W.L. Brunson.

The request was granted and the Sumterville church became a station church with 151 white members and 300 black.

Another interesting relic hanging on the wall near the petition is a copy of the Santee Circuit budget of 1824 listing Green Swamp's contribution as $84.33½. The money was used, said the report, for "traveling expenses and quarterage" for the minister.

Preserved in a cabinet is a baptismal dress worn by infants of the Chandler and Kirven families since the turn of the century.

A relic of great interest that may be seen on another wall is an old, old copy of the "Rules for Sumterville Methodist Female Benevolent Working Society." This society, according to the record, was organized in 1833 with 21 charter members. It was the first Methodist "Women's Aide Society" in Santee Circuit and its purpose was "to raise money to paint the church and to aid in the support of the superannuated preachers of South Carolina."

Dues were twenty-five cents per quarter, or a dollar a year. Members met on Saturday for not less than three hours and not more than four. At the meetings they studied the Bible and other religious books and had discussions on what they read. They also made garments to be sold "in John Ramsey's store" to make money for their projects.

Charter members were Sarah Capers Glenn, Jane D. Moses, Martha A. Walsh, Elizabeth D. Glenn, Lucy K. Macon, Martha A. DuBose, Elizabeth Ballard, Margaret A. Bostic, Maria M. Huitt, Sarah W. DuRant, Mary N. DuRant, Sarah Mellett, Louisa Williams, Mary A. Bowen, Eliza A. Williams, Theresa A. Wilder, Caroline M. Brunson, Sarah Daniels, Elizabeth Flowers, Mary Williams, and Eugenia P. Poole.

On one wall of the Archives Room is a grouping of pictures of the church buildings used by Trinity through the years. The first shown is that of the "white wooden church," the first at the present location. This has been described as "a neat building, capable of seating approximately four or five hundred persons on the lower floor and a hundred or so in the gallery." The minister preaching the dedication sermon, Rev. Hartwell Spain, referred to it as "this beautiful temple of God."

This church was used until 1885 when it was sold to a Black congregation and moved to the country.

The next picture shows the Red Brick Church begun in 1885 to accommodate a growing congregation. Participating in the ground breaking for this church was little Eugenia Hoyt, daughter of the C. Isadore Hoyts; James H. Dingle, D.J. Winn, J.D. Craig, J.B. Roach, F.A. Treadwell, R.W. DuRant, A.J. China, F.H. Folsom, C.M. Hurst and the minister, Rev. H.F. Creitzburg. It was dedicated in 1888.

The Red Brick Church was known as the First Methodist Episcopal Church, but some time during the years of its use the name was changed to Trinity Methodist Church, South. Pictures of the interior of this church may also be seen in the display. They show the dark woodwork and windows of Victorian colored glass. Above the pulpit was the rounded dome-like ceiling painted blue with gold stars to represent the heavens. The stars were painted by Mrs. C.M. Hurst.

In the Archives Room are two chairs used in this church and a beautiful marble baptismal font made by Mr. W.P. Smith, a member of that church; and his granddaughter, Mrs. Harry Smith, left this priceless heirloom to Trinity. It was placed in the Archives Room in 1975.

Nearby is the picture of the next church building erected by the membership now grown very large. The history of Trinity states that the "Red Brick Church" was torn down and ground was broken for the new sanctuary, which was known as the "Buff Brick Church," in 1911. Participating in this ceremony was again Eugenia Hoyt, then Mrs. W.A. Thompson, with her young son, W.A. Thompson, Jr. The dedication of this beautiful church building was on September 28, 1913.

The last service held in this church building was on May 29, 1960. In the early morning of June 10, the lovely buff brick sanctuary was destroyed by fire. Plans had already begun, however, for erecting a larger plant to meet the needs of the large membership. The picture of the magnificent building now being loved and enjoyed by Trinity United Methodist Church completes the wall display of photographs which show the growth of this historic church.

Some items in the Archives Room that were salvaged from the fire are some Bibles, The Dorsal Cloth, some candlesticks, hymn books and pictures.

A unique exhibit in the Archives Room is the "Birthday Bower" used first by Mrs. J.W. Cox, who organized the Beginners (Kindergarten) Department of the Sunday School and remained the superintendent of this department until 1956. When a member of the department had a birthday, he or she had the privilege of sitting in the "Bower" on the Sunday nearest the "great day" and how it delighted the little hearts to receive the special attention!

Other departments organized in those early years were the Cradle Roll (Nursery today), organized by Mrs. W.A. Brown; the Primary, Junior and Intermediate Departments, formed by Mrs. A.M. Broughton, Mrs. J.C. Cormell, Miss Hattie Phillips and Mrs. C.E. Hurst. Mementoes of these classes have been preserved through the years.

In 1912 the first adult classes were organized. The men, under the influence of the pastor, Dr. D.M. McLeod, began the McLeod-Wesley Bible Class, which was a very dedicated group. In 1921 this class sponsored an enlistment campaign to interest more men in Sunday School work. On the Sunday designated to climax the special drive, there were 600 men and boys present. A picture of this occasion may be seen in the Archives Room, as well as in the room where the class now meets.

The other class organized in 1912 was the Mizpah Bible Class for women, with Mrs. E.W. Vogel as president. This class has been noted through the years as one that has helped the needy, comforted the bereaved, cared for the sick and contributed generously to all causes fostered by the church.

Kept in loving care in the Archives Room is a quaint little bonnet with collar and cuffs, all from the uniform of Miss Mamie Chandler, who went out from Trinity as a deaconess to engage in Home Mission work. She was graduated from Scarritt College, Nashville, Tennessee, in 1939. She first attended this school in

1923 and after working for a number of years, she returned to complete her courses.

Miss Chandler served in educational work in several states. Her last assignment was at East Carolina College for Women in Greenville, North Carolina, where she was instrumental in establishing a Youth Center, which was dedicated to her and named in her honor. Her portrait hangs in the Center.

Prominently displayed in the Archives is a picture of Miss Rosalie Brown, a missionary from 1922 to 1962 in Brazil. She was supported by the Woman's Missionary Society of Trinity.

There is also a large scrapbook containing a brief biography and some of the experiences of Miss Brown. First in the book is a picture of this beloved daughter of Trinity seated on the steps of the Rosalie Brown Building in Brazil.

Her work in Brazil was primarily that of teaching English and Bible in secondary schools, though she did supervise a kindergarten for a while.

Contained in the book is a Certificate of Service for 39½ years spent in Brazil, signed by the president of the Board of Missions of the Methodist Church, president of Woman's Division of Christian Service and the executive secretary.

In the book also are a number of family pictures from past years, a missionary magazine published in Brazil, clippings from Sumter papers, a 1954 church bulletin used on "Rosalie Brown Day" and other items of interest.

Another scrapbook is devoted to the life of Sallie Bell Reynolds, the very first missionary sponsored by First Methodist Church (now Trinity).

She went to China in 1892 and taught piano for five years in McTyeire School for Chinese girls in Shanghai. Although she was married in 1897 to Gilbert Reid and was no longer sponsored by the Sumter church, she spent many more years in China with her husband.

Carefully and attractively displayed in the Archives Room are numerous other scrapbooks containing pictures of Sunday School classes and Daily Vacation Bible Schools. Some of these have been prepared by the children themselves. A visitor to the Archives Room may peruse some old newspapers of Sumter which contain articles concerning special events at Trinity through the years.

Special copies of **The Southern Christian Advocate**, a 1951 copy of **The Methodist Advocate** featuring on the front cover the Boyle Bible Class, another men's class that has been a great Christian witness in Sumter are on display.

There are church bulletins from 1919 and the original picture of the "white wooden church." (The one on the wall is a copy.)

Two very old hymn books without music have been kept. The pulpit Bibles from both the red and buff brick churches have been preserved. A very valuable treasure in the Archives is a copy of the Quarterly Conference minutes of the years from 1879 through 1882.

All who love Trinity will want to see the large scrapbook that contains a step-by-step account of the growth of this great church beginning in the 1700's and concluding with a description and picture of the present magnificent sanctuary and other buildings used in the work of the church. This history, carefully prepared by Lena Hill and Katie Allen, follows the development and expansion of each organization, telling of the significant Christian outreach as it has grown through the years.

Along with history are many pictures of interest, such as the picture of the five Scouts who received the God and Country Award during the last worship service held in the buff colored church on May 29, 1960. There are also pictures of the fire that destroyed this lovely sanctuary 12 days later on June 10.

There is a list of pastors who have served the congregation through the years, from 1851, when it became a station church, until the present time with pictures of some of the more recent ones.

Included also is a history of Trinity's Mission established in the South Salem area in the 1930's. Sometime after this mission outgrew its usefulness, Trinity Community Center was founded on Newberry Street. These accounts are accompanied by snapshots showing work done in the Mission and Center including a picture of Miss Connie Herbert, first director of the Center.

The memorabilia found in the Archives Room at Trinity United Methodist Church will bring back to the older members memories of the past and will furnish to the younger generations information. To all they will be an inspiration to continue building on the foundations laid by those who often in the face of great difficulties, made Trinity the great blessing it is today to Sumter and surrounding areas.

Military Museum

Completed recently is the only military museum for the Army National Guard in this state.

In the museum will be housed a large collection of weapons, a part of South Carolina's historic background.

The weapons that will be stored and displayed in this museum have been collected through the years by history-minded Sumter citizens, including Mr. Lewis E. Leavell, Jr., and others.

The largest collection so far, however, is that of Mr. William E. (Billy) Brunson, who began collecting at the age of nine. Through the years he has added to his store of military memorabilia which he has carefully preserved in a room over his garage.

Mr. Brunson has two characteristics that have led to this invaluable collection — his love of history and his great enthusiasm for collecting.

His ancestors were among the first settlers in South Carolina with four Brunson names inscribed on the Revolutionary Association for Public Defense — South Carolina Association. Therefore he has been possessed with a great interest in the history of his state and country during those early days, as well as a special interest in the types of weapons used in the Revolutionary War.

His great-grandfather fought in the War Between the States, and when very young he fell heir to the carbine used by this ancestor in that war.

That gun whetted his appetite, and the desire for more weapons grew. In a few years he was not only collecting firearms of every kind but was making cannons of many sizes and kinds based on historic research.

His collection today possibly covers every type of weapons used in the military history of this country. And in addition to weapons, he has war relics of nearly every kind used during South Carolina's eventful history. He is especially proud of his set of South Carolina guns, containing at least one of every type made in the old Palmetto Armory in Columbia in 1852. Included in his collection are a number of uniforms worn in actual conflicts.

The South Carolina National Guard plans to have on display for the public battle flags, side and shoulder arms, long arms, artillery shells, cannons, military documents and other artifacts of the state's military history.

On permanent loan by First Federal Savings and Loan is a picture of Thomas Sumter painted by Ray Davenport, Sumter artist, who is nationally known.

The Museum, a brick structure adjacent to the Armory, will be known as Gamecock Artillery Headquarters, 151 Field Artillery Brigade, authorized by T. Eston Marchant, Adjutant General of South Carolina.[153]

Brunson is in demand for the reenactment of battles fought in South Carolina in the past. His military rank is Artillery Sergeant, 2nd Regiment, South Carolina Line, Continental Establishment. (Coincidentally this is the same rank in the same regiment held by his great-great-great-grandfather in the Revolutionary War.) During the Bicentennial he took part in the reenactment of many Revolutionary War engagements. Dressed in his

2nd Regiment uniform, he fires cannon salutes and demonstrates in other ways the actual battle scenes. More recently he has fired salutes, using one of his authentic Revolutionary cannons, in the reenactment of the Battle of Singleton's Mill, Poinsett Park, at the dedication of a marker by the Clarendon County Historical Society.

He also took part in the dedication of a marker and later of a Park at Dingle's Mill, scene of the memorable battle on the outskirts of Sumter at the close of the Civil War.

Thus the use of some of these weapons brings to the mind of many today the hard-fought battles of the past.

Lt. Col. Hugh M. McLaurin, III, Executive Officer 151st Field Artillery Brigade SCARNG, says that the museum will make necessary announcements as to times for visits by groups or individuals.

PART IX. EDUCATION

Morris College

With "Preparing the student of today for the challenge of tomorrow" as its aim, Morris College was opened in 1908 as Sumter's first college.[154] It was authorized by the Educational and Missionary Convention of South Carolina (Baptist).

In the beginning when free schools were scarce and Negro children had few opportunities for an education, this school offered three levels of training – elementary, high school and college.

Under the first president, Dr. E.M. Brawley, the curriculum provided a liberal arts program, "normal" training for the certification of teachers, and a theological course.

Dr. John J. Starks became president in 1912 and courses leading to the Bachelor of Arts degree were added, the first two recipients being graduated in 1915. Under the able leadership of Dr. Starks, the college became well established.

Succeeding Dr. Starks in 1930 was Dr. I.P. Pinson and for tw two years Morris operated as a junior college. However, in 1932 it again advanced to senior college status and continued to grow.

After Dr. Pinson's accidental death in 1939, Dr. J.P. Garrick was elected president. This distinguished scholar and religious leader served the college well for seven years, assisting in the beginning of the Pinson Memorial Library, and he was instrumental in increasing the enrollment. Upon his resignation in 1946, he was named president emeritus.

Taking the place of Dr. Garrick was Dr. H.H. Butler. Though death ended his term of office in two years, he was able to accomplish much. The Pinson Memorial Library was completed and two other buildings, financed by the Federal Government, were built.

After Dr. Butler's death, a few months elapsed before another president was found. During that time, Dr. J.W. Boykin served as acting president until Rev. O'Dell Richardson Reuben was elected to the presidency in 1948.

Before coming to Morris as professor of theology in 1947, he held pastorates in Allendale and Ware Shoals. In 1945 and 1946 he was awarded bachelor of divinity degrees from Benedict and Oberlin Colleges. He received the S.T.M. degree from Oberlin in 1947 and in 1955 was given an honorary L.L.D. from Allen University and an honorary Ph.D. from Benedict.

Death ended the presidency of Dr. Reuben after 22 years of outstanding leadership. During his presidency the college grew in all directions. The physical plant was expanded by the addition of a number of buildings, including the Butler Education Building, the Garrick-Boykin Gymnasium, the Mable K. Howard Building, the Student Center, four cottages on campus, two off-campus dwellings, an athletic stadium, Danniells Hall, Dining Hall – Dormitory, Dobbins-Keith-Whitener Hall, the Wilson Booker Science Hall.

An endowment of a quarter of a million dollars was raised and the college program changed and expanded to meet present-day needs.

Dr. Henry E. Harden succeeded Dr. Reuben and after three years resigned. Supplying the position of the presidency (1973-1974) was Dr. Jesse W. Taylor. In 1974 Dr. Luns C. Richardson was elected president and is currently leading the college in notable growth.

Morris College, through its history of more than threescore and ten years of growth, has had strong support from many Baptist organizations, alumni, friends of education in many places and the Sumter business community. Thousands of dollars have been raised with the result that this instituion now rests on a sound financial base.

The provision of a strong foundation in liberal arts with additional courses that will develop skills useful in the successful pursuit of some gainful occupation has been established. The curriculum provides preparation for medicine, nursing, law, theology and graduate study.

Though the college seeks to give the best possible educational background to its graduates, its first interest is in the religious welfare of its students. Various on-campus organizations enhance a spiritual atmosphere in the school, and students go out to serve in the community churches. Morris College is deeply concerned with the development of moral and spiritual values in young people and gives priority to this phase of its program.

Public Education Has Interesting History

It was not altogether neglect on the part of the Colonial government that free schools had a slow start in Sumter. Provision was made in the state for free schools as early as 1792, but there was no law for levying taxes for education until much later. The financial burden was so great that the general public could not afford to operate schools. Those who were able sent their children to private schools, and the poor had no opportunity for an education.

There were many private schools in the city of Sumter, as well as in the county. Perhaps the last such institution was run by the Sumterville Academical Society on land furnished by John B. Miller on the corner of Washington and Liberty Streets. It was opened in 1837 and closed in 1867, the building later being destroyed by fire.

One record states that Sumter's first public school was opened in a five-room building on East Hampton Avenue, with R.P. McQueen as principal. From another source it is found that James Diggs Wilder was principal of a five-room school on East Hampton Avenue until 1888.

It was in that year that a vote was taken to allow the city to have a school district separate from the county. In May 1889, the newly formed district leased the A.J. Moses home on Washington Street for white pupils. The Board of Commissioners consisted of John Kershaw (chairman), R.O. Purdy, R.D. Lee, C.C. Brown, Altamont Moses, W. Alston Pringle, Jr. (secretary).[155]

First principal was J.B. Duffie, and teachers were S.H. Edmunds, Mary H. Girardeau, Mrs. L.E. Steinmayer, Miss E.C. Davis, Miss Gertrude Waddill, Miss Virginia Ingram, and Miss J. Florence Hurst.

In the black school, Rev. J.B. Smith was the principal and the teachers were Miss M.A. Savage, Miss Jennie E. Walker, and Miss Rowena Andrews.[156]

At that time the population of the city (estimate) was 4,500; those between the ages of six and 21 numbered 1,100. Pupils enrolled were: white, 361; black, 370. Average salary paid teachers per month, including the principal, was $37.00.

One of the requirements in the curriculum as stated in the minutes of the school board was: "Satisfactory results in Language can be obtained only when the teacher regards every recitation, every reading lesson and its interpretation, each step of instruction in arithmetic, etc., as a language lesson, that the ultimate purpose of language teaching may be achieved with certainty . . . There has been much writing, the work of the grade affording themes for compositions . . . "

Another notation in the minutes for the 1890-91 year gives reason for the high standing of the Sumter system in those beginning years: "Our aim has not been to secure large graduating classes, but efficiency and thoroughness and pupils have been promoted only when they have shown themselves prepared for the work."

In 1892 a school building unique in architecture was erected on what was known as Monument Square on the corner of Washington and Liberty Streets, which was the property of the Ladies' Monumental Society and had been the site of Sumterville Academy.

This new building, however, was inadequate for the growing enrollment. In 1889 Lincoln School was built on Council Street for black children and it, too, was inadequate. So crowded it was that it was necessary to hold double sessions for a number of years.

In 1924 Savage-Glover was built and named in honor of two of the early teachers. A larger building was constructed on the Lincoln School property in 1936.

The city public schools were divided into two districts – District 1 and District 17 – with each district having its own trustees and its own elementary schools.

In 1895 Superintendent Duffie resigned because of bad health and S.H. Edmunds was unanimously elected to fill his place. Some of his first recommendations were that Latin begin in the seventh grade, that two medals be purchased for honor graduates and that diplomas be presented to graduates.

In 1903 a lot was bought on the northwest corner of Monument Square for a new building. It was completed in 1904 and was designated as the "high school."

In 1907 Lincoln was remodeled and later more land was added. A lot was purchased on Calhoun Street and a school built there for boys. Military training was added to the curriculum for this school.

The 11th grade was added to the system in 1914 and in the meantime more courses had been added. Sumter students gained special recognition in the colleges they attended.

In 1915 plans were made for a new girls' school to be built between Washington and Hampton Schools on Monument Square. This building was to serve also as an Administration Building. It was formally opened January 19, 1917.

Plans were approved in 1924 for a new Boys' High School on the corner of Purdy and Haynsworth Streets and the school on Calhoun became the Girls' High School. The one that had been used for high school girls became Central Elementary.

Always alert to the needs of pupils, Dr. Edmunds and the School Board authorized in 1914 a program of music instruction under the initiation and direction of L.C. Moise. From the beginning definite requirements were set up for a program that was difficult enough to present a challenge to the students and to inspire study on their part.

Since the music in the elementary grades was under the direction of the classroom teachers, afternoon and night classes were arranged for these to receive special music instruction.

Choruses and glee clubs were organized for boys and girls in the high schools in separate groups, of course, since at that time boys and girls were in separate schools. In later years, Moise recalled that one of his greatest joys was a chorus of 300 girls who learned many classical and semi-classical songs. He noted that the high standing of the Girls High School, with Miss Linnie McLaurin as principal, made this feat possible.

Even that early, under the tireless efforts of Moise, there were orchestral groups and bands in the various schools.

Dr. Joseph McGlothlin, president of Furman University, said, "When people in other parts of the state think of Sumter, they think of music."

And through the years that tradition has continued. Sumter's bands and choruses still stand high in the musical contests held in the state.

Were L.C. Moise living today, he could take great pride in his contribution to the city schools of Sumter, that of introducing music into the system and his tireless effort in making it an important part of the curriculum. Other talented musicians have carried high the torch that he lighted more than a half-century ago.

More and more expansion was seen from year to year in the system. Families attracted by the schools moved to Sumter. United States Commissioner of Education Claxton issued a bulletin around 1922 on Sumter's schools. This bulletin attracted the attention of school and college personnel, editors and others interested in the best in education.

Dr. Edmunds continued as superintendent until his death in 1935, and his works have truly lived after him.

The new high school building for boys and girls on Haynsworth Street was formally opened in 1939 and was dedicated to him. It was given the name, Edmunds High School.

In the years since Dr. Edmunds, several have served the schools well in the capacity of superintendent.

Completing the 1935-36 session after the death of Dr. Edmunds in October, was Miss Linnie McLaurin, esteemed principal of the Girls' High School for many years.

Since that time the schools have been led into greater growth and worthwhile achievements by several qualified superintendents; namely, W.T. Loggins, W.H. Shaw, E.R. Crow, James L. Blanding, John Southwell, L.C. McArthur, and Harold D. Patterson (presently serving).

A very important innovation began in the high schools of Sumter in a small way in the 1940's, but it soon grew into a full-scale guidance program. One of the first directors was Miss Ethel Burnett, who gave wise counsel to many boys and girls, helping them to solve problems and meet crises in their lives. Soon, she was joined by other counselors. She has now retired, but the work goes on, proving a very worthwhile part of the educational development of boys and girls.

In place of the military training that Dr. Edmunds introduced for the boys' future, Sumter High now has the Air Force Junior ROTC program. With the official name, "Aero-Space Education, it is designed to provide meaningful military training . . . of benefit to the student and of value to the . . . Air Force."

Sumter was one of 19 schools in the U.S. to qualify for this program in 1966. In 1968 the group at Edmunds and the one at Lincoln composed a unit, the largest in the United States.

The school lunch program in District 17 has proved one of great importance. The District for a number of years has had a centralized lunch program (one of the few in the state) for the 19 (in 1968) schools in the system. This program is designed to serve two purposes: "Educating the child in basic foods needed for good nutrition and providing an adequate meal away from home."

Interest in physical training and sports has grown through the years. Outstanding football, basketball, and baseball teams for the boys have made excellent showings in interscholastic contests. Girls, too, have shown great interest in basketball and softball, and these teams, too, have stood well in competition. Other sports include track, tennis, and golf.

In 1965 pre-primary work was begun in Sumter School District 17 with 40 pupils and three workers. Dr. L.C. McArthur, superintendent at the time, was instrumental in launching this new program. Soon there were three centers in the system and since then others have been added.[157]

In the 1960's money became available to provide a career laboratory to serve Sumter High, Furman, Hillcrest, and Mayewood (the last three in District II). More and more courses are being offered and students are being prepared for the business world.

Sumter schools began in 1967 a program of Special Education which has for its purpose "to provide the opportunity and assistance for a child to learn good work habits at an early age, to place before him an immediate goal of obtaining a job, and to instill in him pride and a realization of the dignity of work."

Extracurricular activities give students opportunities to pursue involvement in their individual interests. Student Councils give training in self-government; the National Honor Society offers additional incentives for improvement in scholarship and character growth; the Quill and Scroll recognizes those with special writing talents; other clubs, such as French, Science, etc., give further study for students with special subject interests. Publications – newspaper, yearbook, magazine – have all excelled through the years. The magazine recently has received nationwide recognition. The radio club also serves a useful purpose.

A plan for complete desegregation of the schools was worked out by the system and approved by HEW for the year 1970-71.

District 17 operates a large fleet of buses that travel thousands of miles each month transporting students to the various schools in the district.

Contained in a report of the district schools for the years 1959-1974, a statement of the purpose of the schools as adopted by the board of trustees is that "public education can and should benefit the individual person . . . the state and nation," that "each person should be enabled to live a useful and satisfying life," that "the schools should strive to develop in young persons the factors . . . essential for rich personal living, for sound choice of and successful work within a vocation, for noble and gratifying relationships with their fellowmen, and for a responsible citizenship." [158]

These principles are much the same as those upon which the school was founded 91 years ago.

A sketch of Miller School (once Winn School), District I, follows:[159]

Shakespeare's picture in **As You Like It** of the " . . . whining school-boy with his satchel and shining morning face, creeping like a snail unwillingly to school," did not apply to the boys and girls who attended the old Miller School in days gone by. Instead they recall with delight the days spent in that unusual school.

Back in 1902 a tiny one-room school located "just across Shot Pouch Branch" was known as the Winn School since it was situated on land deeded by D. James Winn. A few still remember "the good old days" at this little school. Mrs. P.E. Chatham recalls the good teachers that she had in this little house of learning, which it truly was. She can still picture Miss Evie Wilson, one of those beloved teachers, riding to school on her bicycle over roads that were sandy or muddy. Mrs. E.M. Brogdon remembers, too, her days in this school.

Dr. Herbert Haynsworth was superintendent of education in those days and his visits to the school are remembered. Mrs. Chatham says that many professional and businessmen and women who have made a name for themselves locally or in other places received their first education at Winn School.

Others who taught there include Miss Fannie Sumter (later Mrs. H.L. Tisdale), Miss Mayo Rees and Miss Hannah Fraser, who was in charge of the little school with about 15 "scholars," when it was moved in 1922 to a site on Miller Road and enlarged to two rooms. More pupils were enrolled and Miss Mattie Gibson was elected as assistant teacher. For a short time, the school was known as Boulevard.

A little later the name was changed to Miller in honor of Edwin Fraser Miller, who had been a trustee possibly from the beginning of Winn. He has been described as "a saintly Christian gentleman."

The grounds on which the new building was located were at first treeless, with no shrubbery. Later Mrs. Alice Leavell, one of the teachers, began the work of planting shrubs to beautify the grounds.

Gradually the enrollment increased, necessitating the addition of more rooms, until there were seven rooms and seven teachers with over 200 pupils.

Pupils attending were from the Broad Street area, including the children's home, and from North Main Street. Those living at a distance were transported in a bus driven by Mr. Ervin Brunson.

The building was heated with potbelly coal stoves. On very cold days the pupils sat in groups around the stove to read. Miss Jennie McLeod, first grade teacher, would take off the shoes and socks or stockings of the little children and dry them on a rainy day.

Lunch was prepared by three ladies of the community – Mrs. Drayton, Mrs. Ham and Mrs. Proctor – in a tiny room in the back of the building at first. Later the front porch was closed in as a lunchroom. Plates were served from the stove and the pupils ate in their rooms. Some of the former students recall today that at one time the containers of food were brought to the classrooms where the plates were served. The menu included such things as soup, beef stew, salad, hot chocolate.

There was no plumbing; therefore, the "rest rooms" were across a ditch at the back of the school grounds. (This ditch was often a problem for the teachers.)

For some years Miller was a part of what was known as District I of the city school system, which included also Wilder,

Lemira and Jordan. With J.D. Blanding as superintendent, it was run somewhat as a demonstration school, putting into practice many of the ideas advanced in the educational philosophy of what was known as "progressive education." Adviser for the school was Dr. Henry Harap of Peabody College, Nashville, Tennessee, who visited the school two or three times each year. He met with the faculty and set up guidelines to be followed in the curriculum and visited the classrooms to observe the progress being made.

The school was well equipped with record players, projectors, screens and other items needed as aids in teaching. Teachers and patrons had barbecue suppers and other money-making projects to pay for the equipment the teachers wanted. Between two of the rooms was a sliding wall that could be raised to make a larger space for chapel, night programs, movies (every two weeks) and other activities planned for the whole school and/or visitors.

A scrapbook was prepared by Mrs. Earle Brooks during the 1941-1942 session, containing pictures taken by Mrs. Heyward Crowson, a patron and friend of the school. These pictures give some idea of the activities of the school. Classes produced plays for important occasions, and pupils enjoyed decorating the rooms in keeping with the meaning of each important holiday.

Members of the faculty that year were as follows: first grade, Miss Jennie McLeod; second grade, Mrs. Brooks; third grade, Miss Madge Montgomery; fourth grade, Mrs. Frank Bostick; fifth grade, Miss Lucie Ann Cuttino (now Mrs. Eldridge); sixth grade, Mrs. Leavell; seventh grade and principal, Mrs. DeWitt Brunson.

Some others came in each week to teach special subjects. The special music teacher was Mrs. Julia Warren Hoar and teaching art was Miss Rosa Wilder. Miss Cornelia McLaurin taught Bible each week. To encourage pupils to learn, she gave a Bible to each one who memorized 10 Bible verses.

Trustees in 1941-42 were, in addition to Mr. Miller, Dr. C.J. Lemmon (vice chairman), R.K. Wilder (Chairman), H.G. Osteen, Earle Rowland, F.M. Moise, S.L. Roddey, W.B. Upshur, and S.K. Nash.

Each teacher taught reading, writing and arithmetic, as well as many other valuable subjects through the medium of meaningful activities. Mrs. Brooks, for instance, had a clean-up corner in her room. Her report on this project with a picture was published in *Primary Activities,* a national magazine.

Because of the prevalence of colds, read the report, the second grade decided to establish a health corner, where each pupil would be inspected each day for neatness and cleanliness. They used the boards from large packing cases for the wall, which they lined with oil cloth. They made shelves for basin, pitcher, soap, comb, etc., by placing boards across orange crates. A "nurse" chosen by the class would inspect each pupil each day and if there was any deficiency found, it was made right at once. Obviously many lessons were learned by this activity.

Another "learn by doing" project, the report of which was also published in the magazine, was a "home unit" carried out by "Miss Jennie's" first grade. The class decided to "build" a room and make it as "homey" and pretty as possible. They used large boxes in which window glass had been packed for the framework. Cardboard was placed on the inside walls and painted pink. The outside was painted white. The dressing table was an old desk cut down and the stool was a grape box. An old rocking chair was found that would fit into the space.

They had a real child's bed with mattress and covers and the doll's cradle was made from a grape box. All the furniture was painted light blue with pink upholstering.

The children did the housekeeping and so doing acquired valuable helps in personal and social behavior learned from their reading books.

The second grade had a school store where they sold "real things for real money."

Countless teaching projects suitable to each grade were thus carried out. However, occasionally one would "miss the mark." Mrs. Bostick laughingly tells of one such incident. One of her boys was completing a bird house when Dr. Harap paid a visit.

"Why are you making a bird house?" the boy was asked.

"Because Mrs. Bostick made me," was the surprising reply.

Then he was asked if he thought the opening was large enough for a bird and the reply was just as unexpected.

"Done killed the bird and stuck it in."

According to former teachers and pupils, school life at Miller was a round of excitement. Every teacher took her pupils on field trips as learning situations or as recreation. Sometimes they went to Mason's Pond, where the wading was good. They often followed nature trails to gather specimens of plants, insects, etc., for their studies in science. Then there were picnics, when it was warm, and Easter egg hunts. Inside they were interested in giving plays, some for the public; and always there were interesting activities preceding the Christmas holidays.

There were games on the school grounds, too, supervised by the teachers. Some of the boys enjoyed playing football, though the equipment and rules were far simpler than those used now by the sophisticated teams and leagues in high school. Smaller children liked to jump rope. Of course, all these athletic activities were used to teach fairness, teamwork and other lessons.

Enthusiasm for school ran so high that pupils living nearby would meet their teachers at school a week before the opening date each fall to clean the rooms, paint the blackboards, put up decorations, making the building have an inviting appearance. They would end their work with a walk to Shot Pouch.

In 1941-42, because of the beginning of World War II, the boys were so stirred with a patriotic desire to serve that they put on a scrap iron drive. This proved a very successful project and again taught valuable lessons.

After Mrs. Brunson left (around 1943), Miss McLeod became principal and remained in that position as long as Miller was a school. In 1949 it was absorbed in Willow Drive School and the old building was later demolished.

Thus ended the life of a school that played an important role in the educational history of Sumter. But the memories of that school still linger in the minds and hearts of all who were in any way touched by its influence from the days of the little one-teacher Winn School till the last day spent at the beloved school on Miller Road.

Mrs. Brooks' words concerning the school seem to express the opinion of others who spent some of their teaching years there: "Miller School will always be dear to my heart. We had such wonderful children to teach. The parents were so cooperative. The teachers were so united and cooperative. I've never before or since seen anything to surpass the atmosphere of that school. My years there will always be a happy memory."

Many men and women living in Sumter today, when reminiscing of their first school days which they spent at Miller, express thoughts in keeping with the words of Charles Lamb, "My joyful school days" in his poem "Old Familiar Faces."

Beginning And Development Of Sumter School District No. 2

The earliest schools in Sumter County, as in all of South Carolina, were privately owned and administered for those who could afford to pay the price. People in less fortunate circumstances were left without any educational opportunities.

In 1811[160] the state passed a law authorizing the establishment of public schools; but even then, progress was very slow. Funds were too low and many parents were unwilling to send their children to other than private schools or academies of which there were many in Sumter County.

Eventually, however, small schools, most of which had only one teacher at first, and very meager equipment, sprang up here and there. Records of only a few are available and most of those records are incomplete.

One early Sumter County school with an interesting history is the old Providence School which, according to tradition, had its beginning in an old log house near where the present Baptist parsonage stands. Among the first teachers were Miss Mary Broadway (Mrs. Caleb Osteen) and Miss Esther Osteen.

The first school building was a barn-like structure, built possibly in 1878 with Miss Mary Mason as the first teacher. After this structure was burned, another was erected on land given by Ed L. Hodge.

Among the first trustees were James T. Brogdon and Drane Tindal (the name of the third not available). Later Carl Pack became a member of the board.

The school grew from a one-teacher to a two-teacher institution as more pupils were able to attend, and at the time when it was closed, through consolidation of schools in District 2, there were several teachers. Instruction went through the ninth grade only; and by some agreement, those who wished to do so and were able to provide transportation, completed the high school course in the Sumter schools.

Many now living in the county taught at one time in this school and those who did not live in the community were boarders with the James T. Brogdons until their home burned. At least two of the teachers in the school were pupils there, also. Miss Theola Brogdon (Mrs. E.W. Hook) went through the ninth grade at Providence and then went back after high school in Sumter and college to teach and serve as principal for a number of years.

Mrs. H.M. Brunson (Miss Lilla Mae Newman) also finished the courses available at Providence and went to Sumter for the remainder of the high school grades. After college she returned to Providence and taught for some time.

Mrs. Brunson tells of attending another small school in a neighboring community, known as Lawrence School, located on land donated by the Lawrence family. She was the instructor in this one-teacher school for two years.

Brogdon, Hodge, Pack, Tindal, Brunson, Newman, Britton, Jones, Lawrence, Geddings, and Osteen families were among the patrons of these two schools.

In another part of the county was the Baker school located on the old Brewington Road. Land for this school was donated by Dr. Chandler Baker. This, too, was a one-teacher school at first. Mrs. M.J. Moore (Miss Flora Edens) tells of teaching in this school in 1911, and describes the building as having an alcove, cloak rooms, and two school rooms that could be thrown together, with a wood-burning stove in each. For any night performance in the "auditorium" (the two rooms opened together) candles were used for lighting. She recalls that home economics and agriculture were taught on a small scale after the second teacher was added. Since there was no lunch program at that time, pupils had lunch baskets which they left in the cloak room, sometimes to their regret.

Some of the families attending this school were Jones, Brown, McLeod, Odom, Andrews, Bradham, Rogers, Howell and Edens.

This building was used for many years for a Sunday School in the community.

Near the Scarborough lumber camp was a one-teacher school known as Rocky Bluff. Mrs. Moore ran this school for some time. It was made of rather rough boards running up and down on the framework.

Some of the Baker school pupils attended this school at one time, and in addition to these, several families were represented, including Hatfield, Pope, Hinson, Josey, Joyner, Davis, Scarborough, Revill, Outlaw, and Wells.

Mrs. Moore tells of her teaching experience at the Lewis Road School, a little one-room shack near Green Swamp, and recalls that she boarded with Mrs. Ed Lewis.

Near the Myers place was the Brown School attended by Mrs. Moore. Miss Mary Hugh Fraser (Mrs. Miller Fraser) and Miss Jennie Richards were the teachers she remembers.

All of these early schools were equipped with wood-burning stoves, homemade desks, and recitation benches. Those attending, both teachers and pupils, either walked or rode in buggies or wagons. Teachers' salaries ranged from $40 to $50 a month in most of the schools; however, expenses were not very high. In many cases teachers were "boarded" in the homes of the pupils.

The pursuit of knowledge was not easy in the old days, but the desire to learn on the part of many was so great that no sacrifice was too extreme and no inconvenience was too discouraging to deter them in obtaining whatever education was available.

After years of the one- and two-teacher schools throughout Sumter County, the picture began to change gradually.

The first real venture in the idea of consolidating small districts was born in the mind of Col. John J. Dargan. He prevailed on the patrons of Districts 8, 9, 10 and 11 in Stateburg Township to consolidate their schools into one large institution. Thus, he founded the General Sumter Academy in 1905, the first experiment in consolidation in the state. The old plantation home, Acton, former home of Francis Kinloch, was used by the school.[161]

Colonel Dargan, who was superintendent of the Academy,

initiated some other "firsts" in connection with his school. Acton was large enough to accommodate some of the girls who wished to board, and the boys who wished to stay near the school were accommodated at Marston, the Dargan home. Others were transported to school by two covered wagons drawn by two mules with a teacher in each. Thus the first "bus" system was begun in South Carolina. He was determined to provide for country children an education as adequate as that enjoyed by city children.

There were six teachers on the faculty, and a curriculum commensurate with the requirements of the State Board of Education was made available for the fortunate students who attended this school. Strict discipline was maintained and the atmosphere for learning was ideal.

Another "first" initiated by Colonel Dargan was what he called an "annex" in education, the teaching of agriculture. He secured some land nearby and established a demonstration farm. He received aid from the government to the extent of 20 acres of land, stock and fertilizer.

One of the first teachers was J. Frank Williams, who taught mathematics in the morning and agriculture in the afternoon. Mr. Williams later became Sumter County's first Farm Agent and the first in the United States.

In 1911 Acton burned, but a new building was constructed and this pioneer of educational advantages continued until 1928 when a wider consolidation of schools had been effected and Hillcrest was built for that part of the county.

Under a new constitution adopted in 1895 giving all districts in the country the power to levy taxes for educational purposes, Pinewood and Mayesville built commodious schools for their white children. In smaller communities schools of lesser size and fewer conveniences were built since their taxable income was less than that in the towns.

For the most part, the schools built for the Negroes were smaller. However, there were two adequate schools in the county built by the Northern Presbyterian Church, Ebenezer near Dalzell and Goodwill near Black River (Brick) Presbyterian Church. A third such school was built in Mayesville by a Northern organization in 1882. It was known as the Mayesville Institute. Emma Wilson was sent by the philanthropists to run the school and it was often called by her name. It is now an elementary school in the Mayesville District and is housed in an adequate modern building.

Sherwood was built in 1937 for the convenience of pupils in the extreme eastern part of the county.

Besides schools for whites and blacks, there were schools in the county for Turks since they were not allowed to attend white schools for a number of years.

According to laws enacted by the General Assembly in 1951, state aid was provided for construction and the state soon began providing funds for transportation. In a short while, School District No. 2 was formed by the County Board of Education. The 25 school districts in Sumter County were consolidated. A Clarendon County District, children from which had been attending the Pinewood school for years, was included in the new District 2.

The first trustees for this district were J.E. Mayes, C.W. Goodman, A.M. Burroughs, H.E. Kirven and W.A. Brown. The first district superintendent was Hugh T. Stoddard. Assistants in the administration of the district were Roland Windham, Fred Wells (later with District 17), and George James.

Many of the small inadequate schools were closed and new schools were built, especially for the Negroes. Some of these were Manchester, Eastern and Ebenezer, providing an accredited program for black students.

Mayesville and Sherwood were consolidated, forming Mayewood. Hillcrest and Furman are the other two high schools in the county.

Integration began in 1964 and total integration became a reality a few years later. Many of the new Negro high schools are now middle schools which prepare students for the three high schools. Ebenezer and Shaw Heights send students to Hillcrest for high school work and the other high schools receive students from other middle schools.

Recently a special honor came to Ebenezer school which once had a reputation for unruly conduct, but under the supervision of Principal Girard J. Myers and a faculty of well-trained and understanding teachers, the picture has changed. Out of 1,003 state elementary and secondary public schools, Ebenezer, with a student body of 900, was chosen as "an exemplary state school" by the State Department of Education, which has asked WRJA-TV to prepare "a documentary film about the school, its teaching and faculty."

Sumter School District 2 has put much stress on the cultural development of the pupils. Each of the schools has had its band where boys and girls received musical training and in 1962 an all-district band was organized. This band has maintained a creditable rating in state competition since that time.

Another special program sponsored by the District is the Lookout Program for Gifted and Talented Students.

Typical of the high schools in the district is Hillcrest, the oldest of the three. It began in a small building in the northwestern part of the county in 1926, approximately 25 years before District 2 was formed.[162]

In addition to regular courses for a well-rounded academic program, the school offers special courses as electives; and there is a well-trained guidance department, members of which counsel with students as to the best courses to take and they give advice and guidance in solving problems.

Students receive valuable training through extracurricular activities such as the Student Council. Membership in the National Honor Society offers an incentive to students to maintain a high standing in scholarship, leadership, service and character. There are also numerous special interest clubs, a few of which are Quill and Scroll, Future Farmers of America and Future Homemakers of America.

There is also a strong athletic program including the major sports in which the school's teams compete with those of other schools.

Dr. James Blanding was the first principal of the school and Mrs. Fannie Dinkins began teaching at Hillcrest when it was begun in 1926. She returned in 1962 to teach math and science. It has been said that she had a "profound influence" on those whom she taught.

Other superintendents, principals and teachers have made valuable contributions in making Hillcrest a strong institution of learning.

History Of Private Schools

In the early history of Sumter County, private schools played a major role in the educational program. Many such as Claremont Academy and Dr. John Roberts Academy in Stateburg were in the county.

In the city were also many such schools, one of the last before the establishment of the public school system was the short-lived Sumter Military Academy and Female Seminary.[163] The history of this school is of unusual interest.

The president of this institution was Clarence J. Owens. With a Master's degree from Columbia University, he was also instructor in English Language, Literature and Moral Science. He came from Orangeburg, having been at the head of O.C.I. (Orangeburg Collegiate Institute).

The school offered quite a broad course of study, with the following as faculty members: W.A. Buckner (A.M., University of Missouri), ancient languages; D.A. Bradham (B.S., South Carolina Military Academy), mathematics; Miss E.E. Cooper (Barhamville College), history and literature; L. Clifton Moise

(A.B., South Carolina College), modern languages.

There was also a business department with O.F. Hunter (B.S., South Carolina Military Academy, Atlanta Business College) as principal. The aim of this department was "to train young men and young women to be bookkeepers, typewriters and stenographers and to equip them for the practical duties of life."

In the music department the Virgil Method was to be used. It was guaranteed to teach pupils: "How to think, how to practice, how to memorize, how to play, how to teach." This must have been indeed an unusual program! The aim given was to "make intelligent and artistic piano players in less time than can be done by any other course of instruction." Included in the course in addition to piano were lessons in voice, violin, mandolin, guitar. A chorus class and an orchestra were also planned.

Director of this department was Miss Annie P. Ewell (Virgil's Conservatory of Music in New York), and her assistant was Miss Rosa Gillespie (Sumter Conservatory of Music).

An art course was taught by Miss Mary Wilson (Limestone College, Wesleyan Female College).

A course in elocution was taught by Miss D.A. Sarling (Emerson School of Oratory, Boston). "It should be the aim of the orator," emphasized the description of the course, "to convey beauty, truth and goodness to the hearer. The importance of this subject in a girl's education cannot easily be overestimated."

Physical culture, also taught by Miss Sarling, had as its chief end "reposeful and dignified bearing, grace and ease of manner."

For the boys, the military training in the school was of utmost importance. Carried in the explanation of the course was the idea that "the perfect man must be developed physically, mentally and morally." And military exercises were said to be the "best all-around bodily culture." This philosophical thought was aded: "He who would govern must first have been governed."

D.A. Bradham (B.S., South Carolina Military Academy) was the commanding officer, as well as an instructor in mathematics. This course was also based on a very lofty aim. "The students are impressed with the importance of thinking out all propositions for themselves; the teacher explains the principles, and requires the pupils to solve the problems, even by new methods, if they can, thus throwing them upon their own resources and responsibilities, giving them self-assurance and confidence."

The science program, including physics, physiology, chemistry, geology, astronomy, was under W.W. Smoak, Jr. (B.S., South Carolina Military Academy), who was also booked to teach philosophy.

Foreign languages offered were Greek, Latin, French, German.

In addition to staff members listed were J.M. Brailsford, Jr. (A.B., Orangeburg College), principal of the preparatory department; Miss Belle Walker, registrar; Jesse E. Chandler, librarian; Hall T. Capers, secretary.

There were to be two written examinations each year – intermediate and final – with each student required to make 60 as a passing grade. These examinations were to be "thorough and rigid," and reports would be issued each month on deportment and class standing.

Plans called for the use of the old Sumter Institute as the main building and dormitory space for approximately 80 girls and female teachers. A barracks would be constructed, it was said, for the boys. However, this plan did not materialize. The young men occupied the main building and the girls lived in what was known as the Monaghan House on South Main Street. The music students used the Sumter Conservatory of Music, which included a recital hall, class and practice rooms.

Announcement was made that there would be two literary societies for both sexes, a YMCA and a YWCA. A journal was to be published by the students. How many of these plans were carried out is not known.

Students were required to wear uniforms. For cadets, fatigues, one gray blouse coat, one pair of gray trousers, one West Point cap. For winter the ladies were to wear Confederate gray, trimmed in black braid and state buttons; for spring a skirt of blue brilliantine, waist of white India linen and lace. Black oxfords, student caps and gloves to match completed the outfits.

Fees included $5 matriculation; $8 board per month; $4 tuition per month. Special departments required additional charges.

How many students matriculated during each year is not known, but they came from neighboring communities, as well as from a greater distance. There were some local students also enrolled.

From the DuRant section of Sumter County came at least two brothers, Edgar P. and John C. DuRant. They stayed with their cousins, the McLaurins, and attended as day students.

Upon graduation, John returned to his home community and became a prosperous farmer. Edgar, however, went on to dental school in Atlanta. When his course there was completed, he began the practice of dentistry in Mayesville. After a few months he moved to Sumter where he built up a very successful practice in which he served his community for 47 years.

Emile Moses, a local "boy," chose the military for his career, making a name for himself and his hometown. He became a general in the Marine Corps, for many years commandant of the

Marine Base on Parris Island. Some years before his death, General Moses retired and went to California to live.

William Cuttino and J.B. Wilder were two other Sumter boys, graduated from the Academy. Cuttino became a successful accountant in his hometown and J.B. (Doc) Wilder, for many years, was connected with the Post Office.

J.C. Brodgon, coming from the lower part of Sumter County, returned to the Brogdon community after graduation and became an influential figure there and in other parts of the county.

Though the Sumter Military Academy had a very short life (two years), it had the distinction of putting on the gridiron Sumter's first football team, with L.C. Moise as its coach. Some recollections concerning this first squad (1901) were given some years ago by Coach Moise. He remembered that during that year, he was not at all well since he had not completely recovered from a very serious illness. He even found it necessary to walk with a cane, and at times he was unable to call practice.

He mentioned that the student body was very small (the only reference found as to the size of the school) and, consequently, there were few who could "make the team." There were few, if any substitutes. Since the school could provide no financial aid, the boys themselves found it necessary to "chip in" to buy needed equipment.

It seems that there was a practice field on the grounds of the Academy, but games were played on the old race track "just beyond the Judge Green place on North Main Street." The field being open to the public with no fences to bar onlookers, voluntary "fees" .were collected when the hat was passed. Moise recalled that "these free-will offerings were disappointing. When the count was "something like 70-0," the coach instructed his captain to stop counting.

The game with the large boys on either the freshman or "scrub" team of South Carolina College was another story.

In 1902 Emile Moses (later General Moses) was the coach and the team was "undefeated and unscored on." The squad finished the season in a blaze of triumph, "in sharp contrast," said Moise, "to the Academy which folded up the following June."

There was also a baseball team during one year at least. Practically nothing is known, however, of its success. Essentially the same boys made up both teams.

Those who prepared the first catalogue enthusiastically praised the location of the school, saying: "Sumter is a beautiful, rapidly growing, healthful city of extensive and diversified manufacturing interests and has the best of most everything.

"The admiring gaze of the State is turned toward Sumter . . . "

Seemingly with all things in its favor, the Academy might have been an institution of note, bringing credit to Sumter. Instead it has come down in history as an unsuccessful venture.

After the public schools became available, private schools were no longer needed, as public education was free for all.

However, in the last decade, several private schools have begun operating in the area. The history of two of these which are typical will be traced. One is in the city and one in the county.

WILSON HALL

Wilson Hall, which began in 1967, is the realization of a dream of many in the area. It bears the name of one who not only dreamed, but worked that such an institution of learning could become a reality. This man was the late John S. Wilson, whose enthusiasm and dedication to the cause of education inspired others to join hands in the building of a school of which Sumter can be proud. [164]

The school is located in the western part of the city on Wise Drive on a 15-acre tract of land donated by Jimmy and Willie Dinkins. The first building of the complex completed was for the lower school or elementary department.

During the first year there were 87 pupils, in grades one through six and six teachers.

In the third year a second building was completed and the school offered a full 12-year college preparatory program. There were 470 students and 26 teachers.

A dedicated Board of Trustees worked tirelessly and wisely to effect this phenomenal growth. Chairman of the Board was George C. James, who was ably assisted by Paul Bullock, D.G.F. Bultman, E.C. Dunn, Burke Watson and J.D. Dinkins.

At first the tuition fee for an elementary pupil was $425 and $450 for a high school student. However, that amount has been considerably increased since that time.

The school has ample space with classrooms, laboratories, office space, a library well stocked with reading materials, faculty and student lounges.

Acting principal of Wilson Hall for the first two years was Mrs. Dorothy Compton, but for the third year a headmaster, J.T. McCorkle, was secured. He came highly recommended. He was followed later by Mr. Charles Quick. After Mr. Quick resigned, Mr. Eugene Nalley became headmaster and is still serving in that position.

The school has a well-rounded curriculum offering all the courses needed for college entrance. There are included courses in music, dramatics and art for students gifted in these areas.

Such extracurricular activities as a newspaper, a yearbook and various clubs claim the interests of many students.

Wilson Hall sponsors an athletic program, including football, basketball, baseball, track, soccer, tennis and golf.

Students participate in all testing programs offered for the establishment of norms. Requirements of the State Board of Education are met.

Graduates from this school stand well in college work wherever they go.

THOMAS SUMTER ACADEMY

"In the rolling hills of Santee
Proudly does she stand,
Our dear school, our Alma Mater
Finest in the land."

Thus the first stanza of the school song reflects the school spirit found at Thomas Sumter Academy, one of Sumter County's independent schools. This school was begun in 1964 in a building which was erected in 1925 and used by Hillcrest High School until 1958, when a new plant was built for that school. When the district no longer had use for the structure, it was bought by a group of citizens.[165]

Six years later, when Thomas Sumter Academy was organized, interested patrons and friends renovated the building and equipped it for use by the Academy, which was named in honor of Gen. Thomas Sumter, that great patriot of Revolutionary fame for whom the county and city of Sumter were named.

Mrs. Frances Dinkins was the first head of the school and through her marked ability and efficiency, it was established on a strong foundation. The beginning enrollment was 180, with grades one through ten. The following year there were eleven grades and in the third year a twelfth was added. Though the enrollment continues to grow, each class is limited to 25 pupils.

Trustees J.E. Davis, Jr., chairman; E.M. DuBose, vice chairman; Miss Martha White; I.P. Pitts; J.M. Brabham and A.W. James, ex officio member, tirelessly worked in improving the school in every way possible.

Five new classrooms, increasing the capacity to 450, were added. What was formerly the Francis Marion Academy in the Bethel community became a branch of Thomas Sumter under the same trustees and administration. The brick building owned by Bethel Baptist Church houses one section each of grades one through six, with a capacity of 150.

Headmaster is C.E. Owens, III.

Tuition cost at first was $400 for elementary pupils and $425 for grades seven through twelve, but it has increased greatly since the beginning. To 12 outstanding students, scholarships are provided by interested friends of the school. These scholarships are based on academic qualifications and need.

Thomas Sumter operates a number of buses, some of which are driven by high school boys with the same regulations as required by public schools. One route accommodates pupils on the south side of Sumter, to the branch at Bethel, and two serve those going to the main campus. There are also car pools from other areas.

A college preparatory curriculum is offered which requires four years each of English, mathematics, science, social studies and three years of French, with an additional course in creative writing. In addition to these requirements, there is a rich program of electives: United States government, French IV, analytic geometry and calculus, Home Economics I and II, Elementary and Advanced Bookkeeping and Accounting, two years of typing, vocabulary and word study, pre-algebra, general math, and general science. Thus those who are not college-bound may find courses to fit them for work after high school.

In order for students at Thomas Sumter to have a well-rounded education, many extracurricular activities are sponsored. There is, first of all, a very active and enthusiastic Student Council.

Other organizations in which students participate according to their wishes and qualifications include the National Honor Society, the Anchor Club, and Quill and Scroll.

At the end of the year, outstanding staff members from the three publications are honored by appointment to the Quill and Scroll Society. This society is not formally organized at Thomas Sumter, but serves only as a way of recognizing those who have done excellent work for the publications. There are in addition to these some special interest clubs.

Students publish each six weeks an excellent printed newspaper, "The Green and Gold." Once a year, a literary magazine, "Calliope," is produced, containing creative writings submitted by students in their English classes. "The General," portraying the life of the school through photography and copy is published each year.

The school gives no financial support to these publications; through various projects the students raise funds to cover the entire cost.

Sports, too, play an important role in after-school activities. In the fall the boys play soccer. Basketball is the chief winter sport. Boys and girls varsity and junior varsity basketball teams compete with those from other independent schools.

A testing program is administered throughout the school. Elementary pupils take all recommended tests; grades 7-10 take National Education Developmental tests. Juniors are given P.S.A. and the National Merit Scholarship Tests; seniors, the College Board, S.A.T. and Achievement Tests.

Eighty percent of the Academy's graduates attend college, and many have received worthwhile scholarships.

The school participates in various academic programs throughout the state, such as the Furman Scholarship program and Wofford's King Teen.

Other statewide programs in which Thomas Sumter participates are Boys' State and Girls' State.

Thomas Sumter is a member of South Carolina Association of Independent Schools and is accredited by that group. Mr. Owens is a member of the Southeastern Headmasters' Association.

In stating his philosophy, Mr. Owens said that in his opinion "a school should provide the opportunity for each child to learn in a Christian environment, receiving an education best suited to his individual needs and abilities."

The same educational ideal is expressed in a quotation from the Handbook: "Matters of policy related to academic requirements, standards of decorum, dress and general attitudes are based on those principles that experience has proven to be the best means to create the environment in which a child may be motivated to truly grow in wisdom and stature, and in favor with God and Man."

PART X. MILITARY

Sumter's Company K, Symbol Of Courage

"None excelled us in morality, in patriotism, fixedness of purpose, or power of endurance, as fully evinced by what we did and suffered for a cause par excellence."

Thus wrote W.J. Andrews as he lived over again those days and nights and weeks and months of privation and danger endured by the brave men of Company K, Twenty-third Regiment South Carolina Volunteers. All except two of this company were either killed or captured in the Civil War.

In 1909 Andrews planned a reunion of the surviving members of Company K at the courthouse in Sumter, and only nine of the few still living were able to attend. In his account of the reunion, Andrews named those present with their ages as follows: Joseph H. Lewis, 82; D.R. McCallum, 75; J. Grier White, 74; F.M. Brown, 72; D.W. Josey, 67; Albert H. Weeks, 67; Ervin J. Player, 66; Welburn J. Andrews, 65; Samuel R. Fraser, 62.

In order that future generations might have a full knowledge of the services rendered the South by Company K during the war, Andrews wrote the account, put together from recollections of those present at the reunion and from bits of information sent by others who were still living but unable to meet. And what a stirring saga of heroism, sacrifice and bloodshed! It seems fitting for those living today to look back to that day in April, 115 years ago when the war finally came to an end.

Company K, composed of 100 men, was organized in Sumter in 1861 with Thomas D. Frierson as captain. Other officers were the following: Lucius P. Loring, first lieutenant; Francis H. Kennedy, second lieutenant; David R. McCallum, third lieutenant; Stephen D.M. Lacoste, first sergeant; H.M. Browne, second sergeant; J. Grier White, third sergeant; Priestly Colclough, fourth sergeant; Leighton B. Wilson, fifth sergeant; J.P. Norton, first corporal; A.G. Murphy, second corporal; S.M. Dinkins, third corporal; Charles A. Stiles, fourth corporal.[166]

When the company reached Charleston it was attached to a regiment commanded by Colonel Hatch to do picket duty. Sometime in December these men were formally mustered for State Coast defense and quartered on the Georgetown Road.

At first, camp life was not burdensome. Except for the grief of being absent from loved ones, the "boys," as soldiers were called, lived very comfortably in their encampment. Having little to do, they went squirrel hunting during the day, and at night they sat around a large fire in the open and swapped "tall tales." They had plenty to eat with boxes from home and the abundance of fish and oysters they could get nearby. The most unpleasant circumstance of camping was the ever present plague of sand fleas.

After several months of this more or less leisurely existence, however, conditions began to change. In May of 1862 Company K was reorganized, becoming the Twenty-third South Carolina Volunteers with Captain Lucius P. Loring in command. Other officers included D.R. McCallum, first lieutenant; H.M. Browne, second lieutenant; J.H. Cooper, third lieutenant; J. Grier White, Priestly Colclough, Moultrie Wilson, Legrand Joye, J.L. Norton, Samuel M. Dinkins, Charles A. Stiles and Thomas W. McDonald were the non-commissioned officers.

Soon the regiment had a foretaste of what was to come. The enemy began to shell their encampment. One man was killed. However, quiet soon reigned again. Company K was then quartered in Charleston in the Second Presbyterian Church yard where it remained for several weeks. Then suddenly the command went out for all those on furlough or sick leave to return at once. After only a few days the Twenty-third Regiment was ordered to Petersburg, Virginia.

From that time on these men were in the thick of the fray. It was one encounter after another and in each one the Twenty-third showed great bravery and Company K did not falter in the face of danger.

Life was hard even when there was no fighting. The fare consisted mostly of "Beef, good, bad or indifferent. Occasionally a little bacon instead; flour and salt (coffee played out); sometimes hard tack (a cake of flour and water minus salt and soda) and poor beef composed the ration."

Andrews tells of one time when the company was issued flour for five days and told to cook bread in two hours. They used every conceivable utensil, such as flat rocks or pieces of barrel heads. It was there that "ramrod" bread was made famous. Some wrapped the dough around the ramrods, while they stuck in the ground at an angle, turning at intervals to insure an even baking process.

After one forced march the men were weak from hunger and there was no food. Colonel Benbow sent deputies out to gather ears of mutton corn from a nearby field. Each soldier received nine ears which he ate with relish. There was an apple orchard in the neighborhood, too; and though the apples were green, some ate these – to their discomfort.

One of the greatest inconveniences was the lack of good water at times. Whenever they found a spring of fresh cool water, they were delighted, but those "finds" were few.

Sleeping accommodations were often far from comfortable. Many times they slept in the outside with only leaves for a bed.

Other inconveniences often had to be endured. On one occasion the men were told when starting on a march to leave their baggage, that they would find it when they returned that night. But while they were away a band of marauding Yankee soldiers came by and burned everything they possessed. Andrews describes graphically the result of this incident: "Picture to yourself a body of men forced to wear the same clothing day after day, week after week, and month after month, without change, trodding daily along dusty roads, at times sloppy, the rain wetting and sun drying them . . . "

One of the first disastrous battles fought by Company K was just beyond Bull Run. This battle was won by the Confederates, but Company K lost three men – Tom Britton, George Josey and John Scarborough. There were 19 wounded. Captain D.R. McCallum, with the assistance of Private Nichols, searched the battlefield all night to find the wounded of his company.

Twenty-third Regiment fought at Sharpsburg, where Cornelius Baker was killed. The next encounter with the enemy was at Kinston. From there they marched to Wilmington and from there to Charleston by rail. They encamped on Sullivan's Island.

Leaving Charleston in June of 1863, they went to Meridian, Mississippi, and on to Jackson, where encampment in the trenches was very hard and some of Company K became ill.

After leaving Jackson, they went to Mobile, Alabama, and on to Savannah, Georgia, where they camped for a short time. It was then back to Charleston and Mt. Pleasant. In September 1863, they went to Sullivan's Island, where they sent weekly relief to Fort Sumter. Their duty there was "both hard and arduous" for the enemy kept up a constant bombardment of the fort.

In January of 1864 the Twenty-third Regiment went to Wilmington where they did some picket duty for six months. In June of that year the unit was sent back to Petersburg, Virginia. There "things warmed up, hot and fast." John Buddin and E.R. Josey of Company K were wounded; Sumter DuRant was killed.

The fighting was hard, with the Confederates outnumbered eight to one. The Southerners had no protection from the enemy fire. With iron spoons and tin plates, they were able to dig out the earth in the preparation of rifle pits and holes large enough for the men to get into by doubling up. In some places the enemy line was not more than 30 yards away. When spades, shovels and pickaxes were made available, however, their breastworks were built. Cotton sacks containing sand were placed on top in such a manner as to protect and still afford a peephole for the sentinel to use in reporting movements of the enemy.

On July 28, 1864, the Twenty-third Regiment moved somewhat to the right and for six weeks or more the men were never able to sleep from 1:00 a.m. to daylight. Sometimes they were so overcome by loss of sleep that they would nod between the shots of the mortar. They were shelled eight to ten o'clock every morning and about two hours each evening.

When it was learned that the enemy was sinking a mine under their breastworks, the Confederates made attempts to countermine, but without success. Then the explosion came. The description given by the author can best convey the horror wrought by this enemy tactic:

"The part blown up was lifted in solid mass and thrown over in adjacent rear. Some four of five companies of the Twenty-second Regiment were buried in the ruins. Companies on the right and left were stunned and captured. Colonel Fleming, of the Twenty-second Regiment, was so completely buried that, though diligent search was made for three days, his body was never found. Our removal to the right was a merciful providence for otherwise the Twenty-third Regiment would have met the fate of the Twenty-second in its stead."

The fighting continued for days in the vicinity of Petersburg with several of Company K suffering wounds and one, Jim Richbourg, being killed. In the thick of this fierce fighting, Sumter had an artillery company with Hugh Garden as captain, who was replaced by Lt. Alexander McQueen. The mortars, trained on the crater, sent shells that were true to aim, killing many of the enemy who were entrenched there. As a result, scores of Yankees surrendered.

As the Twenty-third Regiment was advancing toward the Crater, Dwight Shaw of Company K was killed. Another tunnel was mined from the Federal to the Confederate lines, extending under the breastworks of the Confederates and on July 30, 1864, there was an explosion and the Federal forces advanced. Fighting raged the whole day and near sunset five privates of Company K – Morgan Baker, Mack Huggins, Joe Lewis, William Prescott and Welburn J. Andrews – advanced through seven companies "within fifteen paces of the bluecoats, where a fierce conflict was going on." After William Prescott, Joe Lewis and Mack Huggins were wounded, "The struggle was then between Morgan Baker, W.J. Andrews and three bluecoats." The result of this fray? The answer can best be given in the words of one who was there:

"We carried away 500 prisoners (black and white) together with a few Indians from the West. And oh! what a spectacle to behold! in this Crater, 30 or more feet deep and more than 100 feet in length. More than one of the Twenty-second Regiment was taken out alive, where he had been buried under the debris all day . . . Then the burying of 500 human beings in this Crater and around it."[167]

The regiment was later moved a mile or two away to a less trying position. Since they were a little farther from the enemy, they had a respite for a little while from the fear of being shot down at any moment. However, other conditions were bad. They had to bring their wood at least a quarter of a mile and for food they had one pint of wheat flour, a fourth-pound of bacon, salt and peas. Hardly an adequate diet it would seem.

While still at the Crater (October 12, 1864), Albertus White was very severely wounded, but under the care of Doctors Murry and Dick and with the nursing of Andrews (who had been ill with chills and fever) at the Confederate State Hospital in Petersburg, he recovered sufficiently to be allowed to go home. Andrews states that eggs bought for White cost $10 a dozen.

These tortured men remained in the trenches until the last of February or first of March, 1865, when they were moved to a position west of Petersburg and quartered in log cabins. Thinking that they would have here a much needed rest, the men in Company K began patching their clothes.

But the rest was all too short. On March 24, they were marched in quick time to Petersburg and on to their breastworks near Appomattox River. They were there ordered to hold the Yankee Fort (Steadman), which had been captured. Here Lieutenant Scarborough was wounded and William Gregg was killed. Both of these were in Company K.

As the Yankees advanced, the Confederates on the right began to retreat. The orderly of Company K, though wounded, refused to retreat and he, with a few others, including Andrews, was captured. They were taken to General Meade's headquarters where they were put on cars to be taken to the prison at City Point. The commissioned officers were sent, it was thought, to Johnson Island; while the non-commissioned officers and privates were taken to Point Lookout, Maryland. Soon other prisoners from Company K began arriving, and over twenty of this company were imprisoned. There they remained till April 8.

Those not captured in Twenty-third Regiment continued skirmishing with the Yankees without rest day or night until the surrender of General Lee at Appotmattox Courthouse. At the Battle of Five Forks, William Randal was killed and the remainder of Company K, except Joe Lewis and Randolph Bracy, were taken captive. It was in this battle that the Twenty-third Regiment was sacrificed to save the remainder of the army.

Point Lookout Prison, where the prisoners of Company K were confined, was located on an "extreme point of land between the Atlantic Ocean on the east and Chesapeake Bay on the south and west." Surrounding the prison was a high wooden wall. Within the wall was a ditch known as the "dead line," for if a prisoner crossed that ditch, he was shot with no questions asked.

The captives were put in tents arranged in rows facing each other. They were lined up each morning for roll call. Between sunrise and sunset they were permitted to walk outside of a gate on the bay side, but the gate was closed at sunset.

Their daily food consisted of two meals, mostly of bean soup and baker's bread.

"Brackish" water came from wells eight or ten feet deep. One bright spot in the whole melancholy picture was that Major Brady, commander, was kind to the prisoners.

When the prisoners were harassed by the guards, Major Brady allowed the captives to form their own guards, allowing these to have separate quarters and extra rations. There were 100 of these guards with two lieutenants and one sergeant. Several of Company K were on the guard. Their rations included sugar, coffee and tobacco.

Another advantage granted the prisoners was the opportunity to study. Some ladies from New York sent school books to Major Brady, who furnished a house to be used as a school and gave to prisoners who were educated an extra ration daily to teach the illiterate. The plan worked well and many who had no education were taught to read, spell and write.

The Confederate Government, assisted by some ladies from Baltimore, sent clothing to needy prisoners. Alonzo Morgan, son of Rev. Jesse Morgan of Sumter, was on the committee to help distribute these clothes.

After the surrender of Gen. Joseph E. Johnston, the paroling of prisoners began. The number of Confederates at Point Lookout was approximately 25,000. They were released according to the length of time they had been in prison, those having been there longest being paroled first. They were given transportation as far toward home as "conditions warranted."

Three Sumter men – John Brunby (sic), Morgan Baker and J. Grier White – apparently Andrews must have been with these three since he tells most of the experience in the first person – left prison by steamer for Charleston. From Charleston they traveled by South Carolina Railroad to Orangeburg, walking from there to the Congaree River, where they were able to pay a man with a boat to take them across. Luckily they spied a hand car on the trestle. They were given a lift to Kingsville, where they met Marion Lafar, railroad agent, who gave them a free ride to Sumter. They reached town between 12 and 1 o'clock on the first Sunday of July, 1865.

Experiences of Company K, Twenty-third Regiment, South Carolina Volunteers are typical of what thousands of others from Sumter, other parts of South Carolina and other states of the South suffered in those four dreadful years of war. Hundreds sacrificed their lives, others carried on their bodies' wounds received on the battle front; still others suffered as long as they lived from disease caused by exposure and lack of food, all for a cause they deemed to be just and right. What examples of patriotism, honor and courage these men set for their descendants!

(It has been learned that there is evidence that J. Grier White wrote the booklet giving the activities of Company K and that W.J. Andrews printed the first edition. That would clear up the dilemma as to the three who made the trip back to Sumter after the war. The first printing was done in Richmond, Virginia. The reprint was done by Wilder and Ward Offset Printing in Sumter.)

Potter Delayed At Dingle's Mill

Having a strong flavor of the heartless marches of Col. Banastre Tarleton, Maj. James Wemyss and other British officers during the Revolutionary War in the Sumter District, was the notorious raid of Gen. Edward E. Potter and his army as they came from Charleston toward Sumter, looting and burning property of their fellow Americans.

Potter left Georgetown on April 5, 1865, with a force of 2,700 fighting men, including five regiments of foot-soldiers, a cavalry unit and two pieces of artillery. In Williamsburg County, near Black Mingo, a small group of old men and boys bravely diverted the march of the "fire-fiend" band by destroying bridges across the Black River, thus giving the people along the way a little more time for preparation.

Women and children in Potter's path were all but defenseless. Old men, too feeble to enter the army, very young boys and wounded or sick soldiers, home for recuperation, were their only protectors.

Imagine the anxiety burdening the hearts of these brave women as they heard reports of the ruthless barbarity of this conglomerate band of marauders. But these women, inured to hardship and suffering by four years of constant subjection to the harshness of war, knew that somehow they would meet this crisis when it came. Yes, these were the women who had sent their fathers, husbands, brothers, sons or sweethearts to the front to fight, for a cause they believed with all their hearts to be right and just. They had endured hunger, oftentimes lacking the barest necessities. Clothing had worn threadbare and there were practically no medicines. Herbs and roots had to suffice if illness struck a family.

Be it ever to their credit that they never complained, though "they passed long days and nights of terrible suspense, fearing, knowing it was but too probable that any moment might bring them tidings of woe, that on some distant battlefield lay the lifeless forms of those whose presence alone seemed to make life worth living."

Patriotism ranked high on the scale of virtues among these women. In one part of the state a Yankee soldier was heard to say, "Confound these women; those 'Rebels' would have given up long ago if it weren't for them." Their heroism can only be lauded, for it could never be truly measured.

Now as reports kept coming of the advance of the enemy, they realized the imminence of a new danger – the destruction of their very homes, the loss of whatever possessions they had left, and perhaps peril to life itself.

Arrival of the enemy in Sumter was delayed briefly when Col. Tom Conners, with about 40 of the Clarendon Militia, destroyed the bridges over Pocotaligo on the northern outskirts of Manning, forcing Potter's engineers to take time to replace them.

However, on April 9, the Northern Army was on the march again. One example of the destruction that lay in the path of the bluecoats will typify what was to be feared. After they had passed the John B. Brogdon plantation just south of Sumter, practically nothing was left in the way of food and farm products. Barns containing over 1,000 bushels of corn, as well as peas, fodder, rice, bales of cotton, were all burned, while the hordes of freed slaves following the army looked on with jeers and shouts of fiendish delight. General Potter himself rode nonchalantly along, paying little attention to these acts of revenge perpetrated by his men.

In the meantime, frantic preparations were being made to meet the foe and protect the town. Col. George W. Lee issued an order through Adjutant T.B. Fraser for the 2nd Regiment (what remained of it in the city) to assemble for duty. This contingent consisting of only 80 men was under the command of Capt. David R. McCallum.

The urgent call for help brought to the scene Colonel Conners of Manning with about 40 men; Col. James Pressley (his arm in a sling) from Mayesville with his troops (100 men) and supplies from railroad cars; Colonel Caldwell of Kentucky from Nelson's Ferry across Santee with about 120 infantrymen; Capt. Alex Colclough, enrolling officer at Camden, with 100 reinforcements. Thomas R. Brown of the Reserves provided 60 recruits.

Two usable pieces of artillery were available. A brass 12-pounder was commanded by Lieutenant Pamperya, a French soldier of the Washington Artillery of New Orleans, who left a local hospital to help in the emergency. Fifteen volunteers stood by him. The other piece of artillery, an old field piece, an iron gun, was manned by a detachment of 15 under the command of Lt. W.A. McQueen, son of the beloved pastor of Sumter's First Presbyterian Church. A third piece commanded by Sergeant Dunbar proved useless. (It is said that two boys – Andrew Buchanan and J. Blanding Jones – hastily brought burning torches from a nearby cabin in a desperate but fruitless attempt to fire this third gun.) One very young lad, D. James Winn (14), considered a very good shot, was stationed in a ditch, where he bravely played his role.

Defenders when counted totaled only 575. What was this small band against Potter's army of 2,700 men in fighting condition, followed by undisciplined hordes bent on destruction? But refusing to count the cost, the few went forth with courage and determination to meet the enemy.

It was decided that the only place suitable for the encounter was at Dingle's Mill, three miles south of Sumter. In preparation for the battle, "the floodgate of the mill was raised so as to flood the swamp below the dam and make it difficult for the enemy to cross." Thus it was the intention of the Confederates to force the oncoming soldiers to cross on the narrow causeway which they hoped to be able to hold. Here the guns were set up and camouflaged by pine saplings and brushes. Pamperya and McQueen made ready to greet with gunfire those attempting to cross. As someone said, "Leonidas and his men at the Pass of Thermopylae deserved no more the laurel wreath of fame than did that little band of Confederates who fought and died at the Battle of Dingle's Mill."

As the first line of the enemy force entered upon the causeway, Lieutenant Pamperya opened fire, the first shot almost taking "the head from General Potter's shoulders" and announcing to him in no uncertain terms that he would be resisted to the death. McQueen's gun spit forth its small shot, and under this surprising barrage the enemy halted in their confident advance. The shots were heard as far away as Stateburg, telling anxious loved ones awaiting in their homes that resistance was being offered to the foe.

The Northern general quickly commanded his artillery, which was much superior to that of the Southerners, to answer the shots. He massed his troops at the end of the causeway and ordered them to advance, but they were turned back by the Sumter riflemen. At this critical moment, C.H. DuRant spotted a Union soldier coming to the causeway from behind the mill house. A well-aimed musket ball caused this man to "reel and fall" and Colonel Pressley ordered the mill house burned to avoid its use as protection for the enemy.

Lieutenant McQueen continued to hold back the enemy forces until he fell at his post. Pamperya helped thwart a second attempt of Potter's men to cross the causeway. Shots ringing back and forth from the two sides, "Rebel" yells, falling branches caused a state of utter confusion. But the Confederates, through sheer determination, continued to hold back the enemy, though their ammunition soon began to run low.

After about two and a half hours of desperate fighting, the Yankee Colonel Cocoran, guided by a traitor, who it was believed had formerly worked at the mill, came by a devious and little known way through the swamp, leading the 108th New York Regiment of White troops.and approached the defenders from the rear.[168] Discovered by an "inexperienced but determined" band of men under the command of Col. George W. Lee, they were met by "murderous fire." However, the brave little band of Southerners, finding themselves surrounded, were forced to give up the fight.

In the last moments of fighting, Pamperya was still standing, bravely and calmly, waiting till his final effort would do the most good. When the Federals were scarcely 50 yards away, he fired his last shot. In answer, the enemy opened fire on him, though a Federal officer tried to restrain his men, exclaiming, "Spare that man, don't fire at him, for he is too brave to die." But the cry came too late. He fell at his post almost immediately.

The battle was over – and so was the war, for it was on that day, April 9, 1865, that General Lee surrendered at Appomatox, though the news did not reach this part of South Carolina till some time later.

Potter now had an open road to Sumter, a town that he considered important in his raid of destruction, because of its rich cotton lands, its position on the railroad between Wateree and

Florence, where were trapped locomotives and freight cars, its hospital facilities and its munitions depot.

Before moving into town, however, the Yankees took time to bury their dead (26 of their men had been killed). They placed the bodies in large graves over which they burned limbs and fence rails.

While their men were fighting, women and children in the town were frenziedly preparing for the worst by hiding food and valuables in the most unlikely places. As for the clothes, each person put on as many garments as possible. Dr. Anne King Gregorie records in her **History of Sumter County** that Mrs. McKagen, who was living at the time on the corner of Washington and Liberty Streets, put her meat supplies in the loft of the chicken house, her silver and linen in holes under the house, and much of the clothing into a large piano box which was converted into a couch for her daughter-in-law, who was ill with pneumonia.[169] Some residents took their treasures into the swamps for hiding. Capt. Robert Andrews saved a four-horse wagonload of Dr. China's valuables by concealing them in Cedar Bay. Many other ruses were used for the protection of property.

Then zero hour struck! Potter, with his well-trained soldiers and his motley crew of followers, reached the city. His cavalry rode up Main Street and into Liberty, thus announcing his arrival. One camp was near the depot, another is said to have been on the back of the lot where McLaurin Junior High School now stands and a third was on Liberty Street. Potter and his staff set up headquarters, it is believed, in the Altamont Moses home on Washington Street.

The work of destruction began at once with the burning of the depot, railroad shops and cotton warehouses. Groups went from house to house, seeking contraband weapons, or so they claimed. In reality they were on the search for food, clothing, money and other valuables. Countless stories have been told of how the members of families were tortured in one way or another, when it was difficult for these ruthless invaders to find the objects of their search.

Some of the troops followed the railroad to Mayesville, where they destroyed seven boxcars and a bridge. Another group went toward Manchester. Tracks, trestles and boxcars for six miles on each side of Sumter were destroyed and in the town itself, four locomotives and several boxcars were burned. The new Sumter jail and the old one, which had been made into a town hall, were also burned. The courthouse was damaged and the furniture ruined. These are only samples of the violation of life and property that went on and on.

One of the first acts of the invaders was to collect all the

Negroes in the town – men, women and children – and take them to the depot where they were put under guard. When Potter left town, practically all were lured into following him with the promise of "40 acres and a mule," a promise which, of course, was not kept. In order to feed the multitude of approximately 1,000 from Sumter along with the thousands collected along the way, he allowed his men to confiscate food and livestock as they passed through the country.

After the Federals left Sumter, Mr. Augustus Solomons and Mr. A.J. Moses went out to the battle site to attend to the burial of the Confederate dead (12 were killed in the battle). One unknown Yankee soldier, who died while the troops were in Sumter, was buried in the Presbyterian churchyard, it is said. Some years ago his remains were placed in the Sumter cemetery.

Potter meanwhile continued to blaze a destructive trail westward, establishing headquarters in the Richard Singleton mansion in the High Hills of Santee, with his regiments camping along the road to Stateburg. In this area they followed their same pattern of destruction. Homes, barns, ginhouses, and other buildings were burned, while the inhabitants were treated with contempt and molested in an even worse manner. Some were even killed, one young man being buried under the corner of the Singleton house.

In an incomplete report of his raid, Potter listed as destroyed 32 locomotives, 250 cars, 100 cotton gins and presses, 5,000 bales of cotton, more than 1,000,000 feet of lumber and vast stores of government supplies. After this report there was continued devastation in the area with several skirmishes between the Northern regiments and small Southern detachments, who were trying vainly to protect their possessions.

A letter written by "Aunt Maria" Haynsworth, as she was called by her family, stated: "It was the General's orders that private property should be respected." That was a tribute paid to General Potter that has come down through generations of the Haynsworth family; though in most places his orders were disobeyed, credit must be given where credit is due.

One example of his personal intereference with the threats of some of his men was at Spring Hill, where he drove them from the home where an aged woman was ill. He ordered his surgeon to treat her, and he offered her medicines and food that she needed so desperately.

Another case when he intervened in a threat of pillage and death was at "Milford," the beautiful home of Governor Manning. A mob of soldiers entered the mansion from the rear and a sergeant had his gun aimed at the head of the Governor when someone shouted, "The General is at the front door!" Manning, turning his back on the mob, went to the front door to meet General Potter.

When the general spoke admiringly of the lovely home, the Governor replied, "It was built by a man from New England by the name of Potter, and I suppose a man from New York by the name of Potter will destroy it."

The General's reply was, in part: " . . . that is not my intention. Your place shall be protected."

At last the horrors of war came to an end, but never would those who suffered through those days of fighting, pillaging and burning forget the atrocities perpetrated by the enemy. Peace was proclaimed, but well did the womanhood of Sumter and South Carolina know the price paid for that peace.

"Sumterites, a valiant people, ready to fight for their homes and to die for their beliefs, now began the long struggle to rebuild from the ashes of their beloved city."

Shaw Air Force Base

How many remember when there was no Shaw Air Force Base? When almost 40 years ago this gigantic military city that has meant so much to Sumter County in so many ways did not exist?

"The site selected for the Base is a tract of 2,828.4 acres seven miles west of Sumter on Highway 76, the road to Columbia. Without the roads it is composed of 2,797.75 acres," so ran **The Herald** account.

This school was designed to be one of the largest in the Southeast and the land on which it was to be constructed was selected by the Air Service. It consisted of 28 tracts, the largest owners being Mrs. Lily M. Levi, Wyndham Manning, the Friersons and W.C. and J.E. Eldridge.

After the officers of the Southeastern Air Corps Headquarters had looked over the sites around Sumter, they wrote the Chamber of Commerce, asking if the city and county could procure options for the land. General Weaver stated that "he considered it one of the best sites to be found anywhere for an Army flying school base."

The projected date for the completion of the facility after the preliminary transactions (which took place in May) was November 8, 1941; and engineers estimated that the cost would be approximately two and a half million dollars.[170]

Credited with much of the effort to get the school for Sumter were Chamber of Commerce Secretary Bill Thompson, C.P.

Gable, John J. Riley, City Manager J.A. Raffield, Mayor F.B. Creech, John A. McKnight and others.

Mayor Creech, in announcing the good news, urged the citizens to welcome those who would come with the school to the community in a "truly Sumter spirit."

The school was named in honor of 1st Lt. Ervin David Shaw,[171] who was shot down over France, July 9, 1918.

The base at first was a basic flying school, with the first class arriving December 25, 1941. This was the first school in the United States to train pilots for night flying and landing without lights.

Shaw, after the war, was made a separation center for thousands of men being released from the service.

There was fear for a while that this base would be abandoned, but instead it became one of 85 bases to be kept. In 1945 it became headquarters for the training of Nationalist Chinese crewmen to fly B-25 airplanes.

After this program was completed, in 1948, it became Shaw Air Force Base. Two years later it was assigned to the Tactical Air Command and became the home of the Ninth Air Force.

The base has made national headlines more than once. In 1962, for instance, Shaw-based reconnaissance pilots made low-level flights over Cuba, photographing the Russian missile sites, for which the 363 Tactical Reconnaissance Wing received a unit citation from President Kennedy.

Shaw Air Force Base has meant much to the Sumter Community. Many who were stationed at the Base while in service, upon retirement have come back to Sumter to make their homes. There is a close relationship between the personnel at the Base and those in the Sumter community in business, educational, religious and cultural life.

PART XI. GENERAL ORGANIZATIONS

The 4-H Program Beneficial For Boys And Girls

For more than 50 years, Sumter County youth have had educational and recreational opportunities afforded by 4-H Clubs, and many adults have enjoyed the privilege of leading these clubs. The local 4-H program is sponsored by the United States Department of Agriculture, the Extension Division of Clemson University and Sumter County. Extension Agent T.B. Tillman and his associates direct the program in a very efficient manner; but without volunteer leaders, the outstanding work done by the young people in these clubs could never be successfully accomplished.

The good received in 4-H clubs by boys and girls from nine to 19 cannot be measured, and the satisfaction that leaders derive from their efforts is great indeed.

Several in Sumter County have been asked to give an evaluation of the program as gleaned from their participation as members and/or leaders.

Charles Brunson recalls with pleasure his days as a 4-H'er. His interest was swine and with 35 or 40 others had a wide-awake club, guided by leaders Tillman, Baker and McNair. Work involved in his project required much time, but it was all very worthwhile and enjoyable, as he remembers.

For Mrs. Ralph Gates, teaching sewing and cooking to girls has been a great joy. For years she led a club in her community, through which her girls won trips and scholarships for the good work that they had done. She has received national recognition.

Another, who for a number of years successfully led a group of young people in club work in Wedgefield, is Mrs. Reginald Goodman. From 10 to 15 youngsters were present for every meeting, choosing as their project the beautification of their town.

One of the most popular of 4-H projects is the Horse Club,

which involves both boys and girls. Various types of horses are owned and shown by the young people. Among these are the Tennessee walking horse, the three-gaited saddle horse, the quarter horse and ponies.

Each summer the horse owners spend a week at Camp Bob Cooper at Santee, where they receive basic training in caring for their horses. They are also instructed in the proper way to ride a horse and in the techniques that have proven most successful in showing their horses. But there is much fun for everybody during this stay at camp in addition to the training.

There are two horse shows during the year in which the boys and girls take part. One is during the Sumter County Fair and one in the summer. In these, the owners compete for ribbons and prizes. During the Fair they also exhibit the various kinds of riding equipment and other projects.

A very interested and enthusiastic leader in this work for many years was Mr. Derle Lowder. In recognition of his work, Mr. Lowder received the County Alumni Award in 1973 and the State Award in 1972.

Mr. Lowder said that it is very rewarding, not only to see the boys and girls under his leadership performing with skill and winning prizes for their efforts, but also to feel that he has been instrumental in instilling principles of good judgment and responsibility that will contribute to the building of character as these young people grow to maturity.

There are 4,000 boys and girls involved in 4-H Club work in Sumter County. Other phases of the work include livestock, clothing, food and nutrition, poultry, and woodwork.

Overall coordinator of 4-H work is now Mr. Ellis Watson and his assistants are Mr. Larry McKenzie, Mrs. Chalys Clarke and Mrs. Doloris Keller.[172]

Eastern Star Home Provides Loving Care

Attractive and inviting, the Eastern Star Home on North Main Street stands as the culmination of cherished dreams, carefully laid plans, and determined effort on the part of many interested persons.

Acting on faith that sometime, somehow their dreams would become a reality, in 1946 the Order of Eastern Star of South Carolina began collecting funds for a Home. And after four years (in 1950) enough money had been raised to begin work; while in the same year the annual assembly, considering the several sites that had been offered for the Home, decided upon the one in Sumter as the most suitable. Preparations were begun immediately for the erection of the building.

Late in the year 1951, the Home was completed and the doors were opened January 1, 1952, with Mrs. Beulah Evans in charge as the first matron. The first guest arrived February 1.[173]

Although the original building had only 12 guest rooms, plans provided for additional space to be added as soon as sufficient funds were available. In 1956 these planned additions were completed, and the Home now has 15 guest rooms, an infirmary unit with space for four patients, a large den, a sitting room, a television room, an adequate dining area, a chapter room where visiting chapters may have programs for those unable to attend regular chapter meetings (this room may also be used as a large dining room when the occasion demands), a roomy kitchen with a large utility room adjoining, a comfortable and attractive room for the matron, a small diet kitchen near the infirmary, wide halls that lend an air of spaciousness. If there is need, more guest rooms will be built in the future.

The Home is a non-profit institution operated by the 205 chapters of the Order of Eastern Star of South Carolina. Each member of each chapter makes a yearly contribution of $1.50 for its support. Those living in the Home are guests in every sense of the word, since they bear no part of their expense. Only Eastern Star members are eligible. Though the doors are open to both men and women, only two men have been guests at any time.

Having general supervision in the operation of the Home is a board of trustees consisting of 13 members from the state at large, together with Executive Director A.E. Garrenton. Mr. Garrenton served on the board for ten years, the limit of service in this capacity, before being elected as executive director.

One example of the thoughtful care that went into the planning of the Home is that all the guest rooms are single; consequently, each guest can enjoy privacy and quiet relaxation when she so desires, or she can meet with others to play games, watch television, or enjoy companionship as she wishes. Rooms are very comfortable, convenient, and "homey."

Furnishings throughout the building, donated by chapters or individuals, include some handsome antique pieces, as well as some more modern. All blend in excellent taste.

Chapters from every part of the state bring fresh vegetables and fruits in season, the surplus being kept in large freezers; articles of good clothing; or other equipment or commodities that can be used to advantage.

A trophy, on display in the sitting room, will be given to the chapter showing the most interest in and making the greatest contribution to the Home during the year.

Mrs. Johnny Baker, who has been in charge as matron for three years, with the aid of two cooks and five maids, keeps the Home spotless, prepares wholesome well-balanced meals for the well and carefully planned diets for the sick, and does all the other chores connected with housekeeping.

Those coming to the Home must be able to care for themselves; however, if they become ill or disabled, they receive the best of care. When there is a patient in the infirmary, someone stays on 24-hour duty to care for her. Seriously ill patients are taken to Tuomey Hospital for treatment.[174]

The building is surrounded by beautiful grounds. In the front are flowers, shrubbery, and lawn grass.

The back premises are large enough to afford a place for those who wish to walk for exercise. In a prominent place is a stone altar where are carved an open Bible and the symbols of Eastern Star as a reminder of the high principles upon which the Order is based.

The 13 guests now residing in the Home are from different parts of the state. They are listed with the chapter and town from which they come:

Mrs. Neally Addy, Brandon (92), Greenville
Mrs. Nell Anderson, Seneca (5), Seneca
Mrs. Anna B. Curran, Stella Vitae (99), Charleston
Mrs. Ella Dees, Azalea (192), Charleston
Mrs. Mary DuBose, Sumter (188), Sumter
Miss Olive Jones (147), Walterboro
Miss Lucile Kelly (59), Columbia
Mrs. Carrie Lancaster (130), Anderson
Mrs. Anna Renfrow, Beauclare (20), Sumter
Mrs. Gertrude P. Stokes, John Francis Gray (219), Anderson
Mrs. Ada Thomas, Mary P. Outz (1), Greenwood
Miss Ada Underwood, Beauclare (20), Sumter
Miss Sarah Walker, Community (13), Islandton

At present there are two vacant rooms for which applications are being considered.

In Evergreen Memorial Cemetery, the Home owns 36 lots in which those who have no family or home may be buried. Five have been laid to rest in this plot.

The same spirit that prompted the building of this Home is manifested in every comfort and convenience provided for those living within its walls. A compassionate concern for those who need loving care was the motive that inspired the dreams and consummated the plans for this lovely place which the guests gladly call "home."[175]

(Written in 1968.)

Golden Agers Enjoy Life

"What do we live for, if it is not to make life less difficult for each other," said George Eliot.

And surely it was such a sentiment that was the origin for Golden Age Clubs.

The purpose of these clubs is to afford older people an opportunity to share with others, bringing joy into other lives and thereby finding happiness for themselves.

The Golden Age Club of Sumter received the inspiration for its beginning through Mrs. R.D. Graham, who during a visit in Mooresville, North Carolina, was impressed with the accomplishments of such a club there.[176]

It was in 1957 when Mrs. Graham conceived the idea of having a club for older citizens in Sumter. At that time, Harry Bryan was director of the Parks and Recreation Department, and he entered wholeheartedly into the plan for organizing a Golden Age Club. After several organizations had been contacted for support in the venture, the V.F.W. Auxiliary agreed to sponsor the new group. During the first year, Mr. Bryan served as director of the club, there being no elected officers. On Thursday of each week the new club met in the Recreation Center for diversified programs planned by the director, with light refreshments at each meeting.

When the second year began, the group became more fully organized with a slate of officers, and activities continued in the same manner.

In 1964 because of certain changes in the Parks and Recreation Department, the Golden Age Club found it expedient to obtain some other meeting place.

At this time the Golden Age Club was able to purchase through the influence of Mrs. Martha Graham an old home built around 1845 by Hasell Dick. It was known as the Dr. Frank K. Holman Cottage and stood for many years on the southwest corner of North Main and West Calhoun Streets. In 1931 it was moved to West Calhoun and used for business purposes.

In 1966 this typical antebellum townhouse of classical design was moved to 436 West Hampton Avenue on a lot that had been previously bought by the Golden Age Club.

To move the house, the moving company found it necessary to remove the wings from the central part of the house and replace them after the building was established in its new location. Mrs. Graham stated that the move was very skillfully and satisfactorily made.

In 1970 the Sumter County Historical Commission placed a marker on the quaint little house. [177]

The next task was to furnish the new home of the Golden Agers. The response from friends was prompt and generous. Manufacturing plants, other businesses, clubs and individuals made donations of tables, chairs, kitchen equipment and other items needed in a club house.

The building contains two club rooms, a dining room, a kitchen, a game room, and a room at the back used for storage. All rooms are comfortably heated and attractively arranged. A few other organizations, upon request, use the buildings for meetings.

Continuing the custom of years, the club still meets every Thursday morning. Sometimes there is a planned program; for instance, once a month the telephone company presents a program, usually showing a film. At times there is a devotional program, and at other times the theme is patriotic. Always there is a social period with a meal served.

Once each year the Pilot Club serves a dinner and gives a variety program for the pleasure of the members. At Christmas time the club has an especially enjoyable affair.

There are various table games which the members enjoy greatly. Some of these are bridge, checkers and bingo (favorite). At the rear of the house is sufficient space for some outdoor games such as shuffleboard.

Expenses, including taxes, insurance and utilities, though rather heavy, are borne by the members themselves. Twice each year they have a sale of handmade articles, as well as cakes, pies, cookies, preserves and other "goodies" contributed by the members.

Mill ends donated by a cloth manufacturing plant in the area are made into children's dresses, aprons, pillow cases, rugs, throws and other articles designed by the ingenuity of the members. These are sold at the semiannual bazaars.

Mrs. Graham said, "We like to do things for others, too; so we send throws to the Veterans' Hospitals for use by amputees." Frequently the club sends remnants and scraps to the State Hospital and Hopewell Home to provide a pastime for patients who are able to do some hand work, reported Mrs. Graham. The club members often remember the Salvation Army with gifts, also.

Lack of transportation to and from the club house has been at times a definite handicap. For a long while the Star Cab Company transported those who did not have a means of travel. When it became necessary for this company to cease this service, for a time some of the members had difficulty in getting to the meetings. However, the Junior League came to the rescue, graciously offering to assume the responsibility of transportation, thus solving a real problem.

"The pale greens of spring and the dark greens of summer are wonderful, but they are made for the harvests of autumn." So the autumn of life is really the Golden Age and these Golden Agers, having made their contributions which are being enjoyed by those in the springtime and summer time of their lives, deserve the best.

Relief Commission

The economic depression that rocked the country in the late 1920's and 30's was felt in Sumter County not only in the closing of banks and the failure of businesses . . . many even felt the cruel pangs of hunger and cold.

At first the only relief available was that provided by the county for those taken to the "Poor House," which was really a few crude huts on the outskirts of the city off North Main Street in the location where the Eastern Star Home now stands. Space there was limited and numbers of destitute families suffered for help. The town also employed a city nurse, Miss Antonia Gibson, who was dedicated to her task of caring for the sick; but her funds were so limited that she was greatly handicapped in her work. It is said that she had $2.50 a month to provide milk for newborn babies.

In 1927 two young ladies – Misses Edgar and Edna Rosnick – came from Salvation Army Headquarters in Florence to help minister to the needy. From their small salaries they rented a house on North Washington Street in which to live. Discouraged by the tremendous need and the scarcity of funds, they decided to return to Florence. Before leaving, they approached Robert T. Brown in tears, telling him that for three days and nights a line of hungry men, women and children had stood in front of their house, begging for bread which they could not provide.

They expressed their reaction to the needs in Sumter to the right person. Mr. Brown immediately began making plans to relieve a situation that he had been unaware of in his town and community. Obtaining from these ladies descriptions of five of the worst cases, he went to H.G. Osteen, who gladly published the needs of these families on the front page of **The Item.** When citizens of Sumter learned of the great needs, they began bringing contributions. Each day **The Item** published the plight of needy families and the amounts of donations coming in, thus keeping before the public the progress of the program.

In the meantime Mr. Brown was instrumental in organizing

what was known as the Sumter County Relief Commission with Brice Waters of the Boad of Trade (Chamber of Commerce) as secretary-treasurer. The Commission consisted of one representative each from the City Council, County Board of Commissioners and County Delegation, as well as the pastors of all white churches in the county.[178]

The second-story rooms of the R.T. Brown Tire Company (now Hughes, 116 North Main Street) were turned over to the workers as a collection and distribution center. In the meantime two other helpers from the Salvation Army in Florence came to Sumter to help in the work of the Commission.

Donations of money, food, clothing, and fuel poured in steadily as people learned of the suffering in the county. Contributions were kept in four accounts – food, clothing, fuel and drugs. Stores gave generous discounts and sold commodities on lenient terms. Not only the wealthy sent gifts but those of more moderate means gave what they could.

As cases were reported from all parts of the city and county, the Salvation Army workers and Miss Gibson investigated to ascertain where the needs were most urgent. According to Mr. Brown the work was carried on in a Christian spirit with workers feeling the leadership of God in investigations and giving help.

As the program progressed, it was found that many mothers could work if there was a place for their children. The next step then was the renting of a house that could serve as a home for several families where some mothers cared for the children while others went to work. The first building obtained was the old Haynsworth home on the corner of Salem and Haynsworth (where Mrs. R.B. Bultman now lives). Later the large Martha W. Graham house, on a ten-acre plot of land on Broad Street (where the School District 17 office later stood), was used and as many as 25 lived there as a temporary home.

Some of the cases were heartbreaking. In one instance there was an old man with five little children living in a hut with a clay chimney at one end. The other end had fallen and there was just room near the chimney for the six to huddle in front of the fireplace with no covering at night except sacks.

In another cabin there was an old man who had been in bed so long that he was covered with sores and his only companions were two little girls, one six and one three.

These are only two of the heartbreaking cases of poverty and illness found in the county when investigations were made.

Under the leadership of R.T. Brown, who gave in generous and unselfish devotion to the task of ministering to the hungry and sick, of his time, talents, and material possessions, the Sumter County Relief Commission continued its work until the mid-

30's when the Salvation Army set up headquarters in Sumter and the Department of Public Welfare was established. The good done by this commission can never be fully realized and appreciated.

Around 1931 the ERA was funded by the federal government with Brice Waters as the director. People were appointed as "visitors" to go out into the county to find those needing aid. At first the "visitors" included Adele Minahan, Caroline McElveen, Rekah Francis, Gussie Williams, Ruth Parker, and Stella Dabbs.[179]

Then in 1935 the Department of Public Welfare came into being with Mrs. Florence Bolger as director. She served 31 years, directing the work with a staff at one time of 24. In the 1960's the Department of Health, Education and Welfare was created and is still administering help to those in need in the county.

Outreach Of Salvation Army

"Frontiers have always been the concern of armies – whether to attack or defend them, whether to expand or hold them. But the concern of the Salvation Army is not with geographical boundaries. This unique organization, structured on a military pattern, is concerned with the frontiers of faith and spiritual, emotional and physical well being of all men."

In order to hold the frontiers already gained and to expand the victories won, the Salvation Army carries on a many-faceted ministry dedicated to the physical, social and religious welfare of men, women and children of every race, color and creed in 69 countries and geographical areas.

Sumter's Citadel, located on Kendrick Street, is engaged in typical Army activities, touching the lives of many needy people.

One project of this Corps, which has been a most worthwhile venture, is the Salvation Army Graham Emergency Children's Shelter, housed in a 100-year-old home (once a parsonage of the First Baptist Church), donated for the purpose by the Graham family, with arrangements made by Mrs. R.D. Graham of Sumter.

The aim of this Shelter is to provide a temporary home for children who suddenly become homeless, and are sometimes in danger, until they can be placed in permanent homes. The idea took shape when the immediate need of four children was reported to Captain Chastain, who took these four into his own home until other arrangements could be made.[180]

Obviously such a project is costly, not only in work, which the Salvationists gladly do, but in money as well. What is the financial cost? Who pays for this service for which there is a definite need as all will agree?

The home was overcrowded and was later torn down and a new brick home large enough to accommodate 20 children was erected. This new home, too, is known as the Martha Graham Children's Home.

Perhaps there may be people who are unaware of the existence of the Salvation Army until they see the kettles on the street at Christmas time, where volunteers ring the bells or play music, inviting the passersby to give coins to bring cheer to needy families. True, that is one phase of the Army's work because it seeks to minister to every need of man.

However, holding fast the religious purpose for which Gen. William Booth founded the Army more than a century ago in the slums of London, it has many arms of service through which it reaches out to save the lost. General Booth's words were, "Go for the lost, and go for the worst."

And this is the Army's ultimate aim. A project such as the Emergency Shelter is only one of the many agencies in Sumter and elsewhere used to fulfill this purpose.

According to the December 9, 1965, issue of **The Wall Street Journal**, the Salvation Army had at that time a budget of $100 million a year and operated almost 2,200 facilities of various kinds in this country alone.

To show something of the tremendous outreach of the Army in many parts of the world, a listing of some of its facilities in 1968 is given here: 220 rehabilitation centers, 400 centers for the homeless, 10 institutes for the blind, 30 centers for alcoholics, 145 children's homes, six leprosaria, 17,000 religious and neighborhood centers and outposts.

It is a deplorable fact that work has been closed in many Communist countries. In Cuba, for instance, the government has removed the children from the children's homes, leaving them empty.

The philosophy of the Salvationists differs from other agencies in that it always responds immediately to emergencies. As has been said, " . . . central to the Army's philosophy is to meet the needs as immediately as it can. If you need help, you won't be put on a waiting list." And it is equally true that it meets the needs of anyone regardless of the extent of his condition. Garry Moore of television fame, who has been a member of the advisory board of the Army in the New York area, says, "It's my favorite charity because they take people nobody else will touch. They take care of people who are lost – even filthy bums. They never say no to anyone."

The same issue of **The Wall Street Journal** states: "Such work requires a rare breed of men and women who can spend their lives amid the worst sort of degradation – and still not lose all faith in mankind."

The words of Maj. Mary Davis, a dedicated Salvationist in New York, give the secret of being able to work under such conditions. "They need someone to love them, and I don't think I could love them enough . . . but," she continued, "I prayed I could love them enough and it was easy."

In comparison with the amount of work done, the Army is small. Throughout the world there are only about one million members, with 25,000 of these as officers. Most of the members are "soldiers," people whose church is the Salvation Army.

Officers receive housing and a small salary, while soldiers receive no pay from the Army. They work at regular jobs but, while carrying out Army activities, they wear the uniform.

Each unit has a local Advisory Board consisting of volunteers who represent various walks of community life.

In addition to their work in the regular centers, Salvationists are always on hand to help in natural disasters and other such emergencies. For example, emergency units supply coffee, soup and sandwiches to firemen during major fires, and aid those driven from their homes with food, used clothing and bedding.

Some of the Army's institutions charge a small fee to help defray expenses, but many phases of the work depend entirely upon charity.

Officers receive their training in the Army's two-year schools, four of which are in the United States, one for each of the territories into which the Army divides the country. For these schools a high school diploma is the only educational requirement for admission; however, many have earned college degrees before beginning officer training.

The curriculum in the officers' schools includes Bible study, homiletics and theology as the major courses.

A few case histories may serve to emphasize the dedicated service that the Salvation Army renders:

"An elderly gentleman without a family was living alone in a rooming house. Day after day went by with no visitors, nothing to do, nothing to look forward to.

"Then he was invited to a nearby Salvation Army Center with a special program for senior citizens. Now he is there every day. He runs errands, sings in the Glee Club, sets original verses to popular music for the club. His step is sprightlier. He smiles often. Life has become meaningful again."

"George, a nearly illiterate young man with deformed hands had spent most of his years behind bars. He couldn't get a parole because he had no chance for a job. This institution felt that he could not be trained to work. He was assigned to empty garbage cans.

"Then the Salvation Army stepped in. They gave George a chance to learn how to work. Eventually he got a job as maintenance man in a hospital. He is now supporting himself."

"Jacqueline, 10, was sent to a Salvation Army summer camp because her activities in the city were very limited. Her mother died when she was seven and she was being raised by a maternal aunt. Her adjustment in school was poor. Her first few days at camp were very difficult, but gradually the counselor won her confidence. During her stay at camp she gained 3½ pounds."

Each day the Salvation Army reaches out a helping hand to many, many persons – the Skid Row outcast, the prisoner, the parolee, the hospital patient, the disaster victim, servicemen and women, youth in need of guidance, the unwed mother, and many others.

The Army, striving to meet necessity wherever and whenever it arises, needs and merits strong reinforcements in order to answer the ever-increasing calls for help that come daily.

Sumter takes pride in giving opportunities to young people for physical, mental and spiritual growth, and one of the chief projects designed for this purpose is that of the Salvation Army Boys' Club.

This organization is affiliated with the Boys' Clubs of America, a movement of phenomenal scope and influence in the great task of helping boys become great men and strong leaders for the future.

The history of Boys' Clubs of America reaches back more than 100 years, the first group having been started in 1860 in Hartford, Connecticut, by some ladies who were possessed with a deep concern for boys wandering on the streets and with a vision and love that prompted them to take action. Rooms were provided where these boys could come and find a warm place to play games.

These groups were called for convenience "boys' clubs," and the idea caught fire, becoming a national movement with clubs in towns and cities throughout the country, providing recreation and training for boys six to eighteen.

No longer is the purpose of Boys' Clubs of America to keep boys off the streets and give them a place for recreational activities, but the scope has widened and the purpose of these clubs now is "to promote the health, social, educational, vocational and character development of boys."

It was with this purpose in mind that interested citizens of Sumter began the Sumter Boys' Club in 1972, the first meeting place being 15 Telephone Street. This location was chosen because of the prevalence at that time of juvenile delinquency in that area, and as a result delinquency has been greatly reduced.[181]

The meeting place was soon moved to an old building on Kendrick Street, but in September of the same year, the building was burned by an electrical fire. After one or two other moves the club established temporary headquarters at the old City Jail. Of course the work has been hampered by lack of adequate space.

However, a much better day for the club is here. The Salvation Army, after receiving approval from the United Way, which furnishes aid for the Boys' Club, undertook a capital fund drive. Success marked this effort with the raising of $300,000, a part of which has been used in the construction of a new headquarters building.

Land was purchased on Belk Street in the Boulevard Road area of the city. The new 12,600 square foot building, standing on a nine-acre lot, is complete. The Boys' Club is now becoming established in these spacious quarters.[182]

The building has the following accommodations: a senior game room for youth 13 and above, a junior game room for those from six through twelve; an exercise and weight-lifting room, a library and meeting room, a shop, a club room, a photo lab, a kitchen, locker rooms for boys and girls (girls also use the facilities two days a week), offices for directors, storage rooms, and a gymnasium.

The program planned for the club has many and varied activities. For the building of strong bodies there are various types of athletics and gymnastics; such as baseball, football, basketball, soccer, tennis, track, karate, etc. Special emphasis is placed on good health and physical fitness. There are eye, ear, blood pressure and dental checks.[183]

Some of the educational offerings planned are courses in beginning auto mechanics, beginning electronics, woodworking and carpentry, first aid, reading, debating, newspaper work. There are also opportunities for those interested in art, music, photography, puppetry, etc.

There are special events such as field trips, picnics, tournaments, parties and a week's summer camp for boys and one for girls.

The Sumter Boys' Club has a membership goal of 1,000. Most of the financing comes from membership fees and the United Way.

The club rooms are open from 9:00 to 9:00 Monday through Friday, 9:00 to 7:00 on Saturday and 2:00 to 4:00 on Sunday. Friday night from 7:00 to 9:00 is family night each week.

True is the saying that, "A man never stands so tall as when he stoops to help a boy." And the men of Sumter are lending valuable help in a very worthwhile cause.

Sumter Mental Health Association, One Of First Four In State

Organized in 1950 by Bobby Lovvern and Chaplain Milton Kempson from the State Hospital in Columbia, the Sumter Mental Health Association was one of the first four in South Carolina. The organizational meeting was held at the Coca-Cola Meeting Room.

Mrs. Carolin Foxworth had worked with G. Werber Bryan, Mrs. Kathryn Holdom, Mrs. Bessie Forrester and Mrs. Ethel Weinberg in forming plans for the organization. Others present for this first meeting included Mrs. Martha Graham, Mr. Harry Ryttenberg, and Mrs. John Hoar.[184]

Among those serving as president of the local association throughout the years have been Rabbi Aaron Levy, William Snow, William Brubeck, John S. Hoar, Johnny Parker, Dr. John Schenkel, Mrs. Sue King, Mrs. Foxworth, Mrs. Myrtis Logan, Mrs. Eloise Courtney, Olin Richbourg, Mrs. Laura Ayers, Fred Schiffley, and Miss Mary Ann Gregoire.

The local association has had no regular meeting place, but it has met regularly, carrying on a most significant educational program at first through the P.T.A. with the help of Miss Elsye McKeown, who worked with the Educational Division of the South Carolina Department of Mental Health. She made a great contribution to the medical health program in the state. She received the Distinguished Service Award from the state association for her contribution during the fifties and sixties, before moving to Atlanta.

In 1954 the Sumter Mental Health Association was instrumental in organizing the South Carolina association, the first office of which was in Sumter. Moving spirit in the forming of the state association was G. Werber Bryan, with the help of the Jaycees and Miss Nettie Marlowe (later Mrs. Harry Bryan). Bryan was the first president of SCMHA and his brother, Harry R. Bryan, was the first executive director. The first newsletter of the state association was "It's True," edited by Mike Karvelas, also of Sumter.[185]

Another valuable service of the association was the work done in helping to bring in 1960 a mental health expert, M.R. Newton, psychologist, to work with the schools of Districts 2 and 17. He did much toward pinpointing child problems and showing the treatment to be used in solving these problems through the organization of the Child Study Project, which received the Gold Star Award for the best such project in the nation.[186]

Influence was exerted by the local association in the establishment of a Mental Health Clinic, which operated from a small building with a trailer annex on East Calhoun, serving Sumter, Clarendon, Lee and Kershaw Counties. This Center was opened in 1963 under the directorship of Dr. Robert N. Milling. In 1971 a new $300,000 mental health center was built on the northern corner of the short block fronted by Lafayette Drive, East Calhoun and Magnolia Streets. After Dr. Robert N. Milling resigned, Dr. Glen N. Burgess became new director. Later Dr. Glenn Ayers, who came as a psychiatrist in 1965, became director. It is said that he should have special recognition because of his dedication to his work in the clinic and also for the great help he has been to the association in an advisory capacity.[187]

The Sumter Association was the first to receive a service award from the state association. It was also the first to form a social club for former patients. This organization, named the Fellowship Club, was designed for the rehabilitation of returned patients or out-patients of the Mental Health Center or the State Hospital. It was organized in 1964 with Mrs. Logan as director, assisted by Mrs. Marion Pitts (coordinator), Mrs. Robert Jones, Mr. Jones and Mrs. Dorothy Tanner.

After-care programs in which many volunteers participate continue to be among the most significant phases of mental health work of the local association. This work is carried on locally and also rendered at the various facilities operated by the State Hospital in Columbia.

Many from Sumter County have made countless contributions to mental health on the local, state and national levels.

In addition to his service in Sumter County and as organizer and first president of the state association, Bryan has served as a director of the national association. He received the Distinguished Service Award from the state organization and for many years has served on the South Carolina Mental Health Commission. Recently the G. Werber Bryan Psychiatric Hospital, off Farrow Road in Columbia, was named in his honor.

Mr. Hoar received recognition in 1979 for his work in the area of legislation and public affairs for the past 30 years. He is a recipient of the D.S.A. from the State Mental Health Association which he served as president. He has also served on the National Board of Directors.

The contributions made during her life by Mrs. Logan to the cause of mental health on local and state levels could never be counted. Her interest in the mentally ill extended from children to the elderly. She was responsible for Camp Logan for mentally ill children and was instrumental in having the children separated from adults at the South Carolina State Hospital. She directed a volunteer service program on local and statewide levels. She established the Logan Foundation of Santee-Wateree Mental Health Center. She, too, was a recipient of D.S.A. from S.C.M.H.A.

Mrs. Foxworth, senior volunteer for the Santee-Wateree Center since 1974, deserves special recognition for her untiring efforts in the interest of mental health. As a school principal, she was especially interested in the mental problems of children. As a charter member of the Sumter Mental Health Association, she has worked tirelessly in promoting programs undertaken by this organization.

In 1978 she received the highly deserved Outstanding Chapter Volunteer Award presented by the South Carolina Mental Health Association, with the Commendation for her "special achievements, one being the training and orientation of volunteers at the Santee-Wateree Mental Health Center."

Others receiving the D.S.A. for outstanding performance include Harry R. Bryan, M.R. Newton, and Miss McKeown.

The Sumter Mental Health Association has made countless other contributions to advancement in the field of mental health. In a recent speech to the Palmetto Rotary Club, Dr. William S. Hall, state commissioner of mental health, spoke of the Sumter area as being "supportive and innovative" in the development of mental health care. He said also, "Sumter and Sumter County are the cradle of the volunteer mental health movement in South Carolina."[188]

Stateburg Literary And Musical Society

As a successor to the Claremont Society which was organized in 1786 by Gen. Thomas Sumter, Dr. Richard Furman and other prominent men of the day for the purpose of establishing an Academy, the Stateburg Literary and Musical Society was begun in 1885 under the influence of Col. John Julius Dargan. In response to his invitation, 13 interested men and women met at his home, Woodville, on May 22, 1885, and on that day was born an organization that became the "cultural outlet for the people" of Stateburg and later attracted people of like mind from other sections of Sumter County.[189]

Organized with the lofty purpose of promoting "interest in literature and music as essential to gracious family living and a cultured community, and to better understanding of the culture of other countries," the society has continued for almost a century to attract those who desire to have a cultural environment in which to live.

Those who were present at Woodville on that day so long ago were W.J. Rees, Mr. and Mrs. H.L. Pinckney, Col. and Mrs. Dargan, Mrs. Sumter, Miss Minnie Rees, N.R. Pinckney, Mrs. Burgess, Miss Lizzie Anderson, Wallace Anderson, and Miss Mary Childs.[190]

At first it was thought best not to have a formal organization with elective offices. The plan was to name at each meeting a man to act as chairman at the following meeting and to serve as president of the society until the next man took over. One duty of the presiding officer was to appoint a gentleman and a lady "to prepare and report to the society at its next meeting a list of readers and subjects for the entertainment of the Society at the meeting following this report . . . "

The group also agreed that no one should refuse to entertain the Society when asked. The meetings at first were fortnightly, but later changed to a monthly schedule. W.J. Rees presided at the first meeting.

After 10 meetings under the original plan, members decided to adopt a constitution and have duly elected officers. Therefore, on October 2, 1885 (the 11th meeting), with Col. Dargan in the chair, a constitution was presented by J. Singleton Moore and each article was accepted by the group.

This constitution officially declared the motto to be "Muscam et Musam Meditamus" ("We meditate on music and the Muse") and the purpose or object of the organization "to create through study a love for literature and music."

The article on membership provided that a prospective member must make written application and this application would be voted on (by secret ballot) at least one meeting after the presentation of application. The membership was limited to 25, and a new member could be received only when a vacancy occurred. And in order to assure regular attendance, the constitution required that a person be dropped from the roll if he or she missed three regular meetings without submitting to the president a valid reason (in writing) for his absence. Active members were those who attended meetings and served on programs. Associate members could attend meetings only by invitation.

The constitution further provided for the election of a president, vice president, and secretary-treasurer. These three officers were to be elected annually (by ballot) for a term of one year, with no one being allowed to hold the same office for more than two years. When the constitution was later amended, the provision was added that a nominating committee of three be appointed by the president to present names of nominees at the March meeting, and after nominations from the floor (if any) were made, the vote was to be taken.

There were only two standing committees: one on the "program of study for each year." This committee of five was responsible for presenting the program to the Society for approval and acceptance. The other committee was on membership, the duty of which was to investigate the eligibility of prospective members.

The last article in the Constitution read: "The Articles, Rules, and Regulations herein prescribed may be suspended on motion and by unanimous consent of the Society. Special meetings may be held at the call of the President."

The first officers elected were Col. John J. Dargan, president; Mr. H.L. Pinckney, vice president; Miss Lizzie Anderson, treasurer; Mr. W. Waties Rees, secretary; and Mr. W.J. Rees, critic.

Members present at the organization meeting, in addition to officers named above, were as follows: Dr. W.W. Anderson, Mrs. W.W. Anderson, Miss Katie Anderson, W.W. Anderson, Gordon Bradley, M.M. Bradley, Sam Bradley, DeSaussure Bull, H.B. Bull, Mrs. DeSaussure Bull, Dr. H. Burgess, Mrs. H. Burgess, Miss Ammie Burgess, Miss M.M. Childs, Miss Belle Caldwell, W.H. Darby, Mrs. J.J. Dargan, Miss Addie Burgess, and Miss Julia Burgess.

For the first six years, the presidents were men. After Col. Dargan served a half-year, the gavel was turned over to Dr. J.C. Spann for the last half of the first year. He was followed by W.W. Rees for the first half of 1887; then Col. Dargan assumed leadership again, serving until the end of 1889. Mr. Mark Reynolds was president for the next two years and Col. Dargan again took over the leadership.

During 1894-95 there was no record kept. Miss A.H. Burgess became president in 1896 and for a year the Society functioned as a "Round Table Society."

It was about this time, for some unrecorded reason, the male membership fell by the wayside, but for more than fourscore years the enthusiasm of the ladies has for the most part been kept alive.

From 1907 to 1919 the Society was known as "The Stateburg Rural Improvement League." Then in 1920 the Society again took its original name and Mrs. E.N. Sullivan was the president. There are no minutes available for the next several years.

Others leading the society through the years until 1949, when the 64th anniversary was observed, were Miss Henrietta Dargan, Mrs. T.H. Rogers, Mrs. J.J. Dargan, Mrs. J.L. Frierson, Mrs. L.E. Leavell (twice), Mrs. J.F. Williams (twice), Mrs. S. Oliver Plowden (twice), Mrs. Stanley F. Morse, Mrs. Paul K. Bowman, Mrs. Mark Reynolds, Jr., Mrs. Wyndham Manning, Mrs. E.E. Rembert, Mrs. Lee H. Thomas, Mrs. Fred B. Beck, and Mrs. Willis D. Ryan.

The Stateburg Literary and Musical Society had its first typed Yearbook for the year 1930-31. On the front of this yearbook and somewhere near the beginning of all succeeding yearbooks may be seen, in addition to the usual information, the following from Henry Timrod:

"No fairer land hath fired a poet's lays
Or given a home to man."

During the year of this first printed yearbook there were still two men connected with the Society as Honorary Members – J.D. Blanding and E.S. Dunbar. The following year the Rev. G.H. Harris was added to the fast disappearing male "population," and he remained loyal to the group for several years.

Beginning with 1933 a subject to be studied for the entire year was presented by the program committee to be approved and accepted by the Society. Each month the program centered around the theme selected. This plan was continued with a few exceptions through 1959-60.

To illustrate the serious dedication of the group to intellectual and cultural improvement and to a greater knowledge of the cultures of other countries, a few of these subjects are here listed:

"Some Literary Centers of the English-Speaking World"
"Statesmen, Music, and Customs of Many Lands"
"Operas and Oratorios"
"Italy"
"Modern Achievements"
"Famous Women"
"Latin America"
"Peace and Post-War Planning"

These few will suffice to show the ambitious intent of these intellectual and artistic women (and a few men) of Sumter County to improve the community and lay a cultural foundation for coming generations.

And for the most part, members adhered strictly to these yearly themes in planning the monthly programs. For instance on the subject "Famous Women," papers were given at the various meetings on George Eliot, Elizabeth Barrett Browning, Edna Ferber, Mary Roberts Rinehart, Jane Adams, Sara Delano Roosevelt, and Sumter's own Dr. Sophia Brunson.

Based on the theme "Modern Achievements" were papers and discussions on Amelia Earhart, Ann Lindberg, Life and Compositions of George Gershwin, sketches of other famous composers, Art and Artists, et cetera.

Sometimes special speakers were invited to discuss some phase of the subject for that particular year. Dr. James McBride Dabbs, for instance, spoke on "Modern Poets."

One of the most interesting themes studied in the attempt to understand the culture of other lands was the one on "Italy." The monthly subjects varied from history to religion to social life to literature to art to music. Some of the papers given had such titles as "Rome at the Time of Nero," "The Nature and Extent of the Papal Power," "Social Life in Rome at the Time of the Caesars," "Selections from **Quo Vadis**," "City of Cremona, Great Fiddle Makers, Stradivarius, Antonia," and "Venetian Art and Architecture."

Since the members were resolved to "Meditate on Music . . . ," there were always musical selections of one form or another in keeping with each theme. "Music in Song and Story." As a part of the program on Russia, "The Volga Boatman" was given, and selections from Beethoven and Mendelssohn were played on the program about Germany.

Another interesting manner in which the theme of a program was emphasized was by the way in which members answered the roll call. At one meeting during the year when English Literature was studied, each member answered with a quotation from Tennyson. At another each gave one of Kipling's works. And at still another each was asked to answer with a quotation from the Brownings.

On and on the list of yearly themes and monthly topics could go, but these few will suffice to impress the reader with the wide scope of interests possessed by members of the Stateburg Literary and Musical Society. Though members enjoyed the fellowship at the meetings, this has always been far from a social club.

There were a few times when the monthly meetings did not follow the subject for the year. Often at the December meeting the Christmas spirit prevailed and subjects were chosen to carry out that idea. One year there was a paper given on the Holy Land and Christmas Carols were sung. On another December program there was a paper on "Christmas in Legend and Story."

Another variant in the trend usually followed was "Husbands' Night and Anniversary." These special meetings were in October and quite often an outside speaker was invited.

In 1935 the 50th anniversary – a day of special significance – celebration was the outstanding social event of that year, enjoyed by the whole community.

The site for this event was "Marston," the home of Mrs. S.O. Plowden and her mother, Mrs. John J. Dargan, widow of Col. Dargan, founder of the Society. Much effort seemingly was put into preparation for the affair.

Special guest speaker was Dr. J. Rion McKissick, at that time dean of the department of journalism at the University of South Carolina.

In order to call to mind the outstanding achievements of the Society's 50-year history and to stimulate interest in future accomplishments, members presented a pageant, "Through the Years." The cast of characters included: Mrs. J. Frank Williams – "The Day We Celebrate"; Mrs. Mark Reynolds – "The Future."

A musical program was given by Miss Vivian Ellis, teacher of music at Winthrop Training School.

Concluding the program was an impressive candle-lighting ceremony led by Mrs. Plowden.

Mrs. Dargan, the only charter member present, was given a brass candlestick, holding a lighted taper in memory of the founder.

If the 50th anniversary was a special occasion, the 75th was special, special. Fittingly it, too, was celebrated at Marston, the home of Mrs. S.O. Plowden, daughter of the founder. The year was 1960.

Mrs. W.A. Brown, president, called the meeting to order; and Miss Julia Reynolds, program chairman, introduced the guest speaker, Dr. Dan Hollis, professor of history at U.S.C.

"Memories," "Last Night," and "The Last Rose of Summer" (as an encore) were sung by Mrs. W. C. Eldridge, accompanied at the piano by her mother.

After party dainties were served, with Mrs. J.M. Barnwell pouring punch, Mrs. Plowden lit the candles on the two-tiered birthday cake, saying: "That first group, gathered in Woodville home that summer evening, May 22, 1885, hardly realized the spark they were lighting would kindle into a flame that would grow and glow with inspiration for many years to come."

Mrs. P.K. Bowman paid the following tribute to the charter members after reading their names: "These voices eloquent of the past have been stilled. The echoes, the memories, the influence will always linger.

"The passion for the beautiful life reaches its height and most radiant beauty through the cultivation of the intellect. Life is not likely to give to us any richer intellectual stimulus ruled by high undaunting purpose than that of those charter members of the Stateburg Literary and Musical Society.

"We pay tribute again to these people whose noble vision, passions, and zest have passed safely to us and will pass through us to posterity."

A toast, given by Mrs. L.E. Leavell to the memory of Col. Dargan, follows in part: " . . . Col. Julius Dargan, imbued with the love of the finer things of life – literature, music and art – sent out the clarion call that summoned the charter members to gather at his home, Woodville, for the first meeting of the Stateburg Literary and Musical Society on May 22, 1885.

"No higher tribute could be paid to his love for truth and beauty than the words inscribed on his tomb taken from Shelley's 'Alastor':

'Every sight and sound from the vast earth and ambient air
Sent to his heart its choicest impulses.
The fountains of divine philosophy
Fled not his thirsting lips and all of great
Or Good, or lovely, which the sacred past
In truth or fable consecrates, he felt
And Knew.' "

The first custodian of Records was appointed in 1937. The first to hold this office was Mrs. Plowden, who carefully and lovingly kept all important records until recently when Mrs. L.W. Leavell was appointed to succeed her. Mrs. W. Loring Lee, Jr., is now custodian for the papers that have been written and presented to the Society.

Time has gone on and so has the Stateburg Literary and Musical Society. It has passed many milestones since the 75th anniversary and the total years of its history have reached 95. Some changes have come in the procedures and programs; the Constitution has been amended a few times; but the original plan of organization has remained much the same during its long and fruitful life.

Replacing those who first had a dream of promoting a more refined community, have been others in the generations that have come and gone who have continued to foster the high ideals inspired by their predecessors and have passed on the torch to today's Society members. They in turn have accepted the legacy by becoming associated with this historic organization and are keeping it alive for the coming generations.

PART XII. MEN'S ORGANIZATIONS

Post 15 American Legion Dedicated To Service

Organized September 2, 1919, Post 15, Sumter's Chapter of the American Legion, has been for the past 61 years dedicated to the service of country and mankind even as many of them were when they answered the call in 1917 to risk their lives in World War I and as many others were in other wars in which America has been involved.[191]

There were 15 charter members in Post 15, but the desire to have an organization through which these valiant men could continue to be of service drew others and 58 years later there were 925 loyal members.

In 1977 the Post, desiring to give special honor to veterans of World War I, planned a special meeting to be held in the American Legion Home. Thirteen of the veterans living at that time were present for the occasion. These were as follows: John W. Bailey, Charles E. Bradham, M.M. Brice, George H. Bultman, W.M. Crawford (Post Commander of Post 15), H.C. Edens, Sr., J.M. Edens, Sr., R.E. Galloway, J. Howard Kidd, Willard E. Kinzle, Waverly B. Levy, W.T. Nixon, and George D. Shore, Jr. (charter member Post 15).

Sumter Post 15 has made a notable impact on the life of Sumter through various activities, especially of the youth of the area. One of the outstanding contributions is through the gift of scholarships. One year four were given for study at the University of South Carolina-Sumter to students selected by the USC-S Faculty Scholarship Committee.

So pleased with the results from these scholarships, the following year Post 15 decided to give eight scholarships to the University and four to students in the Sumter Area Technical College.

It was also suggested that the Post pay expenses for one 4-H member each from Clarendon, Lee and Sumter Counties in 1977 for the National Convention in Chicago, Illinois.

One year the theme for the national organization was "The American Legion – It's Great to Belong" and that will be the theme for every year for members of Post 15, for their enthusiasm is spontaneous and wholehearted at all times.

This organization is supportive of the American Cancer Society programs, gives school awards to high school seniors, has reactivated the Sons of the American Legion program.

Perhaps the best known and most popular of Post 15 is the sponsoring of American Legion Baseball teams. It has sponsored more regional and sectional tournaments than any other Post in South Carolina. These tournaments draw teams from many places, such as North Carolina, Georgia, Alabama, Florida, Puerto Rico, and the Canal Zone.

Plans are now in the making for the Legion World Series to be held here in 1981.

In 1977 Post 15 celebrated the 50th anniversary of American Legion baseball in Sumter with a banquet attended by a large crowd of former coaches, players, Legion members and fans. The celebration was held at the Sumter County Exhibition Center.

All players and coaches during the 50 years were listed in the souvenir program booklets. Almost 500 former players were listed.

"John J. Riley was the dominant figure in the Post 15 baseball program from its inception as organizer and coach. In his honor, the City of Sumter dedicated the municipal facility, Riley Park, in his honor.

"Another outstanding coach of the P-15's, as he dubbed them, was W. Bernard "Bernie" Jones, who resigned after a successful tenure, turning the coaching duties over to the present coach, Hugh Betchman, who has also run an outstanding program." These comments were made by Robert Moise, who has great interest in Sumter's sports programs.

Other coaches through the years were Ellie Brunson, "Hutch" Hutchinson, Jim Partin, Harry Stokes and Larry Weldon.

Douglas W. Purdy is the present Legion baseball committee chairman and was instrumental in getting the 1981 American Legions World Series for Sumter.

Sumter Post has stood high in the national organization, having furnished many outstanding general officers; namely, three past Department Commanders – George D. Levy, Martin Rosefield and Oral Cox; two national committeemen; a District Commander; a Zone 4 Commander. Other men of distinction from Post 15 include a Medal of Honor Winner and Speaker of South Carolina House of Representatives.[192]

This post has held a place of honor in the state. It consistently wins the Community Service Award, and in 1977 was the recipient of the Post of Distinction Award. Honors named are indicative of the distinctive service rendered by Post 15 of the American Legion, and the tradition of service begun more than a half-century ago continues.

BPOE Original Goal Was To Help Others

Built upon the cardinal virtues of charity, justice, brotherly love and fidelity, the Benevolent and Protective Order of Elks had its beginning on Feb. 16, 1868.[193]

The original idea of such an organization was born in the heart of Charles Vivian, son of a clergyman in England, who came to New York to seek a place for himself in the world of the theatre and music. And though he was successful in these endeavors, his heart led him toward a more worthwhile goal – that of helping others who might be in need.

Seeking a symbol for their organization, he and his friends, who were moved by the same motive as he, decided upon the elk, after reading from a scientific article. The author described the animal as "strong in defense of its own, timorous of wrong doing and possessing other qualitites that man might emulate to his benefit."

Thus BPOE became an organization that was destined to grow, slowly at first it is true. However, as time passed, though Vivian died in 1880 at the age of 34, the increase of the number of clubs gained momentum, no doubt because of the altruistic spirit that prevailed among the members.[194]

Times have changed and needs are somewhat different, but the Order has never ceased to uphold its original purpose – to exemplify the virtues upon which it was built – charity, justice, brotherly love and fidelity.

Club 855 was organized in Sumter Nov. 25, 1935[195] with Shepard K. Nash as the first Exalted Ruler. The Sumter Club met at first in whatever meeting places were available, but soon purchased the beautiful home on the corner of Broad and Salem, which had been built by Thomas Wilson, a well known lumber magnate of Clarendon and Sumter Counties.

This lovely three-story home proved to be an excellent meeting place for the Club with plenty of room for all activities. However, in 1967 they decided to sell the home and buy a 100-acre plot at Second Mill. Since the dam had collapsed, the drained lake was proving a health hazard and the Club hoped to restore the area.

In 1971 the contracts were signed for the construction of the new club building. After the home on Broad Street was sold, the Club met in temporary quarters above the old Lawson Drug Store on North Main Street.

The Club is now enjoying its new building at Second Mill.

Following the motto of BPO Elks, Club 855 has done much for the improvement of life in Sumter. Having a special interest in Boy Scouts, the Club built a Scout Hut, ground for which was broken Mar. 18, 1859, on Club property adjacent to the swimming pool. Chairman of the Scouting Committee at that time was Dr. E.J. McGinnis. Under the direction of Harry Ryttenberg, a member of the committee, ground was cleared and Exalted Ruler John Henry Thomas lifted the first shovelful of dirt. Many businesses in Sumter contributed materials and money in this good cause and the hut was dedicated July 13 of the same year.

Scouts have been encouraged in many other ways by the Lodge. It feted Elk-sponsored Boy Scout Troop 332 after members of this troop won 249 out of a possible 250 points for camp standards maintained during their stay at Camp Coker that year.

Annually BPO Elks Club 855 followed the custom of entertaining Scouts with a banquet. Highlight of the banquet in 1962 was the presentation of the Eagle Scout award, the highest rank a Scout may reach. Recipient that year was Mike Twombley, Senior Patrol Leader of Troop 332. He also received a Scout watch from the Troop.

At this banquet were in addition to Boy Scouts, Cubs, Girl Scouts, Brownies and Sea Scouts.

Another service of the Elks for young people is a scholarship program, initiated for those maintaining a high scholastic average and having a financial need.

Other groups of boys and girls for whom the Elks have worked is the Sumter County Association of Retarded Children, March of Dimes and Youth Government Day in Sumter.

At least two significant programs have been a part of the emphasis of the Elks on current affairs. In 1958 the Sumter Elks paid tribute to the press and radio personnel of Sumter, Lee and Clarendon Counties, at which time the keynote speaker was the Hon. John J. Riley, U.S. Representative and a member of the Elks Club 855. Some of his remarks could well have been made in 1980. For instance he began his speech with these words: "Americans are placing entirely too much reliance on central government." Another statement pictures a situation that is true today: "The debt has gone to fantastic proportions, so much so that the bankers are charging high interest rates . . . "

Another phase of special emphasis of the Elks has been that of patriotism. In Flag Day ceremonies one year Sumter Club joined with other Elks in South Carolina in celebration. The speaker reminded the audience that 1,800 Elks Lodges pay tribute to the American flag.

He called attention to the patriotic programs promoted by Elks during World War II and the Korean conflict in establishing centers for service men, assisting in care of hospitalized veterans and supporting many other worthwhile programs for patriotic causes.

With Woodson W. Hurt as the present Exalted Ruler, BPOE 855 continues cooperation with the 2,000 and more Elks Clubs in the United States in a program of help and hope for handicapped children, of interest in improved higher education, of provision of aid to servicemen and veterans, of loyalty to the American government, of help in disaster relief and of other avenues of service.

Cain's Mill Club Began In 1929

One of Sumter's oldest social clubs for men is the Cain's Mill Club, organized in August of 1929 with 50 members.

First officers were R.D. Epps, president; W.O. Cain, vice president; James Cuttino, secretary-treasurer. The first board of directors consisted of R.D. Epps, W.O. Cain, James Cuttino, R.F. McLellan, R.E. Wilder, J.E. Stoudenmire and E.P. DuRant.[196]

The club purchased from R.B. Cain, the Cain's Mill property in Privateer Township for the sum of $6,500 with $2,250 as the initial payment. The property consisted of a club house, a mill-house, a 177-acre lake and surrounding land with a total of 286 acres.

The president and treasurer were authorized by the club to mortgage the property to obtain the money to complete payment of the debt.

Directors drafted bylaws for the organization that set up regulations for the use of the property. These were accepted by the club and have been closely followed through the years.

Plans were made to repair the dam so that fishing could begin.

The rules allow any member, members of his family living in the home or any visitors in the home to fish. They further ruled that each catch must not be more than 15 flatfish and five trout. No member may invite more than 12 guests each year and no member is to fish oftener than twice each week.

Dr. S.H. Edmunds made a motion that no fishing should be done on Sunday, and the motion was carried.

The first caretaker of the club house was May Holliday and her pay was $15 a month. Presently caring for the property is Carl Nesbitt, who lives with his mother nearby. His father preceded him as caretaker.

Five ponds feed into Cain's Mill Pond and the club has lost the dam two or three times; therefore, there is a committee responsible for regulating the water level.

Another sport that members enjoy is duck hunting, and baiting is allowed to a limit.

The pond has an occupant that is often heard, but seldom seen. An alligator has made this water his home for a long time, but he makes no trouble for the fishermen.

During the Depression, the club house was burned and each member was assessed $20 to begin a fund for rebuilding. Members cut cypress poles from the area and peeled them with a drawing knife for the building, and a new club house was soon completed. It is very attractive and comfortable. Someone built a lovely brick fireplace and Dr. E.P. DuRant built a picnic shed nearby. In the club house are several deer heads owned by Dr. DuRant and donated to the club by his son, Dr. Eddie DuRant, Sr.

Outsiders may use the property for picnics or parties if recommended by a member. A fee is charged and a written permit must be obtained from the secretary. No alcohol is to be used.

The club has five supper meetings each year. Sometimes they prepare their meal and sometimes it is catered.

At first wives were invited only once a year – on Ladies' Night. Now, however, they may attend every meeting.

A committee of four men, with an elected chairman, plans the supper for all. After supper the ladies meet in one room where they have a program planned by the wife of the chairman of the supper committee. Sometimes they have a musical program, sometimes a speaker and sometimes a program on crafts or other interesting projects.

The men have their business meeting, along with some banter or joking, no doubt, in the other room.

No alcohol is ever allowed at any of the meetings or on the premises.

For the December meeting, the ladies and gentlemen meet together and sing Christmas carols.

The Cain's Mill Club now has 65 members, which is the limit. A prospect must be suggested by a member and he is put on the waiting list. When his time comes, he is voted on by the membership. There are now 13 on the waiting list, with one having waited for five years.

Only two of the charter members are now in the club – Hugh

L. Palmer and Charley B. Jenkins.

Present officers of the club are as follows: John Brabham, president; John Graham, vice president; J.B. Baker, secretary-treasurer.

The Property Committee is composed of: John Creech (chairman), Tilly Cuttino, James Mallard, Stan DuBose, Robert James, and Warren Carroway.

Composing the Fish and Dam Committee are Steve Creech (chairman), Bubba James, John James, Dick Lee, John Pate, and L. Lawrence.

On the Board of Directors are L. Lawrence, Dick Lee, Jim Mallard, J.T. James, III, Steve Creech, and Will Shaw. They are replaced two at a time each year.

Claremont Lodge No. 64

Entwined with the history of Sumter County during many decades has been the story of Claremont Lodge No. 64, and well it might be, for Free Masonry is an honorable institution that goes back beyond the discovery of America and has had a marked influence on society in this country from almost the beginning.

In fact, it is doubtful just when the Order began. According to an old Masonic charge, it is said to be an "ancient and honorable institution; ancient, no doubt it is, as having subsisted from time immemorial; and honorable it must be acknowledged to be, as by a natural tendency it induces to make those so who are obedient to its precepts . . . To so high an eminence has its credit been advanced that in every age, monarchs themselves have been promoters of the art; have not thought it derogatory from their dignity to exchange the scepter for the trowel; have patronized our mysteries and joined our assemblies."

Though there are recorded instructions given to candidates in the "reign of the Saxon King Aethelstan (c. 894-940)," there were no doubt changes made through the years and the first organization of the institution which came from England to America was the formation of the Grand Lodge of England, at the Appletree Tavern in London in 1717. Possibly the first Lodge in this country was organized in Boston in 1733.

From an account printed in the **South Carolina Gazette** the first organization in this state was in Charles Town on October 28, 1736.[197] This Lodge was known as Solomon's Lodge No. 1. From that time other Lodges were formed throughout the state at intervals, some lasting until the present time and others continuing for only a short time.

The first appearance of a Masonic organization in Sumter County was an ancient York Lodge No. 52 in Salem on Black River, formed in 1807.[198] Most records of this organization have been lost, but it seems that it was moved to Sumterville in 1817, its name changed to Sumterville Lodge No. 26, and suspended in 1826.

In the meantime, another short-lived Order was formed in the western part of the District, known as Manchester Lodge No. 52, lasting from 1823 to 1830.

There is no record of any other Order of Free Masonry in Sumter County until 1854. By this time, Sumterville had become a thriving town of four hotels – the old China Tavern, Webb Clark's Hotel, Graham and Brother Hotel (near the railroad station), and a hotel owned by Benjamin Mitchell. There were four churches – Baptist (1813), Methodist (1827), Presbyterian (1830) and Roman Catholic Church of St. Lawrence, Martyr (1849). Col. James D. Blanding was intendent (mayor) at that time.

In the office of Judge of Probate William Lewis, located on the ground floor of the Old Courthouse, on July 6, 1854,[199] the first meeting of Master Masons was held with the following present: J.J. Ling, James P. Robertson, H.E. Wideman, Jonathan Brogdon, E. Walker, Dr. W.W. Brunsön, Napoleon Lewis and James Bell. The purpose of this meeting was to organize Claremont Lodge No. 64.

Although a slate of officers, consisting of Henry E. Wideman, W.M.; James P. Robertson, S.W.; and George Hall (absent), J.W. had been chosen, when St. David Lodge No. 72 in Darlington, which had been asked to sponsor the Lodge, came together for a dispensation of the new organization, a different slate of officers was elected. The problem was resolved after considerable confusion, and the organization was completed in January 1855 under special dispensation, with the following officers: W.W. Brunson, W.M.; James Bell, S.W.; Napoleon Lewis, J.W. Then in the following April, the final dispensation was consummated with some additional officers, including W.W. Alston, treasurer; W.J.N. Hammett, secretary; J.T. Green, S.D.; R.S. Mellett, J.D.; R.S. Webb, steward and F.M. Andrews, tiler.

A monument to the first Worshipful Master, Dr. W.M. Brunson, may be seen at his grave in the old Joseph Barton White Cemetery on the east side of the Camden Highway. It is inscribed with beautiful tributes to the memory of one who was evidently greatly respected, honored and loved.

From the beginning, the Lodge had difficulty finding a suitable meeting place. First they rented an Odd Fellows hall, then a building from Noah Crane, each for a short period of time.

The next arrangement was the purchase of the third story of a building owned by Mr. Winn, located on the corner where the Sumter Dry Goods now stands. Later when the building needed repairs, because the Lodge still owed money on the purchase, Mr. Winn was unwilling to comply with the request for such repairs. Meetings were then held in a building owned by T.D. Foxworth. In 1877 or '78 a new meeting place was found – a hall belonging to Gen. E.W. Moise. However, when arrangements for this place proved unsatisfactory, the Lodge obtained use of the hall belonging to the International Order of Good Templars.

Finally, a new Masonic Temple was constructed on West Liberty Street. It was owned by a corporation known as the Masonic Temple Company with Masons probably owning much of the stock and was rented to the Lodge and other fraternal organizations. The Temple was finally ready for occupancy in 1893, and Claremont Lodge felt that they had finally found a permanent meeting place. But, alas, this arrangement, too, was unsatisfactory. Almost at once, structural defects began to appear and the company felt unable to make repairs. In 1898 Richard I. Manning bought the shares of the other stockholders, but apparently, the situation was not improved.

In 1913 the Lodge arranged a five-year lease of a new building that was being erected on the corner of Main and Dugan Streets by "Brother" Perry Moses, Jr., who named it the "Alston Building" in memory of his friend and fellow Mason, Alston J. Stubbs, who had died.

After 16 years on the third floor of this building, the Lodge, because of lack of funds to build a fire escape required by an ordinance of the City Council, moved back to the old Masonic Temple (owned at that time by Neil O'Donnel) where it remained until a fire on January 8, 1943, damaged the building, destroying many of the valuables owned by the Lodge, among which were photographs of Past Masters, ceremonial paraphernalia, the old Master's chair, and other relics that the Lodge had collected during the 89 years of its existence.

Once again Claremont Lodge No. 64 began its search for a meeting place – a place that could afford some feeling of permanency to the organization. The search continued until 1959 when at long last, after more than 100 years, it obtained a place it could call "home." Together with Sumter Lodge No. 364, it erected a beautiful and commodious Masonic Temple on Alice Drive in that year. Since then, the two Lodges, as well as all Masonic-related organizations, hold their regular and special meetings there.

In the years gone by, Claremont Lodge took part in the laying of cornerstones of many of Sumter's important buildings.

In 1872 the invitation was accepted to share in the ceremony for the Market and Town Hall.

A description of this building might be of interest since it no longer stands, having been destroyed by fire in 1892. A two-story wooden building, it was located on North Main Street at the site of the old City Hall and Sumter Theater building. On the north and south were alleyways. On either side of a wide hallway on the first floor were stores. At the back of the building were open markets or stalls, separated by latticed partitions, used for the sale of meat, vegetables and other produce.

On the second floor of the building was a large hall, furnished with chairs and having a "stage" at one end, used for the presentation of plays and concerts.

Renovations were made in the building in 1890, providing quarters for the City Police and erecting a hall tower where a bell was installed to be used as an alarm in the case of fire.

Other cornerstone ceremonies in which Claremont Lodge No. 64 took part included that of the Confederate Monument on "Monument Square." This monument was erected through the efforts of the Ladies Monumental Association, directed by Mrs. Andrew Jackson Moses, who had had seven sons in the Confederate Army.

When Mrs. Moses became too feeble to continue the work, the task was taken up by her daughter, Mrs. Charles Moise, who in turn was succeeded by her daughter, Miss Dulce Moise, under whose leadership the project was completed.

Rev. John Kershaw, Episcopal rector of Sumter, issued an invitation on behalf of the Commissioners of the new Graded School of Sumter to the Lodge to have charge of the laying of the cornerstone of the new school building, also on Monument Square. This ceremony took place on October 19, 1891.

The Lodge was, of course, in charge of the very colorful ceremony in connection with the laying of the cornerstone of the Masonic Temple (mentioned above). For this occasion there were many officers present, as well as 79 members of Claremont, 99 visiting Masons representing 19 nearby Lodges, and visitors from Lodges in Virginia, North Carolina, New York, Wisconsin, Georgia, and Maryland.

In 1893[200] the cornerstone was laid for the new brick City Hall and Opera House, which was built at a cost of $35,000.

Claremont Lodge was called on for laying the cornerstone of two other new buildings in Sumter – the First Baptist Church and the new Sumter County Courthouse.

As Claremont Lodge members enjoyed some happy occasions with the town, they likewise shared some trying times through the years. Together they weathered many storms and won some hard-earned victories.

Scores of Masons left their homes and businesses to join the Confederate Army. In fact, it became necessary for the Lodge to seek a dispensation to suspend their monthly meetings during these months.

In the years after the war, people in Sumter suffered terrible financial straits, as was the case all over the South. The Lodge was forced to accept the due-bill of one of its most active and prominent members for his life membership dues. Few new members were inducted because there was no money for dues.

Though in great financial difficulty, the organization lent a helping hand to others through its Committee on Charity which worked tirelessly aiding the hungry and sick.

Again the Lodge was equal to an emergency when World War I began. Fees of members in the service were waived, generous subscriptions to the Red Cross were raised by the "Brethren," War Savings Stamps were purchased by the organization. The same patriotic response was found in World War II. Aid for the British Medical Societies was solicited, the American Red Cross again received generous gifts, the sale of War Bonds was promoted, and many other unheralded deeds were done through these critical times in Sumter and elsewhere.

Some unique and interesting events in the history of Claremont Lodge have been recorded. During the first year of the organization, the membership contracted with Rev. John Mood of Charleston (grandfather of Dr. Julius Andrew Mood), who was not only a Methodist minister but also a manufacturing jeweler and silversmith, for a set of jewels for the Lodge. The price to be paid was $60. The jewels were delivered, approved and purchased. Ten years later (1865) when Potter's men made their raids through Sumter, they ransacked the Lodge hall, among other places, stealing the jewels along with other valuables. The Lodge began collecting money for another set, but contrary to all expectations, they received a report in January of 1867 that the jewels had miraculously fallen into the hands of a "Worthy Brother," Joseph Seymore, a jeweler in Syracuse, New York. In November of that year, H. Claremont Moses returned the jewels to the Lodge "in the name of Brother Joseph Seymore." In appreciation, the Lodge passed a resolution naming Joseph Seymore as an honorary member of Claremont Lodge No. 64. These jewels were later burned as was mentioned earlier.

Another unusual occurrence was the presentation to the organization of a silver square and compass by Colin C. Manning, a member of the Lodge who came into possession of them in Italy, where he was staying because of illness in his family. As he was walking down a street in a strange town, homesick and miserable, he happened to notice these Masonic symbols hanging in the window of a curio shop. Going in, he learned that the owner had inherited the shop from his father who years before had bought the jewels, along with a Masonic pin and apron, from the effects of a refugee from Brazil. The Brazilian had once been governor of his province, but because of political revolutions was forced to flee for his life, coming to Italy where he had died in poverty. The Masonic emblems were among his possessions which were sold after his death.

Manning purchased the square and compass and sent them to his Mother Lodge in Sumter.

Another unusual gift that came to the Lodge was a gavel, made of mastodon ivory 50,000 years old, presented by "Brother" Noble Dick of Fairbanks, Alaska. This gavel was one of the few relics not destroyed by the fire in 1943.

Always patriotic, Claremont Lodge was ready to share in any worthy national cause that was being promoted. For instance, in 1858 a South Carolina lady (Miss Anne Pamela Cunningham of Laurens), daughter and sister of a Mason, called upon the Masonic Fraternity in her state to donate toward the purchase of Mount Vernon, the home of George Washington, that it might become a national possession. Claremont, along with other Lodges in the state, cooperated wholeheartedly in this worthwhile enterprise.

In another national project, S.K. Nash, Worshipful Master of Claremont, was delegated to represent his organization at a meeting in Washington, D.C., in March 1932,[201] regarding the George Washington National Memorial Monument, the bicentennial celebration of the former general and President's birth having been held on February 22 of that year. (Washington took his first step in Masonry before he reached 21 and became a Master Mason soon thereafter.)

Minutes from time to time listed the passing of Lodge members, but space forbids the mention of any except those who received special notation. The first of these was William H. Girardeau, "one of the most beloved and respected members of the Lodge," whose funeral was in April of 1879. He is described as "going through the chairs" until 1869 when he became Worshipful Master. His death was said to have been a "sad blow to the Lodge."

In the record of November 23, 1893, the death of R.M. Jones, "our Tiler," was mentioned, and he, too, was praised as being "one of the most faithful Members."

The death of "Brother" John M. Barwick in 1932 meant the loss of a "fine instructor of candidates," who "possessed the qualities of patience and tact to a remarkable degree." Special resolutions were passed in his memory, which stated that the "Lodge had lost a faithful and diligent member – one who exemplified in his daily life the principles and tenents of Masonry . . . "

Another member who was mourned greatly was John S. Kennedy, who was especially appreciated for his service as "Tiler," an office which he held for 22 years.

Other Lodges were organized in Sumter from time to time; namely, Sumter Lodge No. 120, America Lodge No. 352, and Sumter Lodge No. 364, but the first two consolidated with Claremont after only a few years.

Because of transportation problems Masons in the Salem area felt it expedient to organize an Order with the meeting place in Mayesville. This Lodge, known as Utopia Lodge No. 303, was established in 1913 with five members of Claremont, five from Mannville No. 232 and others. First officers of this Lodge included George C. Warren, W.M.; R.L. Grier, S.W.; L.C. Tisdale, J.W.; J.W. Montgomery, treasurer; J.E. Goddard, secretary; R.L. Kahn, S.D.; W.T. La Coste, J.D.; W.J. Thames and E.F. McCoy, stewards, and Charles Richardson, Tiler.

Utopia No. 303 was very active, having as many as 69 members at one time during the nine years of its existence. Since the problem of transportation was essentially solved in 1922, Sumter County having paved many of its roads, this organization merged with Claremont.

It seems that another organization known as Salem Lodge No. 141 was formed in Mayesville in 1868 with Guy L. Warren as Worshipful Master at that time. The only other record available concerning this Lodge was that of 1875 when the Worshipful Master was Harvey J. Wilson. Other members mentioned at that time were G.A. Andrew, secretary; H. Dickson Corbett, P.M.; J.W. Hudson and C.R.F. Baker. It is not known whether this Lodge expired or merged with Claremont.

Although the Lodge carried out very serious assignments and made many worthy contributions to the life of the city and county, there were recreational periods as well, when the members had fellowship with one another. They enjoyed suppers, picnics and other gatherings where good eats were the "thing of the day." Some of the places of refreshment in the old days were Hotel Marion (where Kress's store now stands), the Jervey House (on northeast corner of Liberty and Harvin Streets) and the Jackson Hotel on South Main (about where Kimbrell's Furniture Store is now located). The traditional feast of St. John's was generally observed in those early years.

For a while Masons sponsored a DeMolay chapter in Sumter to which belonged a number of worthy boys of Masonic connection. These boys were trained in character according to Biblical precepts. An energetic Eastern Star Chapter sponsors a girls group known as Rainbow Girls and helps support a comfortable home for the aging in Sumter.

And so Claremont Lodge No. 64, supported by similar groups, continues to be a part of the life of Sumter. Perhaps as never before society needs today forces such as these which are founded on principles of honor, uprightness and faith in God. There are countless "isms" that are subtly creeping in to undermine the foundations upon which America was built. Free Masonry has declared its war on these influences in the following words:

"Masonry abhors Communism, Fascism, and any form of dictatorship as being repugnant to its conception of the dignity of the individual personality, destructive of the basic human rights which are the Divine heritage of all men and inimical to the fundamental Masonic tenets of faith in God."

Columbia-Sumter Hunting And Fishing Club

"Doubt not but angling will prove to be so pleasant, that it will prove to be, like virtue, a reward to itself." – Isaac Walton

Fishing and hunting are favorite pastimes with most men. Some fish for relaxation. They like to go out alone and meditate as they wait for the bite that sometimes never comes. Others like to join a group in a spirit of competition, each vying for the honor of catching the greatest number of innocent victims or receiving the acclaim for the size of the prize fish caught.

The same motives lure hunters into the woods. But whatever the reason many men enjoy these sports.

One such group to which a number of sportsmen belong is the Columbia-Sumter Hunting and Fishing Club. The Columbia group organized themselves some 50 years ago and a bit later Sumter enthusiasts joined the organization. There are now 62 members – 31 from Sumter and 31 from Columbia.

In the beginning, dues were $10 a year, but gradually they have been increased until the present member pays $160 a year – except those who have reached the age of 70. They enjoy honorary status.

The club has hunting and fishing rights on a body of water known as Big Lake bounded by Dowd's Lake, the Santee River, Santee Reservation and Lake. It is near the Clark Plantation and Manchester, and the complete area where they have rights contains 83,000 acres. The property is leased by Georgia-Pacific for timber rights until 1983. From this company the club secured hunting and fishing privileges.

They have a club house where groups meet at times for a fish fry, but most of the fishing is done by individuals or small groups. They fish mostly for bass and bream.

Hunting is done in the summer and fall when usually the water is low and hunters can walk through the wooded area and cross small streams. The usual game sought is deer or wild turkeys. At present, however, there is a moratorium on turkey-hunting. The supply became limited and restocking was necessary. The moratorium will extend through four more years.

There is a hunting committee that makes a schedule which members are required to follow. Hunting is done once a week – one week on Wednesday afternoon and one on Saturday afternoon.

In spite of restrictions, however, men in Sumter feel it is to be a real privilege to belong to this club, which has the same appeal that it had many years ago.

Fortnightly Club – Unique Organization

Enjoying continuous prestige for more than 60 years, the Fortnightly Club has had as members many of Sumter's most illustrious citizens. It is even today counted an honor to be asked to join this famous literary organization, which has a restricted membership.

In the paper which he gave at a meeting of the group, Harold Moise related the high points of the club's history. This paper serves as an important source for information given in this article. Other sources include the few sets of minutes that have been preserved and some of the papers given by members at meetings. Minute books for only a few years of the club's existence are extant, and slightly more than a hundred of the many, many papers (only about 15 percent) that have been written for the meetings are still available.

The Fortnightly Club was organized in 1914, 1915 or 1916 (the exact date uncertain), for the purpose of "broadening of interest and knowledge through discussion of any phase of thought: religion and partisan politics alone excepted." From the beginning, the objective of the club was implemented by the presentation of a paper by a member of the club, usually the host, at the beginning of each meeting, the presentation being followed by a general discussion of the topic introduced.

From a paper given by H.A. Moses at a meeting in 1952, it was learned that Father N.A. Murphy, "a delightful and lovable priest of the Catholic Church," originated the idea of such an organization. He first shared his thoughts with his friend, H.R.

Van Deventer, who may be remembered by some as an important official of the Sumter Telephone Manufacturing Company. The two then approached Hubert G. Osteen, publisher of **The Sumter Daily Item**, and Dr. J.A. Mood, an outstanding physician of the city. The four proceeded with the organization, which in the beginning was designed with a membership of 20. The limit was soon changed to 25, and that has been the number kept through the years.

Charter members, according to Mr. Moses' paper, were the following: Father N.A. Murphy, H.R. Van Deventer, Hubert G. Osteen, Dr. J.A. Mood, L.C. Moise, George D. Levy, W.B. Daughtry, J.B. Jenkins, Dr. H.A. Mood, Dr. S.H. Edmunds, E.C. Haynsworth, H.C. Haynsworth, Dr. S.C. Baker, Davis D. Moise, I.C. Strauss, David Kline, R.B. Belser and R.O. Purdy. If there were 20 in the beginning, two are not named in this list.

The following were early members, but according to another listing they were not charter members: J.J. Brennan, Mark Reynolds, C.M. Hurst, H.A. Moses, R.D. Epps, Dr. George W. Dick, Dr. C.J. Lemmon, Dr. Harry L. Shaw, Dr. Milton Weinberg.

Other early members were Dr. R.B. Furman, Arthur S. Harby, G.A. Lemmon, A.C. Phelps, George L. Ricker, Dr. J.M. Wells and George D. Shore. These could have been charter members, but were not designated as such in available records.

Bylaws require that papers be limited to 30 minutes, unless the president allows extra time in view of the importance of the subject. An integral part of the program is the discussion of the topic presented by the main speaker. Each person is required, however, to restrict his comments to six minutes with no second privilege for the floor. By common consent those wishing to speak must stand and be recognized. This custom is not included in the bylaws. From the minutes read, some of which were written in great detail, it seems that discussions are very lively, as well as informative.

In the beginning, refreshments at the meetings were very simple, the host using $5 from the treasury to pay for coffee and sandwiches. After some years, Dr. Julius Mood, host on one occasion, served hot hominy and fried chicken. That marked the end of the coffee-sandwich routine. It was said that Judge R.O. Purdy set the pace and the dinners became very bountiful and elaborate affairs.

Annual dues of $10 are paid by the members and this takes care of incidentals.

The club has had various meeting places, the first being the Elks Club, then over Mitchell's Drug Store on the corner of Main and Hampton. Other places used include the assembly room on the second floor of Central School Building; the Claremont Hotel; the Coca-Cola Community Center; Julian's Restaurant (in the building now occupied by Maxwell Brothers and Blackwell Furniture Company on Main Street); the YWCA, in the same location; Frank's Restaurant; the Downtowner; the Plantation Restaurant. At least once it met in the Synagogue and in the Episcopal Parish House. Occasionally it has met in the home of the host.

Each year the club entertains the wives of the members in a very special "Ladies Night" affair. The theme of this gala event is "Thus Hand in Hand Through Life We'll Go."

Topics for papers and discussions have covered a wide scope of interests, ranging from the light and humorous to the philosophical and profound.

In May of 1929, H.C. Haynsworth spoke on "Russia, the Land of Autocracy and License." A few sentences from this paper will serve to illustrate the feelings of some as early as the 1920's concerning the problems facing today's world: " . . . A land of mystery, seeking what it could appropriate from age-old civilizations, it has drawn a veil across its own customs, life and soul. Even during the reign of Peter the Great, who drafted artisans, scientists, and philosophers from Western Europe for his own purposes, the outlanders had to leave Moscow at sundown and go into a suburb especially reserved for them."

" . . . Autocracy invades the personal liberty of the people, ostensibly for their own good."

At a meeting in 1942 another paper was read concerning Russia and during the discussion Maj. William Reynolds made the terse comment – "We'd better watch Russia . . . "

In a discussion following a paper on the topic "The Primary System in South Carolina," given by H.G. Osteen on October 24, 1942, A.S. Merrimon, one of Sumter's prominent lawyers, a special guest at the meeting, made a prophetic comment concerning "the growing encroachment of the federal government on States' Rights." He said, "We can be sure that the federal government is going to regulate all elections for the filling of federal offices."

F.M. Moise gave a paper in 1936 concerning the "Menace of Marijuana." He said that that harmful drug was then a real problem and was a growing menace for young people especially. He classified its source as a hempweed growing all over the country.

W.E. Covington spoke at one meeting on the intriguing title, "Frankenstein Monster – Labor Unions," saying, "implications of growing might were presaged with forboding of serious troubles in the future."

A listing of a few other topics will give an idea of the great variety of interests manifested by members: "Bret Harte," "Winston Churchill," "Moses," "Sons of Abraham," "Sports," "Bob White Quail," "Taft-Hartley Law," et cetera, ad infinitum.

Typical of the humor displayed at times, was a paper by C.M. Hurst entitled, "Who's Who in the Fortnightly Club," in which he gave amusing thumbnail sketches of the first president, Dr. J.A. Mood, three other early presidents and one of the colorful members of the club, George D. Shore. The whole of the sketch of the first will be given here and some excerpts from the last.

DR. J.A. MOOD

"Our president – son of a clergyman, was born in North Carolina, whither the father had gone as a missionary. His parents were South Carolinians, and the accident of birth in a foreign land does not make him an alien. A kitten, born in an oven, does not thereby become a biscuit. It will be a repetition of history should North Carolina claim him as she does in the case of Andrew Jackson. A charter member – first and only president, he has so guided the affairs of the club that its permanence seems assured.

"He is president for life, because he possesses the only gavel in the Club. What a sorry figure would a president cut without that symbol of authority? And why incur the expense of a gavel while we have a member who owns one in fee simple and is willing to wield it free of charge? In former years a pocketknife rapped to order. But we have evolved beyond that primitive stage and must not retrograde.

"The gavel turns the trick. May he never lose it for thus saith the wizard of the cave 'so long as ye retain the gavel; so long shall ye reign – Lose it and the dynasty shall totter and fall.' Political honor thrust upon him made him Mayor – then Chairman of the City Board of Education. He served as surgeon, with rank of major, in the Spanish-American War. At Chickamauga he fought mosquitoes, filth and disease. When the Spaniards were sufficiently punished, he returned to less strenuous pursuits of peace. The memories of that campaign are the delight of his life. His reverential regard for his commanding General grows with the years as becometh a good soldier."

GEORGE D. SHORE

"He hails from North Carolina, which some geographer taught him, was a valley of humility between two mountains of conceit

— not being of humble disposition he came to South Carolina, wiped the tar off his heels in a goober patch and proceeded to learn the art of conceit. His progress had been phenomenal . . . Rapidly acquiring the refinements of civilization, he was admitted to the Fortnightly Club and now we do not know how we could get along without him. He is "agin the government" always. You can't get him on your side of an argument. He stops, listens, and takes the opposite view. George came near getting into the poet's corner, but his keen sense of humor, and homely philosophy got him into a niche where he sits alone, the foremost wit of our Club."

The Fortnightly Club is indeed a unique organization.

Jaycees' Creed Inspires For Service

In this crucial period in the history of America the Jaycee Creed could well be the foundation upon which all those in authority might build their service. The Creed reads as follows:

"We believe: That faith in God gives meaning and purpose to human life; That the brotherhood of man transcends the sovereignty of nations; That economic justice can best be won by free men through free enterprise; That government should be of laws rather than of men; That earth's great treasure lies in human personality; And that service to humanity is the best work of life."

Inspired by the idea that young men should become more actively involved in public affairs thus developing leadership abilities, 32 young men in St. Louis, Missouri, on October 13, 1915, organized the Young Men's Progressive Civic Association, later known as the National Junior Chamber of Commerce, the name later becoming the Jaycees.

More clubs were formed and with a meeting of 29 such groups across the nation, the national association was officially organized in 1920.

In 1944 the U.S. Jaycees joined with six other nations to form the International Jaycee Association.

The South Carolina Jaycees became an organization in 1930.

It was in 1940 that the Sumter Jaycee Chapter was formed with Robert Graham as the president. [202]

Since many of the young men went into military duty when World War II began, the organization became inactive. However, it was reactivated in 1946, with G. Werber Bryan as president.

Jaycees have four main objectives; namely, (1) to make the community a better place in which to live; (2) to develop leadership among the membership; (3) to offer education, recreation and social activities to men of similar age; (4) to give young men a voice in the affairs of the community, state and nation.

In keeping with the spirit of these objectives the Sumter Jaycees plan and carry out around 50 projects a year. Among these are the following: manning the Salvation Army Kettle, recruiting blood donors, taking underprivileged children on shopping tours at Christmas, helping in the "Get Out the Vote" campaign, planning a bicycle rodeo, arranging the Sumter Generals semi-pro football games, planning a teenage safe driving road-e-o, sponsoring the Miss Sumter Pageant, arranging the Christmas parade, sponsoring the Iris Festival, and planning "Drug Awareness Days."

The Jaycees of South Carolina began searching in the 1950's for a permanent home. Of the seven chapters that put in bids for the privilege of furnishing the home, Sumter was the winner. The Chapter set to work to find a location and raise funds. As a result a $12,000 building was erected on Alice Drive on a lot that had been used by the city as an airport.

Sumter has been closely allied with the state association. In 1958 Richard Moses was state president and in 1960 another Sumter member, Ramon Schwartz, headed the South Carolina Jaycees, and there have been members from Sumter on the S.C. Jaycee Executive Committee almost every year. In 1959 Richard Moses was a national vice president.

In May of 1974, leaders of the local chapter held groundbreaking ceremonies for the Jaycee Hut on Pine Street at Church Street which had been in the planning stage for 14 years. Richard P. Moses, assisted by Steve Creech, turned the first shovel full of dirt. Other enthusiastic members on hand to take part in this long-awaited event were Roger Heim, Willie Grate, Mike Blake, Frank Williams and Joe McElveen. As president that year, McElveen appointed a hut committee to make plans for the completion of the building.

Funds for the project were solicited from persons and businesses in the community and the response was most gratifying. Since its completion the hut has been used to great advantage by the Jaycees, filling their needs and desires; and it is often used by other groups as well.

Each year the Jaycees in Sumter celebrate D.S.A. and Bosses Night, at which time the Distinguished Service Award is given to an outstanding citizen in the community (not a Jaycee) chosen by members of the association. The following have received this honor since the beginning of the custom: Buford Mabry (1949), Robert E. Graham (1950), D.B. James (1951), H.N. Hutchinson (1952), Harry Bryan (1953), James Pritchard (1954), Mike Karvelas (1955), Richard Moses (1956), Ramon Schwartz (1957),

Billy Priest (1958), Bobby Richardson (1959), Robert K. Galloway (1960), W. Burke Watson (1961), S.L. Roddey, Jr. (1962), Billy Harris (1963), Robert Vetter (1964), Robert Royall (1965), Arthur Bahnmuller (1966), John R. Parker (1967), James P. Nettles, Jr. (1968), G.B. McEwen, Jr. (1969), Charles H. Hughes (1970), Don Barber (1971), T.R. Mims, Jr. (1972), T. Eugene Spann (1973), Mike Blake (1974), Steve Creech (1975), J. Grady Locklear (1976), David Smith (1978), W. Burke Watson, Jr. (1979).

In 1970 the Jaycees began the custom of selecting the outstanding Boss of the Year. Those who have been thus honored are as follows: G. Werber Bryan, Arthur Bahnmuller, John Miles, S.L. Roddey, Jr., James P. Nettles, Sr., W. Burke Watson, C. Bob Ray, Fred Schiffley, William B. Sanders and Jim Cooper.

Jaycees make their influence felt in Sumter in countless ways. They give unselfish service both as individuals and as an organization.

Progressive Club Is Unique In Formation And Existence

Tucked away in a wooded spot near Cain's Mill sits a modest little building that may not attract even a passing glance from the passer-by.

However, this is a very important place for a number of men in the area.

Activities twice a month bring real life to the inconspicuous surroundings, as it is the meeting place of the very wide-awake Progressive Club, a group of 20 men who meet regularly for friendly banter, an exchange of ideas and, perhaps most important of all, a delicious supper prepared by the members.

This club was begun more than a half-century ago in a most informal manner as described by the one who was the originator of the idea, Bill Raffield: "On January 6, 1919, I was discharged from the Army as a cook. In this simple statement lies the origin of the Progressive Club. As I did not want to forget what I had learned about cooking, I thought that some regular practice would help. I discussed with several friends the idea of having supper out in the country once in awhile. They were all for it, so we had our first meeting at McCray's Mill. With the rice ready-cooked, we carried chickens to fry. There was plenty of wood so we had no problem getting fire to cook with."

He went on to say that the most disagreeable part was "getting the pots and pans clean." At first these were brought from his home.

After meeting several times at McCray's Mill, the men ran into a financial problem. The person who had the mill in charge began charging for the use of the grounds. In looking for a more suitable location for their outings, they decided on White's Mill.

It then became the consensus of the group that a permanent organization was desirable. Therefore in 1925, "The Cook Your Own Club" was formed with the following members: James Bradley, Hughes Bradley, George Bultman, Harry Bultman, Archie Crumpton, W.T. Nixon and Bill Raffield. Raffield was elected first president.

According to the bylaws adopted, there would be no drinking at any of the meetings and no discussions of religion or politics.

When word of the good times these men were having got around, applications for membership began coming in. As more members were added, the need was felt for a new place for meetings. The use of the Monaghan house at Cain's Mill was obtained. The members soon decided, however, that they wanted a permanent place for their own. Leasing a small lot from the Cain's Mill Club, they bought some inexpensive lumber and hired some carpenters to work under the supervision of the building committee, consisting of George Bultman, Crumpton and Raffield. Soon they had a small club house, not fine they felt, but comfortable.

Because the building was small, the membership of the club was limited to 18. Later, after the addition of 10 feet on the front and the purchase of 20 homemade chairs, the number was increased to 20, the number of the present membership.

For a while only makeshift equipment was used for cooking and lighting, but eventually electricity was installed and a gas stove was purchased.

Somewhere along the way the name was changed to the Progressive Club.

As time went on, applications for membership increased; therefore, the club found it necessary to screen the applicants by a process still followed. When a member dies or moves away and a vacancy thus occurs, a replacement is proposed. A name is presented and it is decided by a vote whether the applicant is eligible for membership according to the standards of the club. Members desire to keep a congenial group, each of whom enjoys the company of the others.

For each meeting – first and third Tuesday night of every month except July and August – two men prepare the supper and two are responsible for the program.

The order of procedure at the meetings calls for the invocation and the meal; after that the Pledge of Allegiance is given, followed by the Lord's Prayer. The secretary calls the roll and reads the minutes of the meeting that was held 20 years previously.

Then comes the planned program. These programs are varied. There may be a guest speaker, using some timely topic, or a paper may be given by a member. Occasionally there is a debate or a quiz program.

Through the years, the club has celebrated on special occasions with a Ladies' Night. These times always prove highlights for the members.

There is always much amicable "give and take," the "cooking committee" for the meeting receiving the brunt of the jokes, especially when the meal is "extra good." The better the food, they say, the more complaints are voiced – all in fun.

Many Sumter County men have enjoyed the activities of this club through its 53-year history. Some have died while members, including James Bradley, George Bultman, Harvey Bultman, H.A. Davis, Marion Doughty, F.K. Ellis, John Evans, Jr., J.R. Fidler, George James, Robert Jennings, Motte Lawrence, Dr. Sam Mitchell, Bert Montague, M.B. Morrow, Jack Pate, William Raffield, Harvey Tiller, and Yates Yeadon.

Plaques have been placed on the wall in memory of most of these. Those who have died more recently will be memorialized in the same way.

Some have moved away; while some are no longer able to hold active membership because of ill health and are known as honorary members. Those are W.N. Bradford (now deceased), H.D. Carlisle, J.M. Cooper (now deceased), and Archie Crumpton.

Present active membership is composed of the following: E.D. Brunson, Archie Caughman, Arland Compton (new member), Pitts DeLorme, H.L. Eure, Dr. R.D. Guilds, S.A. Harvin, Graham Hill, H.C. Humphries, J.H. Humphries, Victor Jones, Buford Mabry, Leon McDonald, Eugene McIntosh, Thomas McJunkin, Hugh McMillan, James Nettles, I. Byrd Parnell, W.C. Plowden, and Melton ("Boots") Tisdale.

The Progressive Club has brought much enjoyment to many people and the founder merits the gratitude of all who have had the privilege of being in the circle of friendship thus afforded. One member expressed no doubt the sentiment of all when he said, "We feel we have the best club in the U.S." [203]

Sumter Rotary Club

February 23, 1980, marked the 75th anniversary of Rotary International, an organization dedicated to service. Rotarians are ceaselessly seeking opportunities for service and exploring more avenues by which they can better serve others.

This great organization began with a vision of four men — Paul Harris, a lawyer, and three others who met that day in Chicago, Illinois, without knowing what to do at first to bring their dream to reality. They were seeking through fellowship to improve the businesses they represented and to find ways to help themselves and others.

For 75 years, Rotarians have been bringing the dream of these four to fruition. The organization has had phenomenal growth. There are now 853,000 members in 18,374 clubs in 153 countries and geographical regions.[204]

The Sumter Rotary Club was organized by the Columbia Club late in the fall of 1921 under the leadership of Dr. S.H. Edmunds, Dr. J.A. Mood, Mr. H.G. Osteen and perhaps a few others.

The application for a charter carried 24 names. Dr. Edmunds was elected president of the new club and Mr. S.L. Roddey, secretary.

Since the county at that time was chiefly agricultural, most of the meetings were devoted to subjects related to agriculture and the improvement of the community.

One of the highlights each year was the meeting at which the graduates of the city school were entertained.

The Rotary Educational Fund was one of the first projects of the Club. Several members contributed a small sum to give the fund a start and then each member added each week to his meal ticket ten cents to increase the amount. This fund now has assets of $43,000, and hundreds of boys have been helped through college. The Club at the present has 25 outstanding loans to students in college or to young people who have finished college and are in the process of repaying loans. Recipients are urged to repay the loans as soon as possible so that the money may be used by others.

Each year, however, a loan of $1,000 is made to medical-related study. This is not to be repaid if the student gives two years of full service to Tuomey Hospital.

The Club is involved in many civic projects. It has furnished the material and manpower for building two cabins at the YMCA camp for boys in Manchester Park. The camp is named Camp Mac Boykin for a former president of the Rotary Club, now deceased. He left a considerable sum to support the project.

The Club invests annually a sum of more than $600 to support work with indigent and crippled children, both white and black.

In many other areas Sumter Rotary has made its influence felt by the citizens of Sumter. A non-partisan, non-sectarian group, it promotes general fellowship and thoughtfulness of others. The organization is an excellent training center for constructive leadership.

To individual members the Club furnishes opportunities for service, for developing talents and capacities for leadership, a greater knowledge of world affairs, encouragement and support in the conducting of business, a wider circle of friends, opportunities to fulfill those noble and unselfish desires that help to make the world a better place.

Membership in Rotary is composed of a representative from each representative business and profession in the community. Members are required to attend all weekly meetings. One who is absent from four successive meetings without a valid reason will lose membership. However, he may make up the absence by attending a meeting elsewhere during the week preceding or following the absence.

The ideal upon which Rotary International is built may be expressed in the slogan of the Sumter Club – "Service Above Self." Every Rotarian strives to apply this ideal to his personal, business and community life.

Sumter Boy Scout Program Records Remarkable History

Sixty-six years ago, on February 8, 1910, Boy Scouts of America was incorporated, an event that has been of the greatest importance in the lives of boys in this country.

Boy Scouting was founded in England by Lord Baden-Powell in 1908 and the following year the idea was brought to America by L.D. Boyce.

As early as 1914 there was a Scout Troop in Wedgefield with Henry Strange recorded as a tenderfoot at that time. In 1915, the record states, there was a troop in that town with Rev. John R. Hay, Presbyterian minister, as scoutmaster.

The late Wendell Levi, it is said, was scoutmaster in the city of Sumter in the same year, but that troop was not registered. Edward Buck was a tenderfoot in that troop.

In June of 1916 the first registered troop was formed in Sumter with John Craig Hurst as Scoutmaster, and committeemen were H.L. Scarborough, H.L. Birchard (secretary of YMCA) and R.T. Brown. At this time, 52 Scouts were listed and the troop was sponsored by the YMCA.[205]

After World War I, Wendell Levi returned to Sumter and became Master of Scout Troop No. 1, serving from 1919 till 1922. At this time the troop was composed of 32 Scouts.

In 1920 Troop No. 2 was organized with Shepard K. Nash as

the Scoutmaster. A group of interested citizens sponsored this troop.

More and more interest was manifested in the Scouting program in Sumter. In 1921, being a Scout was an honor that all boys coveted and there was always a waiting list of those desiring to join. In that year the Sumter troop won practically all prizes in the round-up held in Florence. They totaled 297 points out of a possible 300.

A booklet of regulations was printed for Troop No. 1 around 1924. It was prepared by Lewis G. Beaty. Included in the 12-page booklet were instructions on conduct, uniforms, meetings, duties of officers, dues, court of honor, test examiners, delivery of messages, forms of speech, complaints, message forms, rank requirements, etc.

Regulations required that meetings open with the presentation of the colors accompanied by the bugle with the Scout oath following. Each meeting was to be closed with the Scout benediction and taps.

Sumter District was organized in 1938, with Frank Clarke, first chairman.

Cubbing for boys eight to eleven was begun in 1930. Ranks in cubbing were Bobcat, Wolf, Bear, Lion and Webelos. The first Cub pack in Sumter was organized in 1939, with Alfred Scarborough, Sr., as Cubmaster. Records of that year show four active Scout troops.

With the belief that the Scout movement was "the best character building and citizenship training program for boys ever evolved," a group of men who were willing to spend time and effort to help equip boys to face life, organized the Pee Dee Area Council in 1928. However, Sumter did not become a member of the council until later.

The Kiwanis Club took great interest in Scouting; and in 1925, 48 Kiwanians built Camp "Kiwabek" near Pocalla, where in 1927 Scouts from Camden, Timmonsville and Summerton were invited by the Sumter Troops for a Rally. (This camp burned in 1939.)

Sumter joined Pee Dee Area Council in 1938 and began taking part in all the activities sponsored by that organization, including the camping trips at Camp Pee Dee and later at Camp Coker.

In fact, camping formed a very important part of Scout training. A quotation from a printed pamphlet sent to boys before the camp will give some idea of the activities. "The day is divided into periods: swimming, hiking, games, test-work, merit badge work, leathercraft, wood carving, archery, outdoor cooking, nature work, making of small articles, bead work, work, rest, devotions, campfire and other things too numerous to mention."

A clipping from a 1940 newspaper tells of the great progress by Sumter Scouts in a few months' time. It states that at the Court of Honor, 123 honors were given, a record that attracted much interest from other districts. Thirty-six promotions and 87 merit badges were conferred. Nineteen were promoted to second class; nine, to first class; three, to Star Scout; four, to Life Scout; one, to Eagle Scout.

It was reported in 1941 that a citizens committee to promote the Boy Scout movement in Sumter had been formed.

According to another newspaper clipping, the Flaming Arrow Patrol of Troup 38 (formerly No. 1), had excelled in practically all the camp activities and had been rated the honor patrol of the camp.

A permanent camp on Lake Marion of the Boy Scouts of Sumter and Clarendon Counties was dedicated in 1950 as Camp Henry Shelor in honor of the one who gave the land, part of the cost of erecting a modern cabin, and much of the work of completing the project.

On December 6, 1951, the Kiwanis Club entertained a number of Scout executives and Boy Scouts. It was brought out in the report on this event that Scouting affords "the finest education in self-protection, whether in a burning building, in the woods, or lost in a swamp." It was said also that Scouts are educated in Patriotism, Americanism and love of parents, home, church, and city in a way that appeals to a growing boy."

According to another news release there were in 1952, ten troops in the County sponsored by the following: Elks Club, Veterans of Foreign Wars, the Lions Club, First Presbyterian Church, Trinity Methodist Church, The American Legion, Pitts Presbyterian Church, Shaw Air Force Base Chapel, Mayesville Presbyterian Church, and Oswego churches.

On August 8, 1952, Sumter welcomed its first full-time Scout executive, Frank Yandell. He was employed to get more Scouting to more boys in Sumter District.[206]

As a training in patriotism, a parade was organized on November 3, 1952, for the purpose of reminding citizens to go to the polls and vote. In the parade were 25 Scouts and 100 Cubs.

As an indication that the Boy Scout program continued to grow, in January 1955 four members of a rural troop, sponsored by Hebron Presbyterian Church, received the God and Country Award, and six became Eagle Scouts. The conferring of six Eagle awards at one time set a record for Troop 343, for the Pee Dee Area Council and possibly for the state and nation.

Eight months later, 27 Sumter Scouts were advanced in rank, four receiving the Eagle Award at a Court of Honor at Trinity Methodist Church.

Reports show that interest in Scouting in 1956 continued to grow. More and more boys were formed into troops, more advancements in rank were noted, more merit badges and awards were won. Jamborees, camping, sailing trips, and other activities gave Sumter boys not only much valuable training, but also many hours of enjoyment. And the same was true in 1957. In February of '58, some 90 Scouts were advanced in rank.

Similar records have been reported through the years since that time.

It would not be possible in this short sketch to name all the individuals in Sumter who have advanced through all the ranks of Scouting. Let it be said only that the young men, and older ones too, who have had the training Scouting can and does give are ready to accept the challenge implied in the words of M.S. Lumjansky: "As long as America has Scouts and Scouters, our nation will have a supply of adequately trained boys and men upon whom she can depend in both War and Peace."

Nor is it possible to mention all the fine men of Sumter County who have dedicated themselves to the cause of Scouting – "who have been willing to train themselves and to give unstintingly of their time and effort that the boys of today might be well equipped to face and solve the problems of tomorrow." Only the "pioneers" have been named. One other, who has been called the Dean of Scoutmasters in Sumter and who has served as a leader in Scouting for many years, is Wilbert Bernshouse. Many tributes have been paid this one for his years of dedicated service to the boys of this area.

To all who have been Scoutmasters, Edgar A. Guest says, in part:

"There isn't any pay for you,
You serve without reward,
The boys who tramp the fields with you but little could afford,
And yet your pay is richer far than those who toil for gold,
For in a dozen different ways your service shall be told."

Sumter County Game And Fish Association

Inspired by an article written by Harry R.E. Hampton in "Woods and Waters," a column running in **The Columbia State** many years ago, Mac Boykin invited a group of about 20 like-minded sportsmen to meet in June, 1931. The place of meeting was the old Board of Trade room in the City Hall. Present at the meeting were Mr. Hampton and Zan Heyward, a writer who was also interested in hunting and fishing.

The result of this meeting was the organization of the Sumter County Game and Fish Association. Enthusiasm for the project spread to Columbia, and the Sumter group was instrumental in the organization of the South Carolina Game and Fish Association, and the Sumter organization became known as the Sumter Chapter of the state association.[207]

Other chapters were formed and all began working together on a program of education with a view to interest sportsmen in game and fish conservation and propagation.

Sumter County Chapter, through the work of the county delegation, secured the passage by the legislature of a law providing for game wardens to be appointed by the directors of the Game and Fish Association.

For a number of years before the Game and Fish Association was formed, one-half of the taxes paid by hunters went to the schools. The Association was able to change this tradition by securing from the county those taxes for use in protecting and propagating game in the county. However, these moneys are no longer designated in this way.

With the help of free labor obtained through the Emergency Relief Act passed by Congress, some of the streams of the county were cleared of debris and stocked with fish from the government hatchery.

Appealing to the county board and the legislative delegation for help, the Sumter County Game and Fish Association was able to have lands that had been sold for taxes during the depression transferred to its use for a period of 20 years in a reforestation project. Accordingly two tracts were taken over by the Association, and with the help of the American Legion Post in Sumter, converted into forestry projects.

Another interest that claimed the attention of this organization in the early days was the propagation of quail from eggs distributed by Mr. Emory W. Clark, owner of Milford Plantation.

Farmers were able to get several hundred quail for restocking sections that had become depleted.

The Sumter County Game and Fish Association, under the able leadership of Will Plowden, H.Q. Jones, Alwin Burns and others, organized the Gamecock Field Trial Association. This association brought to Sumter the National Amateur Field Trials where some of the finest pointers and setters in the nation were shown.

The Field Trials have been through the years and still are of great interest to many in Sumter. Ernest Newman is one of the well-known judges in the association, judging in events in many states each year, including national championships.

In the interest of forming state parks in the Southern states,

Mac Boykin, president of the Sumter County Game and Fish Association, went to Washington with State Forester H.A. Smith and others. The trip was very successful, resulting in the securing of Poinsett State Park, containing 1,000 acres of land. It has since been developed into a very attractive resort.

Certainly one of the greatest accomplishments of the Game and Fish Association in the early days was the acquisition and development of the Poinsett Forest Area, containing 28,800 acres. Through the assistance of Maj. Loring Lee and Clarence Haynsworth, with additional help from Sen. Thomas H. Beck, this tract was acquired under definite agreements and work began in the process of making it a rest area for migratory birds.

The officers of the association, with the cooperation of Mayor F.B. Creech and City Council, secured the Tilghman Forestry Nursery (now named for Mr. Creech), the largest pine nursery in the world at that time.

Though the members of the Game and Fish Association worked with great interest to give Sumter County the advantages now enjoyed by all, it is the consensus that Mac Boykin, the first president, should be given the thanks of all who knew of his untiring efforts for the association and the county.

For the organization of the Sumter County Game and Fish Association in 1931 there were 114 charter members.

The historical facts here given were found in "Historic Sketch, Sumter County Game and Fish Association," distributed at the spring meeting of the association, March 22, 1945. (This booklet was furnished by Rembert Skinner.)

Since that 1945 meeting, the association has continued to carry out projects in the interest of hunting and fishing in Sumter County.

There are still two meetings a year – spring and fall – with an interesting and educational program planned for each. Membership at present is approximately 150. Dues are $17.50 for a family and $10.00 for an individual membership.

Present officers are Burke Watson, Jr., president; Bill Elliott, vice president; F.B. Cheech, III, secretary-treasurer. Board members are Charles H. Andrews, III, Richard M. White, Lathan Roddey, Blaise Lareau, Robert Hutchins, David McCracken, Frank Holloway, John James, Eddie DuRant, Jr., and William Davis.

Projects of recent date include a landing light at Pack's Landing and a display of antique duck decoys. Each year the Mac Boykin Open Bass Fishing Tournament is held. The winner has his name engraved on a large trophy that is displayed on a rotating basis in the sporting goods stores; and small trophies are given also.

Sumter Kiwanis Club Organized in 1922

With "We Build" as a general theme, Kiwanis International has made its influence for good felt through many years in all parts of the United States and in other countries as well.

Always looking for opportunities to enlarge its scope of activities and service, Sumter organized a Kiwanis chapter in 1922.[208] This new chapter was sponsored by the Kiwanis Club of Columbia. The organizational meeting was held at the Claremont Hotel on the evening of June 20 of that year. Lieutenant Governor of the Carolinas District Alva M. Lumpkin presided over the meeting, which was attended by visitors from Columbia and other parts of the state.

The first slate of officers for the Kiwanis Club of Sumter included the following: H.L. Scarborough, president; Dr. H.L. Shaw, vice president; John B. Duffie, secretary; A.M. Broughton, treasurer. S.A. Harvin, Sr., George W. Hutchinson, T.C. McKnight, H.A. Moses, Rev. W.E. Thayer, B.C. Wallace and R.B. Waters were chosen as directors.

The charter was presented to this club, which was No. 802 in Kiwanis International, approximately four months later, on October 5. Lieutenant Governor Lumpkin was again master of ceremonies in the absence of Gov. W.B. Merrimon.

The initial thrust of the club toward meeting needs in the vicinity was work with and for the youth. They purchased pigs and corn for 4-H Clubs to start them on the raising of hogs for shows and for sale. Another interest was providing suppers for the entertainment of children in the community. During one year they provided such entertainment for as many as 1,500.

The club undertook the worthy endeavor of lending money to student nurses, an outgrowth of this being a health program for needy children. Other youth work was with Boy and Girl Scouts and baseball teams and leagues.

In 1954 Kiwanians organized and sponsored a Key Club at Edmunds High School. This club has continued through the years to hold an important place among high school boys. A similar club was chartered by the Kiwanis Club at Hillcrest in 1963, and the third such organization was formed at Wilson Hall in 1969. A Kiwanian attends meetings of Key Clubs and encourages them in their various projects which they plan and execute through their own efforts.

Though services for young people exercised first claim on the early interest of the Kiwanis Club of Sumter, their work has extended into many other fields. There is, for instance, a division of their activities known as Citizenship Services. Working in this field are committees on Agriculture and Conservation, International Relations, Public and Business Affairs, Support of Churches in Their Spiritual Aims, and Endowment.

To raise funds for the many worthwhile services, the club has sponsored several money-raising projects. A sizable sum was realized from one of these — a circus brought to Sumter several years ago.

Kiwanians enjoy a fellowship luncheon meeting on the first and third Fridays of the month at Sunset Country Club. There is always a special speaker for the occasion, and selected Key Clubbers are invited as guests.

Each year there is a national convention held alternately in different sections of the country, and the local club sends a delegate or delegates, according to the distance and the financial status at the time.

Published in Chicago, Illinois, is "Kiwanis," a monthly magazine, the voice of the National Association.

When a Kiwanian completes 25 years of service in the organization, he is awarded a certificate of honor, and every five years thereafter he is similarly honored.

The Sumter Club has a distinctive characteristic in that within the club is an inner circle composed only of past presidents. So far as is known this is the only such organization of Kiwanians. There are no dues required, and the club meets once each year for a time of reminiscing and fellowship.

Many of the members of this "club within a club" have passed on and some have moved away. However, a listing, showing the year in which each served as president of the Kiwanis Club of Sumter will call to mind those to whom honor is due:

H.L. Scarborough (1922-23), Harry L. Shaw (1924), R. Brice Waters (1925), John B. Duffie (1926), F.B. Creech (1927), F.K. Hirsch (1928), John D. Lee, Sr. (1928), J.M. Eleazer (1929), H.A. Moses (1930), J.A. Raffield (1931), W.E. Bynum (1932), J.J. Brennan (1933), E. Murr Hall (1934), S.F. Stoudenmire (1935), E.W. Hartin (1936), H.A. Davis (1937), P.J. Gallagher (1938), C.E. Hurst (1939), W.Y. Yeadon (1940), R.H. Tucker (1941), Alfred Scarborough (1942), J. Cliff Brown, Sr. (1943), Frank A. McLeod, Sr. (1944), H.I. Mercer (Vidalia, Georgia), S.K. Nash (1945), J.A. McKnight (1946), L.E. Purdy (1947), J.C. Hughes (1948), B.L. Williams (1949), E.P. DuRant (1950), H.C. McLaurin (1951), F.K. Holman (1952), K.E. Ward (1953), E. Frank Bostick (1954), John B. Pate (1955), I.D. Elmore, Sr. (1956), Harry Ryttenberg (1957), Archie L. Caughman (1958), M.W. Edwards (1959), Lester W. Allen (1960), Roland H. Windham (1961), Herman D. Rubin (1962), W.J. Snyder, Jr. (1963), John S. Wilson (1964), Fred E. Brogdon (1965), Marion Moise (1966), G. McBride Dabbs (1967), George A. James (1968), and I. Byrd Parnell (1969).

And the work of this worthwhile organization continues.

(written in 1970)

Sumter VFW Post 3034 Influential

Post 3034 VFW, Sumter County, was organized in 1934[209] through the influence of John L. McInnis, at that time Deputy Chief of Staff for the Department of North and South Carolina.

At the organizational meeting held at the County Courthouse, J. Motte Lawrence was elected as the first Post Commander. For this meeting there were present 150 veterans, but when the charter was issued the enrollment had risen to 228.

The following year the Ladies Auxiliary was organized with a membership of 79.

During the first years of existence of Post 3034 the number o of veterans enrolled fluctuated considerably and the Ladies Auxiliary disbanded in 1938.

When McInnis became Post Commander in 1942, interest revived; and after he had served for four terms, the enrollment had increased. Attendance at meetings reached as many as 180. A building fund was begun and the Ladies Auxiliary was reactivated. Service activities were begun with a marbles tournament for the city schools children.

In 1948, while Riley Jackson was Post Commander, the Evans home at 25 E. Calhoun Street was bought for $18,000 and the Post was able to make a down payment of $8,000 with monthly payments of $200 to be paid until the debt was liquidated. The enrollment at this time had reached 521.

Climaxing the 1949-50 term of Commander T.H. Davis, Jr., was the winning of the Community Service Plaque, an honor that was repeated many times thereafter.

In 1950 membership was reported to have reached an all-time high of 835. This was the time of the Korean conflict when many of the members again donned their uniforms. At this time, R. Kirk McLeod was leading the organization.

During the 1951-52 command of Robert O. Purdy, III, a building bond issue was begun with a view to providing more adequate quarters for the increased membership.

A committee was appointed to seek property upon which to build a Post Home. During the 1952-53 term, a lot containing approximately three acres off Highway 76 West was purchased and building plans were drawn. The property on East Calhoun was sold to Hurst Funeral Home for $16,000 and the sum applied to the cost of the new Post Home, which was begun on December 7, 1953, and dedicated April 9, 1954. At this time Ernie Carima was Post Commander.

Post 3034 Veterans of Foreign Wars has rendered countless services to the young people of Sumter through the many years of its existence. Services that it has initiated and contributed to include: a scholarship fund for worthy students, a safety patrol for the students, an essay contest, help for the high school newspaper, repairs and painting of the trophy case in the high school, sponsorship of a fund for mentally retarded children and a Voice of Democracy Contest for boys and girls. These services are symbolic of the interest in the youth of the Sumter community and show cause why over and over the Post has received the Community Service Award. At least two from Post 3034 have served as state commanders – Robert O. Purdy, III, and Wendell M. Levi.

The work of Post 3034 continues for disabled Veterans as well as for the youth of Sumter. Present commander is Mr. James Heater and the membership is approximately 360.

YMCA Has Rich Heritage

"This is the story of a building and of people. It is the story of an old building and young people."

Thus began a series of articles by Robert Moise in 1966-67 concerning the passing of an old friend, the first Sumter YMCA.[210]

This beloved "home" of Sumter's youth was a towering three-story brick structure on the corner of Liberty and Sumter Streets. What it lacked in beauty was made up in appeal to the young people of that era. The gymnasium, known as "the largest and finest in the South," was the place where there was always something for everyone – ping-pong, swimming, handball, and many other attractions for the boys of Sumter. They loved it.

The lobby was at first the most popular meeting place for committees and other groups that were not too large to be comfortably seated.

There were rooms where young men from the surrounding farms and other places could live while working in Sumter. Among these were Clint Brogdon, Jake and Rock Chandler, John Mahon, Bob Nettles, Fred Ortman and three that roomed together – S.L. Roddey, F.B. Creech, and W.E. Bynum.

A look at the beginning of this "home" of so many of Sumter's citizens will bring to mind some of those outstanding men who worked and sacrificed that a place might be provided for the education, physical and spiritual training and recreation of Sumter's boys.

It was back in 1910 that an organizational meeting of the Young Men's Christian Association was held at the Armory Hall over what is now Brody's Department Store on West Liberty Street. Those present set the seemingly impossible goal of raising $35,000 over a 10-day period for the purpose of erecting and equipping a building for the primarily religious training of Sumter's 2500 young men and boys. It is said that this movement did much to create lasting harmony among the religious groups of the city.

That historic meeting called together most of the prominent citizens of the community. Richard I. Manning (later governor of South Carolina) was toastmaster. Other outstanding citizens of that era who were present to lend their support included Dr. J.A. Mood, T.A. Clarke, Thomas Wilson, C.G. Rowland, W.B. Boyle, R.O. Purdy, E.L. Witherspoon, C.M. Hurst, G.A. Lemmon, T.B. Fraser, G.W. Dick, W.M. Graham, and J.H. McKeiver.

The first board of directors, Dr. S.H. Edmunds, president, guaranteed payment of the first mortgage. Others who signed a mortgage for $16,500 were H.L. Scarborough, C.M. Hurst, L.D. Jennings, R.F. Haynsworth, R.I. Manning, E.C. Haynsworth, and G.D. Shore.

In the early years the religious aspect of the "Y" was stressed. Many outstanding religious leaders spoke on Sunday afternoons to well-attended gatherings of young men.

For years the "Y" was said to be the focal point for all athletics in the city. In 1914-15 the earliest basketball team on record was trained by Coach White. Members were S.K. Nash, L.C. Bryan, P.E. Chatham, D.G.F. Bultman, H.E. Drevenstedt and Joe Chandler.

From that time the Sumter YMCA was the source of many championship teams in basketball, swimming and other sports.

Another highly rated accomplishment of the "Y" was the Better Citizenship program known as Boys' Week. The contest extended over a period of seven months, with each boy keeping strict records signed by his parents, Sunday School teacher, school teacher, and the YMCA General Secretary. The city's first boy mayor was R.F. Haynsworth. The first councilmen were Alwin Burns and I.D. Elmore, Jr. Other members of this "administration" were as follows: Miller Jackson, recorder; Robert Moise, city clerk; Wilson Greene, board of trade; Joe Dean, chief of police; Henry Flowers, Danny McKeiver, Cody Palmer, Frank

McLeod, Stan Stoudenmire, policemen; George Hurst, III, fire chief; Mac Moise, assistant fire chief; Earle Beatson, manager Rex Theater; Lee Rogers, superintendent of water works; Wallace Hinds, Harry Bryan, Magnus Munson, Eddie DuRant, board of education; Tubby Gibson, postmaster; John Lee, Jr., assistant postmaster; Cornelius Wise, health officer; William Belser, city attorney; Phil Booth, YMCA secretary; Billy Rogers, YMCA physical director; "Flop" Shaw, YMCA business manager; Earl Elmore, YMCA swimming director.

The first general secretary of the "Y" was Harry L. Birchard. After serving for some years, he moved away and was succeeded by a Mr. Todd, who was followed by Cuttino McKnight in 1921. Under McKnight's leadership the athletic program was greatly expanded. In 1930 he was forced to move West because of his heath.

Austin M. Francis was the successor to McKnight, and it was under his leadership that the "Y" enjoyed some of its greatest accomplishments.

Under his leadership the swimming program reached a high mark of excellency. At the pool hangs a plaque noting some of his achievements.

The basketball program made an outstanding record while he was secretary of the YMCA. At one time the national basketball championship was held by his team. Other sports programs were developed and many, many boys received worthwhile physical training.

Following Francis was Carl Link, a professional YMCA worker under whose guidance many winning teams in various sports were trained.

He remained until 1949. Among others serving as general secretary in the old "Y" were Charles Nooney and Bobby Richardson. In 1961 Bob Vetter, a young youth worker from New York, came as secretary.

In 1966 the old "Y" building that had been the "home" of so many boys and young men for approximately a half-century was demolished and many looked on with nostalgia for the "good ole days."

But the story of the YMCA of Sumter was far from ended when the old 1910 building was no more. A fund was raised under the leadership of the late Shepard Nash and Julian Buxton. There was also an E.C. Kneece bequest for its successor.

A beautiful and spacious modern Sumter Family YMCA has been built on Willow Drive, with Robert Vetter as first general secretary. In 1968 Jack Harvie succeeded Vetter.

Under his leadership, in 1961, an expansion program was begun. The YMCA complex now has two gymnasiums, a swimming pool, courts for handball, basketball and other indoor sports, indoor and outdoor running tracks, a game room, club rooms, a fitness center and other facilities.

In the new wing of the building is a lovely chapel, dedicated to Mrs. Mary Warren. On the wall is a plaque reading: "In gratitude to Mrs. Mary Burgess Warren for her many years of wise and devoted service given to the women of Sumter."

There are instructional programs for yoga, baton twirling, modeling, cooking, sewing, parent-child programs, fitness for overweight, as well as normal persons and for adults and families.

The "Y" also directs a camping program, both day and resident. Camp Mac Boykin in Manchester Forest, known as the "All-American Camp," offers an outstanding program for boys and girls seven to twelve. Each summer many boys enjoy the facilities offered by the "All-American Camp" or Camp Mac Boykin in Manchester Forest, made possible by a trust fund furnished by a real friend of Sumter's boys, the late Mac Boykin. In addition, there is the Camp Counselor program for 14- to 16-year-old youths who think they would like to be camp counselors.

Through a trust fund, the "Y" issues scholarships each year to 120 children.

A summer care program with arts and crafts, sports and other forms of recreation is held for six hours a day. One of the outstanding programs of the YMCA is the swimming classes for special education students, taught by Mrs. Charles Cuthbert.

The "Y" is under the leadership of a professional staff consisting of the following: Woodie Thomas, general director; Morris Peltz, director of fitness; Sollie Till, director of P.E.; Bill Whatley, director of aquatics; Frank Neal, director of the fitness center.

The officers of the board of directors is composed of: William H. Price, past president; L. Stanley DuBose, president; Mrs. E.C. Kneece, vice president; Mrs. W.H. (Dot) Weishun, secretary; Alvis J. Bynum, treasurer.[211]

Thus the YMCA continues as "Sumter's Finest Center for Fun, Fitness, Sports, Camping and Recreation." [212]

PART XIII. WOMEN'S ORGANIZATIONS

American Legion Auxiliary

A very efficient "Aide" to the American Legion, the American Legion Auxiliary is composed of (a) mothers, wives, sisters, daughters and granddaughters of members of the American Legion or (b) of men and women who lost their lives in World War I, World War II, the Korean War or the war in Vietnam or (c) veterans who have died since being honorably discharged and women who are veterans themselves.

There are more than 13,000 local units in the United States, the territories and six foreign countries.

The American Legion Auxiliary was established by an act of the First National Convention of the American Legion in 1919, and its program has always been the furtherance of the American Legion's program of service to the community, state and nation, implemented through more than 20 national well-constructed plans.

The National Headquarters of the Auxiliary is in Indianapolis, Indiana, in a spacious and imposing headquarters building. The Auxiliary is organized into state departments, multi-county districts and local units, with officers and committee chairmen in each.

The Sumter Unit No. 15 had its charter approved January 29, 1922. The Unit has had some of Sumter County's leading women to serve as officers. The first president was Mrs. E.W. Dabbs, Jr., and currently the office is held by Barbara Kirk (Mrs. Harold G.).[213]

Mrs. Kirk believes that the programs and service possibilities are so varied that each member may find something in which to become interested and involved.

The program that is of prime importance in every level of the Auxiliary is the rehabilitation of disabled veterans. The family of a veteran who is in the hospital or unable to work becomes the special interest of the Auxiliary. One program that has proved of great value in South Carolina is the special Gift Shop program at the Columbia and Charleston Veterans' Hospitals. The program is helpful not only as a financial asset, but it brings cheer at the Christmas season for the Veteran and his family.

Another program in which the disabled veterans themselves become involved is the Poppy Program. Hospitalized veterans make the poppies which are sold by volunteers during Memorial Day weekend. The proceeds are used exclusively for the veterans hospitals. Last year over $2,600 was donated in Sumter County through this endeavor.

Special emphasis is placed by the Auxiliary on services for the children of veterans. One of these emphases is the Americanism program. The Auxiliary considers patriotism of paramount importance in the education of the youth of the land. Respect for and use of the flag are stressed with children and adults. The local unit places flags in the various schools upon request. An Americanism Essay Contest is sponsored annually by Unit No. 15 with three monetary awards offered. And the first place winner receives also a beautiful medallion.

As suggested by the national organization, Unit No. 15 also contributes toward sending a social studies teacher to an annual graduate-credit seminar offered by Freedoms Foundation at Valley Forge, Pennsylvania. This seminar offers a three-week session with lectures structured to assist the teacher in classroom effort to increase the understanding of, faith in and support for the American system of government.

There are efforts made to help young people understand legislation, National Security, conservation, foreign relations and other important features of the American way of life.

As a part of this program, American Legion Post 15 and Auxiliary Unit No. 15 send each year selected boys and girls to Boys State and Girls State. This program gives high school boys and girls a week of training in government affairs, teaching them in a concrete way the responsibilities and privileges that American citizens have.

The needy children of the community, especially the children of veterans, receive help from the Auxiliary. They are provided clothing, as well as dental and other health care through the help of this organization. And Unit No. 15 contributes toward the Children's Heart Fund, sponsored by the National Auxiliary. Through this program children receive heart operations which they would never be able to receive otherwise.

Scholarships and loans are also arranged for the education of needy children.

Ever seeking ways to promote education of the children of America, the American Legion and the Auxiliary initiated American Education Week in the schools a number of years ago with the purpose of acquainting parents with the educational advantages afforded by the schools.

Mrs. Kirk explains that Unit No. 15 endorses the National Auxiliary's Foreign Relations program which helps to fight communism in a designated country each year by contributing toward the building of schools, improving homes, roads and general living conditions.

Members of the local unit keep informed through the Legislation and National Security committees as to bills being considered in Congress and they are urged to keep in touch with Senators and Congressmen, giving them their views on these bills. And members are urged to vote in all elections.

Individual members of Unit No. 15 are ever looking for opportunities to serve. They work in their churches, help in literacy work, assist in the annual Special Olympics Program for Handicapped Children, visit in the nursing homes and the Green House and answer many other calls for service.

Other officers of the Unit are as follows: Peg Ray, vice president; Dot Wright, parliamentarian; Carol Black, secretary; Fay Lowe, treasurer; Lucile Crawford, chaplain; Myrtle Wright, historian; Jessie Cook and Inez Brabham, sergeants-at-arms.

Auxiliary Brought Joy To Patients

"If you can anticipate the needs of a patient and work well with others, there's a place for you on our team."

No doubt such an idea was in the minds of a few generous, kindhearted, sympathetic women in Sumter almost 50 years ago when they made plans to organize themselves and others into the Woman's Auxiliary of Tuomey Hospital to "exist as long as agreeable to the governing board of the Hospital."

The hospital itself was still quite young, having begun in 1894 with Baker-Dick Infirmary. A short time later Dr. Julius A. Mood founded his ten-bed hospital. In 1908 Dr. Dick and Dr. Baker with their associates built what was then known as the Sumter Hospital, and a few years later the Mood Infirmary was consolidated with this institution which later became one wing of the present Tuomey Hospital.

Though these early medical centers, both the Mood and Baker-Dick, sponsored nursing schools, there was need for additional assistance in patient care. Sensing the need and seeing an opportunity for service, these public spirited young women brought to reality their dream of an organization "to assist the governing board of the Hospital by general interest in the needs of the institution." [214]

Any woman residing in Sumter County was eligible for membership if her name was presented by a member and she paid the annual dues of $1. Anyone paying $25 became a life member and the recipient of all privileges of membership.

Meetings of the organization were held quarterly – January, April, July and October. Place of meeting was "preferably at the Hospital, as it would thus be more convenient, if necessary, to confer with the Superintendent, or one of the physicians of the Board."

At the organizational meeting officers were elected to serve for the 1924-25 term. These included Mrs. Pringle Brunson, president; Mrs. Mitchell Levi, vice president; Mrs. Ferd Levi, secretary; Mrs. W.I. Whitehead, treasurer. Members of the first Board of Directors were Mrs. Julius A. Mood, Mrs. Hugh C. Haynsworth, Mrs. S.C. Baker and Mrs. Robert D. Graham.

Committees were named to be responsible for helping meet pressing needs connected with the care and comfort of patients. These four committees – Investigating, Purchasing, Sewing and Sunshine – were appointed by the president, with the first named serving as chairman.

The Investigating Committee, composed of three members, with Mrs. William Moran as the first chairman, carried out the responsibility of visiting the hospital "singly at least twice a month, without notice and at irregular times" and reporting findings to the executive board. Through consultation with the superintendent, they could also ascertain shortages of linens or other supplies that the Auxiliary would be able to provide. Any complaints concerning procedures in the hospital were to be reported to the president of the Auxiliary, who in turn would report to the Board of Physicians.

Mrs. Yates Yeadon, chairman, with the other two members of the Purchasing Committee, would get estimates for large purchases, reporting same to the executive board. The committee was instructed to make small purchases as economically as possible and make reports to the board.

The Sewing Committee, consisting of five members, distributed to the members of the Auxiliary materials for bed shirts, sheets and pillow cases with directions on how to make them. All donations were to be marked before being sent to the hospital and they were also to be examined by the president for approval. This committee was "the medium through which all gifts from the Auxiliary to the Hospital shall be delivered, and would keep an accurate record of all articles sent with dates of sending and acknowledgments from the Secretary of Board of

Physicians." Serving as first chairman of this important committee was Mrs. Margaret S. Burgess.

To "bring sunshine to the patients well enough to see them, by a few minutes conversation, a little reading, a trifle attention, or any help of a sympathetic nature which might lighten the burden of the sick, or make the hours seem shorter" was the satisfying privilege of the Sunshine Committee. This group, with Mrs. T.H. Siddall, Sr., as the first chairman, was composed of four subcommittees appointed each month by the chairman, "two of whom shall visit the hospital once a week." Before visiting patients, however, they were to learn from a nurse or the superintendent the condition of each one to be visited as nothing was to be done which would result "in the slightest harm."

This was a very active committee, according to Mrs. R.D. Graham. She remembers that special attention was given to accident victims, especially those from out of town. They wrote letters for them and showed friendliness to these strangers in various ways.

Bringing sunshine to children was one of the most enjoyable duties of the committee members. Tots were delighted with the toys, story and picture books, puzzles, etc., brought by their kindhearted friends. There was one child, Mrs. Graham recalls, who was in the hospital for months recovering from burns. This little one, as well as many others, tore at the heartstrings of Auxiliary members, many of whom were mothers with special love for children.

Helping the various committees in their voluntary aid to the hospital were two nurses in the county. These provided background information concerning the patients, information that was necessary for bringing the best results from their efforts. One of these dedicated nurses was Mrs. Lula Boykin Exum, who was beloved throughout the area. It was she who laid the groundwork for the present very efficient Sumter County Health Dept. The other who assisted the organization was Miss Antonia Gibson, City Nurse, whose name in Sumter was and is still remembered as a symbol of selfless devotion to the task of alleviating physical ills of young and old among the less privileged families in the city.

In 1933 the Auxiliary disbanded. Since more nurses were being graduated from the nursing schools and more supervisors were being employed in the hospital, the need for help from the volunteer group was no longer urgent. However, these busy housewives and mothers had gladly shared their time and talent, giving approximately ten years of dedicated service to the hospital staff and bringing joy and comfort to scores of patients.

An organization that is different from the Woman's Auxiliary of Tuomey Hospital, fully as dedicated and broader in scope, is the Woman's Auxiliary to the Sumter-Clarendon Medical Society composed of the wives of the physicians who are members of the Society. This organization was formed in 1923 and is still active.[215]

Sumter has furnished four presidents: Mrs. William Stuckey, Mrs. C. Benton Burns, Mrs. Davis D. Moise, and Mrs. Barney L. Williams, Jr.

Business And Professional Women's Club

Desirous of having a Business and Professional Women's Club in Sumter, Mrs. Myrtis Osteen contacted the Gastonia, North Carolina, Club for information as to the organizational procedure. Her request was referred to the Columbia Club, from which two members visited Mrs. Osteen.

After two preliminary meetings with much publicity and many contacts made by Mrs. Osteen, Miss Adele Moore and a few others, the organizational meeting was held on April 16, 1953, with 33 local women attending. Since the charter would not be effective until July 1, it was decided to leave the charter list open till that date.

First officers elected were as follows: Audrey S. Mercer, president; Adele L. Moore, first vice president; Dell D. Spears, second vice president; Reba Gerrald, recording secretary; Sadie Hodge, correspondence secretary; Lucile Mims, treasurer; Annie Laurie Ethridge, parliamentarian.[216]

From the beginning, the Club held monthly meetings and dues were set at $7.50.

Chief goal of B & PW Clubs is involvement for women. All programs, projects and other activities are geared toward this end. Since 1962 the club has had representation at all National Conventions; while State and District meetings have been attended since 1959. Thus the members are kept informed as to the achievements of other clubs.

Objectives of the club include the elevation of standards for business and professional women, the promotion of their interests, the fostering of cooperation among women in their undertakings, business and professional, and the opening of new opportunities for women through industrial, scientific and vocational activities.

Through this organization, women are ever seeking to serve their communities. They offer scholarships to career women who want to acquire more academic skills.

The Sumter Club sponsored the formation of a Nike Club, a program for high school girls, at Wilson Hall in 1970. The purpose of this club is to prepare its members for a smooth and successful transition from school environment to the college or the working world. "We Strive to Succeed" was chosen as the motto. It was inspired by B & PW's emblem, Nike, which pictures the winged goddess of victory.[217]

Another service of the local club is assistance in manning the Salvation Army Kettle at Christmas time.

Each year the club chooses a Career Woman of the year. Other local clubs are asked to make nominations. More recently the club decided to alternate with the choice of a Young Careerist. The first Young Careerist chosen was Priscilla A. McLeod. In 1977 the choice was Jane Luther Smith, a very talented musician. She has studied in many schools and with well-known masters. She has given concerts in several cities and states, Canada and England.

In 1978 Mrs. Emily Sanders Edens was the recipient of the honor. Mrs. Edens has made an enviable record in the business world. She is director of marketing and public relations at the National Bank of South Carolina and is also a vice president of the bank. She was chosen because of "her significant achievements in her career area and her outstanding contributions to her community."

Last year the club honored as the "Outstanding Career Woman of Sumter, 1979," Mrs. M.F. ("Sunny") Korn. Mrs. Korn is well known for her interest in the protection of animals. She is currently serving as administrator of the local Society for the Prevention of Cruelty to Animals and Humane Education Center. It was largely through her efforts that this center was established. She also serves on the board of directors of Korn Industries, the Furniture Library in High Point, North Carolina, Sumter Little Theater, Sumter Gallery of Art and the Sumter-Shaw Community Concert Association.

Others who have been named Career Women since the program began in 1959 are the following: Mrs. Mary B. Warren (1959), Mrs. Ruby Gallman (1962), Mrs. Katie L. Allen (1963), Mrs. Ruth Sanders (1964), Miss Ethel Burnett (1965), Mrs. Ethel Turbeville (1967), Miss Elvera Mingroni (1969), Miss Lucile McKiever (1971 – now deceased), Mrs. Clara Elmore (1975), and Mrs. Ellen S. Rogerson (1977).

Each year B & PW holds a Civic Night at which time other civic clubs are represented and a special program is presented. For instance, in 1974 the presentation was a very impressive patriotic program, "Birth of a Nation."

At the October 19, 1978, meeting the Sumter Club celebrated

its 25th anniversary, using as a theme, "At the Threshold of New Horizons."[218] Special recognition was given the Continuing Charter Members – Miss Lillian Burkett, Miss Louise Burkett, Mrs. Louise W. Butler, Mrs. Reba L. Gerrald, Mrs. Edna G. Grumbles, Mrs. Ammie LeCoq, and Mrs. Myrtis G. Osteen.

Outstanding Club Members, who have received the Audrey S. Mercer Award were also honored. Listed in chronological order, they are: Mrs. Ammie LeCoq, Mrs. Jennie Cormell, Mrs. Marie Wheeler, Mrs. Martha T. Calahan, Miss Christina Geddings, Mrs. Eleanor James, Miss Eva Boykin, Mrs. Rubie O. Davis, Mrs. Louise Butler, Mrs. Elsie L. Martin, Mrs. Ethel Turbeville, Mrs. Dortha G. Machen, Miss Louise Burkett, Mrs. Jill L. Hailey, Mrs. Celeste T. Rivers, Mrs. Ellen S. Rogerson, Miss Emily R. Sharp, Mrs. Serena Ferguson, Mrs. Brenda L. Crowley, and Miss Barbara R. Mandot.

The Sumter Business and Professional Women is a part of a strong national organization which had its beginning in 1919. It is built on high ideals of the professional status of women and is activated by a consuming desire to be of service to others as is expressed in the last lines of **The Collect** by Mary Stewart.

"And may we strive to touch and to know the great common human heart of us all, and, oh, Lord God, let us forget not to be kind."

Civic League Once Active

Once upon a time (and this is not a fairy tale), when Mayesville had five doctors, two drug stores, three banks, a department store, a gift shop, a jewelry store, a hotel, four passenger trains stopping every day, several grocery stores, a candy kitchen, and other indications of a thriving town, there was a very active Civic League, affiliated with the State Federation of Women's Clubs.

This organization was formed for the purpose of making Mayesville a clean, attractive, progressive center for those living in the community. A constitution was adopted, providing for the usual officers, a time for meeting, and dues of 50 cents each year. The only requirement for membership was a promise to abide by the constitution and pay the dues.[219]

Some of the tangible accomplishments of the League were a "summer house" around a well in the town cemetery, regular clean-up day for yards and streets (with prizes offered for the best results), a cement coping on two sides of the school yard, the planting of silver maples along the street in front of the Presbyterian church. Some of the residents, reminiscing about those days, said that the yards were really swept clean and the children took pride in picking up paper on the streets.

Influence of the group was brought to bear on the mayor and town council for help in the beautification of the streets and schoolyard, including a request that garbage be collected regularly. There was also a petition presented to the town council asking that they contact the County Supervisor and urge him to have work done on the road between Mayesville and Sumter. Many remember the days when that road was a sandbed in dry weather and a series of mudholes in the rainy season. The bridges over 'Scape O'er and Rocky Bluff Swamps were narrow wooden affairs which were rough and unsafe in the best of times.

Petitions were sent to the county delegation asking for their support in the General Assembly on bills having to do with compulsory education, medical inspection, juvenile courts and anti-racing legislation.

A medal was offered for the best essay submitted by a pupil of the school on the topic, "Civic Improvement in Mayesville."

To raise money for the various projects, the League sponsored recitals given by visiting musicians, lectures on timely topics, suppers, a silver tea, etc.

One project that brought in "around $50" (according to the minutes of a meeting) was a "Trip Around the Islands of the Sea." Several homes represented the different islands, and those "taking the trip" paid an entrance fee for each "island" where there were appropriate decorations, entertainment, and refreshments.

The project that seemed to create most enthusiasm and was most profitable from a financial standpoint was a May Carnival. A parade featuring children with wagons, bicycles, and doll carriages was the opener for the festivities. A prize was given for the "vehicle" having the most colorful decorations.

For entertainment there was a "booth to throw at cats," a fish pond provided for the children to "fish" for prizes after the payment of a fee, and a Maypole dance.

A candy booth was available where homemade goodies could be bought. Ice cream and cake were sold during the afternoon; each could be purchased for five cents. At night there was a supper consisting of chicken, rice, pickles, and bread, the price of each plate being 25 cents.

The exciting climax of the carnival was the crowning of the May Queen. Votes were sold during the week at the two drug stores and the Post Office for one cent each. Results were posted each day so that the young men might see how their chosen candidates were running. When the final day came and all votes were counted, it was found that the winner was Miss Netta Corbett, who was sponsored by P.M. Tiller, whom she later married.

Miss Minnie Chandler (later Mrs. Thames of Sumter, now deceased) was second and automatically named maid of honor. Winning third place was Miss Carrie Anderson (now deceased).

The amount of profit realized from the event was reported as $138, a sizable sum in those days.

The only members of the League still surviving are Mrs. T.H. Newman and Mrs. P.M. Tiller.

Some who are no longer living, but have close relatives in Mayesville or in Sumter include: Mrs. F.J. Bass, Mrs. J.D. Blackwell, Mrs. J.F. Bland, Mrs. W.M. Bradley, Mrs. Henry Burgess, Mrs. W.S. Chandler, Miss Alice Cooper, Mrs. E.W. Mayes, Mrs. S.W. Pringle, Mrs. C.D. Cooper, Sr., Mrs. W.G. Thomas, Mrs. R.J. Mayes, and Mrs. E.G. Spencer.

Contributions Of YWCA To Life In Sumter

The YWCA has been, through the years, one of Sumter's most active organizations. The beginning dates back to 1924 when Dr. S.H. Edmunds, chairman of the board of directors of the YMCA, saw that the women of the city needed a Christian organization similar to the YMCA.

He consulted with Cuttino McKnight, at that time secretary of the YMCA, and they appointed seven outstanding women to consider the idea of such an organization. These seven were Miss Linnie McLaurin, Mrs. Mary B. Warren, Mrs. R.C. Forrester, Mrs. A.T. Heath, Mrs. O.H. Foley, Mrs. T.B. Fraser and Mrs. C.L. Cuttino.[220]

After due consideration, it was decided to rent the former home of Miss Eliza Cooper on Church Street for headquarters. The YMCA gave some financial assistance in paying expenses. Memories of Miss Cooper as a teacher of youth lent special significance to the choice of the home.

Mrs. Laura Lebby served as hostess at first and many women enjoyed their meetings. Mrs. Myrtis Osteen, one of the pioneer members of the group, recalls how they prepared simple suppers for 15 cents each and delighted in the fellowship. However, the groups were small at first and the "home" was open only three or four times a week.

As the years passed, the membership grew and the need was felt for the enlargement of the program.

In 1929 the local YWCA became affiliated with the national organization, which had for its objective the promotion of "growth in Christian character and service through physical, social, mental and spiritual training."

The pioneers in the movement in Sumter raised $4,000 to

pay for more spacious quarters and to obtain a secretary from National Headquarters to direct the activities.

In January of 1930 they were able to engage Miss Eva Strawbridge as a temporary director. Then in September of the same year, Miss Martha Robeson came as official secretary. They moved in 1930 to North Main Street.

Miss Robeson remained until 1940 leading the group very efficiently. During those years many leading women in Sumter carried on the work under her leadership and the YWCA had a wholesome influence on the girls and young women of the community.[221]

As the organization grew, many others became leaders. Some of these were Miss Lula Harvin, Mrs. E.M. Hall, Mrs. William H. Stender, Miss Lillian Tisdale, Miss Mary Amerson, Miss Maud Bateman, Mrs. James Douglas Blanding, Dr. Sophia Brunson, Mrs. J.S. Cormell, Miss Goldie Gaston, Mrs. Peter Handte, Miss Daisy Jennings, Mrs. Jenkins Knight, Mrs. J.A. Middleton, Mrs. H.M. Parker, Miss Priscilla Shaw, Mrs. Robert P. Turner, Miss Fannie White, Miss Rebecca Reid, Mrs. Gladys Jackson Knight, Miss Sallie Rembert.

The YWCA carried on for a while a program of recreation, education and worship through two clubs – senior and junior – with Miss Lois McKnight as president of the senior group and Miss Ruby Lawrence (Mrs. Hicks), the junior. Those assisting with the seniors were Miss Irene White, Miss Rosalie Neyle (Mrs. Kenneth Beck), and Miss Nelle Commander (Mrs. D.E. Milling). Assistants for the junior club were Miss Gertrude Cotton (Mrs. D.L. Belvin), Miss Ethylene Dennis (Mrs. Harold Wilson), Miss Thelma DeWitt (Mrs. G.B. McEwen). Adviser for the group was Miss Teresa Chandler (Mrs. Harry Davis).[222]

One of the enjoyable activities sponsored by the YWCA in the early years was an annual celebration of May Day, with all the traditional "trimmings."

After the quarters on North Main Street became too small, the YWCA made several moves, the last headquarters being a spacious colonial home donated by W.B. Burns to the organization on North Washington Street.

From 1967 to 1969 the YMCA, which had built a beautiful headquarters building on Willow Drive, planned expansion including "Family Services." The YWCA, having decreased in membership for a number of reasons, members were offered special Family Night membership if the property was sold and funds given toward the expansion. The adult group accepted the offer.

As years have passed and changes have been wrought in many facets of life in Sumter and elsewhere, programs and activities of YWCA are based on objectives that are different in some respects from those around which the organization began, but the underlying purpose is essentially the same.

Headquarters building is now on South Washington Street, and one of the aims for the future is to provide a new home for the organization.

Another project has been the completion of Dignity Village, an up-to-date, comfortable apartment complex for the elderly, handicapped and/or disabled. This structure, with the cooperation of HUD, is on Blanding Street. This project is an indication of the strong desire of the YWCA to be of service to the community.[223]

Some of the activities of 1979 included: 1. Leadership workshops designed especially for teens; 2. Job Corps recruitment with W.I.C.S. and Church Women United; 3. Statewide leadership training for YWCA volunteers; 4. Development of the pilot busing project for senior citizens and/or handicapped.

Board of Directors for 1979-80 include: Casey Reiling, Cassaundra Anderson, Brandolyn Clanton, Laura New, Waltene Vaughn, Theo Moore, Angela O'Hara, Irene Knauff, Evelyn Gadson, Mary Relihan, Ph.D., E. Lee Craig, Wanda Witherspoon, Nora Greenlee, Nancy Wilson, Lenora Haas, Jean Gray, Rosa Riley, Valeria White, Cecily Graham, Jessie Coleman, Mary Gillard, Dorothy Chatman, and Betty Stover.

These come from education, business, industry, news media, medicine, etc. The overall purpose and work of the Sumter YWCA can best be understood as it is summarized in a letter written by County Attorney G. Werber Bryan, which letter will be quoted here in part:

"To Whom It May Concern:

"As requested I have looked into the policies, projects and program of the Young Women's Christian Association of Sumter. It is a character building organization which has been recognized as being interested, fundamentally, in the well being of girls and women of all ages. That includes furnishing an opportunity, for all who wish to avail themselves, to become self-confident and self-sufficient in the American system as practiced in the United States. This objective of well being for girls and ladies of all ages includes, for the asking, help to achieve stable physical and mental health through the practice of strong, reliable moral principles common to all Christian religions throughout the world.

"The YWCA is an on-going organization in Sumter. It has sustained support from young and older ladies from all socio-economic levels of the Sumter Community . . . It furnishes a wholesome setting of complete freedom of expression under well-informed leadership and guidance. I think it deserves the support of the Sumter citizenry . . . "

Sumter's Girl Scout Program

Girl Scouts are welcomed each year as they ring doorbells and offer for sale their delicious cookies.

But selling cookies is far from the extent of their activities. Proceeds from the sales of the cookies help with expenses involved in their various activities, chiefly camping.

Back in 1945 Rotary Club sponsored the first Girl Scout troop in Sumter, with 12 members. Leader of this group was Miss Dorothy McCullough. The second troop was sponsored by the Kiwanis Club.

Scouting in those days was directed by a county troop board under the direction of Mrs. Martha Graham, with Mrs. J.H. McLean serving as volunteer trainer.

In 1957 a committee was formed to investigate the possibility of having the Sumter troops join the Congaree Council. Serving on this committee were Mrs. Reuben Brody, Mrs. Samuel Lipsey, and Mrs. O.P. Tanner. After extensive study, the Sumter County Girl Scouts gained membership in 1960 in the Council, making the Congaree a five-member council. Since that time, other counties have been added. Responsible for the development of the Sumter County Girl Scout program were Mrs. Hazel Pate, Mrs. C.B. Burns, Mrs. Carolyn Summerour and Mrs. Harrison Harp.

Today there are in the Sumter area three Neighborhoods of Scouts – Shaw, Sumter, and Fannie Ivey, with a total of 44 troops and more than 500 Scouts. The Shaw Neighborhood, with Mrs. Stella Bailey as chairman, has 12 troops with 120 members; Mrs. Fannie Ivey (deceased since this writing) is chairman of the Neighborhood that bears her name. In this Neighborhood there are 18 troops, with 175 girls from six through 18; the Sumter Neighborhood, with Mrs. Gail Stark as chairman, has 14 troops with 200 Scouts. Each troop, of course, has a leader who directs the activities.[224]

Troops are divided into four age groups. Brownies are from grade one through grade three; those in grade four are juniors; cadets are ages 12 through 14; girls from 15 to 18 are seniors.

Troops meet once a week with programs lasting two hours, through the fall, winter and spring; but there are no regular meetings during the summer.

Their programs consist of ceremonies, songs, crafts. The girls are taught career exploration and are trained in the social graces.

Emphasis is on spiritual development.

The Scout program is geared to the development of each girl to her greatest potential. Scouts are inspired to strive for the highest standards of character, conduct, patriotism and service. They are commended for accomplishments and are thus encouraged to work toward improvement.

In many ways these girls serve their communities through the schools, the churches and in other ways. They help collect trash from the streets. They work in landscaping yards and streets, planting bulbs for beautification. They help with the Special Olympics held each year for handicapped children.

During July and August they enjoy Day Camps which last for several hours five days a week for two weeks. The charge for these camps is $11.00 for members and $11.50 for non-members. The Sumter and Fannie Ivey camps are held on the grounds of St. Christopher Episcopal Church. The Shaw Neighborhood camp is at Shaw. Former Sumter Day Camps were held at the cabin and pond of Mr. C.C. Goodwin near Shaw Field.

Camp Congaree is open during the summer for those who can attend; however, those wishing to attend need to register some time ahead in order to have a place. There are paid counselors there all summer to direct the programs.

Proceeds from the sale of cookies, some from United Way and other donations help pay the expenses for the year-round Scout program.

Scouting is a great program for any community and it would be worthwhile to have every girl engaged in the activities of Girl Scouts. Sumter County is fortunate to have such widespread interest among both girls and adults.

Much credit is due those dedicated women who have given and are giving time and talents in leading young girls, instilling in them the highest standards of living and inspiring them to give in return their service to others.

Great Things Undertaken And Achieved By DAR

With the motto, "God, Home and Country," the National Society Daughters of the American Revolution undertakes great things and achieves great things. And the theme for 1979-1980, "A Tapestry of Service," further demonstrates the underlying purposes of this important body of patriotic American women.

The National Society was founded with a threefold purpose: (1) "To perpetuate the memory and spirit of the men and women who achieved American independence"; (2) " . . . to promote as an object of primary importance, institutions for the general diffusion of knowledge"; (3) "to cherish, maintain and extend the institutions of American freedom, to foster true patriotism and love of country and to aid in securing for mankind all the blessings of liberty. It was granted a charter by the U.S. Congress, signed by President Grover Cleveland in 1896.[225]

The National Society now has over 209,000 members. It is headquartered in Washington, D.C., in a complex of magnificent buildings near the White House. The connected buildings fill an entire city block and are visited each year by thousands of people to browse through the Museum Gallery, the Genealogical Library, the Historical Research Library and other interesting rooms.

The work of NSDAR follows three main objectives: historical, educational and patriotic.

Sumter's Home Chapter, founded in 1900, is an integral part of this great national organization.

Organizing members of this chapter were as follows: Miss Edith M. DeLorme, regent; Mrs. Jeannie Baker, vice regent; Miss Catherine Moses, secretary; Mrs. Virginia Phelps, treasurer; Miss Dulce Moise, registrar; Mrs. Marian Kershaw Carson; Mrs. Armeda C. Emanuel; Miss Caroline Moses; Miss Rebecca Schwerin; Mrs. Clara Childs; Mrs. Isabel Moise; Miss Eleanor R. DeLorme.

South Carolina DAR is divided into six districts and Sumter is in District V. The present District Director is Mrs. Marilyn Ayers of Sumter's Home Chapter.

A committee was appointed at the 72nd Continental Congress to aid and encourage the "preservation of our rich heritage in the fields of art, crafts, drama, literature and music." The program thus established gives opportunity to all state and local chapters for activity.

In the educational phase of the program, DAR offers many scholarships in nursing, as well as medical and occupational therapy. During the past year these scholarships amounted to $41,000. There is also in the program an $8,000 American History scholarship.

Several schools are supported by NSDAR. The South Carolina chapter helps support the national school at Tamassee in Oconee County.

This school had 30 buildings on 790 acres. The chapters furnish food, clothing and an education to 250 boarding students and classroom instruction to 250 day students. Sumter's Home Chapter has a part in this worthwhile endeavor, as well as in many other activities.

Work among the Indians is another important interest of DAR. One year, more than $100,000 was given for scholarships and clothing for Indian children.

Conservation and energy problems concern the members of DAR and they find many opportunities for service in these areas.

In addition to cooperative efforts in conjunction with NSDAR, states have their individual projects. For instance, South Carolina is undertaking the furnishing of a parlor in the Old Exchange and Customs House in Charleston, which was deeded to "the Order of Daughters of the American Revolution in and of the State of South Carolina to be held by it as a historical memorial in trust . . . "

In this project Sumter's Home Chapter is asked to participate with donations of money and/or suitable objects for the room.

Chairman of Old Exchange and Custom House restoration project for District I is Mrs. Herbert Rosefield of Sumter.

Through the years many have served as regents of Sumter's Home Chapter, some serving for more than one two-year term. Names available are as follows: Mrs. S.C. Baker, Mrs. E.S. Booth, Sr., Miss Sophia Brunson, Mrs. H.M. Stuckey, Mrs. P.D. Aman, Mrs. S.C. McKeown, Miss Catharine Bass, Miss Louise Burkett, Miss Ammie Wells, Mrs. Robert Purdy, Mrs. J.H. McLean, Mrs. John D. Pate, Mrs. M.V. Dawkins, Mrs. Perry Moses, Mrs. Dorothy Lennox, and Mrs. Marilyn Ayers. [226]

The first yearbook was prepared for the use of the chapter by Miss Catharine Bass during one of her terms as regent.

The present officers of the local chapter are as follows: Mrs. H.A. Rosefield, regent; Mrs. Harvey W. Tiller, vice regent; Mrs. W.S. Heath, chaplain; Mrs. John B. Duffie, rec. and cor. secretary; Mrs. A.M. Kendrick, treasurer; Mrs. A.M. LeGrand, registrar; Mrs. J.H. McLean, historian; Miss Ruth Lyon, librarian.

The programs for the year follow themes suggested by the three objectives of NSDAR – historical, educational and patriotic. For some of these meetings there are special speakers.

All meetings are held at the John Rutledge Sumter House.

The Daughters' Book Club

Reading maketh a full man, conference a ready man, and writing an exact man. – Bacon.

And what could fulfill this philosophy of Sir Francis Bacon better than a book club which encourages the reading of many books, the discussion of these books and the writing of many papers giving facts and opinions concerning the books or their authors.

In Sumter's early days many with a desire for improving their minds through reading formed clubs for this purpose. There were three such groups to which belonged ladies of keen intellect, studious habits and mental curiosity.

The oldest of these three was the Woman's Literary Club, organized in 1906. It met on Thursday afternoon. According to Miss Julia Reynolds, whose mother, Mrs. Mark Reynolds, was a member of this club, the ladies were encouraged in forming the club by Rev. H.H. Covington, rector of the Church of the Holy Comforter.

A list of charter members is not available, but a yearbook of 1909 gives a listing of officers and members, most of whom doubtless were members in the beginning.

Officers that year were Mrs. Covington, president; Miss Kate Furman, vice president; and Mrs. W.W. Rees, secretary-treasurer.

Other members at that time were Miss Edith DeLorme, Mrs. S.H. Edmunds, Miss Annie Graham, Mrs. E.C. Haynsworth, Mrs. Hugh Haynsworth, Mrs. W.H. Ingram, Mrs. C.W. Kingman, Mrs. R.I. Manning, Mrs. R.C. Richardson, Mrs. George Shore, Sr., Mrs. T.H. Siddall, Mrs. S.M. Spann, Mrs. John Rutledge Sumter, Miss Elizabeth Lemmon.

This club received materials from the Extension Department of the University of South Carolina, and that particular year they had set for themselves the study of Shakespeare.

Through the years this club has continued its ambitious undertakings, though today they sometimes have visiting speakers instead of following the requirement of writing and presenting a paper at each meeting.

The next club in point of age has met from the beginning on Wednesday afternoon and is thus sometimes called the Wednesday Book Club, but its official name is "The Book Club." It was organized in 1923.

Some of the earliest members were Mrs. Dozier Lee, Mrs. Fenwick Murray, Mrs. Shepard Nash, Mrs. Earle Rowland, Mrs. Scott Rumph, Miss Elizabeth White, Mrs. Itly Wilson.

The youngest of the three early clubs was organized in 1933 and followed a slightly different program of study. Known as The Current Literature Club, it had as its objective the keeping up with trends in modern writing. This club has now disbanded.

Some members of this club were Mrs. Robert Bland, Mrs. J.P. Booth, Jr., Mrs. Belton Boyle, Sr., Mrs. Fred Heath, Mrs. M.F. Korn, Mrs. Ashby McElveen.

For many years it followed its program with interest and enthusiasm making a worthwhile contribution to the reading interests of the community. However, it is no longer in existence.

These early literary-minded mothers must have shown great skill in creating interest in reading for they set a precedent that has been followed by their descendants.

In more modern times daughters and daughters-in-law of those book lovers have devoted themselves to the same pursuit of knowledge. They have a very active club known as The Daughters' Book Club.

They meet on Tuesday afternoon of each month and follow much the same program used by their mothers.

Their constitution limits the number to 18 and when there is a vacancy a "daughter" is presented and voted on by ballot. No "daughter's" name is presented who is a member of another book club.

Charter members of the club were as follows: Mrs. Thurston Bagnal, Mrs. Lauren Booth, Mrs. Richard Burns, Mrs. Wilson Greene, Jr., Mrs. William Harritt, Mrs. Sam Hunter, Jr., Mrs. Louise Jumper, Mrs. Frank McLeod, Jr., Mrs. Kirk McLeod, Miss Margaret McElveen, Mrs. Cordes Palmer, Mrs. Mary Rembert, Miss Annette Roddey, Mrs. Scott Rumph, Jr., Mrs. Glen Sharp, Mrs. Nora Jane Throckmorton, Mrs. Melton Tisdale, Mrs. John Wilson.[227]

First officers were Mrs. Wilson Greene, Jr., president; Miss Margaret McElveen, vice president; Mrs. Sam Hunter, Jr., secretary-treasurer.

Present officers of The Daughters' Book Club are Mrs. Frank McLeod, Jr., president; Mrs. Henry Bynum, vice president; Mrs. Glen Sharp, secretary-treasurer.

Each member pays annual dues of $5.00. This money is used for the purchase of books for the club's use.

For the club programs members present original papers. Each member is required to give a paper in alternate years. To show the wide interest of these members, a few of the subjects treated in the past may be listed: a paper on Germany, the Life and Works of Leonard Bernstein, a paper on Graphology-Handwriting Analysis, Life of Eliza Lucas, Charles Dickens. At some meetings there are outside speakers.

Instead of the regular meeting in May, the club has a luncheon. In May 1980, the living mothers and mothers-in-law of members were invited. These included: Mrs. Robert Bland, Mrs. E.T. Broadwell, Mrs. J.P. Booth, Mrs. Belton Boyle, Sr., Mrs. Sydney Burgess, Mrs. W.B. Bynum, Mrs. M.F. Korn, Mrs. Ashby McElveen, Mrs. Francis Moise, Mrs. S.W. Rumph, Mrs. Itly Wilson, Mrs. Marion Zemp.

Members of The Daughters' Book Club are enthusiastic in the work of their club, and the intellectual growth suggested by Sir Francis Bacon continues in Sumter from generation to generation.

First In The World

Bethel Home Demonstration Club, organized in 1915 by Mrs. Mary Lemmon McCoy, Home Demonstration Agent, was officially declared in 1962 as the oldest such organization in the world.

After a careful check of evidence and research through the U.S. Department of Agriculture, it was determined that the Bethel Club was the first and was so declared.[228]

Charter members of this club were as follows: Mrs. Bruce R. Barkley; Mrs. G.L. Broadway; Mrs. Dwight Cain; Mrs. Harry Cuttino; Mrs. R.B. Furman; Mrs. J.N. Griffin; Mrs. S.A. Harvin, Sr., vice president; Mrs. William Haynsworth, president; Mrs. Hannah Ingram; Mrs. J. Dargan Jones; Mrs. J.M. Kolb; Mrs. Silas Kolb; Mrs. George Nettles; Mrs. Henry Pritchard; Miss Tallulah Ramsey; Mrs. H.H. Wells; and Mrs. G.M. Zeigler.[229]

In recognition of the honor accorded this club, the Sumter County Historical Commission placed a marker on the old Bethel School grounds in September of 1962.[230]

The inscription reads as follows: "Here in Bethel Community, in March 1915, the first Home Demonstration Club in the world was organized by a group of women under the leadership of Mrs. Mary Lemmon McCoy, Home Demonstration agent, Sumter County Extension Service of Winthrop and Clemson Colleges, State of South Carolina." The names of charter members follow on the marker.

Mrs. Ralph Gates, who has been an active and efficient president of the club for many years, led the members in getting data to prove the authenticity of the origin of the organization and was instrumental in furthering plans for the erection of the marker.

Six of the original 17 members were still living at the time of the erection of the marker and those who were able attended the dedication ceremonies.

Mrs. S. Oliver Plowden, who was influential in the Home Demonstration Club movement in the state, aided in research for the marker.

Mrs. Gates introduced the county and state dignitaries who were present for the occasion.

Many Homemakers' Clubs In County

"To cooperate with others for the common ends of a more abundant home and community life."

Thus reads the concluding point in the creed adopted by the South Carolina Extension Homemakers Council; and from the beginning of Home Demonstration work in Sumter County, this purpose has motivated the women to endeavor to make their community the "best of communities," though at first there was no South Carolina Council and there was no creed as such.

That first little group in the Bethel community, with Mrs. William Haynsworth as president, working hand in hand to improve their homes, were entirely unaware of the influence their efforts would have on other women of the county, state, and even beyond. Little did Miss Mary Lemmon (later Mrs. McCoy) and the 17 charter members of that "first Home Demonstration Club in the world" realize that they were launching a movement that would be so far-reaching as it proved to be as time went on.

Since 1915 when the Bethel Club was organized, the work has grown from year to year.

Many leaders, known at first as Home Demonstration Agents, but now called Home Economists, have advanced the work since Mrs. Mary Lemmon McCoy organized that first club.

In 1954 the clubs began serving every citizen instead of farm women alone.

An important general goal of the Council requires that "each Homemaker should serve as a volunteer teacher-leader in her community to reach low-income homemakers with information in nutrition and health . . . " The response to this goal has indeed been praiseworthy. Members of the various clubs have engaged in such services as urging parents to have children immunized against disease; sponsoring programs to bring cheer to the elderly and sick; soliciting help for families that had lost homes by fire; teaching nutrition to low-income families; helping with special drives.

Goals set for the third department of work – Citizenship, Civil Defense and Conservation – involved the wholehearted cooperation of club members with other agencies in creating a "more beautiful Sumter County" and in informing through special interest meetings all family members of the importance of preparedness in case of emergencies.

Each club member was held responsible for making her own home and surroundings attractive. In order to give concrete aid in the beautification program, clubs made a special study of plant material and native plants that could be used to advantage, and in two centers demonstrations in proper pruning were given.

Good citizenship was stressed by the displaying of flags and the giving of the pledge and salute at all club meetings. A study of pending legislation was undertaken and contacts (by letters or visits) with legislators were made.

All members of clubs studied the "Family Survival" lessons and each club taught the course to others in the community.

Homemakers clubs would naturally focus their efforts on improvement of family life, setting as a goal the teaching of "family stability through understanding one's self and extending to the less fortunate a helping hand." Accomplishments in this area were very similar to those realized in Community Service, since a well-adjusted family is concerned with the community as a whole, as well as with its own well being. Good homes naturally form the nucleus for good communities. Such services as providing inspirational programs and recreation for shut-ins and arranging tours, picnics, parties for the less fortunate were some of the activities undertaken.

One of the most important phases of the Council's outreach is in the area of health. The chief goal of this department of work has been to dispense information among the low-income and less fortunate families concerning proper nutrition and to urge people to take advantage of clinical services – tests, examinations, etc. – offered by the county health agencies. Clubs accomplished much in attaining this goal by cooperating at all times with the various agencies in putting on drives and ministering to those in need of health care.

Interests of Homemakers extend far beyond the borders of Sumter County. Ever eager to learn ways of improving their services, Council members have in their program an International Relations Department. They have made a study of customs in other nations through letters exchanged with members in four different countries and through subscriptions to "National Notes."

In striving for the accomplishment of the second goal in the area of safety, clubs studied poisonous plants, berries and insects, together with the antidotes for these poisons. Members were urged to study causes of pollution in water and air and the proper precautions.[231]

At present there are 14 Home Extension Clubs in the county with 240 members. Officers include Mesdames Bessie Ridley, Anna Blanding, Nadine Geddings, Mary Barrett, Pat Gates, Bessie McLeod, Teresa Glass, Ruth McGill, and Jacqueline Cummings.[232]

From a look at the diversity of Homemaker's interests, the ambitious goals set and accomplishments recorded, one can readily see that Sumter County Extension Homemakers Council exerts no small influence in the life of city and county alike. Someone has said that "Leadership is the process of helping people do the worthwhile things they want to do." In what better way can the leadership of this organization be described?

Garden Clubs Of Sumter

"If you would have a mind at peace,
A heart that cannot harden
Pick up your hoe and spade tomorrow
And grow yourself a garden."

Sentiment expressed in this little verse filled the hearts of many citizens of Sumter from the beginning of its history. And in 1927 a group of garden lovers, prompted by a great desire to "Make Sumter More Beautiful," decided to promote a program for "The Advancement of Gardening." The result of their efforts was the organization of the first garden club dedicated to the improvement of homes and public property in the city.

This organization was called the Sumter Garden Club, and it began with the following 14 charter members: Mrs. D.G.F. Bultman, Mrs. Julia Lester Dillon, Mrs. Ann Nash Dunn, Mrs. John D. Lee, Sr., Mrs. C.J. Lemmon, Mrs. R. Leland Moore, Mrs. Perry Moses, Sr., Mrs. F.A. McLeod, Sr., Mrs. R.C. Williams, Mrs. Arthur Harby, Mrs. Fred Levi, Mrs. W.L. McCutcheon, Mrs. I.C. Strauss, and Mrs. Allston Stubbs.[233]

The first members chose for themselves one purpose: "improvement in civic beautification, and the seeking of knowledge on How to Grow, What to Grow, and Where to Grow," and under the leadership of Mrs. Williams, president, they pursued this purpose with enthusiasm.

Other officers who played no small part in the leadership of the club the first year were Mrs. Dunn, vice president; Mrs. Stubbs, treasurer; Mrs. McLeod, secretary. Mrs. Dillon, Mrs. Henry Barnett, and Mrs. Strauss composed the executive committee.

During the first year, programs featured such subjects as the growing of annuals, perennials, roses, and iris; the control of garden pests; artistic arrangement of flowers; and other phases of gardening.

As the years passed new members joined the club; while its work and influence grew.

The first flower show was held October 5, 1928, and since that time the Sumter Garden Club has continued to sponsor or assist in sponsoring one or more shows each year.

The year 1930 marked the organization of the Garden Clubs of South Carolina, with Sumter Garden Club as a charter member. In this year also, the club became affiliated with the South Carolina Federation of Women's Clubs and Owner Rose Society.

In 1931 two other areas of study and promotion were added to the general program of the club – Landscape Design and Bird-Life. In the latter area, the club encouraged an extensive educational program, putting up Bird Sanctuary signs at the northern and southern entrances to the city, and presenting to the Public Library a copy of "Carolina Bird Life" by Spruitt and Chamberlain.

Mrs. Julian Buxton, because of her interest and accomplishments, was chosen State Bird Chairman in 1951 and National Bird Chairman in 1955 and again in 1957.

A highlight of 1934 was the sponsoring of a Junior Garden Club, with Mrs. A.T. Heath, Jr., acting as chairman of this project. This year also marked the first Garden Club Center in South Carolina, located in a cottage on the grounds of Mrs. Leland Moore's home.

Approximately ten years after the beginning of the Sumter Garden Club, the Iris Seal was designed by Mrs. Dillon and used by the club as a means of promoting interest in the Iris Gardens and in raising money for other civic endeavors.

Although through the war years the club was inactive since members were engaged in the war effort, it was reorganized with an increased membership and renewed enthusiasm, and during the following years, much hard work was done and many valuable services were rendered by the club. Proof of these achievements was shown in 1950 when Sumter Garden Club received from the Garden Clubs of South Carolina first place award for best report of work done.

One of the most far-reaching and valuable achievements has been the sponsoring of other clubs. The impressive list of clubs, organized by gardeners who at one time were members of Sumter Garden Club or a club organized by a member of Sumter Garden Club, follows:

Garden Makers (1946) by Mrs. Frank Chandler, Mrs. Edwin Boyle, and Mrs. Julian Buxton.

Poinsett (1946) by Mrs. Victor Barringer and Mrs. Frank Chandler.

Iris (1950) by Mrs. C.E. Hinson of Poinsett.

Bland (1950) by Mrs. Henry P. Moses.

Gay Gardeners (1950) by Mrs. Ann Nash Dunn.

Evening (1960) by Mrs. C.E. Hinson and Mrs. A.D. Alcott, of Poinsett.

Azalea (1958) by Mrs. Hinson and Mrs. Alcott.

Perhaps the most significant advance toward civic improvement came in 1950 in the organization of the Council of Garden Clubs of Sumter, with the following officers: Mrs. Edwin Boyle, president; Mrs. Ernest Newman, vice president; Mrs. C.E. Hinson, secretary-treasurer.

The Sumter County Council of Garden Clubs has become a vital part of life in Sumter. Its membership has been on a steady rise and, at present, is close to 400.

A quotation from an address by Mrs. Bradley Morrah before the Garden Club of South Carolina seems fitting as a description of the Council's accomplishments:

> "Coming together is the beginning;
> Keeping together is progress;
> Working together is success."

Each club continues to function as a separate unit, planning programs according to the interests of the members.

The Council of Garden Clubs, after much dedicated effort, realized in 1964 a long cherished dream of having a Garden Club Center large enough to accommodate all the clubs with their varied activities, as well as events sponsored by the council. Mr. Edwin Boyle and other interested citizens and groups assisted in the enterprise.

The Center, located on a hill overlooking Swan Lake, is a beautiful structure, planned and furnished with expert and loving care. At the front is a spacious and well-appointed meeting room. There is also a library containing numerous books, magazines, and pamphlets dealing with all the facets of garden club work.

Most of the lovely furniture was donated by Williams Furniture Company (Georgia-Pacific) through the courtesy of W.E. Covington.

The Center is known as the Alice Boyle Center, having been dedicated to the late Alice D. Boyle, a faithful member of the Sumter Garden Club. An excerpt from the history of the Sumter Garden Club attests to the fact that she was most deserving of the honor:

"Our club had a very Special Award bestowed on our beloved and deserving Alice D. Boyle. The Garden Club of South Carolina gave Alice this special Achievement Certificate of Merit for Exceptional Achievement in the Garden Club Movement of South Carolina.

"No individual could be more deserving of this high award. Alice became a member of the Sumter Garden Club in 1931 . . .

In 1946 Alice helped organize the Garden Makers Club, in 1949-50 Alice was Flower Show School Chairman, and worked to organize Garden Council and has served as Council President, President of Sumter Garden Club, President of South Carolina Judges Club and was the first accredited judge in Sumter Garden Club . . . a member of American Camellia Society, South Carolina Camellia Society and South Carolina Rose Society . . . Chairman of the *National Gardener* magazine . . .

"Every member of all Garden Clubs in Sumter feels there has never been a time when Alice Boyle was asked to help in any way, that she has ever said 'No' . . . " She served from 1953-1957 on the National Board as national circulation chairman for the publication *National Gardener.*

In the Center hangs a metal plaque in memory of Mrs. Julia Lester Dillon, who was truly the inspiration for all garden club work in Sumter. She was instrumental in organizing the Sumter Garden Club in 1927 and was its guiding light as long as she lived. Her counsel and encouragement were constantly sought and always followed by members of the Club.

Since its organization, the Council of Garden Clubs has sponsored many worthwhile projects, always with the purpose in mind of making Sumter a clean, attractive, beautiful city to be enjoyed by citizens and visitors. These projects have included Flower Shows, Holiday House Tours, Horse Shows and others.

Another worthwhile service rendered by the Council was the dedication on March 28 of a Blue Star Memorial Highway Marker on Highway 378 in tribute to all those who have served, are serving, or will serve their country in the armed forces. This highway was designated as one of the many Blue Star Memorial Highways throughout the United States and the first in South Carolina. The name comes from the blue star in the service flag, and the marker adds to roadside beautification.

Today the fame of Sumter's beautiful gardens and streets is widespread. In the winter many varieties of camellias, for which Sumter is noted, are found in numerous yards. At the same time a wealth of daffodils, jonquils, snowdrops, and narcissi attract passersby. In the spring visitors to the city are impressed with the colorful dogwood, wistaria, red buds, Japanese magnolia, and other flowering trees and shrubs. Banks of azaleas flash their varied colors; while pansies, violets, petunias, candytuft, thrift present their more modest but equally lovely charm. There are gorgeous rose gardens, too, in summer and fall; and dahlias are a favorite in many home gardens.

"Conserve Today for Our Heritage Tomorrow," theme for the 1973-'75 biennium of the Garden Club of South Carolina, under the leadership of Mrs. Clara Elmore, is in keeping with the purpose for which this influential body was organized in 1930 at Rosehill, Aiken.[234]

This purpose was "To promote the love of gardening among amateurs, to protect and promote the growth of our native trees, wild flowers and birds and to encourage civic planting and civic beauty."

The president's message sent to all clubs in August of 1973 was not only a summary of the scope of work sponsored by the Garden Club of South Carolina, but also an excellent indication of the enthusiasm, knowledge and ingenuity of that president, Clara Elmore of Sumter.[235]

She came to Sumter as the wife of I.D. Elmore and at once became a part of her adopted city, entering wholeheartedly into the life of the community.

With gardening, landscaping, flower arranging and cone craft as hobbies, she naturally became interested in garden club activities, joining the Bland Garden Club in 1950. In 1951 she was elected as president of this club for a two-year term. Again in 1969 she was chosen as president. In the meantime she served as president of the Garden Club Council of Sumter, being one of the two permanent board members of the Council. She was co-chairman of the Alice Boyle Garden Center Building Fund and Building Committee.

Before becoming president of the Garden Club of South Carolina, she served as the Garden Center Chairman for that organization, also as second vice president and on a number of committees.

Though it would be impossible to elaborate on all the many projects to which she has devoted interest, time and personal endeavor in her garden club activities in Sumter, a few will be mentioned.

As chairman of Grounds Committee, she spent countless hours working with others from the various garden clubs in planting shrubbery and flowers in the Sumter Cemetery, relieving the lonely feeling usually associated with cemeteries.

She was chairman of the committee that planned, developed and maintained the mini-parks that have added much to the attractiveness of streets and vacant lots in Sumter. These club members put much work into this project for the Tri-Centennial celebration and many of the lovely little spots are still being tended by various club members. So successful was this project that Sumter received fourth place with $750 in the national contest.

During the forty-third state convention of the Garden Club of South Carolina, meeting that year in Charleston, Mrs. Elmore received the Special Award, "the highest award given to an individual for meritorious statewide accomplishments in line with State Garden Club objectives such as horticulture conservation, birds, civic and roadside beautification." Special mention was made in the citation of her efforts in regard to Mini-Parks and old Cemeteries and her work with the Governor's Beautification Board and with the "Pitch-In Program."

At the same convention, Mrs. Elmore received the Rose Reedy Civic Beautification Award for her work in 1970. She was the first recipient of this "engraved Silver Bowl Award." Thus as a member of the Sumter Garden Club Council and as an active participant in beautification projects, she has brought honor to Sumter and the garden clubs that have a part in the project that gained statewide and nationwide recognition.

By study and attendance upon symposiums, she has become a member of the Nationally Accredited Judges Club of Sumter and a Master Judge in South Carolina.

As a token of appreciation for her service, Mrs. Elmore received the Outstanding Achievement Award from the Sumter Chamber of Commerce in which she is chairman of Beautification. This phase of the Chamber's work has as its purpose "To motivate and assist other civic groups toward the goal of total beautification of the city and county of Sumter." The inscription on her plaque reads: "In recognition of the honor she has brought to Sumter County by her outstanding leadership in the area of beautification throughout the state of South Carolina."

As a vital part of Garden Club work in Sumter is the Nationally Accredited Judges Club, made up of Nationally accredited judges in the Sumter area. Members of this club must: be a member of a garden club, attend study courses, stand examinations, exhibit and win blue ribbons in horticulture and artistic design. The judge must attend symposiums every three years in order to keep accreditation.[236]

Members of the Sumter club are Mrs. Frank J. Bryan, Mrs. C.B. Burns, Mrs. Charles Cuttino, Jr., Mrs. E.W. Dabbs, Mrs. LeRoy Davis, Mrs. Wortham W. Dibble, Mrs. I.D. Elmore, Jr., Mrs. J.P. Gerald, Jr., Mrs. C.E. Hinson, Mrs. John S. Marshall, Jr., Mrs. C.G. Mason, Jr., Mrs. J.H. McLean, Mrs. Henry P. Moses, Mrs. Ray V. Segars, Sr., Mrs. H.J. White, and Mrs. T.M. White, Sr.

Student judges: Mrs. H.J. Archie, Mrs. C.E. Longberry, Jr., Mrs. R.C. Whittle.

Junior Welfare League Fills Many Local Needs

It is very likely that relatively few people in Sumter realize the wide scope of service rendered by the Junior Welfare League. Indeed there are few areas of need not touched by this very active and public-spirited organization.

The purpose for which the League was organized in 1934 gives some idea of the variety of channels through which the volunteer members take part. It reads as follows: "To foster interest among its members in the social, economic, educational, cultural, and civic conditions of their community and to make efficient their volunteer service." [237]

At a time when help was sorely needed in the community, 12 young ladies sincerely desired to become involved in meeting the needs that were so prevalent during those depression days. Therefore the League was organized by these 12 – Allene Bland, Mary Baker, Martha Brice, Margaret Clarke, Annie Peyre Chandler, Mary Clowney, Rekah Francis, Mary Ellen Harvin, Martha McInnis, Allene O'Donnell, Louise Skinner and Priscilla Shaw. Assisting in the organization was the Junior Welfare League of Camden and Mrs. Winthrop Palmer, then national president of the Junior Welfare League of America.

In order to add strength to the organization for the work that needed to be done, they invited others and soon doubled their number.

The next problem faced by the group was how to raise funds to carry on their work, and this problem they faced bravely and enthusiastically. As time went on they sold magazines, Christmas cards, shrubbery; they sponsored antique, fashion and puppet shows; they had bridge tournaments, art exhibits, booths at the Sumter County Fair, delicatessen sales. The list of projects could go on and on as these wide-awake young ladies used their talents to bring in the needed funds for all the things they wanted to do for those in need. And the needs were too many to name.

In their first years as an organization, members made large donations to the Child Health and Welfare Association, provided hundreds of school lunches before the government took over that program. A delivery room was outfitted at Tuomey Hospital. For many years a scholarship fund was used for worthy nurses; much medical help was provided for needy children, such as money for operations and eyeglasses; for two years the League operated a Camp Sumter and then helped with the opening of Burnt Gin for handicapped children; they sent a girl to

Montreat College; they furnished transportation for a crippled child to attend school each day. These were some of the many thoughtful and helpful services the League gave.

It was decided in 1952 to establish a Community Guidance Center which later became known as the Family Welfare Service. For the support of this service the League established a snack bar and store at Tuomey. This proved a tremendous help for the families of patients, doctors, nurses, other employees and sometimes even the patients themselves.

In 1967 the Canteen, an outgrowth of the snack bar, was opened for business on the first floor opposite the business office. Here one may purchase fountain drinks, coffee, hot chocolate, milk, juices, sandwiches and other "eats." League members operate the Canteen on a voluntary basis, for the most part. Proceeds support the Family Welfare Service, which serves children in many ways. It furnishes transportation and supervision for weekly dental clinics, thus relieving the school nurse for special duties. Working as a part of the Service is a clothing committee that collects clothes for more than 100 elementary children each year. Members also aid teachers in special classes in drama, music and art.

Another phase of service is to members of the Golden Age Club, furnishing transportation for members to and from the Club on Hampton Avenue.

At Christmas time, the League has worked with other groups to distribute food to needy families.

The Scholarship Fund, sponsored by the League, has assisted many deserving students to attend college.

The Junior League has monthly meetings at which members gain additional ideas for service in the community.

There are certain restrictions for membership. Invitations are issued each year for women at least 25 years of age to join. Those who accept the invitation, known as "provisionals," serve a training period, at which time they are given a course in city government and service needs in the city. At the end of the training period, they are tested for their eligibility to be confirmed. Each member is required to accept certain responsibilities.

The Junior Welfare League was organized as a service club and it completely fulfills its mission in the community.

Neighborhood Club Honors Charter Members

For years the Neighborhood Club of Shaw's Crossroads has brought joy to many hearts. This unique club grew out of a gesture of kindness and neighborliness when a new bride, Mrs. Brogdon, moved into the community. Wishing to welcome her, Mrs. W.L. Currie invited all the ladies from the vicinity to come to her home to greet the newcomer.

A little later a similar gathering was called at the same place to honor two newlywed couples, Mr. and Mrs. Willie Reames and Mr. and Mrs. Willie Shaw.

Those two gatherings put an idea into the mind of Mrs. H.D. Shuler (Florence Shaw). She suggested that all the ladies of the community begin a sewing club. There was unanimous agreement, and she invited all to her home for the first meeting. Mrs. Ed Pringle was co-hostess for this meeting, which was in February, 1931. Some of the gentlemen in the community said the club would not last a month. But those 17 ladies who gathered that afternoon so many years ago knew they were beginning something that would bring great pleasure to them, and they entertained no doubts as to the success of their plan. Each month they came, rain or shine, sleet or snow; and as others moved into the neighborhood, they too joined the club.

In later years, as one charter member, Mrs. Currie, reminisced, she expressed her memories in poetic form:

"How well we remember the first day we met,
Neighbors all gathered to welcome a dear loving bride in our midst —
Who had left both father and mother.

"The meeting was pleasant and each one rejoiced
Getting out in the beautiful weather,
It was something new in our neighborhood,
For the women to all meet together!

"One precious neighbor was overrejoiced;
Her heart was filled with delight.
The meeting had given her so much joy
She scarcely slept any that night!

"And so a neighborhood club was formed
By two of our dear ladies fair
To meet just once each month of the year
And miss it we would not dare!

"We have met in sunshine,
We have met in rain,
In snow and icy weather,
But always each and everyone
Were happier meeting together.

"So let us go on in the same old way,
Meeting rejoicing together

For there's no better way to show our love,
Than meeting and eating together."

The members at first brought sewing, fancy work, mending to feel that they were not spending idle moments, but soon they left the work at home and just enjoyed the time spent at these monthly get-togethers. Sometimes they had contests or games, but now they just chat, sharing experiences, ideas and neighborly advice.

But time has never been wasted by these devoted friends. They have been constantly planning ways to help one another. Newcomers are always welcomed; new babies are showered; bride-elects are entertained. In times of sorrow, sympathy is poured out through kind and loving deeds.

Each July the club has a picnic for all the families of members. For years, Pocalla was the scene for this joyous occasion. Then Poinsett Park was chosen as the site. Recently the crowd has gathered at the Singleton-Watt pool and picnic area.

The December hostess each year has a Christmas tree. All members bring gifts which are numbered. Then each draws a number and receives a gift.

Mrs. Shuler was hostess for the 25th anniversary of the club, but all members brought food which was served buffet from the lovely dining table.

As the years have passed, many former members have moved away, but they still consider themselves a part of the club and attend meetings whenever possible. There are approximately 25 who live in the Shaw's Crossroads community and in other nearby places who are still active in the club, attending meetings and entertaining.

At a meeting in 1973, for which Mrs. Aleada Weldon was hostess, the only two surviving Charter members — Mrs. Currie and Mrs. Shuler — were honored. They were presented lovely gold pins engraved with the name of the club and the date of its beginning.

Mrs. Currie read the following poetic tribute to the friends who have been bound together with lasting ties of friendship and love:

OUR NEIGHBORS

Dear neighbors of mine,
I love each of you,
For your wonderful work
And the kind things you do.

We have lived here together
Through many years.

We've had many sorrows,
And shed many tears!

The dear ones we loved
Whose faces we can't see,
Are waiting and watching
For you, and for me.

But oh, we've been blessed,
In so many ways
God has given us sunshine,
And lengthened our days!

So let us be faithful,
In all that we do,
Stand close by each other
And always be true!

Let us labor and trust,
Each day do our best
While the sun in its beauty
Sinks down in the west.

When our work here is ended,
And we enter our rest,
May we meet altogether
Where each shall be blest!

Sumter Pilot Clubs

With the motto of Pilot International, "True Course, Ever," as an inspiring incentive, the Sumter Pilot Club came into being. A group of business and professional women met on April 5, 1939, at the Nurses Home of Tuomey Hospital and under the sponsorship of the Florence Club, organized the Sumter Club, the eighth in District 5.

Present to give helpful hints and discuss the role of service clubs were Mr. Claude E. Hurst of the Kiwanis Club and Mr. George D. Levy from the Rotary Club.

A second meeting was held on April 11, when the following officers were elected to lead the young club in its initial activities: Lula B. Exum, president; Bea (Sharpton) Heuttig, first vice president; Maude (Bateman) White, second vice president; Nelle (Commander) Milling, recording secretary; Lenore Gaston, corresponding secretary; Norine Moore, treasurer. Directors chosen were Martha Graham, Teresa (Reese) Davis, Ruth Sanders, Louise Earle, "Peak" (Britton) Aycock, Ada Snyder.

On April 14, 1939,[238] the charter was granted and the

following 27 signed the document listed in the order of signing: Lula B. Exum, Lenore Gaston, Pearl Golden (Lofton), Martha Graham, Maude Bateman (White), Stella M. Hurst, Ruth Redfern Jennings (Sanders), Ada Snyder, Elizabeth Parrot Blanding, Reese Chandler (Davis), Minnie McBride, Gussie H. Williams, Lucile B. McKeiver, Lois B. Raffield, L. "Peak" Britton (Ayecock), Julia Obenshain, Norine Moore, Beatrice Sharpton (Heuttig), Ernestine S. Curtis, Nina M. Phelps, Florence B. Bolger, Nelle Commander (Milling), Louise Y. Earle, Bessie W. Forrester, Ida Brunk, Martha Robinson, Elizabeth White.

Charter Night was observed with a banquet at the Claremont Hotel on September 25 of the same year. In the intervening months, nine new members were added. These were Corrine Schwartz, Corrine Riley, Christine Britton, Isadore Teicher, Ester Breeze, Thelma Chappell, Edith Haddon, Elizabeth Norris, Susie Raffield Cox.

And thus with full sails the Sumter Pilot Club, the largest in District 5 at that time, began its exciting, successful journey. Activities have been many and varied. It would not be possible to recount all the worthwhile contributions made by this organization to the life of the community. The listing of some, however, will give a hint of the services rendered by members, inspired by such themes as "Trailblazing for New Horizons," "Principles of Freedom – Our Trust," "Progress Through Gifts of Time and Talent," "Leadership Through Service," "Hands and Hearts United in Service" and others of a similar tone.

Some of the activities that have engaged the interests of these dedicated women will be mentioned under three categories – money-making, civic and charitable.

In order to have funds for the various objects supported by the club, it was necessary to carry on some fund-raising endeavors. One such project was the selling of stationery and Christmas cards. The first big undertaking was the barbecue supper begun in 1946 by Ruth Lawrence and her group who had been given the responsibility of projecting an idea that could be used from year to year as a means of adding funds to the treasury. This venture was unbelievably successful and was used each year until 1966. That year the Pilot Cookbooks were sold as a money-making project. In 1973 the idea of a Christmas Fair or Bazaar was conceived, and from the beginning was a great success. In 1975 this project netted the club $2,345.71.

Services rendered to others, some in conjunction with other civic clubs and some initiated by the Pilots have been varied and far-reaching. A few will be listed to give some indication of the scope of influence of this active organization.

A contribution was made toward the purchase of an iron lung, a project sponsored by the Elks. In cooperation with the South Carolina Forestry Division, the Pilot Club sponsored a picture, "The River." In cooperation with the A.A.U.W., Sumter Pilots set on foot a movement to begin a Domestic Relations Court in Sumter. Representing the Pilots in this endeavor were Lula Harvin and Bessie Forrester. The Pilot Club assisted the Rotarians with the Red Cross Drive; they have also worked with the Lions in their assistance to the blind. Members also showed an active interest in the U.S.O. while it was in Sumter. When French students were brought to Sumter by the Kiwanis Club, Pilots entertained them with a luncheon and distributed sourvenirs, symbolic of South Carolina. They have cooperated with the American Cancer Society, the Tuberculosis Association, the Sumter County Crippled Children's Society, and other groups.

The Sumter Pilot Club not only helped other groups, but initiated and accomplished many services in addition. One of its loving deeds was helping the Golden Age Club move to its permanent meeting place and from time to time has entertained the Golden Agers with luncheons and parties on special days. Another project of the club was to furnish a room at Solomon's Home and to plan parties for the residents there. Those at the Eastern Star Home are also remembered with parties, and the patients at Hopewell and Hampton are sometimes cheered by visits of thoughtful Pilots.

They encouraged a movement to have agents in the sheriff's department trained in dealing with drug abuse.

During World War II, club members spent countless hours, making surgical dressings, doing home nursing, holding nutritions classes, organizing Red Cross classes for high school students, doing air raid warden service, holding first aid classes, sponsoring volunteer recreational activities. They even went in small groups to Charleston to welcome soldiers coming home from the battlefront. Perhaps the most lasting contribution made for the soldiers was to raise $3,500 for a memorial tablet that was erected on the courthouse grounds, bearing the names of those killed in service. This memorial was dedicated in 1949. Then in 1973 names of casualities in the Vietnam War were added and a memorial service for these was sponsored by the club.

An important contribution to the cultural life in the area was the forming of the Sumter-Shaw Community Concert Association.

To encourage patriotic enthusiasm, this public-spirited organization supplied flags to the YMCA, Thomas Sumter Academy, the Golden Age Club, Francis Marion Academy and other public places. They sponsored the sale of war bonds and stamps.

For the improvement of the educational status of Sumter County, the club sponsored a project to help stamp out illiteracy. Pilot "Peak" Britton took a course in the Laubach Method of teaching reading, the slogan of which was "Each One Teach One." She then conducted a workshop which was attended by a number of Pilots and other interested ladies in the community. These became the teachers. The project proved very successful, with a number of illiterates learning to read.

Another worthwhile and thoughtful gesture on the part of the club was to erect a granite marker at the grave of Miss Antonia Gibson in tribute to her sacrificial service to the community in caring for the sick and needy.

In addition to time given willingly and spent profitably for the good of the town and surrounding areas, members of the Sumter Pilot Club have given of their means to help in needy causes. They have consistently made contributions to the Salvation Army, Girl Scouts, Hope, Meals for Millions, March of Dimes, the Antonia Gibson Scholarship Fund, Child Health and Welfare, the Rehabilitation Fund, projects sponsored by Pilot International, and other projects.

The club donated a child's bed to Tuomey Hospital, three reclining chairs to the new wing of the hospital, sheets and other furnishings to the shelter for children under the care of the Sumter County Civil and Domestic Relations Court. In 1974 they set up a Loan Closet, containing such items as wheelchairs, walkers, etc., for the use of Sumter County residents. Some of the items they bought and others they have solicited from others.

One of the members of the club, Mrs. Martha Graham, gave a home to be used by the Salvation Army. The club furnished a day-room for young men at Shaw, contributing chairs, lamps, pictures, a rug. Packages of clothing and other necessities were sent to a town in France that was accidentally bombed by Americans during the war.

On and on the list could continue of causes to which Sumter Pilot Club as an organization and individual Pilots, as well, have contributed.

Through the interest and aid of this organization, other civic clubs have been formed. In 1967 Pilots organized an Anchor Club at Thomas Sumter Academy with 32 charter members. On October 17 of that year, the charter was presented to the first president, Barbara Cook, by Nelle Milling, president of the sponsoring club.

In 1949 Sumter Pilot Club assisted at the organization of the Pilot Club of Orangeburg, with 24 charter members. The charter was presented to the president of the new club, Annie Laurie Blanton, by the governor of District V, Marjorie Knox of the sponsoring club.

The Evening Pilot Club in Sumter was formed in 1972. Charter night was held on April 17 of that year with the president of Pilot International, Mrs. Frances Keever, as guest speaker. The charter was presented to Elizabeth B. Nettles, president of the new chapter by Frances Carlisle of Charleston, District V governor. Eleanor W. James was president of Sumter Pilot Club.

Others who served as first officers of the new club were Margaret Brown, first vice president; Anne Stokes, recording secretary; Margaret Fortner, treasurer; Mary Schellin, Johnnie Brogdon, Emily Jackson, directors.

Among the outstanding contributions of this club to the community was the presentation of 12 flags to the Sumter County Historical Society Museum-Archives. These are flags used during the Revolutionary War period by the various military units.

The Evening Pilot Club continues to serve the community in true Pilot fashion.

During the year 1948-49, the Sumter Pilot Club assisted in the organization of the League of Women Voters.

Regular programs of the club have been varied and enjoyable. A few of the highlights may be mentioned. Exchange students of Edmunds High School were guests at different times. Guest speakers, including doctors, educators, ministers, businessmen appear on the program from time to time. Interesting papers are given by members of the club. Occasionally a timely film is shown.

In addition to regular meetings, there are many special events. Each year Civic Night is celebrated with representatives from other civic clubs as guests.

One year all civic clubs in Sumter held a joint luncheon meeting with about 350 people present, as a kick-off for the United Appeal Fund. On this occasion, Sen. Ernest F. Hollings was the speaker.

The 25th Anniversary of Sumter Pilot Club was celebrated on April 30, 1964, at the Elks Club. By way of recalling their first meeting, the charter was presented by Maude White and the Code of Ethics was read by Florence Bolger. "Peak" B. Aycock paid tribute to the deceased charter members – Lula B. Exum, who died January 1, 1953, and Minnie McBride, whose death came on March 25, 1956. Sixteen charter members were present for this happy occasion.

Three times District V Convention has been held in Sumter – 1941, 1959, 1967. The meeting in 1959 was a very special event since Ruth Lawrence of the Sumter Club was district governor and Annie Lee Blackmon was secretary.

The 1967 convention drew approximately 250 representatives from 21 clubs throughout South Carolina. Sumter Pilots were assisted in entertaining by clubs from Bishopville, Camden, and Hartsville.

One of the many highlights of this meeting was the joint convention and civic night banquet. Speaker on that occasion was Mrs. Mabel B. Breen of Galveston, Texas. Another enjoyable feature was a musical program by Pilot Norajane Throckmorton, accompanied by Mrs. Eugene Matthews.

The first yearbook for the Sumter Pilot Club was arranged in 1944 by President Lenore Gaston. A newsletter, "The Chatter Sheet," was begun in 1960.

During the forty-one years since it was organized, many honors have come to Sumter Pilot Club as an organization and to individual members, as well.

In 1956 Sumter Pilot Club received the Achievement award for the "Club of the Year," an honor based on outstanding work on local and international projects, membership, attendance and activities. Iantha Reese was president that year.

The 1952-53 scrapbook of the club won first place in the state. This was the third consecutive year that this honor had come to the Sumter Club.

In 1957 another honor, announced at the International Convention was given to the "club having the longest record of no resignations." Sumter had 35 months without a resignation.

The Governor's Golden Half Century Club received Sumter as a member. This club was one of 13 that organized a club during the Golden Anniversary year of Pilot International.

At the 1963 convention of Pilot International Sumter Club received the Safety Award, having worked in numerous safety programs.

Many individual members of the club have been honored for outstanding achievements. Three – Maude White, Ruth Lawrence and Marjorie Knox – have served as District V governors.

In 1952 the staff of the **Sumter Daily Item** decided to recognize women in Sumter who contributed much to the improvement of the community. The first to be named "Woman of the Week" by **The Item** was Pilot Priscilla Shaw, who had just been elected mayor of Sumter, an honor that had or has been conferred on no other woman. Other Pilots receiving the recognition of "Woman of the Week" were "Peak" Aycock, Gussie Williams, Elizabeth White, Goldie Gaston, Lenore Gaston, Nina Phelps, Florence Bolger, Jane Hamer Brooks, Rosalie Rayle, Maude White, Helen Blanding, Portia C. Myers, Ada Snyder, Elizabeth Bryan, Julia L. Dillon, Iris Edens, Norine Moore, Annie Laurie Ethridge, Martha Graham, Dr. Sophia Brunson, Ruth Sanders, Mary Warren, and Ruth Lawrence.

Other members of the Sumter Pilot Club who have been honored for various reasons include the following: Ruth Sanders, chosen by the Business and Professional Women's Club as "Professional Woman of the Year" in 1965; Ethel Burnett, given the same honor in 1966; Mary Warren, given Y.W.C.A. Life Membership; Rosalie Rayle, voted South Carolina "Mother of the Year"; Martha Graham, 35-year pin for service to Sumter County Chapter of American Red Cross; Evelyn Kirkland, the McKnight Award for fostering good relations between Shaw and the Sumter community; Antonia Gibson, the only woman to receive the Health Award, a silver service for Outstanding Service to her community; Evangeline Thompson, the Florence Hall Award for Notable Achievement in working with mothers of pre-school children; Helen Purdy, an award for her work with the Sumter County Heart Association.

The 1970-71 yearbook was dedicated to Martha W. Graham and Martha S. Sibert, "In recognition of outstanding community service in true Pilot tradition of 'Sympathy for Humanity.' "

Sumter Pilot Club has given special recognition to some of its members by bestowing upon them status of Honorary Membership which recognizes "meritorious achievement in Health, Welfare, Education, Religion, Arts and Science or any other endeavor related to the unselfish advancement of human affairs." In 1940 this honor was bestowed upon Miss Elizabeth White, an artist; Mrs. Nina Phelps was added in 1953 for her enthusiasm for all civic work and her years of social welfare work; the honor was given Mrs. Reese Davis in 1960 for her interest and work in all civic activities of the community. Mrs. Martha Graham, Dr. Sophia Brunson and Miss Antonia Gibson were also thus honored.

At a recent convention of Pilot International held at Myrtle Beach, Pilot Mary T. Blanchard received the highest award that a Pilot can receive, the Mildred Henry Davenport Award. This honor, symbolized by a silver vase, is given to the Most Outstanding Pilot in the state.

On April 28, 1976, Sumter Pilot Club held its final meeting of the 1975-76 year with President Mary Hinson presiding. The program, planned to honor charter members, was presented by past presidents.

Past presidents present to give highlights of their terms of office were Maude White, Ruth Lawrence, Alice Rappe, Elizabeth Bryan, Virginia Mood, Iris Edens, Mary T. Blanchard, Marguerite Newton, Katherine Foxworth, Eleanor W. James, Marjorie Nettles, Jean Reames, Elizabeth Kennedy, Lenore Gaston, Iantha Reese, and Ethel Burnett.

Sumter Pilot Club plays an important role in Pilot International which was organized in 1921 when 40 executive and professional women met in Macon, Georgia. They announced as their purpose "to do our part in boosting and putting over any movement for the betterment of the cities in which we exist." Forty years later there were some 430 clubs with approximately 13,000 members in the United States, Canada, England, France, Bermuda and Japan, united for the same purpose.

Since that time (1961), the organization has continued to grow and exert an untold influence for good through the affiliated clubs and their loyal members.

UDC Nourishes Historic Interest

Dedicated to the task of keeping alive the memory of those who laid down their lives in defense of the Southland more than 100 years ago are the faithful women of the South, descendants of those heroes of the Confederate War. Banded together in a strong organization, the United Daughters of the Confederacy, they have missed no opportunity to give honor to those who fought a losing battle and returned home to support their families through years of disappointment, frustration, and privation, as well as those who gave their lives on the battlefields.

Sumter has two very active chapters of the UDC, chapters that have not only kept before each generation the sacrificial devotion of their ancestors, but have made countless contributions to life in the community. In tribute to those who began these chapters, these pages will hark back to those earlier days.

Named in honor of one of Sumter's illustrious soldiers of the War Between the States, Lt. Gen. Richard Heron Anderson, better known as "Fighting Dick Anderson," the first chapter was begun in 1896.[239] This chapter is one of the oldest women's clubs in Sumter and was the 75th UDC Chapter in the nation.

Leading spirit in the move to form the patriotic organization was Miss Caroline Moses (later Mrs. M.J. Moses of Colorado). Others among the 12 charter members were Miss Edith DeLorme and Mrs. Nina Moise Phelps.

Following the pattern of the first UDC chapter, the Dick Anderson Chapter outlined as its chief purposes: "to spread a knowledge of Confederate history; to help perpetuate the brave deeds of the men and women of the 1860's; to care for the needy veterans and their families; to assist with educating descendants of these men and women."

It would not be possible to enumerate all their contributions to many phases of community life. In their effort to advance the education of the young people, they have given historical writings to the various libraries, contributed to educational funds, provided scholarships for students in the county, sponsored writing contests in the City Schools on subjects related to the Confederacy and given prizes for the winners. They have shown tangible interest in caring for the needy among veterans and their families, and made generous contributions to hospitals. Much interest in Southern history they have instilled in their fellow citizens by setting up monuments, shrines and memorials of other kinds. Among these is a marker to commemorate the Battle of Dingle's Mill. They have cared for the monument erected in the Sumter Cemetery in memory of the dead and for the Confederate Monument on Monument Square.

In 1979 plans for an attractive park on Highway 521 near the site of the Battle of Dingle's Mill came to fruition – plans that had been in the making under the untiring efforts of Myrtis Ginn Osteen (vice president at the time) – with a most impressive dedication service in memory of those who gave their lives in this battle.

The featured speaker was W. Loring Lee, Jr., a descendant of Col. George W. Lee, who was a commander in the battle. The speaker has received a Military Cross of Honor.

In the days when there were still "old soldiers" of the Civil War living in the county, this chapter held a dinner for them every year, giving to each of them a "Cross of Honor." They continued to make these awards to descendants of the Confederate veterans, who fought through the years in other wars.

The Dick Anderson Chapter of the UDC is unusual in that it is a chartered organization. When the Confederate Monument Association began to grow weak, their books, papers, funds and property were "willed" to the UDC's. In order for them to accept the inheritance, however, it was necessary for them to have a charter, which was granted to them in 1897.

The property received was known as Monument Square. This square on which was erected many years ago the Confederate Monument is bounded by Liberty, Washington and Hampton. The deed received by the Dick Anderson Chapter leased the land to the City of Sumter for use of its schools for 99 years.

In 1927 the Sumter Chapter of the United Daughters of the Confederacy was founded by Mrs. C.L. Stubbs.[240] At the organization meeting, Mrs. Mauldin, state president, was the inspirational speaker.

First officers of the chapter were as follows: Mrs. C.L. Stubbs, president; Mrs. R.L. Gantt, vice president; Mrs. W. Harry Smith, recording secretary; Miss Florence Hurst, corresponding secretary; Mrs. L. Brunson, treasurer; Mrs. B.O. Cantey, historian; and Miss Lou Pate, registrar.

Mrs. Stubbs held the presidency in a very efficient manner for many years and was in office at the time of her death in 1944.

Sumter Chapter served the community in many civic and benevolent projects from its beginning. They awarded numerous scholarships to grandsons and granddaughters of Confederate Veterans. One of their interesting projects had to do with the planting of an oak in memory of Gen. Robert E. Lee on the campus of the Boys' High School (now Haynsworth Campus of Sumter High School). The tree was actually planted by Gen. N.G. Osteen, himself a Confederate Veteran.

The chapter also has sponsored a service each year for the Confederate dead on Memorial Day in the Sumter Cemetery.

The Sumter Chapter has kept alive the memory of those who fought for their beloved Southland by presenting historic programs such as the one on "The First Nurse Who Wore a Red Cross." This program pointed out the sufferings of the soldiers because of scarcity of medicines and doctors.

Another revealing program was on "Spies of the Confederacy." This program included the stories of two young women and several young men who were willing to risk their lives to serve as spies and successful spies they were.

Many other programs planned and presented well helped the membership to have a great feeling of gratitude to those who served the Confederate cause with sacrifice and devotion.

This chapter observed its 50th anniversary in 1977 with a program on flags, climaxing with the presentation of a five by seven foot flag to Wilson Hall. [241]

Under the able leadership of Mrs. Louise A. Parker, the Sumter Chapter has won many honors in the State and District Divisions.

Three times they have won the silver pitcher for the most outstanding report in South Carolina.

The chapter has had the privilege of presenting four Military Crosses of Honor, one to Miss Essie Rivers, a member of the chapter.

Scholarships amounting to $1,000 have been given over the past four years, and many awards have been earned by patriotic work done.

The Sumter Chapter is one of the largest in the state with excellent attendance and one of the most active. In the past ten years, membership has increased 53%.

Each year a reception is held to honor state and local officers and real daughters. Awards are presented members for their continuing contributions in service to the chapter's work.

And so the good work begun by these two chapters of the United Daughters of the Confederacy goes on, keeping the memory of those valiant men who left home and loved ones to defend the cause they believed to be right warm in the hearts of those who love the South and its culture.

PART XIV. ATHLETICS

PARD Plays Important Role In Sumter County

In a study of recreational opportunities in the city of Sumter made in 1948 by the planning staff of the National Recreation Association, assisted by various municipal, public school and private agency officials, it was found that the city at that time had a population of 26,400, with a potential increase to 41,000 in the next decade. Recommendations were made that consideration be given to the "broadening and extension" of the recreation program in use. Some of the existing recreational centers were described as excellent, but there was a deficiency noted in extent of provision of facilities for active and passive recreation for the population, with no provision for future population growth.[242]

It was recommended that the City Council, Board of Education and the Park and Recreation Board should plan for "substantial increases" to the amount of $1.60 per capita expenditure for recreational expansion.

Since the time of this report, interest in the city's recreational program has grown at a tremendous rate and at the present time the per capita expenditure for recreational purposes for all ages is $30.32. The population is now 60,000.

The recreational program in Sumter really began in the 1930's when the W.P.A. opened Jenkins Center, with Mrs. Ethel Disher and Mrs. Marie Phillips as workers. They taught nutrition, crafts, as well as a pre-school program. Later the program included activities for all ages.

The Parks and Recreation Department was organized in 1947 with Harry Bryan as director.[243] Soon afterward, Memorial Park Center was given by the Heaths to the white youth of Sumter. From this point a recreation plan for the city of Sumter began to take shape.

Jenkins Center on Oakland Avenue, for which the Jenkins family gave the land, was for white children. The W.P.A. building was used. The black children were provided a center in the U.S.O. building. Then Birnie Center was opened for the Blacks on South Purdy. Pearl Brinson was one of the first workers there.

Then came Silver Center on Silver Street. The land was given by Korn Industries. Iris Edens was first director of this center.

In the summers of the 1950's and 1960's, the Elks Pool was used to develop swim teams. Next to Columbia and Abbeville, those teams were the best in the state. Since the mid-1950's, there have been accelerated summer programs in all areas. There is a nine-weeks program for arts and crafts, music, art, and special events.

The Department now operates several year-round centers. Memorial Park for teenagers; Crosswell, all ages; South Sumter, all ages; Birnie, all ages; Jenkins, all ages; Lafayette, senior citizens; Spectrum, senior citizens. However, there are at least three sections in which there is no center – the northern section of the city, Stonehill, and the east side of Lafayette.

The department operates two camps – art at Mill Creek and Shaw-Sumter Day Camp at Shaw.

Beginning the second week of June, special accelerated programs extend over an eight-weeks period for the accommodation of every part of the city and county. These include SKIB (baseball), soccer, softball, tennis, slow pitch for men and women, art and pottery classes, gym, kindergym and kinderart square dancing for teenagers and adults, disco lessons, needlework, cake decorating, yoga, flower arranging.

PARD also sponsors Gamecock field trials, a horse show during Iris Festival, horse show seminar and camps. Sumter Parks and Recreation Department develops and directs projects at county facilities on contract. At Mill Creek there are camping clubs, parties at night, wagon train reunion.

There is an arts festival in both July and February. At Spectrum, quilting is taught and the senior citizens have a gift shop where they sell their handmade articles. They also enjoy luncheons at that center.

All year, basketball and volleyball are available in District 17 facilities, with school coaches in charge. There is a planned program of athletic events. Another interesting offering is the teaching of dog obedience.

The city appropriates money for staff and equipment at the centers. Participants are also taught recycling and clean-up procedures.

At intervals there are competitive sport exhibitions. Creativity is stressed.

Directed by Sim Wright, PARD operates under three sections: parks, headed by Walter McGee; athletics, directed by Gary Stuber; program coordination by Mary Hinson.

South Sumter Park, located at South Sumter and Atlantic Streets, serves over 10,000 people under the direction of Larry Reynolds. It is the newest center and is well equipped for both active and passive recreation. Other parks available for use are Palmetto, Swan Lake, Memorial, Dillon and Crosswell.

There is great need for a park or center at Hilldale, which has no recreational facilities. That, no doubt, will be the next center to be provided. There is need, too, for a modern building for inside recreation to be used by the young people of Sumter. Their teen canteen was sometime ago given to the Sumter County Council on Aging for the use of the elderly. Hence the youth of the city have no place to meet for indoor recreation or activities.

Last year the city bought for the Parks and Recreation Department the old Sumter home next to Memorial Park to be used for meetings of clubs, civic and historical organizations.

Sumter has achieved an excellent record in providing recreational facilities for citizens of all ages. It received First Place rating in the state for two years, 1977, 1978, and even greater service is seen for the future.

Outstanding Sumter Athletes

Athletics is a world apart. It thrives as much on legend as on fact or heroic deeds - of which there are an abundance. This section is a summary, partly recollection; therefore, the writer has taken certain liberties. For instance, Miss Nicholes has been forced to exclude many deserving individuals from her sketches - such as artists and practitioners - simply because they are still living. (Hers is history; this is for fun!) This section in the book looks at the present as well as the past.

Sumter has always been a sports-oriented town. It has one of the largest high schools in South Carolina, one of the nation's leading YMCA's, and outstanding private school participation. Having produced an abundant crop of outstaning individual athletes, this brief summary will necessarily be confined to those who achieved national recognition. This is painful to the writer, because there are so many more brilliant athletes who should be recognized - but space does not permit.

Sumter's earliest athlete to capture national attention was Allan Ralph "Buck" Flowers. Little "Buck" at only 5'7" and 152 pounds was the star of one of Georgia Tech's most successful football teams - the Golden Tornado of 1920. A triple-threat back, he ranks statistically with the all-time greats of football, and in addition was a premier defensive player.

Comparing the records of Flowers and the immortal "Red" Grange, the "Galloping Ghost," is revealing. In Grange's final year at Illinois he ran and received passes for 1332 yards - and he was not a passer or a kicker. "Buck" gained 1423 yards on the ground plus passing, kicking off, punting, and drop-kicking (now a lost art). W.A. Alexander, who along with John Heisman coached him at Georgia Tech, paid this tribute to "Buck" Flowers: "The best kicker who ever lived." In addition, Tech lore has it that in his career at safety, no runner ever ran over or by him! The 1920 team allowed only 16 points scored while pounding the opposition for 312 points in a low-scoring era.

A brief look at what statistics are available from that era establishes this great athlete's stature. In 1920, Flowers ran from scrimmage 80 times for 819 yards, or 10.2 yards per carry. He ran back punts for 429 yards. In this era of low scoring, he ran for 48 points, added six passing, and drop-kicked 13 more. His 85-yard punt and 44-yard drop-kick were the longest of the year.

His performance against powerful Auburn is legendary: punt returns of 82 and 75 yards; punting average of 55 yards; touchdown runs of 31, 82, and 65 yards. Sportswriter Morgan Blake wrote this account of the game in **The Atlanta Journal**:

> "The Auburn Tiger came up from the Plain yesterday with jaws sharpened and maw hungry for Tech. As he writhed in death agony on Grant Field when the battle was over, he made one last request: Please Omit Flowers."

"Buck" Flowers was inducted into the College Football Hall of Fame, Sumter's only native to be so honored. It was indeed an honor, because at the time of his selection in 1955, only 88 players and 39 coaches were named in 85 years of football.

Flowers attended Davidson College as a freshman before transferring to Georgia Tech. It is interesting that a gridiron teammate at Davidson was Sumterite Alwin C. "Buck" Burns. "Big Buck" and "Little Buck" were indeed a formidable backfield combination for the Wildcats. Burns ran over opponents and Flowers ran around them!

Today "Buck" Flowers - the best of his time - is a retired insurance executive and lives in Birmingham.

(Credit for the above information on "Buck" Flowers goes to the late F. Jenkins Knight, a Sumter writer for **The State Magazine**, Oct. 16, 1955.)

Sumter produced other notable athletes during the pre-World War II period, but there is little documentation on most. One of the near-greats was Richard Wright. Said to be one of the greatest natural athletes of the period, he was an all-sports superlative. Like "Buck" Flowers he entered Georgia Tech to play football but - tragically - died before his potential could be realized. Some thought his gridiron ability rivaled that of even the great Flowers.

Local historian E. Murr Hall remembers the town's first "big league" baseball player to be Joe Villanue. He was a pitcher and played about 1897 - 1900. That is all we know.

Pat Crawford, a local boy, made it to the major leagues and played in a World Series with the New York Giants. According to C.V. "Bit" Wilder, Crawford was an outstanding first baseman and pinch hitter. Wilder says that Pat Crawford refused to play baseball on Sundays because of his religious beliefs, which might have had some effect on his career as a professional.

Other local baseball players of that era who played professionally but never rose to the major leagues include M.W. "Billy" Edwards, Marion Wilder and his brother "Bit," an all-around athlete of great ability. There are undoubtedly others, but sources have not come forward to identify them.

This summary would not be complete without a look at the years after World War II.

Sumter's preeminent athlete of the modern era has to be baseball star Robert Clinton "Bobby" Richardson of the New York Yankees. Robert - as he was known until the New York sportswriters inevitably changed it to "Bobby" - was what you call a "natural." As a youngster he excelled in all sports, being one of the best basketball and ping-pong players around. He was signed by the Yankees immediately upon graduation from Sumter High School in 1953, weighing in at 5'8" and 158 pounds. In spite of his small stature, Richardson worked his way up through the Yankees "farm system" by perfecting his God-given ability through dedication and hard work. By 1957, he had established himself as a member of the Yankees during their glory years - the best team in baseball. The Yankees won the American League pennant every year except one - 1959. During this span they won 3 World Series with "Richie" at second base. His teammates included baseball immortals Mickey Mantle and "Yogi" Berra, along with Roger Maris, who broke "Babe" Ruth's hallowed home run record in 1961 with 61 homers.

Acknowledged one of baseball's outstanding infielders, little Bobby also left some batting marks on the books. He hit for a .302 average for the 1962 season, his best season's batting average in the majors.

By far his best World Series performance was in 1960 when he was named the outstanding performer. In that Series he became one of only ten players to hit grand-slam home runs; he had most runs batted in (6) and most in a World Series (12). He tied the World Series record by hitting two triples in one game and also tied the World Series record for most runs scored - 8. Despite these heroics Pittsburg won the Series on Bill Mazeroski's famous ninth inning homer in the seventh game.

In his final season with the Yankees before retiring - 1964 - he set a World Series record for most hits with 13. That season he had led the mighty Yankees in hits with 181. A fixture in the lineup at second base, Bobby seldom missed a game, setting American League records for most times at bat.

During his final three seasons with New York he was selected American League second baseman for the All Star game against the National League's finest.

Richardson retired from baseball at the height of his career after the 1964 season and devoted his time to public relations and religious work. He also accepted the position of head baseball coach at the University of South Carolina where he built the Gamecocks into a national power before resigning to follow his real calling - Christian evangelism.

An internationally respected Christian leader, he lives in Sumter with his wife, Betsy.

Sumter produced two other New York Yankees during this period. The late Bobby Jordan, a heavy hitter from Sumter High, and football - baseball star, Ingram Haley of Furman High School signed contracts with the Yankees. Haley left Furman University (where he was a football and baseball athlete) to play professional baseball. The two Sumter youngsters played on the same club at Binghampton, N.Y., one season.

Former American Legion P-15 players who signed professional baseball contracts were Mike Steen with the Texas Rangers, Toy McCord of Manning with the Chicago White Sox and Vic Smith with the Minnesota Twins.

Although none of these players rose to the majors, being selected was a tribute to their abilities.

Neck-and-neck with "Bobby" Richardson in national exposure is the superb football player, Freddie Solomon. He had a brilliant gridiron career at Sumter High School where he was named All-Everything in post season selections. Freddie devastated North Carolina's Tar Heels in the 1970 Shrine Bowl game and was named the outstanding player. Solomon was simply in a class by himself as a high school running back.

Sought after by virtually all major college football powers, he decided to attend the University of South Carolina, which resulted in a power struggle between U.S.C. and the Atlantic Coast Confefence. Subsequently, Solomon enrolled at Tampa University where he also enjoyed a brilliant career.

Drafted by the Miami Dolphins of the National Football League as a wide receiver, Solomon saw limited action. Miami coach Don Shula traded him to San Fransisco where he has become the Forty Niners' premier pass receiver and kick returner. A six year NFL veteran, Solomon has regained his high school and college reputation as a "game breaker" - capable of scoring any time he touches the football. Mentioned as a Pro Bowl prospect, stardom is nothing new but Solomon is first and foremost team oriented. In an interview with Robbie Evans in **The Sumter Daily Item** he said, "I am a team player. If they want me to catch the ball, throw it or run with it (he did all three in a game against the Atlanta Falcons), I'll do it to help the team win.

"I'm still improving as a player. I'm still learning as a wide receiver. I look at every game as a test."

Sumter fans are confident Freddie Solomon will pass any test.

Sumter can also claim one of Solomon's San Francisco teammates: Archie Reese, a graduate of Mayewood High School and Clemson University where he was an All Atlantic Coast performer at tackle.

A three-year veteran of National Football League play, Reese has been used in several positions by the Forty Niners. Playing his first two seasons at defensive end, he was used in 1980 as a defensive tackle and, at times, nose tackle. Reese was named defensive captain for the entire 1980 season. "It's a real honor," he says, "especially since my teammates picked me." Being a standout on a young, improving team, Reese will undoubtedly be given the acclaim that was his through Mayewood and Clemson.

Sumter is proud of Archie Reese.

Another Sumter athlete of great ability who should be mentioned is Tommy Hughes. Excelling at every sport he tried, Hughes had an outstanding high school career. He was named All-State in football and basketball and was captain of the South Carolina Shrine Bowl football team in 1943.

Good enough to be offered a football scholarship to Notre Dame by the great coach, Frank Leahy, Hughes was the first Sumter player so honored. However, World War II was in full swing, and he went into military service. Following discharge, Hughes accepted an athletic scholarship to Duke University where he starred in 1947 - 1949. This was before the professional football draft. Hughes was, however, "invited" to play football for the Washington Redskins following his senior season at Duke.

Tommy Hughes showed equal ability as a basketball player. A three year starter for Duke's Blue Devils, he was an All-Conference selection at guard.

During his senior year at Duke, the Associated Press selected its first All-America basketball team. Hughes was good enough to be nominated by the sportswriters in his area. He was selected by those who had seen him play many times and realized his uncommon abilities and fierce competitive instincts. The squad included at forwards Cousy of Holy Cross, Dickey and Ranzino of N.C. State; centers, Groza of Kentucky and Macauley of St. Louis; Jones and Beard of Kentucky, Lavelli of Yale, and Hughes at guard. Any way you look at it, that's pretty fast company to be keeping!

Playing for a small college, Joe Kirven "made it big" as a Little All-America selection for Presbyterian College in 1953. A 1949 Shrine Bowler at Edmunds High School, Kirven played offensive and defensive end from 1949 - 1953. He was co-captain and voted best athlete at the Clinton, S.C. school which is a member of the small college NAIA league. An outstanding pass receiver and sure tackler, this solid 180 pounder was also named to the national Pi Kappa Alpha team which included all major colleges. Kirven is now associated with the Sumter City Schools as an administrator.

In addition to Freddie Solomon, Sumter boasts one other high school All-America, and possibly two, as we shall see later!

This All-American is Clarke Bynum, and he won his fame with the Barons of Wilson Hall School. He probably had more national media exposure than any high school athlete in the history of the state. Standing 6'7" tall, he literally wrote the record books at Wilson Hall.

Under the guidance of Coach Jerry Faulkner, Bynum was a starter for four years. During that span the teams' record was 105 wins against 14 losses, his senior team winning 30 games against a single loss! Wilson Hall only lost two home games during those four years. During those four years, Wilson Hall won three South Carolina Independent School state championships, losing only once as runner-up during Clarke's junior season.

Clarke Bynum holds the Wilson Hall career scoring record of 2,227 points, and during his senior year averaged 21 points and 11 rebounds. In his senior year he made numerous All-America teams. Some of the more prestigious were **Parade** magazine, **Popular Sports** and **Street and Smith**. In addition, he played in the McDonalds' Capitol Classic, the first player from our state to particiapte in that all-star event.

Bynum comes from a rabid Sumter basketball clan. His father, Henry C. Bynum, and uncles, W.E. "Billy" Bynum, Jr. and Alvis J. Bynum, were all outstanding local players. Uncle Billy Bynum's son, Will, was an All-Southern Conference forward who led Virginia Military Academy to the NCAA playoffs and played professionally in Europe.

Recruited by virtually all major colleges, Bynum cast his lot with the Clemson Tigers. (Incidentally, Coach Faulkner also joined the Tigers as an assistant coach.) His freshman season at Clemson was a learning process. He performed well and his legions of local fans continued to predict a second rise to stardom.

The second possible All-American performer was James Farmer. Farmer was a two-sport standout at Sumter High School in 1940 and 1941. A hard-throwing pitcher for Sumter's American Legion and high school teams, he signed a professional baseball contract with the Cleveland Indians in 1942. Shortly afterwards, Farmer went into the Navy and served on LST's in the European Theatre (participating in the Normandy invasion) and in the liberation of the Pacific. Following his stint in the Navy, he took a brief fling at baseball but never regained his old form.

As a pile-driving fullback, he made a name for himself and Sumter High School football. Leading Sumter to a state championship, he received several post season honors, among them All-Southern. Local sports authority Ralph "Hank" Wilson (who cleared the way for Farmer as blocking back) claims that Farmer also made All-America. Farmer doesn't remember that, so we'll go with Hank who **does** remember! **Voila**! The problem is solved and we have another All-American!

James Farmer now lives in Summerville where he has been Chief of Police since 1952.

In tennis the Hodgin brothers, Charles "Chuck'. Hodgin, Jr. and Mark, have a spot by themselves.

"Chuck" won the S.C. High School championship four years in a row - a record. During this period he was always ranked in the top 20 nationally. Ranked eighth in the nation as a 14 year old, he once defeated John McEnroe, current U.S. and Wimbledon Champion. A 1981 Phi Beta Kappa - Magna Cum Luade graduate of U.S.C., he has accepted a position with a prominent accounting firm in Columbia.

Mark was also unbeatable as a high school player, winning the state championship as a sophomore and junior. He was unable to defend his title as a senior because of a serious illness. Despite his illness, Mark went on to The College of Charleston where he played number two position as a sophomore.

Sumter produced a national table tennis champion in the person of Oliver Stubbs. Stubbs had won the North Carolina State Championship in 1950 and the South Carolina Championship in 1950 and 1951.

He entered the 1951 All-American Table Tennis Tournament, a national amateur event, and was seeded second. The tournament was held at the Sheridan Plaza Hotel in Chicago. Young Stubbs won five matches, defeating the favorite, Leonard Schatke of Chicago, for the national title.

No ping-pong player from Sumter has even come close to Oliver Stubbs' record. As far as we know, none from South Carolina has, either.

This summary is expanded to briefly catch a few highlights of Clarendon and Lee County athletics—since those counties were a part of Sumter District before "seceding."

First there is Felix Anthony Blanchard, Jr., the incomparable "Doc." He was raised in Bishopville - which he called home. His mother, Mrs. Felix A. Blanchard, and sister, Dr. Mary Elizabeth Blanchard, are now Sumter residents.

Playing for Army on the best football teams ever to come from West Point, "Doc" Blanchard was simply devastating. He played fullback on offense and linebacker on defense. A slashing runner, he was almost unstoppable; and he was also an excellent pass receiver and punter. At 208 pounds, he was a punishing tackler.

In the three years Blanchard played for Army, the cadets never lost a game, and were national champions in 1944 and 1945. A scoreless tie with Notre Dame in 1946 gave the national title to the Fighting Irish.

"Doc" Blanchard's honors were so numerous that only some of the important ones will be given:

He was awarded the Heisman Trophy symbolizing the best player in football in 1945 - the only South Carolina native ever to win the Heisman and was named to every All-America team.

He was awarded the James E. Sullivan Memorial Award honoring the amateur doing the most to advance the cause of sportsmanship. No other football player had ever been selected.

He was inducted into the National Football Hall of Fame, and the S.C. Athletic Hall of Fame.

Retiring in 1971 after 25 years in the Air Force, "Doc" Blanchard now lives in San Antonio with his wife, Jody.

(We give credit for the Blanchard data to Will McKenzie writing for **The Sumter Daily Item.**)

Another athletic standout from Sumter District is C.R. "Dick" Harvin, now a Sumter business executive. A native of Manning, Harvin was a three-sport star at Georgia Tech. His prep competition had been at the Darlington School in Rome, Georgia, where he won letters in football, baseball, basketball, and track.

Entering Georgia Tech in 1947, the 210 pound speedster lettered in football, baseball, and track. He won nine varsity letters at Tech; freshmen not being eligible at that time.

Harvin played end on both offense and defense for the Yellow Jackets. He was selected on several All-America teams, including **Look** magazine, Grantland Rice, and Associated Press second team.

Drafted by the San Francisco Forty Niners to play football and the Philadelphia Phillies for baseball, Harvin solved the problem by pursuing neither. While still in college he had married Carole Lita Keith, daughter of a Georgia Tech coach, Dwight Keith. Professional football did not fit into his plans, and he opted for a career in business. Except for service in the Korean conflict, he has lived in Sumter since graduation.

Harvin chuckles that he achieved many of his goals early at Georgia Tech. On his first play in football, he caught a touchdown pass (against Vanderbilt), in his first baseball game he hit a home run; and in his first track meet he won his event, the 60 yard dash (in an indoor meet at Chapel Hill). That's not bad for a country boy from Manning, S.C.!

Harvin ran the 100 yard dash (9.9 seconds), the 440 yard relay, and threw the discus and shot as a member of the Yellow Jacket track team.

Now an oil jobber in Sumter, Dick Harvin is active in church and civic affairs.

Another product of Sumter football is Wayne Mass. An Air Force dependent not born in Sumter, Wayne played three years for Edmunds High School (1960 - 1963) and considered this his home town. An offensive tackle, he was a Shrine Bowl selection and was **Coach and Athlete** magazine's prep honorable mention All-America.

Mass went on to Clemson University where he was again a star at offensive tackle. Coach Frank Howard called the 6'4", 245 pound athlete one of the best, if not **the** best offensive tackle at Clemson in his 35 years there. But best of all, Mass was an honor student.

An All-Conference selection at Clemson, he was named to several All-America teams including **Playboy** magazine's and Dell Publishing Company's. From college he moved on to professional football. Drafted in 1967 by the Chicago Bears as an offensive tackle, Mass also played for the Miami Dolphins and New England Patriots before retiring from the NFL in 1972.

Another All-American who calls Sumter home is Harvey W. Achziger. A Sumter businessman, he came to us via military duty at Shaw Air Force Base where he married Mary Lou McLean and settled here.

Achziger was a four-sport standout at Colorado State from 1949 - 1953. At 6'3" and 260 pounds, he starred at defensive tackle for the Aggies. His play earned him a spot on the 1953 INS All-America team.

In addition he lettered in basketball, wrestling and track (discus).

After graduation, he played defensive tackle for the Philadelphia Eagles, 1953 - 1954, before being called by the Air Force. He became a jet pilot and also played football where he was an All-Air Force selection. After a brief return to professional football following separation from the Air Force, Achziger returned to Sumter.

A final note on the athletes of Sumter District:

George Turbeville from Turbeville was known as the fastest pitcher in these parts. He flashed to the top, playing with Connie Mack's famous Philadelphia Athletics, then wound up his career with the Brooklyn Dodgers, according to my sources. It was said that George threw hard and played hard, and nobody knows how good he really could have been.

Clarendon County was the birthplace of Althea Gibson, queen of the tennis world in the 1950's. Born near Silver, she moved away at an early age. The first black champion, she literally dominated women's tennis in 1957 and 1958. During those big years, Althea Gibson was United States and Wimbledon singles champion and captured the Wimbledon women's doubles title as well.

Contributed by Robert B. Moise

PART XV. THE ARTS

Art Guild

The Sumter Art Guild has been instrumental during its relatively short history in awakening among Sumter residents a wide interest in the study of art and an appreciation for art at its best.

In the early 1960's, Mildred White (Mrs. J.F.), a newcomer to Sumter, began teaching art with about 20 pupils in her class. Among these was Eva Kirven (Mrs. T.J. – now deceased), who was desirous of creating a livelier interest in the arts among the residents of Sumter County.

These two, after talking over the prospects, decided to take steps to form an organization of art lovers. The first meeting was held at the home of Mrs. Kirven in 1966, and the two were joined by six young men – Ray Davenport, Bob Jones, Jimmy Milling, Roland McCollum, Lad Chandler and Sam Fiorini.

Thus the seed was planted and by much work on the part of these eight enthusiasts, a meeting was planned. There were approximately 30 present at this organizational meeting held at the C & S Bank on Liberty Street and the Sumter Art Guild became a reality. [244]

Chosen as the first officers were the following: Mrs. Eva Kirven, president; Mrs. Mildred White, first vice president; Mrs. Katie Damron, second vice president; Roland McCollum, treasurer; Lad Chandler, recording secretary (alternate, Miss Thelma Gaston); Bob Jones, corresponding secretary (alternate, Al Gibbs).

Inspired by the purpose of the Guild – "to promote an interest in the arts and eventually to establish a local gallery for local and traveling exhibits," members immediately became actively involved. By 1967 the membership had grown to 79. Monthly meetings were held, alternating between programs and business meetings. For the programs, outstanding artists were scheduled, bringing to the members valuable information and stirring in them a desire to work for improvement both for themselves and for the Guild.

From the beginning, the Guild sponsored sidewalk shows for the encouragement of participants and inspiration of viewers. These shows became a tradition as a part of the Iris Festival and Arts Festival – "Summerthing."

In addition there have been three annual exhibits – one for members and two for the public. These were held at first in such places as the basement of the courthouse, the old Mayflower restaurant, empty stores and other available locations.

Another early project of the Guild was the sponsoring of an art class at the Burns Education Center in the old YWCA. To interest young people in the study of art, the Guild also promoted exhibits in the elementary and high schools, giving awards and ribbons.

In 1968 the Guild presented an exhibit of 57 works of local artists as part of the opening of the new Sumter County Library.

Though always busy with different projects, the dream of an art gallery was always foremost in the minds of members; so in 1969, they decided that was the year to obtain their goal. Even though they had nothing definite in mind, they began to raise funds. They worked diligently preparing pieces of art for what they called a "raffle." Each person who would make a donation of $20 would receive a piece of artwork. From this project they raised $980.

In the meantime, someone suggested the old Carnegie Library building on Liberty Street as a likely place for the gallery. Someone approached Dr. L.C. McArthur, superintendent of School District 17, that owned the building. He suggested that the Guild appoint a board of directors to consider the matter with the trustees of the school.

The following public-spirited citizens agreed to serve on this board: Messrs. Marvin Trapp, Hubert Osteen, Phillip Wittenberg, Olin K. McDonald, Gene Matthews, M.F. Korn, Jim Eaves, Walter Sharpe, Mrs. Charles Propst and Mrs. Lyman Quincy. (These together with the officers of the Guild became the first Board of Directors of the Gallery.) [245]

Through the efforts of these, who served as volunteers, an agreement was reached with School District 17 to lease the building.

Members set to work with a will, remodeling, renovating, painting. Approximate cost of repairs was estimated at $10,000.

On January 4, 1970, the old library building became the Sumter Art Gallery. A dream had come true! On exhibit for the opening was the South Carolina Art Collection, containing some of the best paintings, sculptures and other works of art. Many dignitaries of Sumter and other parts of the state were on hand for the occasion.

Since that day many exhibits by local artists and famous artists from other places have been on display and art lovers from Sumter and elsewhere visit the Gallery for the shows.

For a number of years Mrs. Margaret Britt served as director of the Gallery. When she resigned in 1977, she was followed by Mrs. Jane Walker for a short while. The director now is Mrs. Laura Ayers. The Gallery has been very fortunate in having dedicated and most efficient lovers of art as directors.

After seven years in the Carnegie Library building, the Gallery is now in its own home, the historic home of the late Elizabeth White, Sumter's own acclaimed artist. The home is being restored to its original mid-19th century charm.

Opening attraction for the 1977-78 season, first in the permanent home of the Gallery, were paintings by P. Buckley Moss, a noted artist from Virginia.[246]

And the work goes on and interest grows. The Sumter Art Guild is continuing the fulfillment of its purpose, to "Propagate, support and foster interest in art and to create an opportunity for our community artists to engage in cooperative artistic enterprises." And the Art Gallery, for which they have diligently worked, is the complete fulfillment of an ambitious, unselfish dream.

Sumter Art Association Chartered In 1925

Sumter has a very active Art Association which was begun November 13, 1925,[247] following a tea given by Miss Elizabeth White and Mrs. Paul Aman in the library of the Girls' High School, honoring Mrs. Edna Reed Whaley, well-known artist of Columbia, on the opening day of the exhibition of her oil and watercolor paintings in Sumter.

Charter members of this association besides Miss White and Mrs. Aman were Mrs. Henry Barnett, Miss Ruth Barnett, Mrs. Loring Lee, Mrs. T.C. McKnight, Mrs. S.W. Rumph, Mrs. C.L. Stubbs, Miss Marie White, and Mrs. Itly Wilson.

The Association was off to a good start with much enthusiasm expressed. Elected as first officers were Mrs. Aman, president; Mrs. McKnight, vice president; Miss Barnett, secretary-treasurer; Miss E. White, art critic.

A constitution was adopted at the June meeting of 1927, with necessary bylaws, one of which limited the membership to 50, setting nine for a quorum. The minutes of this meeting mentioned Mrs. Ferd Levi, Mrs. Lee Scarborough and Mrs. A.C. Phelps as members. There may have been others admitted before this meeting. Others listed during 1927 were Mrs. George Shore,

Mrs. G.A. Lemmon, Mrs. A.C. Phelps, Mrs. John Wilson, Mrs. Arthur Harby, Mrs. A.H. Forrester, Mrs. H.M. Stuckey, and Mrs. Fenwick Murray. Thus it can be seen that enthusiasm for this organization spread rapidly, bringing in more and more members.

It was decided that unless there was a special invitation from some member, the regular meeting place would be the YWCA.

In those early years there were many outstanding speakers from various places. Some of these were Miss Dora Gray, interior decorator from Columbia; Anna Heyward Taylor, artist; Lafaye, architect; Dr. Thomas, Rock Hill.

Programs were on such subjects as: "The Furniture of the Middle Ages," "England's Georgian Period," "Colonial Homes in New England," "Etchings," "Art Appreciation – Pictures Every Child Should Know," and "Landscape Painters of America."

Other activities of the Art Association toward the beginning covered a variety of interests. At one meeting the group decided to endorse the plan suggested by Mrs. E.W. Dabbs for the beautification of county roads; they raised a fund for the library; delegations represented the association at a meeting of the County Federation of Women's Clubs; programs were carried out for the beautification of Sumter. In February of 1927, the Art Association united with the music clubs in giving a Colonial Party to raise money for a Memorial Fund.

As the years passed, many worthwhile programs and projects were carried out, making art an integral part of the cultural life of Sumter.

In 1973 the constitution was revised and the membership limit was set at 75 regular members, which the Association now has. There are also 24 associate members; and the following are honorary members: Mrs. Jenkins Knight, Miss M. Priscilla Shaw, Mrs. James F. White.

Officers for 1979-80 were Mrs. S.A. Harvin, Jr., president; Mrs. M.L. Lawrence, vice president; Miss Myrtle DesChamps, corresponding secretary; Mrs. Bartow Shaw, recording secretary; Mrs. Charles Cuttino, Jr., treasurer.

Some of the more recent programs have been on "A Talking Tour of Old Homes Around Stateburg," "English Brass Rubbings," "Exhibition of Miss White's Work," "Slides of Alaska," and "Jewelry."

The Sumter Art Association, for more than half a century, has meant much toward the beautification of homes and the development of artistic tastes of young and old in the county. Interest continues to grow and plans are in the making for additional activities.

Municipal Band In Sumter As Early As 1848

Sumter people as far back as the record goes, were lovers of music of all kinds. As early as 1848 there was a band in Sumterville. When the Grand Division of the Temperance Union of South Carolina held its quarterly celebration in the town, it is said that "it was escorted from Town Hall to the Methodist Church in an 'imposing and gorgeous procession,' the rich velvet collars and handsome emblems of office contrasting effectively with the white collars and variegated rosettes of the Sons (the Sumterville Order)." The march was accompanied by the music of the Sumter Brass Band, supplemented by the performance of an "Amateur Band." The account in **The Banner** reported that "music again disturbed the silence," but it neglected to say to which band the comment referred.

A year later at the dedication of Temperance Hall, the old Presbyterian Church having been remodeled for this purpose, the Sumter Band played and was recognized for "interest added to the occasion by their music."

Just how long this band was in existence is not clear, nor who was the director. The only person whose name is known to this writer as a member of this early musical group was Lewis D. Hope, a native of Germany. Injured in a mishap that occurred while he was carrying the mail by stage from Sumterville to Gadsden, he died in 1850.

In 1871 a brass band consisting of 18 members, was organized in Sumter by H.M.C. Knopff, a German music teacher, who at that time was giving lessons on a number of instruments.[248] He is said to have conducted the Sumter Orchestra also, and another of his accomplishments was tuning pianos in the community.

Charter members of this band included such men as B.R. Nash, a businessman from North Carolina; M.F. Hewson, an Englishman who belonged to "the garrison"; Jerry Croghan, a native of Ireland; Fritz Bultman, a shoemaker who had come to this country from Germany, where he had served four years in the army of the King of Hanover; J.C. Herrington, apparently a native of the Sumter community; A. Morris, a Jewish barkeeper.

Knopff's Brass Band and Orchestra performed frequently, no doubt, at the Music Hall, which was completed in December 1872.

The next band in Sumter was known as the Schumacher Band, organized and directed by W.S. Schumacher, with about 28 members. This organization was active here in the early 1900's and it evidently lasted for several years.

One person remembers that this was an excellent band, giving concerts of the highest calibre each week on the "Green." The bandstand stood where Central School once stood, and the surrounding area was known as "the Green." Smaller children sometimes skipped around the square to the beat of the music. The late James Graham was drum major for this band.

Mr. Schumacher was said to have "played the violin beautifully," and in addition to directing his band, he conducted a very fine orchestra. His orchestra played for the wedding of young Graham to Miss Gertrude Knight in the old Trinity Methodist Church.

According to one source, one of the violins used by this eminent musician was made by the late W.J. McKinney, Jr., of Mayesville, who used wood from seven foreign countries in fashioning the instrument. Around 1911, this violin was said to have again been in the possession of Mr. McKinney, who sold it to the late M.B. Wilson, Sr., in Mayesville. It is now owned by M.B. Wilson, Jr., a retired English professor at Clemson University.[249]

Attorney Arthur H. Wilder recalled that, at one time, five members of his family played in the Schumacher band. They were his father, Arthur, who was adept at the French horn; and four uncles, James G.R. (Richard) Wilder, trombone; R.K. (Kendrick) Wilder, cornet; Julian D. Wilder, bass drum; and Robert Eugene Wilder, baritone horn.[250]

Those who remember Mr. Schumacher picture him as resembling Paderewski and say that he and his wife, a very attractive lady, possibly came from the Midwest. This latter idea, however, is mere conjecture.

It is not known how many years beyond 1915 the Schumacher Brass Band was active, but in 1924 another band came into being. In that year Frank A. Girard came to Sumter as a music teacher and organized a Community Band. A native of Philadelphia, Pennsylvania, he received his education in that city and gained experience by playing in bands and orchestras in the greater Philadelphia area.

His coming to Sumter has an interesting sidelight. His brother-in-law, S.C. Miller, was traveling in the South for a business firm and when he reached Sumter, he telephoned his family to come on down that he had found the "garden spot of the world." Taking Miller at his word, the entire family came at once and established their homes in Sumter.

Many young people studied under the talented young Girard; and as they became proficient, they were added to the band or the orchestra which he also conducted.

The band held regular practice sessions in the old Opera House or Music Hall, and the town people were privileged to hear good music in scheduled concerts. The group also provided music for special occasions such as the Confederate Memorial Day programs and the "Trolley Parades." Outdoor concerts were given in Memorial Park, which was completed in the early 1920's.

One special show was staged to raise funds for uniforms. This affair must have been a financial success, for members were soon after decked in smart maroon-colored uniforms that added much to the appearance of the group.

Girard's band had a far-reaching reputation as a very talented group. It was frequently invited to play at out-of-town functions, such as the opening of the Cooper River Bridge in Charleston and the bridge at Georgetown. The orchestra played for commencement exercises at Mayesville for many years.

Numbers of Sumter men belonged to the Girard band at one time or another. Some of these may be listed (in most cases with the instrument played) as follows: John Evans, bass drum; George Bultman, French horn; Robert Walker, tenor saxophone; Alva McDonald, trumpet; Snookie King, saxophone; Robert Warren, saxophone; Delmar Wadford, clarinet; William Tisdale, clarinet; Marvin Brown, saxophone; Robert Mooney, bass horn; Theodore and Jimmy DuBose, saxophone; Julius Stubbs, trombone; William C. Baldwin, trombone; Francis James, baritone horn; Claude Hurst, trumpet; Doug Youngblood, French trumpet; Jobie Dixon, drum; Burgess Bultman, drum; Morris Mazursky, trumpet; Fletcher Ellis, base horn; Gerald Carrigan, saxophone; W.M. Hodge, alto horn; H.C. Carlisle, tenor saxophone; Bob Jennings, trumpet; Clifton Brown, trombone; Charles Girard, trumpet; Joe Dean, alto horn; Robert LeNoir; Ingram Blanding; Don Harby.

Small groups from the band or orchestra were sometimes selected to play for special occasions. For instance, Don Harby, Ingram Blanding, Doug Youngblood, Robert Warren, Robert Mooney and Professor Girard played the score for the silent movie "The Hunchback of Notre Dame" when it came to Sumter.

This band, directed by Girard, was the last full-time Municipal Band.

James Pritchard, band director in Sumter School District 17, formed a community band for summer concerts at Memorial Park in 1953.

Director Pritchard was well qualified to conduct such a band. He received his A.B. degree at Newberry College and later studied at Juilliard School of Music in New York City, completing his Master's degree there. He received special training in Berkshire Music Center in Massachusetts, later playing in the Air Force Band in England, France and Germany. One season was spent with the Southern Symphony Orchestra. He recorded for Masterworks records. Clarinet, saxophone, and bassoon were the chief instruments played by this talented musician, and on one occasion he was clarinet soloist at Carnegie Recital Hall in New York.

His programs were always well balanced with sacred music, marches, classical numbers, old favorites and currently popular tunes. Soloists were featured on most of the presentations. At one Trolley Parade he featured "The Three Pigs," with George Foxworth as narrator. One instrumental soloist was Jimmy Burns, playing "Soliloquy for Trumpet" by Morrissey. On another program, James Cuttino sang, and on another Valerie Powell was featured in a modern interpretive dance. In one of the last concerts of this band, Bill Chada was soloist for the "One-Finger Polka." There was always something special included to please the audience, which sometimes numbered as many as 400.

The Pritchard Band was composed of adults, college students and high school boys and girls. In 1954 there were 50 members, with 10 fewer in 1955.

The emphasis on the summer community band was on "recreation, the enjoyment of playing together, etc., but at the same time making an attempt to produce the best musical result."

Since Mr. Pritchard was leaving Sumter to take a position at the University of South Carolina, this highly successful band gave its last concert in 1958.

After this concert, there was no community band in Sumter for approximately 12 years. But in 1970, Patrick Veltre, retired director of the Ninth Air Force Band, agreed to direct the newly organized Community Concert Band sponsored by the Parks and Recreation Department.

There was a promising outlook for this band with a well-chosen slate of officers. Serving as president was Harvey Ackerman, a 1950 graduate of Edmunds High School.

After a few years, however, interest lagged. Those attending the concerts seemed to have other interests. Finally PARD decided to discontinue the Community Band; but there is a possibility that a new band will be organized in 1981 and Sumter music lovers will have an opportunity to participate.

Sumter's Interest In Art Grows

Although early settlers of Sumter County were interested in other ways of expressing their love of beauty than in painting and sculpture, the county produced or welcomed as adopted sons or daughters some talented artists who were counted among the great.

As wealth increased and more elaborate homes were built, a desire for suitable decorations and taste for the fine arts grew. Perhaps the first form of art that gained popularity was portrait painting, and one of the first works of art done by a native of Sumter County was a self-portrait by Chancellor Thomas Waties [251] of the High Hills of Santee. This painting won widespread recognition, and a portrait of one of his daughters was of equal value.

It was customary for portrait painters to travel on what was once called the "King's Highway" between Camden and Charleston, stopping in the plantation homes of the wealthy along the way to paint portraits of members of the families. One such artist was William Kennedy Barclay, a Charleston native, who was a well-known painter in Camden in the 1830's. He is known especially for a portrait of Thomas Salmond of Camden, which hung in the cabin of the **Thomas Salmond**, a river steamer carrying passengers and freight between Camden and Charleston and making frequent stops at Sumter's Landing.

In 1838 James Devaux, also of Charleston, having won recognition for a portrait of John Laurence Manning done in New York, was invited to "Milford," the spacious home owned by the Mannings in the Sandhills, to paint other members of the family. He remained into the following year, busily engaged in turning out some of his best work.

Well known for "landscapes in oil colors and miniature painting on ivory" was Mrs. Catherine Ladd, an art instructor in the Bishopville Academy, in 1835. She is also given credit for having designed the first Confederate flag.

Young ladies were sent to "finishing" schools in ante-bellum days to become "accomplished." One student, Mary Hooper Anderson, who later married Frederick L. Childs, was found to have unusual talent, having inherited the interest from her father, William W. Anderson, who made an exceptionally fine drawing of Chancellor Waties from a miniature. Among Mrs. Child's paintings are a portrait and two pictures of Marden, the lovely home of Chancellor Waties. One of these pictures of Marden is now owned by Mrs. S.M. Rhodes, Jr., of Mayesville, who is great-great-great-granddaughter of the Chancellor. She was formerly Harriett Tisdale of Sumter.

Coming from Tennessee in 1837 upon the invitation of Col. John B. Miller to visit in his home, Corn Hill Plantation, was William Harrison Scarborough, the artist who painted more portraits of people in Sumter than any other. Among those who posed for him, besides Colonel Miller, were Judge and Mrs. John Smyth Richardson, William S.G. Richardson, Judge and Mrs. Franklin

I. Moses, Dr. Thomas W. Baker, Bishop William Capers, Mrs. W.F.B. Haynsworth, Franklin Moses Mikell, Mrs. S.R. Chandler and Dr. W.W. Anderson.

Born in Stateburg, nephew of Bishop Capers, was Albert Capers Guerry,[252] Sumter's first native artist of note. Guerry was married in 1867 to Miss Gertrude Wilson, said to be the daughter of an English artist. One of the Guerry children was reared by J. Harvey Wilson of Mayesville, no doubt because times were hard, especially for artists. A portrait of the Rev. Donald McQueen, done by Guerry, received much favorable comment.

Many itinerant artists set up shops in Sumter in the 1850's and painted pictures of all who wished them. One of these, trying to boost his business, used the slogan: "Death is abroad and may take away your friends at any moment."

Some artists were skilled in various crafts. Isaac B. Alexander, for instance, was known primarily for his painting of excellent miniatures which in 1838 were advertised for their "delicacy of finish and accuracy of expression." He was also a jeweller and silversmith and repaired guns and pistols.

A native of Charleston, but a resident of Sumter, Charles W. Davis was said to be "a young man of much genius and taste." For the Charleston Fair he cut from paper a plan of Charleston and Savannah and carved a wooden chain from a solid block with a pen knife. He also worked out a method of making ambrotypes, which are taken on glass, and specialized in "stereoptican views" which were once a very popular type of entertainment in the home. Through further experimentation, he developed a method of "mirroring and graining" his ambrotypes so as to make the pictures stand out on the glass in bold relief.

Although many of the portraits and other paintings of these and other artists of the past have been lost in fires that have destroyed many of the old homes, some are still preserved and treasured by people of Sumter and elsewhere.

Today the Sumter Art Association, the Sumter Art Guild and the Sumter Art Gallery are keeping alive an interest in art through programs, art classes and exhibits. Many adults, young people and children are working creatively and demonstrating marked talent in all types of art and crafts.

In the 20th century, two Sumter artists are widely known throughout the nation. A sketch of each of these follows:

MISS ELIZABETH WHITE

Among 20th Century Sumter artists, Miss Elizabeth White has received wide acclaim by art critics and art lovers in many lands. Her paintings in oil, charcoal and crayon are well known and appreciated, but she is best known for her black and white etchings.

This artist has left for posterity something of the beauty of Sumter County, as well as that of more distant places. Having spent much time in the mountains and on Pawley's Island, she has portrayed many realistic scenes inspired by both. She also displayed great talent in her paintings of historic country life. Her character studies of individuals show the touch of a real artist.

Miss White's interest in painting was awakened when she, as a child of four years, received from her grandfather, the late Anthony White, a watercolor paint box. When she was old enough, she began the study of art in earnest, spending parts of five winters at the Pennsylvania Academy of Fine Arts. She had the privilege later of studying under Wayman Adams, famous portrait painter of New York, and Alfred Hutty, a master of the art of etching, in Charleston.[253]

For a while she taught in Sumter High School and was art teacher at the University of South Carolina for three years, before she decided to give all of her time to the occupation that she loved best.

Her parents died when she was still quite young and she was taken into the home of her grandfather and was cared for by her aunt, Miss Marie White. The mid-nineteenth century home on North Main Street became hers after the death of her grandfather and aunt. Her studio was the original outside kitchen of the quaint old home, which was built, it is said, by Dr. John Independence Miller, an early druggist in Sumter.

From time to time, she took advantage of opportunities for further study. She spent some time at Tiffany Foundation, Oyster Bay, Long Island. And she also had the privilege of spending three summers at the McDowell Colony in New Hampshire. This colony was made possible by the gift of the master musician, Edward McDowell, and developed by his widow. Here talented writers, musicians and painters of note came on invitation to work independently in their chosen fields of endeavor under perfect conditions.

The modern trend in art showing a disregard for standards set by disciplined artists of the past was regarded by Miss White as a grave error.

As mentioned above, Miss White's specialty was the black and white etching.[254] She said that this is most difficult and should not be undertaken until the painter has become skillful in the use of other media.

Her etchings of old churches, plantation homes, scenes of

nature are known all over the world. They have been shown in the Smithsonian Print Gallery in Washington, D.C., and in Venice, Italy, during the Biennial Exhibition, sponsored by the National Academy and Society of Etchers.

Miss White's home is now the home of the Sumter Gallery of Art. Thus through her paintings and the home that she loved, her memory will continue to be in the hearts of those who knew her in the home and those who know her through her contributions to beauty and art.

CHARLES MASON CROWSON

Shown in the Columbia Museum of Art have been many distinguished portraits painted by Charles Mason Crowson, whose untimely death in February of 1973 ended in its prime a life of great artistic talent.

It was Crowson who installed in the East/West Galleries "The Face of American History" from the National Gallery, the exhibition that "featured the launching of Columbia's Museum of Art . . . " How fitting that he should be honored by a showing of his art in the same Galleries!

Charles Mason Crowson was born in Sumter April 29, 1916, the son of J.W. Crowson and Eleanor Mason Crowson, and the grandson of the well-known Sumter inventor Charles T. Mason.[255] His mother having died when he was only 10 days old, he was reared by an aunt, Miss Fannie Mason, growing up in the old Mason home. The home was owned by his aunt, and another, Mrs. Jessie Moon Myers, who with her husband, Girard J. Myers, Sr., and two children, lived in one part of the home. Therefore, Charles was very close to his two cousins – Girard, Jr., and Jessie Mason Myers.

After graduation from Sumter High School (Boys), he entered the University of South Carolina where he received his degree. He then went to New York to continue his study of art at the Art Students League under George Bridgeman and Frank Dumond.

In New York he became the protege and close friend of the late Howard Chandler Christy, "one of the world's most famous illustrators."

In New York, Crowson began his professional career, painting his first commissioned portraits in 1938 and 1939.

He next went to Roanoke, Virginia, where he painted at least 20 portraits before returning to South Carolina and making Columbia his home for some years. There he was engaged in painting many South Carolinians. He later lived for a while in

Atlanta, Myrtle Beach and one year at Montego Bay, but wherever he lived, he was always busy with his brushes.

Charles began drawing as soon as he was old enough to hold a pencil, remembers his cousin, Jessie Myers. In fact, she has kept some of his early drawings and one can readily see that even as a very small boy he showed unusual talent.

One of his classmates at the University of South Carolina, John A. Crawford, Jr. (now professor in State University College, New Paltz, New York), said that even in those first years of training he was "struck with awe at the magical effects he was able to achieve with paint and brush . . . It was clear to me that Charlie had an extraordinary talent!"

At the age of 23, young Charles painted a self-portrait which remained for some years at the home of his grandfather, at whose death it was brought to the home of Miss Jessie Myers, where it now hangs.

Though conscious of his innate ability, Crowson did not depend on talent alone. Long hours of persistent labor he spent in developing his gift. He believed firmly in the necessity of continuous effort if he would be a successful artist.

He said that most of his subjects posed for two-hour sessions from four to six times. The first sitting was usually just a social occasion that he might become acquainted with the subject, studying his personality in a relaxed mood, for "naturalness and animation are the paintable things," he believed.

This approach proved a strong point in his phenomenal success as a portrait painter. According to Carolyn Hodges, who had the privilege of knowing him, "The laughing eyes of a child, the sparking eyes of a debutante, the piercing eyes of a patriarch – they are all expressed on canvas by Charles Mason Crowson, one of the nation's top portrait painters." She continued her tribute to his art, speaking of the great variety of his subjects – "mischievous children, airy teenagers, handsome matrons, businessmen, fishermen, sportsmen, teachers, lawyers, doctors." When the wife of a surgeon at Mayo Clinic saw the portrait of her husband painted by Crowson, she said, "If I saw nothing but the hands in the portrait, I would know it was my husband."

Crowson is said to have painted more than 450 commissioned portraits, in addition to countless others done for friends and for himself. His subjects represented 20 states, the District of Columbia and Jamaica.

His portraits of doctors hang in hospitals in Columbia, Camden, Conway, Winnsboro, and Charleston.

In the State House in Columbia are portraits of George Washington, John Rutledge, Sol Blatt, Mendel Rivers, and Chief Justice Eugene Blease.

Sumter treasures a full-length portrait of Gen. Thomas Sumter, done by her native son, Charles Mason Crowson.

His portraits of great educators may be seen in the University of South Carolina, Columbia College, The Citadel, Clemson, The University of Virginia, the National Guard Institute of Washington, Columbia Theological Seminary in Atlanta, the U.S. Military Academy at West Point. Some of these especially liked by his admirers include Dr. Francis Wright Bradley, who held several positions of distinction at the University of South Carolina; Dr. Leonard T. Baker, former president of the University; Dr. Wil Lou Gray, founder of the South Carolina Opportunity School.

His portraits of artists and writers are also outstanding. These include three of his friend Howard Chandler Christy and one of Dr. Chapman Milling, author of **Singing Arrows**.

Many of his works have been done posthumously, such as George Washington, General Sumter and others. These required, said Crowson, hours of research in family records and in the close study of photographs.

Crowson's works have been exhibited at the famous New York Galleries, art centers of Miami and Palm Beach in Florida, the Charleston Museum of Art. His one-man shows were seen in the Columbia Museum of Art and private galleries in Columbia, Roanoke, Virginia, Greensboro, North Carolina, and Sumter. He held membership in the National Arts Club and the Art Students League in New York.

Little Theater A Community Asset

"The Sumter Little Theater represents community theater's true spirit – dedicated people of all ages overcoming obstacles of cramped, uncomfortable quarters and lack of funds to put on theatrical productions," said Bob Talbert, former columnist for **The State**, in 1964.

Having begun in 1949 with that spirit, Sumter's thesbians, motivated by genuine love of the dramatic arts, are still carrying on in 1971 with the same spirit. Though the acquisition of a new theater building in the fall of 1968 relieved the situations of "cramped, uncomfortable quarters," the financial burden still weighs heavily.

The history of Sumter's Little Theater movement really goes back before World War II. Several plays were produced before it became necessary to discontinue the organization because so many were being called away from Sumter to join the Armed Services.

In 1948, Harry Bryan, City Recreation Director, was instrumental in forming a steering committee to revive the idea of a Little Theater. Serving on this committee, in addition to Bryan, were four who had been active in the earlier organization – Mrs. Herbert Moses, Mrs. Lyman Quincy, J.B. (Red) Baker, and Mrs. Margaret McKeown. Things began moving at once. An organizational meeting was held in the old YMCA and H. Glen Oetgen was elected the first president.[256] (Others who have served as president since that time include Harry Bryan, Mrs. Agnes Drevenstedt, Mrs. Margaret McKeown, Don Furman, John Hoar, Marvin Trapp, and Walter Sharp.) The 1949 Board of Directors, apparently the first, was composed of John J. Riley, J.Whitney Cunningham, T. Doug Youngblood, Mike Karvelas, Mrs. Agnes Drevenstedt, Mrs. Alma Terrell, Mrs. Margaret McKeown, and Miss Lula Harvin.

Those first few members began work in earnest. Each week they presented a play over radio, adapting short stories or writing original script.

Realizing the need for a professional director, officers and directors consulted the University of North Carolina, where interested students were trained for such work. Since there was no money on hand to pay a director, a fund-raising campaign was implemented, the result being a sum of $2,000 raised in two weeks. This was enough to obtain someone for three months.

In the meantime, the university had recommended the perfect choice – James Moos. This personable young man, having been a prisoner in Germany during the war, saw the hunger for wholesome entertainment among the other prisoners and decided that he would dedicate his life to the work of bringing happiness to others through the medium of dramatic art. His three-month contract with the Sumter group lengthened into three years and under his direction, hidden talents were developed to the point where plays of the highest caliber were produced.

After Moos left, Jack Priest, who had served as technical director for some years, became the production director. Priest had valuable experience, gained in Little Theater work in Dallas, Texas. After three years, the group, finding the financial burden of paying a professional director too heavy, became "strictly amateur" as someone expressed the situation; however, "amateur" in this case has no derogatory implication. Productions have always shown a professional flavor. Local directors include Mrs. Beth Bond, Mrs. Shirley Housen, Miss Betty Kennedy, Mrs. Margaret McKeown, Mrs. Irene Schlesinger, D.J. Cerra, Don Furman, Henry Martin (music), C.J. Milling, Jr., Mr. and Mrs. Herbert Rosefield, Tom Prewett and Mrs. Kate Damron.

During the first years the theater had no place to call "home."

Performances were staged in auditoriums of District 17 schools, in the American Legion Home, the Coca-Cola Community Center, the National Guard Armory and even the County Courthouse. Props, costumes and other "valuables" that were collected for the different plays were stored in members' homes or wherever there was an available space. These devotees of art, however, surmounted every obstacle with determination and good humor.

Finally permission to use a part of the old Miller School was received from District 17. Under the skilled direction and with the hard work of Jack Priest, the building was renovated and put into usable condition. Two rooms, thrown together, formed the auditorium, which had the capacity of approximately 100. The stage extended to the wall so that actors entering and leaving were often forced to go outside regardless of the weather. The building afforded also a lobby, a place for storage and a green room. For the benefit of any who may not understand theater parlance, a green room in old theaters was "a waiting room for players between cues and scenes." This original use has been somewhat extended nowadays to include a place for meetings and social chats. Seats for the auditorium were some that had been discarded by the Sumter Theater.

This building was used until the fire marshal ordered it closed in 1965. That era of the theater's history ended in a blaze of glory with the superb production of "The Sound of Music." Acting, even in the many "bit parts," was excellent; the music was delightful. The play as a whole was said to have "sparkle and verve."

For a period of three years, more or less, the membership spent most of their time and effort in collecting funds for a new theater. In a building on Sumter Street, rented for a short time, they produced one play, "Mary, Mary." But the Board of Directors and officers decided that it was the better part of wisdom to concentrate on the goal that had been theirs from the beginning – to possess a home of their own, constructed according to their plans.

At long last, their dream came true! In the fall of 1968,[257] the Sumter Little Theater became a reality. Constructed of cement blocks, the new building stands in the western part of Sumter on land donated by the city. The building has a seating capacity of 250. The stage is spacious, allowing room for any type play undertaken and eliminating crowding in the wings (an advantage not enjoyed before). The stage is also equipped with two revolving platforms that facilitate change of scenery.

In addition to the auditorium, the building has a lower and upper lobby, dressing rooms, a make-up room, a wardrobe room and three rest rooms.

Though the membership was able to collect generous gifts and pledges, the financial strain continued for some time.

The first offering of the Little Theater, after it was organized, was "You Can't Take It With You." So successful was this production that the membership increased during 1949 from 22 to more than 300, with ages ranging from seven to 70. People of the community soon learned that there was work for all who would volunteer. Enthusiastic thespians worked diligently and cheerfully whether they were behind the footlights or behind the stage. Quickly did each newcomer realize that a suitable set, an authentic costume, skillful make-up and correct lighting effect were just as necessary for a successful production as the role of an actor.

Many plays with foreign background have been produced by this organization with great success. One that will be long remembered by producers and audience was "Teahouse of the August Moon," the scene of which was laid in Okinawa. This was indeed a technical triumph, requiring all the ingenuity, skill and plain "know how" that the backstage crew could muster. For the bamboo curtains, Boy Scouts were enlisted to cut bamboo vines from the swamps; for Ikinawan holiday and festival customs, somebody spent countless hours poring over books and pictures; for the proper performance of a little nanny goat that ate dutifully from a helmet on top of a jeep, Jim Kronberg faithfully fed Nanny (Fija dayo in Japanese) grapes (that was her favorite food) from a helmet for weeks before the play. The "admirable and deft" direction of the play, the excellent acting of the cast, as well as the surprisingly successful work of the backstage crew made "Teahouse of the August Moon" truly a professional performance.

Another hit production was "The King and I," which was indeed an ambitious undertaking. English and Siamese fashions of the mid-nineteenth century called for costumes that required 600 yards of fabric and the work of 25 seamstresses. Make-up artists gave just the right touch to the complexions of the Siamese. This play, as one newspaper stated, was "theater magic." One hundred and 80 people were involved and thousands of hours of work were spent on this stupendous performance.

The versatile artists of Sumter showed their skill in handling historical drama in the presentation of "Elizabeth the Queen." Again the backstage artists won applause for the elegant costumes, the "stage within a stage" adaptation of the Elizabethan theater, as well as the spectacular lighting effects. Actors showed rare perceptive skill in portraying thoughts and feelings of characters they represented. Altogether the production was hailed as an "Achievement."

Gilbert and Sullivan, all-time favorites, have been favorites, too, of the Sumter performers. They have produced for the delight of their audiences "The Gondoliers," "H.M.S. Pinafore," and "The Mikado."

"Theater in the round" or the arena-type of presentation has been used with great success by the Sumter Little Theater. This technique dates back to Greece some 2,500 years ago. It was introduced in Sumter by James Moos at the same time it was becoming popular in such cities as Dallas, Atlanta, Jacksonville; the play used was "The Man Who Came to Dinner," which was so well received that the same method has been used in other plays that lent themselves to the method. In the arena-type production the actors are on a level with the audience in an informal setting, with no backdrop, no conventional scenery, the illusion being created by the actors.

The theater group has gone "on the road" several times. "Blithe Spirit" was presented in Manning; "Saint Joan," one of the theater's more difficult productions, was taken to Bishopville. For this play, seven scenes were used, and it has been called a miracle of production for the stage crew to take flats for these seven scenes to another town and set them up at the proper time without a hitch.

Hillcrest School invited the players to present Dickens' "A Christmas Carol" there in December of 1951.

Children (actors and audience) have not been forgotten in the planning of the Sumter Little Theater. Such plays as "Cinderella," "The Pied Piper," "Alice in Wonderland" (sponsored by the Junior Welfare League) might be named as well as other plays with roles for children, such as the musicals, "Oliver!" and "The King and I."

It would be too lengthy an undertaking to list all the hit productions of the Sumter Little Theater in its lifetime. However, mention must be made of the Sesquicentennial Pageant presented at Riley Park. It was written by Director Moos and it told the story of Sumter from 1800 to 1905. A cast of 300 was needed to portray the 15 scenes of life in the community during these years.

Various traditions are always a part of any organization. One that has been enjoyed from "way back" by members of Little Theater is the informal party after each production when cast and stage crew relive the problems, mistakes (if any), humorous episodes connected with rehearsals and performance. There is always some form of entertainment also at these get-togethers — a one-act play, a recording or something of special interest.

The South Carolina Arts Commission gave assistance in financing the new theater and set up standards for the organization —

under the leadership of Mrs. Katie Damron. Each Wednesday night at the theater building was a clinical session for those who wished to learn something of the work involved in producing a play. Assisting Mrs. Damron in these training classes was an experienced director for each of the countless tasks necessary for a finished performance. The idea was stressed again and again that every play is a community project. Director Moos believed that one reason for the theater's popularity was the fact that "Mr. John Q. Public acts in one show or builds scenery or ushers. The next time, he's out in the audience letting his next door neighbor entertain him."

Time goes on and so does the Sumter Little Theater. By the time one play becomes a part of history, another is in the mill. Since "Oliver!" was successfully produced as the first play in the new theater, many successors have been recorded and the future holds promise of even greater triumphs.

(Written in 1971.)

PART XVI. MISCELLANEOUS

Camp Alice, An Efficient Tuberculosis Sanitorium

At one time in the not-too-distant past when tuberculosis was widespread in this area, as well as in many other parts of the state and country, Sumter operated a very efficient sanitorium for the treatment of this dread disease.

This sanitorium was near the corner of what is now Alice Drive and Wise Drive, but at that time, this was a very quiet location in a rural area on the outskirts of the city.

The treatment center, known as Camp Alice, was built in 1916 by H.J. Harby and named for his daughter Alice, who was a victim of a disease.

When the camp began, it had a capacity of 16 beds, eight for white patients and eight for black. There were some private rooms and some wards. By 1942 the capacity had been increased to 26 beds – 16 for whites and 10 for blacks.[258]

Mr. Harby continued as president until his death in 1938. At that time his son, Hal W. Harby, became president and gave of his time and effort to the management of the camp until it closed.

Taking over the nursing supervision of the camp in 1923 was Mrs. Minnie McBride, a registered nurse who was very efficient and widely experienced. Assisting Mrs. McBride was Miss Gibson, a colored nurse who was professional and competent. There was a good cook in the kitchen and several maids kept the rooms and wards spotlessly clean. It was said that the food was excellent.

Operating costs of the sanitorium came from an endowment fund given by Mr. Harby and from other bequests. These funds were supplemented by the city and county, as well as by those patients who were able to pay for their treatment. The yearly cost of the facility amounted to approximately $10,000.

The eight months prior to the closing of the camp in August 1941 for much needed repairs, the facility had a total of 3,047 patient days. This number of patient days was higher than in the whole of 1923.

Patients were sent to State Park and other treatment centers during the months required to make the needed repairs.

Many loyal supporters of the camp gave generously to help with the work. Kennedy Brothers made a donation of 1,500 bricks; Sumter Brick Works gave $16; Shaw Lumber Company added $25 to the fund; Williams Furniture Company donated a dresser, a bed, a table and six chairs.

Other thoughtful gestures showed that the town was very much in sympathy with the work being done to improve the camp for the comfort of the patients.

The Sumter County Chain Gang, under the supervision of Mr. B.M. Oliver, did a thorough job of clearing the area where the camp was located, removing dead trees and stumps.

An article in **The Sumter Daily Item** of Jan. 17, 1942, stated: "The road to the camp will be paved when the money is available. It has already been placed in the state road system."

The treatment at the camp included plenty of fresh air. Patients spent much of their time on screened porches. Some patients were confined to their beds, and some did not recover though they received the best of care.

Patients ranged in age from teenagers to those past middle age, the majority belonging to the older group.

Ministers visited the camp regularly to read to the patients and to talk and pray with them.

When tuberculosis became less prevalent, the officials of the camp felt that it would not be economical to keep the center open for only a few patients. Therefore Camp Alice, which had served such a worthwhile purpose for a number of years, closed its doors. The property was sold and the proceeds were added to the endowment fund begun by Mr. Harby.

Patients are now sent to State Park or treated at Tuomey Hospital. Camp Alice, Inc., with Mr. Henry Shelor as president and Mr. Murr Hall as secretary-treasurer, was formed to use the Camp Alice fund where needed. Each year Tuomey receives from $3,000 to $5,000 for the treatment of lung patients. The fund also assists eight or ten patients to go to State Park each year.

At a time when there was a great need for the care of tubercular patients, Camp Alice was a great blessing, both to those patients who could pay their expenses and those who were unable to pay. The county holds and will continue to hold the name of Mr. Harby in high regard for his contribution toward providing treatment for those suffering from any lung problems.

Sumter County Library Located In Civic Center

"Reading maketh a full man," said Sir Francis Bacon over 300 years ago, and this truth is of equal significance today.

However, twentieth century men, women and children have a much greater opportunity to read than did man in Bacon's day, since more reading materials are being written, published and made available to the public than ever before.

In the beautiful library, located at the Civic Center site, citizens of Sumter County have easy access to thousands of books, numerous periodicals and many other types of reading matter.

Much thought went into the planning, building, and equipping of this library in order that it might be adequate, comfortable and attractive. The outside presents a striking modern appearance, and the inside is even more handsome.

On the first floor is the spacious reading lounge for adults. The entire front is made of glass paneling, with colorful draperies, blending with the decor of the room. The walnut furniture includes comfortable chairs, which are inviting to visitors wishing to relax and browse, as well as to those who come for more serious reading or research; while the carpeted floors insure a quiet atmosphere for all.

Book stacks in the area contain adult fiction, biography and other non-fiction books, in addition to ample reference material from which data on any subject may be found.

Young people at the age of 14 may, with their parents' permission, use this adult area.

Also on the first floor is a county extension department, not open to the public, for servicing the Bookmobile which goes throughout the country on a regular schedule for the convenience of those who may not be able to come to the library. Adjacent to this department is a porte-cochere where the Bookmobile may be loaded and unloaded in any kind of weather.

An outside entrance leads to the children's department on the second floor. This room is equipped with slant-topped reading desks and small chairs to accommodate the youngsters. A glass-paneled front is made attractive with lovely and appropriate draperies. Here, too, the floor is carpeted and the furniture is of walnut. Lower book stacks that can be easily reached by the smaller folk contain juvenile reading materials to appeal to the tastes of all.

The building also contains a meeting room where programs of various clubs may be scheduled, with library-sponsored meetings having priority. Office space and a processing area are provided, as well as rest rooms on both floors.

Now available for use are 79,561 books and 28,650 for distribution through the Bookmobile. The present circulation has reached 165,043 and there are 21,241 registered borrowers. There are also pieces of artwork in circulation.

The Sumter County Library is supported for the most part by a local two-mill tax and state aid. Through the State Library Board, however, comes a little federal assistance. Cost of the new building was $317,679, with the site being donated by the city and county.

Use of the library is free to all city and county residents and/or taxpayers, with a nominal fee of $3 for non-county residents. Every borrower is issued a card which must be presented each time a book is obtained. A brochure containing library rules is also provided each borrower.

An added convenience for the users of the library is that the location affords ample parking space, paralleling Harvin Street.

Head librarian is Mr. Chapman J. Milling and assistant is Mr. Ware G. Martin. Mrs. Walter Ivey is children's librarian.

Chairman of the board of directors is Mr. Robert O. Purdy and vice chairman is Mr. Grady Locklear. Secretary is Mrs. Carolin Foxworth, and Mrs. Philip Palmer is treasurer. Other members of the board are Mrs. Hugh C. Humphries, Jr., Mr. Franklin Robinson and Mr. William B. Sanders.

"Sumter County's magnificent library," said Mr. Milling, "is an invitation for the public to use and enjoy books and periodicals in comfort and in beautiful surroundings. And I should like to add," he continued, "a personal invitation from all of us, who are charged with the responsibility of providing library service, to each one to come and enjoy this fine facility."

BIBLIOGRAPHY

BOOKS

Andrews, W.J. *Sketch of Company I, 23rd South Carolina Volunteers.* Whittet Shepperson. Richmond, Va. Reprinted by Wilder, Word Offset Printing, 105 North Harvin Street, Sumter, S.C.

Bass, Robert D. *Gamecock.* New York: Holt, Rhinehart and Winston.

Bass, Robert D. *Swamp Fox.* Henry Holt and Company. Jan. 1959. Printed in the United States of America.

Blanding, A.L. M.D. Compiler and Editor. *Blanding-McFaddin Families.* Jacobs and Company. Clinton, S.C.

Cousar, Dr. James E. *Physician Turned Planter.*

Garlington, J.C. *A Biographical Encyclopedia of Contemporaneous South Carolina Leaders.* 1902. Garlington Publishing Company. Spartanburg, S.C.

Gregorie, Anne King. *History of Sumter County.* 1954. Osteen Davis Publishing Company, Sumter, S.C.

Haynsworth, Hugh Charles. *Haynsworth-Furman and Allied Lines.* 1942. Osteen Publishing Company, Sumter, S.C.

"Historic Sketch of Sumter County Game and Fish Association"

The Historical and Descriptive Review of the State of South Carolina, Vol. III. Charleston, S.C. 1884.

"History of Church of the Holy Comforter"

King, Joe M. *A History of South Carolina Baptists.* R.L. Bryan Company, Columbia, S.C. 1964.

McCoy, Azile Mellette (Mrs. Hazel). "History of the Oswego Section of Sumter County."

McGrady, Gen. Edward. *Cyclopedia of Eminent and Representative Men of South Carolina, Vol. II.* Reprint Company, Spartanburg, S.C.

Moses, Herbert A. *The Early Minutes of the Sumter Society of Israelites.*

O'Neall, John Belton. *Bench and Bar of South Carolina, Vol. I.* Charleston, S.C. S.G. Courtenay & Co., Publishers. 1859.

Plowden, Mrs. Theodosia. *The Stateburg Literary and Musical Society, 1885-1949.*

Ramsay, David Green. *History of South Carolina, 1670-1808.* Reprint Company, Spartanburg, S.C.

Ramsey, Ralph H. Jr. Green. A.H. Bulletin University of the University of South Carolina. Aug., 1922.

Reppy, J. Fred. Joel R. Poinsett, *Versatile American.* Duke University Press, Durham, N.C. 1935. 281 pp.

Scott, Edwin. *Random Recollections of a Long Life, 1806-1876.* Charles A. Calvo, Jr., Printer, Columbia, S.C. 1884.

Shaffer, E.T.H. *Carolina Gardens.* Huntington Press, N.Y. 1937.

Snowden, Yates, Ed. *History of South Carolina, Vol. IV.*

Snyder, Mary Cuttino. *Swan Lake Gardens and Mr. Bland.*

Stroud, Agnes Blanding, Compiler and Editor. *The Book of Remembrance 1846-1941, Vol. II.* The Wed E. Reid Co., Italy, Texas.

Stubbs, Thomas McAlpine, *A History of Claremont Lodge No. 64, 1854-1949.*

Ibid. Early History of Sumter Churches.

MAGAZINES

Names in South Carolina
The Southern Christian Advocate

NEWSPAPERS

The Sumter News (of 1866)
The Sumter Tri-Weekly Watchman
The Sumter Watchman
The Banner
The Evening News
The Sumter Daily Item
The Columbia State
The Sumter Herald
The Charlotte Observer
The Winston-Salem Twin-City Sentinal

MISCELLANEOUS

Bradham, Miss Lila Mae, Paper on Sumter Mental Health Association.
Broün Family Records (from paper given Sumter County Historical Society by Mrs. T.D. Broün and Matthew Singleton Broün
Cemetery Records.
Church Records (from minutes, bulletins, printed programs, etc.)
Courthouse Records - Sumter County Courthouse.
Curtis, Horace, City Manager, List of Intendants-Mayors and of City Managers.
Dabbs, Thomas M. Paper on John K. Crosswell read before The Fortnightly Club.
Dick, Dr. Russell. Dick Family Records.
Dinkins, William; Dinkins, Mrs. Frances Mellette. Dinkins Family Records.
DuBose, Vermelle Montgomery (Mrs. T.A.) and Jordan, Ada Montgomery (Mrs. Forest L.) Montgomery Family Records.
Eaves, James M. Information on Chamber of Commerce.
Files of Myrtis Ginn Osteen and Gertrude McLaurin Shaw.
Hoar, John S. Paper read before The Fortnightly Club on George Washington Murray.
Letters: Mrs. Louis Tolleson, Greenville, S.C.; Mrs. John Jay Philips, Sumter.
Loring, Marsena Brunson. Scrapbook. Lent by Mrs. W. Loring Lee.
Map: Downtown Sumter: Made by William Leonard Brunson, surveyor, in 1817. Reproduced in 1981 by H.S. Willson, R.L.S.
Map: Sumter County Showing locations of Historical Markers. Made in 1980 by Lewis E. Leavell, Jr.
Minutes of Sumter City Schools.
Moise, Harold. Paper read before The Fortnightly Club giving history of the Club.
Moise, Robert B. Paper read before The Fortnightly Club on Dr. Warren G. Burgess.
Muldrow, Lucile Rhodes (Mrs. J.E.). Rhodes Family History.
Propst, Dr. Charles R. Paper read before The Fortnightly Club on Neill O'Donnell.
Purdy, Judge Robert O. Paper on Early Sumter read before The Fortnightly Club.
Richardson, Elizabeth Buford. History of Bloom Hill Richardsons furnished by Robbie Hickman.

Shaw, Dr. Ervin B.; Shaw, Harvey; Shaw, Russell R. Shaw Family Records. (Information on the children of John Calvin Shaw, Jr., based on Davis Elias DuRant Bibles in possession of Mrs. Ralph Gandy and Mrs. Charlie Harmon, the death certificate of Leonard Shaw. Newspaper account of death of Jack Shaw, Clelia Florence Shaw, daughter of Cora Shaw.) Facts furnished by Miss Catharine Bass.
Smith, Sherman. Tape - Tour of Sumter County Museum - Archives.
Yearbooks, Bulletins, Printed Programs and other written information on Businesses, Clubs, and other organizations.

Footnotes

1. Anne King Gregorie, *History of Sumter County*, p. 124.
2. *Ibid*, p. 431.
3. A.H. Green, Ralph H. Ramsey, Jr., Sumter County Economic and Social, p. 28.
4. Edwin Scott, *Random Recollections of a Long Life*, p. 28.
5. Gregorie, p. 123.
6. E.T.H. Shaffer, *Carolina Gardens*, p. 289.
7. *The Sumter Daily Item*, Sesqui-Centennial Issue, May, 1950.
8. A monument to Graham was placed near the scene of the fire and later moved to intersection of Main and Warren Streets.
9. Thomas M. Stubbs, from *Names in South Carolina, Vol. V.*
10. *Ibid.*
11. *The Sumter Daily Item*, May 17, 1950.
12. Chamber of Commerce Program of Work.
13. *The Historical and Descriptive Review of South Carolina*, p. 2.
14. *The Sumter Daily Item*, May 17, 1950.
15. Information from Mrs. Harry Berger.
16. Gregorie, p. 490.
17. Pamphlet "75 Years of Service."
18. Information from Henry L. Martin.
19. Gregorie, p. 354.
20. *Ibid*, p. 459.
21. Records of First Presbyterian Church.
22. John Belton O'Neall, *Bench and Bar of South Carolina, Vol. I.*
23. *Ibid.*
24. Gregorie, p. 362.
25. A.L. Blanding, (Editor & Compiler), *Blanding-McFaddin Families*, p. 12.
26. *Ibid*, p. 16.
27. Gregorie, p. 355.
28. *The Sumter Daily Item*, September, 1975.
29. Family Records.
30. Files of Myrtis G. Osteen.
31. Mary Cuttino Snyder, "Swan Lake Gardens and Mr. Bland."
32. *Ibid.*
33. Gen. Edward McGrady, ed. *Cyclopedia of Eminent and Representative Men of South Carolina, Vol. II.*
34. Family Records.
35. *Ibid.*
36. Records of Grace Baptist Church.
37. Family Records.
38. Former Pupils and Others.

39. *The Sumter Daily Item*, Feb. 23, 1981.
40. Records of Holy Cross Presbyterian Church.
41. Family Records.
42. Records of First Presbyterian Church of Sumter.
43. American Legion Post 15 Records.
44. Records of Holy Cross Presbyterian Church.
45. City Records.
46. Records of Kiwanis Club.
47. Records of First Baptist Church of Sumter.
48. *The Sumter News*, June 14, 1979.
49. *The Historical and Descriptive Review of the State of South Carolina, Vol. III.*
50. Family Records furnished by Mrs. F.S. Nance, granddaughter.
51. Records of First Baptist Church of Sumter.
52. Family Records from granddaughter, Miss Sarah DuBose.
53. Family Records.
54. Records of the Church of the Holy Cross, Episcopal.
55. J.C. Garlington, *A Biographical Encyclopedia of Contemporaneous South Carolina Leaders.*
56. Minutes of the Board of Education of the City Schools.
57. Records of First Presbyterian Church of Sumter.
58. Hugh Charles Haynsworth, *Haynsworth-Furman and Allied Families*, p. 132.
59. His letters in the Caroliniana Library in Columbia.
60. Personal Memories.
61. Haynsworth, p. 120.
62. *Ibid*, p. 132.
63. Gravestones at Bethel Baptist Church.
64. Family Records.
65. City Records (Sumter).
66. Haynsworth, p. 79.
67. *Ibid*, p. 84.
68. *Ibid*, p. 87.
69. *Ibid*, p. 89.
70. *Ibid*, p. 89.
71. Family Records.
72. *The Sumter Daily Item*, July, 1980.
73. *Ibid*, Sept. 10, 1976.
74. Letter from daughter, Mrs. John Jay Philips, Sumter.
75. Letter from sister, Mrs. Louis Tolleson, Greenville, S.C.
76. *Ibid.*
77. Personal Interview.
78. Information from son, Fred McLaughlin.
79. Minutes of Board of Education, Sumter City Schools.
80. Family Records.
81. *Ibid.*
82. *The Sumter Daily Item*, Sept. 10, 1976.
83. Gravestone at Bethel Baptist Church.
84. Minutes of Academical Society.
85. Records of First Baptist Church of Sumter.
86. Gravestone.
87. Clipping from *The Sumter Daily Item*, supplied by son, Perry Moses, Jr.
88. Family Records.
89. Paper by Dr. Charles Propst.

90. Records of Sumter City Schools.
91. *The Sumter Daily Item*, Feb. 22, 1975.
92. *Ibid.*
93. Gravestone, Church of the Holy Cross, Episcopal.
94. Information furnished by Miss Julia Reynolds.
95. Personal Interview.
96. Gregorie, p. 9.
97. *Ibid*, p. 39.
98. *The Charlotte Observer*, Feb. 6, 1955.
99. *The Winston-Salem Twin City Sentinal*, July 28, 1953.
100. Family Records, furnished by George Decatur Shore, Jr. (Deceased, April 1981.)
101. Family Records.
102. "History of Sumter County Historical Society."
103. *The Sumter Daily Item*, Feb. 27, 1974.
104. *The Columbia State*, Feb. 28, 1974.
105. Family Records (furnished by Josephine Williams Wilder) (Mrs. A.H. Sr.)
106. *The Sumter Daily Item*, Nov. 20, 1952.
107. Gregorie, p. 161.
108. *Ibid*, p. 276.
109. *Ibid*, p. 185.
110. *Ibid*, p. 223.
111. *Ibid*, p. 284.
112. *Ibid*, p. 196.
113. Church Minutes.
114. *Ibid.*
115. Interview with pastor, Rev. J.L. Gillison.
116. Herbert A. Moses, *The Early Minutes of the Sumter Society of Israelites.*
117. Notes from Anniversary sermon by the pastor, the Rev. T.L. Johnson.
118. *Southern Christian Advocate*, July 18, 1955.
119. Church Minutes kept by John C. Chandler.
120. Church Records.
121. *The Sumter News*, Aug. 30, 1979.
122. Minutes of Santee Baptist Association.
123. Church Records.
124. Church Records.
125. Information from Mrs. B.L. Britton.
126. "History of the Church of the Holy Comforter."
127. Church Records.
128. Paper written by Rev. J.W. Wilder, former pastor.
129. Church Minutes.
130. Interview with pastor, The Rev. Franklin Delano Colclough.
131. Interviews with the pastor, the Rev. Alvin Haigler and Mrs. F.H. Suber, Sr.
132. Information furnished by Mr. Roland Chewning, church officer.
133. Facts from paper written by James Haynsworth for the Anniversary Celebration.
134. Member of family that owned Bloom Hill Plantation before it was purchased by William Richardson.
135. From office records furnished by William M. Crawford.
136. Personal tour of cemetery.
137. Herbert A. Moses, *The Early Minutes of the Sumter Society of Israelites.*
138. From the files of the late W.F. Bultman.

139. Records of the late George D. Shore, Jr.
140. Gregorie, p. 325.
141. *Ibid*, p. 362.
142. Information from McLaurin family.
143. Wells family records.
144. Information from Robert Graham.
145. In records of Mrs. Francis M. Cain, Sr., present owner.
146. Data furnished by Josephine Williams Wilder (Mrs. Arthur H., Sr.). Facts fully authenticated.
147. Agnes Blanding Stroud, Editor & Compiler, *Book of Remembrance, 1846-1941.*
148. Records of the late Paul K. Bowman.
149. Files of Myrtis G. Osteen and tapes prepared by Sherman Smith.
150. *Ibid.*
151. *Ibid.*
152. Minutes of Sumter County Historical Society.
153. Information furnished by William E. (Billy) Brunson III and Lt. Col. Hugh McLaurin III.
154. *The Sumter Daily Item*, Sept. 10, 1976.
155. Minutes of Board of Education, City Schools.
156. *Ibid.*
157. *The Sumter Daily Item*, Sept. 10, 1976.
158. *Ibid.*
159. Information from former faculty members.
160. Gregorie, p. 175.
161. *The Sumter Daily Item*, Oct. 15, 1939.
162. Facts learned at 50th Anniversary Celebration.
163. *The Sumter Daily Item.*
164. Interview with Headmaster J.E. McCorkle.
165. Interview with Headmaster C.E. Owens III.
166. W.J. Andrews, *Sketch of Company K, 23rd South Carolina Volunteers.*
167. *Ibid.*
168. *The Sumter Daily Item*, June 25, 1979.
169. Gregorie, p. 270.
170. *The Sumter Daily Item*, May 18, 1951.
171. *Ibid.*
172. Clemson Extension Agency.
173. *The Columbia State*, June 22, 1966.
174. Interview with matron.
175. Visit to Home.
176. Information from Mrs. R.D. Graham.
177. Approved by the State Department of Archives and History.
178. Interview with R.T. Brown.
179. Interview with Mrs. Florence Bolger.
180. Information from Mrs. R.D. Graham.
181. *The Sumter Daily Item*, May 2, 1972.
182. *Ibid*, May 10, 1976.
183. Interview with Dr. Robert R. Hirschberg.
184. Interview with John S. Hoar.
185. Files of Myrtis G. Osteen.
186. *The Sumter Daily Item*, Sept. 26, 1967.
187. Paper by Miss Lila Mae Bradham.
188. *The Sumter Daily Item*, July 12, 1980.
189. *The Columbia State*, June 5, 1960.

190. Historical Sketch, Mrs. Theodosia Dargan Plowden.
191. *The Sumter Daily Item.*
192. *Ibid*, March 18, 1969.
193. Pamphlets and other information furnished by Michael Karvelas.
194. *Ibid.*
195. From charter in Elks Club Headquarters at Second Mill.
196. Minutes of Club furnished by J.B. (Red) Baker.
197. Thomas M. Stubbs, *A History of Claremont Lodge No. 64*, p. 21.
198. *Ibid*, p. 4.
199. *Ibid*, p. 9.
200. *Ibid*, p. 31.
201. *Ibid*, p. 49.
202. *The Sumter Daily Item*, Jan. 29, 1965.
203. Interviews with members.
204. Booklet - Golden Anniversary Programs.
205. *The Sumter Daily Item*, Oct. 1, 1973.
206. Interview with Wilbert H. Bernshouse.
297. "Historical Sketch of Sumter County Game and Fish Association."
208. *The Sumter Daily Item*, June 21, 1969.
209. Brochures and Newsletters from Michael Karvelas.
210. Published in *The Sumter Daily Item* in serial form.
211. Interview with Director Woody Thomas.
212. Brochures on activities at the YMCA.
213. Facts furnished by Mrs. Harold G. Kirk.
214. Information from Mrs. R.D. Graham.
215. Information from Miss Catharine Bass and Mrs. C.B. Burns.
216. Files of Myrtis G. Osteen.
217. *The Sumter Daily Item*, Oct. 15, 1971.
218. *Ibid*, Oct. 20, 1978.
219. Historical Data furnished by Mrs. P.M. Tiller (deceased).
220. Files of Myrtis G. Osteen.
221. Letter from Miss Martha Robinson.
222. *The Sumter Herald*, Oct. 1934; May 8, 1930.
223. Information from Mrs. Theo Palmer.
224. Interview with Mrs. Stella Bailey, Co-Chairman of the Fannie S. Ivey Service Unit.
225. Information furnished by Mrs. Herbert A. Rosefield, present regent of the Sumter Home Chapter.
226. Minutes of the Sumter Home Chapter.
227. Minutes of Club.
228. *The Sumter Daily Item*, March 29, 1962.
229. *Ibid.*
230. Approved by the South Carolina Department of Archives and History.
231. Information from Mrs. Evangeline Thompson, former director in Sumter County and Mrs. Ralph Gates.
232. Clemson Extension Office.
233. Yearbook.
234. Information from Mrs. I.D. Elmore.
235. *Ibid.*
236. Facts from Mrs. C.B. Burns.
237. *The Sumter Daily Item*, June 23, 1970.
238. Records, yearbooks, current information from members.
239. Files of Myrtis G. Osteen.
240. *The Sumter Daily Item*, May 17, 1950.

241. Facts from Mrs. Louise Parker.
242. Report of National Recreation Association in pamphlet form.
243. Records of PARD furnished by Mrs. Mary Hinson, program coordinator.
244. *The Sumter Daily Item*, Jan. 19, 1970.
245. *Ibid*, Aug. 16, 1969.
246. *Ibid*, July 24, 1978.
247. Minutes of Art Association.
248. Gregorie, p. 432.
249. Information from H.C. Wilson of Mayesville, brother of M.B. Wilson, Jr.
250. Information from Mrs. Arthur H. Wilder, Sr.
251. Gregorie, p. 423.
252. *Ibid*, p. 428.
253. Family Records.
254. Gregorie, p. 429.
255. Family Records furnished by Miss Jessie Myers.
256. Records furnished by Mrs. Lyman Quincey and others.
257. *The Sumter Daily Item*, Oct. 15, 1969.
258. *Ibid*, Jan. 17, 1942.

APPENDIX

GOVERNORS FROM SUMTER DISTRICT

James B. Richardson	1802-1804
Richard I. Manning	1824-1826
Stephen D. Miller	1828-1830
John Peter Richardson	1840-1842
John L. Manning	1852-1854
Franklin I. Moses, Jr.	1872-1874
John Peter Richardson	1886-1890
Richard I. Manning	1915-1919
Thomas Gordon McLeod	1923-1927

INTENDANTS OR MAYORS OF SUMTER, SOUTH CAROLINA 1871 -

Minutes of the meetings of the governing body of Sumter, South Carolina are on file at City Hall for the period beginning May 15, 1871.* From these records the following information has been gathered:

Town of Sumter

Election Date	Intendant
May 15, 1871	Capt. E.C. Green
September 11, 1871	Capt. Green resigned Replaced by Guignard Richardson
April 12, 1872	Guignard Richardson
February 13, 1873	Richardson resigned Replaced by A.W. Suder
April 15, 1873	A.W. Suder
April 20, 1874	A.W. Suder re-elected
April 16, 1875	A.W. Suder re-elected
April 17, 1876	A.W. Suder
April 17, 1877	Dr. J.J. Bossard
April 23, 1878	Dr. J.J. Bossard
April 14, 1879	Capt. William R. Delgar
April 19, 1880	George W. Reardon
April 20, 1881	George W. Reardon re-elected
April 11, 1882	Horace Harby
April 10, 1883	Col. J.D. Graham
April 18, 1884	Col. J.D. Graham
April 14, 1885	Marion Moise
April 16, 1886	Major Marion Moise
April 16, 1887	Major Marion Moise

January 9, 1888 "Town of Sumter" changed to "City of Sumter;" "Intendant" became "Mayor;" "Wardens" made "Aldermen."

(2-Year Terms)	**Mayor**
April 16, 1888	Julius A. Mood, M.D.
April 10, 1890	R.O. Purdy
April 14, 1892	B.G. Pierson
April 17, 1894	B.G. Pierson
January 29, 1895	Special Election
February 11, 1896	Special Election
April 20, 1896	Dr. J.J. Bossard
April 12, 1898	H. Frank Wilson
April 10, 1900	A.B. Stuckey
April 23, 1902	A.B. Stuckey
April 14, 1904	Dr. George W. Dick
April 12, 1906	W.B. Boyle
January 23, 1907	Special Election
April 22, 1908	W.B. Boyle
April 12, 1910	L.D. Jennings
June 11, 1912	
August 13, 1912	L.D. Jennings
August 13, 1918	L.D. Jennings
April 27, 1920	
August 8, 1922	L.D. Jennings
August 15, 1924	R.D. Epps
August 10, 1926	
August 14, 1928	J.A. Raffield
August 12, 1930	
August 11, 1932	F.B. Creech
August 14, 1934	
August 11, 1936	F.B. Creech
August 9, 1938	
July 30, 1940	F.B. Creech
August 11, 1942	
August 8, 1944	E.B. Boyle
August 13, 1946	
August 15, 1948	W.E. Bynum
August 8, 1950	
August 12, 1952	M. Priscilla Shaw
August 10, 1954	
August 14, 1956	S.A. Harvin
August 12, 1958	
August 9, 1960	Clifton G. Brown (resigned 5-21-64 to accept appointment to State Development Bd.)
August 14, 1962	

May 22, 1964	Morris D. Mazursky
August 11, 1964	Robert E. Graham
August 11, 1966	
August 13, 1968	Robert E. Graham
August 11, 1970	
August 8, 1972	Richard P. Moses
June 4, 1974	
June 18, 1976	W.M. Hodge
June 6, 1978	
June 17, 1980	W.A. McElveen, Jr.

*We have no records on the meetings declaring election results during 1882, 1883, 1884, and 1885. This information was obtained from records at Caroliniana Library, University of South Carolina, by R.E. Graham.

BUSINESSES, 1950 AND EARLIER

Alderman Drug Company
A & P Food Stores
Ammons, B. Refrigeration and Air Conditioning
Appliance & Television Center
B.J. Barnett, Inc.
Belk-Stroman Company
Berger's, Inc.
Black River Electric Corp.
Booth-Boyle Livestock Company
Boyle Farm Supply Company
Boyle Motor Company
Bradham & Co.
Bradham Insurance Agency
Brody's Department Store
Brown-Watson, Inc.
Burgess-Brogdon Building Supply
W.B. Burns & Sons
Burress, M.C. & Son, Wedgefield
W.E. Bynum Lumber Company
The Capitol
Carolina Coca Cola Bottling Company
Carolina Furniture Works
Carolina Hardware Company
Carolina Power & Light Company
Central Insurance Agency
Central Production Credit Association
Charm House, Fabrics of Sumter
Cities Supply Company
Claremont Oil Company
Commander, J.P. Company
Credit Bureau of Sumter
Creech Holding Corporation
Creech Lumber Company

Crosswell & Company
Crosswell Home
James Cuttino & Son
Dragon Fly Company
H.C. Edens Enterprises, Dalzell, S.C.
Edens Lumber Company
Eldridge Realty Company
Evans Manufacturing Company
Tom Evans Garage
FCX Farm and Garden Center
Federal Land Bank Associates of Sumter
First Federal Savings & Loan Association
Flower & Gift Shop
Fort Roofing & Sheet Metal Works
Frank's Servicenter, Inc.
Galloway & Moseley
Georgia-Pacific Corp., Williams Furniture Division
F.E. Gibson & Sons
Goodwin Buick AMC, Inc.
G & W Real Estate
Hapco, Inc.
H.J. Harby Trust Fund
Harvin Laundry and Cleaners
Harvin Packing Company
Hill Furniture Company
Hill Plumbing Company
Hodge Properties
Hodge Real Estate and Insurance Company
Holland Office Equipment Company
Home Federal Savings and Loan Association
Hughes, Inc.
Hurst-Sexton Furniture Company
Jack's Department Store
James, DuRant, Matthews & Shelley
Job's Mortuary
Keith's of Sumter Dry Goods
Kirby's Sales and Service
Kirkland Cleaners
H.E. Kirven Lumber Company, Pinewood
Knight Bros., Inc.
Korn Industries, Inc.
S.H. Kress & Co. 5¢ & 10¢ Store
Latham Oil Company
Lenoir Store, Horatio
Liberty Motors
Merritt Veterinary Supplies, Inc.
Mills Electric Company
Moise Insurance Company
B.L. Montague & Company
Morris College
Henry P. Moses Company
Perry Moses & Son Real Estate and Insurance, Inc.
McDaniel-Sigmon Roofing Company
McElveen, W.A. Pontiac Dealer
McLaurin Farms, Wedgefield

McLaurin-Nettles, Inc.
National Bank of South Carolina
Nu-Idea School Supply Company
Osteen-Davis
Osteen Publishing Company
Owens & Shuler, Inc.
Pack's Landing, Rimini
Palmer Funeral Home
Palmer & Mallard, C.E., Inc.
Palmetto Pigeon Plant
J.C. Penny Company
Peoples Natural Gas of S.C.
Piedmont Auto Parts
Piggly-Wiggly
Pilot Life Insurance Company
Plywood Company
Radio Communication Service, Inc.
Radio Station, WFIG
Richardson Marble and Granite Works
Riley & Company
Rowland Warehouse Company
RuVelle, Inc.
Sanders Glass Company
Santee Print Works
Schwartz Dress Shop
Seaboard Coastline Railroad
Seaco Music Store
J.H. Seale & Son
Sears Roebuck and Company
Shaw Lumber Company
Shaw Manufacturing Company
Shelley-Brunson Funeral Home
Sifco Industries, Inc.
Silver Moon Restaurant
South Carolina National Bank
Southern Coatings and Chemical Company
Suburban Propane Gas Company
Sumter Airways
Sumter Builders Electrical Contractors
Sumter Casket Company
Sumter Concrete Company
Sumter Cut Rate Drug Store
Sumter Daily Item
Sumter Dairies, Inc.
Sumter Electric Rewinding Company
Sumter Frozen Foods, Inc.
Sumter Insurance Agency
Sumter Laundry & Cleaners
Sumter Machinery Company
Sumter Office Supply
Sumter Petroleum Company
Sumter Printing Company
Sumter Radio Shop
Sumter Theatre
Sunset Country Club

Tuomey Hospital
D.E. Turbeville & Associates, Inc.
Union Bus Terminal
United Way of Sumter County
Veterinary Hospital
Ventu-Lite Custom Products
Waters Greenhouse and Flower Shop
Western Auto
Young's Food Stores, Inc.

LEGENDS FOR MAPS ON JACKET

BATTLE OF DINGLE'S MILL — 1
SC 251, 1.5 miles S of Sumter.

BETHEL BAPTIST CHURCH — 2
Near intersection of S-43-77 and S-43-251.

BIRTHPLACE OF MARY McLEOD BETHUNE — 3
US 76, Mayesville.

CHURCH OF THE HOLY CROSS, STATEBURG (EPISCOPAL) — 4
SC 261, Stateburg.

EARLY CHARLESTON ROAD — 5
At intersection of US 76/378 and SC 261, NE side, approximately 9 miles W of Sumter city limits.

COL. DAVID DuBOSE GAILLARD — 6
ENGINEER OF THE PANAMA CANAL
SC 261, approximately 20 miles S of intersection with US 76/378 at Fulton Crossroads, about 4 miles W of Pinewood.

GREEN SWAMP METHODIST CHURCH — 7
W. Liberty St. Extension, beyond Swan Lake, Sumter.

HIGH HILLS BAPTIST CHURCH — 8
S-43-488, off SC 261 N of Stateburg.

LENOIR STORE — 9
S-43-37, Horatio.

REMBERT CHURCH — 10
SC 43, about 1 mile N of Sumter County line in Lee County.

RICHARD RICHARDSON — 11
3 miles W of Pinewood, just off SC 261 at St. Mark's Church.

SALEM (BLACK RIVER) PRESBYTERIAN CHURCH — 12
SC 527, approximately 4 miles from Mayesville.

ST.MARK'S EPISCOPAL CHURCH — 13
3 miles W of Pinewood, just off SC 261.

SITE OF MANCHESTER — 14
SC 261, approximately 8.5 miles S of its intersection with US 76/378.

GENERAL THOMAS SUMTER | 15
SC 37 at its intersection with SC 488, between SC 261 and SC 441, approximately 2 miles W of Shaw Air Force Base.

GENERAL THOMAS SUMTER MEMORIAL ACADEMY 1905-1911 | 16
SC 441 at Hillcrest, 11 miles E of Sumter.

WILLIAM TENNENT | 17
Intersection of US 76 and SC 261.

SITE OF FIRST HOME DEMONSTRATION CLUB | 18
Near intersection of S-43-77 and S-43-251 (Near Bethel Baptist Church).

MARKERS IN THE CITY

DIGGS WILDER HOUSE | 1
25 South Magnolia Street.

20 KENDRICK STREET | 2
Circa 1855.

CHARLES MOISE HOUSE | 3
432 North Main Street.

HENRY HAYNSWORTH HOUSE | 4
41 Haynsworth Street.

HASELL DICK-DR. FRANK K. HOLMAN | 5
436 West Hampton Avenue.

THE ELIZABETH T. BUFORD HOUSE | 6
523 West Hampton Avenue.

CLARA LOUISE KELLOG | 7
S.W. Corner, S. Main and Dugan Streets.

THIS SCHOOL SITE | 8
N. Washington Street, near intersection with Liberty Street, Sumter.

THE SUMTER INSTITUTE 1867-1901 | 9
Corner of Washington and Calhoun Streets, Sumter.

SUMTER COURT HOUSE | 10
Court House grounds, Main Street, Sumter.

ADDENDUM - ATHLETICS - See Page 569

Helen Carroll - Olympian

Not a native, but a longtime Sumter resident, Helen Carroll has top standing in aquatic sports. Mrs. Carroll was a member of the 1932 Olympic 400 meter freestyle relay team that won a gold medal at the Los Angeles games. Previously, she had won the National Junior 100 yard AAU freestyle championship and placed second to the great Helene Madison in the National Senior Girls Championship.

David F. McInnis - Diver and Coach

Attorney David F. McInnis must be rated as Sumter's top diver since he attained national ranking. He attended the University of North Carolina where he became the dominant diver in the Atlantic Coast Conference. He won the conference championship for one and three meters in 1956 and 1957. In 1957 McInnis was NCAA honorable mention All-American.

Following graduation at Chapel Hill, he coached swimming and diving at Sumter, Conway, and Columbia and was freshman diving coach at the University of South Carolina while attending law school.

McInnis represents Sumter in the South Carolina Legislature where he is Chairman of the House Rules Committee.

In recognition of his accomplishments, McInnis is presently a nominee to the South Carolina Athletic Hall of Fame.

Aquatic Sports

Other outstanding divers who earned recognition were Ralph "Hank" Wilson, five-time State Senior Men's Champion, Carolinas and Georgia high school champion, Southeastern AAU Champion and fourth place winner in the AAU National Junior Championship; Robert Hirshberg, Southeastern Conference Champion at the University of Georgia; the late Leslie Boney, and Willis Beall, Southern Conference champs at the University of South Carolina.

Sumter produced a host of outstanding swimmers and divers under the tutelage of the late Austin M. Francis and others. Among these were Southern Conference champions F.M. "Nick" Moise, Jr. (butterfly) and Deuward Bultman, Jr. (relay) at the University of North Carolina; and Ed Garris, only five-time winner of the James Austin Francis trophy as Sumter's outstanding swimmer. "Nick" Moise was team captain at Duke.

Edwin C. Cuttino was the early superstar of the local program, excelling in swimming and diving, winner of numerous Carolinas and Mid-Atlantic AAU titles. Many others were outstanding; among those that come to mind are Guy Battle, "Bud" Burgess, James Brown, the Propst brothers - Julian and "Pap," Randy Bradham, Raymond Baker, Charles Penney, Phelps Bultman, J.L. Mooneyhan, "Sambo" Roddey, Cody Palmer, Harry Parker, P.D. Hammond, Jimmy Bryan, Danny McKiever, Scott Rumph, Scriven Brunson, Jimmy Moise, Dick Warren, Joe Warren, Roddy Rappe, John Marshall, and Buddy Hodge, to name a few.

Outstanding females of that period included Sally Nash, Andrena Owens, Iris Hill, Dorothea Bultman, Libba Andrews, Helen Ulmer, Lucy Barringer, and the Dollard sisters - Ann and Betty.

Annette Roddey - Golf Champion

Annette Roddey's record stands alone among Sumter golfers. Perennial champion at Sunset Country Club, Miss Roddey has won four South Carolina Women's Championships. To crown her achievements, she became Sumter's only member of the South Carolina Golf Hall of Fame in 1981. Frequently the qualifying medalist, Miss Roddey won the Women's South Carolina Association Championship in 1955 and 1960. She followed this by winning two WSC Seniors titles - 1970 and 1973.

A founder and first secretary of the WSGA in 1948, subsequently president, she has also been president of the Women's Carolinas Golf Association and S.C. representative to the Southern Golf Association.

Mike Holland

Bishopville golfer Mike Holland has attracted considerable attention on the Tournament Players Association tour. An All-American at the University of South Carolina, his top finish was winning the 1981 Disney World National Team Championship with partner Vance Heafner. Obviously an excellent team player, Holland paired with Marion Fowler of Lake City to win successive Carolinas Golf Association 4-ball championships.

Dr. Edmund M. McDonald - Hall of Famer

The Benedict College Athletic Hall of Fame has inducted Sumter dentist Edmund M. McDonald in its initial selections. Born in Sumter, Dr. McDonald played football for Lincoln High School, attended Morris College for one year, then enrolled at Benedict. Playing two years for the Tigers at center and his final two years at end, the 180 pound athlete was a "sixty minute man," going both on offense and defense. He was honored for his play as a senior by being named All-American by the *Pittsburg Courier* in 1938. He was also a varsity tennis player at Benedict.

Following graduation, Dr. McDonald taught at high schools in Georgetown and Columbia, S.C. He received his master's degree from Columbia University in health and physical education in 1941. He then entered Meharry Medical College in Nashville where he received his degree in dentistry. Dr. McDonald has practiced his profession in Sumter since then.

Terry Kinard - All American

In this Year of The Tiger, it is appropriate to honor Sumter's latest All-American, Terry Kinard. Even though this book has gone to press, we wish to honor Clemson University's junior free safety. The outstanding defensive back for Clemson's 12-0 National Champions, Kinard was the only defensive back to make All-American in the school's history. With another year of eligibility, this gifted athlete was a first team selection of the Association Press, NEA, and the Football Writers - an absolutely astounding accomplishment.

A devastating tackler, Kinard is already third in career interceptions at Clemson. Incredibly, he finished second on the Tiger team in tackles in 1981 with 92, highest ever by a secondary back.

At Sumter High School, Terry played quarterback, but according to coach Eddie Weldon, he could have played any position. He was a starter for Sumter's basketball team, and Weldon says he could have played for Clemson, but his first love is football.

Sumter is expecting more great things from Alfred Terrance Kinard - both on and off the field.

Anthony Rose

Aiding and abetting Kinard in his attack upon enemies of the Tigers was Anthony Rose - an unsung starter for Clemson in its drive for the championship. Anthony Rose is the All-American type person from Mayewood High School. Defensive back *par excellence,* he has earned his share of honors for Sumter and Clemson.

Finale

As this goes to press, the San Francisco Forty-Niners have just won professional football's Super Bowl, with Freddie Solomon and Archie Reese leading the way (see page 569). How good are Archie Reese and Fast Freddie Solomon? Just ask the Cincinnati Bengals and other old pros in the NFL!

Also participating in the Super Bowl was defensive end Eddie Edwards of Cincinnati. A Mayesville native, Edwards did not play football here. He played two years at Arizona Western Junior College, transferred to the University of Miami, Florida, and from there to the Bengals.

See Page 619, Appendix

JOEL ROBERTS POINSETT
1779-1850
CEMETERY, CHURCH YARD, CHURCH OF THE HOLY CROSS,
STATEBURG, (EPISCOPAL)
S.C. 261 Stateburg

Born in Charleston, S.C., Statesman, Diplomat, Author, and Naturalist. Educated in medicine, military science, and law.

Traveled extensively in Asia and Europe. United States Commissioner. Concerned with the independence of South American colonies. U.S. House of Representatives, First U.S. Minister to Mexico and Secretary of War in Van Buren's cabinet. From Mexico he introduced to this country a species of the Euphorbia plant, later named Poinsettia in his honor.

ERECTED BY SUMTER COUNTY HISTORICAL COMMISSION
1960

(On back panel)

Sacred to the memory of Joel R. Poinsett, who departed this life on the 12th day of December, 1851, in the 73rd year of his life. A pure Patriot, an Honest man and a good Christian.

Sacred to the memory of Mary, the relict of the Honorable Joel R. Poinsett, who departed this life on the 9th day of November, 1857, in the 76th year of her age.

ERECTED BY SUMTER COUNTY HISTORICAL COMMISSION
1960

The above inscriptions were taken from the graves of Poinsett and his wife, adjacent to this marker.

INDEX

B

C

D

F

H

I

J

K

L

M

Mc

N

O

P

Q

R

S

T

U

V

W

Y

Z